PRACTICAL HANDBOOK

FOR

THE STUDY OF THE BIBLE

AND OF

BIBLE LITERATURE

INCLUDING

BIBLICAL GEOGRAPHY, ANTIQUITIES, INTRODUCTION
TO THE OLD AND THE NEW TESTAMENT,
AND HERMENEUTICS

BY

DR. MICHAEL SEISENBERGER

ROYAL LYCEUM, FREISING

TRANSLATED FROM THE SIXTH GERMAN EDITION

BY

A. M. BUCHANAN, M.A. (LONDON)

AND EDITED BY

THE REV. THOMAS J. GERRARD

NEW YORK
JOSEPH F. WAGNER

𝔑𝔦𝔥𝔦𝔩 𝔒𝔟𝔰𝔱𝔞𝔱

    REMIGIUS LAFORT, S.T.L.

                Censor Librorum

𝔍𝔪𝔭𝔯𝔦𝔪𝔞𝔱𝔲𝔯

    ✠ JOHN M. FARLEY, D.D.

                Archbishop of New York

NEW YORK, October 1, 1911

THE UNIVERSITY PRESS, CAMBRIDGE, U. S. A.

EDITORIAL PREFACE

THIS book is offered to the English-speaking peoples as a small contribution towards the realization of the great and noble aims of the reigning Sovereign Pontiff, Pope Pius X. The heroic stand which he has made for the preservation of the Word of God, commands at once the sympathy and admiration of all the faithful. Just as in the realm of philosophy he has insisted on the true personality and dignity of man, and as in theology on the true transcendence and majesty of God, so also has he in the realm of biblical science insisted on the Divine Character of the Inspired Word.

When the Church speaks officially through the Sacred Congregations, she does not argue with her children. She teaches them. She says, plainly, what is the truth concerning the Divine Revelation. Then, after the Church has spoken, the work of the theologians and critics begins. It is their office to justify the Word of the Church to men. Hence, the remark of those who say that their errors have been condemned, but not refuted, is pointless. The functions of condemnation and refutation are quite distinct, and pertain to different spheres of the Church's action.

A translation of Dr. Seisenberger's work has been asked for, as providing a bird's-eye view of the biblical question from the Catholic standpoint, suitable to the exigencies of the present day. It is a handbook for the hard-worked parochial clergy. It is an introduction for the Seminary student. Yet, although it is merely a synopsis, it is enriched on every page with ample references to the more specialized works — a detailed list of which is appended to the book — so that the reader who wishes to pursue any given subject more deeply has the material at hand without further search.

The treatment in the book itself, however, will be found amply sufficient for dealing with that ever-increasing number of souls who pick up rationalist conclusions anywhere and everywhere, and are thus, somewhat needlessly, disturbed in their faith.

The editor would beg, with all deference, to call attention to a theological distinction which would seem to have come into prominence since the author first wrote his book, and which does not appear to have been made sufficiently clear even in the latest edition. It is the distinction between inspiration and revelation. All the Bible is inspired, but not all the Bible is revealed. A sacred writer, for instance, might write down an account of an event as he had seen it or heard it from an eye-witness. The source of his information is purely natural. In writing it down, however, he does so under the influence of that supernatural charism which is known as inspiration. On the other hand, he might have the knowledge infused into his mind directly by God. Such was the way in which St. Paul received the information for his classical passage on the Holy Eucharist. That was a revelation. And, since he was moved by the Holy Spirit to embody it in one of his epistles, it was also a part of inspiration. The distinction is necessary, if one is to understand the difference between Catholic plenary inspiration and Protestant literal inspiration.

The Douay version of Scripture has been generally adopted, but there are about three or four places where this did not literally agree with the German version used by the author. These cases have been rendered by a literal translation of the German.

THOMAS J. GERRARD.

HERRENWIES, BADEN-BADEN.
    Feast of SS. Peter and Paul, 1911.

CONTENTS

First Part

THE HOLY LAND

GEOGRAPHY

Second Part

THE HOLY PEOPLE

BIBLICAL ARCHAEOLOGY

A. *Outlines of the History of Israel*

B. *God, and the Gods, in Israel*

C. *The Religious Institutions of Israel*

CONTENTS

First Section

HOLY PLACES

I. THE TABERNACLE

THE SACRED FURNITURE AND UTENSILS

II. THE TEMPLE

(a) *Solomon's Temple*

(b) *The Second Temple*

Second Section

HOLY PERSONS

Third Section

SACRED RITUAL

I. SACRIFICES

(a) *Bloody Sacrifices*

(b) *Unbloody Sacrifices*

Fourth Section

SACRED SEASONS

Third Part

HOLY SCRIPTURE

DECREES OF THE HOLY SEE RELATING TO HOLY SCRIPTURE

INTRODUCTION TO THE BIBLE

First Part

ORIGIN OF HOLY SCRIPTURE, OR HOLY SCRIPTURE AS THE WORD OF GOD

INSPIRATION

THE CANON OF HOLY SCRIPTURE

Second Part

GENERAL INTRODUCTION. THE BIBLE AS A WHOLE

THE ORIGINAL TEXT OF HOLY SCRIPTURE

TRANSLATIONS OF THE BIBLE

Third Part

SPECIAL INTRODUCTION. THE SACRED BOOKS CONSIDERED SINGLY

The Books of the Old Testament

First Section

Second Section

From the Entrance of the Israelites into Chanaan to the Division of the Kingdom

CONTENTS

Third Section

Fourth Part

INTERPRETATION OF HOLY SCRIPTURE (HERMENEUTICS)

First Section

THE MEANING OF HOLY SCRIPTURE

Second Section

OF DISCOVERING THE MEANING OF HOLY SCRIPTURE (HEURISTICS)

Third Section

EXPLANATIONS OF THE TEXT

MAPS AND ILLUSTRATIONS

FIRST PART

PRACTICAL HANDBOOK FOR THE STUDY OF THE BIBLE

INTRODUCTION

THE Christian religion, and with it the whole civilization of Christian nations, is based upon Israel. The modern world, which calls itself Christian, is inseparably connected with the people of Israel, and the new Covenant between God and man, instituted by Christ, is only the extension and development of the old Israelite Covenant. Out of Israel proceeded the Saviour and salvation for the whole world. "Salvation is of the Jews" are words used by Christ Himself in His conversation with the Samaritan woman (John iv. 22). Amidst the Israelites grew up the body of literature also, that both Jews and Christians venerate as "Holy Writ." What Greece and Rome received from the East they passed on with their own additions to the West, and thence the benefits of salvation have been spread abroad over the whole world.

Not only believers, but also unbelievers, study Holy Scripture with peculiar interest. The former do so for their own edification, to strengthen their faith and to find means to defend the truth; the latter often show even greater zeal, if possible, in their efforts to undermine the foundations of faith. No one can attain to a full comprehension of the documentary evidence for our faith without taking into consideration the circumstances of the early history of the Jewish race and the course of events affecting this people.

Therefore, before beginning to discuss Holy Scripture, we propose to give some account of the Holy Land, including a sketch of the history and religious institutions of Israel. Then we can proceed to discuss the Bible and its interpretation.

THE HOLY LAND

GEOGRAPHY [1]

1. SITUATION OF PALESTINE

IF Israel was the nation chosen by God to preserve the true religion and to be instrumental in the salvation of mankind, — and for the present we shall assume this to be the case, — then it was but fitting that a suitable habitation should be assigned to this people, where it might live its own life and fulfill the task assigned to it. No country could be found better adapted to this purpose. (1) Palestine resembled a lofty fortress, shut off and protected on all sides from hostile invasions. In the north Lebanon formed a strong boundary; on the west was the sea, the stormy breakers of which made approach on that side almost impossible; the south and the east were protected by deserts. In this way the inhabitants of this country

---

[1] Apart from the sacred writings themselves, we derive our knowledge of the geographical features of Palestine from the works of some Greek and Latin authors who mention the East, and especially the little Jewish nation. Chief among these are Strabo the geographer, and the Elder Pliny; but Herodotus, Diodorus of Sicily, Plutarch and Tacitus also supply information. Allusion must be made, moreover, to the *Onomasticon* (Name book) of Holy Scripture, compiled by Eusebius and translated into Latin by Saint Jerome (printed by Vallarsi among Saint Jerome's works; *cf. Onomastica sacra*, ed. de Lagarde, Göttingen, 1887). Descriptions written by travelers, and especially by pilgrims in biblical countries, are also important. The earliest pilgrim's book is the *Itinerarium Burdigalense*, the author of which was an unknown Christian from Bordeaux, who visited the Holy Land about 333 A. D.; but the *Peregrinatio s. Silviæ Aquitanæ* (385–388), Rome, 1888, and the *Peregrinatio s. Paulæ*, by Saint Jerome, are almost equally old. The *Hodœporicon s. Willibaldi*, Eichstädt, 1881, contains an account of a journey made by this saint in the years 723–727. *Cf. Itinera hierosolymitana*

were cut off from intercourse with the world and its errors, and were able to live in peace and to serve the true God undisturbed. (2) Palestine lay in the center of the civilized world as known to the ancients. Its seclusion was not absolute, for it was surrounded by civilized countries, viz., Assyria and Babylonia, Phœnicia and Egypt, Greece and Italy. Jerusalem lay midway between Babylonia and Athens and between Ninive and the mouth of the Nile. The chief trading routes skirted the boundaries of Palestine and the great trading cities of Tyre and Sidon, Damascus, Ninive and Babylon were all in its neighborhood. Thus it was possible for God's chosen people to enjoy all the benefits of civilization without being forced to share its disadvantages. (3) The position of Palestine was favorable to its future task. Its central situation between the three continents of the ancient world was carefully adapted by Providence for the speedy dissemination amongst all countries of the tidings of the Messianic kingdom, when the time for redemption should come. Such a position was of the utmost importance at a period when almost all journeys were made on foot, apart from scanty intercourse by means of caravans, and navigation, which was carried on with great difficulty. Nowadays it is scarcely possible to form any idea of the obstacles to travel and transport that existed in antiquity.

sæc. IV–VIII ex recensione Pauli Geyer (Corp. script. eccl. lat. Vindob., T. xxxviiii.), Leipz., 1898. Many pilgrims' books have come down to us from the Middle Ages, and of the more recent books of travels we may mention particularly the works of Niebuhr, Seetzen, Chateaubriand, Schubert, Geramb, Robinson, Tobler, Mislin, Sepp, Dixon, Schegg, Messmer, Socin, Keppler, Fahrngruber, Liévin, Bädeker-Benzinger and Rückert; also Meistermann's Nouveau guide de Terre Sainte avec 23 cartes et 140 plans, Paris, 1906. — Atlas Scripturæ sacræ, auctore R. de Riess, ed. 2, Friburgi, Br., 1906. M. Hagen, S.J., Atlas Biblicus, Paris, 1907.

Architectural remains and pieces of sculpture that have come down to us from early times are also interesting, but very few remains of this kind have been preserved in Palestine. Further information regarding the sources of our knowledge of biblical geography may be obtained by referring to the Catholic Encyclopedia; Roehricht, Bibliotheca geographica Palæstinæ, Berlin, 1890; Cheyne and Black, Encyclopædia biblica, London, 1901; Hastings, "A Dictionary of the Bible," Edinburgh, 1898–1902; Vigouroux, Dictionnaire de la Bible, Paris.

Ezechiel v. 5: "Thus saith the Lord God: This is Jerusalem, I have set her in the midst of the nations, and the countries round about her."

Ezechiel xx. 6: "I lifted up my hand for them (the Israelites) to bring them out of the land of Egypt, into a land which I had provided for them, flowing with milk and honey, which excelleth amongst all lands."

Deuteronomy iv. 6: (The heathen are to say of the Israelites,) "Behold a wise and understanding people, a great nation."

Cf. Gen. xii. 7; xiii. 14; xv. 7, 18; xvii. 8; xxvi. 4, etc.; Deut. xxxii. 8, etc.; xxxiii. 28, 29.

2. EXTENT

In its configuration Palestine falls into two parts, being divided by the Jordan into a large region lying to the west of the river and a smaller one lying to the east. The country to the west of the Jordan is Chanaan, properly so called, stretching from Lebanon in the north to the Arabian desert in the south, and from the Jordan on the east to the sea on the west. The smaller district east of the Jordan was formerly called Galaad or Gilead,[1] and, in the time of Christ, Peræa; it extends from the range of Hermon on the north to the Arnon on the south, which river flowing from the east falls into the Dead Sea. On its eastern side this district is gradually merged in the great plain of the Euphrates. Between these two regions lies the valley of the Jordan, now called El Ghor = the depression. Palestine extends, therefore, from latitude 31° N. to beyond 33° N., and from longitude 52° E. to beyond 54°E. Its length from north to south is approximately 150 English miles and its breadth from east to west 125 miles. Its total area is about the same as that of the kingdom of Belgium.

3. NAMES

The oldest name for the chief part of the country was Chanaan. This name was borne by Cham's fourth son, the ancestor of the Chanaanites, who occupied all the land west of the Jordan. The name Chanaan therefore excludes the dis-

---

[1] גִּלְעָד is interpreted as meaning "the rugged region," from גָּלַע rough, rugged; but the traditional meaning is "hill of testimony" (see Gen. xxxi. 21, etc.).

trict eastward of the Jordan, but includes Phœnicia, and when in course of time the Chanaanites were driven to the northwest as the Israelites settled in the country, only Phœnicia retained the old name of Chanaan. ("The woman of Chanaan," Matt. xv. 22.)[1] Other names are: the Land of Israel, because it was inhabited by the descendants of Jacob or Israel; Land of the Hebrews, i. e. the descendants of Heber, or the people from beyond;[2] Land of Yahweh (God), because the country was always to be regarded as belonging to God in a peculiar degree, and He permitted the Israelites to dwell in it under definite conditions; Land of Juda, because from the time of David and Solomon onwards the tribe of Juda was pre-eminent, and because the exiles who returned from the Babylonian captivity belonged almost exclusively to this tribe, so that the people came to be known as Jews, and Greek and Roman writers speak of the whole country as Judæa. The Jews call Palestine the Holy Land because it belonged especially to God and was sanctified by God's presence in the Temple; and Christians give

[1] It is possible to derive Chanaan from *kana'*, to bend, to settle down, and thus Chanaan would mean the low-lying land, as opposed to *'aram*, the high ground (Maurer, *Lexikon*). The early inhabitants might have been called Chanaanites, the low-landers, and in this case the name of the founder of the race would not have been Chanaan, but would simply be unknown. This interpretation is, however, inaccurate. Chanaan is a mountainous country and Aram is chiefly a plain watered by rivers; hence Aram cannot mean "high ground," and the origin of the word is doubtful. We may therefore assume that the name of the founder of the race was transferred to the country inhabited by the race. — As the Phœnicians were traders, the Israelites often called all merchants "Chanaanites."

[2] Ewald derives the name from *Heber*, but it seems better to connect it either with *'abar*, to pass over, or with *'eber*, beyond. The name seems to have been originally given to the Israelites by the heathen inhabitants, because they came from beyond the Jordan. They generally spoke of themselves as the Children of Israel. "Israel" means "God fighteth," — a very suitable name for the community of believers, who were constantly assailed by enemies and seemed again and again to be on the verge of destruction, but nevertheless outlasted all their foes, because God fought for and with them. Thus the followers of God under the new dispensation are known as the "Church Militant." *Cf.* Wellhausen, *Isr. u. jüd. Geschichte*, 15. The struggle described in Gen. xxxii. 24, etc., when Jacob's name was changed to Israel, probably signifies that Jacob's descendants would be punished for their repeated resistance to God's commands, just as Jacob was lamed in wrestling.

it the same name because it was the scene of our Lord's life and death. It is called the Land of Promise (Heb. xi. 9), or the Promised Land, because God promised it to the patriarchs as their dwelling place. Lastly, the name Palestine comes from *peléschet* or Philistine-land; this name was originally given only to the strip of coast on the southwest inhabited by the Philistines, but the Greeks and Romans, who visited the coast before they penetrated inland, applied the name to the whole country.

4. CLIMATE

Lying as it does in latitude 32°, Palestine has a mild climate, and suffers neither from excessive heat nor from extreme cold. The seasons differ from one another less than they do with us, and in Holy Scripture as a rule only two seasons, winter and summer, are mentioned. Winter lasts from the beginning of November until March, but is not so cold as ours. It sets in with the early rains (*jore* or *chariph*), which soften the ground and facilitate the sowing of the winter crops (barley and wheat). Rain continues to fall intermittently during the following months, and occasionally snow is seen, but seldom lies more than a few days; the earth hardly ever freezes. February is the wettest month of the year. Corn reaches its full height in March, and after the late rains (*malgosch*) at the end of this month the summer crops are sown.[1] The corn grown in winter is harvested in April and May, and then the summer sets in, during which rain seldom falls; the earth soon loses its verdure and most of the brooks dry up. The heat increases rapidly and is very oppressive in August, when the thermometer often rises above 100° Fahrenheit. The nights, however, are cool and there is abundant dew. The days vary in length from ten to fourteen hours. In December the sun rises a little before seven and sets about five; in June it rises a little before five and sets soon after seven.

---

[1] The farmers anxiously await the rain, for it causes the floors to be filled with wheat and the presses to overflow with wine and oil (Joel ii. 24). Job boasts that men waited for him as for rain and they opened their mouth as for a latter shower (xxix. 23).

5. CONFIGURATION [1] *features*

Almost the whole country is hilly, as it is crossed by off-shoots of the Lebanon range. Lebanon itself (= the white mountain) lies to the north of Palestine and belongs not to it but to Syria; Little Lebanon (*Antilibanus*) to the east and Hermon, about 10,000 feet high, with its summit always covered with snow, likewise belong to Syria. Between these two ranges lies a broad, deep valley called Cœlosyria (κοίλη Συρία = hollow Syria) which never formed part of Palestine.

1. Offshoots of Mount Lebanon form the hill country westward of the Jordan. The most conspicuous heights in the north are Thabor (1850 feet), and the promontory of Carmel (1800 feet above the Mediterranean). Farther south, in Samaria, are Garizim and Ebal, both about 2500 feet high, and still farther, near Jerusalem, the Mount of Olives reaches a height of about 2650 feet, while some points near Hebron, quite in the south, are 2800 feet above sea level. The whole range is intersected by numerous valleys, the broadest being the plain of Esdrelon, watered by the brook Kison. Towards the east the mountains terminate abruptly with the valley of the Jordan, but towards the west they sink in a succession of terraces down to the sea. Along the coast is a flat strip of fertile land, known as the Plain of Saron, where the Philistines dwelt.

2. The mountains east of the Jordan are a prolongation of the Little Lebanon range, and are from 1300 to 2200 feet above the sea. On the east they sink gradually down to the great plain of the Euphrates, but on the west the descent to the valley of the Jordan is steep and abrupt. The high ground is intersected by several deep valleys, along which rivers flow, the chief being the Jabbok and the Arnon.

3. The valley of the Jordan runs nearly due north and south between these ranges of hills and extends from the foot of Hermon to the Dead Sea, and even beyond it, being shut in by steep hills on either side. Its length is about 125 English miles,

---

[1] A fuller account of the configuration of Palestine will be found in J. Wimmer's *Palästinas Boden mit seiner Pflanzen- und Tierwelt*, Cologne, 1902.

and its breadth varies from 6 to 13 miles. Its climate is mild,
and its soil more fertile than that of the hill country. The
Jordan (*Hajjarden,* the descending) rises on Mount Hermon
and is the chief river in the Holy Land; owing to the rapid
slope of the land it flows very quickly, and contains about
thirty waterfalls; it is not navigable. Quite in the north, not
far from its source, it flows through the small, swampy Lake
Merom, and ten miles further on it enters the beautiful Lake
of Genesareth. The lake is over 600 feet below the sea level,
is 14 miles long and 6 broad, and has sweet, clear water, abounding in fish. Its banks are picturesque, though now desolate. In
our Saviour's time they were covered with prosperous villages,
which He took pleasure in visiting. The Jordan leaves the lake
by a cataract at its southern end, being by this time a stream
about 40 feet broad and 7 feet deep. It does not flow in the
middle of the valley, but keeps along the eastern side, until after
a further course of nearly 80 miles it enters the Dead Sea.
This lake, called by the Arabs *Bahr Lut* or Lot's Sea, lies 1300
feet below sea level, and is 47 miles long and 10 miles across.
It is shut in by high, barren walls of rock, and is justly called
the Dead Sea, as no vegetation is visible anywhere near it and
no fish can live in it. The water is of a grayish green tint,
not quite transparent, and it contains 25 per cent of salt. It
is therefore more brackish than sea water and of a greater
specific gravity than the human body. The lake is divided into
two very different parts by a promontory stretching out from
the eastern shore. The northerly part is on an average 1100
to 1300 feet deep, while the southern part, which forms about
a quarter of the whole lake, is only 13 to 16 feet in depth.
This smaller part appears to be of later formation than the
rest, and it seems probable that the soil, permeated as it is
with resinous substances, was at some period set on fire, possibly
by lightning, and it gradually burnt itself out.[1]

[1] The subject has been discussed in a periodical called *Gäa* (1897, nos.
7 and 8, pp. 402, etc.) and the writers of the articles tend to ascribe the
present state of the lake to the action of an earthquake. *Cf.,* however,
Natur und Offenbarung, 1900, no. 3, and also Elbert, *Entstehung und
Geschichte des Toten Meeres.* In any case we see the results of punitive

This resulted in the formation of a depression over which the water of the northern part of the lake poured. It would seem that the water acquired its extreme saltness only after this occurrence, as it has since then been brought into contact with the bed of rock salt to the south of the lake. The biblical account of the catastrophe is given in Genesis xix. According to it four towns, Sodom, Gomorrha, Seboim and Adama, stood on a fertile plain to the south of the lake, and were destroyed in the time of Abraham, while Segor, a smaller city, was spared.[1]

6. NATURAL PRODUCTS

In consequence of Israel's want of faith and God's curse, Palestine is at the present time barren and unproductive. Formerly, however, it was a very fruitful country, capable of supporting four or five million inhabitants, whereas now it has scarcely 800,000.[2]

The natural causes of the present desolation are: the destruction of forests, which has caused the former abundant supply of water to diminish (Deut. viii. 7) ;[3] the numerous wars and

action on God's part, as recorded in Holy Scripture. Nature is God's instrument.

[1] Since 1900 a steamer, built in Hamburg and carrying thirty-four passengers besides cargo, has been plying regularly along the Dead Sea, which had been deserted for thousands of years. It has opened up trade between Jerusalem and Kerak, the old capital of the Moabites, which has a population of 1800 Christians and 6000 Mahometans, and is the only town of any commercial importance situated east of the Jordan.

[2] According to Fr. Liévin, and also Bädeker-Benzinger, *Palästina*, fifth ed., Leipzig, 1900, the population consists of about 440,000 Mahometans; 200,000 Jews, mostly immigrants in the last few years; 50,000 Christians, half of whom are Catholics and the other half Greeks not Uniates; and the remainder includes Armenians and Druses and a few Protestants. The population is only a quarter as dense as that of Germany.

[3] " For the Lord thy God will bring thee into a good land, of brooks and of waters, and of fountains, in the plains of which and the hills deep rivers break out." Even in the time of Esdras and Nehemias the high ground must still have been covered with forests, for in Nehemias viii. 15, we read the command to " Go forth to the mount and fetch branches of olive, and branches of beautiful wood." When forests are cut down the springs and brooks dry up, the banks of which are mentioned in Leviticus xxiii. 40, as the places where the willows grow.

devastations with which the country was harassed; and the
Turkish supremacy, which has always proved hostile to progress.
In spite of all this, however, Palestine still shows traces of
great fertility.[1]

Palestine is poor in minerals. There are some iron mines
in the north, and rock salt is found in the south, near the
Dead Sea, but these are almost all the mineral products. The
vegetable kingdom is abundantly represented.

At the time when the Scriptures were written the natural
fertility of the soil was increased by the extraordinary care
with which it was cultivated. Plots of ground were protected
against wild animals by hedges and walls and against floods
by being laid out in terraces. Artificial means of irrigation
were everywhere employed (cisterns, channels and ponds) wherever the natural water supply was deficient. Wheat and barley
were grown in great quantities, rye and oats were unknown.
The corn surplus was so large that much could be exported, and
the Phœnicians especially imported from Palestine the large
amount of grain that they required (cf. Acts xii. 20). Palestine
was very rich also in vineyards, and even now the vines often
grow to the height of trees and bear bunches of grapes weighing several pounds. There was no dearth of lentils and beans,
and flax was plentiful, though it is doubtful whether cotton
was cultivated. Among the trees with foliage may be mentioned
the fig, the olive, palms, pomegranate, apple (tappuach), oak,
terebinth, acacia, tamarisk and sycamore; they furnished the
ordinary wood used for building purposes; among conifers the
cypress and the cedar, the wood of the latter being used for
buildings of the highest class. Many shrubs abounded, such
as the oleander, myrtle, mandragora and hyssop.

According to Leviticus x. and xi., animals were divided into
four classes, — (1) the larger land animals, (2) water creatures, (3) birds, (4) other animals.

(1) The first class is subdivided into cattle (behema), i. e.

_____

[1] The sect of the German Templars have in modern times succeeded
in raising very fine crops in various places; e. g., near Jaffa and Jerusalem. The same is true of recent Jewish settlers in both the east and the
west of the country.

tame domestic animals, and beasts of the field (*chajjath haarez*), i. e. wild creatures. Of the domestic animals, oxen, sheep and goats were bred in great numbers,[1] so that every year many thousands of them could be sacrificed and killed for food. Cattle were used in agriculture, for plowing, for threshing out the corn, and for drawing wagons. Many asses were kept, intelligent animals, on which people generally rode, though they were also employed in drawing the plow and in working the larger mills. Camels, or rather dromedaries with one hump (animals with two humps occur only in the heart of Asia), served then, as now, to carry merchandise and travelers on long journeys. Horses were not much used until the time of David. Dogs were generally despised as savage and bloodthirsty and as resembling wolves (Ps. lviii. 7); it is only in the book of Tobias and in the New Testament that there is any mention of dogs as domestic animals. Swine were not kept at all.

Many wild animals were used for food, such as stags, antelopes or gazelles, and ibexes. The hare was regarded as unclean. Mention is made of the following savage beasts: the wild boar, the bear, the wolf, the lion, the panther, the hyena, the lynx and the jackal.

(2) Only such fish were eaten as had fins and scales. The Lake of Genesareth abounded in fish and at the time of our Lord many of the people in that neighborhood lived by fishing. In this region fish served as the usual relish eaten with bread (*cf.* Matt. xiv. 17).

(3) There were many pigeons, wood pigeons and turtledoves in Palestine (Ezech. vii. 16), and partridges, swallows and cranes were well known; hens are only mentioned in the New Testament. Birds of prey were numerous, and were all regarded as unclean. Birdcatching was common, but when a bird's nest was discovered it was forbidden to take with the young ones also

---

[1] In spring the cattle were driven out to pasture and left out during the whole summer, until the approach of winter. At night they were collected into a fold, a space surrounded by a low wall, at the entrance to which one of the shepherds kept watch all night. Such folds were often very large, and afforded room for several flocks under different shepherds. Similes from pastoral life abound in Holy Scripture, and our Lord speaks of Himself as the Good Shepherd, John x.

the mother bird (Deut. xxii. 6). In this way the various species were preserved.[1]

(4) Other creatures are divided into four classes, according to Leviticus xi. 20, etc.: (a) animals that walk upon the earth, such as the weasel, the mouse and various kinds of lizards; (b) those that creep on their belly, such as worms and all kinds of snakes; (c) small creatures with wings, such as grasshoppers (four varieties of which are mentioned in Lev. xi. 22 as edible), flies, gnats, wasps and bees; the latter abounded, although no attention was paid to bee-keeping, and honey was frequently eaten; (d) small creatures with many feet, such as beetles, ants, spiders and scorpions.

7. PLAGUES OF COMMON OCCURRENCE

Under this heading four things may be mentioned:

1. The Samum, a hot wind that prevails in the desert and is dangerous to life. It is injurious owing to its being very hot and dry, and it carries a quantity of fine dust with it. Men try to avoid it by throwing themselves flat on the ground, as it always blows a few feet above the earth.

2. The plague, which formerly visited Palestine very frequently and caused great loss of life. For the last few years the Holy Land has been spared this visitation.

3. Leprosy,[2] at one time very common throughout the East, but now of less frequent occurrence.

4. Locusts, a kind of grasshopper, capable of breeding in incredible numbers, so as often to overspread and devastate whole districts. Joel ii. 3, "The land is like a garden of pleasure before it, and behind it a desolate wilderness."

---

[1] In Lev. xi. 13–16, and Deut. xiv. 12, etc., the following birds are mentioned as unfit for food: the eagle, the griffin, the osprey, the kite, the vulture, the raven, the ostrich, the owl, the sea mew, the falcon, the screech owl, the cormorant, the ibis, the swan, the pelican, the purple water hen, the stork, the heron, the lapwing and the bat (among the ancients the bat was always reckoned as a bird).

[2] For full information regarding this disease, that is still prevalent in Palestine and elsewhere, see *Die Kath. Missionen*, 1902, 1903.

8. Dwellings, Food and Clothing

1. The Patriarchs lived as nomads in tents resembling those
of Bedouin Arabs at the present time. Covers made of goats'
hair or sometimes of linen were stretched over several uprights
and fastened down to the earth by means of pegs at the sides.
As a rule a curtain divided each tent into two apartments, one
for the men and the other for the women and little children;
occasionally there was a third apartment for the servants. Sometimes the women occupied a separate tent. A cluster of tents
round that of the chieftain, now called the Sheikh, formed a
village.

In mountainous parts of the country caves were often used as
dwellings, or artificial caves were hollowed in the rocks. The
Horites to the east of the Jordan were so called from their
living in caves (*chor* = cave). An entrance was often built in
front of the cave, so that the dwelling consisted of two parts.
The house of the Holy Family in Nazareth seems to have been
of this kind. Caves served also as places of burial, and were
then closed with a stone; such was our Lord's grave. *Cf.* also
Gen. xxiii. 9; Matt. viii. 28; John xi. 39.

2. The houses of the settled population were then as now
built of clay bricks, which were seldom baked, but only dried
in the sun; hence the buildings did not last long. The houses
of wealthy persons were built of hewn stone. The beams were
mostly of sycamore wood, i. e. the wood of the fig-mulberry
tree, which often grows to an enormous size. The walls were
lime-washed, and the floors were of clay, firmly stamped down.
As a rule a house had but one story and a flat roof, on which
the occupants could walk about and follow their employments,
especially in the cool of the evening. In order to prevent them
from falling down, it was often necessary to have a parapet
or a trellis round the roof (Deut. xxii. 8). Often there was
an upper room on the roof. A staircase led from the roof down
into the house or else to the road outside.

The door of the house was secured with a wooden bolt having
openings in it, into which a large key fitted, with a movable iron

tip, so that the bolt could be moved backwards and forwards. Above the door a text of Scripture was inscribed (Deut. vi. 9). The windows were not glazed, for glass was very costly, but they were latticed, and there were fewer of them than in our houses. One indispensable article in every house was a candlestick, — a wooden stand supporting a lamp. A hand mill was to be found in almost every house.

3. The food of the people consisted chiefly of grain. Wheat supplied the daily bread, and only the poor ate barley bread. Unripe grain was often cooked in oil, but as a rule it was ground to flour and baked into bread, which very frequently was unleavened, such as is still common in the East. The loaves were round or long in shape, about the size of a plate, and of the thickness of a finger. They were not cut but broken at meals. Bread was the chief article of food, hence in the Lord's Prayer we ask for " our daily bread." As a relish the Israelites often ate fruit or fried fish, although there was no lack of meat. Only very poor people or strict penitents ate locusts (Lev. xi. 22; Matt. iii. 4).

The ordinary beverage was water. The dearth of water in the East causes a draught of fresh water to be regarded as a great boon, hence a special reward is promised to the giver of it (Matt. x. 42; xxv. 42). As the water was seldom quite fresh, but drawn from cisterns, the common people in summer quenched their thirst (Num. vi. 3; Ruth ii. 9) with a sour drink (*chomez*) made from dates, into which they dipped their bread. The upper classes drank wine (*jajin*), which was no doubt mixed with water.[1] They had also an artificial wine (*schekar, σίκερα, sicera*) prepared by fermentation from grain, fruit or honey, with the addition of spices.

4. They usually took two meals daily, at noon and in the evening. The latter meal seems to have been the more important, as the solemn Paschal supper had to be celebrated at night (the meal at which the Holy Eucharist was instituted); also the wedding feasts were held in the evening (Matt. xxv.

[1] The Greeks and Romans drank wine much diluted with water. *Vinum temperatum* consisted of one part of wine to three parts of water.

1–13).[1] Both before and after a meal it was customary to wash the hands. In early times people sat at table (Judges xix. 6: "They sat down together and ate and drank"), but afterwards it became the fashion to recline on cushions,[2] leaning on the left arm, and using the right to carry the food to the mouth. The feet, that were of course bare, were stretched out at the back.

Triclinia

5. The clothing worn by the Israelites was commonly a tunic (*kethoneth,* χιτών, *tunica*) with a cloak or upper garment (*beged*) over it. The tunic was made of linen or woolen cloth and reached to the knees; it had very short sleeves or none at all. A coat that came down to the ankles and wrists was considered a festival garment (*kethoneth passim,* Gen. xxxvii. 3). The tunic was held in place by a girdle round the waist. Over it was worn the cloak, a square piece of cloth, which frequently served also as a bed covering. At its four corners were tassels fastened to a blue cord (*arba kanphoth* = fringes. Num. xv. 38). The feet were shod with sandals, and a band formed the headgear; women wore a veil. Isaias speaks of the vanity of women in dress (iii. 16–23). "The daughters of Sion are haughty, and have walked with stretched-out necks, and wanton glances of their eyes, and made a noise as they walked with their feet and moved in a set pace. . . . The Lord will take away the ornaments of shoes and little moons, and chains and necklaces, and bracelets, and bonnets, and bodkins, and ornaments of the legs and tablets, and sweet balls, and earrings, and rings, and jewels hanging on the forehead, and changes of apparel, and short cloaks, and fine linen and crisping pins, and looking-glasses, and lawns, and headbands, and fine veils."

The present state of the native population is very depressing. Their dwellings are mostly mud huts with flat roofs, and it is only through the narrow doorway that light and air can penetrate into them. The fellah generally owns a small plot

---

[1] The Greeks and Romans also took their chief meal (δεῖπνον, *cena*) in the evening. The midday repast was a lighter meal, more like our breakfast or luncheon, hence it was called *prandium,* i. e., early meal (πρὰν = πρώην, early, connected with πρωί).

[2] *Triclinia,* so called because there was generally room for three persons. These couches had no backs.

of land, on which he grows wheat, barley and a few vegetables. He may possess also some olive and fig trees, and perhaps some sheep, goats and fowls, an ass, a horse or a camel. The work of a fellahin family is divided between the husband, who looks after the land, and the wife, who does everything else. Thus the chief burden falls on the weaker sex. The woman has to provide the meals, which, simple as they are, involve fetching water, preparing fuel by mixing chaff with animals' dung, grinding the corn at the handmill, and making and baking the bread. She has moreover to make all the clothing, and carry a child on her back while she does her work.

The meals are very simple; the chief article of food is bread, mostly unleavened and newly baked, and as a relish a few olives or onions, figs or grapes; sometimes rice with sour milk. Meat is seldom seen. The ordinary beverage is water, generally drawn from a cistern, and only on festive occasions is a cup of coffee produced. Amusements as we understand them do not exist, with the sole exception of tobacco smoking. No one can be called well to do, although so very little is required to maintain a family. The chief reason for this deplorable state of affairs is that the taxation is very heavy. The tenth part of all that the land produces is claimed by the government. For every sheep, goat and pig three piasters (about 12 cents) must be paid yearly, and in addition there is a land tax of four piasters (16 cents) on every piece of land worth 1000 piasters ($40.00). All non-Mahometans have to purchase exemption from military service, and according to Liévin each man has to pay yearly 38 piasters ($1.50). Besides all this there are tolls on bridges and roads, customs duties, death duties, trade taxes, etc. Moreover the manner of collecting the taxes makes them more oppressive; all taxes, but especially the tax on land produce, are generally leased — the man who accepts the contract paying a fixed sum to the government and then collecting the tax for himself, in doing which he is often assisted by armed men, and tales of atrocities are by no means uncommon. The fellah is often obliged to borrow money from usurers, who charge from 100 to 200 per cent interest. Turkish officials seldom draw a fixed salary with any regularity, and each tries to wring money out of his unhappy subordinates to make up for his own arrears of salary. In this way there is no end to the extortions.

The European immigrants, who are now fairly numerous, are in a far better position, and are engaged in trade and in opening up means of communication. Their profits increase rapidly. The chief exports are oranges, oil and wine, while every kind of European produce is imported. It is hoped that considerable impulse to progress in Palestine and Syria will be caused by the Anatolian railway, which, when completed, will serve as a connection between the countries near the Euphrates and those of the West.

9. Inhabitants before the Israelites

Before God's chosen people settled in Palestine, the land had already had Semitic and afterwards Chamitic inhabitants. Tribes of Chanaanite origin had come into the country possibly from the northwest, but more probably from the east, and had mingled with the earlier Semitic population and had adopted its language and lost their own. Abraham and his descendants likewise lost their Aramaic dialect and acquired that of the country, which on their account was designated Hebrew.

To the old Semitic inhabitants of Palestine belonged the following tribes: (1) the Pherezites, mentioned in Gen. xiii. 7, as living near Bethel; (2) the Raphaites (*Rephaim* = giants), in the district east of the Jordan (Gen. xiv. 5); (3) the Enakites (*Anaqim* = long-necked), who were also men of great stature, living near Hebron in the south. They were to a great extent exterminated by Josue (Num. xiii. 22, 28; Jos. xi. 21); (4) the Hevites or Avvites (*'Avvim,* Deut. ii. 23), who came into conflict with the Philistines and were subdued by them. They seem not to have been akin to the Philistines, but to have been of the same race as the Hevites of Chanaan (see p. 21); (5) the Kenites (*qenim,* Gen. xv. 19), who lived in the southeast, but now and then were in alliance with the Amalakites, whose lands lay still farther south (I Kings, xv. 6). To the same race belonged the Rechabites, a small tribe who lived by breeding cattle (they are mentioned in Jeremias xxxv.), and also perhaps the Cenezites and the Cedmonites (Gen. xv. 19). Melchisedech, king of Salem, was undoubtedly a Semite, but his lineage is unknown.

The greater part of the country, however, before the coming of the Israelites, was occupied by the Chanaanites, descendants of the fourth son of Cham. Chanaan had eleven sons (Gen. x. 15–18), and the tribes descended from six of them settled along the seacoast in the northwest. The Greeks called them Phœnicians from the color of their skin (φοίνικες, from φοίνιξ, reddish purple). The tribes descended from the other five sons settled in Palestine itself. They were:

1. The Hethites, descended from Cheth, Chanaan's second son. They lived in the south of the country. It was from them that Abraham bought a plot of land as a burial place (Gen. xxiii.). Like the Amorites they spread over the Holy Land, and founded a great empire in the north, with two principal cities, Kades on the Orontes and Karkemisch on the Euphrates. The Hethites are compared as warriors with the Egyptians in IV Kings, vii. 6, and in early Egyptian records there is mention of wars between the Egyptians and the Heta or Hethites. Rameses II (about 1350), called by Herodotus Sesostris, was forced to ratify peace with them by marrying a Hethite princess. The Hethites were a source of danger to the Assyrians also, until Sargon took Karkemisch in 717, and destroyed their power. That they were of Chanaanite origin is proved by their worshiping Baal and Astarte.[1]

2. The Jebusites, descended from Jebus, Chanaan's third son. They lived in and round Jerusalem, which was at that time called Jebus.

3. The Amorites, descended from Amor, the fourth son, are mentioned as living in the south, near the Dead Sea, but they settled also far to the north, in the country east of the Jordan.

4. The Gergesites were descended from Girgas, the fifth son of Chanaan; their abode is unknown.

---

[1] See Sayce, " Fresh Light from Ancient Monuments," pp. 96–99. It is possible that the Hethites ought to be identified with the Hyksos. Sayce, however, regards the Hyksos as Western Semites.

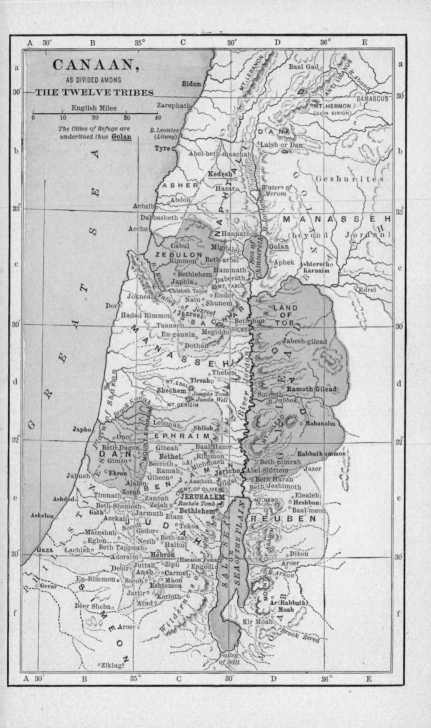

CANAAN,
AS DIVIDED AMONG
THE TWELVE TRIBES

English Miles

0   10   20   30   40

The Cities of Refuge are underlined thus **Golan**

A   30'   B   35°   C   30'   D   36°   E

a

30'

b

33°

30'

c

30'

d

32°

30'

e

30'

f

Baal Gad
Sidon
Zarephath
MT. LEBANON
R. Abana
ANTI LIBANUS
DAMASCUS
MT. HERMON
(SION SIRION)
B. Leontes
(Litany)
Tyre
Abel-beth-maachah
Laish or Dan
D A N
Kedesh
Hazar
Waters of Merom
Geshurites
ASHER
Abdon
Achzib
Dabbasheth
Accho
Hannathon
M A N A S S E H
(beyond Jordan)
Cabul
Migdalel
Golan
ZEBULON
Rimmon
Beth-arbel
Aphek
shteroth Karnaim
Bethlehem
Hammath
Japhia
Daberath
Chisloth Tabor
MT. TABOR
Edrei
Jokneam
Endor
Dor
Nain
Shunem
LAND OF TOB
Hadad Rimmon
Jezreel
Beth-shan
M A N A S S E H
Taanach
Megiddo
GILBOA
En-gannin
Jabesh-gilead
Dothan
Thebez
Tirzah
MT. EBAL
Shechem
Josephs Tomb
Ramoth Gilead
Jacobs Well
MT. GERIZIM
Succoth
R. Jabbok
Mahanaim
Lebonah
Shiloh
Japho
Ono
E P H R A I M
Beth Dagon
Gibeah
Baal-Hazor
Gimzo
Bethel
Rimmon
Rabbath ammon
D A N
Ai
Michmash
Beeroth
Ramah
Anathoth
Jericho
Beth-nimrah
Abel Shittem
Jazer
Ekron
Gibeon
Gilgal
Beth Haram
Ajalon
Beth Jeshimoth
Zorah
MT. OF OLIVES
Elealeh
Timnath
Zelah
JERUSALEM
MT. NEBO
Heshbon
Ashdod
Zanoah
Rachels Tomb
Baal-meon
Beth-Shemesh
Bethlehem
Askelon
Gath
Jarmuth
Etam
R E U B E N
Azekah
Socoh
Tekoa
Mareshah
Gedor
Beth-zur
Eglon
Nezib
Halhul
Dibon
Gaza
Beth Tappuah
Lachish
Adoraim
Hebron
Aroer
Juttah
Z
Gerar
Debir
Anab
Ziph
Carmel
Engedi
R. Arnon
En-Rimmon
Socoh
Maon
Ar (Rabbath) Moab
Jattir
Eshtemoa
Beer Sheba
Arad
Kerioth
Kir Moab
Aroer
Brook Zered
Ziklag?
Valley of Salt

A   30'   B   35°   C   30'   D   36°   E

5. The Hevites, descended from Chev, the sixth son, lived in the north, near Lebanon.

Besides the Semitic and Chanaanite tribes, the Philistines had settled in the south, before the time of Abraham;[1] they were a Chamitic people (Gen. x. 14; xx. 2, etc.) that had migrated from Kaphtor.[2] Their chief towns were Gaza, Asdod (Azotus), Ascalon, Gath and Accaron.

All these tribes were governed by rules of their own; almost every district had a king.

10. Palestine as divided among the Israelites

When the Israelites entered the Promised Land under Josue, the previous inhabitants were either conquered or driven out, and some were exterminated by God's command as a punishment for their sins. Then the country was divided among the twelve tribes as their possession. The tribe of Levi, whose duty it was to attend to the worship of God, received no land, but the members of that tribe were distributed over the whole country and occupied forty-eight towns. The tribe of Joseph received two portions, as Ephraim and Manasses were adopted by Jacob (Gen. xlviii. 5). (1) The territory assigned to the tribe of Juda lay in the south. (2) Westward of it was that belonging to Simeon, the weakest of the tribes. (3) To the north of Juda lay Benjamin. (4) the tribe of Dan, that was very numerous, lived at first between Juda and the Philistines, but as its territory was too small, and constant fighting was required for its defense, part of the tribe migrated northwards and settled near the town of Lais, which was thenceforth called Dan. (5) Ephraim, a large tribe, occupied the center of the country. (6) To the north of Ephraim dwelt half the tribe of Manasses,

[1] In the Septuagint the name Philistine is rendered Ἀλλόφυλοι, strangers, so possibly it ought to be connected with the Ethiopian word *falasa*, to travel or wander. "Pheleschet" is therefore the strangers' land, and if this be correct the Philistines did not belong to the original Semitic or Chanaanite population.

[2] Kaphtor was a strip of coast to the east of the delta of the Nile. It must not be identified with Crete, nor with Cappadocia, as is done in the Septuagint and the Vulgate versions of Amos ix. 7. The Philistines certainly came from Egypt.

the other half having been left by Moses in the northern part of the country east of the Jordan. (7) The tribe of Issachar lived round the plain of Esdrelon. (8) The tribe of Zabulon settled to the west of the Lake of Genesareth. (9) The tribe of Aser lived near Mount Carmel. (10) Nephtali occupied the northernmost part of the country. (11) Ruben dwelt in the south of the district east of the Jordan, and (12) Gad in the north.

In the period following the captivity this division of the country fell into disuse, as the majority of those who returned belonged to the tribe of Juda, and thenceforth the whole nation became known as Jews.

At the time of our Lord, under the Roman government, the land west of the Jordan was divided into three parts; viz., Judæa, Samaria and Galilee. The country east of the Jordan was called Peræa.

11. Description of Places

I. *Judæa*

1. *Jerusalem*,[1] formerly called Salem, then Jebus, then Ælia Capitolina (under the Roman Emperor Hadrian) and now El Kuds, the holy (its Mahometan name), is situated on an uneven slope, divided from northwest to southeast by a depression, which Josephus calls the Tyropœon, and surrounded by valleys on the north, south and west.[2]

[1] יְרוּשָׁלַיִם = either "vision of peace" or "foundation of peace," according to the derivation of *jeru* from a verb meaning "to see" or from one meaning "to found." In the hymn *Cœlestis urbs Jerusalem, beata pacis visio* the former derivation is accepted. The dual form seems to refer to the upper and lower cities. As early as 1400 B. C., in the cuneiform inscriptions of Tell el Amarna, the name of the town was Urusalem. The Assyrian form is Urusalimmu.

[2] Upon two ridges of unequal height,
  That front each other, stands Jerusalem,
  Through which there runs a narrow vale, whose site
  Divides the town in two, and severs them.
  Three sides a steep ascent the town defends,
  But on the fourth you go, nor seem to rise,
  And this plain side, which toward the north extends,
  By loftiest ramparts more defended is.
    Torqu. Tasso, Jerus. Delivered, III, 55, trans. K. James.

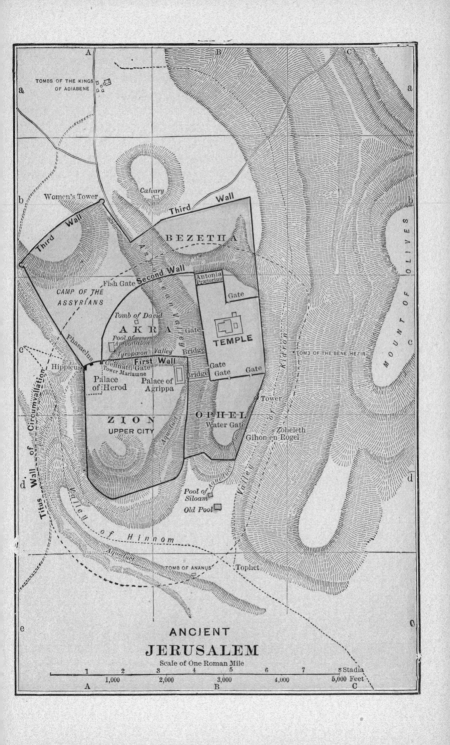

ANCIENT
JERUSALEM

Scale of One Roman Mile

1   2   3   4   5   6   7   8 Stadia
1,000   2,000   3,000   4,000   5,000 Feet

The town originally did not extend beyond Mount Sion on the southwest, and consisted of the stronghold of Sion and the old city clustered about it. It was here that David dwelt. Solomon enlarged the town and built the Temple, which occupied a large area on the low hill called Moria, situated northeast of Sion and due north of Ophel.[1]

After the captivity the second Temple was erected on the same site, and the restored city retained its former limits. Antiochus Epiphanes built a fortress to the north of the Temple, on the Hill of Akra (II Mach. iv. 12), in order to dominate the Temple. Round this fortress a new quarter of the town gradually arose, and as it was on a lower level than Sion, it was known as the Lower City.[2]

Herod I, who had a mania for building, effected great changes in the fortress of Sion, the Temple and Akra, which he called Antonia. It was here that our Saviour was brought before

---

[1] Recent explorers have sought Mount Sion in the east of the city, though this is contrary to tradition, their reason being that we often read that the Lord dwelleth on Sion, and this must refer to the hill on which the Temple stood. The periodical entitled *Das Hl. Land* (Cologne, Oct. 1, 1896, p. 77) contains, however, the following important information: " The most recent discovery in the topography of Jerusalem is that of the steps of the city of David. It is scarcely possible to doubt that these are the steps of the city mentioned in Nehemias iii. 15 and xii. 36. These newly discovered steps are on the southwest hill, not on the southeast, but where the former hill slopes down in an easterly direction towards the Tyropœon, on the west side of the valley. They could only lead up to the southwest hill. Hitherto about fifteen steps have been found. . . . The problem of Mount Sion is therefore approaching its solution, and in all probability the traditional Sion will win the day, and the theory of the southeast hill will be proved erroneous." — If we occasionally read that God dwelleth in Sion, Sion stands for Jerusalem, just as the Vatican often means Rome, and the Seine Paris. The name is also used figuratively for the theocratic Jerusalem. (The steps mentioned in Neh. xii. 36, can hardly be the same as those referred to in iii. 15, but were steps in the city wall.) Gatt, a missionary in Gaza, who knows Jerusalem very thoroughly, in a work on the hills of Jerusalem defends the traditional position of Sion, and Rückert does the same. In a recent work Gatt aims at justifying the traditional view and at establishing it more firmly.

[2] According to Mommert (*Topographie des alten Jerusalems*, Leipz., 1903), an upper and a lower city existed as early as the time of Josue. Mommert does not locate David's stronghold in the upper city of Sion, but on the Hill of Akra, which he thinks was included with the upper city at a very early period under the general name of Sion.

Pilate, and from this place of His condemnation He carried the cross to the place of His execution outside the city.[1]

To the north of this fortress, on the hill Bezetha and also to the west of it, a new quarter has gradually sprung up, called the suburb or new town.

Jerusalem as it now is, situated in a barren, rocky region, has a desolate and lifeless appearance, and makes a gloomy impression upon those who behold it. The words of Jeremias' lamentation are even more applicable now than they were after the Babylonian devastation: " How doth the city sit solitary that was full of people! " (Lam. i. 1.) The population has, however, increased rapidly in the last few years, and has risen from 20,000 to 66,000 (1905). Of these 45,000 are Jews, 8000 Mahometans, 6000 Greeks (Orthodox Church), 2500 Latins, 950 Armenians, 800 Protestants, 250 Uniate Greeks, 150 Copts, 100 Abyssinians, 100 Jacobite Syrians, 50 Uniate Syrians and a few Maronites. During the nineteenth century twelve Catholic churches and several chapels were built in Jerusalem, but of the thirty existing Catholic places of worship only three are of ancient origin; viz., the Church of the Holy Sepulcher, St. Anne's, and the Grotto of the Agony; the rest have all been built since 1840. (The schismatic Greeks possess thirty-four churches and chapels, the Russians five, all newly built, and the Protestants four. *Cf. Das Hl. Land*, 1897, p. 37.) Since 1892 there has been a railway connecting Jerusalem with Jaffa. At the present time the still existing " Pools of Solomon," which he made to the south of Bethlehem, are being reconstructed so as to supply again the capital with water. The watercourses will follow the same lines as they did three thousand years ago.

The following places in and near Jerusalem are familiar to us, as their names occur in Holy Scripture:

(a) *Golgotha*, i. e. place of a skull (*golgotha = golgoltha,* the Aramaic form of the Hebrew word *gulgoleth*. The Evangelists translate the name as κρανίου τόπος = *calvariæ locus*). The name is certainly not derived from skulls of executed malefactors. They would not have been allowed to lie about, as contact with a corpse or any part of one caused legal uncleanness.

---

[1] On this subject Father Barnabas Meistermann wrote a well-grounded argument in favor of the Catholic tradition regarding the holy places in Jerusalem. The same religious has written very careful monographs on the grave of Our Lady, on Thabor, Emmaus, Arimathea, and the home of John the Baptist (*Ain* = Karim St. John in the mountains). Several writers have attempted to prove that by Pilate's Pretorium is meant, not the fortress Antonia, but Herod's palace on Sion. If this were correct, would not the tradition regarding the Way of the Cross have to be abandoned?

The spot must have borne some resemblance to a skull, and have been bare and somewhat raised. It was here that our Saviour redeemed us by His death on the Cross. At that time the place was outside the city, and, according to an unbroken tradition, lay to the northwest of it. After our Lord's death Jerusalem was extended in this direction and so Golgotha came to be included within the city wall. Hence the Church of the Holy Sepulcher, which contains the place of the Crucifixion, is now within Jerusalem.[1]

From the point of view of accuracy the question may be asked whether, as our Lord was crucified "without the gate" (Heb. xiii. 12; *cf.* Matt. xxvii. 33, John xix. 15), the city wall at that time included or excluded the site of the present church of the Holy Sepulcher. Three walls may be considered:

(1) David's wall, which only surrounded Sion, and this, according to tradition, was the western hill.

(2) The wall of Ezechias and Manasses, restored by Nehemias after the Captivity, and still forming the city wall in our Lord's time. It branched off from the earlier wall and surrounded the city on the west, north and east, terminating at the Temple.

(3) Herod Agrippa's wall, begun about 43 A. D. The second wall is the one that we have to consider. Those who defend the literal accuracy of the text maintain that it was possible and even probable for the place of crucifixion to have been outside this wall. Their opponents hold that the second wall must have enclosed the site of the church of the Holy Sepulcher, as Jerusalem was then very populous. The difficulty has now been solved, and the question decided in favor of the text. In 1883 remains of the second wall were discovered, showing quite plainly that it did not include the site of the church. (Keppler, *Wanderungen, etc., im Oriente*, 208.)

(*b*) On the southern plateau of Mount Sion, outside the present Sion Gate and not far from the Christian cemeteries, is a huge building containing a mosque, in which, according to Mahometan tradition, King David is buried. There is probably no truth in this tradition.

Christians, on the other hand, assert that the room where the Last Supper was eaten used to be here, and tradition identifies the place further with the room where our risen Saviour

[1] Mommert has proved beyond all question that Constantine's basilica contained our Lord's sepulcher, Golgotha with a church called the Martyrion on it, the chapel of Saint Helena and the Finding of the Cross.

appeared to His Apostles in Jerusalem, and where the Holy
Ghost came down upon them. Finally we are told that it was
in this neighborhood that Mary, the mother of our Lord, lived
and died, for which reason the space to the north of the above-
mentioned building has been called the *Dormitio b. M. V.* It
was acquired in the autumn of 1898 by the German Emperor
William II, who presented it to the German Catholics, and a
church and a Benedictine Monastery have been erected on this
site.[1]

It is certain that from the very earliest times of Christianity
until 1551 there was a church here, Sancta Sion, the original
parent church of the world.[2]

(c) The Mount of Olives (*har hassethim*), so called from
the numerous olive trees with which it was formerly covered;
now only a few remain. It lies to the east of the town, about
a quarter of an hour's walk from it.

(d) Between the town and the Mount of Olives lies the
Valley of Josaphat with the brook Cedron (Kidron). The name
Josaphat (i. e. the Lord judgeth) seems to be very ancient,
although its use cannot be actually traced farther back than
to the time of Eusebius and Saint Jerome. The Cedron (i. e. the
dark or cloudy) receives water only from rains; its source has

---

[1] The monastery was given over to the German Benedictines on March
21, 1906; the church was opened in April, 1910.

[2] Of sources of information regarding the history of this site we mention as very important the following: Diekamp, *Hippolytos v. Theben*,
Münster, 1898, p. 96, etc.; Zahn, *Dormitio s. virginis u. das Haus des
Joh. Marcus* (*Neue kirchl. Ztschr.*, X, 5) ; Lagrange, *La dormition de la
s. vièrge et la maison de Jean-Marc*, in the *Revue biblique*, 1899, IV, 589.
It may be assumed that the house of John Mark's mother, where Peter
took refuge (Acts xii. 12), is identical with the room of the Last Supper, the room where our Lord appeared to the Apostles, and the room
where the Holy Ghost descended upon them; it is possible that Our
Lady too sought shelter there. Nirschl opposes the theory, based on
K. Emmerich's visions, that Mary died and was buried in Ephesus. We
may, however, very well believe that she joined Saint John there and remained there for some time, as is related in the visions of K. Emmerich.
J. Niessen, in a work entitled *Panagia Kapuli* (Dülmen, 1906), upholds
the unsatisfactory theory that Mary died at Ephesus. (*Panagia Kapuli*
= the Gate of the B. Virgin, is a little house situated to the south of the
ruins of Ephesus.) Bardenhewer and Lübeck do not agree with Niessen
on this point.

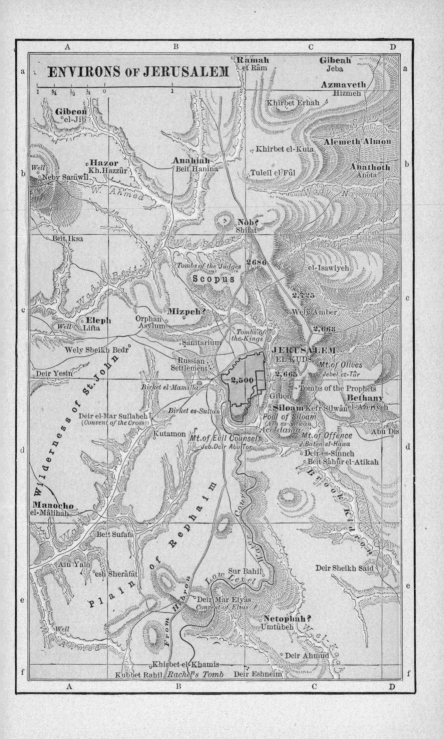

ENVIRONS OF JERUSALEM

A B C D

Ramah
et Râm
Gibeah
Jeba
Azmaveth
Hizmeh
Khirbet Erhah

Gibeon
el-Jib

Alemeth Almon

Khirbet el-Kuta

Hazor
Kh.Hazzûr
Anahiah
Beit Hanina
Anathoth
Anôta
Neby Samwil
Tuleil el-Fûl

W. Ahmed

Beit Iksa
Wady es Semar
Nob?
Shfat

el-Isawiyeh

Wady en Nar

Tombs of the Judges
2,680
Scopus

Wady Beit Hanina
2,725
Wely Amber

Eleph
Lifta
Mizpeh?
Well
Orphan
Asylum
Tombs of
the Kings
2,663

Wely Sheikh Bedr
Sanitarium
JERUSALEM
EL-KUDS
Mt. of Olives
Jebel et-Tûr

Deir Yesin
Russian
Settlement
2,500
2,665
Tombs of the Prophets

Birket el-Mamilla
Gihon
Bethany
el-Azeriyeh
Siloam Kefr Silwân
Pool of Siloam
Ain es-Silwan
Abu Dis

Birket es-Sultan
Aceldama

Deir el-Mar Sullabeh
(Convent of the Cross)
Kutamon
Mt. of Evil Counsel
Jeb. Deir Abu Tor
Mt. of Offence
J. Baten el-Hawa

Wilderness of St. John
Deir es-Sinneh
Beit Sâhûr el-Atikah

Manocho
el-Mâlihah
Brook Kidron

Beit Sufafa
Plain of Rephaim

Ain Yalo
esh Sherâfat
Sur Bahil
Deir Sheikh Said

Well
Low Level
Deir Mar Elyâs
Convent of Elias
Netophah?
Umtûbeh

From Hebron
Well

Deir Ahmud

Khirbet-el-Khamis
Kubbet Rahil Rachel's Tomb Deir Eshneim

A B C D

long been dry. Its course begins near Jerusalem and its mouth
is in the Dead Sea, but usually the river bed is quite dry.

(*e*) Gethsemane (the oil-press) was a lonely farm on the
western foot of the Mount of Olives, beyond the brook Cedron.
Beside it was a garden, whither Jesus withdrew before His
Passion.

(*f*) The Valley of Hinnom is to the south of Jerusalem.
The depression begins in the west and continues round Sion,
terminating in the southeast at the village and spring of Siloa,
and joining the Cedron Valley. It was here that the idolatrous
Israelites once offered their children to Moloch. From the
name *gehinnom* the word *gehenna,* hell, has been formed, and
in later times the Jews, mindful of the fires of Moloch and
the shrieks of the victims, applied the name of this abhorred
spot to the place of suffering of the damned.[1]

(*g*) On the eastern slope of the Mount of Olives lay the little
villages of Bethphage (house of figs) and Bethany (*beth anija*
= place of low ground), both familiar to us in the life of
Christ.

2. *Bethlehem.*[2] This little town, the birthplace of David
and of Christ, lies two hours' journey to the south of Jerusalem,
and is situated on the northern slope of a hill running east
and west. The Grotto of the Nativity lies to the east, at a
little distance from the town. Above it a church has been
built, and there is a monastery near it.

The latter is divided into three parts, one of which belongs to the
Latins, one to the schismatic Greeks and the third to the Armenians.
The Catholics have a little church of their own near their monastery, —
it is dedicated to Saint Catherine and serves as a parish church.[3]

[1] Hinnom seems to have been the name of some man, perhaps a Jebu-
site, as the designation *ge bene Hinnom* also occurs. *Cf.* Vigouroux,
Dict.

[2] i. e. house of bread, probably because much grain was grown in the
neighborhood.

[3] This church was rebuilt in 1880, by the assistance of the Emperor
of Austria, and it was consecrated on Aug. 18, 1882. In Bethlehem there
are still some descendants of the Crusaders, who call themselves Vene-
tians, and speak chiefly Italian. The Catholic community numbers 4000
souls. The rest of the 8000 inhabitants of Bethlehem are Greeks, and a
few Armenians and Mahometans. A very small part of the population

The Grotto of the Nativity and the large church dedicated to our Lady once belonged to the Catholics, but were seized by the Greeks, the church in 1758 and the Grotto in 1847.[1]

3. *Hebron* (= fellowship) lies in a beautiful mountainous region, six hours' journey south of Bethlehem. The town is well known from the history of Abraham and David. At the present time it has 10,000 inhabitants, who are almost all Mahometans. There is a mosque on the east of the town, containing the graves of the patriarchs. An hour's journey north of Hebron is the Valley Mambre, where Abraham dwelt for some time.

4. On the southern boundary of Chanaan was the town of *Beersabe* (= seven springs), which is often mentioned in Holy Scripture.

5. *Jericho,*[2] a very ancient city of the kings of Chanaan. It lay seven hours' journey to the east of Jerusalem, at some distance from the Jordan. Now it is deserted, and only ruins mark the site of the former city, and a tiny village called Riha reminds us of its name.

6. *Anathoth,* the birthplace of the prophet Jeremias, was a priestly city, one and one-half hours' journey north of Jerusalem.

7. *Rama,* now Ram, lay three hours' journey north of Jerusalem.

8. *Bethel,* now Beitun, the place where Jacob saw the ladder from heaven, is four and a half hours' journey north of Jerusalem. After the separation of the two realms it belonged to Samaria, and became one of the chief seats of idolatrous worship (*cf.* Amos vii.).

9. *Silo,* a little north of Bethel, now a place of ruins called

is Protestant; this denomination has a church and a school of its own. There are no Jews in Bethlehem.

[1] The well-justified claims of Latin Christians upon the holy places are almost all jeopardized by attacks made by schismatics. On Nov. 4, 1901, several Franciscans were severely injured in the Church of the Holy Sepulcher, as also happened on Jan. 22, 1907, in Saint Mary's at Bethlehem.

[2] i. e. the fragrant (from רוּחַ), not the moon-city (from וְרֵחַ). The neighborhood of this town formerly abounded in fragrant plants, such as balsams and rose trees.

Seilun, was the resting place of the Tabernacle at the time of the Judges.

10. *Emmaus* (see Luke xxiv. 13). It is now a village called Kubeibeh, and is situated 60 furlongs (three hours' journey) to the northwest of Jerusalem.[1]

11. *Lydda,* now Ludd, is mentioned in Acts ix. 33. It is believed to have been the birthplace of Saint Georgius, and lies ten hours' journey westward of Jerusalem. Near it is Ramle, which tradition identifies with Arimathea, although many people believe Rama near Jerusalem to be Arimathea.[2]

12. *Joppe* or *Jaffa,* a town on the Mediterranean; the place where Jonas took ship in order to flee to Tharsis. The town has 45,000 inhabitants, and is still, as it was in the Middle Ages, the usual landing place for pilgrims, although the stormy sea and the sunken rocks make the harbor unsafe.

[1] The name = *chammath,* to be hot, is equivalent to Thermæ. The district was formerly rich in springs. The Franciscans now have a church and a friary, and the German Holy Land Society has acquired some property there. Kubeibeh or Kubebe is, according to Haneberg's *Archäologie,* to be identified with Gabeon, frequently mentioned in the Old Testament, but its position is disputed. The above statement is based upon a tradition that goes back to the time of the Crusades. The Franciscans believe Kubeibeh to be the Emmaus mentioned by Saint Luke, and so do various other writers; but there are several other opinions on the subject. Some identify Emmaus with the present Amwas on the plain to the east of Jaffa. Eusebius and Saint Jerome both say that this place, which is also called Nicopolis, was the Emmaus of the Bible. It is, however, too far from Jerusalem, being at a distance of 176 furlongs, or nearly nine hours' journey, and so it cannot be reconciled with Saint Luke's account. Sepp thinks that the present Kulonieh (Colonia), about 30 furlongs from Jerusalem on the way to Jaffa, may have been Emmaus, but there is no tradition supporting this theory, and Kulonieh is too near. The Greeks believe Abu-Gosch, the ancient Kariathiarim, 60 furlongs from Jerusalem, to be Emmaus, but this view also is unsupported by tradition.

The Codex Sin. reads in Luke xxiv. 16, 160 furlongs, and not 60. Tischendorf and others regard this as an intentional alteration. After careful observations and personal investigations in Palestine, Belser has pronounced himself opposed to the Nicopolis theory, and in favor of Kubeibeh, chiefly on account of its distance from Jerusalem. The reason why Eusebius and Saint Jerome preferred Nicopolis is probably that in their time Emmaus-Kubeibeh was destroyed, devastated and forgotten. *Cf.,* however, Knabenbauer, *Comm. in Luc.,* p. 632.

[2] Ever since 1296 the Franciscans have had a mission at Ramle; in 1902 their chapel was transformed into a beautiful church.

II. *Samaria*

The central portion of Palestine derives its name from the town that was once the capital of the northern kingdom.

1. *Samaria* (Hebr. *schomron,* Gk. Σαμάρεια and afterwards Σεβαστή, which name is still retained, though the natives pronounce it Usbuste). The town was built by Omri, king of the northern State, about the year 930 B. C. It was situated on a hill which the king had bought from a certain Schemer, called in the Septuagint Σεμήρ, and in the Vulgate *Somer* (III Kings xvi. 24). It remained the capital for two hundred years, but was destroyed in 722, though subsequently rebuilt. Herod I enlarged it, and gave it the name of Sebaste in honor of the Emperor Augustus.[1]

At the present time it is only a village with 500 inhabitants. Among the ruins of the old town those of the Church of St. John the Baptist are conspicuous. According to tradition his body was buried here. Thirza (i. e. grace), which served for a short time as a royal residence, may have been in the neighborhood; perhaps it should be identified with the modern Tejazir, thirteen miles northeast of Sichem.

2. *Sichem* (Hebr. *schekem* = ridge or stretch of land) was the central point of the Holy Land, and lay fourteen hours' journey north of Jerusalem, between the hills Garizim and Ebal, the former being to the south, the latter to the north of the town. Sichem is mentioned as early as the time of Abraham and Jacob. After the division of the kingdoms, Sichem was the residence of the kings of the northern State. In Apostolic times it was generally called Neapolis, the new city, probably because it had been almost completely rebuilt under Vespasian. The modern name Nablus comes from Neapolis. The town now contains 25,000 Mahometan inhabitants. A small body of Samaritans, about 200 in number, still live at the foot of Garizim.

3. *Cæsarea,* situated on the west coast, and therefore known

---

[1] σεβαστὴ = augusta; σέβω, σέβομαι = to honor; σεβαστός = honored, honorable = augustus.

as Maritima, to distinguish it from Cæsarea Philippi, was built
by Herod I, and raised by Augustus to the dignity of an imperial
city. In Roman times the procurator of the province generally
lived here. Saint Paul was a prisoner here for two years. After
the destruction of Jerusalem, Cæsarea was regarded as the capital,
and very early became a bishop's see. In the eighteenth century
some part of the town was still inhabited, but now it all lies in
ruins.

III. *Galilee*

In the north of Chanaan the Israelites lived in the midst of
pagans, and hence this part of the country received the name
gelil haggojim = the heathen district, in Greek Γαλιλαία
τῶν ἐθνῶν, or simply Γαλιλαία (Is. viii. 23; I Mach. v. 15;
Matt. iv. 15). Its chief towns were:

1. *Nazareth* (from *nezer,* flower, hence Nazareth = city of
flowers) is never mentioned in the Old Testament. It lies on
a hill in southern Galilee, six hours' journey southwest of the
Lake of Genesareth. From very early times pilgrims have
visited Nazareth, and it soon possessed several churches, and
was a bishop's see in the Middle Ages. Since the fourteenth
century the little town has been decaying. In 1620 the Franciscans restored the Church of the Annunciation,[1] and in 1720
a friary, and then some other houses, arose from the ruins.
Nazareth has now 11,000 inhabitants, mostly Catholics.

2. The little town of *Naim,* now scarcely more than a village,
lay three hours' journey southeast of Nazareth.

3. *Cana,* now a village with 600 inhabitants, and known as

---

[1] The *casa santa,* or house of the Holy Family, is venerated at Loreto
in Italy. According to the legend it was brought to the west in 1291,
first to Dalmatia, and in 1395 to Loreto. A basilica has been built over
it. Many people have doubted whether it is genuine; the following are
the reasons for believing it to be so: (*a*) By permission of Pope Pius
IX in 1861 the Roman antiquarian Bartolini caused some stone and
mortar from the *casa santa,* and also some from the foundations of the
house at Nazareth, to be chemically examined, and they proved to be
exactly similar, whereas such stone and mortar are not used in Italy.
(*b*) In Kresser's work, *Nazareth, ein Zeuge für Loreto* (Graz, 1908), evidence is adduced to show that the house of the Holy Family was in
Nazareth until 1291, but vanished after that date. (*c*) Father Poisat,
S.J., in the *Univers,* 1907.

Kefr-Kana, is an hour and a half's journey north of Nazareth. This village, rather than the more distant Kana-Eldschelil,[1] ought to be regarded as the place where our Lord wrought His first miracle. It is believed to have been the birthplace of Saint Bartholomew the Apostle.

4. On the west coast of the Lake of Genesareth is the city of *Tiberias*, built by Herod Antipas and named after the Emperor Tiberius. It is now called Tubarich, and contains 8000 inhabitants of various creeds.

5. Not far away, and also on the west coast of the lake, was the village of *Magdala*, now Medschdel, which is thought to have been the birthplace of Saint Mary Magdalen.

6. Also in the same neighborhood was *Bethsaida*, the home of several of the apostles, but it cannot now be identified. Another Bethsaida with the additional name Julias ('Ιουλίας, -αδος, after the daughter of Augustus), lay on the northeast shore of the lake. The feeding of the five thousand took place near there.[2]

7. *Capharnaum*, our Saviour's favorite town, was on the north-west shore of the lake. In Saint Jerome's time it was still a town, though decaying. In the sixteenth century it was a heap of ruins, and now every trace of it has disappeared, so that its very site is a matter of discussion (*cf.* Matt. xi. 23).[3]

IV. *The Country East of the Jordan*

The southern part of the region east of the Jordan was formerly called Galaad or Gilead, and the northern part Basan; but at the time of our Lord the whole province was known as

---

[1] Sepp follows the *Onomasticon* of Eusebius in regarding Kana-Galil, four hours' journey north of Nazareth, as the scene of our Lord's first miracle. This is a mistake, for tradition always pointed to Kefr-Kana. *Cf.* Josue xix. 28.

[2] Sepp and Guthe think the Bethsaida on the northeast shore was the only town of that name, but they have many opponents.

[3] Most authorities regard the ruins at Tell-Hum (Sepp derives this name from τελώνιον, place of tribute) as marking the site of the ancient Capharnaum. Sepp prefers to identify it with Chan-Minieh, which lies farther south, not far from Medschdel, although he thus is at variance with the old pilgrims' reports and with Josephus.

Peræa, i. e. the land beyond, πέραν τοῦ Ἰορδάνου. At that period it was divided into three portions: (1) In the north were the five districts known as Gaulonitis, Ituræa, Auranitis, Trachonitis and Batanæa, these being the Greek forms of the Semitic names Golan, Jethur, Hauran, Trachona and Basan. (2) In the center eight towns, viz. Philadelphia (Rabbath Ammon), Raphana, Gerasa, Duim, Pella, Scythopolis, Gadara and Hippus, had formed a league with the more distant cities of Kanatha and Damascus, so that the Evangelists speak of the region as Decapolis, i. e. the ten cities. (3) The southern portion was Peræa in the narrower sense of the word, and, together with Galilee, was governed by Herod Antipas.

The best known towns in this country are:

1. *Cæsarea Philippi* in the north, originally called Paneas, so named from a cave in the neighborhood dedicated to the god Pan. The town was enlarged by Philip the Tetrarch and named Cæsarea, with flattering reference to Augustus. A mere hamlet known as Banias now stands on the site of the former city.

2. *Gerasa,* now Dscherasch, and Rabbath Ammon (= Philadelphia), now Amman, are situated farther south, in what was once Decapolis.

3. *Hesebon,* a very ancient royal city, lay opposite to Jericho, not far from the Jordan.

4. Still farther south, near the Dead Sea, was the fortress *Machærus,* in which, according to Josephus Flavius, John the Baptist was put to death (Jos. Fl., *Antiq.,* XVIII). Near it was Callirrhoe, a place with hot springs, where Herod I, towards the end of his life, vainly sought a cure for his disease.

5. *Dibon,* on the plain north of the Arnon, was sometimes claimed by the tribe of Gad and sometimes by that of Ruben. It is now in ruins, but is occasionally mentioned because one of the earliest Hebrew monuments, a triumphal column of King Mesa of Moab, dating from 896 B. C., was discovered here in 1868.

This column is 1.13 meters in height, 0.7 meters in breadth and confirms the statements contained in IV Kings iii. 4, etc. It was first seen by Klein, a German missionary. In 1869 Clermont-Ganneau, a Frenchman, took a cast of it. After that, the Bedouins broke the stone, but the black basalt is so extremely hard that it was possible to collect the fragments and convey them to Paris, where they are preserved in the Louvre.

6. *Madaba,* thirteen miles east of the north end of the Dead Sea, was generally reckoned as belonging to the land of Moab, but in Josue xiii. 9 and 16 it is ascribed to the tribe of Ruben. Later on it became a bishop's see and contained several churches.

This town long lay desolate, but is now again inhabited by 800 schismatics and 400 Latin Christians. During the process of rebuilding a Greek church, among the ruins of an ancient basilica, a mosaic map of the Holy Land was discovered, dating from the sixth century A. D. It originally covered the whole floor of the basilica from wall to wall, and was a most important find. *Cf. Revue biblique,* 1897, II, 165.

It is quite possible that, as the prophecies seem to suggest, Palestine is destined to play an important part in the salvation of mankind. It seems to exert a wonderful attraction, not only upon many Jews, but also upon Christian nations, who are drawn towards this cradle of Judaism and Christianity. From east and west, Asiatics, Europeans, and Americans; Armenians, Copts, Greeks, Russians, and Latins; Catholics and Protestants, — all are eager to acquire settlements in the Holy Land. The most energetic in this respect are the Russians, who far surpass all other nations in the number of pilgrims who yearly visit the Holy Land, and also in founding schools and other establishments, especially in the northwest of Jerusalem. There can be no doubt that their zeal is aimed against Rome.

SECOND PART

THE HOLY PEOPLE

BIBLICAL ARCHÆOLOGY

A. OUTLINES OF THE HISTORY OF ISRAEL

1. TRADITIONAL AND MODERN ACCOUNTS OF THE HISTORY OF ISRAEL

A. *Traditional Account*

THE people of Israel are descended from the Patriarchs Abraham, Isaac and Jacob. Abraham, the founder of the race, was born at Ur in Chaldea, and with his whole family he migrated to Haran in Mesopotamia, where his father Thare (Terach) died. Being a worshiper of the one true God, he left Haran, which was an idolatrous city, and about the year 2080 B. C. betook himself with Lot, his nephew, to Chanaan. Lot parted from him and became the ancestor of the Ammonites and the Moabites. Abraham had several sons, who founded various tribes of Arabs; viz. Ismael, son of the Egyptian woman Agar, and the twelve sons of Ketura; but by his first wife, Sara, Abraham had only one son, Isaac. God made a covenant with him for the preservation of the true religion among his descendants, and for the eventual redemption of mankind by means of a Saviour to be born of his line. The two sons of Isaac, Esau and Jacob, founded the nations of the Edomites and the Israelites respectively. Through the action of Joseph, one of Jacob's twelve sons, the families of Israelites went to Egypt before 1800 B. C. and remained there a considerable time, becoming very numerous. Being oppressed, they were led back out of Egypt by Moses, and lived for many years as nomads in Arabia. They received the divine law on Sinai, and concluded a covenant with Yahweh, whereby they became the chosen people of the one true God, chosen to receive His revelations, thus being raised above all other nations.

Finally they entered the Promised Land from the east, and expelled the earlier inhabitants or subjugated them, exterminating some as a punishment for their sins. Thenceforth they lived under the rule of judges, until Saul, of the tribe of Benjamin, was made their king. He was succeeded by David, of the tribe of Juda, and David by his son Solomon. During the reign of Roboam, Solomon's son and successor, ten tribes fell away from David's dynasty and founded another kingdom in the north, in Samaria, with kings of their own. This northern kingdom was destroyed by the Assyrians in 722 B. C. and the majority of its inhabitants were carried off to Assyria. One hundred and thirty-four years later the southern kingdom with Jerusalem, the capital, was plundered by the Babylonians (588 B. C.), the magnificent temple was destroyed, and the inhabitants were taken in captivity to Babylon. When the Persians took this city in 538 B. C., the Jews were allowed to return home, but not all availed themselves of this permission.

Those who returned rebuilt the Temple, and gradually regained their national and religious self-confidence. Two men in particular, Esdras and Nehemias, did very much to restore a settled state of affairs; Esdras induced the people to renew the covenant with God on the basis of the Mosaic law; Nehemias attended to the revival of the external political order. After the fall of the Persian Empire the Jews became dependent first upon the Egyptian Ptolemies, and then upon the Syrian Seleucidæ. In the second century before Christ they recovered their freedom after a severe struggle, and thenceforth had kings of their own nation. After 64 B. C. they gradually became subject to the Romans, who in the year 70 A. D. destroyed Jerusalem and put an end to the existence of the Jewish State. Since that time the people of Israel have been scattered all over the world, but have nevertheless preserved the purity of their race almost unimpaired throughout this long period. The present number of Jews is about eleven millions.[1]

[1] The history, religion, literature and customs of the Jewish people, from the earliest times to the present day, have been discussed very fully in the " Jewish Encyclopædia " in twelve volumes, published in New York and London, 1901–1906; 605 writers, mostly Jews, contributed to the work.

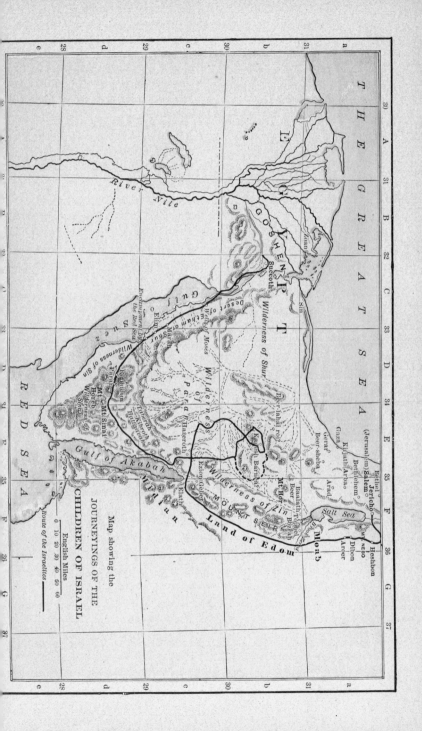

Map showing the
JOURNEYINGS OF THE
CHILDREN OF ISRAEL

English Miles

0 10 20 30 40 50 60

Route of the Israelites

B. *Modern Account of the History of Israel*

Rationalistic criticism accepts the foregoing account of the history of Israel only partially. According to it, no nation knows anything of the founder of its race, and therefore the stories of Abraham, Isaac and Jacob, and their immediate descendants, as recorded in Scripture, is to be regarded as purely mythical and devoid of historical truth.[1]

Owing to the absence of Egyptian testimony it is disputed whether all or any of the Israelite tribes ever lived in Egypt.[2]

Moses is to be recognized as an historical person, who instructed the Israelites in the worship of one God, Yahweh, who was especially adored on Sinai. This god " Yahweh was not originally the universal deity, becoming later the God of Israel; but he was primarily the God of Israel, and much later became God of the whole world" (Wellhausen). It is possible that Moses wrote something, but it cannot be proved; in any case, the Thora, as we now have it in five books, cannot have been compiled by him. The cultus, however, which was connected with the portable Ark of the Covenant, and in some degree the

---

[1] This is an arbitrary assumption, arising from the denial of the supernatural, and of the character of Israel as the people of revelation. The only nation which clung to the true God was not permitted to mix with other races; those who belonged to the kingdom of God could not be permitted to mingle with the subjects of worldly rulers. Therefore this particular nation of necessity had to know the founders of its race, and the sacred records carefully preserved the genealogies and handed them down unaltered. After the Captivity those Israelites who could prove their descent were clearly distinguished from those unable to do so, and the latter could not enjoy the full privileges of citizenship (I Esdras ii. 59, 60). It made a vast difference who belonged to the line inheriting the blessing, and who did not. Other nations perhaps know nothing of their ancestry, but Israel is not like other nations. The name of Abram is actually found on early Babylonian contract tablets, and the position of Ur, his home, now Mugheir on the Euphrates, has been discovered (Sayce, "Records of the Past"). Further details will be found in Dornstetter's work, "Abraham," 1901. In it excellent reasons are given for opposing the attempt to relegate the story of Abraham to the sphere of legend.

[2] Spiegelberg's investigation, however, comfirms the traditional account of the history of Israel.

Thora, i. e. the administration of justice, which was bound up with the cultus, both have come down to us from Moses. The Thora was one of the chief supports of the national life. A priest on Sinai, said by tradition to have been Moses' father-in-law, took an important part in the work of composing it. After leaving the peninsula of Sinai, Israel migrated to the country east of the Jordan, but the date and the route of this migration are unknown. As the population increased, it overflowed into the district west of the river, migrating first after the fashion of Bedouins, i. e. making small but frequent inroads upon the territory of the Chanaanites, but in course of time forming permanent settlements. It is impossible to believe in a rapid conquest of Chanaan by force of arms under Josue's command; probably the Israelites and the Chanaanites often lived peaceably together, as is implied in Judges i. From the Chanaanites, who were superior to the Israelites in civilization, the immigrants adopted many outward forms of civilized life, and recognized their holy places and chief festivals. Through amalgamating with the Chanaanites and other tribes, the Israelites became an agricultural nation — and it is at this point that their real history begins. The reigns of Saul, David and Solomon are all historical, and so is the separation of the kingdom into two parts, Samaria and Juda, and the destruction of these kingdoms by the Assyrians and the Babylonians. The Captivity is also an historical fact; a small remnant of Jews returned from Babylon, and it was not until then that the books professing to be historical, as we know them, were composed.

These books are: First, the *Pentateuch*, which is believed to have been compiled from various older sources, viz. (1) a *Yahvistic* and (2) an *Elohistic* history, so called from the use of the names Yahweh and Elohim to designate God. The former work perhaps dates from about 800 B. C., and was written in the southern kingdom; the latter is of the same date, but was written in the north; (3) the *Deuteronomium*, consisting of the original Deuteronomium (chapters xii.–xxvi.), written in 623 B. C. and some later additions; (4) the " priests' code," written about 500 B. C. in Babylon, and containing regulations for offering sacrifices, purification, etc. (i. e. especially the present book of

Leviticus). The second class of books contains Josue, Judges, Samuel, Kings and Ruth; in the compilation of all of these use was made of earlier records. The Psalms too, and all the other books, but more particularly the so-called writings of Solomon, belong to the period after the Captivity, and nothing remains that can be ascribed to an earlier date except some of the prophetic works, which go back to about 800 B. C.

2. RESULTS

If these theories are correct, then we must conclude:

1. That the Israelite priests, who (IV Kings xxii. 8, etc.) in 623 B. C. under King Josias (Stade, I, 642) are said to have compiled the Law of Moses, or, as Stade calls it, "the Book of Doctrine" (i. e., according to modern criticism, Deut. xii.–xxvi.), and especially Helcias the priest, who "found" it in the temple and pointed it out to the king as the work of Moses, were all liars and forgers. Josias, the king, and the whole nation would in that case have been deceived by a very clumsy forgery, quite easy of detection;

2. That Esdras and Nehemias, who, after the Captivity, strove to revive the national spirit on the ground of the Mosaic Law, "which the Lord God had given to Israel" (Esdras vii. 6), and to renew the covenant between God and His people (Nehem. viii. 1, etc.), were likewise liars and forgers (Stade, I, 16), and the Israelites of that time were deceived, as a recently composed work was read to them and expounded as the Law of Moses, and they were credulous enough to accept it without question;

3. That the whole of Judaism and Christianity based upon it are the outcome of repeated acts of deception and not of divine revelation;

4. That Jesus Christ Himself, who speaks of Abraham as the founder of the race, of Moses as a writer, and of David as a Psalmist, was Himself ignorant, and therefore could not be God.

3. GENERAL REFUTATION

The theories just stated have already won so much popularity among non-Catholic theologians that an adherent of the old traditional doctrine is assumed by them to have no place in the ranks of scholars. The recognition of the post-Captivity origin of the Pentateuch is extolled as one of the most brilliant results of scientific research. It is admitted that for the present these results of " science" cannot be communicated to the general public nor to the young (Stade, I, 11). " Whether the material employed be really historical need not be considered" in teaching " what is called Bible history, . . . which aims at edification and appeals to children." But the " scientific statements are meant for adults, who strive solely after truth and the whole truth." [1]   But let us examine the value of this " truth."

1. The attempts to give a natural explanation for everything and to deny the occurrence of all supernatural intervention of God in human affairs, and especially in the fortunes of the people of Israel, are in direct opposition to any conception of God as the almighty, omniscient and all-good personal Being, who does not allow Himself to be completely cut off from His creatures. These attempts lead, therefore, to Pantheism and Atheism.

2. According to modern criticism the Hebrew race was originally as polytheistic as any other nation; it is true that from the time of Moses onwards Yahweh was regarded as their deity, but Yahweh was in no respect superior to Baal of the Phœnicians, Kemosch of the Ammonites, or Milkom of the Moabites. Every nation had its own particular god, and so had Israel. Modern critics, like the Moabites of old, say, " Behold, the house of Juda is like all other nations " (Ezech. xxv. 8). They maintain that the ancient Jews enjoyed no exclusive position in their relation to God; the existence of other gods was recognized as well as that of Yahweh; Monotheism de-

---

[1] Smith, G. A., " Modern Criticism and the Preaching of the Old Testament," London, 1901, tries to show that the results of modern criticism can very well be used in preaching; that what is important is not names, but the inward reality and types of character.

veloped gradually, and then Yahweh was regarded as the sole ruler, not of Israel alone, but of all nations and lands. The prophets called monotheism into existence, and after the Captivity it won universal acceptance among the Jews, Yahweh being exalted above all other gods.

But how is it that other nations did not ascribe to their gods any omnipotence or universal dominion, any lordship over humanity as a whole? How can we account for the fact that the insignificant little nation of Israel alone attained to this clear view of God? The Jews were not on a level with greater races, such as the Greeks and Romans, in point of civilization or political life, — how could this people not only evolve the idea of there being one supreme God, but cause their worship of this one God to penetrate and influence the whole of their political, religious and social life?

Israel's monotheism is inexplicable unless it was an inheritance (often too lightly esteemed) from remote ages and based upon revelation.[1]

3. The strongest evidence against these theories is supplied by the origin, growth [2] and permanence of Christianity, which, had it been of human origin, would long ago have been destroyed by its bitter foes, so that its continued existence is a proof that it is the work of God. "If . . . this work," said Gamaliel, "be of men, it will come to nought; but if it be of God, you cannot overthrow it" (Acts v. 38, 39).

With its fixed and exalted doctrines and institutions, Chris-

---

[1] That the Israelites' religion was monotheistic before the Captivity is proved by Dr. J. Nikel in his work entitled *Der Monotheismus Israels in der vorexilischen Zeit* (Paderborn, 1893). — Recent excavations in the neighborhood of the Euphrates do not support but overthrow the theory that Israel adopted monotheism at a comparatively late period, in consequence of studying the records of the Babylonians. All their monuments show that the Babylonian religion was polytheistic. How should Israel alone, amidst a number of heathen nations, have actually *become* monotheistic?

[2] Mommsen's "Roman History" was intended to fill five volumes; of these, one, two and three appeared, and then five; the fourth volume is missing. When Mommsen was asked to account for this, he replied that he could not understand the period with which he had meant to deal in the fourth volume — it was to him inexplicable how Christianity had suddenly appeared in the world, spread all over it and transformed it.

tianity has bestowed upon the nations who received it both the highest civilization and supremacy in the world, it has inspired many individuals to make heroic sacrifices, it has formed the noblest characters and has brought untold multitudes to happiness.

4. It is inconceivable that a nation, settled in the midst of the civilized peoples of antiquity, should have remained for centuries without a literature. The Egyptians were very fond of writing and have bequeathed to us a vast literature, going back more than 3000 years before Christ. Scarcely less abundant is the very ancient literature of the countries bordering on the Euphrates, which has recently been discovered. The Phœnicians, the nearest neighbors of the Israelites, are believed to have taught the Greeks the art of writing with letters of the alphabet, and they certainly did this before 1200 B. C., at which period the Greek tribes were already strong enough to carry the Trojan War to a successful end. And yet the Israelites are supposed to have produced no literature before the year 800, if (as Reuss, p. 76, and his followers assume) " the prophets are older than the Law, and the Psalms of later date than both Law and prophets." It is true that the Israelites did not use for writing materials either the papyrus of Egypt or the clay tablets of Babylon and Ninive, but, as beseemed a pastoral people, they employed the prepared skins of animals, and occasionally tablets of stone.

5. Neither Jewish nor Christian tradition knows anything of an Israelite law laid down after the Captivity, but they both acknowledge a law of Mosaic origin. Whoever completely abandons tradition, and interprets Holy Scripture without reference to it, often in accordance with preconceived opinions, arbitrarily invents a history of Israel, and builds on an insecure foundation.

6. It is impossible that an entire nation should allow itself to be deceived with books that made very serious demands upon it, contained severe censures, and even threatened its rejection. If the Jews had composed such books, they would perhaps have revealed and proclaimed to the whole world the honor and glory of their nation, but not its shame. (Just as Christians would not have submitted to the obligation of Confession, but would

have resisted it, had it been imposed, as some maintain, by the
Fourth Lateran Council, and not inherited from Christ and
the Apostles, so the Jews would certainly not have submitted
to the yoke of the law, unless the law had been given by God
through Moses.)

7. The mightiest nations known to history, such as the
Assyrians, Babylonians and Phœnicians, have disappeared in
course of time, or have long ceased to play any part in the
affairs of the world; the descendants of the ancient Egyptians
and Greeks are now obscure — but the small Jewish nation,
although so constantly hated, persecuted and despised, still
survives, and, scattered amongst all peoples, exercises a great
influence. This permanence of the Israelite race, neither increasing nor diminishing in numbers,[1] is inexplicable, unless we
acknowledge that the Israelites were chosen and set apart,
were rejected and yet preserved to the end of time to fulfill the
final purpose of God, — in short, unless we recognize their character as the people of the revelation.

4. Refutation from the Old Testament

The preceding arguments are quite enough to demolish the
fancies devised by spurious scholarship; but it is easy to
quote facts mentioned in the Old Testament which will show
the groundless character of the rationalistic assertions that
we have mentioned. If it can be proved that the Pentateuch
existed long before the time of Esdras or of Josias, and was
regarded as the work of Moses, then the bold speculations of
modern criticism are at once overthrown. Let us now undertake
to prove it.

We may begin by referring to the Book of Judges, in which

---

[1] *Cf.* Ezech. xii. 16. " I will leave a few men of them . . . that they
may declare all their wicked deeds among the nations whither they shall
go." Chateaubriand, in his " Journey from Paris to Jerusalem," remarks
that the Persians, Greeks and Romans have vanished from the face of
the earth, whilst a little nation, whose origin is far more ancient than
the time when these great nations appeared, still lives on, keeping its
race pure. If anything among the nations of the earth bears the stamp
of the miraculous, it is the case with these people.

(viii. 14 [1]) the art of writing is spoken of as something quite familiar and commonplace. The Judge Gedeon, long before the time of the kings, took a young man from Soccoth, who had to write down for him the chiefs and the principal inhabitants of Soccoth, in all 77 men. According to Kautzsch and Cornill this passage forms part of one of the oldest historical portions of the Old Testament. All critics acknowledge as genuine the letter written by David and sent through Urias (II Kings xi. 14); it shows that in the year 1000 B. C. reading and writing were quite common. These are only indirect testimonies, but they show that it is *possible* that the Pentateuch existed long before the time of the prophets Amos, Osee, etc. We can, however, derive much more evidence than this from the Old Testament.

I. *The Original Deuteronomium*

Let us begin by asking what we are to understand by " the book of the law " or, as Stade calls it, the " book of doctrine," found in the reign of Josias (IV Kings xxii. 8, etc.) which the priests are supposed to have forged. Did it really consist only, as is suggested, of fragments of Deuteronomy (especially chapters xii.–xxvi.), or was it the whole law?

1. Immediately after its discovery the book is described as one familiar to all, but hidden away during the time of idolatrous worship. Helcias does not say that he has found a strange book, hitherto unknown, but " I have found the book of the law (*sepher hattora*) in the house of the Lord." It was not indeed the original manuscript written by Moses, but a later copy, which could be read at once without any difficulty. Nevertheless, it was the " book of the (Mosaic) law." [2]

[1] The word " describe," as will be seen from the context, must be taken in its derivative sense, meaning " to write down."

[2] We need not of course assume that every word and sentence in the Pentateuch have come down to us from Moses. The work has no doubt been revised, and additions have been made, and it must have been frequently copied, and the language modified to suit the changes in the speech of the people. The same kind of alterations have been made in our prayers and popular books. Saint Jerome even declared that Moses might be regarded as the author, but Esdras as the *instaurator* of the book; but long before Esdras lived many additions must have been

2. King Josias had not been well instructed in the law during his youth, as idolatry prevailed everywhere. For this reason he was astonished and shocked at the contents of the book, after its discovery, and modern criticism regards this as a proof that the book was altogether new. He must, however, have known of the law by hearsay, as he at once realized his position; and the chief outlines of the law must have been known to him, as, even before the book was found, in the twelfth year of his reign (II Chron. xxxiv. 3), he had begun to reform religion, and was putting down idolatry with vigor. The law was no longer observed, but it had not been quite forgotten, and now the long-neglected work of Moses reappeared, after being hidden in the Temple, as of old in the Tabernacle.

3. The author of the third and fourth books of Kings wrote them, as critics admit, about the year 608 B. C., towards the end of the reign of Josias or at the beginning of that of Joakim. He narrates the history of the kings before Josias in such a way that everything contrary to the book of the law, which Josias and his people solemnly swore to observe, is represented as a breach of the law of Moses. He regards the discovered book as having come down from Moses. Is he so dull as to know nothing about the past? He was alive long before 623. But he certainly knew more than just the book of Deuteronomy. In III Kings xxi. 10 he plainly quotes Lev. xxiv. 16 and Ex. xxii. 28 (witnesses to blasphemy against God and the king). In xxii. 17 he quotes Num. xxvii. 17 (sheep without a shepherd). In IV Kings iv. 16 he distinctly refers to Gen. xviii. 10, and in v. 17 he shows that he knows of the altar of burnt offering in the Tabernacle (Ex. xx. 24). In IV Kings xii. 4 there is a mention of money paid to redeem the living; therefore the law of sacrifice in Num. xviii. 16 was known. In the same way in

---

made to the law as written down by Moses. Vetter acknowledges that the whole Pentateuch has not a common origin, but he ascribes a large part of it to Moses. Hummelauer (*Comm. in l. Deut.*) is inclined to ascribe part of Deuteronomy (xii.–xxvi.) to Samuel, because we read in I Kings x. 25 that "Samuel told the people the law of the kingdom, and wrote it in a book, and laid it up before the Lord." — It is, however, unsafe to disregard the many passages (at least ten) in these chapters which are expressly ascribed to Moses.

xii. 16 trespass and sin offerings are mentioned. In chapter xvii. of this book there are frequent allusions to the clauses of the Covenant which Yahweh made with Israel (e. g. v. 15 and v. 38). In xviii. 4 we read of the "brazen serpent which Moses had made" (Num. xxi. 8, 9). In xxiii. 9 we hear of priests who on account of some transgression shared the food of the other priests, but might not exercise any priestly functions (cf. Lev. xxi. 21, etc.). In xxiii. 21 the Paschal celebration is spoken of, which is certainly mentioned in Deut. xvi, but is far more clearly described in Ex. xii.; Deut. xvi. only becomes intelligible when read with Ex. xii., and must have been written by one who took for granted the knowledge of this chapter. According to Kautzsch, all the passages referred to occur in the so-called "priests' code," which is assumed to have been drawn up in Babylon about 500 B. C. How is this possible, since they were quoted as early as the seventh century before Christ? If then the author of the Books of Kings (who is rightly believed to have been the prophet Jeremias) knew the Pentateuch as a whole in 608, and especially if he knew those portions also which are supposed to have been written during the Captivity, there can be no ground at all for maintaining that Helcias deceived Josias by forging a Deuteronomium, or that Esdras was the first to foist upon the people the "priests' code" as a work of Moses, in or about the year 444 B. C., and that he read it to the people, and induced them, on the strength of it, to form a covenant with Yahweh, or that the Pentateuch was not completed until about 400 B. C.

II. *The Prophets and the Pentateuch*

The ancient prophets, upon the date and authenticity of whose writings even modern criticism has cast no doubt, refer to the Pentateuch again and again, and also to those particular passages which are supposed to have been written during the Captivity.

Isaias i. 11, etc., speaks of the sacrifices, new moons and Sabbaths, in just the same language as Exodus xxix., etc. Leviticus i., etc. (the "priests' code"), Ezechiel (iv. 14, etc.), complain that the people in heathen lands will be forced to eat unclean food (*cf.* Lev. xi. See also Ezech. vi. 4 and *cf.* Lev. xxvi. 30). The same prophet in ix. 6, etc., speaks of defilement from dead bodies, which violates the law in Num. xix. 11, etc. This nineteenth chapter is another of those belonging to the "priests' code" (*cf.* also Ezech. xi. 20 with Ex. vi. 7; Ezech. xxii. 10 with Lev. xviii. 7, 8, 19).

Jeremias insists upon keeping holy the Sabbath day (xvii. 19, etc.) ; Ezechiel does the same (xx. 13, 16, 21, where the violation of the Sabbath is mentioned as a reason for the punishment inflicted upon the people). In spite of this evidence, the critics suggest that the law regarding the Sabbath is derived chiefly from the "priests' code" that was drawn up during the Captivity. Osee, writing about 750 B. C., says (i. 9) that Israel ought no longer to be called God's people: "Call his name Not My People (Lo-ammi), for you are not my people, and I will not be yours." There is plainly a reference here to Ex. vi. 7: "I will take you to myself for my people," which words are now ascribed to the "priests' code." Compare also Osee iv. 4 with Num. xvi., a chapter most of which is supposed to belong to the "priests' code." Compare further iv. 10 with Lev. xxvi. 26. In viii. 12 there is a particularly plain reference to the existence of the Pentateuch: "I shall write to him my manifold laws, which have been accounted as foreign. They shall offer victims, they shall sacrifice flesh, and shall eat it, and the Lord will not receive them: now will he remember their iniquity, and will visit their sins: they shall return to Egypt." This passage affords absolute proof that the "priests' code" existed at the time of Osee. Amos (ii. 4) reproaches the Jews with not having kept the commandments of Yahweh. In iv. 4 he speaks of sacrifices and tithes (*cf.* v. 21, etc.).[1]

Micheas (iii. 11) finds fault with the priests for taking money for teaching, and Ezechiel too (vii. 26) mentions such instruction given by the priests. Now Ezechiel, writing in 594 B. C., might have referred to the Deuteronomium that is supposed to

[1] That Amos must have been acquainted with the so-called "priests' code" has been proved by Vetter. He has proved also that even Hoseas knew the Pentateuch, and that the compilation of it dated back before his time, and before that of the separation of the kingdoms.

have been discovered in 623, for the law occurs in Deut. xvii. 9, etc. But if Micheas also speaks of something forbidden by law, Deuteronomy must be much older than 700 B. C., as Micheas lived under Achaz and Ezechias. The reference in Micheas vi. 15 to Deut. xxviii. 38 affords a similar proof.

When such quotations from the prophets are brought forward as evidence of the antiquity of the "priests' code" and the whole Pentateuch, we sometimes meet with the argument that the code is derived from the prophets! But whence did the prophets take their zeal, their indignation and their reproaches against Israel if not from Moses? How could they blame the people so bitterly, and hurl such denunciations upon them, and threaten them with God's vengeance, if the people had no definite law of God binding upon them? If that were so, the prophets would be simply beating the air.

AN OBJECTION. Cornill says, p. 64 : " Such passages as Isaias i. 13, 14 and Amos v. 21–23 would be almost inexplicable, if the laws in the 'priests' code' had been known to these men and their hearers as a divine command and binding obligation. How could Jeremias utter the words in vii. 22, if he had had before him the books of Exodus, Leviticus and Numbers in their present form? "

Let us examine these passages.

Isaias in chapter i. directs the Israelites to the right path when he says (12) : " Who required these things at your hands, that you should walk in my courts? (13) Offer sacrifice no more in vain, incense is an abomination to me. The new moons and the Sabbaths and other festivals I will not abide, your assemblies are wicked. (14) My soul hateth your new moons and your solemnities, they are become troublesome to me."

Amos v. 21. " I hate, and have rejected your festivities, and I will not receive the odor of your assemblies. (22) And if you offer me holocausts and your gifts, I will not receive them. (23) Take away from me the tumult of thy songs, and I will not hear the canticles of thy harp."

Jeremias vii. 22. " I spoke not to your fathers and I commanded them not, in the day that I brought them out of the land of Egypt, concerning the matter of burnt offerings and sacrifices; (23) but this thing I commanded them, saying, 'Hearken to my voice, and I will be your God, and you shall be my people.'"

It is maintained by some that these passages prohibit sacrifices and festivals, and that the prophets were indignant at such things as being a heathen element in the worship of Yahweh — hence the "priests' code" enjoining such forms of worship (especially Exodus, Leviticus and Numbers in their present form) could not have existed when the prophets used these words. "All these prophets fail to find words enough to express Yahweh's hatred of sacrifice and all formal worship" (Volck, 36).

But any unprejudiced reader will easily perceive that what is condemned as wrong by all the prophets is the merely external worship of God, since He demands not so much exterior homage as interior submission and righteousness of life. The words, however, actually prove that before the Captivity, in the time of Isaias, Amos and Jeremias, the sacrificial worship was regularly performed. If, however, these passages are regarded as sufficient proof that the "priests' code" did not exist in the eighth, seventh and sixth centuries before Christ, the following words from the Psalter, which, according to modern criticism, belongs to a period long after the Captivity (Kautzsch, *Altes Testament, Beilage* 130, etc.) would prove that the code was still non-existent in the fifth, fourth, third and second centuries. In Ps. xlix. (Vulg.) 9, etc., we read: "I will not take calves out of thy house, nor he-goats out of thy flocks. For all the beasts of the woods are mine, the cattle on the hills and the oxen. . . . If I should be hungry, I would not tell thee, for the world is mine and the fulness thereof. Shall I eat the flesh of bullocks? or shall I drink the blood of goats?" Similar passages occur in Ps xxxix. 7, etc., l. 18. Kautzsch (loc. cit., *Beilage* 207) thinks, indeed, that these psalms may belong to an earlier, prophetic period. But if the men who collected the psalms, often, as he assumes, made serious alterations in their original form, and if, when they lived, the exterior liturgical forms of worship were regarded "as the chief and absolutely indispensable proof of a disposition pleasing to God" (ibid. 209), what could hinder these persons from suppressing such passages as these, which must have seemed to them very objectionable?

If, however, the Psalter recognizes and emphasizes the fact that outward sacrifices cannot please God, unless accompanied by the right inward dispositions, ought not the same interpretation to be assigned to the prophets' utterances? (*cf.* Is. lviii. 3, etc.).

5. Refutation from the Samaritan Pentateuch

The mixed race of the Samaritans possessed the Pentateuch, but in a form that differs frequently from the Masoretic text, and has more points of agreement with the Septuagint version, that existed long before the time of our Lord. This fact and the use of the old Semitic characters in which it was written and is still preserved and used by the few remaining Samaritans, are proofs of its great antiquity. When did the Samaritans obtain possession of it?

There are three answers possible to this question.

1. The usual opinion at the present day is that the law became known to the Samaritans about the time of Esdras and Nehemias, or perhaps at the time of Alexander the Great. Josephus Flavius records in his "Antiquities" (XI, viii. 2), that a priest from Jerusalem, Manasses by name, was exiled in consequence of having broken the law, and joined the Samaritans. With the aid of his father-in-law Sanaballat, governor of Samaria, he built a temple on Mount Garizim, and instituted the worship of Yahweh. Josephus says that this occurred in the time of Alexander; but Nehemias relates a very similar story as belonging to his own lifetime (xiii. 28). In speaking of the reprehensible custom of taking foreign wives, he says that even a priest, one of the sons of Joiada, the son of Eliasib, the high priest, had married the daughter of Sanaballat the Horonite, and he adds: "I drove him from me." It seems quite improbable that the Sanaballat mentioned by Nehemias was not the same man as the Sanaballat mentioned by Josephus, and that on two occasions, separated by no long interval of time, a member of the high priest's family should have married the

daughter of a Samaritan ruler named Sanaballat, and was therefore excluded from all priestly duties at Jerusalem. It seems
fairly certain that Josephus has made a mistake; he is not quite
trustworthy with regard to the history of Esdras and Nehemias.
However, whether it was about 430 or about 330 B. C. that a
priest left Jerusalem for Samaria, it is assumed that when the
Samaritan temple was built on Garizim, a form of worship
conformable to Jewish usage was instituted, and that part of
the service consisted in reading the Book of the Law, which this
priest Manasses is said to have carried with him from Jerusalem.

2. According to IV Kings xvii. 24, etc., after the destruction of the northern kingdom in 722, the king of Assyria sent
people from the region of the Euphrates to occupy Samaria,
and they mingled with the remainder of the Israelites. That
some Israelites were left there is clear from Jeremias xli. 5;
II Chronicles xxxiv. 9, 21, and also from the Book of Judith,
which (even if it were not canonical) is certainly based upon
historical traditions.[1] In the sparsely populated country in the
north, wild beasts increased so rapidly that lions made their way
into the villages. This was regarded as a punishment inflicted
upon the heathen colonists for not worshiping Yahweh, the God
of the country, but their own deities. Consequently, a priest was
sent back home from the number of those in captivity in Assyria,
in order to instruct the people in the worship of Yahweh. For
this purpose the priest may have provided himself with a book
of the law, which thenceforth remained in use in Samaria.

3. The Samaritans may have possessed the book of the
law before the separation of the two kingdoms, and have retained
it after that event. Although King Jeroboam drove out the
lawful priests and Levites and introduced the worship of idols,
some faithful servants of Yahweh were no doubt left in the
northern kingdom, as we see, for instance, from the story of
Tobias, which, even if it were purely fictitious, would nevertheless bear witness to the feelings of the population of the north,
as does the activity of Amos and Osee, the prophets, who re-
proached Samaria with having fallen away from the right wor-

---

[1] In the same way some Jews were, after 588, left in Juda, for not all
the people, not, for instance, old men, children and the sick, were removed.

ship and threatened the country with God's vengeance. Nahum, who was zealous for Yahweh's honor, came from the north.

This last explanation seems by far the best; for (a) immediately after the return of the Jews from the Captivity, the Samaritans asked to be allowed to take part in building the Temple, saying: "We seek your God as you do, and have sacrificed to him" (Esdras iv. 2, etc.). They knew, therefore, the religious institutions of the Pentateuch. (b) When their request was not granted, they developed bitter hostility against the Jews, which lasted for centuries, and still existed in the time of our Lord, so that it is inconceivable that they still received and accepted religious books from them.

(c) If they had received the Book of the Law long after the Captivity, through Manasses the priest, it could hardly have been in the old Hebrew script, which the Samaritans have preserved to the present day, but in square characters. According to Jewish tradition, Esdras brought these square characters or Assyrian writing back with him from exile. We read in the Talmud: "The Law was originally given to the Israelites in Hebrew script and in the holy language. It was given the second time in the days of Esra in Assyrian writing." Origen and Saint Jerome adopt this statement. In opposition to this tradition it is useless to argue that the Samaritans received the Pentateuch in the old Hebrew script from the Jews about the year 400 (Benzinger, *Archäologie*, 287), for this statement would first have to be proved.

(d) How can the fact be accounted for that the Samaritans possess only the Pentateuch and a mutilated version of Josue, if they received the holy book from the Jews long after the Captivity? Modern criticism assumes that the historical part of the Pentateuch was united with Josue, Judges, Samuel and Kings, about 561 B. C., so as to form one body of sacred literature; why, then, did the Samaritans receive a comparatively small part of it? And why have they none of the prophetic writings, which at that date had long been held in honor by the Jews?

(e) We have an account of Manasses taking refuge with the Samaritans, and of the building of the temple on Garizim, but there is no record of any transfer of a book of the law. " Neither Nehemias nor Josephus says a word about the Pentateuch in this connection" (Reuss, 381).

(f) In Jerusalem there would have been taken all precautions against allowing the apostate to obtain the holy book. Was it so badly guarded that he could steal it? Would not this theft have been a constant ground of reproach against the Samaritans? There is no trace of anything of the kind.

(g) It would not be to the interest of the apostate priest to take with him, and to introduce into Samaria, a book the precepts of which he had himself transgressed by his marriage, as it would contain his own condemnation.

6. REFUTATION FROM ORIENTAL RECORDS

(a) The chief weapon of the modern critics is " divergence of authorities." When, however, they attempt to apply this principle to the subject of the Deluge they are found to be untrustworthy and wholly misleading. The account of this event, as given in Genesis vi.–ix., is supposed to have been derived partly from the Yahvist and partly from the " priests' code." The Chaldæan Genesis, however, discovered by Smith, an Englishman, in cuneiform characters at Ninive, and published by him, contains all the essential features of the Bible narrative.[1] " Divergence of authorities" ought, therefore, to be applied also to the Chaldæan work, which formed part of the library belonging to King Asurbanipal of Assyria (667–626). If that work is inadmissible, we may say the same of Genesis.

(b) It has been proved that the proper names occurring in the Pentateuch, which in their construction bear witness to monotheism, are not, as Wellhausen asserts, of very late invention, but that names of quite similar meaning (e. g. " my God knoweth," " my God hath heard ") were used long before the time of Moses by some of the western Semites in Asia Minor. These tribes of Arab origin won supremacy over Babylon, and hence similar names occur also in polytheistic Babylon. They

[1] Two other texts of the Babylonian account of the Deluge are in existence.

prove (1) that monotheism belongs to a period long anterior
to the prophets and Moses, and (2) that the five books of Moses
containing these proper names are much older than modern
criticism will allow.[1]

B. GOD AND THE GODS IN ISRAEL

1. Monotheism and Polytheism

In the history of antiquity we everywhere meet with the
worship of God, but as the deity is worshiped differently in
different places, it has been assumed by modern students of
religion that polytheism was the original, and that monotheism
was a later development, as generally what is imperfect precedes what is perfect; the latter developing from the former.
This opinion is, however, erroneous. In the lives of nations, as
of individuals, there may be a falling away from good to bad.
Polytheism is a degeneration of the earliest religion of mankind,
and hints of this decay are given plainly enough in the stories
of a golden age, stories that are of almost universal occurrence
among all nations, and therefore certainly contain a grain of
historical truth. We have, moreover, the generally accepted
axiom that the plural presupposes a singular.

It is indeed true that ancient nations generally worshiped
several gods, but amidst the plurality of gods there is always
a glimmer of the original idea of one true God. Even the name
of this one God exists in similar forms among many nations.
El of the Israelites is the same as *Ilu* of the Babylonians and
Assyrians, *Allah* of the Arabs and *Alloho* of the Syrians. In
the Turin " Book of the Dead," that goes back to nearly 3000
years before Christ and supplies us with the earliest recorded
doctrines of the Egyptians, we read: " There is One most Holy,

---

[1] With all the preceding portion of this section of the book (pp.
37–56) *cf. Lex mosaica*, an excellent work. The authors, eminent English scholars and theologians, succeed in proving that the whole history
of the Jews depends upon the Mosaic Law, which reappears in the prophetic writings. Many other scholars, for instance Cornill who once
supported radical criticism, are now disposed to pay due regard to tradition in many respects.

Creator of the world in its fullness. He sees as you see, hears as you hear, stands as you stand. Suffer me to praise the Architect, who hath made the fullness of the universe; who caused all things on the earth and beyond the world to come into being in due time, who hath fashioned them for me." But when Moses lived there were eight elementary deities recognized by this ancient and highly civilized nation. In Babylonia originally one, and only one, local deity was honored in each town, but a plurality of gods was recognized from the time when the various districts were united into one monarchy;[1] and the deities were all classed together in the same way as the towns and people. The same thing happened in Rome; and this is how polytheism originated.

It is a remarkable fact that we know of no nation, either in ancient or modern times, completely devoid of religious faith. Atheism and materialism have always appealed only to individuals. It is almost equally remarkable, however, that among most nations the worship of the one true God perished, and that even among the most civilized peoples religious worship was perverted. The former fact can be explained only by accepting a very early revelation, which was never completely forgotten, but in remote times was more fresh in men's minds. The latter has several causes:

(1) Man cannot and will not live without God. His religious feelings need satisfaction, and whenever, in consequence of human transgression, the true God is no longer recognized, man seeks his god in the stars, in thunder and lightning, in wood and stone. (2) True religion at all periods has required strict control of the passions. Heathen religions, on the contrary, have taken the sensual inclinations of mankind under their protection, and thus have won ready acceptance. (3) Demoniacal influences have played their part. The fallen angels wished to be equal with God, and having failed in this attempt in Heaven, they tried to win divine honors for themselves on earth. Just as the devil contributed to the sin of the first human beings, so he has promoted the errors of mankind in

[1] Hammurabi became the first overlord in about 2100 B. C., when Abraham left Ur, his native place (Gen. xi. 34; Jos. xxiv. 2).

later periods. The devils would not relinquish the influence that they had once secured in Paradise (Deuteronomy xxxii. 17). The faithless Israelites in the wilderness "sacrificed to devils and not to God"[1] (Psalms xcv. 5). "All the gods of the Gentiles are devils."[2] The Fathers of the Church held the same opinions. (4) Another reason for the repeated lapses of the Israelites into idolatry was the example of the Chanaanites and other heathen neighbors, as all around heathen worship prevailed with its seductive charm. Many kings, too, set a bad example; those of the northern kingdom especially had a political ground for opposing the worship of the true God. If their people had no religious interest in the Temple at Jerusalem and ceased to visit it, they would lose also their affection for David's line, that ruled in Jerusalem (IV Kings xii. 27).

2. WORSHIP OF THE STARS

Probably the earliest form of degeneration undergone by the original monotheism was the worship of stars, known as Sabaism, from צבא = host of the heavenly bodies. It occurred occasionally among the Israelites. In Deuteronomy xvii. 3 it is strictly forbidden, as opposed to the worship of the true God, and the penalty of death by stoning was imposed upon any who practiced it. In the Book of Job (xxxi. 26) the holy man declares that he has never worshiped the heavenly bodies. "If I beheld the sun when it shined, and the moon going in brightness; and my heart in secret hath rejoiced, and I have kissed my hand with my mouth, which is a very great iniquity, and a

---

[1] According to the Hebrew words יִזְבְּחוּ לַשֵּׁדִים this passage means literally "they sacrificed to the destroyers" (from שֵׁד = שָׁדַד, to attack violently, to ruin). The Septuagint translated ἔθυσαν δαιμονίοις, and understood thereby the gods of the heathen, who, in contrast to the true God, could only bring disaster. This is only possible if they are self-conscious beings, hostile to God, viz. evil spirits.

[2] Hebrew אֱלִילִים (from אַל, not) = nothings, *vanitates*. But the Septuagint renders the word δαιμόνια, according to the meaning given it by their countrymen. That the Jews were well aware who was the object of idolatrous worship appears from their designating the prince of the devils by the name of the false god Beelzebub (Matt. ix. 34; Mark iii. 22; Luke xi. 15).

denial against the most high God." From Ezechiel viii. 16, 17 we learn that the worshiper turned his face towards the rising sun, keeping a branch before his eyes, probably as a token of gratitude for the growth of plants. From Jeremias xix. 13 we see that incense was burnt, and from Job (loc. cit.) that it was the custom to kiss the hand to the sun.

3. WORSHIP OF IMAGES

"Thou shalt not make to thyself a graven thing, nor the likeness of anything that is in heaven above or in the earth beneath, nor of those things that are in the waters under the earth" (Ex. xx. 4). The reason for this prohibition was the danger of idolatry that prevailed generally. Especially in Egypt the Israelites had witnessed idolatrous worship, and hence in the wilderness they attempted to worship the true God under the form of a golden calf; just as the Egyptians worshiped the deity under the form of a bull. The same thing occurred in the schismatic kingdom of Samaria. Jeroboam I, who had lived in Egypt in his youth, caused two golden calves to be made, one to stand in Dan, and the other in Bethel, as representations of Yahweh (IV Kings xii. 29). The prophets vigorously opposed this design, and denounced it as being idolatrous (Amos iii. 14; v. 5; Osee iv. 15; viii. 5). Other images of gods were the *teraphim*, little domestic deities, mentioned as early as the times of the Patriarchs and Judges (Gen. xxxi. 19; Judges xvii. 5; xviii. 31), and there was also the statue Kijjun, a representation of the planet Saturn, which the Israelites carried with them in the wilderness (Amos v. 26; Acts vii. 43) and is often identified with Moloch or Kronos.

The prohibition only referred to figures intended to represent the true God or other deities, for in Lev. xxvi. 1, it has the addition "to worship it." Figures having no religious significance were not prohibited; cherubim were set up near the Ark of the Covenant and brazen cattle near the laver in the Temple. At a later period the Jews extended the prohibition to all figures, and would not even allow the Roman soldiers to enter Jerusalem with eagles on their standards. This aversion on the part of the Jews passed on to Islam. It is well known that Leo III, the Isaurian, encouraged iconoclasm among the Christians, in his anxiety to conciliate Jews and Mahometans (726–841).

Other deities, repeatedly worshiped by the Israelites, were of
Chanaanite, Assyrian or Egyptian origin.

4. Chanaanite Deities

1. The chief god, common to all Chanaanite tribes, was Baal
or Bel,[1] i. e. the Lord, and especially the husband. He was
honored as personifying the procreative and propagating principle in nature, but he was also thought of as a natural force
tending both to preserve and to destroy. His worship varied
at different periods and in different places. Therefore there
were several Baals (I Cor. viii. 5, κύριοι πολλοί).

Babylon was the original home of this cultus. In Holy
Scripture there is mention of:

(*a*) Baal-berith = Baal of the Covenant. A temple in Sichem
was dedicated to the god under this name.

(*b*) Baal-semes = Baal as sun-god.

(*c*) Baal-sebub = Beelzebub = Baal of the flies. Under this
name he was worshiped in Accaron (Ekron), a city of the
Philistines. He was believed to have power to bring swarms
of destructive flies and to remove them again. The Israelites
in later times, who detested idolatry, gave this name to the chief
of the devils, and, through the similarity in sound, they seem
often to have called him Beelsebul, i. e. lord of the dwelling,
because he chose human bodies as his habitation, for the name
is given in this form in the Gospels.

(*d*) Baal-peor, probably so called from the hill Peor or
Phegor situated opposite Jericho. This god was worshiped
by the Moabites.

There were originally no figures of Baal, but upright pillars
(*chammanim* or *mazzeboth*) served to mark the sites of his
worship; later, however, he was represented in human form.

---

[1] הַבַּעַל, Chald. בְּעֵל, abbreviated בֵּל; in the cuneiform inscriptions
Bil. After the introduction of polytheism the name was used to designate the chief of the gods, as were the names Zeus and Jupiter. Here,
too, a trace of the primitive monotheism remains. — The frequently mentioned name Marduk (in the Bible Merodak or Merodach) was only another expression for Bel. Marduk was primarily the god worshiped at
Babel.

The so-called Tyrian Herakles is really a statue of Baal. He was known also as Melkart, i. e. the city king. According to Müllenhof (*Deutsche Altertumskunde*, I, 69) Herakles himself is not of Greek origin, but both the legends about him and his cultus came to the Greeks from the East.

2. The chief female deity of the Chanaanites, occupying a position like that of Baal, was Axhtoreth; the meaning of her name is uncertain. Its Greek form is 'Αστάρτη, and in the Vulgate it is spelled Astarthe. Another name for the same goddess is Aschera (אֲשֵׁרָה = happiness). She represents the female principle in nature, i. e. nature herself, as conceiving and bringing forth ever new forms of life. There were originally no real statues of this deity, but wooden columns, called *Ascherim* or *Ascheroth*, marked her cultus. They stood on mountains and hills, or among trees with thick foliage, for which reason the Septuagint and Vulgate translate the word *Aschera* by " wood " or " grove." They generally were placed near the altars to Baal, but were shaped differently from the stone pillars dedicated to the god. Astarte was subsequently often represented as a cow, or as a woman with a cow's head, or with a human head and cow's horns. The worship of this goddess was very obscene; men and women gave themselves up to obscenity in her honor. She had persons specially dedicated to her, *gedeschim* and *gedeschot* (Gen. xxxviii. 15). Christian chastity dedicated to God stands out in beautiful contrast to her worship, which did not, however, originate in western Asia, but was introduced from the lands near the Euphrates, as was probably also the cultus of Baal. From Phœnicia it spread westward to the Greeks and the Romans. Hence Astarte is to be identified with Baaltis or Beltis of the Babylonians (also called Bilit or Mylitta), also with Istar of the Assyrians, with the Syrian goddess Anaitis, with the Greek Aphrodite and the Roman Venus. On account of her cow's horns the western nations sometimes honored her as Luna or Juno, as the horns suggested a crescent moon. The Israelites very early adopted her worship, as may be seen from Judges ii. 13; x. 6; II Kings iii. 4; xii. 10. Out of deference to his Phœnician wives, Solomon afterwards transferred her cultus to Jerusalem.

3. The worship of Tammus [1] seems to have been connected with the service of Baal, and had its chief seat in the Phœnician town of Biblos. This cultus, too, spread from Phœnicia to the west; first to Cyprus and then to Greece, where the god was known as Adonis = my Lord. Under the Jewish kings his worship was introduced into Jerusalem, for Ezechiel says that the women in the Temple mourned over Adonis or Tammus (Ezech. viii. 14). The idea underlying this cultus is the expression of sorrow for the decay and death of the powers of nature in the autumn, and of joy over their re-awakening, as soon as the sun turns again to the north. In spring, therefore, there was a joyful festival and in late autumn a time of mourning, when women especially gave themselves up to sorrow and lamentation over the loss of Adonis. Ezechiel tells us that the Israelites observed the time of mourning, but it cannot be proved from Holy Scripture that they also celebrated the joyful festival.

4. In the Old Testament (first in Lev. xxvi. 30), especially in the books of Kings and Chronicles, but also in the Prophets, we read of a worship on high places which is censured (*bama* = height, plural *bamoth*). It is well known that the Chanaanites, who worshiped nature, preferred to celebrate their rites on natural or artificial hills, which became the scenes of great revelry. The Israelites copied the Chanaanite custom and also chose hills on which to worship their God. This was very natural, as the true God had appeared to them on Mount Sinai; but soon heathen practices and obscenity crept into their ceremonies, and consequently the prophets sternly denounced them, and pious kings destroyed these high places.

5. The two Philistine deities, Dagon and Derketo (Gr. ᾿Αταργάτις), bore some resemblance to Baal and Astarte. Both were represented with the bodies of fish, and human heads and hands. Dagon, the male deity, symbolized water and the procreative forces of nature, which are rendered active by means of water. The female deity, Derketo, is supposed to represent the power of the earth to absorb moisture, and as a result to produce living things.

[1] תַּמּוּז. The meaning of the name is obscure.

It would be reasonable to suppose that the cultus of these deities in Philistæa was connected with its proximity to the sea; but the monuments and records of the lands near the Euphrates show representations of Dagon, proving that the Babylonians and Assyrians also honored this god. That his cultus was not limited to Philistæa appears from the occurrence of the name Bethdagon in the territory of Juda and Aser (Jos., *Antiq.*, XV, 41; XIX, 27). An *Atargateion*, or temple of Atargatis, existed in the district east of the Jordan in the time of Judas Machabæus, and was destroyed by him (II Mach. xii. 26 in the Septuagint). The name Dagon is certainly connected with *dag*, a fish; Atargatis or Derketo appears to be another expression for Astarte, just as Dagon represented one definite side of the Baal worship.

5. ASSYRIAN AND BABYLONIAN DEITIES

1. The god Moloch (i. e. king), also called Milkom or Malkom, is often mentioned in Holy Scripture, and was honored in western Asia as early as the time of Moses. In Leviticus xviii. 21 the Israelites are warned against him. He is generally spoken of as the false god of the Moabites, but Chamos (i. e. ruler), the god of the Ammonites, is identical with him (Num. xxi. 29; Judges xi. 24; III Kings xi. 5); and Orotal (= God's fire) mentioned by Herodotus as the fire-god of the Edomites may also be regarded as the same deity. To please his heathen wives, Solomon built shrines to him on the Mount of Olives (III Kings xi. 7 and 33), but they were intended only for the king's wives and for foreigners in general. The Israelites, however, themselves worshiped Moloch in the valley of Hinnom, south of Jerusalem, as we read in many places, especially in Jeremias. Holy Scripture records also (IV Kings xvii. 31) that the colonists from the Euphrates, who settled in Samaria after the downfall of the northern kingdom, offered children in sacrifice to their national god Moloch, whom they called Adramelech (splendor of the king) or Anamelech (King Anu). This fact shows that the cultus of Moloch, like that of Baal, was introduced from Assyria and Babylonia. It was intended to emphasize one special aspect of the worship of Baal, viz. the honoring of the destructive and therefore fearful forces of nature. That Moloch was well known in Assyria appears from inscriptions on monuments that still exist, on which the name Anamalech (King Anu) very frequently occurs.

The worship of Moloch consisted chiefly in the sacrifice of children. In order to appease the dread deity, people offered him their children, their most precious possession. Even King Achaz (IV Kings xvi. 3) offered his own son to Moloch in the valley of Hinnom. The statue of the god was of metal, and probably in human form; it was hollow inside, and was made red hot with fire. Then living children were laid upon the outstretched arms of the figure, so that they rolled into the open mouth and, falling into the midst of the fire, were burned to death.[1] The idea underlying this cultus is that time destroys all existing things as well as produces them. Hence Moloch is identical with Kronos and Saturn, a god of the west, who devours his own offspring.

2. We read of King Achaz in Holy Scripture (IV Kings xvi. 10) that in the Temple at Jerusalem he set up an idolatrous altar resembling an Assyrian one that he had seen in Damascus, and caused sacrifices to be offered upon it. It seems that he did not intend to honor any particular god by this means, but wished to propitiate the deities in general, who had raised the Assyrians to such power and dignity. "The gods," he said, "of the kings of Syria help them, and I will appease them with victims, and they will help me," but the passage concludes, "whereas on the contrary they were the ruin of him and of all Israel (II Chron. xxviii. 23).

3. In IV Kings xvii. 30 Holy Scripture tells us that the immigrants into Samaria from the east honored the God of Israel as god of the country, but retained their heathen deities as well. Besides Moloch (Adramelech and Anamelech), to whom the people of Sepharvaim (i. e. Sebarim, Ezech. xlvii. 16) sacrificed children, mention is made of (a) Sochothbenoth,

---

[1] Diodorus Siculus describes the statue of this god at Carthage as follows: "There was a brazen statue of Kronos, in human shape, stretching its hands upwards and somewhat sloping, so that children, laid upon them, rolled down and fell into its throat, which was full of fire." Raschi (Jarchi), the rabbinical commentator, says on Jer. vii. 31: "Moloch was made of brass and heated from below. The hands were stretched out and glowed with heat, and the child was laid upon them and burned up, shrieking all the while; but the sacrificing priests made a noise with kettledrums, so that the father could not hear its cries."

(b) Nergal, (c) Asima, (d) Nibhaz (Nebahaz), (e) Thartak. Nothing is known as to the worship of these gods.[1]

6. EGYPTIAN DEITIES

1. In Egypt there was a worship of animals, which were adored as symbols of the deity. The Israelites while in Egypt had become familiar with their cultus, and so in the desert, wishing to honor the god who had brought them out of Egypt, they represented him as a calf, no doubt remembering the worship of Apis. This did not imply a falling away from the true God, and Aaron proclaimed that the ceremony should be regarded as held in honor of Yahweh (Ex. xxxii.). It appears, however, that the people only desired the sensual pleasures connected with the heathen worship and with the sacrifices performed at that time; therefore the occurrence was declared sinful and sternly censured, and was not regarded as a pardonable mistake.

2. In Ezechiel viii. we read that shortly before the destruction of the kingdom of Juda, the Israelites, fearing the Babylonians, tried to win the favor of the Egyptians by again adopting the worship of Egyptian gods. Animal worship revived, this time in direct antagonism to the service of the true God. If Ezechiel's narrative is to be understood literally, this idolatrous cultus was carried on actually in the Temple at Jerusalem; it is, however, possibly not intended to be thus understood. The prophets often denounced a mere inclination towards heathen nations and a

---

[1] According to Erasmus Nagl: Sochothbenoth = Zakmuku Zarbanit, i. e. a solstice festival in honor of Marduk and his spouse Zarbanit; the names may have been abbreviated in the common dialect. The people of Cutha (Assyrian: Kutu, a town north of Babel, now Till Ibrahim) made a Nergal; he was a sun-god, also ruler of war pestilence and hell. The men of Emath (Chamath, Egyptian and Assyrian Chamati, now Chama) worshiped Asima, i. e. the old Chanaanite deity Esmun-Thammus, the god of death and resurrection; Emath is mentioned in Gen. x. 18 as a Chanaanite settlement. The Hevites (Avvites) honored Nibhaz and Thartak. They were a tribe of Chanaanite origin, and so their gods are also Chanaanite (see pp. 19 and 21) (Gen. x. 17). Nibhaz is called in the Septuagint Ἐβλαζέρ, which is probably a corrupt form of Baal-azar= Baal is our help. Thartak seems to be the same as Derketo or Atargatis.

desire to seek help from them instead of from God as worship of heathen deities.

After return not dispose to idolatry

> On account of their obstinate falling away from the true God, Moses had threatened the people with the penalty of exile from the Promised Land and even of losing this land altogether (Deut. xxviii. 63; xxx. 18). These threats were fulfilled when they were carried into captivity; but the punishment had the wholesome result of making the Jews thenceforth abhor idolatrous worship of false gods. After their return from Babylon, they showed so little tendency towards it that every attempt by the Syrian King Antiochus Epiphanes to introduce the cultus of other gods amongst the Jews remained completely unsuccessful.

C. THE RELIGIOUS INSTITUTIONS OF ISRAEL

Religious antiquities are generally discussed under four headings: (1) holy places, (2) holy persons, (3) sacred ritual, (4) sacred seasons.

SOURCES OF INFORMATION

(a) *Principal Sources of Information.* These are primarily the Holy Scriptures, especially the historical books of the Old Testament.

Next in importance are the works, not included in the Bible, of Jewish writers of the same period as the Bible. There are, unfortunately, very few of these, and they are not earlier than the time of Christ and the Apostles. We may mention particularly the works of Philo and of Josephus Flavius, both of whom wrote in Greek.

Philo was born in Alexandria in 25 B. C. He was the son of a Jewish priest, lived in Alexandria and received there a comprehensive Greek education. He employed the knowledge thus acquired in writing books intended to defend and expound Judaism for the benefit of pagan readers. His chief works are: The Life of Moses; The Creation; The Decalogue; Circumcision; Sacrifices.

The writings of Josephus, who bore the Roman cognomen Flavius, are still more important. He, too, was the son of a Jewish priest, and was born in Jerusalem in 37 A. D. His works, written in Rome, far from Palestine, and after the destruction of Jerusalem, are nevertheless most valuable, especially for the later period, of which the Bible does not give much account. They are: History of the Jewish War, in seven books; Jewish Antiquities, in 20 books;[1] two books against the Sophist Apion, and the history of his own life.

(b) *Secondary Sources of Information.* The foremost of these is the Talmud (from *lamad,* to learn, hence the book of learning, or doctrine). For the Jews this is by far the most important book after the Bible;[2] it consists of two parts, the Mishna and the Gemara. The first part, which forms the Talmud strictly so called, is the Mishna (from *schana,* to repeat, hence it is the repetition of the Law). This is in Hebrew,[3] and contains a collection of the earliest Jewish traditions, written down at the end of the second or at the beginning of the third century by Rabbi Juda Hakkadosch, head of the school at Tiberias, in order to preserve them from being forgotten or tampered with.[4] Explanations were added later, and these form

[1] In the "Antiquities," XVIII, iii. 3, Josephus speaks of Christ, in whom he did not himself believe. The passage is as follows: "At this time lived Jesus, a wise man, if indeed we may call him a man; for he was a worker of miracles and a teacher to those who gladly receive the truth. He had many followers, both Jews and Gentiles, and was regarded as the Messias. In consequence of the envy of our rulers he was condemned by Pilate to be crucified. Nevertheless those who had formerly loved him remained loyal to him, for he showed himself to them alive again on the third day. This and many other wonderful things had been foretold concerning him in the writings of the prophets, and hitherto the sect of Christians, taking its name from him, has not ceased to exist." Many critics have pronounced this passage to be a forgery, but it bears every token of being genuine.

[2] The Jews maintain that everything taught by our Lord may be found also in the Talmud; this book, however, is of later origin than the New Testament. It is based not only upon the oral teaching of the Rabbis, but has also written sources. Much in it is pure gold, but intermixed with worthless matter.

[3] i. e. in modern Hebrew, which bears the same relation to biblical Hebrew as is borne by the Latin of mediæval scholars to that of the Roman classical authors.

[4] Rabbi Juda divided his writings into six sections (*sedarim,* arrangements): viz. (1) *seder ser'im* = seed section, containing all relating to husbandry, i. e. explanations of the laws regarding it; (2) *seder mo'ed* = of festivals (Sabbath, Pasch, Day of Atonement, etc.); (3) *seder naschim* = of women, marriage laws; (4) *seder nesigin* = of injuries (damage to property, compensation, trials, etc.); (5) *seder qodaschim* = of holy things (regulations for sacrifice); (6) *seder theharoth* = purifications

the second part of the Talmud, viz. the Gemara (from *gamar,* Aramaic *gemar,* to complete, hence conclusion, completion). This part is in Aramaic and falls into two portions, the Jerusalem and the Babylonian. The former originated, like the Mishna, in the school at Tiberias, and was compiled by Rabbi Jochanan (189–279). It is in the West Aramaic dialect. The Babylonian Gemara is much longer and is in East Aramaic, a dialect akin to the Syrian. It was brought from Babylon, where there had always been many Jews, ever since the Captivity, and where they had famous schools. It was written in the fifth and sixth centuries, and was the joint work of several Rabbis (Asche, Jose, etc.).[1]

(Levitical uncleanness, ablutions, bathing, etc.). The Gemara also, both in the Palestine and in the Babylonian portions, shows the same division into sections.

[1] The Gemara is often called simply the Talmud, so that we hear of the Palestine and the Babylonian Talmud. *Cf. Monumenta Judaica:* I *Bibliotheca Targumica,* II *Bibliotheca Talmudica.* Vienna and Leipzig.

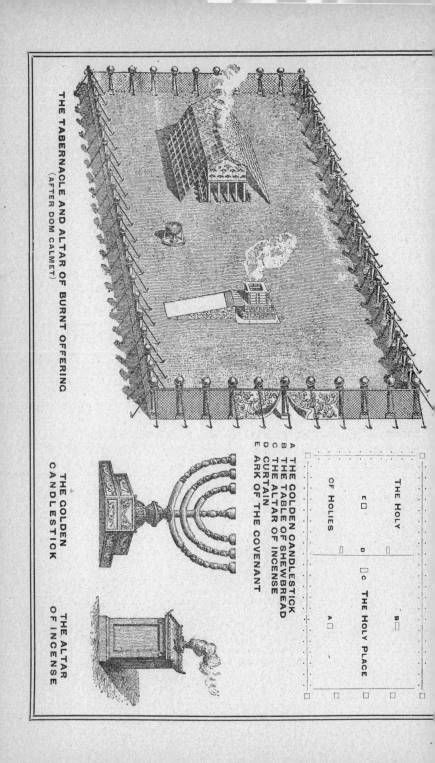

THE TABERNACLE AND ALTAR OF BURNT OFFERING
(AFTER DOM CALMET)

THE GOLDEN
CANDLESTICK

THE ALTAR
OF INCENSE

A THE GOLDEN CANDLESTICK
B THE TABLE OF SHEWBREAD
C THE ALTAR OF INCENSE
D CURTAIN
E ARK OF THE COVENANT

THE HOLY

OF HOLIES

E ☐

☐ B

☐ D ☐ C THE HOLY PLACE

A ☐

FIRST SECTION

HOLY PLACES

I. THE TABERNACLE

1. GENERAL DESCRIPTION

(Exodus xxvi.)

A T God's command Moses employed skillful workmen to
erect a tent temple on Sinai, according to the plan revealed
to him by God. This was called the Dwelling (*mischkan*) or
Tabernacle.[1] This tent was entered from the east and was
divided into two parts, the Holy and the Most Holy places. It
formed a long quadrangle, and its length (interior) was 30
cubits,[2] its breadth 10 cubits and its height 10 cubits; it was
made of a wooden framework, composed of 48 strong planks [3]
or beams of acacia wood.[4] Each plank was covered with gold,
and measured 10 cubits in length and 1½ in breadth. This
wooden frame surrounded the interior on three sides, but on
the fourth side were columns and a curtain. The two side
walls contained 20 planks each, the shorter end wall only 8.

---

[1] In the Vulgate it is called *tabernaculum fœderis* or *tabernaculum
testimonii*. In the Septuagint, σκηνή τοῦ μαρτυρίου; in the Hebrew Bible,
"Tent of the Agreement, Tent of the Testimony, Dwelling of the Testimony."

[2] An ell or cubit is the length from the point of the middle finger to
the elbow = six handbreadths or two spans; about half a yard.

[3] The Hebrew קְרָשִׁים (from קָרַשׁ, to cut off) is generally translated
planks. The word, however, only signifies something cut or hewn of
wood, as in Ezech. xxvii. 6. In the Septuagint it is rendered στῦλοι,
pillars. The Vulgate has (less accurately) *tabulæ*. The word might be
translated beams or uprights.

[4] Hebrew, "wood of schittim." This is the plural of *schittah* = the
genuine acacia, *Mimosa nilotica*. The tree grew to a considerable size
and its wood was very durable and at the same time very light. This
wood was to be used because the acacia is the only tree that thrives in
the valleys of Sinai.

Each plank must have been a cubit in thickness, so that the two at the ends of the shorter wall were flush with those at the ends of the long walls.[1] At the lower end of each plank were two projections [2] which fitted into silver sockets, and on the outer side were strong golden rings, five on each beam, through which were passed the gilded bars that kept all the planks in place, and so kept the whole erection together. On the front side stood five gilded pillars of acacia wood with artistic capitals. These pillars rested on brazen sockets and supported a curtain, through which the Tabernacle was entered. The curtain was arranged thus: At the top of the pillars were golden hooks holding up gilded rods to which the curtain was fastened. In the inside was another curtain dividing the Tabernacle into two parts, the Holy and the Most Holy Places. It hung down from four gilded pillars, resting on silver sockets. The inner portion, which was the Most Holy Place, measured 10 cubits in length, breadth and height; the Holy Place had the same breadth and height, but was 20 cubits in length.

The bare earth formed the floor, nor had the Tabernacle any wooden roof, the place of which was taken by coverings stretched over the framework. These coverings were four in number (Ex. xxvi.).

The lowest covering was the most magnificent. It consisted (Ex. xxvi. 1, etc.) of ten cloths or curtains of white linen, fine but strong, prepared in such a way that on the white ground cherubim could be artistically worked with thread of a violet, dark red and bright red color. Each of the ten curtains was 28 cubits long and 4 wide, and they were joined together in two sets of five, so as to form two large curtains each measuring 28 by 20 cubits, and the whole covering that they

[1] The transport of such solid wooden pillars from one encampment to another must have caused great difficulty, though there was not so much hurry as in our day and in our countries. According to Num. vii. 4, etc., the heavier articles were laid on wagons drawn by oxen.

[2] As beams measuring 1½ cubits in breadth were perhaps difficult to obtain, it may be assumed that each consisted of two parts, firmly fastened together — the "two projections" seem to suggest this. According to the reports of missionaries, however, even at the present time the acacia furnishes very substantial wood for building purposes in China.

formed together was 40 cubits long and 28 wide. We are not told how the five separate parts of each half were composed; but we know that each of the two at the end of the curtains had 50 violet loops, placed opposite to one another, and fastened together by means of 50 golden pins, which gripped them on either side. This covering was arranged over the holy Tabernacle so that the join down the middle lay precisely above the inner curtain. It must therefore have hung down 8 cubits on the two long sides (north and south) and 9 cubits at the back, behind the Most Holy Place. It was probably fastened down to the earth by means of pegs.[1]

The second covering was less precious. It was woven of goats' hair, and was composed not of 10, but of 11 pieces, each of which was 30 cubits long and 4 wide. Its total extent, therefore, was 30 by 44 cubits. It, too, consisted of two parts, the front one being made of 6 pieces and the back one of only 5. These two parts were fastened together by means of 50 loops and 50 brass clasps, so as to form one whole. The part consisting of 5 pieces was spread over the Most Holy Place, and that of 6 pieces over the Holy Place. One piece hung over, and this was folded back and doubled on the front of the Tabernacle, to gain more solidity, so that it measured only 2 cubits, and projected for a space of 1 cubit, so as to form a kind of shelter over the entrance. At the other end of the tent this covering extended 1 cubit beyond the former, and this was the case also at the sides, so that the second covering was a protection to the innermost one, stretching 1 cubit beyond it in all directions. The fastenings, where the two halves were joined together, cannot apparently have been exactly above the entrance to the Most Holy Place, but about half a yard behind it.

[1] If the planks were each 1 cubit in thickness, the covering could not have hung down more than 8 cubits, rather than 9, at the west end. That it hung outside is very probable, as this was, and still is, the usual arrangement for tents, and moreover there would have had to be some special means of securing it on the inner side, and no such thing is mentioned. The pegs (or pins) and cords of the Tabernacle are referred to in Ex. xxvii. 19; xxxv. 18; xxxviii. 20 and 31. The space thus formed under the coverings could be used for the storage of utensils and as a sleeping place (I Kings iii. 3).

The two outer coverings are mentioned in Holy Scripture, but are not fully described. The lower one of these, i. e. the third covering, consisted of rams' skins dyed red,[1] the upper, or fourth covering, of *tachasch* skins.[2] The *tachasch* was probably the sea-cow found in the Red Sea, and now called Manati; some authorities, however, believe that the badger is meant, as tachasch = to penetrate, creep in; and the badger lives in holes in the earth. We may reasonably suppose that the Tabernacle was not always erected with all these four coverings over it, but that often one sufficed. The innermost appears to have been intended chiefly as an ornament; the others served as protections against dust and storms.

The two curtains separating the Holy and Most Holy Places formed each a square, measuring 10 cubits in each direction. They were made of the same materials as the first or innermost covering, but whereas the inner curtain also bore pictures of cherubim, the outer one had none, but was only embroidered in colors.

2. THE COURT OF THE TABERNACLE

(Ex. xxvii. 9, etc.)

The Tabernacle that has just been described was always surrounded on all sides by a court. This was marked off on the outer side by a wall of curtains, 5 cubits in height. The court was 100 cubits long and 50 broad; on the north and south sides stood 20 pillars, and on the east and west sides 10. These had brass sockets and their capitals were covered with silver. Silver rods resting on hooks kept them in place, and supported the curtains, which were made of strong linen, and ran round the whole court, not, however, touching the ground, but being secured on the outer side by means of stakes (Ex. xxvii. 19). Towards the east the curtains projected only 15 cubits beyond the corners, so as to leave in the center a space

---

[1] Vulgate, *de pellibus arietum rubricatis;* Septuagint, δέρματα κριῶν ἠρυθροδανωμένα.

[2] In the Septuagint the name is given as δέρματα ὑακίνθινα; in the Vulgate, *ianthinæ pelles* = violet-colored hides.

20 cubits wide, that served as the entrance. This was closed by another curtain embroidered with colors, 5 cubits high and 20 broad, hanging from four pillars. It took the place of a door.

The holy tent was probably not erected quite in the middle of the courtyard, but nearer to its western than to its eastern end. Philo says that the two sides and the back were all at the same distance, viz. 20 cubits, from the outside boundary of the court, so that the open space in front of the Tabernacle formed a square of 50 cubits.

Modern critics outside the Church declare the whole account of the Tabernacle to be a fiction. "We have to deal here not with historical facts but with unrestrained fancy" (Benzinger, 397). As in later times only the Temple in Jerusalem was the recognized place of worship, and as the performance of religious rites on high places and all sacrifices outside the Temple were strictly forbidden, the authors of the "priests' code" invented the story of the Mosaic Tabernacle, as if Moses wished God to be served in only one place and had made these regulations to secure this end. "It is impossible that an uncivilized nomadic nation could have erected such a magnificent shrine in the wilderness." "An additional argument against the truth of the story is its inexactitude."

On the other hand the Egyptians were skillful craftsmen, and themselves erected temples of similar construction. Why may we not believe that they imparted their skill to the Israelites? The latter nation had not come out of Egypt in a state of destitution (Ex. xxxiii. 24, 25, 29), so it is easy to account for the abundance of costly materials.[1] The wood that they used for building is said to have been that of the genuine acacia or schittah; if the story of the Tabernacle had been drawn from the imagination of men in later times, the wood mentioned would certainly have been that of the cypress or cedar, as known in Palestine. In fact, Philo understands schittah to mean cedar wood. This fact alone is enough to convince us that the Tabernacle really existed and was made on Sinai (cf. p. 69, note 4). The alleged inexactitudes in the description vanish if a right explanation is given, and the "unrestrained fancies" prove to be on the side of the modern critics, who always discover what they want to find.[2]

[1] Cf. also Num. xxxi. 22, where we read that the Israelites plundered the Madianites of the wealth of their mines.

[2] Wellhausen feels obliged to recognize the existence of a tent covering the Ark of the Covenant, but he will not admit that it is identical with the one described in Exodus xxvi. Passages containing clear reference to the Tabernacle, such as Judges xviii. 31, I Kings i. 9, i. 24, ii. 22, xxi. 7, II Kings vii. 6, are arbitrarily pronounced suspicious, and explained as later interpolations (cf. Kautzsch, Altes Testament).

THE SACRED FURNITURE AND UTENSILS

3. Furniture in the Court of the Tabernacle

In the court stood the altar of burnt offering or holocausts, and the laver.

1. The altar of holocausts (Ex. xxvii. 1–8; xxxviii. 1, etc.) consisted of a framework of acacia wood, 5 cubits in length and breadth and 3 cubits in height. The frame was hollow and was filled up with earth and stones, so that the latter formed the altar proper. The wooden sides were covered with brass,[1] and provided at the corners with four brazen horns.[2] Half-way up the altar, i. e. at a height of 1½ cubits from the ground, ran a projecting ledge about a cubit in breadth, having at its outer edge a copper grating or network resting on the ground; brass rings were attached to the four corners. This ledge served for the priests to stand on, so that they might more easily perform their duties at the top of the altar. The fire on this altar, which consumed the victims, was never allowed quite to die out (Lev. vi. 9, 12, 13). "This is the perpetual fire which shall never go out on the altar."

2. The brazen laver, made of metal mirrors (Ex. xxx. 17–21; xxxviii. 8), stood between this altar and the Tabernacle, a little to the south. It is not clearly described in Holy Scripture, but, on the analogy of the great basin in the Temple, we may imagine it to have been shaped like a cauldron, and of considerable size. Probably there were openings and taps at the sides for letting out the water when necessary, as it was used for washing the priests' hands and feet, whenever they entered the Tabernacle, and also to cleanse the flesh of the sacrifice, and the sacrificial vessels and garments if they happened to be

---

[1] נְחֹשֶׁת = something dense or hard; i.e. metal. The name is always given to æs cyprium = cyprian brass, or copper with its alloys.

[2] These horns suggest that the altar and the sacrifices were means of averting the punishments inflicted by God and also attacks from enemies, as an animal defends itself with its horns. Hence "horn" often means power, strength, security, confidence; e. g. I Kings ii. 1; II Kings xxii. 3; Ps. xvii. 3; Luke i. 69. They have nothing to do with the representation of the deity in the form of an ox, as Benzinger imagines.

stained. There was below the laver a base of brass to receive the
water that flowed out of it (Ken).[1] Among the other furniture
of the courtyard we have mention made of pots to hold the
ashes, tongs, forks and censers. Besides there must certainly
have been the apparatus required for slaughtering the victims
and for skinning them; and tables on which the flesh of the
sacrifice could be laid, such as were used later in the Temple.

4. FURNITURE IN THE HOLY PLACE

Three things stood here: the candlestick, the table for the
loaves of proposition or shewbread, and the altar of incense.

1. The golden candlestick (Ex. xxv. 31, etc.) stood sideways

---

[1] The correct explanation of the words in Ex. xxxviii. 8 is doubtful:
נְחֹשֶׁת וְאֵת כַּנּוֹ נְחֹשֶׁת בְּמַרְאֹת הַצֹּבְאֹת אֲשֶׁר צָבְאוּ פֶּתַח אֹהֶל מוֹעֵד: וַיַּעַשׂ אֵת הַכִּיּוֹר
The Septuagint renders them: καὶ ἐποίησε τὸν λουτῆρα τὸν χαλκοῦν καὶ τὴν
βάσιν αὐτοῦ χαλκῆν ἐκ τῶν κατόπτρων τῶν νηστευσασῶν, αἱ ἐνήστευσαν παρὰ τῆς
θύρας τῆς σκηνῆς τοῦ μαρτυρίου. Vulgate: *Fecit et labrum æneum cum basi
sua de speculis mulierum, quæ excubabant in ostio tabernaculi.* It seems
certain that the word צָבְאֹת denotes women who took some kind of
part in the service of the Tabernacle. Knobel (*Ex.*, p. 332) suggests
that these were Levite women, who visited the sanctuary from time to
time, in order to wash, clean and polish it; he says that figures of
such women occur on basins. If he is right, we ought to translate:
"He made the brazen laver and its brazen base with *figures* of serving
women. . . ." But figures of women with brooms, etc., would not
probably be considered suitable for the sanctuary. The Hebrew מַרְאָה,
and κάτοπτρον, mean, not figure, but mirror. It is more likely that
women are referred to, who lived austere lives near the Tabernacle, and
sometimes were employed there, perhaps in baking, and in making the
priests' garments. *Cf.* II Mach. iii. 19, where, in the account of the
plundering of the Temple, mention is made of "shut up" virgins (αἱ
κατακλέιστοι τῶν παρθένων) who sought by their prayers to avert the sacri-
lege. The Septuagint translators must have been guided by some tradition,
when they rendered the Hebrew בְּ (= by, by means of, with) by ἐκ, and
אָבָא by νηστεύω (= to fast, abstain). The sons of Heli were said to have
sinned by behaving in an unseemly way towards such women (I Kings
ii. 22). Jephte seems to have placed his daughter among these women in
consequence of his vow (Judges xi. 31). The mirrors belonging to such
persons might have been attached to the laver, in order that the priests
could always see whether their clothes and faces were properly clean;
but this would probably have been stated in the Hebrew in a separate
clause. It is most likely that these women offered their metal mirrors
as the material out of which the laver was made. This is the Vulgate
interpretation, and Kautzsch takes the same view.

on the south side of the Holy Place. It was of beaten work of the finest gold (therefore not massive), and it had seven branches, the one in the middle rising straight up, and the others being in pairs on either side of it. The central shaft rested upon a pedestal called in Holy Scripture *jarek*, i. e. hip or loin; the name seems to have been selected because there were probably feet lower down, whilst the upper part suggested a body with outstretched arms. On the branches were ornaments like the cup of a flower, consisting of a knob and a blossom. These were placed on the central shaft below the points where the arms branched off, and also at the place where the shaft joined its pedestal. Moreover, each side branch bore three such ornaments, so that there were twenty-two in all. At the upper ends were lamps, but these did not actually form part of the candlestick, and only rested on the seven branches. In shape they probably resembled the ordinary lamps of antiquity; that is to say, they were oval, having at one end a projecting wick and at the other a handle by which they could be carried. At the ends of the seven arms were slight depressions to hold them. The lamps cast their light inwards, towards the " side of the Countenance " on the north. Every morning they had to be taken down to be cleaned, and then were replaced.[1] The purest olive oil was burned in these lamps. As accessories are mentioned (Ex. xxv. 38) golden tongs (probably snuffers) and dishes to hold the snuffers and wicks.

2. The table of the bread of proposition or shewbread (Ex. xxv. 23–30) stood on the north side of the sanctuary, opposite the candlestick. It was of acacia wood, measuring 2 cubits long, 1 cubit wide and $1\frac{1}{2}$ cubits high, and completely covered with sheets of gold. At the top was a projecting ledge of gold (*misgereth* = enclosure) as wide as a man's hand, so that the surface of the table lay below it, and round about this margin ran a golden garland. To the legs of the table four rings

---

[1] It is uncertain whether the lamps burned constantly, day and night. Josephus Fl. (*Antiq.*, VI, iii. 9) agrees with the Rabbis in saying that by day only three were alight, but at night all seven. While Lev. xxiv. 4 states that they were *always* (*tamid*) to be burning, it probably only means that the light ought never quite to be extinguished.

were fastened, through which rods could be passed, so that it might be carried. The rods also were of acacia wood, overlaid with gold. Upon the table lay always twelve thin loaves [1] of the finest wheat flour; they were arranged in two rows of six, and Josephus Flavius assures us that they were unleavened. The Hebrew text calls them "loaves of the Countenance"; the Authorized Version has "shrewbread." Every Sabbath they were taken away and replaced by fresh ones; and the priests ate the stale bread within the sanctuary. At this ceremony the incense near the loaves was burned (perhaps on the altar of incense). The loaves were carried in on (probably two) shallow dishes and set in order; the incense was placed in little bowls. Wine also was brought in (perhaps only on the Sabbath) in special jugs, poured into bowls and then offered as libations, being thrown out on the ground. All these accessories were of pure gold.

3. The altar of incense (Ex. xxx. 1, etc.; xxxvii. 25, etc.) occupied a position in the middle before the inner curtain. It was four-cornered and made of acacia wood, measuring 2 cubits in height and 1 cubit in length and breadth. It had a so-called "roof" (*gag*); i. e. a raised edge ran all round the flat upper surface, and a golden garland was fastened to the edge, as in the table of the shewbread. Below the garland were two golden rings on each side, through which staves were passed for carrying the altar. Horns were fastened to the four corners. The whole was overlaid with gold. Incense was offered on this altar daily, both morning and evening. The ritual was as follows: [2]

A priest took some glowing charcoal from the altar of holocausts and carried it in a golden vessel into the Tabernacle,

---

[1] The number refers to the twelve tribes of Israel, and the offering placed before the Face of God testified that they owed their bread to the Lord's goodness.

[2] Mishna, order Qodaschim, tract. 9; Thamid, chap. v.–vii. According to Isaias vi. 6 it appears that the charcoal was not laid immediately upon the top of the table, which would soon have been destroyed if this had been done, but it was placed on stones; probably pebbles. It is, however, possible that only the censer rested on the altar, although this is contradicted by the Mishna (*cf.* Heb. ix. 4: *habens thuribulum aureum*).

whilst another carried the incense. The first priest scattered the charcoal on the altar, and the second laid the incense upon it. Meanwhile the people stood in the court, engaged in prayer, and then they received the priest's blessing. The incense consisted of four ingredients, which were called collectively *sammim* = sweet perfumes. It had to be salted, and had to be clean and holy, i. e. some salt was strewn over it, as over everything offered in sacrifice; it was not to contain any foreign ingredients, and after it was mixed, was to be used only in the sanctuary. It was forbidden, under penalty of death, to use incense mixed in this particular way for any profane purpose.

5. The Holy of Holies

The ark of the Covenant stood here; it was a chest of acacia wood, covered with gold both inside and outside. Its length was 2½ cubits, its breadth and height 1½ cubits. Round the middle of it ran a garland of pure gold. At the four corners were golden rings, through which gilded rods were passed to enable the ark to be carried; these rods were never to be removed. Inside the ark was nothing but the two stone tables, on which the Ten Commandments were inscribed (Ex. xxvi. 16; Deut. x. 4, 5). According to Hebrews ix. 4, beside the holy ark were kept Aaron's rod, and a vessel of manna.[1] In Deuteronomy, xxxi. 25, etc., we read that the Book of the Law also lay beside the ark. Moses commanded the Levites: "Take this book and put it at the side of the ark of the covenant." מִצַּד אֲרוֹן, ἐκ πλαγίων τῆς κιβωτοῦ, Vulgate, *in latere arcæ.* The book was, as it were, the commentary upon the Decalogue.

---

[1] In Heb. ix. 4 the reading is ἐν ᾗ (κιβωτῷ), which is generally translated "*in* which [ark]." But ἐν, like the Latin *in,* also means near, beside. In Ex. xvi. 33 all that is said of the vessel of manna is that it was לִפְנֵי יְהֹוָה = before the Lord; Sept. ἐναντίον τοῦ θεοῦ. In Num. xvii. 35 (Vulg. xvii. 10) Aaron's rod is commanded to be carried into the Tabernacle for safe keeping. At the time of Solomon, according to III Kings viii. 9 and II Chron. v. 10, there were only the two tables of the law in the ark, but it is possible that for a time the vessel of manna and Aaron's rod, probably cut short, were kept in it also.

Over the ark was the *Kapporeth,* i. e. a cover of pure gold. It was by no means intended merely to close the ark, but had a far higher purpose. This is implied by the fact that it was of solid gold, whilst the ark was only of wood overlaid with sheets of gold, and also by the command that the Kapporeth should be as long and as broad as the ark (Ex. xxv. 17), — if it were only a cover, this would be a matter of course. Its true destination is suggested by the Holy of Holies being called the house of the Kapporeth. The word *Kapporeth* may indeed mean " covering," but it may equally well be translated " place of atonement." [1] The Kapporeth may be explained as God's resting place. At either end of it, and inseparable from it, was a cherub of beaten gold, undoubtedly in human form, but with wings, which were stretched inwards over the ark. The space between the two cherubim on the Kapporeth was considered to be God's abode on earth. It was therefore called the *Schekina* = dwelling. From this spot God made answer to Moses and other leaders of the people, when they consulted Him on important matters.[2] If the question is asked how we are to imagine this presence of God, whether it was perceptible to the senses or only perceptible intellectually, we may reply that the object of the Holy of Holies was to perpetuate the memory of the events on Sinai, and that for this reason we may believe the presence of God to have been perceptible in clouds and fire (Lev. xvi. 2; Is. xxxvii. 15; I Chron. xiii. 6). It is, however, improbable that this presence could always be perceived; as a rule, it was latent, and became visible only on important occasions.

---

[1] The name comes from *Kaphar,* to cover; *Kapper* = to atone, propitiate. On the Day of Atonement every year the solemn ceremony of atonement had to be performed here.

[2] Ex. xxv. 22: " Thence will I give orders, and will speak to thee over the propitiatory, and from the midst of the two cherubims, which shall be upon the ark of the testimony, all things which I will command the children of Israel by thee." *Cf.* Num. vii. 89; Deut. v. 7; I Kings iii. 3.

II. THE TEMPLE

(a) Solomon's Temple

6. INTRODUCTORY

As long as the people of Israel were wandering in the wilderness, the Tabernacle and all its furniture and utensils were carried by the Levites (Num. iv.) from one encampment to another.[1]   After the Israelites had taken possession of the Promised Land, the Tabernacle was erected in various places.   It stood for a long time at Silo, then at Nobe, and later still at Gabaon.   Meantime the ark had been separated from it, and during a war had passed into the possession of the Philistines, but they voluntarily restored it, and it was kept for a time in a private house, and then was placed by David in a specially erected tent[2] on Mount Sion, whence it was transferred to the new Temple.

When the Israelites took Jerusalem from the Jebusites and obtained complete possession of the city, it was proposed to build a Temple to the Lord on Mount Moria,[3] according to the

---

[1] The Tabernacle stood within the camp.   In Ex. xxxiii. 7, etc., we read that Moses erected a " tabernacle of the covenant " outside the camp. Benzinger (p. 370) follows Wellhausen in believing this to have been another tent and not the Tabernacle, which was required to be within it. The matter is, however, explicable in the following way: On account of their rebellious spirit the Israelites were not permitted to be in God's immediate neighborhood, but later on (Ex. xl.) the holy Tabernacle was erected inside the camp, and the tribe of Levi was placed nearest to it, the other tribes were further away, three on each side of it.   To the east was the tribe of Juda, and to the left of Juda was Issachar, and to the right Zabulon; to the south was Ruben with Simeon and Gad; to the west Ephraim with Manasses and Benjamin; and to the north Dan with Aser and Nephtali.

[2] This was no longer the Tabernacle made by Moses, but a new tent, probably made in the same fashion as the Mosaic Tabernacle which remained in Gabeon, having possibly become damaged in course of time. Solomon had it solemnly removed and brought into the new Temple, where it was most likely kept in the upper story above the Holy of Holies.   Allusions to it occur in III Kings iii. 4; I Chron. xxi. 29; II Chron. i. 3, 13; II Mach. ii. 4, 5.

[3] Moria is perhaps = אמוריא = Land of the Amorites.

same plan as the Tabernacle.[1] King David collected a great quantity of materials for this purpose (I Chron. xxix. 2, etc.) and gave them and the designs that he had prepared to his son Solomon, who faithfully carried out his father's wishes. He began to build the Temple in the fourth year of his reign, and completed it in seven years (III Kings vi).

The surface of Mount Moria proved to be too small for the Temple, so huge walls were built up on the eastern side and the space between them and the hill was filled up with earth, and thus a sufficiently large site was obtained (Jos. Fl., *Ant.*, III., iii. 9; *Bell. Jud.*, V, v. 1).

The stone and the cedar and cypress wood all came from Lebanon, as Solomon had made an agreement for this purpose with Hiram, King of Tyre; who supplied also some workmen, well trained in their art. Solomon gave Hiram in return the products of his country, especially grain, oil and wine.

Like the Tabernacle, its model, the Temple was divided into a house and a court.

7. The House of the Temple

(III Kings vi.–viii.; II Chron. iii.–v.; Ez. xl.–xlii., xlvi.)

The Temple proper, called the House (*habbajith*), was built of hewn stone, and measured 60 cubits in length, 20 in breadth, and 30 in height; — these are the inside measurements, not including the thickness of the walls. It had a flat roof. The interior was divided into the Holy Place and the Holy of Holies. The former was 40 cubits long, 20 broad and 30 high; the latter was 20 cubits in length, breadth and height, as the other 10 cubits, deducted from the total height of the building, formed an upper chamber. The masonry was covered on the inside with wooden panels; these were not smooth, but were carved with figures of cherubim, palms, gourds and opening blossoms. Over these very thin plates of gold were fastened with golden nails, so that the carved figures showed through the gold with which they were covered. It is probable that

---

[1] In Wisdom ix. 8 the Temple is called μίμημα σκηνῆς ἁγίας.

some beams of wood were built into the masonry. The ceiling and the floor were also covered with wood and sheets of gold, but no figures were carved upon them.

A door of sycamore wood with five corners,[1] in the middle of the partition wall, formed the entrance to the Holy of Holies. It was 6 cubits in width (Ezech. xli. 3) and was in two parts; they, like the walls, were covered with gilded carvings, and turned on golden hinges. Both halves of the door were usually open, but it was not possible to see into the Holy of Holies, as a curtain of the same kind as that which hung formerly in the Tabernacle (II Chron. iii. 14) shut off all view. The Holy Place was entered by folding doors of cypress wood, but they folded back in two pieces on each side, and were ornamented like the doors of the Holy of Holies. In front of the house of the Temple was a porch 10 cubits in depth, and running along the whole breadth of the building (20 cubits); nothing is stated as to its height in III Kings, but in II Chronicles iii. 4 we are told that it was 120 cubits high. If this be correct, the porch must have been a kind of tower, but as we nowhere else find any suggestion of a tower, the number may perhaps be due to a copyist's mistake. In the porch stood two thick columns, one known as Jakin and the other as Boaz. They were made by Churam of Tyre, a skillful artist (II Chron. ii. 13). They were hollow, cast of brass, measuring 12 cubits in circumference and 18 in height, and on the top of each was a capital specially cast, 5 cubits high, so that the columns and capitals together measured 23 cubits, and this may have been the height of the porch.[2]

---

[1] i. e. a quadrangle running up into a point at the top.

[2] Saint Ephrem gives the following explanation of the names of these columns: "Solomon called the one Jakin, i. e. 'may he establish.' This expresses the wish that the building may stand firm and be strong. He called the other Boaz, i. e. 'in strength,' so that together the names contain a request for strength and permanence" (Opera, ed. Rom. Syr. Lat., I, p. 460). The two names were sometimes taken to be those of people, perhaps of the two artists who made the columns; and both designations, יָכִין and בֹּעַז, actually occur elsewhere as proper names. Another explanation might be: "May he strengthen! with him is strength." Benzinger quite arbitrarily assumes that the columns "were unmistakably copied from the pillars dedicated to Baal." It would be more

All round the outside of the Temple, except at the east or front, ran an annex (*jazua* = spread out) containing three tiers of chambers for the things used in the Temple worship and for storage of supplies. The beams supporting these stories rested on rebatements in the Temple wall at each story; the beams were not built into the wall. As the thickness of the Temple wall diminished by a cubit at each story, the chambers in the annex varied in width. At the basement they were 5, above that 6, and in the third tier they were 7 cubits wide. The height of each story was 5 cubits. If the ceilings are included, we may assume that the whole annex was about 18 cubits in height; the house of the Temple itself, being 30 cubits high, rose considerably above it, and in the upper part of the wall on either side were windows, i. e. latticed openings intended to admit air rather than light. The Holy Place was lighted with lamps, but the Holy of Holies was totally dark. Doors on the north and south sides (Ezech. xli. 11) formed the entrances to the lowest story in the annex, and a winding staircase, beginning close to the door, led up to the apartments above.

8. The Courts of the Temple

1. Round the house of the Temple was the Inner Court for priests. It was enclosed by a wall of hewn stone, covered with cedar wood, and, according to II Chronicles vii. 3, this court (and probably the other also) was paved with stones.

2. The Outer or Great Court for the people seems to have surrounded the Inner Court on all four sides, and it was certainly also enclosed by a wall, as it had gateways with folding doors. Jeremias xxxvi. 10 speaks of the Inner Court as the Upper; it was therefore on higher ground than that of the people, and it is most likely that the house of the Temple, following the form of Mount Moria, occupied the highest part of the hill, and was raised above the court of the priests.

3. The extent of these courts is nowhere stated. As they were only enlarged copies of the court of the Tabernacle, we

reasonable to regard them as copied from Egyptian obelisks, which often stood at the entrance to temples.

may perhaps infer that the inner court was 200 cubits long and 100 broad, and the outer court about double the size.

9. Furniture of the Temple

1. In the Holy of Holies stood the Ark of the Covenant. Apparently no new one was made, but Moses' ark with the Kapporeth and the two cherubim upon it was transferred to the Temple (III Kings viii. 1, etc.; II Chron. v. 22, etc.).[1] Near the ark, however, were stationed two large cherubim, i. e. figures of angels in human form, made of sycamore wood overlaid with gold, keeping watch over it.   Each figure was 10 cubits high and had wings each 5 cubits long.   One wing was stretched out backwards and touched the wall; the other was lifted forwards so as to meet the corresponding wing of the other cherub above the Kapporeth.   The figures stood upright, with their faces turned towards the entrance (II Chron. iii. 13).   The staves for carrying the ark, that were never removed, projected so that their ends could be recognized through the curtain (III Kings viii. 8).

2. In the Holy Place stood: (*a*) The Altar of Incense near the curtain; it was of cedar wood overlaid with gold.   (*b*) Ten golden candlesticks, bearing seven lamps each; the candlesticks were arranged five along the north and south walls respectively.   (*c*) Ten tables of shewbread, five on each side. We have no information regarding the size and shape of all these things; they no doubt differed only in size from those in the Tabernacle.

3. In the Inner Court were: (*a*) The brazen altar of holocausts, 20 cubits in length and breadth and 10 cubits in height. In design it resembled that of Moses, and was filled up inside with earth and stones.   It probably had several projecting ledges, on the uppermost of which the officiating priests stood. It must also have had steps, at least on the east side, as may be inferred from Ezechiel xliii. 17, "and its steps turned

---

[1] As at this time the ark contained only the two tables of the law (see p. 78), it seems probable that Aaron's rod and the vessel of manna and the Book of the Law were kept, with Moses' Tabernacle, in the room above the Holy of Holies.

towards the east." (*b*) The brazen sea or laver was a great round basin of water, 5 cubits high and 10 cubits in diameter at the top. It was cast of brass of the thickness of a man's hand and had an edge curving outwards, beneath which were two rows of gourds as ornamentation. The laver contained 2000 baths, i. e. about 360 hectoliters of water. It rested on twelve brazen bulls, three of which looked towards each quarter of the heavens, and presumably they stood on a brazen base. The water could probably be drawn off as required, by means of taps. It was used for washing the hands and feet, and also the flesh of the victims. We can scarcely suppose that the laver was filled by hand labor; there must have been some sort of aqueduct. Near the altar on the north and south sides were ten brazen stands with brazen basins upon them, intended for the reception of the flesh of the victims. These stands were four-cornered boxes, 40 cubits square at the top and 3 cubits in height. Under each were four wheels, so that they could be moved to and fro when required, and convey the flesh to the laver and the altar. On the sides of these stands were biblical figures, — oxen, lions, and cherubim. The basins on them contained each 4 bath (about 7 hectoliters) and were removable. These stands and basins were not used either in the Tabernacle nor in the second Temple. On the completion of the building the ark was solemnly carried from Sion into the Temple, and the dedication took place (III Kings viii. 1, etc.; II Chron. v. 1, etc.).

Solomon's Temple stood for 416 years (1004–588 B. C.) and was used as was intended during the whole time of the kings of Juda. In 588 it was plundered by the Babylonians and burned with the city of Jerusalem. The holy vessels and furniture, in as far as they were of precious materials, were taken to Babylon.

(b) The Second Temple

10. ZOROBABEL'S TEMPLE

After the Israelites were released by Cyrus, perhaps through Daniel's influence (I Esdras i.), they returned home from the

Captivity in 536 B. C., under Zorobabel's leadership, and at once restored the altar of holocausts on its old site and renewed the daily sacrifices. At the same time they began to rebuild the Temple, but were so much hindered by the hostility of the Samaritans that building operations ceased altogether for fifteen years and were only resumed in 520; the work was then carried on with such zeal that the Temple was ready for consecration in 515. From Esdras vi. 3 it appears that the new Temple was larger in extent than Solomon's,[1] but far less magnificent, owing to the poverty of the Israelites. Moreover, the chief treasure of the earlier Temple, the Ark of the Covenant,[2] was missing, and the Holy of Holies was empty. Where the ark should have stood, a stone was placed, on which the high priest set the censer on the day of Atonement. In the Holy Place was the altar of incense, a golden candlestick and a table for the shewbread; in the court was an altar of holocausts built of stone; and a laver stood between the altar and the porch, somewhat to the south (Middoth iii. 6; cf. Ecclus. l. 3). The Court of the Priests was surrounded by a larger court for the people. In consequence of many costly offerings being made, this temple gradually became more magnificent, and the temple tax of half a shekel (about 30 cents), demanded yearly of every Jew, even in foreign countries, supplied funds for its decoration.

In the second century before Christ, Antiochus Epiphanes plundered and laid waste the Temple and desecrated it by the worship of false gods. Judas Machabæus, after driving out the Syrians, repaired the buildings, as far as they had been injured, caused some of the furniture to be replaced by new, and had the Temple reconsecrated. This was the origin of the feast of the Encænia or Dedication (ἐγκαίνια, John x. 22, or φῶτα). At this time strong fortifications were added to the Temple,

---

[1] It is said to have been 60 cubits high and 60 wide.

[2] According to II Mach. ii. 4, 5, the prophet Jeremias in 588 "commanded that the tabernacle and the ark should accompany him, till he came forth to the mountain (Nebo) . . . and when Jeremias came thither he found a hollow cave: and he carried in thither the tabernacle, and the ark, and the altar of incense, and so stopped the door." But afterwards the place could not be found (l. c., 6, 7).

but nevertheless it was again taken by the Romans under Pompey (64 B. C.), and also by Herod the Great, who by the aid of Roman troops captured Jerusalem (37 B. C.) and stormed the Temple.

11. Herod's Temple

Herod the Great showed his passion for building by enlarging and altering the Temple, although he did not actually rebuild it.[1]

Work on the Temple began in 20 B. C., and in a year and a half the whole house of the Temple had been transformed; all the building being done by priests and Levites, after the materials had been prepared and arranged for them. The courts were finished in ten years, but work on the surrounding buildings was still going on during our Lord's lifetime, and even later.

In the form that it now assumed the Temple area measured a stade, or 500 cubits, in each direction.[2] It was laid out in terraces, so that one court was on a higher level than the other, and the Temple itself occupied the top of the hill. It could therefore be seen from all parts of the city and also from a great distance, and presented a magnificent appearance.

The outermost court was that of the Gentiles. It was surrounded by a high wall with several gates; it contained several halls, and was paved with colored stones. It ran round all the other buildings, enclosing them on all four sides. This huge court was generally filled with a crowd of people, and goods were sold in it as if it had been a market place. It was twice cleansed by our Saviour from this desecration.

Within it, and on higher grounds, being reached by 14 steps,

---

[1] The reason why Herod did not undertake to build an entirely new Temple, which would perhaps have been less costly, was, as many people think, because the prophet Aggæus (ii. 10) foretold that the second Temple should excel Solomon's in glory. Herod's Temple is always spoken of as the second, never as the third.

[2] 1 stade = $\frac{1}{40}$ geographical mile; so 4 stades = $\frac{1}{10}$ mile = 742 meters (nearly half an English mile). The Talmud contains an account of this Temple (tract Middoth); see also Jos. Flavius, *Antiq.*, XV, 11, and *Bell. Jud.*, V, 5.

was the Court of the People, also surrounded by a wall, on which were notices in Greek and Latin, warning the Gentiles on pain of death to go no farther. On the east side this court was entered by Nicanor's Gate, which was very large and magnificent,[1] and is called the Beautiful Gate in Acts iii. 2 and 10.[2] Besides this gate there were several others on the north and south sides, leading into the Court of the People, one on each side into that of the Women and three into that of the Men, for this Court was divided into a square and somewhat lower court assigned to the women, and a higher court for the men; the former lay nearest to Nicanor's Gate.

On the same level as the Court of the Men was that of the Levites, separated from it only by a low fence. In it was the great altar of holocausts, 15 cubits high, and at its lowest projection 40–50 cubits broad, and, somewhat to the south, the huge laver.

The house of the Temple was situated on rather higher ground. It was built of immense blocks of white marble and was richly gilded both inside and outside, and had larger dimensions than the earlier temple. It consisted of a magnificent porch (100 cubits high, 100 broad and 20 deep); the Holy Place (40 cubits long, 20 broad and 40 high) and the Holy of Holies (20 cubits long, 20 broad and 40 high). The Holy of Holies was empty; the Holy Place contained the altar of incense, one golden candlestick and one table for shewbread. At the sides, as in Solomon's Temple, there were three stories containing small rooms. The roof was a low gable, with gilded spikes on the gable.

Such was the Temple where our Lord taught and worked miracles. Beholding it, He foretold its speedy destruction, and that no stone would be left upon another. This prophecy was fulfilled in the year 70.

---

[1] This Nicanor is not to be identified with the Syrian General Nicanor, mentioned in the books of Machabees; it was an Alexandrian Jew who had this gate built.

[2] The *Beautiful Gate* of the Acts, the *Brazen Gate* of Josephus and *Nicanor's Gate* of the Mishna are identical.

At the time of Nehemias [1] the Samaritans built themselves a temple on Mount Garizim near Sichem, which the Jewish king John Hyrcanus destroyed in 129 B.C. Another temple, also built to rival the Temple at Jerusalem, existed at Leontopolis (near Cairo) in Egypt. It was poorly equipped and was pulled down by the Romans under Vespasian.

12. THE SYNAGOGUES

Besides the Temple, but not as substitutes for it, for they were totally different, were the synagogues, συναγωγαί, houses of prayer or assembly. We hear of them only after the Captivity. No sacrifices could be offered in them, and therefore, since the destruction of the Temple, the Jews have had no sacrifices. In the time of our Lord, as at the present day, synagogues existed not only in Palestine but wherever Jews had settled.

The requisites for the establishment of a synagogue are only (1) a cupboard for books on the side of the building towards Jerusalem — in it the parchment rolls of the Holy Scriptures are stored; (2) a lectern; the synagogue is especially the place where instruction is given in the law, and those learned in scripture are required to expound it; (3) seats for the congregation, the sexes being separated, the front row of seats being reserved for those learned in the law; (4) one or more candlesticks to give solemn light on important festivals. To keep order a ruler of the synagogue was appointed; he was assisted by a college of elders, and by a minister who had to attend to the opening, closing and cleaning of the building.

---

[1] *Cf.* John iv. 19. Josephus is in error when (*Ant.*, XI, viii. 2) he says that this Temple was built in the time of Alexander the Great (see p. 52).

Course for Exam.

SECOND SECTION

HOLY PERSONS

13. INTRODUCTORY

SINCE the Israelites quitted Egypt, the firstborn son of every family was dedicated to God for the purpose of attending to His worship (Num. viii. 17; *cf.* iii. 13). Subsequently the command was given that, instead of the firstborn sons, all the males of a whole tribe should be in a peculiar way God's property and look after His service (Num. iii. 41, etc.). This was the tribe of Levi, to which Moses belonged.[1] The reason for this change was probably that the setting apart of the firstborn would have caused excessive disturbances in the maintenance of families; however (Num. iii. 47), in order that the original custom should not be forgotten, every firstborn son had to be redeemed by the payment of a sum fixed by the priest, but not exceeding five shekels.

The task of the tribe of Levi was generally to preserve and continue the work of Moses. The Levites had to keep the Law of Moses free from all falsification;[2] they themselves had to observe its precepts most strictly and instruct the people

---

[1] Fr. v. Hummelauer, S.J., in a monograph on the subject, has attempted to prove the existence of an Israelite priesthood before the time of Moses, that it was transmitted through Manasses from Joseph who had been admitted to the priestly caste of the Egyptians, and then was exterminated on Sinai, because it had lapsed into Egyptian paganism (Ex. xxxii.). This hypothesis might perhaps throw some light on the lists in the early chapters of I Chronicles; but in Ex. xxxii. and xxxiii. the men killed are nowhere described as priests, and the account refers to the whole nation that had sinned through idolatry. It seems, therefore, very unsafe to assume the existence of a priesthood before the time of Moses.

[2] The book of the law was kept in the Holy of Holies, but there can be no doubt that copies existed for the use of the priests and Levites. In Deuteronomy xvii. 18, 19 we read that the king, when he wanted the book of the law, had to apply to the priests of the tribe of Levi. The law had to be read aloud to the people from time to time.

in the observance of the law. It was their business to watch over the manner in which the law was kept, to give verdicts in accordance with it, to hand it down in all its purity to their descendants, and, finally, to provide for the whole worship of God in the sanctuary.

Unlike the other tribes, the Levites received no land as their property in Palestine. God alone was to be their portion. "Levi hath no part nor possession with his brethren, because the Lord Himself is his possession" (Deut. x. 9). There were, however, forty-eight places assigned to them as dwellings in the midst of the other tribes; a list of these is given in Josue xxi. 9–40. Besides these they had pasture ground for their cattle, but no land for cultivation. These forty-eight places were by no means the property of the Levites, who only lived there amidst the other inhabitants.

The tribe of Levi had, however, a sufficient income, at least if the law was faithfully observed. To the Levites belonged all tithes, i. e. the tenth part of all the yearly produce of the fields and gardens, and of all cattle and sheep; and in addition the first fruits, i. e. the first produce of all the fields and gardens, the firstborn of all animals, and the sums paid for the redemption of the firstborn sons. They had also definite shares of all sacrifices.

The duty of attending to the actual worship of God was imposed upon one particular family, viz. the descendants of Aaron. Aaron himself and the firstborn of his family in each generation were the high priests, all his other direct descendants formed the priesthood, and the whole tribe was subject to them. This division of his family corresponds with that of the sanctuary. The high priest had to serve in the Holy of Holies; the priests attended to all the ceremonies in the Holy Place, whilst the Levites were only required to help the priests in the court.

14. THE LEVITES

Levi, the founder of the tribe, Jacob's third son by Lia, had three sons, Gerson, Cahath and Merari, so the tribe was divided into three parts, the Gersonites, the Cahathites and the

Merarites. To these Levites were assigned thirty-five places as their dwellings, and as means of livelihood they had, besides the produce of their herds, a tithe of the produce of all fields and gardens and of all cattle. They had, however, to pay a tenth of this tithe to the priests. They were summoned to take part at the sacrificial meals.

They were admitted to the holy service by means of a special dedication, called *taher* = cleansing. They were sprinkled with water of purification, prepared for the purpose; their hair was cut off, and they washed their clothes. Then they came to the place of the sanctuary, where the people were assembled, with two oxen destined for sacrifice. Here some men of the people, acting in the name of the nation, laid their hands upon the Levites, who on their part laid their hands on the oxen, which were then sacrificed, one being a burnt offering and the other a sin offering. After this ceremony, the Levites entered on their duties.

It is easy to see that the laying on of hands on the part of the community signified that the whole nation was really pledged to God's service and was ready to perform it, but the Levites were the representatives of the people and especially of the firstborn. The Levites on their side acknowledged that they, as sinners, were unworthy to serve the Lord, and deserved death. As, however, in that case there would be no ministers for the sanctuary, they allowed the oxen to die in their stead, and signified that these creatures were their representatives by laying their hands upon them.

The first dedication of the Levites in the wilderness was performed in the manner just described. It is uncertain whether this held good always, or was repeated subsequently. There is no record of a renewed dedication, and so probably the first dedication held good forever.

We are not told anything of a special official clothing being prescribed for the Levites. It would seem that they wore the ordinary dress, both in daily life and when engaged in their sacred duties. In the performance of these duties the Levites were absolutely subordinate to the priests, and were regarded as their assistants (Num. viii. 26). They were forbidden to do sacrifice, and might not touch the furniture of the Holy Place, nor the altar of incense, under penalty of death (Num.

xviii. 3). During the wandering of the Israelites in the wilderness, their business was to keep guard over the Tabernacle, for which reason they were encamped nearest to it, the Gersonites on the west, the Cahathites on the south and the Merarites on the north (Num. iii. 23, 29, 35), whilst Moses and Aaron and the priests were stationed on the east side near the entrance. The Levites had to erect the Tabernacle, and take it down when the march was resumed, and carry the parts of it, when it was taken to pieces, as well as the sacred furniture, which was all covered up. In Palestine they had to guard the Tabernacle and later the Temple, to open and to close it. Every day sixteen Levites kept watch at the gates of the Temple (I. Chron. xxvi. 12), and in the second Temple still more were employed because the spaces were so great and the gates so numerous.[1]

Moreover, the Levites were required to clean the Temple and everything connected with it, to prepare the shrewbread and the cakes used at sacrifices, to procure and look after all the accessories of worship (garments, grain, flour, salt, wine, oil and beasts for sacrifice) and to supply whatever was wanting. Further, they were bound to provide for the music in the Temple and to arrange for the singing. They assisted the priests in slaying and skinning the victims.

Besides serving in the Temple, the Levites acted as judges, and therefore they had to instruct the people in the Law and to punish transgressors in conformity with its precepts. According to I Chronicles xxiii. 4, there were four distinct classes of Levites: (1) ministers of the priests; (2) overseers and judges; (3) porters, or doorkeepers; (4) singers and musicians. They were bound to devote themselves to their official duties between the ages of 25 and 50.[2]

Besides the Levites, there were other men employed in menial work in the Temple, such as cutting wood and carrying water. These were called *Nethinim* = given ones, bondmen (see Jos. ix. 27; I Chron. ix. 2; I Esdr. ii. 43 and 70).

---

[1] The "Officer of the Temple," mentioned in Acts iv. 1, was probably the commander of the guard of Levites.

[2] Numbers viii. 24. In Numbers iv. 2 the age when a Levite could enter upon his duties is mentioned as thirty, but this passage refers to the removal of the Tabernacle during the wandering in the wilderness.

15. THE PRIESTS

Only the descendants of Aaron, Moses' elder brother, belonging to the Cahath branch of the tribe of Levi, were chosen by God to be priests. Aaron had four sons, two of whom, Abin and Nadam, were slain for their carelessness in the service of God (Lev. x. 1), so only the two remaining sons, Eleasar and Ithamar, could pass on the priestly office to their descendants. Not every one belonging to Aaron's family was fit to be a priest; all were excluded who had any bodily defect, who were blind, lame, deaf, or suffering from permanent sores, etc. (Lev. xxi. 16, etc.). No fixed age is prescribed in the Law, but the age appointed for the priests no doubt was the same as that for the Levites. Thirteen of the Levite towns were assigned to the priests as their dwellings.

The maintenance of the priests was provided for by (1) tithes, which the Levites had to give over to them from their tithes; (2) first fruits of field and garden produce; (3) money paid for the redemption of the firstborn, each of whom was redeemed for a sum to be fixed by the priest, but not exceeding 5 shekels; (4) the first male born of all clean beasts had to be sacrificed; the fat was burnt on the altar, but the rest of the carcass belonged to the priests (Num. xviii. 18); (5) the first male born of unclean beasts either had to be killed, or a clean beast, that could be sacrificed, was substituted for it, and the fifth of its value was paid in addition; (6) the skins of all the animals used for burnt offerings, and definite parts of those used in other sacrifices, belonged to the priests. Their sources of income were abundant; they had no taxes to pay and were free from military service. It was to their own interest to preserve a knowledge and the observance of the law among the people; for only thus had they an assured income.

Apart from their sacred duties, the priests wore the ordinary dress of the people, but when engaged in these duties they wore special garments prescribed by law. These were: (1) a tunic [1] with narrow sleeves, reaching from the neck to the ankles, and

---

[1] כְּתֹנֶת, from כָּתַן, to spin, weave.

made of white linen; (2) a head-covering,[1] made of byssus, in
the shape of an inverted flower-calyx, so that it was a kind of
hat; (3) a loin-cloth, also of byssus,[2] probably a large cloth,
such as was worn also by other people beneath the tunic for the
sake of decency (in Ex. xxviii. 42 it is mentioned as covering
the middle of the body), as the ordinary garments reached only
to the knees; (4) a colored girdle, of white, purple, crimson and
dark blue threads, all interwoven. According to the Rabbis, this
was 3 fingers in breadth and 32 cubits in length, so that it could
be wound several times round the body. The priests wore no
shoes, as the sacred places must be entered barefoot.

The priest's office consisted of the following duties: (1) Every
morning and evening he had to put incense on the altar of
incense, near the inner curtain in the Holy Place, and trim the
lamps on the golden candlestick. The old shewbread had to
be removed and the fresh substituted on the table of proposition
every Sabbath.[3]   (2) In the Court of the Temple the priests
offered very many sacrifices on the great altar, where they kept
the fire burning day and night. Every morning after the daily
offering of incense, they blessed the people.   (3) They were
especially bound to uphold the Law of Moses, and therefore it
was their duty to instruct the people in the law and to attend
to the administration of justice (Deut. xvii. 8; xix. 17; xxi. 5);
(4) among their extraordinary occupations were: (a) negotiat-
ing about first fruits and the firstborn; (b) blowing the silver
trumpets at certain festivals; (c) examining lepers and pro-
nouncing them clean, as well as inspecting houses and garments
infected with leprosy; (d) releasing Nazirites from their vows;
(e) performing the ceremony of the offering on behalf of women
suspected of adultery.

Priests were required to be in a state of cleanness whenever
they discharged any part of their office. As long as they were

---

[1] מִגְבָּעָה, Exodus xxviii. 40 and elsewhere. The word is connected with
גָּבִיעַ, a cup, so the head-covering was probably cup shaped.

[2] מִכְנְסֵי בַר, covering of cleanness; it does not mean breeches or
drawers.

[3] Cf. page 75. Descendants of Aaron, who were disqualified from the
sacred service by some physical defect, might eat of the loaves of proposition or shewbread, but only in the court, not entering the Holy Place.

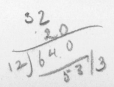

engaged in the sacred service they might not drink wine nor anything intoxicating (Lev. x. 9) and remained apart from their wives (Ex. xix. 14). Even when not employed in their priestly duties, they were forbidden to touch any corpses (Lev. xxi. 1), with the exception of those of their nearest relatives (Lev. x. 6), nor might they wear mourning, for sin and its consequences are an abomination to God, and therefore no reminder of it, such as mourning for the dead would imply, could be tolerated in His priests. If, accidentally, a priest incurred legal defilement, he could not discharge any sacred duty, nor eat anything consecrated, until, after the lapse of a definite time, he had been cleansed by legal ceremonies. The priests were particularly bound to lead pure and blameless lives, as the law prescribed, and the same obligation rested also upon their families, so that even a priest's daughter, who had fallen into immorality, was required to be burned to death (Lev. xxi. 9). It seems, however, that the priests often went astray, for the prophets frequently complain of their setting the people a bad example; e. g. Jer. v. 31; vi. 13; Mich. iii. 11.

16. THE HIGH PRIEST [1]
(Exodus xxviii., xxix., xxxix.)

The head of the priesthood was the high priest, who was always the firstborn of Aaron's race, provided that he possessed the necessary physical and mental qualifications. His exalted position conferred upon him various prerogatives, so that he stood to the other priests in the relation of a father to his sons ("Aaron and his sons"); but it was his duty to live a life peculiarly pure and blameless.

Dress. Over and above the usual priestly attire (tunic, loincloth, girdle and head-covering) an official costume in keeping with his exalted dignity was given to the high priest and worn exclusively by him. If his head-covering be included, this costume also consisted of four parts, viz.:

---

[1] The ordinary name is הַכֹּהֵן הַגָּדוֹל, *sacerdos magnus*, but occasionally he is called הַכֹּהֵן הָרֹאשׁ, *sacerdos princeps*.

1. The *Meîl*,[1] a garment made of dark bluish purple, and worn over the priest's tunic. It had an opening at the top, so that it could be passed over the head. There were no sleeves. On the lower edge it was ornamented with artificial pomegranates made of yarn and twelve [2] golden bells arranged alternately. It probably reached only to the knees, so that the white tunic could be seen below it.

2. The *Ephod*,[3] made of white linen skillfully interwoven with gold and colored threads, dark blue, dark red and bright red. It consisted of two squares of cloth, one covering the breast and the other the back. These two squares were fastened together and held in place by means of shoulder-pieces of gold, on each of which was an onyx.[4] On the two precious stones were engraved the names of the twelve tribes of Israel, six on each. The lower part of the ephod was fastened to the body by means of a girdle of the same materials.

3. The *Choschen*,[5] or breastplate. This was a double square folded in half, so as to form a sort of pocket (not unlike the burse to contain the corporal). It measured half a cubit in each direction, and was made of the same material as the ephod. On the outer side were twelve precious stones set in

---

[1] מְעִיל from מַעַל, upper; hence "upper garment."

[2] This is the number given in the apocryphal Gospel of Saint James. The Rabbis say seventy-two, but this is plainly too large a number.

[3] אֵפוֹד = dress. In every place where the word occurs, not excepting Judges viii. 27 and I Kings xxi. 9, it has this meaning. It never means, as Wellhausen suggests, the figure of a deity, or, as A. Mäcklenburg assumes, a shrine in which to keep pictures. Kayser (*Theol. d. A. T.*, 2d ed., 28) agrees with Wellhausen, and thinks "the figure of God took its name 'Ephod' from the fact of its being covered over." But in that case the high priest too ought to have been called an Ephod. The question is connected with the assertion that the Pentateuch could not have existed as early as the time of the Judges and the first few kings, because representations of the deity existed, and the making of these is strictly forbidden in the Pentateuch. But a violation of the law in the midst of Gentile surroundings is no evidence that it did not exist. There is a proverb to the effect that "clothes make people," but that clothes also make gods is something new. *Cf.* p. 39 and also p. 102.

[4] Heb. שֹׁהַם, perhaps the sea-green beryl. The word means in Arabic "pale." Sept., σμάραγδος, Vulg., *lapis onychinus;* ὄνυξ = finger nail.

[5] חֹשֶׁן from חָשַׁן, to cut off, secure, keep. The meaning is certainly "receptacle," and is correctly rendered δόχιον by the Sept.

gold, arranged in four rows, and bearing the names of the twelve tribes of Israel engraved upon them. At each corner of the choschen was a golden ring. To the rings at the two upper corners were attached little gold chains, having at their extremities golden clasps, by means of which they were fastened to the shoulder-pieces of the ephod, close to the onyx stones. Blue cords were passed through the rings at the two lower corners, and also through two other rings which were sewn on to the edge of the shoulder-pieces of the ephod below the arms. In this way the choschen was fastened to the ephod, both at the top and at the bottom, and so was drawn close to the breast and prevented from slipping out of place.

Inside the choschen the *Urim* and *Thummim* were placed. What they were, is not explained, and the names do not help us; they probably mean " Light and Right " or " Clearness and Truth "; Septuagint, δήλωσις καὶ ἀλήθεια; Vulgate, *doctrina et veritas*. The Jewish authors, Josephus and Philo and the Rabbis, are all at a loss as to the interpretation. It appears from Exodus xxviii. 16, 30, and from Leviticus viii. 8 [1] that some solid thing is meant, which could be put into the choschen and taken out again, and that this served as an instrument whereby the high priest could ascertain God's will in matters of importance. We may be sure that the Septuagint translation δήλωσις and ἀλήθεια has some foundation. The words signify clearing away of doubt and recognition of the truth. The high priest was believed to be inspired and capable of deciding upon the right course of action.

4. The *head-covering* worn by the high priest was, according to Josephus (*Ant.*, III, vii. 7) and Philo, the ordinary covering worn by the priests, with the addition of dark blue ribbon, to which a little gold plate was fastened, having engraved upon it the words " Holy to the Lord " — *qodesch la adonai*. The high priest did not always wear his official dress. As a rule, when he had only ordinary business to transact, he dressed like the other priests, but the ribbon and plate on his head-covering

---

[1] The rational of judgment (*rationale judicii*) " shall be four square and doubled . . . thou shalt put in the rational of judgment doctrine and truth . . . the rational, on which was doctrine and truth."

always distinguished him from them (*cf. Kirchenlexicon,* 2d ed., VI, 168, 169).

Duties of the High Priest. The following duties were assigned exclusively to him: (1) To perform the important ceremonies on the great Day of Atonement. (2) To ascertain God's will by means of the Urim and Thummim, and to make it known. (3) In the administration of justice to give the final decision, from which there was no appeal. (He seems to have presided at trials of important cases, and in the Synedrium.) (4) To watch over everything connected with the worship of God, and over the Levites and Priests. He could, of course, discharge all the priestly functions.

Sanctity of the High Priest. Standing as he did near to God, and above the whole nation and the ordinary business of life, the high priest was strictly bound by the law: (1) to touch no corpse, not even that of his father or mother; (2) at the death of his nearest relatives to show no outward token of mourning and to omit none of his official duties; (3) to take a virgin as his wife, not a dishonored woman, or a widow, or a divorced person.

Tenure of Office. The high priest retained his dignity until his death, if he were not disabled by sickness or old age, and so rendered incompetent to perform his sacred duties. Occasionally two high priests are mentioned as holding office at the same time, but only one of these is to be regarded as really acting as high priest.

17. Consecration of the Priests
(Ex. xxix., Lev. viii., and also Ex. xl.)

The ceremony whereby the Levites were set apart for the service of the Temple was called a purification (Num. viii. 6) (*taher*), but the consecration of the priests, hallowing (*qaddesch*). The consecration consisted of several parts, but, like the purification of the Levites, it falls into two main portions, viz., the actual consecration and the accompanying sacrifices.

1. The consecration was effected by bathing the body, putting on the priestly garments, and anointing. A specially pre-

pared oil was used to anoint the priests' hands, but in the case of the high priest some oil was poured also on his head.

2. For the sacrifices a young bull, two rams, unleavened bread and other cakes were required. The newly consecrated priests laid their hands on all the animals before they were killed. The bull was slain as a sin offering; one ram served as a holocaust and the other as a thank offering. The right ear, right hand and right foot of the consecrated priest were smeared with the blood of the second ram. Whatever was not burnt of the flesh of the thank offering and whatever remained of the bread and cakes was eaten by the new priests as a sacrificial feast.

The consecration was not completed for seven days, but the first day was the most important. On the six other days the anointing was repeated and other sin offerings sacrificed, and on the eighth day the priests entered upon their office.

It was thus that Aaron and his sons were admitted to the priesthood. Whether the same ceremonies were observed in the case of subsequent priests and high priests is not certain. According to the Rabbis [1] all that was necessary for a high priest, on entering office, was to put on Aaron's robes and to offer an unbloody sacrifice (Lev. vi. 14, etc.). The same rule applied to all priests, and no further ceremonies were required. This is quite in harmony with the spirit of the Old Testament. The Holy Spirit had not yet been poured forth, and the idea of individuality had not yet been so fully developed as in the New Testament, and hence the consecration of each priest was unnecessary, as the father of his tribe continued to live in him and his dignity was transmitted by the act of procreation. Just as Abraham's blessing passed on to the whole of God's people, so the consecration of Abraham's family affected all their descendants. In Hebrews vii. 15, 16, emphasis is laid upon the fact that, in contrast to Christ's spiritual priesthood, Aaron's priesthood was propagated according to the flesh, i. e. by procreation. Hence, after the Captivity all were excluded from

[1] Exodus xxix. 29 may be understood to mean that each high priest was to share in Aaron's consecration if he put on the garments of the founder of his line, and if his hands were anointed.

the priesthood who could not prove with certainty that they were descended from Aaron (Esdras ii. 62; Nehemias vii. 64). *Cf.* page 91, on the purification of the Levites. As in time the number of priests increased very greatly, David arranged for their division into twenty-four classes or courses, each under a chief (I Chron. xxiv. 3, etc.), and each course in turn had to officiate in the sanctuary for a week, from Sabbath to Sabbath. The various offices connected with the Temple worship were assigned by lot; and according to the Talmud there was a special superintendent of the lots (*cf.* Luke i. 9).

The Mosaic Origin of the Priesthood and of Levites. — Wellhausen *[Radical critic.]* (*Proleg.*, 121, etc.) denies that the distinction between priests and Levites dates from the time of Moses and claims that Ezechiel did not recognize it as the sharp distinction which the Priests' Code ascribes to it; and so, argues Wellhausen, the Priests' Code did not exist at the time of Ezechiel. In his vision of the restoration of Israel and particularly of the Temple after the Captivity, Ezechiel says (xliv.) that only the descendants of Sadok, who had acted as priests in Jerusalem from the time of David onward, might officiate in the new Temple, but those priests of the tribe of Levi who, here and there in the country, had gone astray and served false gods, should thenceforth (in the persons of their descendants) be admitted to only the lower duties in the Temple worship, as a punishment for their guilt. They had forfeited their priesthood by misusing it in order to worship on high places. Wellhausen thinks that Ezechiel is the first to distinguish priests and Levites, in much the same way as the distinction between Israelites and Gentiles on the one hand, and that between the mass of the people and those engaged in the worship of God on the other, should not be referred to any very remote period. " In the chief part of the Book of Judges there is no mention of any one officially engaged in the *cultus;* we hear twice of sacrifice being offered, but it is by Gideon and Manoah. A priest was not thought necessary. . . . If the priests and Levites living in the midst of the Children of Israel had been so arranged from the time of Moses, they could not have vanished completely in the time of the Judges." In I Kings vi. 15 Levites are indeed mentioned as serving in connection with the ark of the Covenant, but this is regarded as a later gloss.

In answer to all this we may say that before the building of the Temple the divine worship was not organized with the regularity of later times. The constant wars which kept the people in an unsettled state, the novelty of all their circumstances and the prevalence everywhere of heathen customs, which could not but affect the Israelites, did not admit of an orderly observance of religious rites. It was a long time, for instance, before Christianity prevailed in Germany and displaced the heathen customs, traces of which still exist in some places. It is, however, clear from the story of Heli and Samuel that the central sanctuary, first at Silo and then at Nobe, was generally respected, and that a large number of men were already engaged in the religious worship. Saul had eighty-five priests from Nobe killed at one time (I Kings xxii. 18). Even if individuals here and there, following the custom of olden times, offered sacrifice elsewhere in their capacity as heads of families or even as private persons, this might be still tolerated as an ancient custom. Strict centralization was possible, however, and its necessity appeared more and more after the Temple was built, for the isolated sanctuaries in the country had become for the most part the homes of superstition, immorality and idolatry.

In support of his theory, Wellhausen relies: (1) upon the Book of Judges, in the greater part of which (iii.–xvi.) there is no mention of a class of persons engaged in religious observances; (2) upon the same book, which in an appendix (xvii., xviii.) speaks of a priestly function in a way that does not agree with the Pentateuch; (3) upon II Kings viii. 18, where we read that David's sons were priests, which, according to the Pentateuch, they could not have been permitted to be.

In reply it may be stated (1) that other passages of the Old Testament, belonging to a later period, also contain no mention of a priestly class, because there is no reason why such mention should be made in them. For instance, in the first and second sections of the Psalms the words *priest* and *Levite* do not once occur; and yet, according to modern critics, the whole psalter belongs to the period after the Captivity, and Wellhausen even regards it as doubtful whether any psalms of an earlier date exist. Is it possible to argue from the silence of these two sections that there was no legally established priesthood even after the Captivity? No! Therefore it is not permissible to prove from the above-mentioned chapters in the Book of Judges that in the time of the Judges the official priesthood organized by Moses did not exist.

(2) That even in that remote period the tribe of Levi was officially connected with public worship appears as a recognized fact in Judges xvii. and xviii. — the very chapters upon which Wellhausen relies. Michas, an Ephraimite, caused a costly metal statue of Yahweh to be made, and appointed one of his own sons to be priest of this statue and of the little temple erected to contain it. That this was an abuse, arising probably out of superstition, is suggested by the words, " In those days there was no king in Israel, but every one did that which seemed right to himself." Then a Levite named Jonathan came into the district from Bethlehem.[1] Michas persuaded him to remain with him as

---

[1] As Bethlehem was not a Levite town, it has been suggested, as this place is mentioned as Jonathan's home, that he belonged to the tribe of Juda, and that, in the time of the Judges, the word *Levite* did not mean a man belonging to the tribe of Levi, but one of the wandering people, who, being descended from Egyptian priests, practiced all manner of arts (fortune-telling, etc.), like our modern gypsies. Their ancestors are supposed to have left Egypt with Moses, and in course of time they succeeded in securing plenty of money on the ground of their priestly powers. The text of the Book of Judges, however, contains a clear sattement that Jonathan was descended from Moses, and consequently from Levi, Jacob's son. " Jonathan, the son of Gerson, the son of Moses " (xviii. 30). His residence in Bethlehem had nothing to do with

priest, in place of his son, in return for payment, food and clothing, and the Levite consented. Michas felt quite happy at having "a priest of the race of the Levites" with him. Afterwards men belonging to the tribe of Dan, in the course of their wanderings to their new settlement, came to Michas, and violently deprived him of his statue and all connected with it, including the Levite, and erected a sanctuary for themselves in their new home farther north. Thenceforth the Levite was their priest. That the tribe of Levi "was completely destroyed at the first attempt to conquer Chanaan" (Volck, p. 44) cannot be inferred from Genesis xlix. 5–7, as the tribe of Simeon, mentioned in the same verses, continued to exist.

(3) While the sons of David are called Kohanim in II Kings viii., this word cannot here bear its ordinary meaning of "priest." In verses 16–18 the men are named who held posts of honor at court; Joab was commander of the army, Josaphat was recorder, Sadok and Achimelech were priests, Saraias was the scribe, Banaias was set over the bodyguard and "David's sons were Kohanim." As the priests are mentioned in verse 17, the word *Kohanim* must receive another interpretation. The Septuagint renders it αὐλάρχαι. Probably the king's sons held some high offices about the court, that we no longer know. The word is generally translated "princes." By designating the king's sons Kohanim, as if they were priests, the writer suggests that they lived with the king as his confidants in the same way as the priests dwelt with God in the sanctuary. The king represents God's majesty. (*Cf.* I Chron. xviii. 17, where David's sons are called the first at the king's hand.

APPENDIX

THE SYNEDRIUM AND THE JEWISH SECTS

The Synedrium

or Sanhedrin, the Council of the Jews, was, during the closing period of the Jews' existence as a State, the chief religious and political body, having authority to decide on the most important matters in the national life, and claiming also the right to pronounce sentences of life and death. Our Saviour and the Apostles, Saint Stephen also and Saint Paul, were all brought before this tribunal, which was formed on the lines laid down by Moses (Ex. xviii. 25; Num. xi. 16) of seventy of the chief priests, elders and doctors of the law, and met under the presidency of the high priest, generally in one of the side buildings of the Temple, but occasionally in the high priest's house.

Jewish Sects

1. Mention is often made in the New Testament of Scribes, doctors and teachers of the law (γραμματεῖς, νομικοί, νομοδιδάσκαλοι); these per-

---

his descent; possibly his mother came thence, as in xvii. 7 we read that he was "of Bethlehem Juda (מִמִּשְׁפַּחַת יְהוּדָה) of the kindred thereof, and he was a Levite and dwelt there (וְהוּא גָר־שָׁם)."

sons were not connected with the Temple worship in these capacities, but belonged for the most part to the sect of the *Pharisees*, the upholders of the claims and doctrines of orthodox Judaism. Their name comes from *parasch*, to separate, and means " those set apart," those who by their piety and wisdom are conspicuous above the mass of the people. Their reputation was so great that even the priests, who formed the hereditary aristocracy of the nation, found it expedient to join this sect, in order to retain their prestige, and the Council or Synedrium consisted chiefly of Pharisees. They seem to have originated before the time of the Machabees, as they were already strong and influential under Jonathan Machabæus in 144 B. C. (Jos., *Ant.*, XIII, v. 9). Besides the Holy Scriptures they reverenced a particular tradition, which they ascribed to Moses, as the source of the Law; this developed later into the Talmud. The sect was at first worthy of high esteem, but it gradually degenerated, and at the time of our Lord the Pharisees appear as sanctimonious persons, full of uncharitableness, pride and avarice. There were, however, noble exceptions, e. g. Nicodemus (John iii.) and Gamaliel (Acts v. 34). Inasmuch as they were the expounders and teachers of the Law, they received the honorable title of Rabbi = master (רַבִּי, from רַב, much, great = magister).

At the time of Christ there were two famous teachers with a numerous following, — Shammai and Hillel. The former represented the strictest school of thought, especially with regard to divorce; the latter adhered to milder doctrines and practice.

2. In direct contrast to the stern Judaism of the Pharisees were the easy-going views of the party of the *Sadducees*, which had penetrated into Palestine from the west after the Græco-Persian wars. It is impossible not to recognize a connection between the Sadducees and the Epicurean philosophy. In origin and name this sect is generally derived from a certain Sadok, a disciple of Antigonus of Socho (died 264 B. C.). According to another account they called themselves Zaddikim = honest people. It is, however, most probable that they declared themselves to be Sadokides, i. e. members of the high priest's party, for, from the time of David, the high priesthood remained hereditary in the family of Sadok. They accepted Holy Scripture, at least the Pentateuch, but no traditions. They believed in God, but not in angels; declared the soul to be material and mortal, and consequently rejected the doctrines of the resurrection of the body and of future rewards or punishments; moreover they denied the action of Divine Providence. This sect consisted chiefly of rich and powerful persons, for which reason it became influential in the Synedrium, and secured the high priesthood (Acts xxiii. 6, etc.), but it never won much esteem among the nation as a whole (Jos. Fl., *Bell. Jud.*, II, viii. 14; *Ant.*, XVIII, i. 2).

3. The *Essenes* are not mentioned in the Bible, but Josephus and Philo describe them as ascetics, who apparently had added to Judaism the tenets of heathen and especially of the Pythagorean philosophy. Various explanations are given of their name; it may be derived from an Aramaic word *chăsē*, pious, pl. *chasēn, chasajja*. They formed a kind of religious order governed by definite rules and divided into four classes. They conceived of the Deity as the purest light, and the sun they regarded as His symbol. They honored Moses and his law; believed in the

immortality of the soul; observed the Sabbath very strictly but rejected the Jewish sacrificial worship. Their morality was based on love of God and man, and on self-control. For love of God they sought to lead pure lives and always to speak the truth; their love of man showed itself in good will, charitable deeds and community of property. They exercised self-control by despising wealth, honors and pleasures, and many refrained from marriage. They lived partly in settlements of their own near the Dead Sea, partly in the midst of other Jews in towns and villages, supporting themselves by the work of their hands or by agriculture. Their number did not exceed four thousand.

4. A fourth, and probably not numerous sect, was that of the *Herodians*, who are mentioned a few times in the New Testament. They were adherents of the Herodian royal family, and were therefore inclined to favor the Romans, and were hostile to the Jewish religion.

THIRD SECTION

SACRED RITUAL

I. SACRIFICES

18. What could be offered

AS a rule it was required of an Israelite coming to the Temple, that he should not appear empty handed. The gifts which might be offered up in honor of God were partly animal, partly vegetable, and also salt. Only clean, domestic animals could be sacrificed, viz. (1) oxen (bullocks, cows and calves); (2) rams, sheep, lambs, goats and kids; (3) doves (turtledoves and young pigeons = *bene jona*). The latter were sometimes offered by the poor, who could not afford to give more costly creatures, but sometimes they served for the less important sacrifices.[1] The animals for sacrifice had to be without blemish; they might not be mutilated or deformed, blind, or affected with sores or wounds; they must not walk crooked, etc. (Lev. xxii. 19–25). Moreover, they must have reached a certain age; the young must be at least eight days old; sheep and goats were generally sacrificed when a year old, and bullocks when three years old.

The following vegetable products might be offered: (*a*) *grain*, including ears of grain, flour, bread and cakes variously prepared; (*b*) *garden produce*, fruit, especially grapes, wine and olive oil; (*c*) *incense*. Salt was used at all sacrifices both bloody and unbloody. The incense and even the blood were salted.

[1] Leviticus xii. 6: A woman after childbirth had to offer a lamb and a pigeon, or, in case of poverty, two pigeons. Leviticus xv. 14 and 29: Certain defilements required to be cleansed by the sacrifice of pigeons. Numbers vi. 10: A Nazarite who had broken his vow had to sacrifice two pigeons.

Salt symbol of cleanliness

Abel offered father floc

Cain what he didn't wa

The chief sacrifices always consisted of animals. A man doing sacrifice may give what he possesses. The Israelites were originally a pastoral people. (Gen. xlvi. 34: "We are shepherds . . . both we and our fathers.") It was only later that they practiced agriculture also, and hence the sacrifice of animals was always the most important, especially as the sense of guilt finds its serious expression in shedding the blood of the sacrifice. This is implied also by God's satisfaction at Abel's sacrifice, whose faith is extolled in Heb. xi. 4. Abel in spirit beheld the future Redeemer, but Cain did not recognize Him.

Honey and leaven were expressly forbidden.[1]

19. RITUAL OF SACRIFICE

Animal sacrifices were performed in the following way: The animal was brought into the court of the Tabernacle or Temple, for it was forbidden, under pain of death, to offer sacrifices elsewhere. It was tied up to a ring fastened in the earth, and the person offering it laid his hands on its head. (This was omitted in the case of the Paschal lamb, and of pigeons.) The meaning of this ceremony was that the sin of the offerer passed over to the victim, who was to die in place of the sinful man.[2] According to the Rabbis (Otho, *Lex Rabbin.*), a confession of sin accompanied the laying on of hands, the words being as follows:

"I have sinned, have acted amiss, have been rebellious, especially have I committed[3] . . . But I return to Thee full of repentance. May this [i. e. the offering of the victim] be my expiation!" *Cf.* Numbers v. 6, 7.

---

[1] Leviticus ii. 11: "Neither shall any leaven or honey be burnt in the sacrifice to the Lord." The reason is probably that honey by its sweetness symbolized sinful sensual enjoyments, and leaven as the means of fermentation typified that inherited element in human nature which always keeps it in a state of wild passion, viz. sensual concupiscence, which originated in sin and leads to sin. Sin, and all connected with it, had to be excluded from the altar of sacrifice, which was undefiled, a place dedicated to God, raised above the sin-stained earth.

[2] Leviticus i. 4: "He shall put his hand upon the head of the victim, and it shall be acceptable and help to its expiation."

[3] The confession of sins answers a need of human nature and has at all times appeared as accompanying true penance. Adam had to acknowledge his guilt and did so, but Cain refused (Gen. iii. 11, iv. 9). David says of himself, "Because I was silent my pain consumed me." He rightly perceived that sacrifice alone was not enough. *Si voluisses sacrificium, dedissem utique* (Ps. l. 18). Happily for him God sent the prophet Nathan, before whom he acknowledged his guilt (II Kings xii.

Thus laden with the sin of the offerer, the victim was slain on the north side of the altar, generally by the person who offered it, but it might be done by the priest (II Chron. xxix. 24). The priest caught the blood in a vessel, and, according to the kind of sacrifice intended, he sprinkled some of it either on the side of the altar, or on the horns, or on the altar of incense, or even towards the Kapporeth in the Holy of Holies. The rest of the blood was poured out on the ground near the altar of holocausts (Lev. iv. 7). Then the victim was skinned and cut to pieces. Either all the flesh was laid upon the altar and burnt, or only some of the fat was consumed by the altar fire, and the rest of the flesh was cooked and eaten by the priests, or used by the offerer of the sacrifice for a sacrificial feast, or burnt outside the city or encampment.

When pigeons were offered, the priest killed them by breaking their necks, not by cutting off the heads (Lev. i. 15; v. 8).[1] Apparently a cut was then made in one place, and the blood was allowed to drip on the side of the altar. The wings were slightly torn and then the birds were thrown into the fire on the altar. Vegetable offerings were seldom made alone, but generally in conjunction with bloody sacrifices. The procedure was as follows: (1) If the sacrifice belonged to the class of burnt offerings, the priest took only a small portion of the flour, cakes, etc., and burnt it with incense on the altar. The rest belonged to the priest, but had to be eaten unleavened in the Court, after being prepared for food. If the offerer were himself a priest, the whole was burnt. If the sacrifice was a peace offering, one cake out of all that were brought was taken for the Lord and given to the priest; the rest was used by the offerer for a sacrificial feast.

13). The Baptism of John was connected with confession of sins (Matt. iii. 6). It cannot, however, be maintained that under the old dispensation a special confession of sins was a *conditio sine qua non* of forgiveness. Special confession was ordained first by Christ (John xx. 23).

[1] The Hebrew מָלַק means to break off; Septuagint, ἀποκνίζειν; Vulgate, *retorquere ad collum, ad pennulas*. It seems that the neck was not wrung, but violently bent backwards, so that the throat was separated inside from the body, remaining united to it only by the skin.

20. Varieties of Sacrifices

According to the objects brought as offerings, sacrifices were divided into (1) bloody, or slain offerings, and (2) unbloody, or meat and drink offerings. According to the reasons for offering the sacrifices they were distinguished as (1) holocausts, or burnt offerings; (2) peace offerings; (3) sin offerings; (4) trespass offerings.

There can be no doubt that the offerings have a symbolic meaning. In the New Testament we have but *one* sacrifice, which, however, contains all the various sacrifices of the Old Testament, and they were merely foreshadowings of it. The holy Sacrifice of the Mass is a holocaust, — the whole victim, the Lamb, who hung in burning agony on the Cross, is offered up; it is a peace offering — a sacrificial feast takes place, at which Christians appear as God's guests; it is a sin offering, for our sins constrain us to offer this holy sacrifice in order to appease the wrath of God; it is a trespass offering, — making reparation for the wrong done to God, and obtaining reconciliation with one's neighbor, hence the kiss of peace. It is at the same time a bloody and an unbloody sacrifice.

(a) Bloody Sacrifices

21. Holocausts, or Burnt Offerings
(Leviticus i. 3–17, vi. 8–13)

1. *Name.* The Hebrew name for this kind of sacrifice is *ola* = that which rises, i. e. that which rises to heaven from the altar as a fragrance pleasing to God. Still more expressive are the Greek names, ὁλοκαύτωμα or ὁλοκαύτωσις, selected by the Septuagint with reference to the Hebrew word *kalil*,[1] or ὁλόκαυστον, which Philo uses. All these signify that the whole victim was burnt. The Vulgate has adopted the word *holocaustum* from the Greek. The words "burnt offering" are less expressive.

2. *Ritual.* Only male animals could be used for these sacrifices; in fact, in all animal sacrifices males are preferred, as being larger and stronger. Every kind of animal that could be sacrificed at all might be offered. The victims were brought

---

[1] Deuteronomy xiii. 17, xxxiii. 10; I Kings vii. 9; Ps. li. 22.

in, hands were laid upon them, and they were slain, as in all sacrifices. The blood was sprinkled round about the altar. The skins belonged to the priest, who did not as a rule take them off himself, this being done by the offerer. The animal was cut to pieces, its entrails taken out and purified, and then the whole was burnt together on the altar of holocausts in the Court. Only the sinew of the thigh (the so-called sciatic nerve) was removed. The reason for this is stated in Genesis xxxii. 32, "therefore the children of Israel unto this day eat not the sinew that shrank in Jacob's thigh, because He [God] touched the sinew of his thigh and it shrank."

Just as men are not accustomed to eat flesh without bread and drink, so with every holocaust was connected an unbloody addition, a meat and drink offering. The materials and quantities of these offerings varied in accordance with the animal sacrificed. There was no unbloody sacrifice connected with an offering of doves.

The holocaust was the most usual form of sacrifice. Twice daily, morning and evening, a lamb was sacrificed in accordance with the law; and in addition similar offerings were prescribed on various occasions, such as the purification of women after childbirth, of those who had recovered from leprosy, etc. There were also voluntary holocausts (Ps. l. 20), and these might be offered even by Gentiles. According to Philo, the Emperor Augustus had a bull and two lambs offered for himself daily as holocausts in the Temple at Jerusalem.

22. PEACE OFFERINGS

(Lev. iii. 1–17, vii. 11–21, vii. 28–36)

1. The second kind of bloody sacrifice is known by various names; the commonest is *schelem*, or *sebach schelamim* = peace offering [1] = εἰρηνική sc. θυσία (Sept.); the others are *sebach hattoda* = thank or praise offering, *sebach neder* = votive offering, *sebach nedaba* = freewill offering. We may assume that "peace offering" is a general name, and that the

---

[1] The name seems to have been chosen by way of contrast to the sin and trespass offerings, which presupposed a sort of separation between God and man, whereas this sacrifice has a more cheerful character, and man appears as God's guest at the sacrificial meals.

three other expressions designate particular kinds of peace offerings.

2. Every animal regarded as fit for sacrifice could be used as a peace offering; it was not necessary that it should be a male, and for freewill offerings of this kind animals might be taken that had some imperfection in them.

3. The ritual began like that of the holocaust. The blood was sprinkled all round the altar, but from this point the procedure differed. Only four, or, in the case of sheep, five parts of the victim were placed on the altar, viz.: (1) the fatty tissues enclosing the entrails; (2) the fat on the entrails; (3) the two kidneys; (4) the liver, and (in sheep) (5) the fat tail (*'alja*).

The breast (*chase*) and the right leg (*schoq*) [1] were separated from the rest of the flesh, and laid by the priest on the hands of the man offering the sacrifice. Then the priest laid his own hands under those of the offerer, and made a movement forwards (towards the altar and the sanctuary) and back again, — this ceremony was called "waving" (*tenupha*), — then another movement from below upwards, and then down again, which was called "heaving" (*teruma*). After this the pieces of fat were burnt on the altar, and a sacrificial meal followed. The breast (wave offering) and the leg (heave offering) [2] were eaten by the priests, and their wives and children could share the food. The people who offered the sacrifice consumed the rest on the holy spot, being in a condition of legal purity. If the sacrifice was a thank offering, the meal was bound to take place on the day that the victim was killed; if it was a free-will or a votive offering, the flesh remaining over from that day might be consumed on the following morning, but whatever was still

[1] The right hind leg must be meant, for *schoq* means runner, and is used of the thigh of a man's leg, below the loins. The Septuagint reading is βραχίων and the Vulgate *armus* = shoulder. *Cf.* Knobel on Leviticus vii. 32, 33; Scholz, *Altertümer*, II, 175.

[2] *Chase hattenupha, schoq hatteruma.* It seems that sometimes only the breast was "waved" and only the leg "heaved," but sometimes the two movements were connected. Exodus xxix. 26, 27: "take the breast . . . and elevating it thou shalt sanctify it to the Lord . . . and thou shalt sanctify both the consecrated breast and the shoulder." The ceremony signified that the portions of the victim should be devoted to the sanctuary and lifted up to the altar.

left had to be burnt.[1] An unbloody offering always accompanied sacrifices of this kind also.

23. SIN OFFERINGS
(Leviticus iv. 1, etc., vi. 24–30)

1. The third kind of sacrifice bears the same name as the sin = *chattath*, and the very name shows that in this case the victim was offered as an atonement for definite transgressions. These were not, however, intentional, as every intentional violation of the law was punishable with death; but they were rather unintentional faults and certain conditions of uncleanness, which had some resemblance to or connection with sin, such as leprosy, issue of blood. Moreover, at certain times it was required that sin offerings should be made on behalf of the whole people, for it was taken for granted that many unnoticed violations of the law must have occurred.

Before our Lord's coming there was no certain outward means of getting rid of sin, for the so-called "sacraments of the Old Covenant" (circumcision, consecration of priests and Levites, the Paschal lamb and the various sacrifices and purifications) could not of themselves remove sin: they secured only righteousness in the eyes of the law. Hence Saint Paul calls them (Gal. iv. 9) "weak and needy elements." The means of removing sin were the inward acts of faith in a future Redeemer (Heb. xi.) which found expression in prayer and in sacrifice, accompanied with an acknowledgment of guilt. *Cf*. p. 107.

2. The occasions when a sin offering had to be made, can be divided into (*a*) permanent occasions recurring at certain fixed times, and (*b*) unforeseen occasions.

a. The fixed times when sin offerings had to be made were (*a*) the Pasch, (*b*) Pentecost, (*c*) feast of Tabernacles, (*d*) Day of Atonement, (*e*) the New Year's festival, (*f*) the New Moons, i. e. the first day of each month. At each of these seasons a sin offering was made for the whole people, the victim being always a he-goat.

---

[2] The Agape of the early Christians had probably no connection with these sacrificial feasts of the Old Testament, but was an imitation of the Paschal supper, eaten by our Lord and His Apostles before the institution of the holy Eucharist.

b. The unforeseen occasions were much more numerous. As chief of them may be mentioned: (*a*) the purification of a woman after childbirth; (*b*) the purification of a leper or of one suffering from any discharge; (*c*) the purification of a woman with an issue of blood. In these cases doves were generally offered. (*d*) If the high priest accidentally violated any precept in the law, he sacrificed a young bullock, free from all blemish. (*e*) If the whole community had transgressed in the same way, the same offering had to be made. (*f*) In such case the head of a tribe or family offered a he-goat. (*g*) Any individual Israelite atoned for such a transgression by offering a she-goat.

3. With regard to the ritual observed, sin offerings were divided into two classes, interior and exterior. The former were sacrifices in which the blood of the victim was carried inside the Temple or Tabernacle. The latter were sacrifices in which the blood only was taken to the altar of holocausts. The flesh of the victims in the former class of sin offerings was burnt outside the city or the camp. The flesh of the victims in the second class was eaten by the priests, with the exception of the pieces of fat, which were burnt on the altar. Interior sin offerings were the more important; such was, for instance, the sacrifice on the great Day of Atonement.[1]

24. TRESPASS OFFERINGS

(Leviticus v. 15, etc.; Vulgate, also vi. 2, etc.)

1. The Hebrew name for this kind of offering is *'ascham* = guilt. The ritual for it was the same as that for the sin offering, and therefore many archæologists identify the two, and regard *'ascham* only as a particular kind of *chattath*. Those who

---

[1] *Cf.* on this subject Heb. xiii. 10–15, which is explained as follows: It was certainly no mere accident that Christ was crucified outside the city. He died as a sin offering. The Jews were forbidden to eat the flesh of the more important sin offerings; it had to be burnt outside the city. Therefore the author of this epistle calls upon the Jewish Christians thus: "Let us go forth to him without the camp, bearing his reproach " — let us separate ourselves from the Jews, let us share in His sacrifice, even if those who believe not despise.

identify them reckon only three bloody sacrifices. There are, however, differences in the cause for these sacrifices and in their object. (a) The trespass offering was always made for an individual, whilst the sin offering might also be on behalf of the whole people. (b) The chief difference lies in the fact that a trespass offering was always connected with some injury committed to the rights of God Himself or of a man's neighbors; whereas, no such thing was presupposed in the case of a sin offering. The damage done had to be made good, a fifth of the value being paid in addition, and a sacrifice offered.

2. In the Law of Moses several cases are mentioned in which a trespass offering was required. The chief are: (a) If a man keep back or diminish the duties payable to the priests. (b) If he deny the receipt of a deposit, or that he has found or damaged anything. (c) If he unintentionally violate the law to the detriment of his neighbor, and later recognize his fault. In every case, as with the sin offerings, it is assumed that the fault proceeded, not from malice, but from inattention and carelessness.

3. The victim was a ram, sometimes a lamb.

4. *Ritual.* The blood was sprinkled on the altar of holocausts; the fat was burnt on the altar and the rest of the flesh was eaten by the priests within the sacred precincts. Thus the ritual is the same as that of the exterior sin offerings.

The rationalistic theory of sacrifice denies the Mosaic origin of the various kinds of offering and seeks to explain the bloody sacrifice by the act of killing. "At all times people have shrunk from attacking nature. One of the most grievous attacks possible is killing, i. e. suppressing, destroying the life of an animal created by God. As, however, men desired to slaughter animals, and were obliged to do so, they tried to calm their fears at least by restoring to God, i. e. by sacrificing, the blood, in which is the life. As often as they prepared flesh food they gave a befitting share to the Deity. If the feast was particularly solemn, or if many were invited to share it, the Deity received a whole animal. In this way arose first the kind of sacrifice called later peace offerings, but originally referred to as victims or offerings (I Kings iii. 14) and subsequently the holocausts (Deut. xii. 11) developed. In very early times sacrifices of atonement (sin and trespass offerings) were unknown. They arose first out of the consciousness of guilt felt by the people in exile — hence they are mentioned for the first time in the Priests' Code."

All these are arbitrary assumptions. The act of slaughtering was not accompanied by sacrifice (Gen. xviii. 7).[1]

The so-called " Priests' Code " dates, as we have shown on p. 46, etc., not from the time of the Captivity, but from a far earlier period. And quite apart from these considerations, the custom of offering human sacrifices, once prevailing over the whole world, is opposed to this theory. Human sacrifices point to a primeval consciousness of guilt felt by the whole human race, and they certainly belonged to the earliest period, since they were of universal occurrence. On the subject of consuming blood, see page 131, Laws concerning Food.

25. SPECIAL KINDS OF BLOODY SACRIFICES

The Sacrifice of the Red Cow ✓
(Num. xix.)

This peculiar sacrifice was not made either in the Tabernacle or in the Temple, but outside the camp or town. A young full-grown cow, red in color and without blemish, that had never carried the yoke, was chosen and given over to the priest. He had to lead her outside the camp or town, in later times always to the Mount of Olives, and kill her there. Then dipping his finger in her blood, he sprinkled it seven times towards the Tabernacle or Temple. Then the cow's body was laid on a pile of wood, which was set on fire, cedar wood hyssop and scarlet wood being laid upon it. The cow had to be reduced to ashes, which were sifted and then used in the preparation of water for purification. If any one had incurred one of the legal defilements, he had to be separated from the people, and could only be purified again after the lapse of a definite time; the purification consisted of being sprinkled with water containing some of the red cow's ashes. Not only persons, but vessels, houses and tents, were sprinkled with this water and restored to their normal condition,[2] if they had become legally unclean [3] (cf. Heb. ix. 13).

[1] Abraham caused beasts to be slain as soon as the three strangers arrived.

[2] A bunch of hyssop, fastened by a red thread to a stick of cedar wood, was used for sprinkling persons or things.

[3] The red cow seems to represent the people of Israel, that through their repeated unfaithfulness (red symbolizes guilt) had deserved death, i. e. destruction, but through faith in the future Messias and by doing penance might hope for salvation.

Sacrifice for Lepers
(Leviticus xiv.)

When a leper recovered from his disease, he had to show himself to a priest, and if the latter judged him to be cured, he had to bring two living birds, which must be "clean," not birds of prey that eat carrion, and also a bunch of hyssop. One of the birds was killed over living water (i. e. water from a spring or a river) in such a way that its blood dripped into the water, into which the bunch of hyssop was dipped, and the healed leper sprinkled seven times. The other bird was dipped in the same water and then allowed to fly away; this symbolized the recovery of health. Then the man who was healed washed his clothes, cut his hair and bathed his body, and thenceforth he was clean, and might come into the camp or city, though he must not occupy his tent or house for another week. On the eighth day he had to bring a threefold sacrifice,[1] and was then on a level with all the other Israelites.

The significance of the ceremony concerning the two birds was probably this: The leper was to acknowledge that as a sinner he had deserved death, which is "the wages of sin," but he was preserved through the offering of living creatures, which the justice of God accepted as types of a better sacrifice.

The Nazirite Sacrifice *Sacred or set apart*
(Num. vi. 1–21)

Every Israelite could, by a vow, consecrate himself exclusively to God, either for a definite period or for life. Persons bound by such a vow were called Nazirites, i. e. set apart (נָזִיר from נָזַר,

---

[1] Namely, a trespass offering (a ram and one log of oil), a sin offering (a female lamb) and a burnt offering (a ram and three issaron of fine flour). In case of poverty two pigeons might be used for the burnt and sin offerings, and only one issaron of flour was required, but no reduction could be made in the trespass offering, which was required because the leper, during his illness, had been unable to render any service in the sanctuary or to his neighbors; a sin offering was necessary, because he had been prevented from keeping the law in every point, and a burnt offering was his homage paid to God.

to set apart). The obligations incurred by those thus consecrated were threefold: (1) they had to avoid all intoxicating
drinks; (2) the hair of their head must be allowed to grow;[1]
(3) they were forbidden to take any part in mourning for the
dead.[2] If the vow was temporary, it held good for thirty days,
and when these expired the Nazirite had to make a threefold
sacrifice, viz. a sin offering, a burnt offering and a thank
offering.[3] After making the thank offering, the Nazirite cut
off the hair of his head and cast it into the fire on the altar.
If a Nazirite broke his vow, by joining in lamentation for the
dead, or in any other way, he had to offer two pigeons in
reparation, and begin his time of consecration over again.

Nazirites were held in great respect. Saint John the Baptist and
Saint James the Less, the Apostle, were Nazirites; even Saint Paul did
not hesitate to become one for a time.

(b) Unbloody Sacrifices

26. MEAT OFFERINGS

1. A meat offering was not always merely an addition to a
holocaust or a peace offering, but it was often an independent
sacrifice. Just as the sin and trespass offerings stood alone, and
required no unbloody addition, so also there were independent
meat offerings. Such were especially (1) the loaves of proposition or shewbread; (2) the Paschal sheaf; (3) the loaves at
Pentecost; (4) first fruits, i. e. first produce of the soil; (5)
jealousy offerings.

[1] According to I Corinthians xi. long hair was a mark of a subordinate
position and of dependence on another, hence it befitted women.
[2] Death suggests sin and is due to sin, but God is the Lord of Life,
who will bestow eternal life on all that serve Him. Probably also some
heathen superstitions were often connected with mourning for the dead,
as a cultus of the dead was very common among the Gentiles, and whoever took part in it showed a tendency to heathenism.
[3] A sin offering, because during the time of consecration some transgressions of the law might have occurred; a burnt offering, because the
Nazirite wished to show especial honor to God; a thank offering, to express his gratitude for the successful completion of the period for which
he had taken the vow.

In addition to these, which were prescribed by law, there were probably (Lev. ii. 1, etc.) also free-will meat offerings.

2. *Ritual.* Of the meat offerings that accompanied bloody sacrifices, only a small part, about as much as could be grasped with three fingers, was taken as *ascara,* i. e. reminder, *memoriale,*[1] and burnt in the fire on the altar. The rest belonged to the priest. An independent meat offering, especially such as priests had to offer for themselves, was often altogether burnt (Lev. vi. 23), though sometimes only the portion taken as a reminder was put on the altar. As a rule the meat offerings belonged solely to the priests, e. g. the first fruits of fields and gardens (Lev. ii. 12).

27. DRINK OFFERINGS

Only wine might be used for a drink offering, and according to Josephus Flavius it was poured out all round the altar. There were no independent drink offerings, but, in conjunction with meat offerings, they were connected with the bloody sacrifices, viz. holocausts and peace offerings. The quantity of wine used corresponded with the size of the victim. For a bullock half a hin of wine was taken, for a ram one-third, and for a lamb a quarter (Num. xxviii. 14).[2] In the Temple there was an

---

[1] This probably means that the fact of burning these things before God should remind men of the fulfillment of their duty.

[2] The measures for liquids were: (1) the Bath; (2) the Hin, a sixth part of the Bath; (3) the Log, a twelfth part of the Hin. The measures for solids were: (1) the Chomer or Kor; (2) the Letech, half the chomer; (3) the Epha, the tenth part of the chomer; (4) the Seah, one-third of the epha; (5) the Omer (issaron), one-tenth of the Epha (Ex. xvi. 36); (6) the Kab, the sixth of the seah. There are difficulties in reducing these measures to those now in use. Josephus Flavius says (*Ant.,* VIII, 2, 9) that the epha and bath were both equal to an Attic *methetes* (about 8 gallons). The Rabbinical mode of reckoning, which was very inexact, gave the capacity of a Log as = six hens' eggs. This would make the log = nearly half a pint, the hin about five pints, the bath four gallons. The kab would be nearly a quart; the omer nearly half a gallon; the seah 1¼ gallons, the epha (like the bath) four gallons, the letech about 20 gallons and the chomer about 40 gallons. Benzinger follows Josephus and doubles all these quantities, therefore the chomer is equivalent to about 80 gallons, reckoning the log as = one pint, etc. But the contents of six hens' eggs can only be half a pint (*Cf.* John ii. 6); the six water pots at Cana would at this rate have contained between 100 and 130 gallons.

official who superintended the drink offerings, and the requisite wine could be bought of him.

A libation of water was made•on the Feast of Tabernacles (see p. 153). Similar libations are mentioned in I Kings vii. 6 and II Kings xxiii. 16.

28. Jealousy Offerings
(Num. v. 11–31)

When a husband suspected his wife of adultery but could not prove her guilt, he brought her to a priest, with a meat offering consisting of one-tenth of an epha of barley meal. The priest took some of the sacred water from the laver in the Temple Court, in an earthern vessel, mixed with it some dust from the floor of the sanctuary, uncovered the woman's head, laid the meat offering in her hands and pronounced a formula of words, assuring her that if she drank the water, being innocent, it would do her no harm; if she were guilty, it would destroy her body. The woman replied " Amen, Amen." Then he wrote the curse on a roll of parchment, washed the writing off in the same water, took the meat offering, laid an *ascara* on the altar, and finally gave the woman the water to drink.

This ordeal is only apparently hard upon the woman; it must be remembered that as soon as the offering was made she was free from all suspicion. It served to protect her from reproaches and ill treatment; and hence women must often have desired and demanded it.

29. The Temple Taxes

Every Israelite over twenty years of age had to pay half a shekel yearly to the Temple. This tax was payable not only in Palestine, but by all the Jews of the Dispersion. Whoever could not pay it in person, sent the money to Jerusalem through collectors or pilgrims.

Similar offerings for the sanctuary were demanded even by Moses. In Exodus xxx. 12–16 we read: " Every one of them shall give a price for their souls to the Lord, and there shall be no scourge among them. . . . Half a sicle shall be offered to the Lord. He that is counted in the number from twenty years and upwards, shall give the price. The rich man shall not add to half a sicle, and the poor man shall diminish nothing. And the money received . . . thou shalt deliver unto the uses of the tabernacle of the testimony." This seems to have been a single, not a yearly payment. Later the tax was collected from time to time when there was unusual need of money (II Chron. xxiv. 6), but after the Captivity Nehemias required a yearly tribute; he diminished it, however, to one-third shekel, perhaps on account of the poverty of the Jews at that time (Nehem. x. 32). " We make ordinances for ourselves to give the third part of a sicle every year for the work of the house of our God." At the time of Christ the amount had been raised again to half a shekel = a double drachma (Matt. xvii. 23). In the Holy Land the tax was payable in the month Adar (February) ; as it had to be paid in half shekel pieces, and other coins were in use all over the country, places for the exchange of money existed, both in the Temple and in the provinces. Priests and Levites also paid this tax.

The shekel (שֶׁקֶל = weight; in the Septuagint the word is rendered δίδραχμον, in the Vulgate *siclus argenti*) is mentioned as early as the time of Abraham, who acquired a piece of land at Hebron for four hundred silver shekels (Gen. xxiii. 15). Subsequently we hear of half and quarter shekels (Ex. xxx. and xxxviii. and I Kings ix.). Very large sums were reckoned in talents (τάλαντον = balance, weight; Heb., כִּכָּר, circle, i. e. a large silver disc = 3000 shekels). The mina (μνᾶ = weight, Heb. מָנֶה = $\frac{1}{60}$ talent) was a silver coin worth 50 shekels. After the Captivity values were often given in darics, Persian coins; and still later Greek coins also became current, especially the stater and the drachma. The Machabees again had shekels coined, but were not able to abolish the use of western coins. Some of their shekels exist at the present time. Under the Romans their coinage too became current, viz. the as (properly εἴε), denarius (piece of 10 as), quadrans (¼ as), and the lepton (λεπτὸν sc. νόμισμα, little coin, ½ quadrans).

The value of these coins in our money may be determined approximately as follows: The Machabean shekels that have been discovered weigh on an average 14.55 grammes; so that their value is about 60 cents; a mina is worth about $30 and a silver talent about $1800. The daric was of the same value as the shekel. The drachma weighed 4.36 grammes, and was worth about 18 cents, the double drachma about 35 cents, and the stater, four drachmas, about 75 cents, although the Jews regarded the stater as equivalent to their shekel, and so demanded a double drachma as the Temple tax. In the time of our Lord the Roman

as was a copper coin worth about one cent in our money. The denarius was a silver coin, which originally contained 10 as, but in the
time of Christ 16, so that its value was about 16 cents. The Romans
reckoned the denarius as equivalent to the drachma.

II. PURIFICATIONS AND OTHER RELIGIOUS CEREMONIES

30. Legal Defilement

In the Law of Moses certain natural conditions are said to
constitute uncleanness in persons who have made a covenant
with God, and directions are given for removing this defilement. The reason is that these conditions are due to sin and
bear a resemblance to it. They fall into three classes: the defilement of death, the uncleanness of leprosy, and sexual uncleanness.

31. The Defilement of Death
(Num. ix. 11, etc.)

A human corpse defiled (1) the tent or house in which it
lay, all open vessels in that house, and the people living in it
or entering it, for the space of seven days. In the same way
(2) contact with a corpse or bones or a grave made a man
unclean for seven days. (3) The defilement of death was
contagious, for every person and thing touched by the unclean
person became unclean until the evening. (4) The dead body
of an animal caused any one who touched it to be unclean until
the evening.

For the removal of this uncleanness, persons and things had
to be sprinkled, on the third and seventh days after contracting
it, with water of purification specially prepared (from the red
cow). Human beings were required, moreover, to take a bath
on the seventh day, and to wash their clothes. For those who
were unclean until the evening, including the man who performed the ceremony of sprinkling with the water of purification, and any one else who accidentally touched this water,
it sufficed to take a bath and to wash their garments.

According to Benzinger (481) the idea that death caused defilement
was only " the energetic protest of the Yahweh religion against any cul-

tus of the dead, and a most emphatic condemnation of the same." The theory that death was a consequence of original sin was based upon the epistle to the Romans, and then referred by Christian theologians to the Old Testament. Benzinger, however, would do well to turn his attention to the author of the Book of Wisdom (i. 13; ii. 23, 24) and also to Saint Paul (Romans v. 12; vi. 23), who lived under the old Covenant and drew upon Jewish opinions and tradition. The underlying reason is to be found in the recognition of the fact that death, the " wages of sin," is something foreign to human nature, imposed upon it, that must be again removed from it. By this means the desire for release could be kept alive, and it was intended that this should be so. The same holds good of sickness, the most appalling form of which is leprosy, and also of various abnormal sexual conditions.

32. UNCLEANNESS DUE TO LEPROSY

Leprosy rendered every person attacked by the disease unclean. If any one was suffering from a suspicious eruption, he had to show himself to a priest, and if the latter recognized his disease as true leprosy (according to the rules laid down in Leviticus xiii.) and declared it to be such, he was bound forthwith to exclude the unhappy man from all intercourse with healthy people. The leper had to rend his garments (i. e. tear them down a short distance over his breast), uncover his head, muffle up his chin, and cry to every one meeting him: " Unclean, unclean! " His dwelling could only be outside the camp or outside any inhabited place. It very rarely happened that any one recovered from leprosy; but when this occurred, he had again to allow himself to be examined by a priest, and if the latter judged him to be really free from the disease, the prescribed ceremonies had to be performed for his purification, and offerings made as described above (p. 116).

Besides human leprosy, the Mosaic law recognized a leprosy affecting houses and clothes.

Leprosy in a house (Lev. xiv. 33, etc.) showed itself by spots and dents of a greenish or reddish color on the walls. As soon as this was noticed, the owner of the house had to give information to a priest, who, if he thought the condition of the house suspicious, had all the furniture removed, and locked up the house for seven days. If he found on the eighth day that the mischief had spread, he caused the stones to be removed at the suspicious part, the whitewash scraped off, and all that was taken away thrown outside the town or village on to some unclean place. New stones were then built into the wall and the whole was whitewashed. If the mischief appeared again, the leprosy was pronounced malignant, the house was declared unclean by the priest, and had to be pulled down. If, however, nothing fresh showed itself through the new whitewash, the priest declared that the evil was remedied, the house was purified by means of ceremonies resembling those by which a man healed of leprosy was purified, and it could then be inhabited again.

Leprosy of garments (Lev. xiii. 47, etc.) showed itself in greenish or reddish marks appearing on woolen or linen clothes and stuffs, and also on leather. As soon as information was given to the priest, he locked up the suspected article for seven days. If, on re-examining it on the seventh day, he found that the mark had increased, he pronounced the article unclean, and it was burnt. If, however, the leprous mark had grown fainter, the part affected was taken out and burnt, and the article could, after being washed, be used again, provided no new spots appeared.

Much obscurity rests on the nature of this evil. Leprosy in houses may perhaps be identified with a kind of rot, injurious to health, and due to the corrosive action of something resembling saltpeter.[1] Leprosy in clothes may be a kind of mold, caused by damp and want of air, and destructive to woven materials and leather. But there is perhaps an assumption that through want of cleanliness human leprosy can be imparted to houses and clothes, and therefore measures must be taken to prevent the disease from spreading.

33. SEXUAL UNCLEANNESS

1. *Vir, qui patitur fluxum seminis, immundus erit.* A chronic morbid condition is meant. The uncleanness connected with it extended to the persons, furniture and utensils touched by the sick man. Persons so touched were unclean until the evening, and were obliged to wash their clothes and to bathe. Earthen utensils must be broken, wooden ones washed with water.

[1] Father Jullien, S.J., refers to Leviticus xiv. in his account of this rot appearing in the basement of dwelling houses in Egypt.

For the ceremony of purification after recovery two pigeons were required as burnt and sin offerings (Lev. xv. 2–15).

2. *Coitus viri cum uxore ambo immundos reddit usque ad vesperam, ac se et vestimenta aqua lavabunt* (Lev. xv. 16–18).

3. *Homo, qui nocturno pollutus sit somnio, egredietur extra castra et non revertetur, priusquam ad vesperam lavetur aqua* (Deut. xxiii. 10, 11).

4. A flow of blood in women caused uncleanness, as long as it lasted. When it was over, the woman had to present two pigeons as burnt and sin offerings (Lev. xv. 25, etc.).

5. Menstruation made a woman unclean for seven days. Persons and things that she touched were unclean until the evening, and required purification in the way described. On the seventh day she had to bathe (Lev. xv. 19, etc.).

6. After childbirth (Lev. xii. 6–8) a woman was unclean, — for seven days after the birth of a son, and for fourteen days after that of a daughter. Moreover, in the former case she had to remain at home for thirty-three days, and in the latter for sixty-six; i. e. any considerable walks, and especially visits to the sanctuary, were forbidden. When the time of purification expired she had to present a lamb as a burnt offering and a pigeon as a sin offering. If she were poor, two pigeons sufficed.

34. Marriage Laws

1. God Himself instituted marriage as a monogamy, but the original ordinance, according to which marriage is the indissoluble union of one man with one woman, became obscured by sin. Lamech, one of Cain's immediate descendants, had two wives, and among the patriarchs we find the custom of having one or more additional wives besides the real wife. This was especially the case when there were no hopes that the real wife would carry on the race. This custom was not altered by the Mosaic Law, although various regulations show plainly that monogamy was to be preferred. Thus, for instance, in Deuteronomy xvii. 17, one who would probably become king of Israel is recommended not to have many wives. Not much attention was paid to this precept, for Solomon had 700 wives

and 300 concubines (III Kings xi. 3). The Israelites as a rule had, however, mostly only one wife, for whom a sum of money was paid to her parents or relatives when the marriage took place; the practice of giving a dowry did not prevail. The position of women was not degraded, as with the Gentiles. Proverbs xxxi. shows how much liberty and independence a wise wife could enjoy in her household. There is no doubt that monogamous marriages were the rule, and after the Captivity we scarcely hear of bigamy or polygamy. Thus the way was prepared for the New Testament ordinance, which restored marriage to its original condition, and at the same time raised it to the rank of a Sacrament and bestowed upon it a special grace. For only by God's grace is it possible for fallen man to observe the ordinance as God designed it.

2. The following obstacles to marriage are enumerated in the Law of Moses:

(1) Marriage with Gentile women, and especially with Chanaanites, was forbidden (Gen. xxiv. 3; Ex. xxxiv. 16; Deut. vii. 3). (2) Marriage was forbidden between persons closely connected by consanguinity or affinity (Lev. xviii. 6, etc., xx. 11, etc.), i. e. a man might not marry (a) his mother or stepmother, (b) his sister or half-sister, (c) his aunt, (d) his granddaughter,[1] (e) his uncle's wife, (f) his mother-in-law or daughter-in-law, (g) his sister-in-law, (h) his step-daughter and step-granddaughter, (i) his wife's sister, as long as the wife is alive.[2] The prohibitions are only stated as applying to men, not to women, for the latter had no freedom of choice, but submitted to the will of parents or bridegroom.

3. If a married man died, leaving no son, his surviving brother was bound to marry the widow. This custom of Levirate marriage exists also among some heathen nations. According to the Mosaic Law, the eldest son born of such a marriage took the dead man's name. and was regarded as his legitimate son

[1] There is no mention of his daughter, probably because it was taken for granted that such a sin could not occur. The same is most likely true of a niece.

[2] Jacob's marriages were exceptional, for his wives were sisters, but he lived before the law was given.

and heir. The object of this law was to secure as far as possible security of tenure and permanence to each family. If the brother-in-law were unwilling to comply with his obligation, the widow could summon him before a court of justice, and if he still refused, he had to put up with public reviling from the widow, but was not forced to marry her (Gen. xxxviii. 8; Deut. xxv. 5; Matt. xxii. 24).

4. As long as marriage was not a Sacrament, divorce could not altogether be forbidden. According to Deuteronomy xxiv. 1–4, it was permitted:

> "If a man take a wife, and have her, and she find not favor in his eyes for some uncleanness, he shall write a bill of divorce, and shall give it in her hand, and send her out of his house. And when she is departed and marrieth another husband, and he also hateth her and hath given her a bill of divorce and hath sent her out of his house, or is dead, the former husband cannot take her again to wife."

The expression translated "some uncleanness" is in Hebrew *'ervath dabar*, i. e. literally shame or disgrace of a thing, something arousing horror or disgust. The doctors of the law did not agree concerning the interpretation of this passage, and in our Lord's time it was hotly discussed by the followers of Hillel and Shammai. The former thought that it meant any unpleasant fact, giving rise to dislike, such as want of skill in cooking on the woman's part. The latter believed that it referred only to indecencies and particularly to adultery. The first interpretation was the one commonly accepted, and our Saviour protested against this frivolous opinion when He declared adultery to be the sole ground for the dissolution of a marriage, and forbade re-marriage under His new law (Matt. xix. 3–12). Divorce must have been rare; there are very few allusions to it in the Old Testament, and the prophet Malachias (ii. 13, etc.) speaks very emphatically against it. The woman had not the same rights as the man, and therefore was not entitled to claim a divorce for herself. We always read that it was the wife who was divorced.

5. Adultery, i. e. intercourse with another man's wife or betrothed, was punished with death; both parties were stoned (Lev. xx. 10; Deut. xxii. 22–24; John viii. 5). This penalty

was of course inflicted only if the case were brought before a judge. A husband might, in secret instances, adopt the line of action proposed by Joseph, "the just man," and put away his wife privately.

35. CIRCUMCISION

1. *Institution.* Circumcision is mentioned as early as Genesis xvii., where we read that God Himself imposed it upon Abraham and his descendants; it was to be a mark of participation in the covenant that God made with him. The obligation of circumcision was binding not only upon all male descendants of Abraham, but also upon their slaves. Every male child had to be circumcised on the eighth day after birth, and every uncircumcised person was ordered to be exterminated from among God's people, because he was regarded as unclean. In the Mosaic Law this rule is referred to as if it had long existed, not as if it were then laid down for the first time: " On the eighth day the infant shall be circumcised " (Lev. xii. 3).

Circumcision was a painful operation, consisting in the removal of the foreskin by means of a sharp knife. Originally stone knives were used for the purpose (Ex. iv. 25; John v. 2), but later on iron ones. As a rule this ceremony of purification was performed by the head of the household.

Precise instructions as to the manner of fulfilling the divine command are not given in the law. Some details have, however, come down to us by tradition, which was always an adjunct to the written law. The most important are as follows:

1. Any one can circumcise, but it is only to be done by women if no man is present.
2. A Gentile is not permitted to circumcise a descendant of Abraham, and such circumcision by a Gentile is invalid.
3. If an already circumcised Gentile embraces Judaism, a wound is made at the place of circumcision in order to bring out the blood of the Covenant.
4. A sick child or a Proselyte is not circumcised until he has recovered his health. If a child dies before he is eight days old, circumcision is still performed on the dead body.
5. Circumcision is permissible even on the Sabbath (John vii. 23).

The later Israelites generally performed circumcision in the synagogue, and united the naming of the child with it. The latter custom is mentioned in the New Testament, but neither it nor the various blessings and rejoicings of modern Jews are to be traced back to Moses or Abraham, or even to God Himself; they have developed in course of time. The same remark applies to the choice of a godfather, on whose knee the ceremony is performed. This practice seems to have arisen in the Middle Ages and in imitation of the custom at Christian baptism.

2. *Origin of Circumcision.* We find circumcision not only among the Israelites, but also among other nations, especially many Arab tribes,[1] and the Phœnicians, Egyptians and Ethiopians. It is quite possible that the Gentiles adopted circumcision from Abraham and his descendants, but it is maintained, on the other hand, that the Egyptians practiced it before the time of Abraham, who adopted it in Egypt and thence brought it with him to Asia. This latter theory is supported by Herodotus (ii. 104),[2] who states that the " Syrians in Palestine " had learnt from the Egyptians to practice circumcision. But we can scarcely attach much importance to this statement, as Herodotus is only reporting what he was told by the Egyptian priests, and their national vanity often led them to represent themselves as the teachers of other nations.[3] If it is suggested that the Israelites were too isolated and politically too insignificant for the Egyptians to have adopted circumcision from them, it is enough to refer to the honors that fell to Abraham and still more to Joseph in Egypt, to make it appear credible.[4] But even if we assume or

[1] To the present day the Mahometans insist most strictly upon it. It is performed between the seventh and the thirteenth years. *Cf.* Genesis xvii. 15: "Ismael was thirteen years old when he was circumcised."

[2] μοῦνοι πάντων ἀνθρώπων Κόλχοι καὶ Αἰγύπτιοι καὶ Αἰθίοπες περιτάμνονται ἀπ' ἀρχῆς τὰ αἰδοῖα. Φοίνικες δὲ καὶ Σύροι οἱ ἐν τῇ Παλαιστίνῃ καὶ αὐτοὶ ὁμολογέουσι παρ' Αἰγυπτίων μεμαθηκέναι.

[3] Reitzenstein expresses the opinion that in Egypt only the priests and other persons connected with the temples were circumcised, and that the Israelites derived the practice from them. If this were true, however, circumcision would certainly have been limited to the priests among the Israelites also. It seems certain that in Egypt and Arabia from remote times the operation was performed at about the age of thirteen.

[4] It is very improbable that other nations practiced circumcision before the Jews. In the Old Testament circumcision is spoken of as the mark distinguishing the servants of the true God from the worshipers of false gods. In Ezechiel xxxii. 21, etc., all non-Israelites, including a great number of tribes, are spoken of as uncircumcised. Scholz believes that the Egyptians adopted circumcision either directly from Joseph, who was ad-

grant that circumcision was commonly practiced by the Egyptians before the time of Abraham, this does not affect the religious importance of the ceremony. If Abraham learnt it in Egypt, he was being prepared to be commanded by God, at a later period, to introduce it into his own race.

Why did God order the people of the Covenant to be circumcised? What is the religious signification of the rite? Was it meant merely as a sanitary precaution? Philo laid stress on this aspect of it, and Christian archæologists have tried to strengthen this theory by pointing out how much it furthers cleanliness, which is beneficial to the health and diminishes sexual excesses. But other nations living under the same climatic conditions, and not practicing circumcision, were neither less healthy nor less moral than the circumcised for that reason. Circumcision seems to have been ordered because the sexual life had been corrupted by sin. If the human race was to be raised, a purification of this life was absolutely necessary. Circumcision was only a symbol and type of such a purification. The true remedy for the evils that had crept in was supplied by Christ, who restored monogamy, raised marriage to the rank of a Sacrament, and gave His followers the counsel of perfect chastity, at the same time making it possible to practice it by means of the grace that He bestowed. Since then circumcision has ceased to be obligatory. It was a type of baptism, but could not remove original sin.

mitted to their priestly caste, or indirectly, through Arab tribes. Egypt was not always completely cut off from intercourse with foreign countries, as is shown by the reign of Hyksos. If traces of circumcision can really be found on very ancient mummies, the first question to decide is to what period they belong. Among the carvings at Karnak the actual operation of circumcision is depicted, but it should be noticed that it is being performed on two boys of about twelve years of age, which is the age at which circumcision takes place among the Arabs, whereas the Israelites circumcise children of eight days old; hence neither the Egyptians nor the Arabs seem to have been their instructors in this respect. It is possible that the Egyptians adopted circumcision from the descendants of Ismael. *Cf.* Genesis xxi. 21: "This mother" (Agar, the Egyptian) "took a wife for him out of the land of Egypt."

36. Reception of Proselytes

In every age, but especially after the Captivity, strangers, members of other races, have lived among the Israelites. They were called *gerim* = those added. Although every Gentile was regarded by the Israelites as unclean, these strangers were tolerated by the Mosaic law, but they had to pledge themselves to conform to some extent to the worship of the true God. According to tradition, they were especially bound to observe the seven Noachic commandments; i. e. they must refrain from (1) blaspheming the true God; (2) worshiping the heavenly bodies and false gods; (3) murder; (4) incest, i. e. marriage with very near relatives; (5) robbery; (6) rebellion against authority; (7) eating blood and flesh containing blood.[1]

If these strangers desired to attain to the full rights of Israel, they had to seek admission to the Mosaic Covenant by submitting to circumcision, and thereby pledge themselves to observe the whole Jewish law.

At the time of Christ (according to the Mishna and Gemara), the Proselytes of the Gate were distinguished from the Proselytes of Righteousness or of the Covenant. The former lived indeed within the gates of Jewish towns, but were only tolerated, the latter had acquired civil rights, observed all the precepts of the law, and were completely on a level with the Israelites. The Babylonian Gemara tells us that sacrifice and baptism were required in their case, as well as circumcision.[2] This baptism is nowhere mentioned in Holy Scripture and seems to be a further development of the bath that preceded the performance of religious ceremonies. The whole ceremony expresses a desire for purification from sin and to be born again to a new life.

---

[1] These rules of late Jewish origin plainly received their name Noachic from the instructions given by God to Noe (Gen. ix. 3, etc.), relating to the killing of beasts and the eating of blood. That these particular rules have come down from Noe cannot be proved.

[2] The baptism was complete immersion in running water in token of their new birth.

37. Laws concerning Food

The nourishment of which a man partakes is not a matter of perfect indifference, because it influences also his spiritual life. Hence God in His revelation repeatedly laid down rules governing food.

According to God's original ordinance, the human race was to live on vegetables. In Genesis i. 29,[1] grass is assigned to the beasts, and to man the produce of the fields and the fruits of the trees as food. Most commentators are of opinion that in the first few centuries there were no beasts of prey, and human beings ate no animal food.[2] Only after the Deluge were men permitted to eat flesh as well as vegetables, and consequently to kill animals, although it was with the limitation that no blood, or flesh stained with blood, should be eaten (Gen. ix. 3, etc.).

The Mosaic law contains many other limitations, and a number of rules regarding the kinds of flesh food that were permitted, and those that were not.

The flesh of all unclean beasts was forbidden to be eaten. Such included (Lev. xi.; Deut. xiv.) :

1. Of four-footed beasts, (a) all that walk on paws, such as dogs, wolves, foxes and lions; (b) all that do not chew the cud, as swine; (c) all that, though they chew the cud, have hoofs not quite divided. In this way only those quadrupeds are reckoned as clean which both have divided hoofs and chew the cud. These are oxen, sheep, goats, and animals resembling them, such as gazelles, wild goats, stags and fallow deer.

2. Of birds about twenty varieties are declared to be unclean, mostly birds of prey (Lev. xi. 13, etc. *Cf.* p. 12). On the other hand, pigeons, turtledoves and quails are mentioned as clean.

3. All water animals are unclean unless they have fins and

---

[1] The Vulgate text is not so clear in this verse as the original, with which the Septuagint, Peshitto and other ancient texts are in agreement.

[2] A reminiscence of this peaceful age has been preserved in the writings of heathen nations. *Cf.* Virgil, *Georg.*, I, 130; Ovid, *Metamorph.*, XV, 96, etc.

scales. So eels, all creatures resembling snakes, and sala-
manders, are unclean.

4. All creeping beasts are considered unclean; and

5. All insects, except such as walk on four feet and have two
others with which to hop. This exception permitted some kinds
of grasshoppers to be eaten (Lev. xi. 21).

But it was not allowed to eat even clean beasts indiscriminately.
With reference to them it was forbidden —

1. To eat the blood and portions of flesh containing blood
(Lev. vii. 26).[1] This prohibition was upheld in the New Testament (Acts xv.), but since the Middle Ages it has been gradually disregarded by the Church, as the Apostles respected it only
out of consideration for the Jews, intending thus to facilitate
their entrance into the Church.

2. It was forbidden to eat the flesh of any beast that had
died a natural death or that had been killed by some wild animal.
In the New Testament (Acts xv.) it is stated in a still more
general way that the flesh of all strangled beasts ($\pi\nu\iota\kappa\tau\nu\acute{o}$)
(e. g. killed through being caught in a snare) is forbidden.
The reason in both cases is that the blood would have been either
only partially or not at all drained out of the body, whereas when
an animal was slaughtered, it was all removed.

3. Certain fatty parts of oxen, sheep and goats might not be
eaten, because they were destined for the altar of sacrifice, i. e.
they were considered sacred, even apart from a sacrifice (Lev.
iii. 16, 17).[2] Cf. p. 111.

4. A kid might not be boiled in its mother's milk (Exod.
xxiii. 19). Tradition extended this prohibition to every form
of mixture of flesh and milk.[3]

---

[1] The blood is the life. Man cannot bestow life; therefore originally
he was not permitted to kill animals, although this was allowed after the
Deluge. By pouring out the blood man aimed at giving back the creature's life to God, without necessarily always offering a sacrifice.

[2] "All the fat shall be the Lord's. By a perpetual law for your generations, and in all your habitations: neither blood nor fat shall you eat at
all." Streaks of fat in the meat, however, might be eaten.

[3] The reason for this precept is obscure. Luther and others have
thought that it was forbidden to eat any sucklings. Others fancy that
the custom was regarded as cruel. Possibly some heathen superstition
gave rise to this prohibition.

further mention of music,[1] and again after the escape of the Israelites from Egypt.[2]

David was the chief musician among the Hebrews; he played the harp so beautifully that he was able to banish Saul's melancholy by means of it. He introduced music and singing to the sanctuary; 4000 Levites, with Asaph, Heman and Idithun at their head, had to supply it (I Chron. xxiii. 5; xxv. 1, etc.). Solomon and his successors maintained the music, but gradually the interest in it diminished, and Ezechias and Josias had to make new arrangements. During the Captivity it was no longer a joy to practice sacred music (Ps. cxxxvi.),[3] but it was not completely forgotten, for among those who returned home were 200 singers (Esdras ii. 65). Their piety caused David's music to be revived (Esdras iii. 10; Nehem. xii. 27), and thenceforth, as long as the Temple existed, it was always kept up with joy.

2. The chief part of the music seems always to have been singing; instruments served only to support it; i. e. to supply a prelude and an accompaniment, to make a transition from one key to another, and to fill up pauses when the singers rested. It is doubtful whether the Hebrews had melodies, strictly so called. It might be assumed that the singing resembled that somewhat high-pitched kind of recitative that is still heard in the synagogues when the Scriptures are read. This monotonous declamation could hardly, however, be called singing. The headings of the Psalms, too, show that different modes of singing were in use; for instance, in the Masoretic text the heading of the 8th Psalm is " according to the Gathitic tune," and that of

---

[1] Laban says to him: " I might have brought thee on the way with joy, and with songs, and with timbrels and with harps " (Gen. xxxi. 27).

[2] Exodus xv. 1: "Moses . . . sung this canticle to the Lord." Verses 20, 21: "Mary the prophetess, the sister of Aaron, took a timbrel in her hand, and all the women went after her with timbrels and with dances, and she began the song."

[3] " Upon the rivers of Babylon, there we sat and wept, when we remembered Sion. On the willows in the midst thereof we hung up our instruments. For there they that led us into captivity required of us the words of songs, and they that carried us away, said: ' Sing ye to us a hymn of the songs of Sion.' How shall we sing the song of the Lord in a strange land? "

the 21st Psalm is that it must be sung to "the hind of the dawn," i. e. to the tune of a well-known song. It seems probable, therefore, that the songs possessed melody, but harmony was absent, i. e. the union of high and deep voices singing together. Musical notation was unknown.[1]

3. The musical instruments mentioned in the Bible may be divided into stringed and wind instruments and instruments of percussion.[2]

(a) *Stringed Instruments.* Those in use among the Israelites were known as the *kinnor* and the *nebel.* The *kinnor* by its very name suggests a harp, lyre or guitar. It had six strings. The *nebel* was like the *kinnor,* but larger, with 10 or 12 strings. As *nebel* means skin, the sounding-board was probably uneven, or twisted. The instruments called in Daniel iii. 5, etc., the *sabbeka* (סַבְּכָא, σαμβύκη) and *pesanter* (פְּסַנְתֵּרִין, ψαλτήριον) were something like the harp. They were used in Babylon.

(b) *Wind Instruments:* the bagpipe or *ugab* (עוּגָב); the flute, *chalil* (חָלִיל), made of reed or wood; the trumpet, *chazozera* (חֲצֹצְרָה), and the trombone, *schophar* (שׁוֹפָר); according to Josephus, the trumpet was a straight, thin tube of metal, about a cubit in length, with a bell-shaped mouthpiece. It is represented on the Arch of Titus. The trombone or horn (קֶרֶן) was probably originally an ox or a ram's horn, and was afterwards made of metal in the same shape.

(c) *Percussion Instruments:* the tambourine (תֹּף, τύμπανον), a ring of wood or metal, with a skin stretched over it and bells attached to it;[3] cymbals (צְלְצְלִים)[4] two concave pieces of metal, giving a clear note when struck together; the *sistrum* (מְנַעַנְעִים)[5] an oval ring of metal, across which were four metal rods loosely attached to it; the instrument had a handle, by which it was

---

[1] Dancing often accompanied the music, even at religious ceremonies. Even King David danced before the ark (II Kings vi. 14). The two sexes never danced together except at the sacrifices to false gods.

[2] Bow instruments seem not to have been known.

[3] It was held in the left hand and shaken in time, whilst the right hand struck the skin, perhaps with a little stick.

[4] In I Esdras iii. 10, cymbals are called מְצִלְתַּיִם.

[5] Gk. σεῖστρον, Lat. *sistrum*, a sort of gong, used in Egypt chiefly in honor of Isis.

shaken and swung; the triangle (שָׁלִישִׁים), made of steel, and attached to a string, by which it was held; it was struck with a little metal rod.

41. Blessings

Numbers vi. 22, etc., contains the prescribed form of words used in blessing the people. It runs:

" The Lord bless thee and keep thee.

The Lord show His Face to thee and have mercy on thee.

The Lord turn His Countenance to thee and give thee peace."

Every day, after the morning sacrifice and the offering of incense, the officiating priest had to raise his hands and pronounce this blessing over the people assembled and praying in the court, or over their representatives. The people answered: "Amen."

The evening sacrifice was not followed by a blessing.[1]

42. Vows and Curses

1. In Holy Scripture a vow (*cherem*) is the dedication of persons or things to be exclusively God's property. The consequence of it was that the persons must be killed and the things given to the sanctuary or burnt (Lev. xxvii. 1, etc.; Num. xxxi. 17; Deut. ii. 34, xiii. 15).

In the Mosaic law this doom was pronounced upon Israelites who sacrificed to false gods, and even upon whole cities that fell into idolatry (Ex. xxii. 19). Human beings and animals in such towns were to be slain by the sword, houses and goods to be consumed with fire. On account of particularly wicked practices this curse was pronounced against the Chanaanites and subsequently also against the Amalekites, who were probably of kindred race with the Chanaanites,[2] but it was carried out in all its severity only in the case of one city — Jericho. Other town were treated more leniently, and were allowed to remain standing. If

---

[1] So Haneberg, who relies on Maimonides.

[2] Josephus Flavius (*Antiq.*, II, i. 2) is mistaken in believing the Amalekites to be the descendants of Amalech, the grandson of Esau (Gen. xxxvi. 12, 16). They are mentioned long before the time of Esau (Gen. xiv. 7). Philo reckons them among the Phœnicians.

any one retained for himself any part of what was cursed, he himself incurred the curse, and was put to death.[1]

A temporary vow differed from the curse. Under certain circumstances it could be removed. Not infrequently persons, estates, animals and other things, were consecrated to God and to the sanctuary, but they could be redeemed by payment of a ransom. This kind of vow was called *qorban* (*cf.* Lev. xxvii. 1, etc.; Mark vii. 11).

2. Altogether different from the vows and curses of the Mosaic law is the banishment from the synagogues of the later Jews. It implies that a man is excluded from the synagogue and congregation and all intimate dealings with other Israelites (John ix. 22, 34). This sentence was generally pronounced in consequence of some religious offense, especially blasphemy. In the Mishna and by the Rabbis this excommunication is called *Nidduj*.

3. The Jews of the Christian era have extended this excommunication, and they now distinguish three varieties of it, viz. *Cherem* = the Mosaic curse; *Nidduj* = simple excommunication, generally for 30 days; and *Nidduj accompanied by a curse*, often also called Cherem, a solemnly pronounced curse and perpetual exclusion from the congregation.

---

[1] The extreme severity that dominated the Old Covenant was inevitable if the worship of the true God was to be maintained. It was only by the sternest measures that the idolatrous worship, everywhere prevalent, could be repressed and prevented from contaminating God's own little nation (*cf.* Josue vii. 21, etc.).

FOURTH SECTION

SACRED SEASONS

43. THE CALENDAR

THE Israelites had not a solar, but a lunar year; i. e. the calendar was governed by the moon.

A day was reckoned not from midnight to midnight, but from sunset to sunset, perhaps because it is only after the sun has gone down that the crescent moon shows itself in the sky. (This division of time has been adopted by the Church, as festivals and days begin with first vespers and end with second vespers.) The natural day, the period of daylight, was divided at first only into morning, noon and evening; but later into twelve hours, which were longer in summer than in winter. The night was divided into three (Judges vii. 19), and afterwards into four watches, called evening, midnight, cock-crow and morning.[1] The week, a quarter of a lunar month, was based on the story of Creation, as God created the world in six days and rested on the seventh day. With the exception of the seventh, the days had no particular names, they were called simply the first, second, etc. The seventh was the Sabbath = rest.

The church adopted the Jewish week, hence the names *feria secunda, tertia,* etc., in use in ecclesiastical language. The Sabbath has retained its old name, and the first day of the week is called *dominica,* as being the day of our Lord's resurrection. Among heathen nations the days were generally named after the heavenly bodies. This custom probably originated in Babylon, where astrology was practiced. In this respect the Israelites took nothing from the Babylonians.

The month (= moon) corresponds with the duration of the moon's circuit round the earth. It lasted 29 or 30 days.[2] Ac-

---

[1] ὀψέ, μεσνύκτιον, ἀλεκτοροφωνία, πρωΐ (Mark vi. 48; xiii. 35).

[2] Astronomically a lunar month consists of 29 days, 12 hours, 44 minutes and 3 seconds. For want of astronomical knowledge it was impossible to determine this precisely, and people had to reckon from the moment when the new moon became visible.

cording to the Talmud, whoever in or near Jerusalem caught sight of the new moon was bound to notify the fact to the priests in the Temple, who then declared the previous month with its 29 days to be ended, and the 30th day to be the first of the new month. If the sky was too cloudy for the new moon to be seen, the month was ended with the 30th day, and the following day was regarded as that of the New Moon. In very early times no special names were given to the months, with the exception of the first, which was called *Abib* (ear of corn), but during the Captivity the Babylonian names came into use and are still retained by the Jews. These names, the meaning of which is quite obscure, are as follows: (1) *Nisan,* the spring month. The Pasch was kept on the 14th of *Nisan.* (2) *Ijjar.* (3) *Sivan;* Pentecost fell on the 6th day of this month. (4) *Tammus.* (5) *Ab.* (6) *Elul.* (7) *Tishri;* on the 1st fell the civil New Year's festival, on the 10th the Day of Atonement, on the 15th the Feast of Tabernacles. (8) *Marcheshwan.* (9) *Kislev;* the Feast of the Dedication of the Temple, that occurred in winter, was celebrated on the 25th (John x. 22). (10) *Tebeth.* (11) *Shebat.* (12) *Adar.* Sometimes there was a thirteenth intercalary month, called *Veadar.*

As the Pasch had always to be celebrated at the beginning of harvest (about April 1st), and Pentecost at the end of it, the lunar year of 364 days had to be reconciled with the solar year of 365 days, as otherwise the festivals would have been celebrated at the wrong seasons. For this reason about every three years an intercalary month was inserted. The beginning of the year was probably reckoned thus: Towards the end of the 12th month *Adar,* the cornfields were surveyed to see if the barley would be ripe by the middle of the following month, so that the harvest could be begun with the ceremony of offering the first sheaf at the Pasch. If the corn seemed likely to be ripe, the new year began with the next month, but if not, the old year was lengthened by the month *Veadar.* After the Captivity, the decision whether the month should be inserted or not rested with the Synedrium, and the rule was observed that in the Sabbatical year there should never be 13 months.

The new year was originally reckoned as beginning in the

spring, but after the Captivity it became the custom to begin
the civil year with the first day of *Tishri,* in the autumn, whilst
the religious year always began with the first day of *Nisan,* in
the spring. For an agricultural people the beginning of seed-
time seems the most appropriate date for the beginning of the
year.[1]

44. DAILY WORSHIP IN THE TEMPLE

Every morning and evening a lamb a year old was sacrificed
as a burnt offering in the name of the whole people (Ex. xxix. 38;
Num. xxviii. 3). It was accompanied by an unbloody sacrifice
of one-tenth *epha* of wheat flour (rather less than two quarts),
sprinkled with oil, and one-fourth *hin* (about a pint) of wine.
Besides this, fragrant incense was laid on the altar in the Holy
Place every day, in the morning and evening; and in the morning, after offering the incense, the officiating priest had to pronounce Aaron's blessing (see p. 137) over the people in the Court.
According to tradition, at least the twelve so-called Officers of
the Temple must be present at this ceremony, to lay their hands
upon the victim in the name of the people, and to receive the
blessing.

Private sacrifices as a rule followed the usual morning offering.

From the time of David onwards the daily services were made
more solemn by the Levites, who provided music and psalmody.

45. THE SABBATH [2]

1. *Origin.* Keeping the Sabbath day was not peculiar to the
Israelites; we find at least traces of it among heathen nations.
The Babylonians and Assyrians distinguished the 7th, 14th, 21st

---

[1] The Jewish era, reckoning from the creation of man, only came into
general use about the fifteenth century of the Christian era. The Jews
say that 1656 years elapsed between the creation and the Deluge, and
3828 years between the creation and the destruction of Jerusalem by the
Romans. According to them, the birth of Christ took place in the year
3760.

[2] שַׁבָּת is an emphatic form of שָׁבַת, to rest. It designates a particular
kind of quiet and rest.

and 28th days from the other days of the month.[1] A week as a period of seven days occurs among the Hindoos and Chinese and also among the people of Peru. Like the Babylonians and Assyrians, the Germanic nations dedicated the days of the week to various deities, and these names have remained, at least partially, to the present time. The name *šabattu* or *šapattu,* which suggests *Shabbat,* occurs in the cuneiform inscriptions. Among the Greeks and Romans all remembrance of the observance of a day of rest seems to have died out, and they often ridiculed the Jews as idlers.[2] The institution of the Sabbath did not, therefore, originate in the Mosaic Law, as many people assume, but is to be referred to the history of creation. The hallowing of the seventh day was therefore no new thing imposed upon the Israelites on Sinai, but it had been almost forgotten, and consequently they are ordered to " Remember to keep holy the Sabbath day " (Ex. xx. 8. *Cf.* Ex. xii. 16, xvi. 22, etc.).

2. *Duration.* The whole nation was required to rest from sunset of the sixth day to sunset of the seventh. According to tradition, the beginning and the end of the Sabbath were made known by trumpet-blasts in every town in the country.

3. *Mode of Observance.* The observance of the seventh day had both a negative and a positive side ; the former consisted in refraining from work, the latter in particular devotion to God and His law.

(*a*) *Negative Side.* The law does not contain precise instructions regarding the kinds of work forbidden, but the general sense of the ordinance is quite clear from certain passages. In Exodus xxxv. 3, it is forbidden to light a fire for the purpose of cooking.[3] In Numbers xv. 32, we read that picking up sticks

---

[1] We must not, however, overlook the fact that among these nations the days mentioned, and also the 19th, were not days of rest and joy and remembrance of the Creation, but days of penance and atonement. Hence the Sabbath of the Pentateuch can certainly not have been derived from Babylon (see p. 272).

[2] Juvenal, *Sat.*, XIV, 105; Sen. in *Aug. de civ. Dei*, VI, 11.

[3] " Six days you shall do work: the seventh day shall be holy unto you, the sabbath, and the rest of the Lord: he that shall do any work on it, shall be put to death. You shall kindle no fire in any of your habitations on the sabbath day." Food for the sabbath was cooked on the preceding day. Also the lights were kindled before sunset on Friday evening.

on the Sabbath was severely punished.[1] It seems, therefore, that every kind of bodily work, even the most trivial, must cease. Therefore the Jews believed all traveling and trading on the Sabbath to be prohibited.[2] How rigorously the Pharisees observed the day of rest is seen in the New Testament. The Mishna, which contains a special treatise on Sabbath observances, names thirty-nine chief kinds of work (*aboth melakoth = patres operum*), each with many subsidiary occupations (*toledoth = generationes*), which were all prohibited on the Sabbath.[3]

(*b*) *Positive Side.* The Law contains no definite regulations for the positive observance of the Sabbath. In general, the Israelites regarded it as a duty to employ themselves reverently with God and His law. The daily sacrifice in the Temple was doubled [4] and fresh loaves of proposition (shewbread) were provided. Prayers were held in the synagogues, and passages of the law and the prophets were read aloud and expounded. The Sabbath was regarded as a day of rejoicing (Is. lviii. 13; Judith viii. 6; Luke xiv. 1). Cheerful meals were held in the houses, as far as this was possible without cooking on the day itself, and people wore their best garments.

---

[1] The offender had to be put to death. It seems likely, however, that he did not merely collect wood, but, in order to obtain it, either cut down a tree or exerted himself to break down bushes. This at least is the interpretation of the Samaritan Targum.

[2] All that the law enacts with regard to walking is that every man is to stay at home and not go forth out of his place (Ex. xvi. 29). The doctors of the law fixed two thousand cubits, about a quarter of an hour's walk, as the farthest point to which a man might go. In Acts i. 12 the distance of the Mount of Olives from Jerusalem is defined as a Sabbath day's journey. Even at the present day the Sabbath day's journey is marked out in Jewish communities by means of a string or wire. The Jews refused also to bear arms on the Sabbath, often to their own great disadvantage. But in later times they were less strict, and sometimes they availed themselves of the law regarding the Sabbath to practice some stratagem of war.

[3] To carry the smallest burden, even a piece of broken crockery, or a needle or a false tooth, was enough to violate the commandment.

[4] Numbers xxviii. 9. "On the sabbath day you shall offer two lambs of a year old without blemish, and two tenths of flour."

46. THE NEW MOONS

The Israelites kept each new moon as a religious festival. As the date could not be precisely fixed by means of astronomy, it was necessary to choose the day after the first appearance of the new moon; on the day when the moon changes, it cannot be seen, owing to the proximity of the sun. In the Temple this day was celebrated by special sacrifices of several animals with the corresponding meat and drink offerings, in addition to the usual sacrifices (Num. xxviii. 11, etc.). To increase the solemnity, trumpets were blown (Num. x. 10). The day was observed as a Sabbath, although this was not absolutely prescribed, and feasts took place. The new moon of the seventh month (1st of *Tishri*) received particular honor, like the seventh day of the week; it was called the day of the blowing of trumpets; and on it an extra sacrifice was offered, over and above those usually offered at the new moons (Num. xx. 2, etc.). As after the Captivity the civil year began with the seventh new moon, this day is also called New Year's day.

The custom of honoring the new moons has been altogether lost under the new Covenant, perhaps because the Sun of Righteousness has arisen, and so the faint moonlight of the Old Covenant is bound to disappear. The change seems to rest upon instructions given by the Apostles. Just like the observance of the first instead of the last day of the week, the abolition of the New Moon ceremonies marks the freedom of Christians from the Jewish law. Saint Paul writes to this effect in Galatians iv. 10 and Colossians ii. 16, etc.

47. THE SABBATICAL YEAR

(Leviticus xxv.)

Men and beasts, after six days of work, had to dedicate the seventh day to God and spend it in rest; and in the same way, after six years of cultivation and fruit-bearing, the whole country was ordered to keep a year's Sabbath in God's honor, and to rest. During this seventh year no field might be cultivated or sown, no garden and no fruit tree might receive attention. Whatever grew without any action on the part of mankind, was common property, belonging to all without distinction.

The Sabbatical year always began in the autumn, when the usual sowing did not take place.

As during the Sabbatical year no profit could be derived from the soil, it necessarily followed that no creditor could forcibly demand payment of debts during it. In the same way no taxes could be claimed by the government. According to Josephus Flavius (*Ant.*, XIV, x. 6), even the pagan rulers of Palestine always remitted their taxes to the Jews in the Sabbatical year.

On the Feast of Tabernacles in this year, the Mosaic law (Deut. xxxi. 10-14) required that the law should be solemnly read aloud to the whole people by the Levites in the sanctuary.

It is a mistake to suppose (1) that as soon as the Sabbatical year began, every debtor was absolutely released from payment, so that his creditor had thenceforth no claim upon him. The law only states (Deut. xv. 2) that in this year the creditor shall not raise his hand, nor oppress his neighbor therewith, i. e. in this year he is not recklessly to claim his due, as his debtor can have no income. (2) Equally mistaken is the supposition that Hebrew slaves always obtained their freedom in the Sabbatical year. The law (Ex. xxi. 2; Deut. xv. 12) orders their emancipation to take place in the seventh year, i. e. not necessarily in the Sabbatical year, but in the seventh year of their service. Although slavery existed in Israel as well as in the rest of the ancient world, it was of a far milder type than among the heathen (*cf.* also the following).

48. The Year of Jubilee

After seven times seven years there followed one year (no doubt beginning in the autumn) of particular rejoicing. This was called the Jubilee, *schenath hajjobel,* because on the 10th of the month *Tishri,* i. e. on the Day of Atonement of the seventh Sabbatical year, it was proclaimed throughout the country with the sound of trumpets.

1. In this year the whole land rested, as in the Sabbatical year, and might not be cultivated. Thus in two successive years there was no agriculture, but the fertility of the soil was so great that provision could be made, and there was no reason to fear a famine. The rest affected only agriculture; cattle breeding and other business went on as usual.

2. In the year of jubilee all persons, who for any reason had

been reduced to slavery, were set at liberty, if one of their relatives had not previously purchased their freedom. When a man was set free, all the members of his family acquired their freedom.[1]

3. All landed property that had passed into the possession of strangers reverted in the year of jubilee to the original owner or his descendants, without payment. This contributed greatly to the prevention of oppression and destitution among the people.

Josephus Flavius (*Ant.*, II, xii. 3) says that in the year of jubilee all debts were canceled; but there is no mention of this in Holy Scripture, and no stress can be laid upon the statement.

THE YEARLY RECURRING FESTIVALS

49. The Pasch

I. The *Pasch* (Ex. xii.).[2] The first and most important festival in the year was always the Pasch, celebrated on the 14th of *Nisan*. The feast itself and the seven days following it commemorated the delivery of the Israelites from Egypt. On the 10th day of the first month a male lamb, free from blemish, and one year old, was set aside for each family. On the 14th, about sunset (Deut. xvi. 6),[3] the head of the household killed it. If any family was too small to eat a whole lamb, two families might unite for the purpose. A bundle of hyssop was dipped into the blood as it streamed out, and some was smeared on the two doorposts and on the lintel of the house. No bone of the animal might

---

[1] This applied only to the slaves who were Israelites, not to those who were Gentiles. The latter could be bequeathed by a man to his descendants (Lev. xxv. 46). The law disapproved of the enslavement of people of the same race (Lev. xxv. 42. *Cf.* John viii. 33).

[2] פַּסְחָא is the Aramaic name; the Hebrew is פֶּסַה; both signify passing over, sparing.

[3] Exodus xii. 6, " between the two evenings." Various explanations are given of this expression; it probably means that the killing was to take place just at sunset. Before the sun went down, the evening belonged to the 14th, after sunset, to the 15th of *Nisan*. Each evening was divided into two parts, one belonging to the preceding, and the other to the following day. The modern Samaritans sacrifice on Mount Garizim, as soon as the sun has set.

be broken, nor was it cut up, but, after the skin and the entrails had been removed, it was roasted whole at the fire. When it was cooked through, it had to be eaten the same night, with unleavened bread and bitter herbs.[1] All the household took part in the meal; only the uncircumcised were excluded. As the ceremony commemorated the flight from Egypt, all present had to have their loins girt, shoes on their feet, and a staff in their hand.[2] The head of the house had to explain why the feast was held. What could not be consumed must be burnt on the following morning.

When settled conditions prevailed in Palestine a change was made in the ceremony, and all full-grown males were required to attend in the sanctuary. The Paschal lambs were no longer sacrificed in each house, but were killed and eaten near the Tabernacle or Temple. Some of the blood was sprinkled on the altar and the fatty parts were burnt. Pilgrims visiting Jerusalem at the time of the festival received the necessary accommodation gratis from the inhabitants, but it was usual to present the hosts with the lambs' skins. As the number of strangers was very great, many spent the nights in the open air, and ate the lamb in tents.

Whoever was prevented from keeping the feast on the 14th of *Nisan,* by reason either of legal uncleanness or some other impediment, was bound to keep the Pasch on the 14th of the second month, under pain of death.

The Pasch, like all the Old Covenant, though in a special degree, had a symbolical meaning. It represents the sacrifice of Christ, the true Paschal lamb, not one of whose bones was broken on the Cross, and whose blood brings forgiveness to mankind. His death and the sacrifice of the Holy Eucharist obtained thereby are means of salvation for all men. For this reason every one was sentenced to death who took no part in the celebration of the Pasch.

According to the Mishna (Pesach 10), the Paschal rites were performed as follows: In commemoration of God's promise in Exodus vi. 6: " I am the Lord, who will bring you out from the work-prison of the

---

[1] *Merorim.* Apparently these might not be selected at will, but the wild lettuce is meant; for the Septuagint has πικρίδες, and the Vulgate *lactuca agrestis.*

[2] It was not until the institution of the Eucharist that Saint John leant on our Lord's breast (John xiii. 25).

Egyptians, and will deliver you from bondage and redeem you with a high arm . . . and I will take you to myself for my people " — four cups of wine were brought in. After the first cup the roasted lamb with the unleavened bread and bitter herbs was carried in, whilst the 112th and 113th Psalms were sung (in the Heb., 113 and 114). The second cup of wine was now handed round. Then the son asked the father the meaning and significance of the Paschal ceremony (Ex. xii. 26) and the father explained fully that it was held in remembrance of the delivery from Egypt and the sparing of the firstborn among the Israelites. The unleavened bread was next distributed and then the third cup, the " cup of blessing," was handed round; it was so called because meantime the blessing was pronounced over the food, which was now eaten. After the feast the fourth cup of wine was passed round, and at the close the 114th to 117th Psalms were sung. A fifth cup might be added; if so, Psalms 119 to 136 had to be sung.

Our Saviour appears to have instituted the Holy Eucharist after the fourth cup of wine, so that He made the optional fifth cup the " cup of blessing " of the New Covenant (I Cor. x. 6), i. e. the chalice of His Blood. Also the washing of the feet, which was the preparation for the Holy Eucharist, cannot have taken place until after the fourth cup had been drunk, for Saint John says (xiii. 2) : " When supper was done . . . he riseth from supper [ἐκ τοῦ δείπνου] and . . . girded himself," etc. In the same way Saint Paul says (I Cor. xi. 25) μετὰ τὸ δειπνῆσαι = postquam cenavit. The Paschal feast was therefore at an end; now followed the washing of the feet and the feast of the New Covenant, and that was concluded with singing psalms (Matt. xxvi. 30).

II. The Paschal supper was not the whole of the festival, which lasted for an entire week. Connected with the Pasch was the seven days' feast of unleavened bread (*chag hammazzoth*) from the 15th to the 21st of *Nisan*. On the 15th and 21st people refrained from work [1] and assembled in the sanctuary; the other days might be spent in work, provided the weekly Sabbath did not fall upon one of them. On each of the seven days a special sacrifice was offered after the usual daily sacrifice (Num. xxviii. 19–23). Only unleavened bread might be eaten during the whole period, and after midday on the 14th no leaven might remain in the houses.

[1] Leviticus xxiii. 7, 8. " The first day shall be most solemn unto you and holy, you shall do no servile work therein, but you shall offer sacrifice in fire to the Lord seven days. And the seventh day shall be more solemn and more holy, and you shall do no servile work therein." *Cf.* Numbers xxviii. 18. As only " servile work " is expressly forbidden, we may infer that these days were not required to be kept as Sabbaths. For this reason the bodies of Christ and the two thieves could be taken down from the cross on this day (John xix. 31, etc.).

The festival was regarded as the beginning of the harvest. Therefore on the 16th of *Nisan,* the second day,[1] the beginning of the harvest was marked by the offering of a sheaf of barley.[2] Before this offering was made, none of the new harvest might be used.

Significance. We read in Exodus xii. 34 that for some days after leaving Egypt the Israelites were obliged to eat unleavened bread, because, in the haste of their departure, there was no time to leaven the bread prepared for baking. In God's design this historical fact was intended to symbolize a higher thought. Leaven is a type of original sin, and so unleavened bread was suitable food for the sanctified race that had just been cut off from the horrors of Egyptian idolatry. By the yearly recurrence of the practice of eating such bread they were constantly reminded and admonished to keep themselves free from sin. — We need not hesitate to assume that on entering Palestine the Israelites found a festival, resembling this sequel to the Pasch, among the Chanaanites, celebrating the beginning of harvest, but they brought their own ideas into it. The same is true of Pentecost and the Feast of Tabernacles at the close of the harvest. (Compare the Yule feast and the summer solstice feast observed by Teutonic nations on December 25 and June 24. The preachers of Christianity found these feasts already existing.)

50. PENTECOST

(Ex. xxxiv. 22; Lev. xxiii. 15, etc.; Deut. xvi. 9, etc.)

1. From the 16th of *Nisan,* on which the harvest was opened by the offering of the first sheaf, seven full weeks were reckoned, and another festival observed on the 50th day. This was Pentecost, so called because it fell on the 50th day ($\pi\epsilon\nu\tau\eta\kappa\sigma\sigma\tau\dot{\eta}$ sc. $\dot{\eta}\mu\dot{\epsilon}\rho\alpha$) after the beginning of harvest.

2. It was also called the Feast of Weeks (Ex. xxxiv. 22; Deut. xvi. 9) because seven weeks had to pass before it might be celebrated. Another name was the Feast of the Harvest (Ex. xxiii. 16), because as the harvest was then over, it was regarded as

---

[1] Leviticus xxiii. 11, *mimmachorath haschschabbat = altero die sabbati.* The 15th was the first and chief day of the festival, on which people refrained from all heavy work. Knobel and Hitzig regard the 15th as the beginning of harvest.

[2] The law does not specify what kind of grain is to be offered, nor does the Mishna; but there can be no doubt that barley is meant, as it is the first to ripen. According to the Mishna it was not the sheaf itself that was offered, but flour hastily ground from it, and of this an ascara was placed on the altar.

a thanksgiving festival. In Numbers xxviii. 26 it is called the Feast of First Fruits, because two loaves were then offered as the first bread baked from the new harvest.

3. Legal regulations: (*a*) Again on this day all adult males were required to appear in the sanctuary (Ex. xxiii. 16), and they were expected to bring with them free-will offerings according to the abundance of the harvest. In later times this festival was largely attended by foreign Jews, because it occurred at the most favorable season (Acts ii. 9–11).

(*b*) All work, except cooking, had to cease.

(*c*) After the ordinary morning sacrifice, there was another special offering of several beasts with the accompanying meat and drink offerings (Num. xxviii. 26, etc.).

(*d*) Two loaves of wheaten flour were offered as the first fruits of the harvest now just gathered in. These loaves were leavened, hence they might not be burnt on the altar, but were only " waved " and then eaten by the priests. Two lambs were sacrificed as a thank offering.

4. The feast lasted, according to the law, only one day, but modern Jews have added another day.

5. In Holy Scripture this feast appears only as a harvest festival; but it cannot be accidental that it coincides exactly with the season when the law was given on Sinai. We are therefore forced to assume that Pentecost had a double significance: it was the harvest thanksgiving, but it was at the same time a commemoration of the giving of the law, and Jewish and Christian tradition both lay more stress on the latter than on the former significance. *Cf.*, however, H. Grimm, *Das isr. Pfingstfest und der Plejadenkult,* Paderborn, 1907.

51. The Day of Atonement [1]

On the 10th day of *Tishri,* the 7th month, Israel celebrated every year its reconciliation with the Lord. All work was

---

[1] *Jom hakkippurim;* in the Mishna " the Great Day " or simply " the Day," *joma.* The passages of the law relating to it are Lev. xvi. 1–34, xxiii. 26–32; Num. xxix. 7–11. Josephus Flavius refers to it (*Antiq.,* III, x. 3).

forbidden on this day, and the whole nation was required to fast, i. e. to take no food at all, from the evening of the 9th to the evening of the 10th of *Tishri*.

Preparations. This was the day when the high priest performed his chief functions. He was obliged to watch during the whole preceding night, so as not to become unclean according to the law. In the morning he bathed, and put on the simple white dress of a priest.[1] In this attire, without the distinctive ornaments of his rank, he appeared as a penitent. For himself and his house, i. e. for the entire priesthood, he brought a young bullock as a sin offering and a ram as a burnt offering; and from the people he received two he-goats, one to be a sin offering, the other to be turned loose into the desert, and also a ram to be a burnt offering. With these five beasts expiation was to be made for priests and people.

After the ordinary morning sacrifice, the ceremonial peculiar to the day began, and the high priest, standing in the Court of the Temple, before the sanctuary, cast lots for the two goats, to decide which should be dedicated to Yahweh and which to Asasel.[2] The one on whom the lot fell "for the Lord" was destined to be slain as a sin offering; the other who received the lot "for Asasel" was to be forever removed from the abode of Israel.

After casting these lots, the high priest made a confession of sins and then slew the bullock for himself and all the priests. He next took the censer, filled it with coals from the altar, and taking incense with him, passed through the Holy Place into

---

[1] His dress was distinguished from that of ordinary priests only by having a plain white girdle instead of a colored one (Lev. xvi. 4).

[2] The meaning of this name is uncertain; probably it signifies the chief devil (*Gesenii thes.*, 1012; Ewald, *Altertumskunde*, 402; Maurer, *Handwörterbuch;* Knobel on Lev. x.). The name is an intensive form of *'asal* or *'asal*, to separate, connected with the Arabic *'azal.* The full form should be *Asalsel;* in the same way Babel is a shortened form of *Balbel*, and Golgotha of *Golgoltha.* The word denotes the wicked one, who, cut off from others, lives apart. The Arabs still believe that the desert is the devil's abode. *Cf.* also Luke xi. 24, where our Saviour speaks of the unclean spirit as being in the wilderness. In Tobias viii. 3 we read that the devil was banished to a distant desert. It was in the wilderness that our Lord was tempted by the devil.

the Holy of Holies, where he strewed the incense on the coals immediately, so that the cloud of smoke might rise up between him and the Lord, and he might not die. Then he came out again and, taking with him the bullock's blood, he re-entered the Holy of Holies, and with his finger sprinkled the blood once on the front of the *Kapporeth,* and seven times on the ground in front of the ark of the covenant. Then, coming out, he sacrificed in the Court the goat destined for Yahweh, as a sin offering on behalf of the people. He used its blood in the same way, going again into the Holy of Holies. By means of these sprinklings with blood, the Holy and Most Holy Places were purified from the defilements that the priests might have caused in the course of the year. The high priest now returned to the Court, and smeared the horns of the altar of holocausts with the mingled blood of the bullock and the goat, and sprinkled the blood seven times on the ground beside the altar. Thus both the altar and the court were purified.

The high priest next proceeded to set the living goat, destined for Asasel, before him in the Court. He laid both his hands upon its head and pronounced a solemn confession of sin in the name of the people. A man stood ready to drive away the goat, thus laden with sins, into the desert, that it might die or be lost there. All the sins of Israel were believed to vanish with it.[1] The high priest returned to the sanctuary, took off the garments he had worn hitherto, bathed somewhere in the neighborhood, and put on all the attire belonging to his office. Then he went back to the Court, and offered the two rams, that still remained, as holocausts, one for himself and the priesthood, the other for the people. The flesh of the two sin offerings (the bullock and one goat) was carried, after the fat had been burnt on the altar, outside the camp or town, and was there destroyed by fire. Those who performed this duty, as well as the man who had taken the living goat into the wilderness, were required to wash their garments and to bathe before returning.

Other special sacrifices, enumerated in Numbers xxix. 7–11,

---

[1] The man received instructions to throw the goat down somewhere if possible, that it might be sure to perish.

were offered before the usual evening sacrifice.[1] This ended the day's ceremonies.

If we are asked how many times the high priest entered the Holy of Holies on this day, we cannot reply, with Philo, that he did so twice, but we must agree with the Talmud that he entered it four times. First he carried in the incense, then the blood of the bullock, then that of the goat, and lastly he had to fetch out the censer, which, according to the Talmud, he did after the evening sacrifice. In coming out of the Holy of Holies, the high priest was required never to turn his back to the Kapporeth.

It is not difficult, after what has been said, to recognize the significa-tion of this day. It was intended that on the Day of Atonement all transgressions of priests and people should be expiated. The chief feature in the ceremonial was the sending forth of the goat into the wilderness, carrying with him all the sins of the Israelites committed during the year. The wilderness was supposed to be the abode of devils, and by the fact that the sins were sent back thither, they were returned to the devils, from whom they had originally come.[2]

52. Feast of Tabernacles

(Lev. xxiii. 34, etc.; Ex. xxiii. 16; Deut. xvi. 13)

The Day of Atonement was penitential in character, but the Feast of Tabernacles (*chag hassukkoth*), celebrated five days later, was a joyful festival. It marked the completion of the gathering in of all the fruits, and lasted from the 15th to the 21st of *Tishri,* occurring thus exactly six months after the Pasch. Sabbath rest was observed on the first and eighth days, i. e. the 15th and 22d of *Tishri*, the latter being added to close the festival, but not being reckoned as actually part of it; the other days were not ordered to be kept as Sabbaths. All adult males again appeared in the sanctuary, and on each day solemn sacri-fices were offered. On the first day booths of green boughs of

---

[1] One he-goat as a sin offering, one bullock, one ram and seven lambs as holocausts, with the customary meat and drink offerings.

[2] The ceremony called *Taschlich*, observed by the Jews in various countries, still contains a reminiscence of the Day of Atonement. Wher-ever the Jews live near running water (as, for instance, in Vienna), they are in the habit of praying beside it for forgiveness of sins, and after the prayer they throw a handkerchief into the water, or they put their hands into their pockets, as if to take out something which they then pretend to throw into the water. The sins of the preceding year are supposed to be carried away by the stream.

trees were erected in the streets and open spaces, and also on the roofs and in the courtyards of the houses; and these were occupied by the people throughout the festival, though probably only occasionally. This custom commemorated the dwelling of the ancient Israelites in tents, after their departure from Egypt.

According to the Mishna (succah III, 1, etc.) those participating in the festival carried in their hands branches of citrons and palms. Moreover a solemn libation of water was made each day. At the time of the morning sacrifice a priest fetched water from the spring of Siloe in a golden jug, and poured it and wine together into two bowls or pipes near the altar. Music and singing accompanied this ceremony. In the evening the court of the women was illuminated in honor of the feast. It seems that our Saviour referred to these customs when He said (John vii. and viii.) : " If any man thirst, let him come to me," and " I am the light of the world." It is probable that the libation of water had reference to the water from the rock, and the illumination to the pillar of fire in the wilderness.

53. Festivals instituted after the Captivity

After the return of the Jews from Captivity, several festivals were added to those prescribed by the Mosaic law, and some of those then introduced are still observed. We may mention:

1. *The Feast of Purim.* The name comes from the Persian word *pur,*[1] plural *purim* = lots. The Persian governor, Aman, had determined on the death of all the Jews in the Persian Empire, and the 13th of *Adar* had been chosen by lot as the day for this massacre.[2] The murderous plan was frustrated through Queen Esther and her kinsman, Mardochæus. In remembrance of this event, the Jews, first in Persia, but afterwards also in Palestine and elsewhere, celebrated a festival on the 14th and 15th of *Adar,* keeping the 13th as a fast. The celebration consisted in reading the Book of Esther aloud in the synagogues; joyful feasts were held in the houses (*cf.* Book of Esther).

[1] Esther iii. 7. פּוּר Heb. גּוֹרָל = lot.
[2] If it should appear incredible that so many thousands could be murdered at the command of the king, we may remember that between the years 1896 and 1900 in Turkey about three hundred thousand harmless Armenians were butchered by the rabble under the eyes of the Turkish rulers. The ambassadors of the European powers vainly protested against this " Asiatic barbarity."

2. *The Feast of the Dedication of the Temple* (τὰ ἐγκαίνια, Encænia, John x.) was kept every year in commemoration of the purification of the Temple from the idolatrous worship of the Syrians, and its re-dedication by Judas Machabæus in 164 B. C. On the 25th of *Kislev* and on the following seven days the houses in Jerusalem and other places were illuminated; hence Josephus calls the feast φῶτα. There seems to have been no special ceremony in the Temple, but perhaps more sacrifices than usual were offered.

3. *The Feast of Rejoicing of the Law,* on the 23d of *Tishri*. On the last day of the Feast of Tabernacles every year the reading of the Pentateuch was concluded, and on the following day again begun.

4. *The Feast of Wood Carrying* (ξυλοφορία or ἑορτὴ ξυλοφορίων) was, according to Josephus (*Bell. Jud.*, II, 17, 6), celebrated on the 14th of *Ab*, but the Talmud does not mention it. It appears that all who wished to do so carried wood to the Temple on this day, for the maintenance of the fire on the altar of holocausts.

According to Nehemias x. 34, certain families were appointed by lot, at least in the period immediately after the Captivity, to supply wood, and the days on which they performed this duty were, for the persons concerned, days of rejoicing and honor.

Modern Jews observe the following festivals:

(1) The Pasch, 15th to 22d of Nisan.

(2) Lag Beomer, 18th of Ijjar, to commemorate the cessation of a pestilence.

(3) Pentecost, or Feast of Weeks, 6th and 7th of Sivan.

(4) New Year, 1st and 2d of Tishri.

(5) Day of Atonement, 10th of Tishri.

(6) Feast of Tabernacles, 15th to 22d of Tishri.

(7) Rejoicing of the Law, 23d of Tishri.

(8) Dedication of the Temple, 25th of Kislev.

(9) Feast of Purim, 14th and 15th of Adar. And all the Sabbaths of the year.

THIRD PART

HOLY SCRIPTURE

DECREES OF THE HOLY SEE RELATING TO HOLY SCRIPTURE

ENCYCLICAL LETTER PROVIDENTISSIMUS DEUS
November 18, 1893

THE TEACHING OF THE CHURCH

THE God of all providence, who in the adorable designs of His love at first elevated the human race to the participation of the divine nature, and afterwards delivered it from universal guilt and ruin, restoring it to its primitive dignity, has, in consequence, bestowed upon man a splendid gift and safeguard — making known to him, by supernatural means, the hidden mysteries of His divinity, His wisdom and His mercy. For although in divine revelation there are contained some things which are not beyond the reach of unassisted reason, and which are made the objects of such revelation in order " that all may come to know them with facility, certainty, and safety from error, yet not on this account can supernatural revelation be said to be absolutely necessary; it is only necessary because God has ordained man to a supernatural end." [1] This supernatural revelation, according to the belief of the universal Church, is contained both in unwritten tradition and in written books, which are, therefore, called sacred and canonical because, " being written under the inspiration of the Holy Ghost, they have God for their author, and as such have been delivered to the Church." [2] This belief has been perpetually held and professed by the Church in regard to the Books of both Testaments; and there are well-known documents of the gravest kind, coming down to us from the earliest times, which proclaim that God, who spoke first by the prophets, then by His own mouth, and lastly by the apostles, composed also the canonical Scriptures, [3] and that these are His own oracles and words [4] — a Letter written by our Heavenly Father and transmitted by the sacred writers to the human race in its pilgrimage so far from its heavenly country. [5] If, then, such and so great is the excellence and dignity of the Scriptures, that God Himself has composed them, and that they treat of God's marvelous mysteries, counsels

---

[1] Conc. Vat. sess. iii. cap. ii. de revel.

[2] Ibid.

[3] S. Aug. de civ. Dei. xi. 3.

[4] S. Clem. Rom. 1 ad Cor. 45; S. Polycarp, ad Phil. 7; S. Iren. c. hær. ii. 28, 2.

[5] S. Chrys. in Gen. hom. 2, 2; S. Aug. in Ps. xxx., serm. 2, 1; S. Greg. M. ad Theo. ep. iv. 31.

and works, it follows that the branch of sacred theology which is concerned with the defense and elucidation of these divine books must be excellent and useful in the highest degree.

The Intention of the Holy Father

Now We, who by the help of God, and not without fruit, have by frequent Letters and exhortation endeavored to promote other branches of study which seem capable of advancing the glory of God and contributing to the salvation of souls, have for a long time cherished the desire to give an impulse to the noble science of Holy Scripture, and to impart to Scripture study a direction suitable to the needs of the present day. The solicitude of the apostolic office naturally urges, and even compels us, not only to desire that this grand source of Catholic revelation should be made safely and abundantly accessible to the flock of Jesus Christ, but also not to suffer any attempt to defile or corrupt it, either on the part of those who impiously or openly assail the Scriptures, or of those who are led astray into fallacious and imprudent novelties. We are not ignorant, indeed, Venerable Brethren, that there are not a few Catholics, men of talent and learning, who do devote themselves with ardor to the defense of the sacred writings and to making them known and better understood. But whilst giving to these the commendation they deserve, We cannot but earnestly exhort others also, from whose skill and piety and learning We have a right to expect good results, to give themselves to the same most praiseworthy work. It is Our wish and fervent desire to see an increase in the number of the approved and persevering laborers in the cause of Holy Scripture; and more especially that those whom divine grace has called to Holy Orders should, day by day, as their state demands, display greater diligence and industry in reading, meditating, and explaining it.

Benefit of Bible Study

A. *In General*

Among the reasons for which the Holy Scripture is so worthy of commendation — in addition to its own excellence and to the homage which we owe to God's Word — the chief of all is, the innumerable benefits of which it is the source, according to the infallible testimony of the Holy Ghost Himself, who says: *All Scripture inspired of God is profitable to teach, to reprove, to correct, to instruct in justice: that the man of God may be perfect, furnished to every good work.*[1] That such was the purpose of God in giving the Scripture to men is shown by the example of Christ our Lord and of His apostles. For He Himself who "obtained authority by miracles, merited belief by authority, and by belief drew to himself the multitude "[2] was accustomed, in the exercise of His divine mission, to appeal to the Scriptures. He uses them at times to prove that He is sent by God, and is God Himself. From them He cites instructions for His disciples and confirmation of His doctrine. He vindi-

---

[1] II Tim. iii. 16, 17.

[2] S. Aug. de util. cred. xiv. 32.

cates them from the calumnies of objectors; He quotes them against
Sadducees and Pharisees and retorts from them upon Satan himself when
he dares to tempt Him. At the close of His life His utterances are from
the Holy Scripture, and it is the Scripture that He expounds to His disciples after His resurrection, until He ascends to the glory of His Father.
Faithful to His precepts, the apostles, although He Himself granted
signs and wonders to be done by their hands,[1] nevertheless used with the
greatest effect the sacred writings, in order to persuade the nations everywhere of the wisdom of Christianity, to conquer the obstinacy of the
Jews, and to suppress the outbreak of heresy. This is plainly seen in
their discourses, especially in those of St. Peter; these were often little
less than a series of citations from the Old Testament making in the
strongest manner for the new dispensation. We find the same things in
the Gospels of St. Matthew and St. John and in the Catholic Epistles;
and, most remarkable of all, in the words of him who " boasts that he
learned the law at the feet of Gamaliel, in order that, being armed with
spiritual weapons, he might afterwards say with confidence, ' the arms of
our warfare are not carnal but mighty unto God.' " [2] Let all, therefore,
especially the novices of the ecclesiastical army, understand how deeply
the sacred books should be esteemed, and with what eagerness and reverence they should approach this great arsenal of heavenly arms. For
those whose duty it is to handle Catholic doctrine before the learned or
the unlearned will nowhere find more ample matter or more abundant
exhortation, whether on the subject of God, the supreme Good and the
all-perfect Being, or the works which display His glory and His love.
Nowhere is there anything more full or more express on the subject of
the Saviour of the world than is to be found in the whole range of the
Bible. As St. Jerome says, *to be ignorant of the Scripture is not to
know Christ*.[3] In its pages His Image stands out, living and breathing;
diffusing everywhere around consolation in trouble, encouragement to
virtue, and attraction to the love of God. And as to the Church, her
institutions, her nature, her office and her gifts, we find in Holy Scripture so many references and so many ready and convincing arguments
that, as St. Jerome again most truly says, " A man who is well grounded
in the testimonies of the Scripture is the bulwark of the Church." [4] And
if we come to morality and discipline, an apostolic man finds in the
sacred writings abundant and excellent assistance; most holy precepts,
gentle and strong exhortation, splendid examples of every virtue, and
finally the promise of eternal reward and the threat of eternal punishment, uttered in terms of solemn import, in God's name and in God's
own words.

B. *For the Pulpit Orator*

And it is this peculiar and singular power of Holy Scripture, arising
from the inspiration of the Holy Ghost, which gives authority to the

---

[1] Acts xiv. 3.

[2] St. Hier. de stud. Script. ad Paulin. ep. liii. 3.

[3] in Isaiam, Prol.

[4] in Isaiam liv. 12.

sacred orator, fills him with apostolic liberty of speech, and communicates force and power to his eloquence. For those who infuse into their efforts the spirit and strength of the Word of God speak *not in word only, but in power also, and in the Holy Ghost, and in much fullness.*[1] Hence, those preachers are foolish and improvident who, in speaking of religion and proclaiming the things of God, use no words but those of human science and human prudence, trusting to their own reasonings rather than to those of God. Their discourses may be brilliant and fine, but they must be feeble and they must be cold, for they are without the fire of the utterance of God[2] and they must fall far short of that mighty power which the speech of God possesses: *for the Word of God is living and effectual, and more piercing than any two-edged sword; and reaching unto the division of the soul and the spirit.*[3] But, indeed, those who have a right to speak are agreed that there is in the Holy Scripture an eloquence that is wonderfully varied and rich and worthy of great themes. This St. Augustine thoroughly understood and has abundantly set forth.[4] This, also, is confirmed by the best preachers of all ages, who have gratefully acknowledged that they owed their repute chiefly to the assiduous use of the Bible, and to devout meditation on its pages.

The Holy Fathers well knew all this by practical experience, and they never cease to extol the sacred Scripture and its fruits. In innumerable passages of their writings we find them applying to it such phrases as *an inexhaustible treasury of heavenly doctrine,*[5] or *an overflowing fountain of salvation,*[6] or putting it before us as fertile pastures and beautiful gardens in which the flock of the Lord is marvelously refreshed and delighted.[7] Let us listen to the words of St. Jerome, in his Epistle to Nepotian: "Often read the divine Scriptures; yea, let holy reading be always in thy hand; study that which thou thyself must preach. . . . Let the speech of the priest be ever seasoned with Scriptural reading."[8] St. Gregory the Great, than whom no one has more admirably described the pastoral office, writes in the same sense. "Those," he says, "who are zealous in the work of preaching must never cease the study of the written Word of God."[9] St. Augustine, however, warns us that "vainly does the preacher utter the Word of God exteriorly unless he listens to it interiorly";[10] and St. Gregory instructs sacred orators "first to find in Holy Scripture the knowledge of themselves, and then carry it to others, lest in reproving others they forget themselves."[11] Admonitions such as these had, indeed, been uttered long before by the apostolic voice which had learned its lesson from Christ Himself, who "began to do

---

[1] I Thess. i. 5.

[2] Jerem. xxiii. 29.

[3] Hebr. iv. 12.

[4] De doctr. chr. iv. 6, 7.

[5] S. Chrys. in Gen. Hom. xxi. 2; Hom. lx. 3; S. Aug. de Disc. Christ. ii.

[6] S. Athan. ep. fest. xxxix.

[7] S. Aug. serm. xxvi. 24; S. Ambr. in Ps. cxviii. serm. xix. 2.

[8] S. Hier. de vita cleric. ad Nepot.

[9] S. Greg. M. Regul. past. ii. 11 (al. 22); Moral. xvii. 26 (al. 14).

[10] S. Aug. serm. clxxix. 1.

[11] S. Greg. M. Regul. past. iii. 24 (al. 14).

and teach." It was not to Timothy alone, but to the whole order of the clergy, that the command was addressed: *Take heed to thyself and to doctrine; be earnest in them. For in doing this thou shalt both save thyself and them that hear thee.*[1] For the saving and for the perfection of ourselves and of others there is at hand the very best of help in the Holy Scriptures, as the Book of Psalms, among others, so constantly insists; but those only will find it who bring to this divine reading not only docility and attention but also piety and an innocent life. For the sacred Scripture is not like other books. Dictated by the Holy Ghost, it contains things of the deepest importance, which in many instances are most difficult and obscure. To understand and explain such things there is always required the "coming"[2] of the same Holy Spirit; that is to say, His light and His grace; and these, as the royal psalmist so frequently insists, are to be sought by humble prayer and guarded by holiness of life.

THE SOLICITUDE OF THE CHURCH

It is in this that the watchful eye of the Church shines forth conspicuously. By admirable laws and regulations, she has shown herself solicitous that "the celestial treasure of the sacred books, so bountifully bestowed upon man by the Holy Spirit, should not lie neglected."[3] She has prescribed that a considerable portion of them shall be read and piously reflected upon by all her ministers in the daily office of the sacred psalmody. She has ordered that in cathedral churches, in monasteries, and in other convents in which study can conveniently be pursued, they shall be expounded and interpreted by capable men; and she has strictly commanded that her children shall be fed with the saving words of the Gospel at least on Sundays and solemn feasts.[4] Moreover, it is owing to the wisdom and exertions of the Church that there has always been continued, from century to century, that cultivation of Holy Scripture which has been so remarkable and has borne such ample fruit.

A. *In the Early Times*

And here, in order to strengthen Our teaching and Our exhortations, it is well to recall how, from the beginning of Christianity, all who have been renowned for holiness of life and sacred learning have given their deep and constant attention to Holy Scripture. If we consider the immediate disciples of the apostles, St. Clement of Rome, St. Ignatius of Antioch, St. Polycarp, — or the apologists, such as St. Justin and St. Irenæus, — We find that in their letters and books, whether in defense of the Catholic faith or in its commendation, they drew faith, strength, and unction from the Word of God. When there arose, in various sees, catechetical and theological schools, of which the most celebrated were those of Alexandria and of Antioch, there was little taught in those schools but what was contained in the reading, the interpretation, and the defense of the divine written word. From them came forth numbers of Fathers and writers whose laborious studies and admirable writings have justly

[1] I Tim. iv. 16.
[2] S. Hier. in Mic. i. 10.
[3] Conc. Trid. sess. v. decret. de reform. 1.
[4] Ibid., 1, 2.

merited for the three following centuries the appellation of the golden age of biblical exegesis. In the Eastern Church the greatest name of all is Origen — a man remarkable alike for penetration of genius and persevering labor; from whose numerous works and his great *Hexapla* almost all have drawn who came after him. Others who have widened the field of this science mày also be named as especially eminent; thus, Alexandria could boast of St. Clement and St. Cyril; Palestine, of Eusebius and the other St. Cyril; Cappadocia, of St. Basil the Great and the two Gregories, of Nazianzus and Nyssa; Antioch, of St. John Chrysostom, in whom the science of Scripture was rivaled by the splendor of his eloquence. In the Western Church there are as many names as great: Tertullian, St. Cyprian, St. Hilary, St. Ambrose, St. Leo the Great, St. Gregory the Great; most famous of all, St. Augustine and St. Jerome, of whom the former was so marvelously acute in penetrating the sense of God's Word and so fertile in the use that he made of it for the promotion of the Catholic truth, and the latter has received from the Church, by reason of his pre-eminent knowledge of Scripture and his labors in promoting its use, the name of the "great Doctor."[1]

B. *In the Middle Ages*

From this period down to the eleventh century, although biblical studies did not flourish with the same vigor and the same fruitfulness as before, yet they did flourish, and principally by the instrumentality of the clergy. It was their care and solicitude that selected the best and most useful things that the ancients had left, arranged them in order, and published them with additions of their own — as did St. Isidore of Seville, Venerable Bede, and Alcuin, among the most prominent; it was they who illustrated the sacred pages with "glosses" or short commentaries, as we see in Walafrid Strabo and St. Anselm of Laon, or expended fresh labor in securing their integrity, as did St. Peter Damian and Blessed Lanfranc. In the twelfth century many took up, with great success, the allegorical exposition of Scripture. In this kind, St. Bernard is pre-eminent; and his writings, it may be said, are Scripture all through. With the age of the scholastics came fresh and welcome progress in the study of the Bible. That the scholastics were solicitous about the genuineness of the Latin version is evident from the *Correctoria Biblica*, or list of emendations, which they have left. But they expended their labors and industry chiefly on interpretation and explanation. To them we owe the accurate and clear distinction, such as had not been given before, of the various senses of the sacred words; the assignment of the value of each "sense" in theology; the division of books into parts, and the summaries of the various parts; the investigation of the objects of the writers; the demonstration of the connection of sentence with sentence, and clause with clause; all of which is calculated to throw much light on the more obscure passages of the sacred volume. The valuable work of the scholastics in Holy Scripture is seen in their theological treatises and in their Scripture commen-

---

[1] See the Collect on his feast, September 30.

taries; and in this respect the greatest name among them all is St. Thomas Aquinas.

When Our predecessor, Clement V, established chairs of Oriental literature in the Roman College and in the principal universities of Europe, Catholics began to make more accurate investigation on the original text of the Bible as well as on the Latin version. The revival amongst us of Greek learning, and, much more, the happy invention of the art of printing, gave a strong impetus to biblical studies. In a brief space of time, innumerable editions, especially of the Vulgate, poured from the press and were diffused throughout the Catholic world; so honored and loved was Holy Scripture during that very period against which the enemies of the Church direct their calumnies.

C. *In Modern Times*

Nor must we forget how many learned men there were, chiefly among the religious orders, who did excellent work for the Bible between the Council of Vienna and that of Trent; men who, by the employment of modern means and appliances, and by the tribute of their own genius and learning, not only added to the rich store of ancient times but prepared the way for the succeeding century, the century which followed the Council of Trent, when it almost seemed that the great age of the Fathers had returned. For it is well known, and We recall it with pleasure, that Our predecessors, from Pius IV to Clement VIII, caused to be prepared the celebrated editions of the Vulgate and the Septuagint, which, having been published by the command and authority of Sixtus V, and of the same Clement, are now in common use. At this time, moreover, were carefully brought out various other ancient versions of the Bible, and the Polyglots of Antwerp and of Paris, most important for the investigation of the true meaning of the text; nor is there any one book of either Testament which did not find more than one expositor, nor any grave question which did not profitably exercise the ability of many inquirers, among whom there are not a few — more especially of those who made most use of the Fathers — who have acquired great reputation. From that time downwards the labor and solicitude of Catholics have never been wanting; for, as time went on, eminent scholars have carried on biblical studies with success, and have defended Holy Scripture against *rationalism* with the same weapons of philology and kindred sciences with which it had been attacked. The calm and fair consideration of what has been said will clearly show that the Church has never failed in taking due measures to bring the Scriptures within reach of her children, and that she has ever held fast and exercised profitably that guardianship conferred upon her by Almighty God for the protection and glory of His Holy Word; so that she has never required, nor does she now require, any stimulation from without.

RULES FOR THE PRESENT TIME

We must now, Venerable Brethren, as Our purpose demands, impart to you such counsels as seem best suited for carrying on successfully the study of biblical science.

But first it must be clearly understood whom we have to oppose and contend against, and what are their tactics and their arms. In earlier times the contest was chiefly with those who, relying on private judgment and repudiating the divine traditions and teaching office of the Church, held the Scriptures to be the one source of revelation and the final appeal in matters of faith. Now we have to meet the rationalists, true children and inheritors of the older heretics, who, trusting in their turn to their own way of thinking, have rejected even the scraps and remnants of Christian belief which had been handed down to them. They deny that there is any such thing as revelation or inspiration, or Holy Scripture at all; they see, instead, only the forgeries and falsehoods of men; they set down the Scripture narratives as stupid fables and lying stories: the prophecies and oracles of God are to them either predictions made up after the event or forecasts formed by the light of nature; the miracles and wonders of God's power are not what they are said to be, but the startling effects of natural law, or else mere tricks and myths; and the apostolic Gospels and writings are not the work of the apostles at all. These detestable errors, whereby they think they destroy the truth of the divine books, are obtruded on the world as the peremptory pronouncements of a newly invented *free science;* a science, however, which is so far from final that they are perpetually modifying and supplementing it. And there are some of them who, notwithstanding their impious opinions and utterances about God, and Christ, the Gospels and the rest of Holy Scripture, would fain be considered both theologians and Christians and men of the Gospel, and who attempt to disguise by such honorable names their rashness and their pride. To them we must add not a few professors of other sciences who approve their views and give them assistance, and are urged to attack the Bible by a similar intolerance of revelation. And it is deplorable to see these attacks growing every day more numerous and more severe. It is sometimes men of learning and judgment who are assailed; but these have little difficulty in defending themselves from evil consequences. The efforts and arts of the enemy are chiefly directed against the more ignorant masses of the people. They diffuse their deadly poison by means of books, pamphlets, and newspapers; they spread it by addresses and by conversation; they are found everywhere; and they are in possession of numerous schools, taken by violence from the Church, in which, by ridicule and scurrilous jesting, they pervert the credulous and unformed minds of the young to the contempt of Holy Scripture. Should not these things, Venerable Brethren, stir up and set on fire the heart of every pastor, so that to this *knowledge, falsely so-called,*[1] may be opposed the ancient and true science which the Church, through the apostles, has received from Christ, and that Holy Scripture may find the champions that are needed in so momentous a battle?

Let our first care, then, be to see that in seminaries and academical institutions the study of Holy Scripture is placed on such a footing as its own importance and the circumstances of the time demand. With this view, the first thing which requires attention is the wise choice of professors. Teachers of sacred Scripture are not to be appointed at hap-

---

[1] I Tim. iv. 20.

hazard out of the crowd; but they must be men whose character and fitness are proved by their love of, and their long familiarity with, the Bible, and by suitable learning and study.

It is a matter of equal importance to provide in time for a continuous succession of such teachers; and it will be well, wherever this can be done, to select young men of good promise who have successfully accomplished their theological course, and to set them apart exclusively for Holy Scripture, affording them facilities for full and complete studies. Professors thus chosen and thus prepared may enter with confidence on the task that is appointed for them; and that they may carry out their work well and profitably, let them take heed to the instructions We now proceed to give.

Introduction

At the commencement of a course of Holy Scripture, let the professor strive earnestly to form the judgment of the young beginners so as to train them equally to defend the sacred writings and to penetrate their meaning. This is the object of the treatise which is called "Introduction." Here the student is taught how to prove the integrity and authority of the Bible, how to investigate and ascertain its true sense, and how to meet and refute objections. It is needless to insist upon the importance of making these preliminary studies in an orderly and thorough fashion, with the accompaniment and assistance of theology; for the whole subsequent course must rest on the foundation thus laid and make use of the light thus acquired.

Interpretation

Next, the teacher will turn his attention to that more fruitful division of Scripture science which has to do with interpretation, wherein is imparted the method of using the Word of God for the advantage of religion and piety. We recognize, without hesitation, that neither the extent of the matter nor the time at disposal allows each single book of the Bible to be separately gone through. But the teaching should result in a definite and ascertained method of interpretation — and, therefore, the professor should equally avoid the mistake of giving a mere taste of every book, and of dwelling at too great a length on a part of one book. If most schools cannot do what is done in large institutions — take the students through the whole of one or two books continuously and with a certain development — yet at least those parts which are selected should be treated with suitable fullness, in such a way that the students may learn from the sample that is put before them to love and use the remainder of the sacred book during the whole of their lives. The professor, following the tradition of antiquity, will make use of the Vulgate as his text; for the Council of Trent decreed that " in public lectures, disputations, preaching, and exposition,"[1] the Vulgate is the " authentic " version; and this is the existing custom of the Church. At the same time, the other versions, which Christian antiquity has approved, should not be neglected, more especially the more ancient MSS. For,

---

[1] Sess. iv. decr. de edit. et usu sacr. libror.

although the meaning of the Hebrew and Greek is substantially rendered by the Vulgate, nevertheless wherever there may be ambiguity or want of clearness, the "examination of older tongues,"[1] to quote St. Augustine, will be useful and advantageous. But in this matter we need hardly say that the greatest prudence is required, for the "office of a commentator," as St. Jerome says, "is to set forth not what he himself would prefer but what his author says."[2] The question of "reading" having been, when necessary, carefully discussed, the next thing is to investigate and expound the meaning. And the first counsel to be given is this: that the more our adversaries contend to the contrary, so much the more solicitously should we adhere to the received and approved canons of interpretation. Hence, whilst weighing the meaning of words, the connection of ideas, the parallelism of passages, and the like, we should by all means make use of such illustrations as can be drawn from opposite erudition of an external sort; but this should be done with caution, so as not to bestow on questions of this kind more labor and time than are spent on the sacred books themselves, and not to overload the minds of the students with a mass of information that will be rather a hindrance than a help.

The professor may now safely pass on to the use of Scripture in matters of theology. On this head it must be observed that, in addition to the usual reasons which make ancient writings more or less difficult to understand, there are some which are peculiar to the Bible. For the language of the Bible is employed to express, under the inspiration of the Holy Ghost, many things which are beyond the power and scope of the reason of man — that is to say, divine mysteries and all that is related to them. There is sometimes in such passages a fullness and a hidden depth of meaning which the letter hardly expresses and which the laws of interpretation hardly warrant. Moreover, the literal sense itself frequently admits other senses, adapted to illustrate dogma or to confirm morality.

SENSUS, QUEM TENET ECCLESIA

Wherefore, it must be recognized that the sacred writings are wrapped in a certain religious obscurity, and that no one can enter into their interior without a guide;[3] God so disposing, as the holy Fathers commonly teach, in order that men may investigate them with greater ardor and earnestness, and that what is attained with difficulty may sink more deeply into the mind and heart, and, most of all, that they may understand that God has delivered the Holy Scripture to the Church, and that in reading and making use of His Word they must follow the Church as their guide and their teacher. St. Irenæus long since laid down that where the *chrismata* of God were, there the truth was to be learned, and the Holy Scripture was safely interpreted by those who had the apostolic succession.[4] His teaching and that of other holy

---

[1] De doctr. chr. iii. 4.
[2] Ad Pammachium.
[3] S. Hier. ad Paulin. de studio Script. ep. liii. 4.
[4] C. hær. iv. 26, 5.

Fathers is taken up by the Council of the Vatican, which in renewing the decree of Trent declared its "mind" to be this — that "in things of faith and morals, belonging to the building up of Christian doctrine, that it is to be considered the true sense of Holy Scripture, which has been held and is held by our Holy Mother the Church, whose place it is to judge of the true sense and interpretation of the Scriptures; and, therefore, that it is permitted to no one to interpret Holy Scripture against such sense or also against the unanimous agreement of the Fathers." [1]

No Restraint

By this most wise decree the Church by no means prevents or restrains the pursuit of biblical science, but rather protects it from error, and largely assists its real progress. A wide field is still left open to the private student, in which his hermeneutical skill may display itself with signal effect and to the advantage of the Church. On the one hand, in those passages of Holy Scripture which have not as yet received a certain and definite interpetation, such labors may, in the benignant providence of God, prepare for and bring to maturity the judgment of the Church; on the other, in passages already defined, the private student may do work equally valuable, either by setting them forth more clearly to the flock or more skillfully to the scholars, or by defending them more powerfully from hostile attack. Wherefore the first and dearest object of the Catholic commentator should be to interpret those passages which have received an authentic interpretation either from the sacred writers themselves, under the inspiration of the Holy Ghost (as in many places of the New Testament), or from the Church, under the assistance of the same Holy Spirit, whether by her solemn judgment or by her ordinary and universal *magisterium* [2] — to interpret these passages in that identical sense, and to prove by all the resources of science that sound hermeneutical laws admit of no other interpretation. In the other passages the analogy of faith should be followed, and Catholic doctrine, as authoritatively proposed by the Church, should be held as the supreme law; for, seeing that the same God is the author both of the sacred books and of the doctrine committed to the Church, it is clearly impossible that any teaching can, by legitimate means, be extracted from the former which shall, in any respect, be at variance with the latter. Hence it follows that all interpretation is foolish or false which either makes the sacred writers disagree one with another, or is opposed to the doctrine of the Church.

Commentaries of the Fathers

The professor of Holy Scripture, therefore, amongst other recommendations, must be well acquainted with the whole circle of theology and deeply read in the commentaries of the holy Fathers and Doctors, and in other interpreters of mark.[3] This is inculcated by St. Jerome, and still

---

[1] Sess. iii. cap. ii. de revel.; *cf.* Conc. Trid. sess. iv. decret de edit. et usu sacr. libror.

[2] Conc. Vat. sess. iii. cap. ii. de fide.

[3] Ibid.

more frequently by St. Augustine, who thus justly complains: " If there is no branch of teaching, however humble and easy to learn, which does not require a master, what can be a greater sign of rashness and pride than to refuse to study the books of the divine mysteries by the help of those who have interpreted them? " [1] The other Fathers have said the same, and have confirmed it by their example, for they " endeavored to acquire the understanding of the Holy Scriptures not by their own lights and ideas but from the writing and authority of the ancients, who, in their turn, as we know, received the rule of interpretation in direct line from the apostles." [2] The holy Fathers "to whom, after the apostles, the Church owes its growth — who have planted, watered, built, governed, and cherished it "; [3] the holy Fathers, We say, are of supreme authority, whenever they all interpret in one and the same manner any text of the Bible, as pertaining to the doctrine of faith and morals; for their unanimity clearly evinces that such interpretation has come down from the apostles as a matter of Catholic faith. The opinion of the Fathers is also of very great weight when they treat of these matters in their capacity of Doctors unofficially; not only because they excel in their knowledge of revealed doctrine and in their acquaintance with many things which are useful in understanding the apostolic books, but because they are men of eminent sanctity and of ardent zeal for the truth, on whom God has bestowed a more ample measure of His light. Wherefore the expositor should make it his duty to follow their footsteps with all reverence, and to use their labors with intelligent appreciation.

But he must not on that account consider that it is forbidden, when just cause exists, to push inquiry and exposition beyond what the Fathers have done; provided he carefully observes the rule so wisely laid down by St. Augustne — not to depart from the literal and obvious sense, except only where reason makes it untenable or necessity requires; [4] a rule to which it is the more necessary to adhere strictly in these times, when the thirst for novelty and the unrestrained freedom of thought make the danger of error most real and proximate. Neither should those passages be neglected which the Fathers have understood in an allegorical or figurative sense, more especially when such interpretation is justified by the literal, and when it rests on the authority of many. For this method of interpretation has been received by the Church from the apostles, and has been approved by her own practice, as the holy Liturgy attests; although it is true that the holy Fathers did not thereby pretend directly to demonstrate dogmas of faith, but used it as a means of promoting virtue and piety, such as, by their own experience, they knew to be most valuable.

Other Interpreters

The authority of other Church interpreters is not so great; but the study of Scripture has always continued to advance in the Church, and, therefore, these commentaries also have their own honorable place, and

---

[1] Ad Honorat. de util. cred. xvii. 35.

[2] Rufinus Hist. eccl. li. 9.

[3] S. Aug. c. Julian. ii. 10, 37.

[4] De Gen. ad litt. lviii. c. 7, 13.

are serviceable in many ways for the refutation of assailants and the explanation of difficulties. But it is most unbecoming to pass by, in ignorance or contempt, the excellent work which Catholics have left in abundance, and to have recourse to the work of non-Catholics — and to seek in them, to the detriment of sound doctrine and often to the peril of faith, the explanation of passages on which Catholics long ago have successfully employed their talent and their labor. For although the studies of non-Catholics, used with prudence, may sometimes be of use to the Catholic student, he should, nevertheless, bear well in mind — as the Fathers also teach in numerous passages [1] — that the sense of Holy Scripture can nowhere be found incorrupt outside the Church, and cannot be expected to be found in writers who, being without the true faith, only know the bark of sacred Scripture, and never attain its pith.

THE PLACE OF SCRIPTURE RESEARCH AMONG THEOLOGICAL STUDIES

Most desirable is it, and most essential, that the whole teaching of theology should be pervaded and animated by the use of the divine Word of God. That is what the Fathers and the greatest theologians of all ages have desired and reduced to practice. It is chiefly out of the sacred writings that they endeavored to proclaim and establish the Articles of Faith and the truths therewith connected, and it was in them, together with divine tradition, that they found the refutation of heretical error, and the reasonableness, the true meaning, and the mutual relation of the truths of Catholicism. Nor will any one wonder at this who considers that the sacred books hold such an eminent position among the sources of revelation that without their assiduous study and use theology cannot be placed on a true footing, or treated as its dignity demands. For although it is right and proper that students in academies and schools should be chiefly exercised in acquiring a scientific knowledge of dogma, by means of reasoning from the Articles of Faith to their consequences, according to the rules of approved and sound philosophy — nevertheless the judicious and instructed theologian will by no means pass by that method of doctrinal demonstration which draws its proof from the authority of the Bible; "for theology does not receive her first principles from any other science, but immediately from God by revelation. And, therefore, she does not receive of other sciences as from a superior, but uses them as her inferiors or handmaids." [2] It is this view of doctrinal teaching which is laid down and recommended by the prince of theologians, St. Thomas of Aquin; [3] who moreover shows — such being the essential character of Christian theology — how she can defend her own principles against attack: "If the adversary," he says, "do but grant any portion of the divine revelation, we have an argument against him; thus, against a heretic we can employ Scripture authority, and against those who deny one article we can use another.

---

[1] Cfr. Clem. Alex. Strom. vii. 16; Orig. de princ. iv. 8; in Levit. hom. 48; Tertull. de præscr. 15, seqq.; S. Hilar. Pict. in Matt. 13, 1.

[2] S. Greg. M. Moral. xx. 9 (al. 11).

[3] Summ. Theol. p. i. q. i. a. 5 ad 2.

But if our opponent reject divine revelation entirely, there is no way left to prove the Articles of Faith by reasoning; we can only solve the difficulties which are raised against them." [1] Care must be taken, then, that beginners approach the study of the Bible well prepared and furnished; otherwise, just hopes will be frustrated, or, perchance, what is worse, they will unthinkingly risk the danger of error, falling an easy prey to the sophisms and labored erudition of the rationalists. The best preparation will be a conscientious application to philosophy and theology under the guidance of St. Thomas of Aquin, and a thorough training therein — as We Ourselves have elsewhere pointed out and directed. By this means, both in biblical studies and in that part of theology which is called *positive*, they will pursue the right path and make satisfactory progress.

AUTHORITY OF THE BIBLE

To prove, to expound, to illustrate Catholic doctrine by the legitimate and skillful interpretation of the Bible is much; but there is a second part of the subject of equal importance and equal difficulty — the maintenance in the strongest possible way of its full authority. This cannot be done completely or satisfactorily except by means of the living and proper *magisterium* of the Church. The Church, by reason of her wonderful propagation, her distinguished sanctity, and inexhaustible fecundity in good, her Catholic unity, and her unshaken stability, is herself a great and perpetual motive of credibility, and an unassailable testimony to her own divine mission." [2] But, since the divine and infallible *magisterium* of the Church rests also on Holy Scripture, the first thing to be done is to vindicate the trustworthiness of sacred records, at least as human documents, from which can be clearly proved, as from primitive and authentic testimony, the divinity and the mission of Christ our Lord, the institution of a hierarchical Church and the primacy of Peter and his successors.

DEFENDERS OF THE BIBLE

It is most desirable, therefore, that there should be numerous members of the clergy well prepared to enter on a contest of this nature, and to repulse hostile assaults, chiefly trusting in the armor of God recommended by the Apostle,[3] but also not unaccustomed to modern methods of attack. This is beautifully alluded to by St. John Chrysostom, when describing the duties of priests: " We must use every endeavor that the ' Word of God may dwell in us abundantly '; [4] not merely for one kind of a fight must we be prepared — for the contest is many-sided and the enemy is of every sort; and they do not all use the same weapons nor make their onset in the same way. Wherefore it is needful that the man who has to contend against all should be acquainted with the engines and the arts of all — that he should be at once archer and slinger, commandant and officer, general and private soldier, foot-soldier and horseman, skilled in sea-fight and in siege; for unless he knows every

---

[1] Ibid. a. 8.
[2] Conc. Vat. sess. iii. c. ii. de fide.
[3] Eph. vi. 13, seqq.
[4] Cfr. Coloss. iii. 16.

trick and turn of war, the devil is well able, if only a single door be left open, to get in his fierce bands and carry off the sheep." [1] The sophisms of the enemy and his manifold arts of attack we have already touched upon. Let us now say a word of advice on the means of defense.

MEANS OF DEFENSE

A. *Ancient Languages*

The first means is the study of the Oriental languages and of the art of criticism. These two acquirements are in these days held in high estimation, and, therefore, the clergy, by making themselves fully acquainted with them as time and place may demand, will the better be able to discharge their office with becoming credit; for they must make themselves *all to all*,[2] always *ready to satisfy every one that asketh them a reason for the hope that is in them*.[3] Hence it is most proper that professors of sacred Scripture and theologians should master those tongues in which the sacred books were originally written; and it would be well that Church students also should cultivate them, more especially those who aspire to academic degrees. And endeavors should be made to establish in all academic institutions — as has already been laudably done in many — chairs of the other ancient languages, especially the Semitic, and of subjects connected therewith, for the benefit, principally, of those who are intended to profess sacred literature.

B. *Criticism*

These latter, with a similar object in view, should make themselves well and thoroughly acquainted with the art of true criticism. There has arisen, to the great detriment of religion, an inept method, dignified by the name of the "higher criticism," which pretends to judge the origin, integrity and authority of each book from internal indications alone. It is clear, on the other hand, that in historical questions, such as the origin and handing down of writings, the witness of history is of primary importance, and that historical investigation should be made with the utmost care; and that in this manner internal evidence is seldom of great value, except as confirmation. To look upon it in any other light will be to open the door to many evil consequences. It will make the enemies of religion much more bold and confident in attacking and mangling the sacred books; and this vaunted "higher criticism" will resolve itself into the reflection of the bias and the prejudice of the critics. It will not throw on the Scripture the light which is sought, or prove of any advantage to doctrine; it will only give rise to disagreement and dissension, those sure notes of error which the critics in question so plentifully exhibit in their own persons; and seeing that most of them are tainted with false philosophy and rationalism, it must lead to the elimination from the sacred writings of all prophecy and miracle, and of everything else that is outside the natural order.

---

[1] De Sacerdotio iv. 4.   [2] I Cor. ix. 22.   [3] I Peter iii. 15.

C. *Natural Sciences*

In the second place, we have to contend against those who, making an evil use of physical science, minutely scrutinize the sacred book in order to detect the writers in a mistake, and to take occasion to vilify its contents. Attacks of this kind, bearing as they do on matters of sensible experience, are peculiarly dangerous to the masses, and also to the young who are beginning their literary studies; for the young, if they lose their reverence for the Holy Scripture on one or more points, are easily led to give up believing in it altogether. It need not be pointed out how the nature of science, just as it is so admirably adapted to show forth the glory of the Great Creator, provided it is taught as it should be, may, if it be perversely imparted to the youthful intelligence, prove most fatal in destroying the principles of true philosophy and in the corruption of morality. Hence, to the professor of Sacred Scripture a knowledge of natural science will be of very great assistance in detecting such attacks on the sacred books, and in refuting them. There can never, indeed, be any real discrepancy between the theologian and the physicist, as long as each confines himself within his own lines, and both are careful, as St. Augustine warns us, "not to make rash assertions, or to assert what is not known as known."[1] If dissension should arise between them, here is the rule also laid down by St. Augustine, for the theologian: "Whatever they can really demonstrate to be true of physical nature we must show to be capable of reconciliation with our Scriptures; and whatever they assert in their treatises which is contrary to these Scriptures of ours, that is to Catholic faith, we must either prove it as well as we can to be entirely false, or at all events we must, without the smallest hesitation, believe it to be so."[2] To understand how just is the rule here formulated we must remember, first, that the sacred writers, or, to speak more accurately, the Holy Ghost "who spoke by them, did not intend to teach men these things [that is to say, the essential nature of the things of the visible universe], things in no way profitable unto salvation."[3] Hence they did not seek to penetrate the secrets of nature, but rather described and dealt with things in more or less figurative language, or in terms which were commonly used at the time, and which in many instances are in daily use at this day, even by the most eminent men of science. Ordinary speech primarily and properly describes what comes under the senses; and somewhat in the same way the sacred writers — as the Angelic Doctor also reminds us — "went by what sensibly appeared,"[4] or put down what God, speaking to men, signified, in the way men could understand and were accustomed to.

The unshrinking defense of the Holy Scripture, however, does not require that we should equally uphold all the opinions which each of the Fathers or the more recent interpreters have put forth in explain-

---

[1] In. Gen. op. imperf. ix. 30.
[2] De Gen. ad litt. i. 21, 41.
[3] S. Aug. ib. ii. 9, 20.
[4] Summa Theol. p. i. q. lxxx. a. 1 ad 3.

ing it; for it may be that, in commenting on passages where physical matters occur, they have sometimes expressed the ideas of their own times, and thus made statements which in these days have been abandoned as incorrect. Hence, in their interpretations, we must carefully note what they lay down as belonging to faith, or as intimately connected with faith—what they are unanimous in. For "in those things which do not come under the obligation of faith, the saints were at liberty to hold divergent opinions, just as we ourselves are,"[1] according to the saying of St. Thomas. And in another place he says most admirably: "When philosophers are agreed upon a point, and it is not contrary to our faith, it is safer, in my opinion, neither to lay down such a point as a dogma of faith, even though it is perhaps so presented by the philosophers, nor to reject it as against faith, lest we thus give to the wise of this world an occasion of despising our faith."[2] The Catholic interpreter, although he should show that those facts of natural science which investigators affirm to be now quite certain are not contrary to the Scripture rightly explained, must, nevertheless, always bear in mind that much which has been held and proved as certain has afterwards been called in question and rejected. And if writers on physics travel outside the boundaries of their own branch, and carry their erroneous teaching into the domain of philosophy, let them be handed over to philosophers for refutation.

D. *History*

The principles here laid down will apply to cognate sciences, and especially to history. It is a lamentable fact that there are many who with great labor carry out and publish investigations on the monuments of antiquity, the manners and institutions of nations, and other illustrative subjects, and whose chief purpose in all this is to find mistakes in the sacred writings and so to shake and weaken their authority. Some of these writers display not only extreme hostility but the greatest unfairness; in their eyes a profane book or ancient document is accepted without hesitation, whilst the Scripture, if they only find in it a suspicion of error, is set down with the slightest possible discussion as quite untrustworthy. It is true, no doubt, that copyists have made mistakes in the text of the Bible; this question, when it arises, should be carefully considered on its merits, and the fact not too easily admitted, but only in those passages where the proof is clear. It may also happen that the sense of a passage remains ambiguous, and in this case good hermeneutical methods will greatly assist in clearing up the obscurity.

INSPIRATION

But it is absolutely wrong and forbidden either to narrow inspiration to certain parts only of Holy Scripture or to admit that the sacred writer has erred. For the system of those who, in order to rid themselves of those difficulties, do not hesitate to concede that divine inspiration regards the things of faith and morals, and nothing beyond,

---

[1] In Sent. ii. Dist. q. i. a. 3. [2] Opusc. x.

because (as they wrongly think) in a question of the truth or falsehood of a passage we should consider not so much what God has said as the reason and purpose which He had in mind when saying it — this system cannot be tolerated. For all the books which the Church receives as sacred and canonical are written wholly and entirely, with all their parts, at the dictation of the Holy Ghost; and so far is it from being possible that any error can co-exist with inspiration, that inspiration not only is essentially incompatible with error, but excludes and rejects it as absolutely and necessarily as it is impossible that God Himself, the Supreme Truth, can utter that which is not true. This is the ancient and unchanging faith of the Church, solemnly defined in the Councils of Florence and of Trent, and finally confirmed and more expressly formulated by the Council of the Vatican. These are the words of the last: "The books of the Old and New Testament, whole and entire, with all their parts, as enumerated by the decree of the same Council (Trent) and in the ancient Latin Vulgate, are to be received as sacred and canonical. And the Church holds them as sacred and canonical not because, having been composed by human industry, they were afterwards approved by her authority, nor only because they contain revelation without error, but because, having been written under the inspiration of the Holy Ghost, they have God for their Author."[1] Hence, because the Holy Ghost employed men as His instruments, we cannot, therefore, say that it was these inspired instruments who, perchance, have fallen into error, and not the primary author. For, by supernatural power, He so moved and impelled them to write — He was so present to them — that the things which He ordered, and those only, they, first, rightly understood, then willed faithfully to write down, and finally expressed in apt words and with infallible truth. Otherwise, it could not be said that He was the Author of the entire Scripture. Such has always been the persuasion of the Fathers. "Therefore," says St. Augustine, "since they wrote the things which He showed and uttered to them, it cannot be pretended that He is not the writer; for His members executed what their head dictated."[2] And St. Gregory the Great thus pronounces: "Most superfluous it is to inquire who wrote these things — we loyally believe the Holy Ghost to be the author of the Book. He wrote it who dictated it for writing; He wrote it who inspired its execution."[3]

It follows that those who maintain that an error is possible in any genuine passage of the sacred writings either pervert the Catholic notion of inspiration or make God the author of such error. And so emphatically were all the Fathers and Doctors agreed that the divine writings, as left by the hagiographers, are free from all error, that they labored earnestly, with no less skill than reverence, to reconcile with each other those numerous passages which seem at variance — the very passages which in a great measure have been taken up by the " higher criticism "; for they were unanimous in laying it down that those writings, in their entirety and in all their parts were equally from the *afflatus* of Almighty God, and that God, speaking by the sacred writers, could not set down anything that was not true. The words of St. Augustine to St. Jerome

---

[1] Sess. iii. c. ii. de Rev.
[2] De consensu Evangel. l. 1, c. 35.   [3] Præf. in Job, n. 2.

may sum up what they taught: "On my own part I confess to your charity that it is only to those books of Scripture which are now called canonical that I have learned to pay such honor and reverence as to believe most firmly that none of their writers has fallen into any error. And if in these books I meet anything which seems contrary to truth I shall not hesitate to conclude either that the text is faulty, or that the translator has not expressed the meaning of the passage, or that I myself do not understand." [1]

CATHOLIC SCHOLARS

But to undertake fully and perfectly, and with all the weapons of the best science, the defense of the Holy Bible is far more than can be looked for from the exertions of commentators and theologians alone. It is an enterprise in which we have a right to expect the co-operation of all those Catholics who have acquired reputation in any branch of learning whatever. As in the past, so at the present time, the Church is never without the graceful support of her accomplished children; may their service to the Faith grow and increase! For there is nothing which We believe to be more needful than that truth should find defenders more powerful and more numerous than the enemies it has to face; nor is there anything which is better calculated to impress the masses with respect for truth than to see it boldly proclaimed by learned and distinguished men. Moreover, the bitter tongues of objectors will be silenced, or at least they will not dare to insist so shamelessly that faith is the enemy of science, when they see that scientific men of eminence in their profession show towards faith the most marked honor and respect. Seeing, then, that those can do so much for the advantage of religion on whom the goodness of Almighty God has bestowed, together with the grace of the faith, great natural talent, let such men, in this bitter conflict of which the Holy Scripture is the object, select each of them the branch of study most suitable to his circumstances, and endeavor to excel therein, and thus be prepared to repulse with credit and distinction the assaults on the Word of God. And it is Our pleasing duty to give deserved praise to a work which certain Catholics have taken up — that is to say, the formation of societies and the contribution of considerable sums of money for the purpose of supplying studios and learned men with every kind of help and assistance in carrying out complete studies. Truly an excellent fashion of investing money, and well suited to the times in which we live! The less hope of public patronage there is for Catholic study, the more ready and the more abundant should be the liberality of private persons — those to whom God has given riches thus willingly making use of their means to safeguard the treasure of His revealed doctrine.

CAUTION IN DOUBT

In order that all these endeavors and exertions may really prove advantageous to the cause of the Bible, let scholars keep steadfastly to the principles which We have in this Letter laid down. Let them loyally

---

[1] Ep. lxxvii. 1, et crebrius alibi.

hold that God, the Creator and Ruler of all things, is also the Author of the Scriptures — and that, therefore, nothing can be proved either by physical science or archæology which can really contradict the Scriptures. If, then, apparent contradiction be met with, every effort should be made to remove it. Judicious theologians and commentators should be consulted as to what is the true or most probable meaning of the passage in discussion, and hostile arguments should be carefully weighed. Even if the difficulty is after all not cleared up and the discrepancy seems to remain, the contest must not be abandoned; truth cannot contradict truth, and we may be sure that some mistake has been made either in the interpretation of the sacred words or in the polemical discussion itself; and if no such mistake can be detected, we must then suspend judgment for the time being. There have been objections without number perseveringly directed against the Scripture for many a long year, which have been proved to be futile and are now never heard of; and not infrequently interpretations have been placed on certain passages of Scripture (not belonging to the rule of faith or morals) which have been rectified by more careful investigations. As time goes on, mistaken views die and disappear; but *truth remaineth and groweth stronger forever and ever.*[1] Wherefore, as no one should be so presumptuous as to think that he understands the whole of the Scripture, in which St. Augustine himself confessed that there was more that he did not know than that he knew,[2] so, if he should come on anything that seems incapable of solution, he must take to heart the cautious rule of the same holy doctor: "It is better even to be oppressed by unknown but useful signs than to interpret them uselessly, and thus to throw off the yoke only to be caught in the trap of error."[3]

As to those who pursue the subsidiary studies of which We have spoken, if they honestly and modestly follow the counsels We have given — if by their pen and their voice they make their studies profitable against the enemies of truth, and useful in saving the young from the loss of their faith — they may justly congratulate themselves on their worthy service to the sacred writings, and on affording to Catholicism that assistance which the Church has a right to expect from the piety and learning of her children.

Conclusion

Such, Venerable Brethren, are the admonitions and the instructions which, by the help of God, We have thought it well, at the present moment, to offer to you on the study of Holy Scripture. It will now be your province to see that what We have said be observed and put in practice with all due reverence and exactness; that so We may prove our gratitude to God for the communication to man of the words of His wisdom, and that all the good results so much to be desired may be realized, especially as they affect the training of the students of the Church, which is our own great solicitude and the Church's hope. Exert yourselve with willing alacrity, and use your authority and your persuasion

---

[1] III Esdr. iv. 38.

[2] Ad Ianuar. ep. lv. 21.   [3] De doctr. chr. iii. 9, 18.

in order that these studies may be held in just regard and may flourish in seminaries and in educational institutions which are under your jurisdiction. Let them flourish in completeness and in happy success, under the direction of the Church, in accordance with the salutary teaching and example of the holy Fathers, and the laudable traditions of antiquity; and, as time goes on, let them be widened and extended as the interests and glory of truth may require — the interests of that Catholic truth which comes from above, the never-failing source of man's salvation. Finally, We admonish with paternal love all students and ministers of the Church always to approach the sacred writings with reverence and piety; for it is impossible to attain to the profitable understanding thereof unless the arrogance of "earthly" science be laid aside, and there be excited in the heart the holy desire for that wisdom "which is from above." In this way the intelligence which is once admitted to these sacred studies, and thereby illuminated and strengthened, will acquire a marvelous facility in detecting and avoiding the fallacies of human science, and in gathering and using for eternal salvation all that is valuable and precious; whilst, at the same time, the heart will grow warm, and will strive, with ardent longing, to advance in virtue and in divine love. *Blessed are they who examine His testimonies; they shall seek Him with their whole heart.*[1]

And now, filled with hope in the divine assistance, and trusting to your pastoral solicitude — as a pledge of heavenly grace, and a sign of Our special good-will — to you all, and to the clergy, and to the whole flock intrusted to you, We lovingly impart in Our Lord the Apostolic Benediction.

SYLLABUS OF ERRORS

CONDEMNED BY THE S. CONGR. OF THE INQUISITION, JULY 3, 1907.

WITH truly lamentable results, our age, intolerant of all check in its investigations of the ultimate causes of things, not unfrequently follows what is new in such a way as to reject the legacy, as it were, of the human race, and thus fall into the most grievous errors. These errors will be all the more pernicious when they affect sacred disciplines, the interpretation of the Sacred Scripture, the principal mysteries of the faith. It is to be greatly deplored that among Catholics also not a few writers are to be found who, crossing the boundaries fixed by the Fathers and by the Church herself, seek out, on the plea of higher intelligence and in the name of historical considerations, that progress of dogmas which is in reality the corruption of the same.

But lest errors of this kind, which are being daily spread among the faithful, should strike root in their minds and corrupt the purity of the faith, it has pleased His Holiness Pius X, by Divine Providence Pope, that the chief among them should be noted and condemned through the office of this Holy Roman and Universal Inquisition.

---

[1] Ps. cxviii. 2.

Wherefore, after a most diligent investigation, and after having taken the opinion of the Reverend Consultors, the Most Eminent and Reverend Lords Cardinals, the general inquisitors in matters of faith and morals, decided that *the following propositions are to be condemned and proscribed, as they are, by this general Decree, condemned and proscribed:*

1. The ecclesiastical law, which prescribes that books regarding the Divine Scriptures are subject to previous censorship, does not extend to critical scholars or students of the scientific exegesis of the Old and New Testament.

2. The Church's interpretation of the Sacred Books is not indeed to be condemned, but it is subject to the more accurate judgment and to the correction of the exegetes.

3. From the ecclesiastical judgments and censures passed against free and more scientific (*cultiorem*) exegesis, it may be gathered that the faith proposed by the Church contradicts history and that the Catholic dogmas cannot be reconciled with the true origins of the Christian religion.

4. The magisterium of the Church cannot, even through dogmatic definitions, determine the genuine sense of the Sacred Scriptures.

5. Since in the deposit of the faith only revealed truths are contained, under no respect does it appertain to the Church to pass judgment concerning the assertions of human sciences.

6. In defining truths the Church learning (*discens*) and the Church teaching (*docens*) collaborate in such a way that it only remains for the Church *docens* to sanction the opinions of the Church *discens*.

7. The Church, when it proscribes errors, cannot exact from the faithful any internal assent by which the judgments issued by it are embraced.

8. Those who treat as of no weight the condemnations passed by the Sacred Congregation of the Index or by the other Roman Congregations are free from all blame.

9. Those who believe that God is really the author of the Sacred Scripture display excessive simplicity or ignorance.

10. The inspiration of the books of the Old Testament consists in the fact that the Israelite writers have handed down religious doctrines under a peculiar aspect, either little or not at all known to the Gentiles.

11. Divine inspiration is not to be so extended to the whole of Sacred Scriptures that it renders its parts, all and single, immune from all error.

12. The exegete, if he wishes to apply himself usefully to Biblical studies, must first of all put aside all preconceived opinions concerning the supernatural origin of the Sacred Scripture, and interpret it not otherwise than other merely human documents.

13. The evangelists themselves and the Christians of the second and third generation arranged (*digesserunt*) artificially the evangelical parables, and in this way gave an explanation of the scanty fruit of the preaching of Christ among the Jews.

14. In a great many narrations the evangelists reported not so much things that are true as things which even though false they judged to be more profitable for their readers.

15. The Gospels until the time the canon was defined and constituted

were increased by additions and corrections; hence in them there remained of the doctrine of Christ only a faint and uncertain trace.

16. The narrations of John are not properly history, but the mystical contemplation of the Gospel; the discourses contained in his Gospel are theological meditations, devoid of historical truth concerning the mystery of salvation.

17. The Fourth Gospel exaggerated miracles not only that the wonderful might stand out but also that they might become more suitable for signifying the work and the glory of the Word Incarnate.

18. John claims for himself the quality of a witness concerning Christ; but in reality he is only a distinguished witness of the Christian life, or of the life of Christ in the Church, at the close of the first century.

19. Heterodox exegetes have expressed the true sense of the Scriptures more faithfully than Catholic exegetes.

20. Revelation could be nothing but the consciousness acquired by man of his relation with God.

21. Revelation, constituting the object of Catholic faith, was not completed with the Apostles.

22. The dogmas which the Church gives out as revealed, are not truths which have fallen down from heaven, but are an interpretation of religious facts, which the human mind has acquired by laborious effort.

23. Opposition may and actually does exist between the facts which are narrated in Scripture and the dogmas of the Church which rest on them; so that the critic may reject as false facts which the Church holds as most certain.

24. The exegete is not to be blamed for constructing premises from which it follows that the dogmas are historically false or doubtful, provided he does not directly deny the dogmas themselves.

25. The assent of faith rests ultimately on a mass of probabilities.

26. The dogmas of faith are to be held only according to their practical sense, that is, as preceptive norms of conduct, but not as norms of believing.

27. The Divinity of Jesus Christ is not proved from the Gospels; but is a dogma which the Christian conscience has derived from the notion of the Messias.

28. Jesus, while He was exercising His Ministry, did not speak with the object of teaching that He was the Messias, nor did His miracles tend to prove this.

29. It is lawful to believe that the Christ of history is far inferior to the Christ who is the object of faith.

30. In all the evangelical texts the name *Son of God* is equivalent only to Messias, and does not at all signify that Christ is the true and natural Son of God.

31. The doctrine concerning Christ taught by Paul, John, the Councils of Nicea, Ephesus and Chalcedon, is not that which Jesus taught, but that which the Christian conscience conceived concerning Jesus.

32. It is not possible to reconcile the natural sense of the Gospel texts with the sense taught by our theologians concerning the conscience and the infallible knowledge of Jesus Christ.

33. It is evident to everybody who is not led by preconceived opinions that either Jesus professed an error concerning the immediate Messianic coming, or that the greater part of His doctrine as contained in the Gospels is destitute of authenticity.

34. The critic cannot ascribe to Christ a knowledge circumscribed by no limits except on a hypothesis which cannot be historically conceived and which is repugnant to the moral sense, viz., that Christ as man had the knowledge of God and yet was unwilling to communicate the knowledge of a great many things to His Disciples and to posterity.

35. Christ had not always the consciousness of His Messianic dignity.

36. The Resurrection of the Saviour is not properly a fact of the historical order, but a fact of merely supernatural order, neither demonstrated nor demonstrable, which the Christian conscience gradually derived from other facts.

37. Faith in the Resurrection of Christ was in the beginning not so much in the fact itself of the Resurrection, as in the immortal life of Christ with God.

38. The doctrine of the expiatory death of Christ is not Evangelical but Pauline.

39. The opinions concerning the origin of the sacraments with which the Fathers of Trent were imbued and which certainly influenced their dogmatic canons are very different from those which now rightly obtain among historians who examine into Christianity.

40. The sacraments had their origin in the fact that the Apostles and their successors, swayed and moved by circumstances and events, interpreted some idea or intention of Christ.

41. The sacraments are merely intended to bring before the mind of man the ever-beneficent presence of the Creator.

42. The Christian community imposed (*iuduxit*) the necessity of baptism, adopting it as a necessary rite, and adding to it the obligations of the Christian profession.

43. The practice of conferring baptism on infants was a disciplinary evolution, which became one of the causes why the sacrament was divided into two, viz.: baptism and penance.

44. There is nothing to prove that the rite of the sacrament of confirmation was employed by the Apostles: but the formal distinction of the two sacraments, baptism and confirmation, does not belong to the history of primitive Christianity.

45. Not everything which Paul narrates concerning the institution of the Eucharist (I Cor. xi. 23–25) is to be taken historically.

46. In the primitive Church the conception of the Christian sinner reconciled by the authority of the Church did not exist, but it was only very slowly that the Church accustomed itself to this conception. Nay, even after penance was recognized as an institution of the Church, it was not called a sacrament, for it would be held as an ignominious sacrament.

47. The words of the Lord: *Receive ye the Holy Ghost; whose sins ye shall forgive they are forgiven them, and whose sins ye shall retain they are retained* (John xx. 22, 23) do not at all refer to the sacrament of penance, whatever the Fathers of Trent may have been pleased to say.

48. James in his Epistle (v. 14 and 15) did not intend to promulgate a sacrament of Christ, but to commend a pious custom, and if in this custom he happens to distinguish (*cernit*) a means of grace, it is not in that rigorous manner in which it was received by the theologians who laid down the notion and the number of the sacraments.

49. The Christian Supper gradually assuming the nature of a liturgical action, those who were wont to preside at the Supper acquired the sacerdotal character.

50. The elders who filled the office of watching over the gatherings of the faithful, were instituted by the Apostles as priests or bishops to provide for the necessary ordering (*ordinationi*) of the increasing opportunities, not properly for perpetuating the Apostolic mission and power.

51. It is not possible that matrimony could have become a sacrament of the new Law until later in the Church; for in order that matrimony should be held as a sacrament it was necessary that a full theological development (*explicatio*) of the doctrine of grace and the sacraments should first take place.

52. It was foreign to the mind of Christ to found a Church as a Society which was to last on the earth for a long course of centuries; nay, in the mind of Christ the Kingdom of Heaven together with the end of the world was about to come immediately.

53. The organic constitution of the Church is not immutable; but Christian society, like human society, is subject to perpetual evolution.

54. Dogmas, sacraments, hierarchy, both as regards the notion of them and the reality, are but interpretations and evolutions of the Christian intelligence which by external increments have increased and perfected the little germ latent in the Gospel.

55. Simon Peter never even suspected that the primacy in the Church was intrusted to him by Christ.

56. The Roman Church became the head of all the churches not through the ordinance of Divine Providence but through merely political conditions.

57. The Church has shown herself to be hostile to the progress of natural and theological sciences.

58. Truth is not any more immutable than man himself, since it is evolved with him, in him, and through him.

59. Christ did not teach a determinate body of doctrine applicable to all times and to all men, but rather inaugurated a religious movement adapted or to be adapted for different times and place.

60. Christian doctrine in its origin was Judaic, but through successive evolutions became first Pauline, then Joannine, and finally Hellenic and universal.

61. It may be said without paradox that there is no chapter of Scripture, from the first of Genesis to the last of the Apocalypse, which contains a doctrine absolutely identical with that which the Church teaches on the same matter, and that, therefore, no chapter of Scripture has the same sense for the critic and for the theologian.

62. The chief articles of the Apostolic Symbol had not for the Christians of the first ages the same sense that they have for the Christians of our time.

63. The Church shows itself unequal to the task of efficaciously maintaining evangelical ethics, because it obstinately adheres to immutable doctrines which cannot be reconciled with modern progress.

64. The progress of science involves a remodeling (*ut reformentur*) of the conceptions of Christian doctrine concerning God, Creation, Revelation, the Person of the Incarnate Word, Redemption.

65. Modern Catholicism cannot be reconciled with true science unless it be transformed into a non-dogmatic Christianity, that is into a broad and liberal Protestantism.

And on the following Thursday, the fourth day of the same month and year, an accurate report of all this having been made to Our Most Holy Lord Pope Pius X, His Holiness approved and confirmed the Decree of the Most Eminent Fathers, and ordered that the propositions above enumerated, all and several, be held by all as condemned and proscribed.

PETER PALOMBELLI,
Notary of the H. R. U. I.

FROM THE MOTU PROPRIO OF PIUS X

ON THE DECISIONS OF THE BIBLICAL COMMISSION AND ON THE CENSURES AND PENALTIES AFFECTING THOSE WHO NEGLECT TO OBSERVE THE PRESCRIPTIONS AGAINST THE ERRORS OF THE MODERNISTS

IN his Encyclical Letter *Providentissimus Deus*, given on November 19, 1893, our predecessor, Leo XIII, of immortal memory, after describing the dignity of the Sacred Scripture and commending the study of it, set forth the laws which govern the proper study of the Holy Bible; and having proclaimed the divinity of these books against the errors and calumnies of the rationalists, he at the same time defended them against the false teachings of what is known as the *higher criticism*, which, as the Pontiff most wisely wrote, are clearly nothing but the *commentaries of rationalism derived from a misuse of philology and kindred studies*.

Our predecessor, too, seeing that the danger was constantly on the increase, and desiring to provide against the consequences of the propagation of rash and erroneous views, by his Apostolic Letters *Vigilantiæ studiique memores*, given on October 29, 1902, established a Pontifical Council, or Commission on Biblical Matters, composed of a number of cardinals of the Holy Roman Church, distinguished for their learning and prudence, adding to these, under the title of *consultors*, a considerable body of men in sacred orders, chosen from among the learned in theology and in the Holy Bible, of various nationalities and differing in their methods and views concerning exegetical studies. In this the Pontiff had in mind, as an advantage admirably adapted for the promotion of study and for the time in which we live, that in this commission there should be the fullest freedom for proposing, examining, and judging all opinions whatsoever; and the letter also ordained that the cardinals of the commission were not to come to any definite decision until they had taken cognizance of and examined the arguments on both sides, omitting nothing which might serve to show in the clearest light the true and genuine state of the Biblical questions proposed for solution; and when all this had been done, that the decisions reached should be submitted for approval to the Supreme Pontiff, and then promulgated.

After mature examination and the most diligent consultations, certain decisions have been happily given by the Pontifical Commission on the Bible, and these of a kind very useful for the proper promotion and direction on safe lines of Biblical studies. But we observe that some persons, unduly prone to opinions and methods tainted by pernicious novelties, and excessively devoted to that principle of false liberty, which is really immoderate license, and in sacred studies proves itself to be most insidious and a fruitful source of the worst evils against the purity of the faith, have not received and do not receive these decisions with the proper obedience.

Wherefore we find it necessary to declare and prescribe, as we do now declare and expressly prescribe, that all are bound in conscience to submit to the decisions, regarding doctrine, of the Biblical Commission, which have been given in the past and which shall be given in the future, in the same way as to the Decrees of the Roman Congregations approved by the Pontiff; nor can all those escape the note of disobedience or temerity, and consequently of grave sin, who in speech or writing impugn these decisions; and this besides the scandal they give and the other reasons for which they may be responsible before God, for other temerities and errors usually accompanying such oppositions.

Moreover to check the daily increasing audacity of a great many modernists who are endeavoring by all kinds of sophistry and devices to detract from the force and efficacy not only of the Decree *Lamentabili sane exitu,* issued, by our order, by the Holy Roman and Universal Inquisition of July 3 of the present year, but also of our Encyclical Letters *Pascendi dominici gregis* given on September 8 of this same year, we do by our Apostolic authority repeat and confirm both that *Decree* of the Supreme Sacred Congregation and those *Encyclical Letters* of Ours, adding the penalty of excommunication against contradictors; and this we declare and decree, that should anybody, which may God forbid, be so rash as to defend any one of the propositions, opinions or teachings condemned in these documents, he falls *ipso facto* under the censure contained under the Chapter *Docentes* of the Constitution *Apostolicæ Sedis,* which is first among the excommunications *latæ sententiæ* simply reserved to the Roman Pontiff. This excommunication is to be understood as *salvis pœnis,* which may be incurred by those who have violated in any way the said documents, as propagators and defenders of heresies, when their propositions, opinions or teachings are heretical, as has happened more than once in the case of the adversaries of both these documents, especially when they advocate the errors of modernism, that is *the synthesis of all heresies.*

Wherefore, we again and most earnestly exhort the ordinaries of the dioceses and the heads of religious congregations to use the utmost vigilance over teachers, and first of all in the seminaries; and should they find any of them imbued with the errors of the modernists, and eager for what is new and noxious, or lacking in docility to the prescriptions of the Apostolic See, no matter how they may be published, let them absolutely forbid the teaching office to such; so, too, let them exclude from sacred orders those young men who give the very faintest reason for doubt that they hold the condemned doctrines and the pernicious novelties. We exhort them also to take diligent care to put an end to those books and other writings, now growing exceedingly numerous, which contain opinions or tendencies of the kind condemned in the Encyclical Letters and Decree above mentioned; let them see to it that these publications are removed from Catholic publishing houses, and especially from the hands of students and the clergy. By doing this they will at the same time be promoting real and solid education, which should always be a subject of the greatest solicitude for those who exercise sacred authority.

All these things we will and order to be sanctioned and established by our Apostolic authority, aught to the contrary notwithstanding.

Given at Rome at St. Peter's November 18, 1907, in the fifth year of our Pontificate.

PIUS X, POPE

INTRODUCTION TO THE BIBLE

1. GENERAL PRINCIPLES

FROM very early times the Holy Scriptures have been read, studied and expounded both by Jews and Christians, by Catholics and non-Catholics. The results of all their exertions are, however, very various and often in direct antagonism to one another. As it is impossible for two or more opinions to be correct at the same time, it follows that many mistakes have been made.

Whoever desires not to err in studying the Scriptures must not separate them from the Church, but regard them as belonging to the Church, and therefore he must recognize the following truths:

1. Holy Scripture is God's word. But as, in accordance with our Lord's commission (Matt. xxviii. 19), it is the task of the Church to make known to men the whole of God's revelation, Scripture is the property of the Church.

2. The Church has preserved Holy Scripture in its integrity and in all its parts free from falsification.

3. The Church alone possesses the correct interpretation of Scripture.

The statement and proof of the first two truths form the subject of the historical and critical introduction to Holy Scripture, whereas the third is the foundation of Biblical Hermeneutics.

Historical Survey

What we call the historical and critical introduction to Holy Scripture is a product of recent times, and it has become an important branch of knowledge only in the last hundred years or thereabouts.

In early Christian times there was no particular reason for carrying on biblical study as we understand it. People believed and accepted the living traditions, as they were still near the time when the sacred books were written. The heathen, too, did not, as a rule, meddle with the sacred books of the Christians. Celsus aimed his attacks upon their contents, i. e. upon the doctrines of Christianity, and so did Lucian. Much valuable material for our present preliminary studies is scattered about in the works of the Fathers of the Church and of ecclesiastical writers, particularly in Origen (185–254), Eusebius of Cæsarea (270–338), Saint Jerome (331–420, especially in his *De Viris Illustribus* and in the introductions to his Latin translation of the Bible) and Saint Augustine (354–430). Cassiodorus, a contemporary of some of the Fathers, who was first a statesman and afterwards an abbot (c. 470–560), wrote the *Isagoge*,[1] a special work on the Bible, for his religious, and the African lawyer, Junilius, wrote a similar book about the year 550, basing it on Theodorus of Mopsuestia.

In the Middle Ages not much attention was paid to historical and linguistic studies, and for this reason the great mediæval theologians are not of much assistance in supplying the sort of material we need. It is, however, not true that Holy Scripture was unknown at that time. On the contrary, the Bible was the foundation of almost all their learned works, and that the people were familiar with it is proved by the numerous works of art, e. g. stained-glass windows, in churches dating back to the Middle Ages. The Bible was the first book that ever appeared in print (1450), and by 1500 it had been printed over 100 times (Janssen, *Gesch. d. d. Volkes*, I, p. 18). In the Middle Ages the Bible was studied with particular zeal in Spain, where the Christians were obliged to defend their faith against Mahometans and Jews. These circumstances prompted the composition of the *Pugio fidei adv. Mauros et Judæos* by Raimundus Martini, and of many works by the Franciscan Raimundus Sullus. Another Franciscan, Nicholas of Lyra (died 1340), collected and arranged in the prefaces to his postils such information about Holy Scripture as then existed.

---

[1] Migne, *Patres Lat.*, Vol. LXX. The word *Isagoge* is used in the same sense as by Cassiodorus, also by the Dominican Santes Pagninus, 1536.

The Dominican Sixtus of Siena (died 1599) in his *Bibliotheca Sancta,* essayed to defend in an intelligent manner the teaching of the Council of Trent regarding Holy Scripture against the Reformers. Cardinal Bellarmine, S.J., wrote the first book (*De Verbo Dei*) of his great work *De Controversiis Fidei* with a similar intention. Many of the numerous commentators who followed him, especially Salmeron, Serarius and Bonfrerius, wrote works that were to be introductory to the study of the Bible.

What we at present call historical and critical study introductory to Holy Scripture was begun by Richard Simon, priest of the Oratory (died 1712),[1] who opposed the pantheist Spinoza, and Calmet, a Benedictine (died 1757).

2. ARRANGEMENT OF AN INTRODUCTION TO THE BIBLE

An introduction to the Bible may suitably be divided into the following headings:

1. The origin of the sacred books, or Holy Scripture as God's word, — first and fundamental part.

2. The collection of the sacred books, or Holy Scripture as a whole, — second part, general introduction.

3. Component parts of Holy Scripture, or the sacred books considered singly, — third part, special introduction.

[1] Of his many writings the ones to which special reference is made here are his *Histoire critique du Vieux Testament* and his *Histoire critique du text du Nouveau Testament.*

FIRST PART

ORIGIN OF HOLY SCRIPTURE, OR HOLY SCRIP-
TURE AS THE WORD OF GOD

3. GENERAL SURVEY

GOD, who is above all, has communicated to some individuals
particular supernatural knowledge, and this communication is called revelation. Those honored by receiving it made
known the revealed truths to others, partly by word of mouth
(tradition) and partly by writing them down by aid of God's
special co-operation (Holy Writ). As the divine truths were
communicated at different times, they were written down at different times, and in this way several sacred books gradually came
into existence, which, being collected into one whole, are called
the canonical books or Bible. The mark therefore by which
the sacred books are distinguished from others is their divine
origin, i. e. they came into being in consequence of some particular action on God's part, which is called inspiration. The
instrument by which we are assured of the divine character
of the written revelation, or by which we recognize the inspired
writings, is the Canon, i. e. the list of the sacred books drawn
up by the Church.

We have therefore to consider: (1) Inspiration; (2) the
Canon.

FIRST SECTION

INSPIRATION

4. TEACHING OF THE CHURCH ON THE SUBJECT OF
INSPIRATION

It is the teaching of the Church that Holy Scripture owes its
origin not merely to human, but more especially to divine action.

This teaching was formulated last by the Vatican Council in 1870 and stated in the words: *Spiritu Sancto inspirante conscripti (libri) Deum habent auctorem* (Sess. 3, cap. 2). In the same way the Council of Trent declared that God was the author of the books of both the Old and the New Testaments (Sess. 4, *de can. scr.*).[1] Pope Eugenius IV also used similar language in the decree of Union, 1439;[2] and still earlier, at the Second Council of Lyons in 1274, the same fact was proclaimed.[3] *Cf. Decretum Inquis. Rom. d. d. 3d Julii 1907,* Nos. 9, 10, 11.

Evidence in support of this doctrine of the Church is derived from Holy Scripture itself and from tradition.

Holy Scripture itself frequently bears witness to its divine origin.

(*a*) In the prophet Osee viii. 12, God ascribes to Himself the authorship of the Pentateuch: "I shall write to him [Israel] my manifold laws [i. e. far more often than has already been done; Moses is known to have written several times at God's bidding], which have been accounted as foreign." In Acts iv. 24, 25, the 2d Psalm, although composed by David, is ascribed to God: "Lord, thou art he . . . who by the Holy Ghost, by the mouth of our father David, . . . hast said." In Hebrews i. 7 the 103d Psalm is quoted as God's word: "And to the angels indeed he saith: *qui facit angelos suos spiritus.*" In the same way there is a reference in Heb. iv. 4, etc., to Gen. ii. 2, 3, and to Ps. xciv. *Cf.* Acts xxviii, 25; II Tim. iii. 16; II Peter i. 21.

(*b*) Jesus Christ Himself quoted passages from the sacred books, adding that they proceeded from the Holy Ghost: Matthew xxii. 43; Mark xii. 36.

Its divine origin may be recognized in the construction of the Bible.

(*a*) It contains many statements which could not be the outcome of merely human knowledge. This is true particularly of the types and prophecies, many of which were at first obscure and unintelligible, and only gradually became plain and were understood (e. g. Gen. iii. 15; xvi. 21, 22; xlv, 7; Is. vii. 14; xiv. 23; xxi. 1; Luke xii. 32).

(*b*) The Holy Scriptures, although belonging to various periods and

---

[1] *Sacra synodus omnes libros tam veteris quam novi testamenti, quam utriusque unus Deus sit auctor, . . . suscipit et veneratur.*

[2] (*Romana ecclesia*) *Deum veteris et novi testamenti profitetur auctorem, quoniam eodem Spiritu sancto inspirante utriusque testamenti Sancti locuti sunt.*

[3] *Credimus novi et veteris testamenti, legis et prophetarum et apostolorum unum esse auctorem Deum ac Dominum omnipotentem.*

written by many different persons, nevertheless bear a uniform character, and appear as one consistent whole, dominated by the same opinions and having the uniform aim of bringing men to God. One and the same spirit prevails and speaks in all the books of the Bible. " As in Paradise, God walks in the Holy Scriptures, seeking man. When a sinner reads these Scriptures, he hears God's voice saying, ' Adam, where art thou? ' " (Ambros., *de Paradiso*). The Old Testament tells us of the preparations made for saving the lost; the New Testament tells us of the actual salvation; in the one are the promises, in the other their fulfillment. See Hermeneutics, p. 449.

Tradition supplies very numerous testimonies to it.

Thus Clement of Rome calls the sacred books of the Old Testament "true pronouncements of the Holy Ghost"; [1] Justin Martyr says the prophets were inspired by the Logos (*Apologia*, I, 36, 39) ; Clement of Alexandria designates the sacred books " divine utterances " ($\theta\epsilon\hat{\iota}\alpha$ $\lambda\acute{o}\gamma\iota\alpha$) (*Strom.*, IX, 345), etc. *Cf.* Leo XIII, Encyclical, pp. 159 and 175.

5. WHAT IS MEANT BY INSPIRATION

The Church declares God Himself to be the primary author of Holy Scripture. The Councils have not given us any explanation of this doctrine, and so it is left to theologians to give a precise account of what is meant by inspiration.[2] Now theologians understand by inspiration, or *theopneustia*, an action of the divine spirit upon the human mind, whereby the latter is raised so far above its natural powers that its productions cease to be merely human works, but are at the same time divine.

[1] Ep. I ad Cor., 45: $\dot{\epsilon}\gamma\kappa\acute{u}\pi\tau\epsilon\tau\epsilon$ $\epsilon\dot{\iota}s$ $\tau\dot{\alpha}s$ $\gamma\rho\alpha\phi\dot{\alpha}s$, $\tau\dot{\alpha}s$ $\dot{\alpha}\lambda\eta\theta\epsilon\hat{\iota}s$ $\dot{\rho}\acute{\eta}\sigma\epsilon\iota s$ $\pi\nu\epsilon\acute{u}\mu\alpha\tau o$ $\tau o\hat{u}$ $\dot{\alpha}\gamma\acute{\iota}ov$.

[2] See Schmid, *De inspirationis Bibliorum vi et ratione*, Brix., 1885. Dausch, *Die Schriftinspiration*, Frbg., 1891. Leitner, *Die prophet. Inspiration*, Frbg., 1896. Chauvin, *Die Imp. d. Hl. Schr.*, übers. v., *Pletl*, Regensb., 1899. Holzhey, *Schöpfung, Bibel und Insp.*, Stuttgart, 1902. v. Hummelauer, S.J., *Exegetisches zur Inspirationslehre*, Frbg., 1904. Fonck, S.J., *Kampf um die Wahrheit der Hl. Schrift*, Innsbr., 1905. Peters, *Stellung der Kath. Kirche zur Bibelforschung*, Paderborn, 1905. Pesch, Chr., S.J., *De inspiratione s. Script.*, Frbg., 1906. *Cf.* Haidacher, *Lehre d. hl. Joh. Chrysostomus über die Schriftinspiration*, Salzb., 1897. (According to Saint John Chrysostom God is really and truly the primary author of Holy Scripture, and throughout we have to assume a real inspiration, and in exceptional passages also a verbal inspiration. Consequently the Scriptures are completely free from error.) Zöllig, *Die Inspirationslehre des Origines*, Frbg. i. Br., 1902. (According to Origen the literal meaning is of minor importance, and may often be quite wrong, but the mystical sense is the chief matter.)

When they proceed to determine this divine action more particularly with reference to the sacred books, theologians differ.

1. Some give too broad an interpretation of the idea of inspiration, and say that a book originating in a merely human way, without supernatural intervention of the Holy Ghost, may be called inspired, if the Church under the guidance of the Holy Ghost admits it to the Canon, thus confirming its contents and declaring that it contains divine revelation without error. This view leaves practically no scope for inspiration, and it cannot be reconciled with the Church, which declares God Himself to be the primary author of Holy Scripture. The Vatican Council expressly condemned this opinion (Sess. 3, cap. 2). Equally wrong is the theory that inspiration affects only *res fidei et morum*, so that Holy Scripture may contain mistakes on such subjects as science and history, for its aim is not to impart information on matters of this kind, but only to teach men what they must believe and how they must live. In this way God Himself, the primary author of the Scriptures, would be the author of error;[1] and for this reason Leo XIII condemned the theory as false in his Encyclical *Providentissimus*.

Consequitur ut qui in locis authenticis librorum sacrorum quidpiam falsi contineri posse existiment, ii profecto aut catholicam divinæ inspirationis notionem pervertant, aut Deum ipsum erroris faciant auctorem (see p. 176).

2. Too broad also is the opinion of others who say that "inspiration consists in the divine impulse to write, and in preservation from error whilst writing." If God is the primary author of Holy Scripture, His divine influence must do more than merely avert errors; some positive action of God must have made itself felt in the composition of the sacred books.

3. Others have too narrow an idea of inspiration, and assume that every word was a matter of divine communication. Against this theory we may say: (*a*) God's divine influence never de-

---

[1] There are indeed mistaken opinions and doctrines in Holy Scripture, but they are only quotations made for the purpose of controverting them. Such, for instance, occur in Ecclesiastes ii. 24, viii. 15; 1 Cor. xv. 32. This was the reply given to a question referred to the Papal Biblical Commission, Feb. 15, 1905.

stroys human individuality, but is wont only to raise, ennoble and transform nature.[1] (*b*) Every one of the sacred writers has his own particular language; Isaias no less than Jeremias, and Saint John as well as Saint Paul, all reveal their definite character. (*c*) The same event, e. g. the birth of Christ, His Passion and Resurrection, is described in different ways by different authors. (*d*) The sacred writers declare that they have encountered difficulties in their work, and have had to take trouble over it (e. g. Ps. lxxii. 16; Eccles. xii. 9. Sirach in his preface). Accordingly we cannot accept a strictly verbal inspiration,[2] yet we must admit: (*a*) that God gave special revelations to the sacred writers, and that the choice of many most important words and expressions, such as *Elohim, Yahweh, Logos, Sophia, Mashiach*, was made through inspiration; (*b*) that the language of the sacred writers was permeated, raised and ennobled by the divine influence; for just as God is the author of the written word, so is He also of the language (*cf.* I Cor. ii. 13).[3] Therefore the language of Holy Writ is the model most worthy of imitation by preachers.

4. The correct view of inspiration is the following: (1) The Holy Ghost impels the authors to write; (2) He enlightens them, so that they fall into no error; (3) He directs them in the choice of their subject; (4) He assists them in finding language to express their meaning; (5) He imparts to them supernatural revelation with regard to all that they otherwise could not know,

---

[1] It may also be taken for granted that the sacred writers often spoke of things as they saw them, and used everyday expressions, although strictly scientific accuracy would have required other forms of speech. In just the same way modern astronomers speak of sunrise and sunset. Thus bees (Sir. xi. 3) and bats (Lev. xi. 19) are called birds, not in the narrower sense, but in a general way, as winged creatures.

[2] The early Protestants declared that the original text had come directly from God; hence they regarded even the vowel marks and accents of the Hebrew as inspired. This theory had to be abandoned when it became known that these marks had not been inserted before the sixth century.

[3] Pope Leo XIII writes: " He [i. e. the Holy Ghost] so assisted them [the inspired writers] during their writing, that all those things, and those alone, which He ordered, they both rightly conceived in their mind, and wished to write faithfully, and expressed them in suitable language with infallible accuracy; otherwise He would not be the author of the entire Sacred Scripture (see p. 176).

e. g. respecting prophecies; (6) He provides also that the deposit of faith contained in Holy Scripture shall be correctly rendered in various languages, so that inspiration belongs not only to the original text but to every authentic text.

The question whether in the case of the Apostles (as well as in that of the prophets) inspiration was given through the call of God, or whether this affected only their oral discourses, must probably be decided in the second sense. They were told simply to go forth and *preach;* therefore a special inspiration was required to enable them to write. (The first view, that no further inspiration was necessary, is supported by Schanz, Dausch and others; the second by Pesch, Cornely, etc.) Were the inspired persons aware of the divine influence? Not always, or at least not always clearly, as is shown by Caiphas, who prophesied unconsciously (John xi. 51).

SECOND SECTION

THE CANON OF HOLY SCRIPTURE

6. Meaning of the Expression

Ever since the time of the Fathers of the Church, the collection of sacred books has been known as the Canon. The Greek word **Κανών** signifies rule or standard. Two opinions exist as to the sense in which this name is given to Holy Scripture. Some think that it means that these books, as they contain divine revelations, are a rule and standard of faith and life for men. According to this interpretation, therefore, the expression " Canonical Books " means regulating or standardizing books. According to the other opinion, the word " Canon " implies that the collection of these books by the Church constitutes the sole rule or standard for what is to be read aloud in the Church or used generally in church worship; so that it is not permissible to go beyond these books and adopt others. Since the time of Saint Jerome the latter view has been commonly accepted, although the other was emphasized by the earlier ecclesiastical writers.

The list of saints is also called the Canon (as the rule for public veneration) ; hence we have the word " Canonization." In the same way the most important part of the sacrificial prayers at Mass is called the Canon, as it is a standing rule for the priest.

7. OLD AND NEW TESTAMENTS

Some of the sacred books were written before the time of our Lord and the rest after. Therefore they are divided into the books of the Old and the books of the New Covenant, or shortly (following II Cor. iii. 14) into the Old and the New Testament. This use of the word " Testament " is identical with " Covenant," being, in accordance with the usage of the old Latin version of the Bible, the translation of the Greek διαθήκη, by which word the Septuagint generally translates the Hebrew *berith*, Covenant.

The word διαθήκη signifies also a testament or will disposing of property. There is a reference to this meaning in Hebrews ix. 16, etc., where we read " where there is a testament, the death of the testator must of necessity come in." Now the Old Testament came into force with the death of beasts, and was sealed with their blood; the New Testament came into force with the Son of God, and was sealed with His Blood. How much higher is the New than the Old Covenant!

8. FORMATION OF THE OLD TESTAMENT CANON

In speaking of the Old Testament we have to distinguish two canons, the Jewish and the Ecclesiastical; the latter contains some books not included in the former.

In order to come to a correct decision as to the power of the Church to add to the Hebrew Canon, we must go back beyond the present opinions held by the Jews, to the time when they were still regarded as God's people. Their later judgments are no longer authoritative. Let us ask, therefore: How did the canon of the Old Testament come into existence, and when was it concluded?

1. It is hardly possible to give a satisfactory answer to the question relating to the origin of the Old Testament Canon, as we do not know what *criteria* guided the Jews in distinguishing the inspired writings from others and in putting them together. All that we know with certainty is (*a*) that sacred books have in every age been distinguished from those of merely human authorship, and (*b*) that in every age care has been taken to collect the sacred books and guard against their

loss.[1] The charge of the sacred books does not seem to have been laid upon the whole nation, but especially upon the priests (Deut. xvii. 18).

Speaking generally, we may say that the whole literature of Israel after the time of Moses is an outgrowth of the Mosaic law, having this as its foundation and its groundwork.

The beginning of a collection of the sacred books was made under Josue, when the Book of Josue was added to the five books of Moses (Jos. xxiv. 26). In a similar way the other historical books must have been appended to those already existing, since they form an exact continuation of them (Judges i. 1; Ruth i. 1, etc.).[2] At a very early period the prophetic writings were regarded as forming part of Holy Scripture, for Daniel (ix. 2) speaks of them as belonging to the collection of sacred books. In the time of the Machabees the didactic books also were considered sacred, as we read (I Mach. xii. 9) that their holy books were a comfort to the Jews, and this remark would apply particularly to the class of didactic writings. In any case, long before the time of Christ there were three classes of sacred books, as there are now, for in the preface to the Book of Ecclesiasticus or Sirach mention is made of "The Law and the Prophets and the other books" — undoubtedly as of a collection of sacred writings.

2. With regard to the date of the conclusion of the Old Testament Canon, we have to distinguish the Palestine from the Alexandrian Canon. In Palestine the Book of Esdras was excluded from the Canon, according to the Jewish tradition, which is stated by Josephus Flavius, a contemporary of the Apostles. In his work against Apion (I, 8) he speaks of the books which the Jews "regard as divine." He names first "the five books of Moses." "After Moses," he continues, "the prophets who followed Moses recorded the events of their time in thirteen books, until the period when Artaxerxes ruled, who succeeded Xerxes. There are, moreover, four books containing songs in praise of

---

[1] *Cf.* Proverbs xxv. 1. "These are also parables of Solomon, which the men of Ezechias, King of Juda, copied out."

[2] It is, however, not improbable that this connection was made when the sacred books were collected in the time of Esdras.

God and rules of life. Between the time when Artaxerxes lived
and our own, other books have indeed been written, but they
enjoy no such reputation as the above-mentioned, which are so
highly esteemed that no one has dared to alter anything in
them. It is impressed upon all Jews from their birth that
they must believe these to be divinely written, and that they
must hold fast to them, and, if need be, sacrifice life itself for
them." From this passage it appears that in the opinion of
Josephus,[1] in the time of Artaxerxes I, when Esdras and Nehemias were alive, the Hebrew Canon was closed. The Jews in
Alexandria and elsewhere outside Palestine, not knowing Hebrew,
read the sacred books in Greek (Septuagint), not only those
collected by Esdras, but others also, which they must have
regarded as being likewise of divine origin, for they certainly
would not have associated profane with holy writings. The
Jews in Palestine, too, had some sacred books not included
in the strict canon; for in II Machabees ii. 15 they offer to
send more recent books to their fellow countrymen in Egypt.
To some extent, even in Palestine itself, the Greek books were
read in the synagogues. The full Canon of the Old Testament
was not concluded until the grace of inspiration ceased among
the Jews, when the foundations of the Church, the new Kingdom of God, were already being laid, and the Jewish people
were approaching its final rejection.

9. CONTENTS OF THE OLD TESTAMENT CANON

The Church received the sacred books through Christ and
His Apostles. The question therefore arises, what books were
considered sacred in our Saviour's time? Unfortunately we
possess no complete list of them dating from His time or from
the period before His life;[2] but not long after His death

---

[1] We can see from his words that in his time, viz. about 100 A.D., the
Jews had already become exclusive, and recognized only the Hebrew
books, and tried to exclude the Greek.

[2] From II Machabees ii. 13 we learn only that Nehemias added to the
already existing sacred books those of Kings and Chronicles, the writings of some prophets, the Psalms, and the books of Esdras and Nehemias. It is certain that the author of the Book of Ecclesiasticus or

Josephus Flavius (born 37 A. D.) gave a catalogue of them. At a later period Melito of Sardes (about 150 A. D.) and Origen (born 185 A. D.) made very precise statements regarding the sacred books recognized by the Jews of their day. The Talmud, too, gives a similar list.

1. In his already quoted work against Apion (I, 8) Josephus Flavius speaks of 22 books "which are considered divine." It is true that we cannot decide which books he means, as he specifies only " 5 books of Moses, 13 of the prophets and 4 others." His testimony is, however, important, inasmuch as it proves that in his time the Jews recognized at least 22 books as sacred.

2. *Melito* (Μελίτων), Bishop of Sardes, made a journey to Palestine expressly to ascertain from the Jews there what sacred books they possessed. He wrote thence a letter to his brother Onesimus, which has been preserved (Euseb., *Hist. Eccl.*, IV, 26), and in it he enumerates the sacred books of the Jews. The only books contained in the present Jewish canon that he fails to mention are Nehemias and Esther.[1]

3. *Origen's* list corresponds with the present Jewish canon, but the 12 minor prophets are not mentioned, although it includes the two books of Machabees (Euseb., *Hist. Eccl.*, VI, 25).

4. The earliest official list of the books regarded by the Jews as inspired is contained in the Talmud, that was compiled at various times between the third and sixth centuries of our era. It mentions:

   I. *Thora*, i. e. law; the 5 books of Moses.

  II. *Nebiim*, i. e. prophets, viz.:

      (*a*) the early prophets; 6. Josue, 7. Judges, 8. Ruth, 9. two books of Samuel, 10. two books of Kings.

      (*b*) the later prophets; 11. Isaias, 12. Jeremias, 13. Lamentations, 14. Ezechiel, 15. the twelve minor prophets.

Sirach was familiar with all the protocanonical books with the exception, perhaps, of Daniel (*Lit. Rundschau*, 1900, No. 11).

[1] Nehemias was probably reckoned as part of Esdras, and Esther may not have been acknowledged because Melito displayed this book in its expanded Greek form.

III. *Kethubim*, i. e. hagiographa. 16. Psalms; 17. Proverbs; 18. Job; 19. Canticles; 20. Qohelet; 21. Esther; 22. Daniel; 23. Esdras and Nehemias; 24. Chronicles.

If Ruth is reckoned as part of Judges, and Lamentations as part of Jeremias, the list contains only 22 books. Saint Jerome (*prologus galeatus*) arranges the Jewish canon thus.[1] We cannot ascertain from any of these lists which books were regarded as sacred by our Saviour and the Apostles, and yet there is no doubt on the subject, as we shall proceed to show.

10. CONTINUATION. CONTENTS OF THE OLD TESTAMENT CANON, ACCORDING TO THE TEACHING OF THE CHURCH. JUSTIFICATION OF THIS TEACHING.

The Council of Trent (Sess. 4) drew up an official list of the sacred books of the Old Testament. It contains all those already mentioned, and in addition (1) Baruch, (2) Tobias, (3) Judith, (4) and (5) the first and second Books of Machabees, (6) Sirach or Ecclesiasticus, and (7) Wisdom, as well as extensions of Daniel and Esther. As these books do not occur in the canon recognized by the Jews, they have been known since the time of Sixtus of Siena as deuterocanonical, whilst the others are called protocanonical. (The Vatican Council, III, 2, simply renewed the decision of the Council of Trent.)

Had the Church any right to add to the Jewish canon, and to recognize 31 books in the Old Testament instead of 22?[2] The New Testament contains about 270 quotations from the Old, and these are mostly from the Septuagint,[3] so that in the time

---

[1] This is still the Canon of the Jews, except that in modern Hebrew Bibles Ruth and Lamentations are classed among the Kethubim, and with Canticles, Qohelet and Esther form the so-called five *Megilloth* or rolls. They are put together because they are read aloud in the synagogues on certain days, viz. Canticles at the Pasch, Ruth at Pentecost, Lamentations on the 9th of Ab (the day when the destruction of both the first and the second Temple is commemorated), Qohelet on the Feast of Tabernacles, and Esther on the Feast of Purim.

[2] If the single books are counted, there are 46, viz. 39 protocanonical and 7 deuterocanonical.

[3] Saint Matthew has a few quotations from the Hebrew, the other Evangelists practically none.

of our Lord the Hebrew Bible seems to have been less the standard version than the widely spread Greek text of the Old Testament. It was the Greek text that the Apostles used themselves and gave to the Christians, and this text contains the above-mentioned 31 sacred books.

The Jews nowadays pay no attention to this Greek text of the Septuagint, but they esteemed it very highly in the time of our Lord and the Apostles. Originating among the Jews, it was regularly read aloud in the Synagogues, as Justin Martyr (born about 100 A. D. at Sichem) testifies (*Dial. c. Tryph.*, 137). Like the Apostles, Josephus Flavius made use of it in his writings. Even in the third century Baruch was read in the synagogues, and in the Talmud Sirach or Ecclesiasticus is mentioned with the Law and the Prophets.[1] The Church accepted this text and all that it contained from the apostles, and could not give it up, as she retained the apostles' teaching.

That from the very beginning the Church has recognized also the deuterocanonical books of the Old Testament appears from the following evidence:

1. In the Catacombs, used in the time before Constantine the Great as places of assembly for the purpose of worship, there are many representations of scenes from the Old Testament, and among them some from the deuterocanonical books.

There are, for instance, pictures of the men in the fiery furnace, singing the praises of God; of Habakuk bringing Daniel food; of Tobias with the fish, and of his guide Raphael; there are scenes from Judith and Esther. There is, however, scarcely a single subject from the apocryphal books, not even from such as were used in public worship, as e. g. Hermas' "Pastor," and this is a proof that the distinction was clear between the canonical and the apocryphal books.

2. In the disputes between heretics and the faithful quotations from the deuterocanonical books were made and accepted on both sides. Thus, for instance, at the First Council of Nicæa (325), the Book of Judith was treated as canonical (*Hier. præf. in I Judith*).

---

[1] They were regarded by the Jews in Palestine as sacred, though not canonical, whereas the Hellenistic Jews considered them to be inspired and included them in their canon.

3. The earliest Fathers and ecclesiastical writers quote all our sacred books as being quite on a level. Thus Polycarp (*Ep. ad Phil.*, c. 10) quotes the book of Tobias; Hippolytus of Rome comments on the Book of Daniel, including the deutero-canonical portions; Saint Ambrose quotes passages from Sirach or Ecclesiasticus and Wisdom, and refers to these books as *scripturæ*. After the fourth century, however, a few of the ecclesiastical writers began to treat the deuterocanonical books as of inferior importance. This was done by Saint Athanasius and especially by Saint Jerome, who, in his *prologus galeatus,* tried to show that the books not contained in the Hebrew canon were of value only for edification, and could not be used in support of dogmas, and he pronounced them apocryphal. This view never won universal acceptation, and most people continued to abide by the old arrangement. There were some who followed the example of this great scholar until the Middle Ages; even Thomas Aquinas wavers to some extent, and this wavering on the part of individuals led the teaching authority in the Church to fix the canon. This was done by the Council of Trent.

4. That the decision at Trent was not suddenly thrust upon the Church, but was based on tradition, appears from earlier ecclesiastical decisions, which had not, however, been addressed to the universal Church. Exactly the same list of the Old Testament scriptures as the Tridentine was given by Pope Damasus in a decretal of the year 374,[1] by a synod held in Africa in 393, during the lifetime of Saint Augustine, and by Pope Innocent I in a letter to Bishop Exsuperius of Toulouse, in 405.

5. The Oriental sects, severed during the first few centuries from the unity of the Church, agree absolutely with the Church regarding the canon.

11. Origin of the Canon of the New Testament

The early Christians set upon the writings of the Apostles exactly the same value as upon their oral teaching; they recog-

---

[1] The authenticity of this decretal is challenged by Friedrich.

nized both alike as the word of God. But at a very early period some books appeared under pretense of apostolic origin, but not really authentic. Saint Luke (i. 1) speaks of *many* who had written an account of Christ. Precautions had to be taken with regard to these works, and the following principle was found to be a safe one:

As a rule the Apostles wrote only when particular local or personal conditions caused them to do so. Only a few of their works were from the outset intended for general use, such as the epistles to the Colossians and Galatians, and the first Epistle of Peter. In the churches where the apostolic writings had been composed (e. g. Saint Mark's Gospel in Rome), or to which they were addressed, and whither they had been brought by trustworthy messengers, it was the custom to read them at public worship. If then one or another Christian church expressed a desire to possess also some particular book of apostolic authorship, a copy was made and dispatched. No work was accepted as apostolic unless it had the evidence for its authenticity of the Church where it had been written, or to which it was addressed. If no such evidence were forthcoming, the book was not considered authentic, even though it professed to be written by an Apostle.[1]

12. Contents of the New Testament Canon

It is plain from what has been said that not every Christian congregation can originally have possessed every book written by the Apostles. The multiplication and diffusion of the apostolic writings was hindered by well-grounded suspicions of their authenticity, by the poverty of the majority of Christianity, by the difficulties of traveling and of transport, as well as by the danger of persecution. The collections of books must have varied at first, and must have remained so for a longer or shorter time, according to circumstances. After the third century still greater caution was shown on account of heretics, and the Christians, remembering the Apostle's warning in II Thessa-

[1] Iren., *Adv. hær.*, III, iv. 1; Tertull., *Adv. Marcion*, IV, 5; Kaulen, I, 31, etc.

lonians, ii. 14, as a rule were unwilling to depart from the tradition that had come down to them.

Some of the apostolic writings were, however, comparatively soon collected and circulated almost everywhere, so that, as far as we know, there was never any doubt as to their authenticity. These were the 4 Gospels, Acts, 13 Epistles of Saint Paul, the first Epistle of Saint Peter and the first of Saint John. The Apostolic Fathers Papias and Saint Ignatius the Martyr are witnesses to the existence of a collection which probably comprised these books. For Papias speaks expressly of the Gospels (see the Special Introduction), and Ignatius refers to the " Gospel and the Apostles " in exactly the same way as to the Law and the Prophets of the Old Covenant (*Ep. ad Philad.*, c. 5 and 9).

The seven remaining books of the New Testament were known in some congregations from the beginning, but only later found general acceptation. These are the Epistle to the Hebrews, the second Epistle of Peter, the second and third of John, the epistles of James and Jude and, finally, the Apocalypse. (These books may be termed deuterocanonical, on the analogy of the Old Testament.)

In his edition of the Apostolic Fathers, Funk has counted 68 allusions to the New Testament in the Epistle of Barnabas, 158 in the first epistle written by Clement of Rome to the Corinthians, 79 in the second epistle, 53 in the letters of Ignatius, 68 in those of Polycarp, and 29 in the epistle to Diognetus.

Cornely (*Comp.*, 39) points out that Saint Matthew's Gospel was known to all the Apostolic Fathers; Saint Mark's at least to Papias; Saint Luke's at least to Clement of Rome, Polycarp and the heretic Basilides; Saint John's to Ignatius, to the author of the Epistle to Diognetus and to Basilides; Acts to Clement of Rome, Ignatius and Polycarp; Saint Paul's Epistles to different churches were known to almost all the Apostolic Fathers, and the Pastoral Epistles also to Clement of Rome, Ignatius and Polycarp; the first of Saint Peter to Papias and Polycarp; the first of Saint John and the Apocalypse at least to Papias and Polycarp; the second of Saint Peter probably to Clement of Rome and Polycarp, Saint James to Clement of Rome. We ought, however, to remember that the writings of the Apostolic Fathers are few in number, and were not intended for all Christians nor addressed to all; it is therefore surprising that only four short epistles are not mentioned by them, viz. Philemon, second and third of Saint John, and Saint Jude. Thus during the first of the second century the greater and more important books of the New Testament were already well known.

13. The New Testament Canon of the Earliest Churches

If we ask the chief churches of early Christianity, those that were the parents of others, what was their oldest canon of the New Testament, we shall obtain the following information:

1. From the Roman church we have a very ancient list of the books of the New Testament, contained in the so-called *Fragmentum Muratorii*,[1] dating from the second century.[2] It contains all our books of the New Testament, except four epistles (Hebrews, James, first and second of Peter). The earliest Latin translation (*Itala*), which was compiled at least in part as early as the first century, contains all our New Testament books.[3]

2. In the church of Antioch, the Syrian translation, known as Peshitto, dating from the second century, was in general use. This contained all the books of the New Testament with the exception of five (second of Peter, second and third of John, Jude, and the Apocalypse).

It is true that Ephrem the Syrian, writing soon after 300 A. D., quotes the latter books, but they probably did not form part of the original Peshitto, but were added later. The translation of them is certainly of later date than that of the rest of the book. Instead of the Gospels, Tatian's *Diatessaron* was read in Edessa (see p. 210).

3. With regard to Palestine, no catalogue of the New Testament books exists older than that made by Saint Cyril of Jerusalem in the middle of the fourth century. It contains all the books as we have them, with the exception of the Apocalypse.

4. From the church of Alexandria we have the testimony of Clement of Alexandria (150–217), of whom Eusebius tells us

---

[1] For a fuller account see Cornely, *Comp.*, 621; *Introd.*, i. 167.

[2] Zahn fixes 210 as its date. The writer however says that Hermas wrote his "Pastor," "*nuperrime temporibus nostris*," whilst his brother Pius was pope. This can be no one but Pius I (142–157); hence the "Pastor" belongs to the second century, and the "Fragment" is of the same period. It is so called because its beginning and end are missing. M. Schanz believes it to be a translation from a Greek original.

[3] Of course it is impossible that it should from the very beginning have contained *all* the books of the New Testament, as the *Can. Mur.* shows.

(*Hist. Eccl.*, VI, 14) that he made a summary of all the sacred
books, including those of doubtful authenticity. In the writings
that have come down to us he mentions all the apostolic writings except the second Epistle of Saint Peter, and the second and
third of Saint John. He must, however, have known the latter
epistles, as he speaks of the first Epistle as " the greater." His
pupil Origen (185–254) gives (*Hom.* 7, *in Josue*) a list of all
our books of the New Testament; and Saint Athanasius, who
lived somewhat later, is in complete agreement with it.

The Coptic translations, which are of very early origin, dating
probably from the second century, contain likewise all our
canonical books (see Kaulen, I, 40).

5. The practice of the West African church can be learnt
from a list contained in an African manuscript dating from a
period before Saint Augustine, which Mommsen has edited.
Three Epistles, viz., Hebrews, James and Jude, are missing in
this list. From Africa we have also the list given in the *Codex
Claramontanus* (*cf.* p. 231), in which three of Saint Paul's
Epistles are not mentioned (Phil. and first and second Thess.).

The *Codex Claramontanus* belongs to the sixth century, but the list
of the sacred books is copied from an earlier original, dating from the
third or fourth century.

6. The fullest account of the books of the New Testament
is given by the ecclesiastical writer Eusebius. In his " Church
History " (iii. 26) he gives the names of all the books which in his
time were regarded as being of apostolic origin, and he classifies
them thus: (*a*) those universally acknowledged as genuine
(ὁμολογούμενα), (*b*) those decidedly not genuine or of heretical
origin (παντελῶς νόθα), and (*c*) those whose authenticity is
contested.

Under the heading (*a*) he places the four Gospels, the Acts,
14 Epistles of Saint Paul, first of Saint Peter and first of Saint
John, and (though with some hesitation) the Apoclypse. Under
(*b*) the Shepherd of Hermas, the Apocalypse of Saint Peter,
etc., and under (*c*) the Epistle of Saint James, that of Saint
Jude, the second Epistle of Saint Peter, and the second and
third of Saint John.

14. ECCLESIASTICAL DECISIONS REGARDING THE CANON OF THE NEW TESTAMENT

The African Synods already mentioned (p. 202) and still earlier Pope Damasus (374) and afterwards Pope Innocent I, declared all the 27 books, that now form the canon, to be of apostolic origin. As, however, these decisions were not addressed to the universal church, some doubt was still possible; especially as the apostolicity of the Apocalypse was questioned in many quarters, at least in the East. It was not until the Council of Trent (*s. 4 de can.*) that the 27 books of the New Testament "with all their parts, as they are contained in the old Latin Vulgate," were expressly declared canonical for the whole Church.

Supplementary Note. The historical result of investigations regarding the canon of the New Testament is: (1) The apostolic origin of the four Gospels, Acts, thirteen epistles of Saint Paul, the first Epistle of Saint Peter and the first of Saint John has never been doubted. (2) The other books of the New Testament have always been generally considered apostolic, but individuals have doubted their authenticity. (3) From the fourth century onwards all the books of the New Testament, as we now have them in the canon, have been accepted in all parts of the Church. (4) The previous hesitation on the part of some churches to accept certain books of the New Testament proceeded from reasonable prudence, especially with regard to Heretics.

APPENDIX. PROTESTANT OPINIONS CONCERNING THE CANON

These opinions conflict with those of Christians in ancient times. The Reformers began by adhering closely to the canon, but as it was one of their principles that in matters of religion private judgment is the chief authority, differences were inevitable on this point as on others. Karlstadt drew attention to Saint Jerome's view of the deuterocanonical books in the Old Testament, and soon many people declared these books to be apocryphal. Modern Protestants, as far as they still believe in inspiration, adhere to this opinion. With reference to the New Testament, Luther stated that every man could think what he liked about the Apocalypse, and believe what his own intellect suggested. He also spoke against the Epistle to the Hebrews, that of Saint Jude, and particularly that of Saint James, but he did not absolutely reject them. Later Lutherans recognized only the ὁμολογούμενα, and declared the seven others to be apocryphal, although many at the present day have come back to the old opinion. Rationalistic Protestants in quite modern times refuse to acknowledge any inspiration, and then of course the canon plays no part.[1]

Many refuse altogether to accept the dogmatic conception of an Old and a New Testament, but abandon it as a " measure taken from the tool-chest of the Catholic Church," and regard the books hitherto called canonical with many others " extra-canonical " merely as sources of information for the history of religion in general.

15. APOCRYPHAL BOOKS

1. Before the time of Christ, and still more frequently afterwards, books were written which many people believed to be inspired, but which the Church never included in the canon. These are called apocryphal.

The name is borrowed from the religious books of the heathen, which were carefully kept secret (ἀπόκρυφος = concealed). The Christians seem to have regarded all books falsely claiming to be inspired with the same sort of horror as the secret religious writings of the heathen. The word implies, therefore, that these books ought not to be used, but set apart and not read in the churches.[2]

2. Among the *Apocryphal Writings of the Old Testament* we must mention particularly: (*a*) The Book of Henoch, written by Jews in the second century before Christ.[3] (*b*) The Psalms of

---

[1] Three schools of thought regarding inspiration are now distinguished among Protestants: Liberal, Strict (who, like the older Protestant dogmatic writers, believe in verbal inspiration) and those midway between them. Hitherto no one has succeeded in steering a middle course satisfactorily.

[2] Collections of Apocrypha: Fabricius, *Codex pseud-epigraphus, V. T.; idem, Codex apocryphus, N. T.*, Hamburg, 1703–1723; Thilo, *Codex apocryphus, N. T.*, Lips., 1832; Tischendorf, *Evangelia apocrypha*, Lips., Ed. 2, 1876; *Acta apost. apocr.*, Lips. 1851; *Apocalypses apocr.*, Lips., 1866; Hilgenfeld, *Novum Test. extra canonem receptum*, Lips., 1866.

[3] The complete text exists only in Ethiopian, edited by Dillmann in 1853. An imperfect Greek text was found at Akhmim in Upper Egypt.

Solomon, a collection of 18 psalms, that have been preserved in Greek but were composed in Hebrew by pious Jews in the second century before Christ. (*c*) The third and fourth books of Esdras; the third was written before Christ, but the fourth about 100 A. D. (*d*) The Prayer of King Manasses, date unknown. The two last mentioned books, (*c*) and (*d*), were formerly often regarded as canonical, and so are appended to official editions of the Vulgate.

3. *The Apocryphal Books of the New Testament* are very numerous. They fall into two classes: (*a*) those written in support of heresies, (*b*) harmless legends and similar works.

(*a*) To the apocryphal books of the first kind belong:

(1) The Gospel according to the Hebrews, used by the Nazarenes and Ebionites, two sects of Christian Jews. The common opinion of antiquity was that this book was the Hebrew original of Saint Matthew's Gospel but had suffered many alterations. This view was not shared by the sects mentioned, nor by many modern critics.[1] (2) The Gospel and Apocalypse of Peter, and works with Docetic tendencies, written probably in Syria, in the second century. A fragment of the Gospel was discovered in 1892 by Bouriant (*cf.* Zahm, *Das Petrusevangelium,* Erl. and Lpz., 1893). (3) The Gospel of Marcion, a mutilated version of Saint Luke, dating from the time of the second century. The Gospel of Basilides seems to have been a similar work.[2]

(*b*) Among the legends and similar works, which are very numerous, we may mention:

(1) The Protoevangelium of James, brother of the Lord. The greater part of this book is concerned with Mary, the Mother of Christ, and the Wise Men from the East. The story is told in a simple and dignified manner, and it must be very ancient, as Origen was acquainted with it. Many believe the con-

---

[1] Kaulen regards it as a re-written version of the Gospel of Saint Matthew, compiled not later than 100 A. D. Handmann, however, thinks it is of independent origin, though related to Saint Matthew's Gospel. He believes that it was written in Aramaic, translated into Greek very soon afterwards, probably in Alexandria, and kept on strictly Jewish Christian lines.

[2] This is mentioned by Origen, *Hom. in Luc.*, I, 1.

tents of this book to be perfectly true. (2) The Gospel of Nicodemus, extant both in Greek and Latin, a very dignified account of Christ's Passion, was highly esteemed and widely known in the Middle Ages. (3) The *Acta Pilati,* a collection of written documents and reports concerning our Lord's Passion. (4) The letter written by King Abgar of Osroene to Christ and His reply to it. This correspondence cannot be regarded as genuine, for the first Christian King of that district was Abgar VIII, who only ascended the throne in 176 A. D. (5) The *Didache,* i. e. teaching of the Twelve Apostles, written in Syria or Palestine, and discovered in Constantinople in 1884. It is quoted by many of the Fathers, and was often used in ancient times for the instruction of catechumens, but as it does not possess any apostolic credentials, Eusebius (*Hist. Eccl.,* III, 52) classes it among the ἀντιλεγόμενα. It is important on account of its high antiquity, for it probably dates from the first century. It contains 16 chapters in Greek. (6) The Sayings of Jesus, very recently discovered, and belonging probably to the third century. At first it was suggested that these were a part of the λόγια κυρίου, which, according to Papias, formed the groundwork of the Gospel of Saint Matthew (see chapters on Matthew) ; but this view is not tenable. We have only six or eight short utterances, which bear more resemblance to Saint John than to Saint Matthew ; one, for instance, is " I appeared to them in the flesh." The origin of these words is quite unknown (see *Katholik,* 1898, I and II). (7) Tatian's *Diatessaron.* Tatian was a disciple of Saint Justin Martyr ; as the name of his book implies, it is a harmony of all the Gospels ; it was written in Syrian about 170 A. D., and until 400 was used in the churches in Syria, but was then removed and destroyed, because the separate gospels were ordered to be read ; hence not a single Syrian or Greek copy of this work has come down to us.[1]

---

[1] This work, which Ephrem the Syrian still used instead of the separate Gospels, was, as the name implies, translated into Greek, and later into Latin, in 545, by Victor, Bishop of Capua. From the Latin version an old German translation was made in the ninth century, which is one of the earliest existing books in the German language. The Augustinian Ciasca discovered an Arabic text of the *Diatessaron* in Rome ; it was published in 1888 with a Latin translation. The book called "Our

Lord's Testament," discovered and published by Rahmani in 1899, was originally written in Greek, and versions of it are extant in the Syrian, Arabic and Ethiopian languages. It must not be classed with the apocryphal books, but was compiled about 475 from the Egyptian service book, and this again from the 8th Book of the Apostolic Constitutions.

SECOND PART

GENERAL INTRODUCTION — THE BIBLE AS A WHOLE

16. TRANSITION

JUST as the Bible has not one, but many authors, so all its parts were not written in the same language, and the sacred books have not in every case been handed down in the language in which they were composed but often in translations. Thus for centuries the Old Testament was known to the Greeks and Romans only in Greek, but later also in Latin. Accordingly, when we consider the Bible as a whole, we have to consider (1) the original text, (2) the translations of Holy Scripture.

FIRST SECTION

THE ORIGINAL TEXT OF HOLY SCRIPTURE

17. BIBLICAL LANGUAGES IN GENERAL

Holy Scripture was written partly in Hebrew, partly in Chaldee, and partly in Greek; but we do not possess all the books written first in Hebrew and Chaldee in their original language. The greater part of the Old Testament was both composed and preserved in Hebrew. Only some portions of the Book of Esdras (iv. 7–v. 18; xxii.–xxvi.) and about half of the Book of Daniel (ii.–vii.) are Chaldee.

The Books of Judith, Tobias, Baruch, Ecclesiasticus or Sirach, I Machabees and parts of Daniel (iii. 24–90; xiii. and xiv.) and Esther (x.–xvi.) were written in either Hebrew or Chaldee, but were lost in their original form, and have been preserved only in translations, of which the Greek Septuagint is the oldest. The Book of Wisdom, second Machabees and the whole of the

New Testament were written in Greek, and have come down
to us in that language; only the first Gospel was originally composed in Hebrew or Chaldee.

18. HEBREW

I. Hebrew is one of a large group of languages spoken in
Western Asia, and called generally the Semitic languages. They
are divided into four chief branches:

1. *Arabic,* used in the south of the Semitic speaking region.
Closely allied to it is Ethiopian, which, like our languages, is
written and read from left to right, whilst most of the Semitic
languages are written from right to left.

Ethiopian, too, was written from right to left, but the Ethiopians
adopted the opposite direction in imitation of the Greeks (Dillmann,
Aethiop. Grammatik, 1899).

2. *Aramaic* is spoken in the north of the region of the
Semitic languages. It is divided into *Eastern Aramaic,* or *Syriac,*
that appears chiefly in Christian literature, but also, though in
a different form, in the Babylonian Talmud, and *Western Aramaic,* that occurs especially in later Jewish literature (the
Targumim, Palestine Talmud). The *Samaritan* belongs to
the same class. Western Aramaic has from ancient times been
called Chaldee.

3. The *Babylonian-Assyrian* language of the far East appears
from the cuneiform inscriptions, that have now mostly been
deciphered, to have been a Semitic language, akin to Hebrew.[1]

4. From the point of view both of geography and of language,
Hebrew stands midway between Arabic and Aramaic; and
Phœnician or Punic is closely allied with it.

[1] In the *Keilinschriftliche Bibliothek,* Berlin, 1889, etc., Schrader
has brought out six volumes containing most valuable information regarding the history of Babylonia and Assyria, which is so closely connected with the Oold Testament. "At a time when all the resources of
scholarship are marshaled to throw discredit upon the historical character of the Old Testament, divine Providence has confirmed its accuracy
by means of documents which lay forgotten for thousands of years under-
ground, but were only concealed, being indestructible." Thus Kaulen, in
the *Lit. Handweiser.*

With the exception of Arabic, all these languages are at the present time quite or very nearly (Syriac) extinct. Arabic has a script of its own, like Ethiopian and Syriac; Samaritan still uses the old Semitic or Phœnician alphabet, with which the sacred books were originally written. Babylonian-Assyrian has cuneiform characters; Chaldee had at one time, like Hebrew, the old Semitic or Phœnician alphabet, but after the Captivity the "Square-script" was used in writing both languages, being simpler than the old Semitic. It is also called the Assyrian script, and this name refers to its origin in the lands near the Euphrates, not specially in Assyria. The various Semitic languages are as closely connected with one another as are the Romance or the Teutonic languages. There are great resemblances between them both in vocabulary and grammar.

With regard to the importance of the study of these languages see the words of Pope Leo XIII, p. 173.

II. Even in the oldest books, Hebrew appears as a fully developed language, and it retained this character for about a thousand years.[1] With the Babylonian Captivity (about 600 B.C.) the language began to fall into decay, and gradually ceased to be used by the people, giving place to the Chaldee, that they had learnt in exile.

19. CHALDEE

One of the Semitic languages is known by this name because it originally developed in the land of the Chaldæans, i. e. in ancient Babylonia. The Jews used it during and after the Babylonian Captivity, for at the time that they were taken into exile it was the ordinary means of communication between all the Semitic nations, and it remained so even under the Persian supremacy (Esdr. iv.–vii.), and was not much affected by the introduction of Greek under Alexander the Great. According to Nehemias viii. 9, it was necessary to translate the book of the Law, when it was read aloud to the people; hence Hebrew was no longer understood. The small portions of the Bible which are written in Chaldee (= Aramaic, Dan. ii. 4,

---

[1] We know nothing as to the earliest forms of Hebrew, for nothing older than the Pentateuch has come down to us. However, this book with its archaisms is undoubtedly very old (see p. 270), though, as it has frequently been re-written, many of its oldest forms of speech may have been lost. We can recognize three periods in the language, — that of the time of Moses, that of David and Solomon, and that of the Captivity.

אֲרָמִית) form the oldest extant memorials of this language. As in them it displays considerable perfection, it must have been in process of development for a long previous period, of which no records remain. Many of later date still survive, especially from the time of Christ until 500 A. D. To this period belong the *Targumim*, i. e. translations or paraphrases of the Hebrew Bible, which were required for use in the synagogues, and the chief part of the Talmud. At the time of Christ Chaldee was the language usually spoken, and our Saviour Himself used it, as appears from several expressions occurring in the Gospels (e. g. *Talitha qumi, Kepha, abba*).[1]

In the New Testament Chaldee is called Hebrew. John xix. 20, Acts xxii. 2.

20. GREEK

The Greek that we have in the Bible is not the classical Greek, but a dialect that developed after the time of Alexander the Great in the countries that he had conquered, and chiefly in Northern Egypt. It is often called " Macedonian-Alexandrian "[2] or κοινὴ διάλεκτος. The Jews in Egypt translated their sacred books from the original Hebrew or Chaldee into this dialect, and some sacred books were written in it. The whole of the New Testament is in Greek of this kind, because the various writers, though not living in Egypt, adopted the language of the Septuagint, which was known all over the world and used also in Palestine. Biblical Greek has two chief peculiarities: it contains a good deal of Semitic coloring, and in the New Testament many Latinisms. If the Greek books in the Bible are compared with others of the same date, written in the Alexandrine dialect, they all show the same idiom. Language, therefore, is a testimony to the authenticity of the sacred books and the purity of their text. They may be compared with many

---

[1] Sometimes our Lord seems to have spoken Greek, especially with Greeks who wished to make His acquaintance (John xii.). The Apostles, too, understood Greek, though imperfectly. Many people belonging to the western nations were living then in Palestine.

[2] Thumb thinks that the name " Macedonian-Alexandrian " ought to be given up, for the κοινή διάλεκτος became the universal language of the Greek world, after the old dialects had disappeared.

apocryphal writings and papyrus rolls written in Greek that have been discovered in Egypt.

21. ORIGINAL FORM OF THE TEXT OF THE HEBREW AND CHALDEE BOOKS OF THE BIBLE

Hebrew and Chaldee are both written in the "square" script, but the square form of the letters was not the original one, and the earliest sacred writers used the old Semitic alphabet, which is generally called Phœnician, although it was not peculiar to the Phœnicians, but was common to all Semitic nations. We know this older kind of writing from inscriptions and coins belonging to the Assyrians, Babylonians, Moabites and other nations, and also to the Jews. It gradually assumed two forms, as in the west the old script was retained, and in the east a simpler script was adopted.

1. The Jews used the Phœnician alphabet until the time of the Babylonian Captivity, after which they used the new script, which is called the Assyrian, or, from the shape of the letters, the square ☐ script. The sacred books were in course of time re-written from the older script into the ☐ script; this was done perhaps partly during the Captivity.

2. Jewish tradition asserts most positively that Esdras collected and arranged all the extant sacred books, and that he introduced in place of the old Hebrew or Phœnician script the Assyrian or square writing, in the sacred books of course. If this be so, that priest who is repeatedly described in the first and second Book of Esdras (e. g. I Esdr. vii. 6, 11, 12) as "the scribe instructed in the words and commandments of the Lord," must have been engaged, of course with others, in rewriting the sacred books.

In the oldest script the words were not divided, but the text ran on without interruption. Vowel points were unknown in manuscripts until at least the fifth century after our Lord. Therefore, according to our ideas, the earlier text was very defective, and it was only by means of tradition that the reading and understanding of the sacred books could be continued in the Jewish schools. Such schools existed at the time of Christ chiefly in Jerusalem and Alexandria; later on there were schools at Tiberias, on the Lake of Genesareth, and in distant Babylon.

The Phœnician script may be regarded as a variety of the Egyptian hieratic writing, and it is possible that Moses undertook this task of re-writing. As the art of writing was known in the time of the Patriarchs, long before Moses, the Semitic alphabet may have originated in Babylonia. The very plausible theory has been suggested that in the East, at a very early period, a kind of square script was common as well as the cuneiform writing, whilst in the West the so-called Phœnician, originating in Egypt, came into use. It is well known that the Phœnician alphabet was carried to the Greeks, and through them to all western countries.

Kaulen assumes that the Septuagint possessed the sacred books in the Phœnician script. This appears, for instance, from Genesis xlvi. 16, where the Septuagint have Θασαβάν for Esban (אצבן), because they read the Phœnician *Tav* instead of *Aleph*, whereas it would not have been possible to confuse ת with א. Haneberg, however, and Reuss, as also the Talmud, Origen and Saint Jerome, adhere to the traditional opinion, that the square script came into use at the time of Esdras and was used by the Septuagint.[1] That the rewriting into square characters had been completed long before the time of Christ is plain from Matthew v. 18.

The Synedrium removed to Tiberias after the destruction of Jerusalem, and at the same time many Jews migrated to Babylon, as they found many of their own nation there, who had remained after the Captivity.

22. Later Forms of the Hebrew and Chaldee Text

1. In the earlier text only the consonants were written, but in course of time, in order to facilitate reading, marks were introduced to denote vowels. To alter the sacred text as little as possible, these marks were only little dots or lines, placed, as a rule, below the consonants. The practice of using these vowel points originated in the Rabbinical school at Tiberias, and became general in the eighth century.[2] A text provided with marks for the vowels is called "pointed," and the earlier mode of writing is "unpointed." It is certain that in all

---

[1] F. Perles shows, from many mistakes in the text, that the square script was in use at least as early as the third century before Christ. Neubauer, in "The Introduction of Square Characters in Biblical Manuscripts," is of the same opinion.

[2] Saint Jerome complains of the ambiguity of the Hebrew text, so he cannot have known any way of marking the vowels. The Talmud often uses expressions showing that only consonants were written when it was compiled. It was completed in the sixth century.

essentials this vowel pointing renders the meaning of the Bible text correctly, as the Rabbis, to whom we owe it, were guided by uninterrupted tradition.[1] The Hebrew text, however, cannot claim to be so perfectly and absolutely correct as to constrain us, where there are various readings, to disregard all the old translations (Septuagint, Vulgate and Peshitto) and adhere solely to the Hebrew Bible. The Greek, Latin and Syriac texts are actually older than the pointed Hebrew. It is incredible that the text of a dead language, written without vowels, should for centuries invariably have been read correctly even in the smallest details. At the present time it is perhaps generally admitted that the Hebrew text has been corrupted in consequence of similar letters being confused[2] and words wrongly divided. Proper names especially often seem to be corrupt. Thus the name " Nebukadnezar," as it often stands in the Hebrew text, is less like the form " Nabukudurusur " of the cuneiform inscriptions, than is the Septuagint " Nabuchodonosor," which the translators adopted from an earlier tradition. We cannot therefore agree with the Jews and the early Protestants, who generally prefer this text to any translation, nor can we follow Saint Jerome in speaking of an exclusively *hebraica veritas*.

The vowel points may be left out and the passage read in a way differing from the traditional mode of the Jews; and the early translators have in many cases adopted other readings. We must not, however, lay too much stress upon this, as Jewish tradition supports the vowels now in use.

2. The division of the text of the Hebrew Bible into chapters and verses is not original, but comparatively recent. The division into chapters is not older than the fifteenth century. In

[1] There was another less satisfactory method of pointing which came from Babylon. In it the points are generally above the consonants. Both systems are based on the usage of the Syrians, who, about the time of Mahomet, began to add points or dots to their consonantal writing, and later adopted the Greek vowels. (The so-called accents in the Hebrew text were primarily intended as aids to the readers in the synagogues; for us they serve chiefly as marks of punctuation.

[2] In the Phœnician script, Aleph and Tav, Beth and Resch, Jod and Zade resemble one another very closely, and in the square characters He and Cheth, Daleth and Resch, Vav and Nun *finale* are much alike.

the thirteenth century, about 1206, Stephen Langton, who was
Archbishop of Canterbury and died in 1228, began to divide
the Vulgate into chapters, and he was followed by Cardinal
Hugo a Santo Caro, who died in 1262. From the Vulgate the
practice was applied also to the Hebrew Bible, in the fifteenth
century. Cardinal Hugo divided each single chapter into seven
sections, which he lettered a, b, c, d, e, f, g, in order to make
it easier to find any required passage. This method of using
letters of the alphabet is still employed in the missal and breviary.
A number was prefixed to each verse first by Robert Stephanus
(Etienne), a printer in Paris, who in 1551 brought out an
edition of the Bible in Greek and Latin. This arrangement
was soon universally adopted, and the verses were numbered
then also in the Hebrew text.

3. Long before this time, though within the Christian era,
the Israelites had divided the books of the Bible into sections,
which, in the case of the Pentateuch, were called *Parashioth*.
These divisions were made for convenience in reading the Law
in the synagogue; one *parashe* was read on every Sabbath.

The other sacred books are also divided into sections, called
Haphtaroth, serving a similar purpose. There are 85 of them,
for the Haphtaroth do not include the whole text, but only
part of it. They stand in the same relation to the Parashioth
as our epistles to the gospels. There is besides these a division
into *sedarim*, i. e. classes, rows, which is carried through the
whole Hebrew canon. It was made by Jewish scholars to aid
them in making grammatical and critical comments on the
sacred text.

Parash (פָּרָשָׁה, from *parash*, to divide, separate) means a section.
The signification of *Haphtarah* seems to be the same, as it comes from
patar (פָּטַר, to split, divide).[1]

The Pentateuch is divided into fifty-four *Parashioth*, which are called
open or closed, according as they commence at the beginning of a line or
in the middle of it. In Hebrew Bibles we often find marks פ פ פ or ס ס ס
to denote *parascha petucha* = open parash, or *parascha sethuma* = closed
parash, respectively.

---

[1] Theile, *Biblia heb.*, § 1232, says, however, that *haphtarah* means dis-
missal, because it was read at the conclusion of divine worship. Hence
the reader is called *Haphtarah maphtir* = the one who dismisses.

Smaller sections are also marked with פ or ס. Every copy of the Bible was most exact, agreeing with the model even in the number of lines and the shape of the letters.

23. THE MASORA [1]

This name is given to an ancient collection of grammatical and critical remarks on the Hebrew text of the Bible. They were originally handed down orally from generation to generation in the Jewish schools, but as in time the original came to belong to a remote historical past, and it grew increasingly difficult to understand it, the danger of corruption in the text increased also, and consequently these notes were written down. Most of them contain instructions for reading the sacred text, hence the Masora is defined as the record, committed to writing, of the traditional rabbinical teaching as to the form and reading of the Hebrew books of the Bible.

The scholars, who gave rise to the Masora, are called Masoretes, and the text corresponding with their rules is known as the Masoretic.

Of particular importance are the Masoretic notes, which come under the Chaldee heading *qĕri* (= *qĕrê* = " read " or " should read ") and contain corrections of the text. They were always written on the margin of the copies of the Bible, when, in the opinion of the Masoretes, something had come down to them in an inaccurate form. The wrong word in the text is called *kethib* (= written). However, a *qĕri* is not always a real emendation of the text, for not unfrequently the *kĕthib* shows the correct reading. Of minor importance, though not without value, are the often trivial observations on the text of the Bible which occur in the Masora. It notes the number of verses in each book, and states which is the middle word or sentence in it.

For instance a note of this kind on Genesis is: " The number of verses in the book Bereschith is 1534, and the middle of it is: ' Thou shalt live by the sword ' (Gen. xxvii. 40), and the number of its Parashioth is 12." On Jeremias the note states that the book contains 1365 verses, and

---

[1] מָסוֹרָה or מָסוּרָה, *masora* or *massora* = tradition, from the Chaldee מְסַר, to hand down.

the words "And Ananias spoke" occur in the middle of it. Other remarks of this kind are: "In the Pentateuch there are two verses that begin with *Samech,* and eleven verses in which the first and the last letter is *Nun.* . . . There are eight verses in the book in which the word *chattaa* [sin] is construed with *asa* [to do]," etc. The Masora actually states how often each letter of the alphabet occurs in the Bible, — for instance, that *Gimel* occurs 29,537 times.

These remarks so fenced in the sacred text that afterwards it could not be altered, but their comparatively late origin diminishes the value of the notes in the Masora; none of them are earlier than the Christian era. Even if, since the Masora has existed, the Hebrew text in the hands of the Jews has undergone practically no alteration, yet we cannot say for certain that at an earlier period, either soon after our Lord's life or even before it, some error may not have slipped in here and there, which has been perpetuated forever by the Masora. That such errors exist appears frequently from comparison with the Septuagint, as well as from parallel passages in the Hebrew text itself.

For instance, in Psalm cxlv., which is alphabetical, the verse beginning with ‫נ‬ is wanting in the Hebrew, though it exists in the Septuagint, Peshitto and Vulgate: πιστός (נֶאֱמָן) κύριος κτλ.

Joachin (Jechonias) when he ascended the throne was eight years old according to II Chronicles xxxvi. 9, while his age is given correctly as eighteen in IV Kings xxvi. 8. *Cf.* Kaulen I, 77, Cornill, 293, etc.

Antiquity of the Masora. We have no trustworthy testimony from ancient times as to the origin of the Masora. Jewish scholars have asserted Moses himself to have been the author of the Masora, whilst Esdras subsequently added to it. The earlier Christian scholars believed that Esdras, and afterwards the Synedrium, had most to do with writing the Masora. At the present time the universal opinion is that it was the work of Jewish Rabbis, written between the fifth and ninth centuries.

As all the notes in the Masora are not of equal importance, extracts have been made for the convenience of readers, and thus the great and the little Masora came into being.

The Masoretic remarks, only a small part of the whole, occurring in the Hebrew editions of the Bible, are not pointed. As a key to their interpretation we have the *Clavis Masoretica* in Theile's editions of the Hebrew Bible, Leipzig. The whole Masora is printed in Bomberg's Bible (Venice, 1518, and in Buxtorf's (Bâle, 168). The most recent but incomplete edition of the Great Masora was brought out by Frensdorff, Hanover, 1867. The whole mass of Masoretic notes was collected by Ginsburg, 4 vols., London, 1880–1885.

24. Hebrew Manuscripts and Printed Editions

As the Masoretic text is not absolutely correct, it has been necessary to seek means for its emendation. These seemed to be the manuscripts dating from centuries antecedent to the invention of printing, and preserved here and there, especially in synagogues. Many of them have been collected and examined. The scholars who deserve particular recognition for their labors are the following:

1. *Norzi,* an Israelite living at Mantua in the seventeenth century, collected a large number of manuscripts of the Bible and the Masora, and used them in preparing an edition of the Bible that was printed in 1742, in Mantua.

2. *Benjamin Kennicott,* an Englishman, collated over 600 of the oldest and best Hebrew manuscripts and about 40 of the earliest printed Bibles, for the purpose of bringing out a critical text-edition. This appeared in Oxford, 1776 and 1780, in two folio volumes. Notice was taken in it only of the consonants.

3. *Bernardo de Rossi,* an Italian, acquired possession of about 700 ancient Hebrew manuscripts; and in addition he collated many others, in order to construct a text of the greatest possible accuracy. He paid attention also to the pointing. The result of his investigations was published in his work, *Variæ lectiones Vet. Test.*, Parmæ, 1784–88.

All these workers did not, however, attain the end that they desired. They had hoped by examining and comparing so many old manuscripts to be able to form a text differing considerably from the traditional Jewish version. They expected to find one in complete agreement with the Septuagint, from which the Masoretic text frequently varies, although not in the matter of dogmatic importance. These hopes were not fulfilled; not indeed because the Masoretic text is perfectly correct, but because all the manuscripts hitherto discovered only reproduce the Masoretic text, as it was fixed in the early part of the Christian era, in accordance with older manuscripts.

That at this time very particular attention was paid to the Hebrew text, probably because of the strife with Christianity, appears from the Talmud, which was compiled in the fourth, fifth and sixth centuries. It contains precise rules, like those in the Masora, for preventing all corruption of the text of the Bible. As to the date when the present Hebrew text was definitely fixed, the following may be said: The Septuagint and the Samaritan Pentateuch are based upon older versions, since they frequently differ from the Masoretic text. Onkelos and Jonathan (in the time of Christ) differ considerably from it; but on the other hand Aquilas, Theodotion and Symmachus (in the second century) show great resemblance to the Masoretic text, as do the later Targumin. Saint Jerome used a text that was almost identical with our own. We may assume, therefore, that the Jews fixed their text soon after the time of the Apostles. Stade says that this was certainly not done until after the year 70, and then the work was performed in a very slipshod manner, as, instead of collating several texts, the compilers simply put together a copy of the Bible from the manuscripts that they happened to have at hand, and this manuscript thenceforth was the one copied and regarded as containing the settled text. Hence the unequal characters of the various books. Cornill thinks that the Jews fixed their text about the year 90, in Jabne (Jamnia), where there was a famous school, and it was decided at that time which books should be recognized by the Jews, and the Greek books were rejected. Stade and Cornill base their arguments upon Lagarde, who tried to prove that all the Hebrew manuscripts, hitherto discovered, can be traced back to a single original, which was so absolutely regarded as the standard that every mistake and every accidental inperfection was reproduced in each copy.

Strack does not accept this theory.

The Hebrew manuscripts hitherto discovered are not very old. Most of them go back only to the twelfth century, and only one single manuscript, containing the prophetical books, has been found that goes back to 916 A. D., and one, containing the whole Hebrew Bible, was written in 1009. The latter was discovered in the Crimea, and is now in St. Petersburg.[1] The oldest Hebrew manuscript in Germany is the so-called *Reuchlin Codex* in Carlsruhe; it was written in 1105. Hitherto no trace has been discovered of any manuscripts earlier than the Masoretic,

[1] In February, 1903, the news was brought from Cairo of the discovery of a Hebrew parchment manuscript containing the Pentateuch, written in 735 A. D. in Samaritan (or early Semitic) characters.

or written before the Christian era; and it would be only from such that we could hope to construct another text.

Many have a date, but, where this is not the case, the age can be determined from various indications. The manuscripts taken from synagogues are all rolls (*volumina*) and not pointed; those belonging to private persons are mostly books (*codices*) like our own, and contain vowels, accents and Masoretic notes. *Cf.* Cornely, *Comp.*, p. 66.

Of critically important printed editions of the Hebrew Bible, in addition to the works of the three scholars named above, the following deserve mention:

1. The Alcalá Bible, *Complutensis*,[1] is a polyglot, the famous work of Cardinal Ximenez; it was published at Alcalá in 1517. The Hebrew text in it is based upon manuscripts that were purchased for over 4000 golden guldens.

2. Daniel Bomberg's editions, which appeared at Venice from 1518 onwards. The most famous is one that was published under the direction of Jacob ben Chajim, one of the most learned Jews of his time. This and the Alcalá Bible have served as the basis for most of the later editions. They were used in the compilation of the Hebrew text of several polyglot Bibles, published (1) at Antwerp (1569–1572), (2) at Paris (1629–1645), and (3) in London (1657, etc.). The elder Buxdorf, too, based his edition of the Bible (Bâle, 1618 and 1619) upon Bomberg.

3. An amended version of Chajim's text is contained in Johann Leusden's edition, printed at Amsterdam in 1661 by Joseph Athias, and also in Everard van der Hought's edition, Amsterdam, 1705. Upon the latter are based two more modern smaller editions, viz., Hahn's, Leipsig, 1839, and Theile's, Leipzig, 1849.

4. Bär's editions, containing all the Hebrew books of the Old Testament (Leipzig, 1869–1892), were prepared with the use of the Masora, some good manuscripts and the best printed editions.[2]

---

[1] *Complutum* is the older name of Alcalá in Spain.

[2] The Hebrew text of the Psalms, with Saint Jerome's Latin translation made directly from it, was edited in 1876 by Bär, Delitzsch and Tischendorf. *Cf.* with it Ik. Ecker, *Psalterium juxta Hebræos Hieronymi*, Trèves, 1906; a valuable work on the textual criticism of the Psalms.

A new edition of the Hebrew text of the Old Testament, with critical notes by P. Haupt of Baltimore, has been appearing since 1893, published by Hinrichs at Leipzig. The edition is the result of many years' work, and many German and English scholars have collaborated in its preparation. The " genuine " and " spurious " passages are distinguished by the use of ink of various colors. Thus Genesis, for instance, is in eight colors, Josue seven, Esdras and Nehemias nine, and Chronicles in four. Hence the book is known as the " Rainbow Bible." Among the collaborators may be mentioned Cornill, Kautzsch, Stade and Wellhausen.

25. VALUE OF THE MASORETIC TEXT

In the early centuries of Christianity it was often said that the Jews had falsified the Hebrew text, in order to supply themselves with a weapon against the Christians, and that this was apparent from the Septuagint version. Justin Martyr and Origen, especially, brought such charges against the Jews, but Saint Jerome decidedly refused to admit any such suspicion, and no one in fact has succeeded with any certainty in proving the presence in the text of a single intentional falsification.[1]

On the whole, the Masoretic text deserves great respect (*cf.* Leo XIII on the Holy Scriptures, above, p. 167). At the same time it cannot claim that its accuracy is above all criticism, as has already been shown (p. 220). It is very probable that before the Masoretic text was fixed, and whilst the Septuagint was most esteemed by the Jews, the original text underwent somewhat careless treatment. This appears not only on com-

---

[1] In Psalm xxi. 17 the reading *kaari* instead of *kaaru*, which the Septuagint read, is, however, very suspicious. According to the Septuagint, the passage means: " They have pierced my hands and my feet "; according to the Masoretic text: " As a lion my hands and feet." There must have been a verb in the passage, perhaps כָּאֲרוּ (כָּאַר = כּוּר) or כּוּרוּ or כָּרוּ (from כָּרָה) = they have pierced, or סָאֲנוּ (from סָאַן, to dig through).

On the ground of the resemblance between Aleph and Tav in the ancient script, F. Perles (*Analekten zur Textkritik des A. T.*, 1895) proposes to read כִּתְּרוּ = " they have shut in." But what would be the meaning of " they have shut in my hands and feet "? There is a similar passage in Psalm cx. 3, where the allusion undoubtedly is to the eternal generation of the Messias. The Septuagint read " from the womb before the daystar I begot thee," but the Masoretic text " from the womb of the sky in the morning [comes] to thee the dew of thy youth," which has no sense at all.

paring it with the text of the Septuagint, but also from the Samaritan Pentateuch, which is of very early origin, as it is still written in Phœnician characters; in many places it agrees with the Septuagint rather than with the Masoretic text. This text, therefore, and then the early translations (Septuagint and Peshitto especially) are of assistance in criticising and correcting the present Hebrew text.[1]

26. THE ORIGINAL TEXT OF THE GREEK BOOKS OF THE BIBLE

The Greek books of the Bible came into existence at a less remote period than the Hebrew books, but nevertheless the originals, and earliest copies of them also, have long been lost. The originals were no longer extant in the third century as is plain from the writings of Origen, Clement of Alexandria and Tertullian,[2] who complain of difficulties occurring in their copies of the Bible, and of their having to take pains to discover the correct text by comparing parallel passages and other means. Had the originals still existed, it would have been quite simple for these writers to consult them, or to employ others to do so. Tertullian especially would have been able to save himself a great deal of trouble if he could have appealed to the originals against Marcion, who tampered with the Bible.

The early loss of the originals is probably due to want of durability in the Egyptian vegetable paper, which was universally used for writing purposes in the time of our Lord and the Apostles. *Cf.* II John 12. "Having more things to write unto you, I would not by paper and ink, for I hope that I shall be with you." Many manuscripts perished, too, during the persecutions of the Christians. In spite of all this, how-

---

[1] In translating the Bible even Luther preferred the Greek text to the Masoretic, but he did so apparently not so much because he thought the latter less valuable as because Hebrew was not his strong point.

[2] Reference is occasionally made to Tertullian, *De Præscript.*, c. 35, where he states that the Apostles' *authenticæ* still existed in his time at Corinth, Philippi, etc. The word, however, does not mean the Apostles' autograph writings, but only the Greek text as distinguished from the Latin translation.

ever, an attempt to ascertain the correct text is much easier in
the case of the Greek books than in that of the Hebrew, as we
still possess ancient Greek manuscripts dating from the early
centuries. Moreover, the oldest translations are very useful in
helping us to determine the text, and the numerous biblical
quotations occurring in the writings of the Fathers and ecclesiastical authors serve the same purpose. Quotations are not
a very safe guide, as early writers generally quoted from memory, and consequently rendered the text inaccurately.

27. THE GREEK MANUSCRIPTS

In the period immediately following the invention of printing,
whenever a Bible was to be produced the first manuscript that
came to hand was printed; and the more the Bibles were
distributed the more did they seem to differ. The spirit of
rivalry, however, constrained scholars to have recourse to older
and more numerous manuscripts, and thus in course of time
many old manuscripts were brought to light and used.

The older a manuscript the greater is its value, as it stands
closer to the original, and there is less fear of corruption in
the text, which very easily, though it may be unintentionally,
creeps in when a book is frequently copied.

All the ancient Greek manuscripts of the Bible that have
hitherto been discovered are in book form (*codices*); rolls
(*volumina*) have not so far been found. All (with the sole
exception of the *codex Q. Paul.*) are written on parchment.
It was only after the Crusades that paper made of linen gradually came into use.

The word *parchment* is derived from Pergamus, the name of a town in
Asia Minor, where the art of preparing writing material from the skins
of animals was particularly well understood. Parchment was costly, but
it had the advantage of being durable, so that when it was used the
great trouble and expense of frequently copying the sacred books were
avoided and the risk of originating mistakes was diminished. Vegetable
paper is less durable, and the results of using it had been unsatisfactory.

The kind of writing employed in the old manuscripts of
the Bible differs very much from our own. The ancients did

not distinguish small letters and capitals, and until the tenth
century they always wrote with what are called *uncials* or
majuscules, i. e. the letters resembled our capitals and were
not connected with one another. *Minuscules* came into use
only in the tenth century, and thus all the oldest manuscripts are
uncials.[1] Moreover, ancient writers did not divide their words,
and employed no punctuation or accents. In order, however,
to make it easier for the reader to survey the whole, they did
not write *in extenso*, but each page of parchment was divided
into three or four columns. After the fifth century the stichometric mode of writing came into use, in which as much of
the text was written on one line as was to be read in one breath;
this was called a στίχος.[2] Later on, in order to economize
space on the costly material, the end of each στίχος was marked
with a dot or a little stroke, and the writing was continued in
the same line. This was the origin of punctuation. Greek
accents came into general use only after the seventh century.[3]
In some manuscripts, both profane and biblical, it is possible
to see that the accents have been added by a later hand, and
were not inserted by the original writer. The text began to be
divided into words in the ninth century. Its division into chapters and verses is recent, as has been shown on page 218; the
division into chapters dates from the thirteenth, into verses
from the sixteenth century.

28. The Most Important Greek Manuscripts

The number of ancient Greek manuscripts of the Bible
hitherto discovered amounts to about 4000.[4] They have not

---

[1] *Literæ unciales*, literally, letters measuring an inch. *Literæ ma-
jusculæ, minusculæ,* large, small letters.

[2] στίχος = arrangement, row, member, division.

[3] They were intended originally to serve the same sort of purpose as
the vowel points in Hebrew, viz. they were to preserve the Greek pronunciation, which was in danger of being lost, as ancient Greek was gradually
dying out.

[4] Nestle follows Scrivener in giving the number as 3829, but he adds
" most of these are, however, recent." Among them are 127 uncials and
3702 minuscules. Only 30 belong to a period prior to the seventh century. This refers primarily to the New Testament.

yet all been thoroughly examined or printed. It is likely that treasures may still be discovered in various places, particularly in the East, but also in Spain and Italy.

The manuscripts are often only fragments, written on parchment that has been used to bind other books. Sometimes the Bible text has been obliterated, and other works copied on the same sheets of parchment. Such remains are called *codices rescripti,* or *palimpsests.* When the sheets have been used in this way, they have often been separated and fastened together again in different order.

Παλιμψηστός = rubbed off again (ψάω = to wipe, rub). The original writing was wiped or rubbed off, and the parchment then smoothed with pumice stone to make it fit for use again. The old writing is sometimes still legible, but sometimes it has to be revived by means of chemicals. Often it remains illegible, and occasionally the chemicals employed injure the parchment and the writing with it.

For the sake of brevity, uncial manuscripts are generally designated by Greek and Latin capital letters, and recently Hebrew letters have also been used; minuscule manuscripts are numbered. Indices are added to the capital letters to distinguish the manuscripts. Thus J is a palimpsest from Palestine, now in St. Petersburg; Jb is a manuscript in the British Museum; 51 is a minuscule manuscript in Oxford; 422 to 430 are minuscles at Munich. To the books of *pericopœ* also Arabic numbers are assigned, as Evl. 45 in Vienna (a book of the Gospels).

The chief Greek manuscripts are the following:

1. The *Codex Vaticanus,* B. It is in the Vatican Library in Rome. It contains the whole of the Old and New Testaments, with some very small omissions. It is written in three columns and came probably from Egypt, dating from about the time of the First Council of Nicæa (325).

Several printed editions of this manuscript have appeared, but they are not all free from mistakes. The Old Testament was printed in Rome in 1587, by order of Sixtus V. August Mai published the whole codex in 1858, and Vercellone brought out a more accurate edition in 1881 in Rome.

The New Testament was published by Loch at Ratisbon, in 1862, and by Tischendorf at Leipzig, in 1867. An edition of the New Testament, reproduced by photolithography was brought out by Cozza-Luzi in Rome, 1889, and a similar edition of the Old Testament in 1890. We owe this magnificent work to Pope Leo XIII. As some defects could still be detected, Pius X has determined that a still more accurate phototype edition shall be prepared, which will enable every student to see the exact form of Codex B.

2. The *Codex Sinaiticus*, designated ℵ by its discoverer. It was found by Constantine Tischendorf on February 4, 1859, in Saint Catherine's monastery on Mount Sinai. It contains almost the whole of the Old and New Testaments in Greek, and is written in four columns. This codex, like the preceding, belongs probably to the fourth century. It is now in St. Petersburg.

Tischendorf believes this manuscript to be older than the Vatican Codex, but others doubt its being so old. It was printed at St. Petersburg in 1862; and the New Testament was published separately by Tischendorf at Leipzig in 1863, under the title, *Novum Testamentum Sinaiticum*.

3. The *Codex Alexandrinus*, A, in the British Museum in London. It was found on Mount Athos and given to King Charles I of England in 1628 by the Patriarch Cyrillus Lucaris. It dates from the fifth century.

A printed edition of the Old Testament, by Baber, appeared in 1816–1828; one of the New Testament by Cowper, in London, 1860. The missing portions have been supplied from R. Stephanus. A photolithographic reproduction of this important codex has existed since 1883.

4. *Codex C*, also called *Regius* or *Parisiensis*, or *Ephræmi rescriptus*, belongs to the same period. It is in the National Library in Paris.

Originally it contained the whole Old and New Testaments, but in the tenth or eleventh century the writing was obliterated, and the parchment used for a copy of some works of Saint Ephrem the Syrian. Much of what was written first has in this way become illegible. About two hundred leaves are left, containing the greater part of the New Testament. It was printed by Tischendorf, 1843 and 1845.

5. *Codex s. Matthæi Dublinensis rescriptus*, Z. This contains the greater part of Saint Matthew's Gospel, and serves to fill up the voids in other manuscripts. It resembles C, and seems to belong to the same period.

As the name suggests, it is now in Dublin, and was printed there in 1801.

The following manuscripts are stichometric:

6. *Codex Bezæ* or *Cantabrigiensis*, D, belongs probably to the sixth century. It was found in a monastery in Lyons, and

came into the possession of Theodore Beza, one of the reformers, who presented it in 1581 to the University of Cambridge.

This manuscript differs from the other texts in a very remarkable way. As it was found at Lyons, and exactly agrees with the quotations made by Saint Irenæus from the Bible, it seems to be based upon a copy belonging to this bishop (177–202). It has received great attention recently. It was printed by Scrivener in 1864.

7. *Codex Laudianus*, E, contains the Acts of the Apostles. It is named after the English Archbishop William Laud, to whom it belonged in the seventeenth century. It dates probably from the sixth century and is now at Oxford.

8. *Codex Claramontanus*, D_2, belongs to the sixth century, and contains the Pauline epistles. It is now in Paris, and was printed by Tischendorf, Leipzig, 1852. It was brought from the north of Africa, and contains a list of the canonical books (see above, page 206).

9. *Codex Rossanensis*, Σ, found at Rossano in Calabria. It belongs to the sixth century and contains Saint Matthew's and Saint Mark's Gospels.[1]

29. GREEK PRINTED EDITIONS

(a) Cardinal Ximenez in Spain, the editor of the *Polyglotta Complutensis*, was the first to have the Bible printed in Greek. His work contains the whole of the Old Testament in Greek, according to manuscripts of the Septuagint translation, and also the New Testament, which is based on several Greek manuscripts. The Greek text was printed in 1514.

Almost at the same time Erasmus of Rotterdam edited the New Testament in Greek at the instigation of the great printer, Frobenius, at Bâle. His text is defective, as, in order to outstrip the Cardinal, he worked very fast, and used only a few

[1] This codex was only discovered in 1879. It is also called *Codex purpureus*, because the parchment leaves are dyed purple, and the letters are written in gold and silver. It is of artistic and liturgical importance on account of the miniatures in it. Another purple codex of the sixth century, containing a large portion of Saint Matthew's Gospel, and agreeing in its text precisely with Σ, was discovered recently at Sinope in Pontus and placed in the National Library in Paris.

newer manuscripts. Robert Stephanus (Etienne), the great
printer in Paris, in 1546 and subsequent years, brought out
several editions of the New Testament in Greek. These were
based on those of Erasmus and Cardinal Ximenes, also on Codex
D and some later manuscripts.

The fourth edition, published in 1551, was the first in which the verses
were divided.

Stephanus's editions, with a few manuscripts and some old
Oriental translations, formed the foundation of a Greek edition
of the New Testament that was the work of Th. Beza, the re-
former. This appeared first in 1565, and was reprinted several
times.

Great but undeserved attention was paid to the Greek editions
of the New Testament that were published by the Elzevir
Brothers at Leyden, in and after 1624. They contain the text
of the Stephanus and Beza editions, which has many defects,
but as they boldly proclaimed it to be generally accepted and
perfectly free from mistakes (*textum ab omnibus receptum*) it
was held in the highest honor among Protestants for nearly
200 years, and was circulated in innumerable reprints. At the
present time it is not considered important, but it retains the
name *textus receptus*, or *editio recepta*.[1]

(*b*) The polyglot Bibles published during the seventeenth
century in Antwerp (by Plantin), Paris and London, are
modeled on the Alcalá Bible, and, as far as the Greek text
is concerned, are derived from the following sources: The Antwerp polyglot follows the *Complutensis;* the Paris polyglot
simply reprints the Greek text from the Antwerp edition; the
London polyglot follows the text of the Septuagint as printed
in Rome in 1587, and for the New Testament it adopts that of
Robert Stephanus.

Two German scholars, Bengel and Griesbach, deserve especial mention as editors of the Greek text of the New Testament during the eighteenth century. They used many old
manuscripts and produced a text differing considerably from

[1] Even the English Bible Society in its most recent editions has substituted Nestle's text for the *recepta*.

the *recepta*. However, the *recepta* was not set aside, though it lost some of its prestige.

Bengel's edition appeared first in 1734 and Griesbach's in 1775.
They divided the existing manuscripts into families, according to their place of origin, — Constantinople and Syria, Egypt, or the West. They cared less for the number of manuscripts than for the agreement of the different families. A reading was considered correct if it was supported by all the families, and the consensus of two families preponderated over a third. This classification has been upheld even to the present time, especially by Westcott and Hort (see below) and the principle has been further developed.

(*c*) In recent years excellent work has been done by some English and German scholars on the text of the New Testament. We may mention: Karl Lachmann, died in Berlin, 1851; Constantine Tischendorf, died in Leipzig, 1874; Bernard Weiss (Berlin); C. R. Gregory (Leipzig); Tregelles, died in England, 1875; Westcott and Hort (in England).

Lachmann started with the principle that our aim should be, not being guided by the *recepta,* to restore the text to the state in which it was in the fourth century, as we have no means of discovering the original, and as a text of that century can have differed only slightly from it. He hoped that other subsequent workers might gradually be able to restore the text approximately as it was in the second century. His text is based chiefly upon six or eight of the earliest Greek manuscripts and upon the *Itala*. His edition of the New Testament appeared first in 1831, and again in 1842 and 1850.

Tischendorf did not regard Lachmann's method as satisfactory, and thought that we possessed means of going back beyond the fourth century and of very nearly discovering the original text. He used not only all the manuscripts that he could get, but also translations and quotations of the Fathers. His critical edition of the New Testament appeared first in 1841 and 1842; the eighth edition in 1869–1890. (Pocket edition, sixteenth edition, 1887.)

Tregelles, an English philologist, was a Quaker. He adhered to Lachmann's principle as a general rule, but his *apparatus criticus* was far more extensive. His edition appeared in seven parts between 1857 and 1879. Still more accurate is the edition prepared by two Englishmen, Westcott and Hort. It appeared in 1881 and has no references to original sources, but the value of all the critical apparatus collected up to that time is assigned according to Griesbach and Lachmann's principles. These guiding principles are expounded in a special volume bearing the title " Introduction," 1882.[1]

A new and independent revision of the Greek text of the New Testament has been brought out in three volumes by Bernhard Weiss (Berlin, 1894–1900).

A new method of arriving, if not at the original text at least as near as possible to it, was devised by Hermann Freiherr von Soden in Berlin. The text had hitherto been taken from the earliest uncial manuscripts (by Tischendorf also), but von Soden, with the assistance of several friends, tried to trace the alterations in it, and in this way to approach the original. They examined 1716 manuscripts of the Gospels; 521 containing Acts and the Catholic Epistles; 628 containing Saint Paul's Epistles; and 219 containing the Apocalypse; and they studied, besides these, many of the earliest commentaries, to which but little attention had previously been paid. In this way they ascertained that the oldest Greek codices (B and ℵ) represent a revised version of an earlier text. Instead of following the traditional custom of designating the majuscules by capital letters and the minuscules by Arabic numerals, Soden prefers a very much simpler method of using the small letters of the Greek alphabet and the Arabic numerals, in which he will perhaps find others to imitate him. For further information see his work, *Die Schriften des N. T. in ihrer ältesten erreichbaren Textgestalt*, Berlin, 1902, 1903.

The labors of these students have almost completely destroyed the reputation of the recepta, whilst they have established the purity of the Vulgate text.[2]

---

[1] Westcott and Hort distinguish four classes of texts: (*a*) the primitive text, as it left the author's hands; (*b*) a text originating in Alexandria; (*c*) a text originating in Constantinople; (*d*) a text brought from Syria to the West before 200 A. D.

[2] A good and at the same time inexpensive edition is O. v. Gebhardt's New Testament, Leipzig, 1895, based on Tischendorf, Tregelles, and Westcott and Hort. It does not, however, satisfy Catholic requirements on account of Mark xvi. 9, etc., and John viii. 3, etc. Mention may be made of Nestle's cheap edition (3d ed., 1901, Stuttg.) and of Weymouth's (London, 1892). Tauchnitz in Leipzig has published a very convenient Greek and Latin edition, revised in accordance with Griesbach, Lachmann and Tischendorf. It has been approved by the Catholic Consistory in Dresden.

SECOND SECTION

TRANSLATIONS OF THE BIBLE

30. GENERAL REMARKS

Translations of the books of the Bible from the original into another language are of importance, not only as enabling us to ascertain the correct text, but also as aids in interpreting the Bible, for we see from them how early readers understood the meaning of the original. All translations are not of equal value. As a rule, those made from the original surpass those made from another translation in importance and authority; literal translations deserve consideration more than free; and, above all, the old translations have more weight than later ones. Hence particular importance is attached to such as were made before the seventh century.

Early translations are fairly numerous. There are several Greek and Chaldee translations (of the Old Testament); a Samaritan version (of the Pentateuch), some Syriac, several Arabic, one Armenian, one Persian, some Egyptian (Coptic), one Ethiopian, one Slavonic, one Georgian, one Gothic, several Latin and fragments of an Anglo-Saxon version.

The most important are the Greek, Syriac and Latin translations.

GREEK TRANSLATIONS

31. SEPTUAGINT

At the time of Christ and His Apostles the Holy Scriptures were mostly read in a Greek translation made in Egypt for the use of the Jews there. Outside Palestine, and to some extent in Palestine itself, the Jews used this version when they read the Scriptures in the synagogues on the Sabbath. From many quotations in the New Testament it is clear that the Apostles were more familiar with this translation than with the Hebrew text, which did not contain all the sacred books; and, when they converted pagans to Christianity, they gave this version to their converts. Testimony to the respect paid to this translation, and to its universal use, is borne by Josephus Flavius (who always used it himself in his writings), and by Justin Martyr, who, in his conversation with the Jew Tryphon, shows that among the Jews this translation was still accepted in the second century, when he lived (see above, p. 201).

The name Septuagint (LXX) is due to an old story preserved by Josephus Flavius (*Antiq.*, XII, ii. 1, etc.), and by the ecclesiastical historian Eusebius (*Præp. Ev.*, viii. 2). It originated in a letter written by Aristeas, an official at the Egyptian court, to his brother Philocrates, in which Aristeas says that Demetrius Phalereus, chief librarian at the royal library at Alexandria, advised his master, King Ptolemy Philadelphus, to add the Jewish law to the treasures in his library. The king was pleased with the advice, and in order to procure the book of the law, he set 200,000 Jews at liberty, and then sent some men, amongst whom was Aristeas himself, with costly presents to Jerusalem, in order to fetch the book from the high priest. The latter not only gave the book to the envoys, but sent seventy-two learned Jews to Egypt to translate the *Thora*. They were received honorably in Egypt, and sent with Demetrius Phalereus to the neighboring island of Pharos, where they worked at their translation undisturbed. According to the story, each man was shut up alone in a cell, and made a translation by himself, but when all the results were compared, they were found to be exactly the same.

In ancient times this story was universally regarded as true, but it cannot be correct in every detail, for it contains fabulous additions. The truth probably is that the translation was made by Jews in Alexandria, and supplied an existing need, as the Egyptian Jews mostly did not understand Hebrew. An Egyptian king, probably not Ptolemy Philadelphus (285–247), who banished Demetrius Phalereus soon after his accession, but, according to Clement of Alexandria (*Strom.*, I, 22), his father, Ptolemy Lagi (323–285), admitted the Greek version of the Jewish law into his library. This occurrence, flattering to the Jews, has been connected with the production of the translation. Possibly the fact that the sacred writings had been rendered into a heathen language displeased some Jews, and a story was invented to calm their indignation.

In any case the report about the translation of the LXX applies only to the Pentateuch. The other sacred books were gradually translated into Greek in Egypt, and therefore the same name of the LXX was given to them also.

The date of the beginning of the translation may be given as about 300 B. C. Probably it was prior to 286, i. e. to the establishment of the library at Alexandria, for there were many Jews in Egypt ever since the time of Alexander the Great. By 200 B. C. the translation must have been nearly completed, as the translator of the Book of Sirach (Ecclesiasticus) knew a Greek text "of the Law and the Prophets and the other books," and mentions it frequently in his prologue.[1]

Character of the Translation. It is, on the whole, faithful and often almost slavishly literal. The Alexandrians frequently translated the Hebrew text word for word; and in this way their language became very barbarous, beside often distorting the meaning.

The Pentateuch is best translated, and next in order of merit are the books of Josue, Judges, Ruth, Chronicles and Proverbs. Less to be commended is the translation of the four books of Kings, and of Esdras, Nehemias and Esther. Ecclesiastes is translated too literally, Job too arbitrarily. The Psalms and the prophetic writings are unsatisfactory, and the worst translation is that of the Book of Daniel, for which reason the Church did not admit the Septuagint version of this prophet into the Canon, but a later rendering by Theodotion.[2]

Taken as a whole, this translation was and still is of inestimable value. As the first rendering of the written word of God from the little known Hebrew into the widely diffused Greek language, it was the first and oldest instrument by which the civilized nations could learn God's special revelation. The Jews carried this version to the east and to the west, thus preparing the way for the Apostles, preaching and supporting

[1] His prologue shows that he wrote primarily only for Jews, and not, as Loch and Reischl suppose, also for Gentiles.

[2] The Septuagint text of Daniel was consequently lost, and was only recovered in the eighteenth century. It was printed in Rome in 1772, and it is given in the appendix to Tischendorf's edition of the Septuagint.

it. For us it is valuable, because it forms an excellent means for us to control the Masoretic text, and to understand the sacred books. In the Church it has always been highly esteemed, and not a few of the Fathers considered it to be inspired. Many old translations are based upon the LXX, such as the *Itala,* the Coptic, the Ethiopian and the Armenian versions. The Jews pay no attention to it at the present time, but that is due to their hostility towards the Church; at the time of Christ and still later, it was valued very highly by the Jews, even in Palestine, and it was the work of Jews for Jews. The Talmud mentions it frequently with respect.

32. OTHER GREEK TRANSLATIONS

After Christianity was fairly established, the diffusion of the Holy Scriptures increased. Christians had to defend their faith against both Jews and pagans; and in doing so they generally appealed to the Septuagint to prove that the prophecies of the Old Testament had found their fulfillment in Christ. The Jews now often had recourse to the evasive answer that this text was not trustworthy, and only the original ought to be relied upon. They maintained that the LXX writers had not been sufficiently faithful in their translation, and for this reason new translations seemed to be required, although there was plainly no ground for the Jews' complaints, as the LXX version is only too literal.

1. It was probably from motives of hostility to Christians that in the second century *Aquilas of Sinope* in Pontus, a Jewish proselyte, made a translation following the Hebrew so slavishly as to violate all the rules of Greek grammar. For instance, he rendered Genesis i. 1: Ἐν κεφαλαίῳ ἔκτισεν ὁ θεὸς σὺν τὸν οὐρανὸν καὶ σὺν τὴν γῆν. Several passages favorable to Christianity he translated differently from the LXX, although their version was correct. For instance, in Isaias vii. 14, he rendered *alma* not by παρθένος, as the LXX did, but by νεᾶνις. His work was warmly welcomed by the Jews, and the Talmud praises it and calls it the *Targum Agilas.*

2. *Theodotion,* an Ebionite from Ephesus, was the next to

translate the Old Testament into Greek. His work resembles the LXX, and he retained that text whenever, in his opinion, it gave a correct rendering of the Hebrew, and he translated only when the LXX appeared altogether misleading, as, e. g., in Daniel. His intention was therefore to revise the LXX. His translation was held in more esteem by the Christians than that of Aquilas, and his version of the Book of Daniel was admitted to the Canon of Holy Scripture. Theodotion lived in the second century, and Irenæus, writing in 176, knew his work (*Adv. hæreses*, III, 24).

3. *Symmachus*, another Ebionite, made a translation somewhat later. Regarding his date we know with certainty that he wrote after Irenæus and before Origen, as the latter knew his work, but the former did not. He seems to have written before 200 A. D., perhaps in the reign of Marcus Aurelius the Philosopher (161–180).[1] The old writers who mention his translations, say at the same time that they are freer than those of his predecessors; he tried to write good Greek, to remove whatever there was in earlier translations offensive to Western ears, and to avoid what seemed foreign. He cared more for the thoughts than the words. Saint Jerome praises his version and undoubtedly often took Symmachus as his model for his own works, for it is impossible not to perceive a similarity between their versions. When Origen was working at the Bible, he found three other translations besides the four already mentioned, and numbered them 5, 6 and 7. Consequently they are known as *quinta, sexta, septima*. None of them seems to have contained the whole of the Old Testament.

Only fragments of all the translations other than the LXX have come down to us. They were collected by Montfaucon, a Maurist, *Origenis Hexaplorum quæ supersunt*, Paris, 1713, 2 vols., fol. This work has been superseded by Field's *Origenis Hexaplorum quæ supersunt*, Oxonii, 1871–75, 2 vols., 4to.

---

[1] Mercati, *L'età di Simmaco*, Freibg., 1893. The only authority is Epiphanius (*De Ponderibus et Mensuris*, c. 16, 17), who assigns him to this period, but he is not trustworthy.

33. LATER HISTORY OF THE SEPTUAGINT. ORIGEN

The more the Septuagint was used by Christians, the more did its reputation among the Jews diminish, until at last their dislike amounted to hatred and horror.[1] Christians, however, read this text, handed down to them by the Apostles and the first preachers of the faith, in their meetings for public worship, just as they read the writings of the Apostles. As the Christian communities became more numerous, copies of this book had to be multplied, and no ancient work was so frequently copied. The very fact of its wide diffusion was harmful to the text; many various readings crept in as a result of its being so often copied, and many persons who possessed Bibles, especially if they understood Hebrew, ventured to make a slight alteration here and there, which was perpetuated when the manuscript was copied. The condition of the copies of the Bible caused anxiety and sorrow to many Christians, particularly to scholars, as they had to hear the Jews assert, in arguments respecting the faith, that the very book from which Christian doctrines should be proved and Jewish errors refuted was devoid of all authority, as it often differed from the Hebrew text, and the various Greek versions of it did not agree with one another. (The mistake was made of setting too high a value on the Hebrew text, and of assuming that it was quite free from errors.)

In order to put an end to these reproaches, Origen, a learned Alexandrian, undertook a very comprehensive work on the Bible, and collated the various texts. This work, known as the *Hexapla*, was completed in 231. Origen's system of arrangement was the following:

He divided the rolls of manuscript into six columns, or, in dealing with some books of the Bible, into seven, eight or even nine. In the first he wrote the Hebrew text in Hebrew letters; in the second the same text in Greek characters; in the third the literal translation, viz., that of Aquilas; in the

---

[1] Later Jews mourned over the existence of the LXX as over the worship of the golden calf, and said that darkness had enveloped the earth for three days, when this work was completed.

fourth that of Symmachus; in the fifth the Septuagint version, and in the sixth that of Theodotion. In the case of some books other columns were added, containing the *quinta, sexta* and *septima,* so that these parts of the whole may be called *heptapla, octapla* and *enneapla* respectively. In the fifth column, containing the Septuagint, Origen inserted definite marks, intended to show exactly the relation between that version and the original. If he found something added in the LXX that was absent in the Hebrew text, he marked it with an obelus ——:-, signifying that it ought to be omitted; if he detected something left out, he supplied it, generally from Theodotion, marking it with an asterisk * and naming the source whence he had taken what was missing. A metobelus ($\frown$) marked the end of the passage to which the other marks applied.

This great work being of the highest value was received with approval and diligently used. On account of its bulkiness it could not be reproduced, and had to be studied and consulted at Cæsarea in Palestine, where it was kept. Extracts from it were, however, made: (1) Origen himself prepared the so-called *Tetrapla;* i. e. an arrangement of the four best known translations (LXX, Aquilas, Theodotion and Symmachus) in four parallel columns. This enabled the Christians to see where they could safely rely upon the LXX without fear of contradiction, as the other translations gave them valuable indications, and Aquilas was almost a substitute for the original text. (2) At a later date Eusebius, Bishop of Cæsarea, the well-known writer on " Church History," and his friend, Pamphilus, had the Septuagint text, with all Origen's marks and emendations, copied from the fifth column of the *Hexapla,* and these copies were approved by the Church in Palestine. Thus the *Hexapla* and *Tetrapla* fell out of use, and only fragments of them are extant (see p. 239).

Additional Notes. 1. Origen was not the only scholar of antiquity who undertook to revise the Alexandrian text. The same was done by Lucian, a priest and afterwards a martyr (312 A. D.) in Antioch, and by the Egyptian Hesychius, who also suffered martyrdom in 311. They studied the Hebrew text, but referred also to early manuscripts of the LXX. Lucian's revision was used in many congregations in Asia (not in Palestine) and in Eastern Europe; Hesychius', in Egypt.

2. The Alexandrian translation has been preserved in several old manuscripts. The codices B, א and A (*cf.* Cornill, 302), which have been already mentioned, contain probably the purest text. The small editions brought out by Loch (2d ed., Ratisbon, 1886) and Tischendorf (7th ed., Leipzig, 1887) are based upon printed editions of these three codices. L. van Ess, *Vetus Test. gr. juxta 70 interpretes*, Leipz., 1824, 1855, 1887, is printed from the Roman edition of Codex B, 1587 (see above, p. 229).

In 1883 P. v. Lagarde published in Göttingen the first volume of an editions already mentioned, contain probably the purest text. The small inclusive, but unhappily no other volume appeared. The text is that of Lucian, which is given also in the *Complutensian Polyglot*. Between 1887 and 1895 a very carefully prepared edition of the Septuagint in three volumes was published in Cambridge, and a second revised edition was printed, 1895–1899, under the title " The Old Testament in Greek," by H. Barclay Swete. Also by Swete is an excellent " Introduction to the Old Testament in Greek," with an appendix containing the letter of Aristeas (Cambridge, 1900).

3. Origen's autograph still existed at Cæsarea until after 600 A. D., but it disappeared when the Arabs conquered Palestine. Not long before its disappearance the Monophysite Bishop Paul of Tella translated at Alexandria (617) the fifth column of the LXX quite literally into Syriac, inserting all the critical marks (see p. 246). By aid of this translation it is not difficult to restore the Greek text. This Syriac version has been preserved in a manuscript of the eighth century now in the Ambrosian Library at Milan. A photolithographic reproduction of it was published by Ceriani in 1874.[1]

34. CHALDEE TRANSLATIONS OF THE OLD TESTAMENT (TARGUMIM) [2]

When Hebrew ceased to be a living language, it was found necessary to translate the Bible into Chaldee. As early as the

---

[1] A small portion of the *Hexapla*, not including the first column for Hebrew in Hebrew characters, has been found in a palimpsest in the Ambrosiana at Milan. The discoverer was Dr. Mercati, mentioned on p. 239. The manuscript dates from the tenth century, and contains the *Hexapla* of eleven Psalms. It is written in minuscules. The discovery is important for several reasons; e. g. for the reading of the Hebrew in the early centuries of the Christian era, i. e. in the time before the *Masora* was written, and also for the criticisms on the text of those particular Psalms. An account of it was given by Ceriani in the *Rendiconti* of the Lombard Literary Institute, Ser. II, vol. 29. The collections made by Montfaucon and Field (see p. 239) do not of course contain this portion of the *Hexapla*.

[2] *Targum*, pl. *Targumim*, means simply " translation," " interpretation," from *tagam* (= *ta'am*), to be double, *targem* (= *taggem*), to double, used especially of something written — hence to interpret, eluci-

time of Esdras and Nehemias, the people no longer understood the ancient Hebrew (Neh. viii. 8), and so it was not enough to read the Sacred Books in the synagogues of Palestine in the original, but what was read had to be translated into the vulgar tongue, viz. into Chaldee. For a long time this was done orally, but gradually the translations were written down. They must all belong to a very early period, as nowhere can any hostility to Christianity be traced in them. They originated partly in Palestine, partly in Babylon, in the rabbinical schools of these districts. We possess Targumim of all the books in the Hebrew Bible except Esdras, Nehemias and Daniel. The most important Targum is that of Onkelos,[1] and dates from the time of the Apostles. It is limited to the Pentateuch, and is very faithful and free from mistakes. A second Targum, that of the Prophets,[2] is ascribed to Jonathan, a disciple of Hillel, who was a teacher of the law. Apparently this was written during our Lord's life. It is not so accurate as the work of Onkelos, contains many explanatory additions, and might almost be called a paraphrase explaining the text. The pseudo-Jonathan's Targum of the Pentateuch and others of various books of the Bible [3] were the work of unknown authors of later date, and are regarded as less valuable. Nevertheless, as they, too, date from very early in the Christian era, they are useful aids in studing the Hebrew text. It is generally acknowledged that the text used by these later translators differed very little from the Masoretic.

date. Oral elucidation seems to have given rise to the sermon, the edifying explanation of what is written, which is still called *Turgam* by Syrian Christians.

[1] According to the Talmud, Onkelos was a proselyte; he showed great honor to the famous Gamaliel at his death (52 A. D.), so he must have lived in the first century (see Kaulen, I, 115). His *Targum* is printed in the great polyglot editions, and a new reprint of it was published by A. Berliner in Berlin, 1884.

[2] It contains Josue, Judges, Samuel, Kings, Isaias, Jeremias, Ezechiel and the twelve minor prophets.

[3] Namely an anonymous Targum of the Psalms, Proverbs and Job; another of the five "Rolls" (*Megilloth,* i. e. Canticles, Ruth, Lamentations, Ecclesiasticus and Esther); another of Esther and one of Chronicles. For printed editions of the Targums see Kaulen, *Einl.,* I, 114; Petermann, *Linguæ chald. grammatica,* pp. 83–88.

35. SAMARITAN TRANSLATION OF THE PENTATEUCH

The Samaritans were a mixed race, speaking a Semitic dialect of their own, and using the old Semitic or Phœnician writing. They were accustomed to read the Mosaic law (written in Phœnician characters), when they assembled for the worship of God.[1] Just as a translation became necessary for use in the Jewish synagogues, so did the Samaritans too require a translation, for they ceased to understand Hebrew. According to the statements made by the few remaining people of this nation, one was made by a priest named Nathanael, about the year 20 B. C. The ancients were familiar with this work, and Origen often quotes it in his *Hexapla*, and calls it τὸ Σαμαρειτικόν. It became known in the West through Della Valle, a scholar who in 1616 acquired a manuscript of it at Damascus, as well as one of the original. Both dated from the year 1514, and are now in the Vatican at Rome. Another manuscript, also from Damascus, is in the library of the Barberini family in Rome, and still older manuscripts, which are, however, fragmentary, are at Oxford, Cambridge and St. Petersburg.

The Samaritan translation is contained in the polyglot editions printed in Paris and London, and it has been reprinted from them by Brüll, Frankfurt, 1873. This text is based upon one single manuscript of the year 514, which is both recent and defective. Petermann's edition, completed by Vollers (Berlin, 1891), is based on several manuscripts and is therefore very valuable. According to a critique by Samuel Kohn, the Samaritan translation is very literal, reproducing the text of the Samaritan-Hebrew Bible almost letter for letter, with servile fidelity, and betraying a want of knowledge of Hebrew. The original composition probably passed through many hands and underwent many alterations.

36. SYRIAC TRANSLATIONS

The Syrian Church, the first community of Gentile Christians, possessed various translations of the Bible, of which the most important is that known as the Peshitto version. It is certainly not the work of one man. The New Testament alone may have been done by one writer, at least as far as the

[1] With regard to the time when the Pentateuch and the Book of Josue came into the possession of the Samaritans, see above, p. 52.

ὁμολογούμενα are concerned. The writings of the Apostles were read in every church at assemblies for worship, and as the Syrian Church is one of the oldest, the Syriac version of the New Testament must belong to quite the early part of the second century, and the uniformity of the language points to its being the work of one translator. The books of the Old Testament, at least the protocanonical, had existed in Syriac before this time, for in the New Testament Peshitto quotations are made from the Old Testament Peshitto, hence the latter must have been written in the first century of our era; it was translated from the Hebrew text, and is probably the work of several persons, as its language has not the same uniformity and evenness as that of the New Testament Peshitto.

The name כְּשִׁיטְתָא, *Peshittho* or *Peshittha*, is explained in various ways. It seems to be connected with פְּשַׁט (Chald. and Syr. *peshat*), i. e. to spread out, expound, so that the meaning would be the expounded, i. e. translated (Scripture).

The deuterocanonical books of the Old Testament and the ἀντιλεγόμενα of the New were added to the Peshitto before the fourth century, as Saint Ephrem the Syrian (300–380), who did not understand Greek, often quotes from them. That they originally were not included seems probable from notes in some manuscripts of the Peshitto (*cf.* p. 205).

In 1858 Cureton, an Englishman, published some fragments of a Syriac text of the Gospels that is older than the Peshitto in its present form. Bäthgen used his work (1885) in an attempt to restore the Greek text from which the Syriac translation had been made. In 1892, in the monastery on Sinai, a palimpsest manuscript of the gospels in Syriac was discovered that appears to be still older than Cureton's text. This *Codex Sinaiticus Syrus* is called Lewis Codex after the lady who discovered it, Mrs. Smith-Lewis, an English widow. It was photographed *in situ*, and published at Cambridge in 1894, under the title "The Four Gospels in Syriac, transcribed from the Sinaitic Palimpsest," 4to. It was followed by "A Translation of the Four Gospels," by Smith-Lewis, London, 1894, 8vo.[1]

---

[1] See K. Holzhey, *Der neuentdeckte Codex Syrus Sinaiticus*, Munich, 1896. This work contains a thorough examination of the codex, as well as a comparison of it with Cureton's text. Both texts appear, according to Holzhey, to have been translated from the same Greek original; they are not independent translations, but are revised versions of one and the same text, and are older than the Peshitto. Tatian's *Diatessaron* is based upon the Lewis Codex, and is possibly later than the Cureton Codex. Both manuscripts are orthodox; only the genealogy in Saint Matthew in the new Sinai palimpsest seems to have been taken from an

The discoverer made a second journey to Sinai in the spring of 1895, in order, if possible, to fill up the voids in the first edition and to verify some doubtful readings. She published the results of this re-examination of the codex in her work, "Some Pages of the Four Gospels retranscribed from the Sinaitic Palimpsest with a Translation of the Whole Text," Cambridge, 1896. This book contains many additions to the text as first published. The discovery is of great importance in Bible criticism, for this is the oldest Syriac text known hitherto. Unhappily it is very incomplete.[1]

Besides the Peshitto, there are two other Syriac translations, viz.: (a) In the seventh century (617) Paul of Tella, a Monophysite bishop, translated the Old Testament from the LXX. The rendering is so literal as to be very useful in determining the text of the Septuagint at that time (see p. 242). (b) At a still earlier date, about 500 A.D., a suffragan bishop, named Polycarp, translated part of the Bible into Syriac from the Greek. He did so at the instigation of his bishop, Philoxenus of Mabug (= Hierapolis). His version contained at least the Psalms and the New Testament. These two translations were used by heretics (Monophysites).[2]

The Bible was translated into *Arabic* only at a comparatively late date, and then not all at once, nor by one man, but book by book, by various persons. The best known of these translators is Rabbi Saadia Gaon (died 942), an Egyptian. He translated the whole of the Jewish canon of the Old Testament directly from the Hebrew. Not all the books, however, in his translation have been preserved, and some still extant have not yet been printed. *Cf.* Engelkemper, *De Saadiœ Gaonis vita, Bibliorum versione, hermeneutica. Monast.*, 1897. Much older, and therefore more important, are the *Coptic* (Egyptian) translations made from

---

Ebionite manuscript of the Gospels, as, in i. 16, it contains the words, "Joseph begot Jesus." The discoverer of the codex, however, does not agree with this theory, and lays stress upon the argument that the text cannot be tainted with heresy, as immediately after the genealogy follows the account of the birth of Christ from the Virgin Mary by the Holy Spirit. She maintains that the word "begot" has throughout the genealogy the purely conventional meaning "was reckoned legally or socially as the son." It has this meaning in verse 8, where Joram is said to have begotten his great-grandson Ozias, and in verse 12, where the childless Jechonias is said to have begotten Salathiel. *Cf.* also A. Bonus, *Collatio Cod. Lew. c. Cod. Curet*, Oxford, 1896.

[1] It is supposed that the manuscript was revised about 400 A.D., in accordance with a Greek text belonging to the second century.

[2] Printed editions: Ceriani, *Translatio syra Vet. Test.*, Mediolani, 1876, etc.; Gutbir, *Nov. Test. Syr.*, Hamburg, 1664.

the Greek in the second or, at latest, in the third century. Of almost equal value are the *Ethiopian* (fourth century) and the *Armenian* (not much later) versions, both based on Greek originals. Of the *Gothic* translation by Vulfilas (died 381) only some considerable fragments remain. This version, too, was made from the Greek.

37. LATIN TRANSLATIONS

The Itala and the Vulgate

1. In the Western Church from very early times of Christianity, the Holy Scriptures have been read in a Latin version, known as the *Vulgata* (*versio*) in consequence of its widespread use. This translation is taken partly from an older version, that was made soon after the introduction of Christianity to the West, and partly is the work of Saint Jerome.

2. As soon as Christianity was adopted, it was necessary to read the sacred books during divine worship in the vernacular, and this gave rise to the Latin translation. Scarcely any one in the West (except the Jews) understood Hebrew, and only the educated classes knew Greek. Most of the early Christians belonged to the lower classes (I Cor. i. 26) and consequently a Latin version was needed.

Whether divine worship in Rome was originally performed in Latin or in Greek is still an open question. Ferd. Probst agrees with De Rossi in believing the Greek language to have been in use until the end of the fourth century, but Kaulen thinks Mass was said in Latin. Even if Greek was the usual language for the sacrificial rite, the Bible would have had to be read to the people in the vernacular.

3. It is tolerably certain that not only one but several Latin translations existed long before Saint Jerome.[1] The first historical mention of the existence of the Bible in Latin comes from Africa, where Tertullian (160–240), writing about the end of the second century, speaks of such a version as in use among the Christians.[2] Saint Augustine, who wrote later, says that there were many Latin versions, but he preferred the *Itala*

[1] Wiseman and others have supposed that all the Latin texts of the Bible, before the time of Saint Jerome, were only different versions of one original translation made probably in Africa. Cornely shares this opinion, but Kaulen thinks that the translation was made in Rome.

[2] *In usum exiit nostrorum.*

(sc. *interpretatio*) to all the rest, as it was accurate and yet intelligible. Probably he had brought it with him from Italy, and therefore gave it this name.[1] The text used by Saint Augustine was certainly not the same as Tertullian's, as may be seen by comparing their quotations. There were therefore at least two Latin versions known in Africa.[2] In Europe also there were probably several Latin texts in existence, as the patristic quotations do not always agree, and Saint Jerome complains of there being many Latin texts containing great discrepancies.[3]

4. Still there must have been one translation regarded in Italy as better than the rest, as also in Saint Augustine's opinion; for Saint Jerome often mentions a *communis editio* or *antiqua translatio*. Moreover, the quotations made by the Italian Fathers often agree exactly and point to their having used one and the same text; and, as a matter of fact, as comparison shows, this text must have been the one used by Saint Augustine, viz. that of the *Itala*. Saint Augustine's preference must have made itself felt in Italy (*ceteris præferatur*), and so there was what may be called an official text.

5. It is true that to a great extent this translation is lost for us, as in most of the books of the Old Testament it has been replaced by Saint Jerome's translation, that will be discussed later. A good deal, however, of the lost translation can be recovered from quotations made by the Fathers who lived before Saint Jerome, and especially by Saint Augustine. Moreover, many remains of older Latin manuscripts have been found.

---

[1] *De doctrina Christ.*, II, 15: *In ipsis interpretationibus Itala ceteris præferatur, nam est verborum tenacior* [sc. than others] *cum perspicuitate sententiæ.* Burkitt, an English scholar, has tried to show that this *Itala* was not an earlier Latin text, but the work of Saint Jerome in 383 in Rome. Saint Augustine wrote the above words in 397. But if this were the case, Saint Augustine's *Itala* would have contained only the Psalms and the New Testament, whereas he is speaking of the whole Bible.

[2] *Cf.* also Wunderer, *Bruchstücke einer Afrik. Bibelübersetzung in der pseudocyprianischen Schrift exhortatio de pœnitentia,* Erlangen, 1889. This translation agrees fairly with Tertullian, but not with Saint Augustine.

[3] *Præf. in l. Josue: apud Latinos tot* [*sunt*] *exemplaria quot codices.*

As early as the eighteenth century Sabatier of the Congregation of Saint Maur attempted to restore the *Itala* completely from the scattered fragments that remain of it (Paris, 1743). Since his time many discoveries have been made. In Munich part of the Acts of the Apostles, according to the *Itala,* was found on parchment that had once been used to bind books belonging to the monastic library at Freising. This was published by L. Ziegler (*Italafragmente,* Marburg, 1875). That these fragments really formed part of the *Itala* is clearly seen, if they are compared with Saint Augustine. The same may be said of an edition of the Gospels by H. J. White, " The Four Gospels " (" Old Latin Biblical Texts," iii. 1888). This is based upon a sixth-century manuscript belonging to a priest named Valerian; it was found at Freising, and is now in Munich. Tischendorf refers to this manuscript as *q.*

Other parts of the *Itala* from Freising were published by Belsheim and Wölfflin. According to Wölfflin the Freising manuscript belongs to the sixth century. He praises the translation of the *Itala,* and, like Saint Augustine, admires its exact correspondence with the Greek original and the lucidity of its expressions. It aims not so much at correct Latinity, but at preventing " any particle of God's word from being lost." Wölfflin thinks that the oldest Latin translation was made in Africa, because Greek was not understood there, whereas in Rome and Southern Italy Greek was spoken as well as Latin. " When and where it was written will only be stated with certainty after we have acquired a better knowledge of African Latin." Other editions of texts belonging to a period before Saint Jerome, and now generally called collectively *Itala,* are mentioned by Kaulen.

6. The existing remains of the old Latin version enable us to see (1) that it was translated from a Greek text, and, in the case of the Old Testament, from the text of the Septuagint that existed before the *Hexapla;* (2) that it reproduced this text with great accuracy, and might justly be called the *Septuaginta in Latino;* (3) that it was in vulgar Latin, and (4) that it was the work of an Oriental. We may assume that the translator (or translators) belonged to the number of those who preached the faith in the earliest age of Christianity. Rufinus the Presbyter, the friend and afterwards the antagonist of Saint Jerome, intimates that the translation, or at least the beginning of it, must be traced back to Saint Peter. In fact, if the founder of the Roman Church established the order of worship, it seems that he must have taken care to have a generally intelligible text of the sacred books, which were read at the assemblies.

7. The widespread use of the Latin text gave rise to many variant readings in the copies of the Bible, as it did in the

case of the Septuagint. Complaints gradually arose, and increased as time went on, and they caused the energetic Pope Damasus to commission the learned Saint Jerome, who was then living in Rome, to revise and amend the Latin text that was in general use in that city. He set to work at once, and in the same year produced a revised version of the New Testament and Psalms. This version of the New Testament has ever since been used in the liturgy. The Psalms, too, were at once introduced into it, and this text is still found where passages from the Psalms occur in the *Missale Romanum*, as well as in the *Invitatoria* and *Responsoria* of the Breviary. To distinguish Saint Jerome's text from the unrevised version, the former was called the *Psalterium Romanum*. Later on, in 392, Saint Jerome, being then in Palestine, revised the text of the Psalms again with more accuracy, comparing it with the Hexapla version of the Septuagint, for he had discovered Origen's great work in the library of the church at Cæsarea. This new revision was adopted first in Gaul, and hence it is called the *Psalterium Gallicanum;* it is the version given in the Vulgate and in the Breviary (with the above-mentioned exceptions). While he was in Palestine, Saint Jerome revised most of the other books of the Old Testament, collating them with the *Hexapla*, but of this revision nothing has been preserved except the Book of Job (published by Lagarde, *Mitteil.*, II, 189–237), as a still better Latin text was soon afterwards produced.

8. While engaged in the work just described, Saint Jerome conceived an entirely new plan. As during his sojourn in Palestine he had learnt Hebrew and Chaldee very thoroughly, and as he was convinced that the original text was far superior to the Septuagint translation, and in order also to prevent the Jews from being able to argue that the text used by the Church was inaccurate, he determined to translate into Latin, from the Hebrew and Chaldee, the whole of the Old Testament, as far as it existed in the original. In spite of some interruptions, he completed this work in fifteen years (390–405). Unhappily, he had too high an opinion of his Hebrew original, which he often calls *hebraica veritas,* although it was very like the present

Masoretic text, contained many defects, and was in many respects inferior to the Septuagint. However, his reverence for tradition, and also his knowledge that most Catholics were averse to any alteration of the sacred text, kept him from giving free rein to his preference for the Hebrew, and in his translation we find many passages at variance with the Hebrew text. Regarded as a whole, Saint Jerome's work is the best of all the old translations, since it exactly reproduces the meaning of the original, and does so in very perfect language.[1]

9. It did not, however, find ready acceptance everywhere in the Church, as the prefaces to the sacred books reveal. Many objected to the new expressions, and disapproved of the apparent neglect of the Septuagint, which had been used by the Apostles. Saint Jerome had to encounter bitter antagonism in consequence, and a long time elapsed before the new text won favor, as the Church gave no special orders enforcing its use. During the fifth and sixth centuries both translations were in use; some persons preferred the *Itala*, others Saint Jerome's text, and it was only after the time of Gregory the Great that the latter decidedly prevailed, for, although the Pope said in his explanation of the Book of Job that either text might be used, he showed plainly in the course of his commentary that he preferred Saint Jerome's. When the Venerable Bede lived, the *Itala* had already fallen out of use in the churches, and was described as *prisca, vetusta, antiqua*, while Saint Jerome's text gradually came to be known as *nostra* or *vulgata*, and ever since, up to the present time, it has always been used in the Church.

The *Codex Fuldensis* of the New Testament, written about 545, is believed to be the oldest manuscript of the Latin text as revised by Saint Jerome (published by Ranke, Marburg, 1868). Of not much later date is the *Codex Amiatinus*, written in England, 690–716; it is named after the Monastery of Amiata near Florence, where it was formerly kept, but now it is in Florence. It contains the whole Bible with the exception of the Book of Baruch. The New Testament of this Codex was edited by Tischendorf under the title *Codex Amiatinus N. T. interprete Hieronymo*, Leipz., 1854.

[1] Concerning the method of this translation see Hoberg, *De s. Hieronym. ratione interpretandi*, 1886.

10. What has been said shows that the Vulgate consis
the following parts: (a) the protocanonical books of the
Testament (with the exception of the Psalms) accordin
Saint Jerome's translation from the Hebrew or Chaldee;
the deuterocanonical books of Tobias and Judith, also trans
by him directly from the same languages; (c) the Psalms,
the *Itala* but revised twice by Saint Jerome in accordance
the Septuagint; (d) the deuterocanonical books of the
Testament (with the exception of Tobias and Judith), as t
from the *Itala*, and not revised by Saint Jerome (Baru
and II Machabees, Ecclesiasticus, Wisdom); Saint Je
translated Esther x.–xvi. from the Septuagint, and Danie
24–90, xiii. and xiv. from Theodotion; (e) the whole of
New Testament is taken from the *Itala*, but modified by S
Jerome's revision mentioned above.

38. Continuation. The Vulgate in the Middle *

11. In course of time frequent copying, and the many
rections made by the owners, of Bibles led to great diversi*
the copies of the Latin Bibles. Most of the variant read
are due to familiarity with the old *Itala*, and the Liturgy
cially was not without influence upon the text. Charlem
employed his learned chancellor Alcuin in revising the
of the Vulgate, probably in accordance with the oldest m
scripts obtainable (801). In the eleventh century the *
scholar, Lanfranc (ob. 1089), undertook a new emendation,
his text was long considered as the standard for copyists.

12. From the twelfth century onwards the so-called
rectoria came into use, to secure as far as possible the accu
of the text. They originated with Stephen Harding, A
of Citeaux (ob. 1134). He corrected a manuscript of the I
in accordance with a very old Latin copy, using at the s
time the Hebrew and the Greek texts. The revised version
produced was thenceforth the standard text for the w
Cistercian Order. Other Orders and learned bodies follc
Stephen Harding, and every community desired in a sin
way to procure for itself a standard copy of the Bible.

standard copy of the Vulgate used by the University of Paris
was very frequently copied, but as it was by no means free from
mistakes, theologians from the thirteenth century onwards collected various readings, adding notes to say which had the
best claim to preference. These various readings were written
on the broad margins of the Bible texts, and a text containing
them, or even a copy of the *apparatus criticus* without the text,
was called a *correctorium*. Many such *correctoria* are preserved
in various libraries.

13. Towards the close of the Middle Ages two things exerted great influence upon the Latin text; viz., the study of
classical literature and the invention of printing.

The increase of classical studies had the result that in many
places people tried to " improve " the traditional text on classical
lines, because Saint Jerome's language did not savor of Cicero.
Moreover, many wished to make the Latin text conform more
closely to the Greek or Hebrew. Alterations of both these kinds
could be made only at the cost of sacrificing the uniformity and
purity of the text.

The introduction of the art of printing had similar effects.
It is well known that the first book ever printed was the Latin
Bible (Mayence, 1450). By the year 1500 over one hundred
different editions of the Bible had been printed and were in
circulation. In bringing out the earliest editions, there was
no thought of textual criticism, and any manuscript that came
to hand was printed. As competition increased, however, the
publishers had to comply with the taste of the period and have
recourse to Hebrew and Greek. The more numerous these aids
were, and the more various their sources, the greater and more
striking were the diversities in the Latin text, so much so that
the very idea of a Vulgate, i. e. of a generally recognized and
accepted form of the written words of revelation, was almost
lost.

39. CONTINUATION. THE COUNCIL OF TRENT

14. Meantime the Reformation had broken out, and in consequence of it the Council of Trent had assembled. On account
of the dogmatic questions which it had to consider, it was

obliged to begin by determining the sources of the Church's teaching. These were declared to be Scripture and tradition. As from the earliest times in all ecclesiastical business the Holy Scriptures had been used in the language of the Roman metropolitan Church, it was decided not to depart from this practice, but it was obvious that the Latin Bibles varied greatly one from another. It was therefore necessary to point out one book in which the Holy Scripture might be found accurately and truthfully rendered, and such the Council declared to be " the old Vulgate edition, which has stood the test of use for many centuries in the Church." It went on to order that the Vulgate should be regarded as authentic and be taken as the foundation not only at all proceedings of the Council, but also at all the official transactions of the Church, at sermons, catechizing and discussions (*Trid.*, Sess. 4).[1]

15. The expression " authentic " (= trustworthy, demonstrative) implies that the Vulgate contains the right text of Holy Scripture, as that text was written by the authors. Therefore any evidence derived from it on matters of faith or morals must be recognized as valid, i. e. it must not be rejected on the pretext that the Vulgate does not contain the correct text of the Bible. This does not, however, mean that the Vulgate is absolutely free from mistakes and cannot and ought not to admit of any correction, but it only means that it contains no mistakes of such a kind as that a misleading doctrine can be derived from them. This decision was not intended to forbid or exclude the use of the original text, or of other translations.

Leo XIII says in his Encyclical on Holy Scripture: " Although the meaning of the Hebrew and Greek idioms is, as far as substance is concerned, abundantly clear from the words of the Vulgate, yet if there be anything ambiguous or inaccurate introduced therein, an examination of the original language, according to the advice of Saint Augustine, will be if great service."

According to Bellarmine (*De Verbo Dei*, II, 11, ed. Mogunt, 1842) reference should be made to the original (1) when there appears to be a mistake in the written or printed Latin text, (2) when the Latin codices

---

[1] *Sancta synodus declarat, ut hæc ipsa vetus et vulgata editio, quæ longo tot sæculorum usu in ipsa ecclesia probata est, in publicis lectionibus, disputationibus, prædicationibus et expositionibus pro authentica habeatur et ut nemo illam rejicere audeat vel præsumat.*

vary, (3) when a word or thought is ambiguous in the Latin, (4) in order to understand the peculiar use and emphasis of words in the original. Salmeron, who was present at the Council, uses similar language. See Cornely, *Introd.*, I, 458; *Comp.*, 112.

16. As the Vulgate had suffered many alterations in consequence of having been frequently reproduced during a very long period, the Council at the same session ordered that thenceforth only carefully revised editions of the Holy Scriptures, and especially of the Vulgate, should be issued.[1] In this way the arbitrary alterations of editors were to be checked, and a return to the tradition of the Church was pointed out as the right course to pursue in restoring the purity of the Bible text.

By saying " as free as possible from mistakes " the Church wished to guard against " corrections " in the text, which are often only the outcome of private judgment and cause much harm. She declared that the old originals or translations ought to be followed as closely as possible. The appreciative treatment of the oldest discoverable manuscripts, which in our day is a favorite pursuit of scholars, has therefore long been desired and encouraged by the Church.

Catholic scholars at once attempted to comply with the wishes of the Council. As early as 1547 the theological faculty at Louvain caused a text of the Vulgate, restored according to strict rules of criticism, to be published by one of their members, John Hentenius, and this was frequently reprinted. This text did not, however, give universal satisfaction, because it subsequently admitted a number of readings to the margins, and they were likely to raise doubts as to the accuracy of the text itself.

17. Meantime the Holy See had determined to issue an official edition of the Vulgate. After much careful work upon it, this Roman edition appeared under Sixtus V, 1590, and again in a more accurate form under Clement VIII, 1592. As some misprints still occurred in the latter edition, a still more carefully revised reprint appeared in 1593 and 1598. This edition is now the standard edition of the Church, and all new impressions of the Vulgate must agree with it word for word. The Council of Trent imposed upon all printers of Bibles the obligation of

---

[1] *Ut posthac sacra scriptura, potissimum vero hæc ipsa vetus et vulgata editio quam emendatissime imprimatur.*

submitting their Bibles to the bishops and of securing their written approval for the books (Sess. 4, *de ed. et usu sacr. librorum*).

Valentine Loch's Latin Bible (Ratisbon, 3d ed., 1873) is an accurate reprint of this Roman edition, and is issued with the sanction of Karl August, Archbishop of Munich and Freising. In 1861 a careful reprint of the Clementine text of 1593 and 1598 was published by Vercellone in Rome; and this was copied at Augsburg in 1880.

Two English scholars, J. Wordsworth and H. J. White, imposed upon themselves the task of restoring, with the greatest possible fidelity, the Vulgate text of the New Testament as revised by Saint Jerome. In doing so they made use of about thirty old manuscripts, but relied chiefly on the *Codex Bibliorum Amiatinus* (see p. 251). Their edition was printed at Oxford: the Gospels in 1889–1898 and the Acts in 1905. This work, like the attempts mentioned before (p. 233) to restore the Greek text of the New Testament, shows that our Vulgate need not fear criticism. Nevertheless many persons desired to have a new edition authorized by the Church. Such an edition appeared at Innsbruck in 1906; it is the result of very laborious studies, and follows the copy in the Vatican. P. Michael Hetzenauer, *Biblia sacra Vulgatæ editionis.* Large octavo, XXXII, 1143, n. 173.[1]

---

[1] At the present moment the Benedictines are busy in preparing what is to be the new official edition of the Church. (Letter of Pope Pius X to Abbot Gasquet, Dec. 3, 1907.)

THIRD PART

SPECIAL INTRODUCTION — THE SACRED BOOKS CONSIDERED SINGLY

PRELIMINARY REMARKS

IN a Special Introduction each of the sacred books must be dealt with separately, its contents stated, the date of composition and the author discussed, and, if need be, its authenticity and textual purity defended.

When we call a book authentic,[1] we mean that it is really the work of the person to whom it is ascribed. Authenticity is proved partly by internal and partly by external evidence, i. e. partly from arguments derived from the book itself and partly from other testimony.

A book is said to possess textual purity when it has undergone no essential alteration in the course of time, but has in the main been preserved as it left the author.

THE BOOKS OF THE OLD TESTAMENT

1. SURVEY AND CLASSIFICATION

The books of the Old Testament were produced gradually among the Israelites, and the special introduction to it may be divided into four sections, corresponding to the four chief periods of Israelite history.

1. From the beginning of the history of Israel to the close of the Mosaic legislation and the entrance of the Israelites into Palestine about the year 1400 B. C.; origin of the Pentateuch.

---

[1] αὐθεντικός (from αὐθέντης = ruler, originator) means proceeding from the originator, genuine (see p. 254). When the Council of Trent proclaimed the authenticity of the Vulgate, a wider signification was given to the word, as it included genuineness and textual purity.

2. From the occupation of the Holy Land to the separation of the two kingdoms of Juda and Samaria about 920 B. C. (or, according to another view, 932 B. C.). The period when the sacred poetry was at its prime; origin of the books of Josue, Judges, Ruth, Samuel, then of the Psalms, of Job and Canticles, later also of Proverbs and Ecclesiastes.

3. From the separation of the kingdoms to the end of the Babylonian Captivity, 536 B. C. In this period prophecy was at its prime; origin of the works of the four major and of most of the minor prophets.

4. The period after the Captivity to the time of Christ; origin of the books of Kings, Chronicles, Esdras and Nehemias, Esther, Tobias, Judith, Machabees; Aggæus, Zacharias and Malachias; Sirach or Ecclesiasticus, Wisdom.

FIRST SECTION

THE OLD TESTAMENT REVELATION BEFORE THE ENTRANCE OF THE ISRAELITES INTO PALESTINE

2. THE PENTATEUCH

1. *Name.* The only sacred book belonging to the earliest period of Israelite history is the Pentateuch [1] (meaning five books), which is at once the book of the law and the history of Israel. The Hebrew name is *Thora* = law; [2] in the New Testament it is ὁ νόμος.

Our names for the single books, Genesis, Exodus, Leviticus, Numbers and Deuteronomy, are taken from the Septuagint, and were given with reference to the contents; the Vulgate retained the Greek names, only rendering ἀριθμοί by *Numeri*. In the Hebrew Bible and among the Rabbis the names of the five books are taken from the initial word of each. The first

---

[1] Πέντε, five, and τεῦχος, utensil, tool, but in the Alexandrian period also book. The name is properly feminine = ἡ πεντάτευχος βίβλος, but is masculine in Latin, because *liber* is understood. The word *Pentateuch* occurs first in Origen (*Ad Joh.*, IV, 25. Reusch, *Einleitung*, p. 10), and in Latin first in Tertullian (*Adv. Marc.*, I, 10).

[2] הַתּוֹרָה, generally with the article.

is *Bereshith* = In the beginning; the second, *Shemoth* = Names, because it begins "These are the names"; the third, *Vajjiqra* = And he called; the fourth, *Vajjedabber* or *Bemidbar* = And [God] spoke in the desert; the fifth, *Debarim* = Words ("These are the words").

The Pentateuch contains the earliest history of the human race [1] and is at the same time the book of the law governing the people of revelation, who were strictly marked off from polytheistic nations.

The division of the work into five books is probably not due to the author, yet is very old. It is quite certain that the Seventy did not divide it, for the division of the Book of Psalms into five parts is based on the similar division of the Book of the Law.

2. Contents. Genesis (50 chapters) contains the account of the Creation of the world and of man, the Fall of man and its immediate consequences, the Deluge, the dispersion of the human race, the history of Abraham and his descendants to the death of the Patriarch Jacob in Egypt.

Exodus (40 chapters) contains the history of Moses, the departure of the Israelites from Egypt, the giving of the Law on Sinai, and the first arrangements for the worship of God.

Leviticus (sc. *liber*) (27 chapters) consists chiefly of rules for worship and the persons engaged in it.

Numeri or *Numbers* (36 chapters) contains lists of the fighting men and of the Levites, the arrangement of the encampments, several laws regarding the future abode of the Israelites in Chanaan, and Balaam's blessing. The thirty-seven years of wandering in the wilderness are passed over in silence.[2]

---

[1] Interest has been awakened by a book written by Merker, a German officer: *Die Masai, ein ostafrikanisches Semitenvolk*, 1904. This race migrated from the Arabian peninsula into eastern Africa in prehistoric times. They have a monotheistic worship and are acquainted with almost the whole account, given in Genesis, of the early history of mankind, Paradise, the temptation by the serpent, the deluge, etc.

[2] Fr. v. Hummelauer (*Commentarius in Numeros*, Paris, 1899) tries to prove that in Numbers xx. 1–11 we may assume the omission of a considerable part of the original history of these thirty-seven years. "Moses struck the rock twice with his rod." The first stroke had no effect on account of the want of confidence felt by Moses. Then the people all re-

Deuteronomium or *Deuteronomy* (= second law) (34 chapters) emphasizes and partially repeats the previous legislation, and, at its close, contains an account of Moses' last words, his death and burial.

Genesis: 1. Creation, six days' work.[1] 2. Second and supplementary

---

belled against him and remained obstinate for many years (Amos v. 25, etc.; Acts vii. 42, etc.). The sin of Moses was therefore the immediate cause of this revolt, and respect for him led subsequent Israelite writers to suppress the sorrowful events of these thirty-seven or thirty-eight years. (?) When afterwards Moses' confidence in God returned, he again struck the rock, and this time with success.

[1] Revelation tells us nothing as to the interpretation of the *Hexæmeron;* hence there are, on the part of theologians, various opinions regarding it.

(*a*) Saint Augustine and Clement of Alexandria (*Strom.*, VI, 16) assume that the six days must be limited to one moment. (It is true that in Ecclus. xviii. 1 we read: *Creavit omnia simul*, but this may refer to the sudden creation of spirits and of matter out of nothing, which is mentioned in Gen. i. 1.)

(*b*) The literal interpretation is that the days of creation were real days of twenty-four hours each, so that God created the world in the course of six ordinary days.

(*c*) The figurative interpretation is that six days are mentioned in Holy Scripture as employed in various forms of creation because man was ordered to work for six days and to rest on the seventh. In this way the work of creation would not have been the foundation of our week, but the already existing institution of the week would have been the reason for dividing the account of creation into six days' work.

(*d*) The Vision theory is that Adam described the work of creation as having been effected in six days to his descendants, because God in a vision (*tardemah*, as is mentioned in Gen. ii. 21 with regard to the creation of woman) showed him the various results of creation on six successive days. *Cf.* v. Hummelauer, *Schöpfungsbericht*.

(*e*) According to Zapletal the six days' work consists of two parts, — first to third day, creation of places; fourth to sixth day, creation of armies. This explanation is based on the word *zebaam* = their army, Genesis ii. 1. The verse runs: "Completed were heaven and earth and all their army." The Septuagint translated *zebaam* by κόσμος αὐτῶν, and so the Vulgate has *ornatus eorum*. The accurate translation, however, would have been στρατὸς αὐτῶν or πλῆθος αὐτῶν = *exercitus eorum*. The scholastics, following the Vulgate, distinguish *opus distinctionis* (first to third days) and *opus ornatus* (fourth to sixth days); the latter should strictly be *opus exercitus*. Zapletal thinks that the reference is to the heavenly bodies (fourth day), creatures living in water and in air (fifth day), land animals and man (sixth day); these constitute the army or armies. This division corresponds to the six working days of mankind. Zapletal, therefore, thinks the account of creation is not strictly histori-

account of the creation. The first human beings in Paradise.[1] 3. The Fall of man. 4. Cain and Abel. Cain's descendants. 5. Adam's gene-

---

cal, which is a questionable doctrine. Moreover we should notice that the creation of light on the first day is not the production of a place, and that plants, created on the third day, also form part of the army of the earth. Reference is made to the meaning of *zaba* = to move, but it also means to serve (e. g. Ex. xxxviii. 8). God's army is the vast host of creatures occupying heaven and earth (angels, stars, plants, beasts and men). They are witnesses to God's power, and do Him service against those who deny Him.

(*f*) Allusion must be made to a theory that at the beginning the alternating periods of light and darkness were much longer than they now are, so that each of the six days of creation may have embraced thousands or millions of years, since they were God's days resembling God's Sabbath, which still continues. This is called the concordistic theory.

It has the advantage of being capable of reconciliation with the account that evidently purports to be historical. We may also notice Thoene's opinion that the days of creation were probably analogous to the seventh day which is not yet over. As this day is composed of many days of evening and morning, so it may have been in the history of creation.

With regard to the age of the story of creation, Kaulen rightly remarks that it was taken from tradition and placed by Moses at the beginning of his law. The investigations of modern scholars offer no opposition to the theory that the story was brought to the West from their Chaldæan home by the original ancestors of the people of Israel. It differs considerably from the stories of creation handed down by the Babylonians and other nations. The heathen races introduced fanciful polytheistic elements into the tradition, whereas the Bible account is monotheistic and contains the absolute truth, viz. the revelation of God to the first human beings. That this account is connected with the Babylonian legends, now being discovered by means of excavations in Babylon, is quite explicable, for Babylon was the first home of civilization for the human race. *Cf.* Genesis xi.

[1] Wellhausen thinks that this account may be referred to the class of Oriental fables that often contain stories of magic gardens and palaces. He proposes, therefore, to set it aside. May not the reverse be the truth? May not the old tradition of Paradise underlie these Oriental tales? Jeremias (xxxii. 19) declares all human beings to be children of Adam. Such inconvenient evidence is rejected by modern critics as being due to "later interpolations," for they believe that the story of creation must have been composed during the Babylonian captivity. The situation of Paradise has been much discussed. Kaulen places it in Armenia, and Hoberg and Schöpfer do the same; von Hummelauer thinks it was in Babylonia, and so does Pörtner; Hommel refers it to Arabia. In his work on the rivers of Paradise (*Paradiesesflüsse*), 1901, Engelkemper supports the old theory that the Euphrates, Tigris, Indus or Ganges, and Nile are meant, and he assumes that the writer of Gene-

alogy. 6. Decay of morality. Noe and the ark. 7. Deluge.[1] 8, 9. End of the flood. Covenant with Noe, Sem, Cham and Japhet. 10. Noe's genealogy. 11. Building of the Tower of Babel. Dispersion of mankind.

---

sis accommodated his statements to the geographical knowledge of his day. It should, however, be borne in mind that great geological changes have taken place since the time of the first human beings, so that there may have been a river at one time in Asia, the name of which was transferred to the African Nile. Engelkemper declares Eastern Armenia to have been the place where Paradise was situated. Fr. Delitzsch prefers Babylonia, and thinks the rivers of Paradise were channels of the Euphrates. Kaulen's view has found most adherents amongst Catholics, at least up to the present time.

[1] With reference to this event see R. de Girard, *Le déluge devant la critique historique*, Fribourg, 1892, and *Le charactère naturel du déluge*, Fribourg, 1894; also A. Trissl, *Sündfluttheorie und Gletschertheorie*, and *Sündflut oder Gletscher*, Ratisbon, 1893–94. That this catastrophe actually occurred is generally admitted, because the stories regarding it are so widely spread. The existence of about sixty-eight autochthonous accounts of a deluge can be proved, so that here we are dealing with a story known all over the world. There is not the same consensus of opinion regarding the extent of the flood, whether it affected the whole earth and all mankind, or only part of it. Nor are scholars agreed as to whether it was absolutely miraculous, or, in part at least, natural. Schanz, Schöpfer, Hammerschmid, v. Hummelauer and Hoberg, *Erkl. d. Genesis*, all believe that the flood covered only a limited area, but Kaulen emphatically opposes this view, and so do Trissl and Gander.

REASONS for believing that the Deluge was general: (1) In II Saint Peter iii. 5, etc., the Deluge is put on a level with the final destruction of the whole world, which is to be effected by means of fire. (2) What would have been the object of building the ark if Noe and his family could have found safety by migrating? (3) The language of Holy Scripture clearly implies that the catastrophe was general, and it is a general rule in hermeneutics that a passage must be explained literally, as long as there is no absolute necessity for departing from the literal sense. (4) The Fathers and the exegetical tradition of the Church assume that the Deluge was general. (5) The Church does the same in her liturgy.

Most of the objections to the general character of the Deluge are based upon the assumption that it must have been a merely natural event. But the language of Holy Scripture indicates that it was due to God's immediate intervention, and was therefore something miraculous, and this removes all difficulty as to its being possible by natural means; it does not prelude the co-operation of the forces of nature but absolutely assumes it. The same remark applies to reports of other, later events, e. g. the plagues of Egypt. (We must acknowledge that at the present time the theory that the Deluge did not affect the *whole* world, but only the inhabited parts of it, and consequently all mankind, is the *sententia communior* of Bible commentators. It seems, however, scarcely in conformity with the language of the text.)

12, 13. Call of Abram and his migration. 14. His victory over four kings. Melchisidech, King of Salem.[1] 15. God's covenant with Abram. 16. Hagar and Ismael. 17. Circumcision. 18. God's intercourse with Abraham. 19. Destruction of Sodom. 20. Abraham and Abimelech. 21. Birth of Isaac, expulsion of Ismael. 22. Abraham's trial on Mount Moria. 23. Death of Sara. Burial place in Hebron. 24. Rebecca. 25, 26. Ketura, Abraham's death. Ismael's descendants. Isaac and his sons Jacob and Esau. Abimelech. 27. Jacob outwits Esau. 28. Jacob's migration. The ladder from heaven. 29. Jacob with Laban. His wives, Lia and Rachel, Bala and Zelpha. 30. Jacob's children. Compact with Laban. 31. Return of Jacob. 32, 33. Jacob's wrestling with God, Israel; meeting with Esau. 34. Ravishing of Dina, destruction of the Sichemites. 35. Benjamin. Rachel's death. 36. Tribes of the Edomites, i. e. of Esau's descendants. 37. Sale of Joseph. 38. Juda and Thamar. 39–41. Joseph in Egypt. 42–45. He tests his brethren. 46, 47. Jacob and his family migrate to Egypt. 48. Jacob adopts Joseph's sons. 49. Jacob's blessing given to his sons; his death. 50. His burial at Hebron.

Exodus: 1. Enslavement of the Israelites in Egypt. 2. Moses. 3. The burning bush. 4. Moses' mission. 5. Moses and Aaron before Pharao.[2] 6. Increased oppression of the Israelites. 7–10. The ten plagues of Egypt. 12. Institution of the Pasch. Flight from Egypt. 13. Consecration of the firstborn. The journey eastward. 14. Passage of the Red Sea. 15. Canticle of Moses. 16. Murmuring of the people. Quails. Manna. 17. Renewal of the journey. Water out of the rock. Victory over the Amalekites. 18. Jethro comes to Moses. 19. The people at Sinai. 20. The Decalogue. 21–23. Further legislation. 24. Conclusion of the Covenant. 25. Rules regarding the ark of the Covenant, the table for the loaves of proposition and the candlestick. 26. The Tabernacle. 27. The Altar in the Court. 28. The dress of the priests. 29. The consecration of the priests. 30. The altar of incense and other furniture. 31. Sabbath observance. Tables of the Law. 32. The golden calf. 33, 34. New tables of the Law. 35. Free-will offerings for making the Tabernacle and all belonging to it. 36–40. The Tabernacle and its furniture are made.

Leviticus: 1–7. Regulations for the various sacrifices. 8. Consecra-

---

[1] The genuine character of this chapter, formerly rejected by the critics, cannot now be questioned. King Amraphel of Sennaar (Gen. xiv. 1) has been identified with King Hammurabi of Babylon. (See L. W. King's " Letters and Inscriptions of Hammurabi," London, 1901.) Mommert has proved that Salem is the old city of Jerusalem.

[2] Sayce, " Fresh Light from Ancient Monuments " (p. 63), identifies the Pharao of the exodus with Meneptah II, who became king in 1325. Most probably, however, he lived in the fifteenth century and belonged to the eighteenth dynasty. Amenophis II (1461–1436) seems to have been the Pharao of the Exodus. (Miketta has showed that Israel must have entered the country west of the Jordan not later than 1392.) In his account of his victories, Meneptah mentions the Israelites among the tribes inhabiting Palestine.

tion of Aaron and his sons. 9. Aaron's first sacrifice. 10. Punishment of his sons Nadab and Abiu. 11. Clean and unclean beasts. 12. Purification of women after childbirth. 13, 14. Laws concerning leprosy. 15. Sexual uncleanness. 16. The Day of Atonement. 17. Sacrifices to be offered only in the sanctuary. Eating blood forbidden. 18. Marriage laws. 19. Various rules governing the life of the people. 20. Crimes to be punished with death. 21, 22. Cleanness of priests and sacrifices. 23. Holy days to be kept. 24. Loaves of proposition or shewbread. Punishment of blasphemy. 25. Sabbatical year and year of jubilee. 26. Blessing for observance and punishment for transgression of the commandments. 27. Vows.

Numeri or *Numbers:* 1, 2. Numbering of the people and arrangement of the camp. 3, 4. Number and order of the Levites. 5. Sacrifice of jealousy. 6. Nazirites. Aaron's blessing. 7. Dedication offerings made by the heads of the tribes. 8. Dedication of the Levites. 9. Pasch on Sinai. 10. Regulations for blowing the trumpets on special occasions. Departure from Sinai in definite order. 11. Quails for food. 12. Mary's murmuring and its punishment. 13. Spies sent to Chanaan. 14. Murmuring of the people, and their punishment. 15. Laws regarding eating the flesh of animals sacrificed. A Sabbath breaker. 16. Sedition of Core, Dathan and Abiron. 17. Aaron's rod that blossomed. 18. Duties and privileges of the Levites. 19. Sacrifice of the red cow. 20. Mary's death. Want of water. The Edomites refuse to allow the people to pass. Aaron's death. Eleazar made high priest. 21. The brazen serpent. Victory over the Amorites. 22–24. Balaam is required to curse the Israelites, but blesses them instead. 25. Service of Beelphegor and its punishment. 26. Numbering of the people. 27. Law of inheritance. Moses beholds the Promised Land from afar; he appoints Josue to be his successor. 28–30. Rules about sacrifices and vows. 31. Victory over the Madianites. 32. Settlements of the tribes of Ruben, and Gad, and half of Manasses. 33. List of the encampments. 34. Boundaries of the land assigned to Israel. 35. Levite cities and cities of refuge. 36. Marriages within the tribes.

Deuteronomium, Deuteronomy: 1–4. Moses before his death reminds the people what God has done for Israel through him. 5. He repeats the Decalogue. 6. He requires them to love God and warns them, 7, against intercourse with the Gentiles. 8. He impresses upon them the necessity of obedience to God, and 9, 10, reminds them of God's benefits. 11. A blessing is to follow obedience and a curse disobedience. 12. The people are to have one single place of sacrifice. 13. Heathen customs and worship are to be avoided, 14, also the eating of unclean animals. 15. The year of remission. 16. Solemn festivals to be observed. 17. Rules for judges and kings. 18. Levites and prophets. 19. Rights of sanctuary and protection of witnesses. 20. Laws relating to war. 21. Family relations. 22. Immorality and adultery. 23. Various rules of life. 24. Divorce. 25. Levirate marriage, etc. 26. First fruits and tithes. 27. Stones to be erected as memorials. 28. Curses and blessings in proportion to the keeping of the law. 29. Renewal of the Covenant. 30. Be faithful to your God! 31. Moses gives the written Law to the priests and elders, ordering them to read it every seven years to the people. Josue is appointed to succeed him. 32, 33. Moses' song of praise, his prophecy and blessing. 34. Moses dies in the Land of Moab; Josue enters on his office.

AGE AND AUTHORSHIP OF THE PENTATEUCH [1]

(a) Criticism

Both the Jewish and the Christian traditions ascribe to the Pentateuch a very high antiquity, for they regard Moses [2] as its author, and believe that he wrote it about 1500 B. C., or not long after. This was the universally accepted opinion until the seventeenth century. At the present time it is absolutely rejected by rationalistic criticism, and the work, as we have it, is assigned to the period following the Captivity.

The English philosopher Hobbes (ob. 1679), the French writer Peyrère (ob. 1676) and the Jew Spinoza (ob. 1677) forestalled the modern critics. In his "Leviathan," III, 33, Hobbes laid down the principle that we ought to try to ascertain their date of composition from the contents of the books of the Bible, and from internal evidence Moses could not be regarded as the author of the Pentateuch. Peyrère, in his work on Præ-Adamites, maintained that the Pentateuch was the work of several authors. Spinoza (*Tractatus theol.-polit.*, c. 7–10) arrived at practically the same results as modern rationalistic critics, and assigned all the historical books of the Old Testament to the time of Esdras.

A great impetus was given to the new criticism in the eighteenth century by J. Astruc (ob. 1766), a French physician, whose book, *Conjectures sur les mémoires originaux, dont il paroit que Moyse s'est servi pour composer le livre de la Genèse*, was published in 1753. In it he drew attention to the various names for God in the Hebrew text of Genesis. Some portions contain the name Elohim exclusively, others no less exclusively the name Jehovah (*Yahweh*), while in others the names alternate.[3] For this reason Astruc assumes that there were two chief originals, one referring to God as Elohim and the other as Yahweh, and

---

[1] It may be noticed that the Pentateuch is discussed twice in the present work (pp. 37–56, and pp. 265–274). This was unavoidable, as in one place we are dealing with the history of Israel and in the other with the sacred literature. The two passages supplement, and do not contradict, one another.

[2] The name Moses is regarded by Döller, who follows Lepsius and Ebers, as formed from the Egyptian *mes, mesu* = Son. Schenz agrees with Exodus ii. 10 and thinks it is a Coptic word, meaning "drawn out of the water."

[3] e. g. in chapters i., v., viii. 1–19 God is always called Elohim; in iii., iv., x., xii.-xvi. He is called Yahweh. (In the Greek text Θεός and κύριος; in the Latin, *Deus* and *Dominus*.)

these were used by Moses. Astruc thinks that he can detect traces of at least two other originals, so that Moses' work originally contained four columns that were subsequently confused. He does not doubt that Moses was the author.

Astruc's opinions were made known in Germany by Eichhorn (ob. 1827), a Protestant, and gave rise to a violent dispute that has now lasted over one hundred years among Protestant scholars, though Catholics have not paid much attention to it. Eichhorn believed Moses to be the author of the Pentateuch, and imagined that he had combined an Elohim history with a Yahweh history, without removing superfluous passages, had then inserted additions of his own that he wrote from time to time, and shortly before his death had completed the work by writing Deuteronomy. Ilgen (ob. 1834) followed Eichhorn, but thought he could trace no less than 17 originals, 10 of which he ascribed to the first Elohist, 5 to the second, and 2 to the Yahwist. The whole theory as upheld by Astruc, Eichhorn and Ilgen was called the Documentary Hypothesis.

The Fragmentary Hypothesis was the next put forward. In 1802 Vater (ob. 1826) brought out a Commentary on Genesis, in which he expressed this opinion regarding the Pentateuch: The five books are made up of fragments, some large and some small, but originally not closely connected. Genesis, for instance, consists of thirty-nine such fragments, strung together by some one who collected them and was anxious that none of them should be lost. This was not Moses, but a much later writer. Hartmann (ob. 1838) followed Vater's lines, and assigned the formation of the Pentateuch to the time of the Captivity.

It is plain, however, that the Pentateuch is no mere collection of stray fragments, and so the Fragmentary Hypothesis had not many supporters.

Ewald (ob. 1875) in his *Komposition der Genesis*, that appeared in 1823, recognized the principle of unity running through it, and thought it possible to reconcile the variation in the names given to God with its authorship by one man, as he might have used now the one and now the other name with a definite intention. This argument exploded the Fragtary Hypothesis.

The next is known as the Supplementary Hypothesis. Bohlen (ob. 1839), De Wette (ob. 1849), Bleek (ob. 1859), Tuch (ob. 1867), Lengerke (ob. 1857) and Delitzsch (ob. 1890) declared: We must admit that there were two authors, one of whom simply expanded the other's work. The original work was that of an Elohist, the supplementary portions were written by a Yahwist. The former was a priest who lived about the time of Saul; the latter during Solomon's reign.

This Supplementary Hypothesis did not meet with universal approval. Against it was the argument that the Yahwistis portions contain evidence of being original, so that they cannot be regarded as mere additions. Eventually, therefore, scholars came back to the Documentary Hypothesis (Hupfeld, ob. 1866, Knobel, ob. 1863, Schrader, Kuenen, ob. 1891, and Dillmann, ob. 1894). They believed that there were several sources whence the author or authors had derived their information. Moses could not be the author, as the work belonged to a much later period.

J. Wellhausen, Professor at Göttingen, basing his studies on the earlier writings of Reuss and Graf, has worked out this documentary hypothesis most thoroughly, and it owes its name chiefly to him. Stâde, Budde, Cornill, Kautzsch and others have written in accordance with his views. They distinguish four original documents, which were put together to form the present Pentateuch at the time of Esdras and Nehemias or not long after: the first was the work of a Yahwist J,[1] the second of an Elohist E, the third is Deuteronomy D, written and published during the reign of Josias (623) and the fourth authority was the priesthood P, from Babylon. (*Cf.* p. 40.)

In answer to these hypotheses, which are now claimed to be irrefutable and true, the following arguments may be brought forward in

(b) Defense of the Mosaic Origin of the Pentateuch

The claim that the Pentateuch is the work of Moses is not a denial that there are other constituents in it. We may admit that Moses incorporated earlier documents and records into his work.[2] No one can doubt that the use of writing was known at the time of Moses and long before.

There is no tradition among the Israelites of any period when the art of writing was unknown to them. It has been asserted that the prophets Elias and Eliseus (900 B. C.) must have been ignorant of it, as no written works have come down from them, and Amos (after 800) is the earliest prophet whose writings are extant (Benzinger, "Arch.," 289). The Mesa stone, however (896), proves not only that the art of writing was known long before the time of Amos, but also that it had been long in use, for the inscription on the stone shows an unmistakable tendency to cursive script, such as could result only from a long-continued development.[3] At the time of David (1055–1015) there was already a "recorder" at court (II Kings (Sam.) viii. 17, xx, 25), and David himself

---

[1] For the sake of brevity, it is usual to designate these "original documents," to which reference has often to be made, by letters. Klostermann and Strack add as a fifth document the "Law of Sanctity" (Lev. xvii.–xxvi.), which they designate by H. Steuernagel (*Allg. Einl. in d. Hexateuch*, Göttingen, 1900), adds further R = revision and union of the various fragments. This author accepts the documentary hypothesis for the solution of the problem as a whole, but also the fragmentary and supplementary hypotheses for that of individual problems. *Cf.* also Gunkel (Genesis, 1901), who also believes that some one finally edited the whole.

[2] Papal Bible Commission, June 27, 1906.

[3] See above, p. 46.

wrote a letter to Joab and sent it by Urias (II Kings (Sam.) xi. 14, 15). Long before this period there had been communication in writing between Egypt and Western Asia, as Cornill (p. 14) admits. The Egyptians, whose wisdom Moses had acquired, are known as having been fond of writing.[1] Their learned men were called "scribes." The largest extant papyrus (Prisse, Paris) belongs to the time of the Twelfth Dynasty, and partly to the reign of Pharao Snefru, about 2800 B. C. Moses may very well have come into the possession of written documents and have added to them, thus compiling the Pentateuch,[2] and he was certainly not the only Israelite who had acquired the art of writing in Egypt.

Various glosses and additions of later date have undoubtedly been incorporated into Moses' work;[3] such are, e. g. Gen. xii. 6, xiii. 7, xxii. 14, xxxvi. 31, etc.; Ex. xvi. 35 (*cf.* Jos. v. 12). The last chapter (xxxiv.) of Deuteronomy seems certainly to have been written by Josue, as Jewish tradition records. The following arguments support the theory that Moses was the author of the entire Pentateuch:

1. The Pentateuch itself names Moses as its author. Deuteronomy xxxi. 9: "Moses wrote this law and delivered it to the priests." 24–27: "After Moses had wrote the words of this law in a volume, and finished it, he commanded the Levites . . . saying: Take this book, and put it in the side of the ark of the covenant of the Lord your God: that it may be there for a testimony against thee, for I know thy obstinacy." It is also frequently stated that Moses wrote down this or that regulation (Ex. xxiv. 4, xxxiv. 27; Num. xxxiii. 2).

2. The Jewish tradition, which has never been contradicted, always regards the Law as being of Mosaic origin. The various parties among the Jews, the Jewish writers Josephus and Philo, and the whole nation both in and beyond Palestine, are unani-

---

[1] "Every object, down to the roughest bits of stone, was covered with written characters. In public and private life papyrus served as a means of communication." Brugsch, *Aegyptologie*, 87.

[2] *Cf.* Winckler, *Die Tontafeln von Tell-el-Amarna* (5th vol. of the *Keilinschrift. Bibliothek*, Berlin, 1896). This important discovery shows that in 1500 B. C. Babylonian civilization had reached Upper Egypt, for the script and language of these tablets are both Assyrian-Babylonian. News and letters were constantly passing to and fro from the Euphrates to the Nile.

[3] It is possible, however, that many of these remarks nevertheless came down from Moses himself.

mous in declaring the Pentateuch to have been the work of Moses, actually written by him. This tradition points to a long recognized fact. It cannot reasonably be supposed that a whole nation allowed itself to be deceived by forgeries and spurious documents.

3. It has already been shown (p. 48, etc.) that in the literature of the Jews the Pentateuch has always been known and recognized as the work of Moses.

4. Attention has also been drawn (p. 52, etc.) to the fact that the Samaritan Pentateuch is evidence that the book existed at a very remote period in the history of the Israelites.

5. Jesus Christ expressly confirmed the Jewish belief that Moses had drawn up the Book of the Law, when He said (John v. 46, 47) : " If you did believe Moses, you would perhaps believe me also; for he wrote of me. But if you do not believe his writings, how will you believe my words?" *Cf.* also Matt. viii. 4, xix. 7; Mark i. 44, vi. 10, x. 3, xii. 26; Luke v. 14, xx. 28, xxiv. 44; John vii. 19, viii. 5.

6. Other evidence is derived from the structure of the Pentateuch.

(*a*) The work professes to have originated in the wilderness.[1] From the second book onwards it contains constant references to life in encampments. The Tabernacle was made of acacia wood, and the sacred furniture of the same material; there is no mention of cedars and cypresses, to which allusion is made so often later in Palestine. The acacia is the only tree that flourishes in the valleys of the Sinai peninsula and can be used for building purposes (*cf.* p. 69). Some creatures, which might be eaten, occur in the wilderness, but not in Palestine. The hides of the *tachasch* (sea cow) (Ex. xxvi. 14) were unknown to the later Israelites; the only other place where the name *tachasch* is found is Ezechiel xvi. 10.[2] Only an eye witness could know how many palms and springs there were at Elim (Ex. xv.

---

[1] By wilderness we must not understand a sandy desert like the Sahara, but only an uninhabited and uncultivated country.

[2] " I shod thee with tachasch." It is plain that the Israelites in later times were unacquainted with this animal, otherwise the name would have been translated in some way and made intelligible. *Cf.* p. 72. (N. B. The Douay reads " violet-colored shoes.")

27), or which men carried away the corpses of Aaron's sons (Lev. x. 4), etc.

(b) The author knew Egypt very well, and assumed that his earliest readers were equally familiar with it. In Genesis xiii. 10 (where we ought to follow the Peshitto and read *Zoan*), the pasture land near the Jordan is compared with Lower Egypt. In Numbers xiii. 23 we read that Hebron was older than the Egyptian town of Zoan. The Israelites are warned against imitating Egyptian customs (Lev. xviii. 3). The dress of the priests resembles that of the Egyptian priests. In the history of the Patriarchs the description given of Egypt exactly agrees with the accounts taken from the oldest monuments that have been discovered. A few expressions even are given in the Egyptian language.[1] A foreigner, writing at a later date, could not have possessed such knowledge of ancient Egypt. The author and his earliest readers must have been long resident there.

(c) The author and the people of his nation knew practically nothing of Chanaan; and such knowledge as they had was not acquired by personal experience. The Egyptian towns of Pithom, Ramasses (Ex. i. 11), Socoth, Etham (Ex. xiii. 20), Pi Hachiroth, Beelsephon (Ex. xiv. 9), are mentioned as familiar, but it is expressly stated of Hebron, Sichem and Lus that these towns are situated in the Land of Chanaan (Gen. xxiii. 2; xxxiii. 18; xxxv. 6).

(d) The whole legislation takes shape under the eye of the reader. Hence there are regulations for the sojourn in the wilderness, which are modified or extended to suit later circumstances. These modifications are found chiefly in Deuteronomy, which, according to tradition, was composed immediately before the Israelites entered the Holy Land.

(e) The language of the Pentateuch generally resembles that of the later books, but it contains some expressions and forms that point to a very high antiquity. Thus הוא is always used as = *commune*, and so is נער; the infinitive ה or ו is used instead of ות with adverbs לה; the third person plural is ון instead of י, and so on.

---

[1] *Cf.* Sayce, "Fresh Light from the Ancient Monuments," p. 39, etc.

The work must have been rewritten from time to time, for not only would the material substance of the book wear out in the course of centuries, but the language, being a living language, underwent at least some changes, and the old Semitic characters were replaced by the square script. It was unnecessary for many copies to exist, as the Pentateuch was not intended to be a reading book for the people. The chief revision of it, and also of the other books written before the Captivity, probably took place in the time of Esdras and Nehemias. There is therefore some truth in the statements of modern critics, but they go astray when they confuse rewriting and final revision with the first compilation of the law, and deduce their daring conclusions from this confusion.

(f) If Moses, as the lawgiver of Israel, wished to secure permanence for his ordinances, he was almost obliged to leave behind him a written code, which should contain, besides the rules themselves, the motives for their enactment, which were contained in the history of the divine revelations. History and Law were necessarily connected in this work. Moses felt, too, the necessity of leaving a written record behind him as a testimony against Israel (Deut. xxxi. 26, 27).

It might be asked whether Moses, having been born and bred in Egypt, knew the Hebrew language. But Exodus ii. shows plainly that the Israelites, living in isolation in Gessen,[1] had retained the speech of their forefathers, and that Moses, in spite of his position at court, felt himself to be a Hebrew and not an Egyptian.

(g) There is unity, circumspection and system in the composition of the book. It is dominated by the thought that the Israelites had been chosen out from among all the nations of the world to be the recipients of God's revelation, and to maintain the right worship of God, and also that at some period redemption for the whole world should proceed from them. For this reason they had to be cut off from the Gentiles and their polytheistic errors, and were to dwell in Chanaan and faithfully serve their God. Only what can stimulate and establish this thought is admitted into the book. All else is either passed over in silence, or mentioned briefly as of subordinate importance and then set aside.

[1] The Vulgate has *Gessen;* Hebrew *goschen*, Septuagint *gesem*.

(c) Objections

Objection 1. " It has been proved that the accounts given in the Pentateuch of the Creation, the Fall of Man, the Deluge, the institution of the Sabbath, the doctrine of angels and devils, might all have been read as early as 2000 B. C. in the cuneiform records of Babylon. They were borrowed from there and admitted to the Bible, but they are not based upon revelation, and Moses was not their author."

Such views as the above are expressed by Delitzsch and Zimmern.

Answer. These assertions have been refuted in a large number of works by Keil, Nikel, Döller, Kaulen, Hoberg, Hommel, Budde, König, Jensen, Barth, Jeremias, Knieschke and others, but especially by H. Hilprecht (see *infra*, p. 476), who has for a long time been working at the excavations in Babylon. The truth is that the Babylonians derived their information from the same source as the Bible, viz. from the primitive tradition of the human race. But whereas on the Euphrates this tradition was obscured by fantastic and polytheistic additions (e. g. the great flood is ascribed to a whim on the part of the gods, who then themselves became anxious and crouched down like dogs, hurried to a sacrifice like flies, etc.), the account given in the Bible has preserved the dignified purity of the oldest period. The resemblances can be explained by community of origin, the great divergencies by the fall of Babylon into idolatry.[1]

Objection 2. " May not the Law of the Pentateuch have been modeled on that of the Babylonian King Hammurabi, who as early as 2100 B. C. had compiled a collection of laws, remarkable for acumen and wisdom, arranged them in 282 paragraphs, and recorded them on stone? "

Answer. Hammurabi is now generally identified with Amraphel, mentioned in Genesis xiv. 1, who, in Abraham's lifetime, took part in a campaign against Palestine (*supra*, p. 263). His code of laws in cuneiform writing originated in Babylon, but was brought to Susa, the capital of the old kingdom of Elam. In 1897–99 it was brought to light by French excavators. The Dominican Father Scheil, noted for his knowledge of cuneiform inscriptions, published it in French, and Hugo Winkler translated it into German (Leipzig, 1902). The original is undoubtedly one of the most important documents in the history of the ancient world. With extraordinary wisdom the laws regulate the public and private life of the nation, their trade and traffic. They prove that Moses might well have acted as a legislator, several centuries later. A comparison of Hammurabi's laws with the Mosaic decrees reveals some similarities, but there

---

[1] *Cf.* especially Father Keil's learned work on *Babel und Bibel*, Trèves, 1903; also Nikel, *Genesis und Keilschriftforschung*, February, 1903. In a review of the latter work Hehn remarks: "The individuality of the Bible is now universally recognized; that the explorations at Babylon can endanger the interests of religion is already out of the question." In another work Hehn says that we must reject the idea that the institution of the Sabbath was borrowed from Babylon, as in Babylonia nothing analogous to it has been discovered.

can be no suggestion that the latter are modeled upon or borrowed from the former.

Objection 3. " The work contains many parallel passages, which would certainly have been avoided, had it been written by *one* author."

Answer. The chief passages of this kind are the apparently double account of the Creation, Genesis i. 1 to ii. 3 and ii. 4, etc.; and also Genesis xx. and xxvi., where the same story is told first of Abraham and then of Isaac. However, the second account of the Creation would be unintelligible without the first; the two versions supplement each other, but they have different objects. The first is intended to describe the creation of the world, and to throw light on religion and especially on the observance of the Sabbath; the second is concerned with the history of the world, and contains its beginning. With regard to the other passages, it is quite possible for the son to have an experience resembling that of the father under similar circumstances.

Objection 4. " So much obscurity and confusion, so many omissions, mutilations and repetitions occur in the Pentateuch, especially in the three middle books, that we are forced to assume several persons to have been engaged in its compilation."

Answer. But how is it possible to judge a work thousands of years old by our standards, and to require of the author strict conformity to the laws of grammar and logic, as we understand them? Can the chronological order, that is maintained throughout the whole work, be mere confusion? All these difficulties can be removed by unprejudiced exegesis. *Cf. supra,* p. 271 (*g*).

Objection 5. " The alternating use of the names Elohim and Yahweh in speaking of God is alone enough to prove that the Pentateuch is not the work of one author."

Answer. This assertion may be so far accurate that Moses incorporated into his work other documents containing the name Elohim, whereas he himself preferred to use the name Jehovah (Yahweh), which was especially made known to him by God (Ex. iii. 14). The meanings of the two names may, however, be the reason why a single author should use sometimes one and sometimes the other. Elohim is an abstract noun or a *pluralis excellentiæ* of the singular *Eloah.* These two words are derived from the root *alah,* which means in Arabic when intransitive, " to be amazed, to fear," and when transitive, " to honor, to worship," so that the name Elohim denotes a being most apt to inspire fear or most worthy of reverence. (Many think it better not to separate the name from *El.* El is derived from the root *'ul,* to surpass, be strong, and its meaning would be " Strong, Mighty." The plural *Elohim* [1] means in this way " the Mightiest," " the conception of all power."

Yahweh,[2] derived from the verb חוה‎ = היה‎ ‎יהוה‎ means " the Being." It is

---

[1] This plural is, perhaps, a kind of substitute for a superlative that does not exist in Hebrew; but it is more likely that it refers to the three Persons in God, i. e. to the Trinity.

[2] This seems to represent the correct pronunciation. The Jews always read Adonai (Lord) whenever the name ‎יהוה‎ occurs in the sacred books, and the Masoretes gave the word the vowel mark for Adonai, be-

the future *kal* (in the same way as יַעְקֹב, one who waylays, or יִצְחָק, a mocker). Such forms denote a permanent condition. Yahweh is therefore He " who is and who was and who is to come " (Apoc. i. 8), He who has absolute Being from Himself, the Eternal, Unchangeable. As the form suggests also the causative (Hiphil) it might perhaps mean also " He who communicates His Being." [1] In any case the name is Hebrew, and denotes God especially as the Lord of Israel, the God of the covenant, whilst Elohim stands for God as ruler of the world and of all nations. The Gentiles also used the name Elohim (Judges i. 7; Jon. i. 6). When reference is made to God as the Creator and Lord of the world, the name Elohim is generally used; but the name Yahweh occurs when the writer is alluding to the God who has revealed Himself to mankind and especially to Israel. This is in a peculiar manner the Second Person of the Godhead, who was in time to assume human nature. The Yahweh or Adonai or κύριος of the Pentateuch and of all the Old Testament corresponds, therefore, with the Λόγος and κύριος Ἰησοῦς Χριστός of the New Testament.[2] *Cf.* I Cor. x. 9; Heb. xii. 2; Jude 5; Apoc. i. 8.

---

cause it must not be spoken in vain, in violation of the Second Commandment. Thus arose the form Jehovah, which is certainly wrong. The Septuagint did not venture upon any translation; in their time people must already have read Adonai, because they always wrote κύριος in its place (Itala and Vulgate, *Dominus*). That Yahweh is the correct pronunciation is apparent from Theodoretus (*Quæst. ad Exod.*, 15): καλοῦσι δὲ αὐτὸ Σαμαρεῖται IABE.

[1] Hommel derives the name from the old Arabic verb *hawaja* (Heb. *hajah*) and explains it as meaning " He exists, comes into existence, reveals Himself." Cornill refers to the Arabic *hawâ* = to fall, and thinks that the meaning is " He who makes to fall," i. e. the God of storms, who overthrows His enemies with His thunderbolt. Delitzsch considers *El* = goal (as in Heb. *el* =to), but this interpretation is too philosophical to be in keeping with early Semitic ideas. Delitzsch states that the name Yahweh was used in Babylon at the time of Hammurabi (2200 B. C.), but this is generally pronounced to be a mistake on his part. Even if he were correct, it would not destroy the value of Exodus iii. The true God might well communicate to Moses the sense in which He claimed this name for Himself.

[2] Too little attention is paid, even by Catholics, to the fact that God Himself is the originator of Holy Scripture, and chose this name therefore. We consider the human element in it too much, and we keep this in the foreground when we argue from these names that there must have been various authors. It is true that critics do not lay so much stress upon these names as they used to do, but, ever since the time of Astruc the whole criticism of the Pentateuch has depended upon them.

SECOND SECTION

THE PERIOD FROM THE ENTRANCE OF THE ISRAELITES INTO CHANAAN TO THE DIVISION OF THE KINGDOM

3. SURVEY

The second period of the history of Israel may be divided into three parts: (1) The conquest of the Promised Land soon after the death of Moses and Aaron. (2) The time of the Judges, divinely inspired men who ruled the people. (3) The establishment of a monarchy by Samuel, the last of the Judges, and the reigns of the first three kings.

The following are the sacred books belonging to this period:

(*a*) *Historical books:* Josue, Judges, Ruth, two books of Samuel (in the Vulgate, I and II Books of Kings).

(*b*) *Poetical books:* Psalms, Job, Canticle of Canticles.

(*c*) *Didactic books:* Proverbs of Solomon and Ecclesiastes, or the Preacher.

HISTORICAL BOOKS

4. JOSUE

(24 chapters)

1. *Contents.* Chapters 1–12, Conquest of the greater part of the Holy Land. 13–19, Distribution of the country. 20–22, Cities of Refuge and Cities for the Levites. 23 and 24, End of Josue's life, his last counsels and death.

1. Josue assumes the government of the nation, and is ordered by God to cross the Jordan and conquer the country. 2. Israelite spies fall into danger at Jericho, but are saved by a woman named Rahab. 3, 4. The Israelites cross the Jordan dry-shod. 5. Revival of circumcision. 6. Fall of Jericho, and later, 7, of Ai. 8. Blessing and curse at Sichem, according to Deuteronomy xxvii. 2, etc. 9. The Chanaanite kings prepare for resistance. 10. The south of the country passes into the possession of the Israelites through the wonderful intervention of God.[1] 11. After a battle near Lake Merom, the northern part also is

---

[1] Much has been said and written about the standing still of the sun (x. 13). It would be simpler if we might explain the matter naturally, and say: "It remained light so unusually long. that it seemed as

subdued. 12. Survey of the conquered lands. 13–19. The tribes of Ruben, Gad and half of Manasses, having already made settlements east of the Jordan, retire thither, after having assisted their brethren to conquer Chanaan. The other tribes receive land in the west according to their numbers. The tribe of Levi receives no continuous territory. The Tabernacle is set up in Silo. 20–22. The cities of refuge are appointed and forty-eight districts assigned to the tribe of Levi, as had been commanded (Num. xxxv.). 23, 24. The elders gather round Josue, who feels his death approaching; he urges them to be faithful to the law, makes them renew the Covenant with God, and dies at the age of one hundred and ten.

Critics who do not belong to the Catholic Church now reckon the Book of Josue as belonging to the Pentateuch, and thus a Hexateuch is formed, written by various authors, and containing the early history of Israel. In the Book of Josue J, E and P are said to be clearly distinguishable as sources of information. The work displays, however, a uniform independent character; it contains an account of the manner in which the divine command (i. 2, etc.) to take possession of the Holy Land was carried into effect, and at the same time it shows God's fidelity in fulfilling His promises (xxi. 41). This appears also in passages such as xiii. 9, etc., and xx. 8, which would seem unnecessary repetitions of Numbers xxxii. 33, etc., and Deuteronomy iv. 41–43, if this book really belonged to the Pentateuch. The Jewish canon never classed Josue with the Pentateuch, but invariably with the Prophets.

2. *Date and Author.* As the book bears the name of Josue, he is generally regarded as its author; but there are several passages indicating that it is of later date. They are iv. 9, "Josue put other twelve stones in the midst of the channel of the Jordan, . . . and they are there until this present day." x. 14, "There was not before nor after so long a day." xix. 47, "The children of Dan went up and fought against Lesem, and took it . . . and dwelt in it, calling the name of it Lesser Dan."

We must, however, not assume that the book was written as late as the time of the kings. In xv. 63 the Jebusites are mentioned as inhabiting Jerusalem, whilst it is clear from II Kings v. 5–9, that David expelled them, so the book must have existed before David's reign; in fact, it must have been written

if the sun were standing still." The story, however, clearly implies that a miracle took place. How this can be reconciled with the laws governing the universe is as far beyond the powers of mortals to decide as it is to ascertain how water could be turned into wine, or how wine can become the Blood of Christ. In the Book of Job (xxxviii.–xli.) God teaches man not to judge of what is too high for him, as even the natural world contains so many mysteries that he cannot fathom.

much earlier, as in xi. 8 and xix. 28, Sidon is called the chief
city of Phœnicia, and in David's time Tyre had long been the
capital.[1] We may therefore believe that Josue wrote the book,
but some later hand added numerous remarks to it. Such is
the tradition of the Jews and of the Western Church. Or we
may believe the author to have lived not long after Josue, and
to have made use of records written by Josue. Those who favor
the latter theory think that it may have been compiled by
Phinees, son of Eleazar the high priest, and grandson of Aaron,
who is mentioned in xxii. 13, xxiv. 33. In this case the work
would be called the Book of Josue, not because Josue was its
author, but because it contains the history of Josue and his
deeds.

5. The Book of Judges

(21 chapters)

1. *Contents.* Israel is defended by God against the Gentiles
in the Promised Land.

(*a*) *Introduction.* Chapters 1-3. Some of the Chanaanites are spared
and occupy the country with the Israelites. The unfortunate result of
this arrangement is that they become dependent upon the Gentiles, and
idolatry spreads among them also.

(*b*) *Chief portion of the book.* Chapters 3-16. This clearly reveals
the purpose with which it was written, namely to show that the fortunes
of the Israelites varied in accordance with their obedience or disobedience to the law. As often as they rebelled against it, they fell into
slavery, but as soon as they returned to their allegiance they were rescued by the judges. Some of these judges are mentioned very briefly;
a full account is given of others. The most conspicuous are Barak, with
the prophetess Debora; Gedeon, whose son Abimelech aimed at supremacy and was therefore put to death; Jephte and Samson. The last
distinguished himself in the war against the Philistines, new enemies
who had come from Egypt (*supra,* p. 20).

The name Judges (*shophetim,* the same word as *suffetes,* the chief
magistrates in Carthage) does not only imply that these men judged the
people according to the Mosaic law (I Kings vii. 15, etc.), but also that
they had power of government, and led the nation in war. They procured justice for the individual Israelite against the malice of his
own countrymen, and for the whole nation against the Gentiles. They

---

[1] According to the *Kirchenlexikon,* 1st ed., VIII, 430, it had been
the capital since 1209 B. C.

won their position not by inheritance or election, but by their great achievements.

The following judges are mentioned by name: (1) Othoniel (of the tribe of Juda), (2) Aod (Benjamin), (3) Samgar (?), (4) Jahel (?), (5) Debora (Ephraim), (6) Barak (Nephtali), (7) Gedeon (Manasses), (8) Thola (Issachar), (9) Jair (Gad), (10) Jephte (Gad), (11) Abesan (Juda or Zabulon), (12) Ahialon (Zabulon), (13) Abdon (Ephraim), (14) Samson (Dan). The judges (15) Heli and (16) Samuel of the tribe of Levi are not mentioned before the Book of Samuel (I Kings).

(c) *Appendix.* Chapters 17 and 18. Prohibition of worship on Mount Ephraim and its transference by the tribe of Dan to Lais in the north of the country (see p. 103). 19–21. War of the eleven tribes against Benjamin, to punish an offense that had been committed.

2. The *records of time* in this book must not simply be added up, but we must assume that some of the periods were concurrent. According to III Kings vi. 1, only 480 years elapsed from the time when the Israelites left Egypt to the building of Solomon's Temple, but the periods mentioned in Judges alone would amount to almost 400 years, and we have still to take into account the 40 years' sojourn in the Wilderness, 40 years of Saul's reign, 40 years of David's reign and 4 years of Solomon's. It seems, therefore, that the time of the Judges cannot have lasted more than about 350 years, unless perhaps there is some flaw in the text regarding the numbers.

3. *Date and Author.* The book was written in the time of the kings, as in xvii. 6, xviii. 1 and 31, xxi. 24 we read that there was no king in Israel in those days. The author ascribes many evils to the absence of a regular government; and as he seems to have seen no rulers of the type of Roboam and Jeroboam, he must have lived before the division of the kingdom. We may go back beyond the reigns of Solomon and David to that of Saul, because the Jebusites are mentioned (i. 21; *cf.* xix. 12) as still inhabiting Jerusalem. The accounts of the various events are the work not of one, but of several authors. This is proved by the variety in the language.

Debora's song (chap. v.) shows archaisms; the history of Gedeon has always שׁ instead of אשׁר for the relative, and the story of Samson is distinguished by the frequent recurrence of "The spirit of the Lord came upon him."

Whoever collected these stories probably himself added the introduction and the appendix. In the Talmud Samuel is named as the author, and his last speech (I Kings xii. 7, etc.) shows considerable resemblance to the line of thought followed in the Book of Judges.

4. *Objection.* The expression *geloth haarez* = taking away of the land (xviii. 30) seems to refer to a much later date than that of Samuel, for it was not until 722 that the land of the northern tribes passed into the hands of the Assyrians. We probably ought to read *geloth haaron* = taking away of the Ark of the Covenant. This took place in Samuel's time, for the Philistines seized the Ark.

6. RUTH [1]

(4 chapters)

1. *Contents.* This little book tells in four chapters how a poor widow named Ruth, from the heathen land of Moab, became the wife of Boaz or Boas, a wealthy man in Bethlehem. From their marriage Obed was born, and his son was Jesse (Isai), David's father. Thus Boaz and Ruth were the king's great-grandparents.

2. *Motive.* The events related are purely a matter of family history, but there can be no doubt that the book originated in their connection with King David, and therefore has some higher significance. One of its objects seems to be to draw the attention of the Israelites to the fact that God did not absolutely reject the Gentiles, as a Gentile woman was admitted to the line of David, that inherited a special blessing, and she thus became the ancestress of the future Messias.

The readiness with which Orpha and especially Ruth followed their mother-in-law Noemi from their heathen home to the land of Juda must have been due to the virtuous life of Noemi and her family, which contrasted with the barbarous customs of the Gentiles. The reason was that

---

[1] רוּת perhaps = רְעוּת, i. e. Friend. In ancient times this book was often reckoned as part of Judges. The first words suggest that it was an appendix to it: "In the days of one of the judges, when the judges ruled." The Jewish canon now places Ruth among the Ketubim.

they worshiped the true God. When Ruth declared " thy God shall be my God," she acknowledged the excellence of the Israelite religion, and was determined to renounce heathenism. Thus to some extent she deserved the honor of being the ancestress of David, and through him of the Messias.

3. *Date.* Ruth lived about one hundred years before David, and the book was written either during his reign or not long after. His pedigree at the end of the book points to its having been composed after his death, and the words in iv. 7, referring to the custom of taking off a shoe in token of renouncing a claim, with the addition: "That was a custom of ages ago in Israel," indicate a later origin.

4. *Author.* The writer of the book is unknown. The Talmud (*baba bathra f.* 14 *b.*) ascribes it to Samuel, but this is probably wrong. The differences in the language show that the author cannot be identified with that of the Book of Judges, nor with the writer of the Books of Samuel.[1]

7. THE BOOKS OF SAMUEL

In the Vulgate: First and Second Books of Kings

(31 and 24 chapters)

1. *Contents.* These books contain the history of the introduction of monarchy into Israel, and of the first two kings; the first book carries the history to the death of Saul and the second to the end of David's reign. The first twelve chapters give the story of Heli, judge and high priest, and of Samuel.

I Samuel. 1. Elkana, Samuel's father, and his mother, Anna. Samuel is dedicated to God and serves in the Tabernacle at Silo. 2, 3. Heli, the high priest, as a father is weak in his dealings with Ophni and Phinees, his degenerate sons; he is threatened with God's vengeance. 4. War with the Philistines; removal of the Ark of the Covenant. Death of Heli and his sons. 5, 6. The Philistines suffer misfortunes on account of the Ark, so they restore it, but remain masters of the country. 7. Samuel conquers the Philistines and practically becomes supreme. 8, 9. The people demand a king; Samuel yields and anoints Saul. 10–12. Saul is brave, wins respect, and Samuel retires. 13. Renewal of war with the Philis-

---

[1] So Kaulen. Weiss on the other hand believes, with Haneberg, that Samuel wrote the Book of Ruth at Najoth at the same time as the fifty-ninth Psalm.

tines. 14–16. Saul repeatedly disobeys God, and therefore Samuel is forced to anoint David, though very young, to be the future king. 17. David conquers Goliath; his friendship with Jonathan, one of Saul's sons, and his marriage with Saul's daughter Michol. 18–31. Saul's jealousy and hatred of David, whom he seeks to kill. David has to lead a life of adventure. Saul and Jonathan die in battle against the Philistines.

II Samuel. 1–3. David is recognized by the tribe of Juda as king, and takes up his abode at Hebron. Elsewhere Saul's son Isboseth is regarded as king. 4. Isboseth is murdered, and all the tribes accept David as their ruler. 5, 6. He conquers the stronghold of Sion and makes Jerusalem his residence. He sets up the Tabernacle on Sion. 7. David is not allowed to build a temple for the Lord, but receives the promise that his kingdom shall last forever. 8, 9. David sins grievously through lust; he does penance. 10–19. His sons Ammon and Absalom cause him much trouble.[1] 20–23. Other difficulties are overcome. David's gratitude to God. 24. His enumeration of the people through pride, and his punishment for it.[2]

2. *Name.* The books bear the name of Samuel only because he is one of the chief characters in the history, and, especially in the first book, he is the chief actor. He cannot have been the author, as many events are recorded that occurred long after his death. The two books were originally united, but they were divided by the Greek translators, and hence appear as two in the Itala and the Vulgate. In the Hebrew Bible the division was not made until 1518. The Vulgate, like the Septuagint, calls them the First and Second books of Kings, and consequently the other books of Kings, that are of much later origin, are numbered Third and Fourth (see p. 334).

3. *Date.* The work was written after the division of the kingdom, but before the destruction of the northern part; i. e. between 932 and 722. The first statement depends upon the words in I Samuel xxvii. 6: " Siceleg belongeth to the kings of Juda unto this day," the second upon the fact that there is no

---

[1] In chapter xii. 31 the Hebrew reading should perhaps be הֶעֱבִיר ; if we may accept it, it alters the story of David's remarkable cruelty to the inhabitants of Rabbath Ammon, for then we read not of fearful forms of death, but of condemnation to compulsory service. In the parallel passage, I Chronicles xx. 3, the reading should be וַיָּשֶׂם and not וַיָּשַׂר, as Kautzsch and others have it.

[2] Peters is inclined to prefer the Septuagint text to the Masoretic, especially from I Samuel xvi. 1 to xix. 18. The Masoretic text is longer, and seems to contain interpolations, and it is in fact much later than that used by the Septuagint.

allusion at all in the book to the destruction of the northern kingdom.

4. *Author*. The writer is unknown. Old commentators ascribed the first twenty-four chapters to Samuel and the rest to the prophets Gad and Nathan. The character of the work is uniform and it shows design in its composition, so we may regard it as certain that the author, who was probably a prophet living under the kings, made use of the records left by these three men, and skillfully adapted them to suit this work.

5. His *purpose* was to show that both the people of Israel and their kings could find happiness only in obedience to God.

POETICAL BOOKS

8. Old Testament Poetry in General [1]

1. *Varieties of Poetry*. In the sacred literature of Israel lyric and didactic poetry attained a high degree of development. The one often passes into the other; many of the Psalms are didactic rather than lyric, whilst the didactic book of Job contains several lyric passages.

Epic and dramatic poetry do not occur. Epos and Drama would be out of place in the sacred books, as they generally presuppose works of the imagination, which would be inconsistent with the divine revelation that communicates only truth. The Hebrews may have possessed some profane poetry, such as Lamech's defiant war song (Gen. iv. 23), but religious poetry held the place of honor among God's people, as all poetry in general originated in worship.

2. *Rhythm*. Hebrew poems possess a definite rhythm, i. e. a movement regulated in accordance with certain laws, and a systematic structure of the parts of the verse. The parallelism in the clauses is peculiar to Hebrew poets and is very distinctive. The poet is not satisfied with expressing a thought in one clause,

---

[1] Kautzsch, *Poesie des A. T.*, Tüb., 1902, is of opinion that the poetical books are of late origin, mostly after the Captivity, but tradition assigns them to a much earlier period.

but he expresses it again in parallel clauses, resembling one another in meaning and form, and these constitute the verse. For instance:

> My son, hear the instruction of thy father,
> And forsake not the law of thy mother.
>
> Prov. i. 8.

or,

> Then was our mouth filled with gladness,
> And our tongue with joy.   Psalm cxxv. 2.

or,

> [The wicked] shall be as chaff before the face
> of the wind, and as ashes which the whirl-
> wind scattereth.   Job. xxi. 18.

In the Psalms of the Roman Breviary the asterisk, marking the pause to be made in choir, often indicates this parallelism, which is, however, not always complete, one of the clauses being only imperfectly developed. Sometimes the second clause does not contain a repetition so much as a contrast or a new idea. These three kinds of parallelism all conduce to make the meaning clear.

The Hebrew poets were not acquainted with the use of rhyme, and, though rhymed verses occur, it is very doubtful whether the rhyme is intentional or accidental. It is uncertain whether real meters were in use. Recent scholars maintain that a trochaic and an iambic meter can be traced in at least some poems; that there is, for instance, a 12-syllabled trochaic meter in the third Lamentation of Jeremias, and a 7-syllabled iambic in the 111th and 112th Psalms. This theory has not yet been generally accepted. Its acceptance would involve great violence being done to the Masoretic text, as the vowels would mostly have to be altered. More attractive is a theory put forward by J. K. Zenner, S.J., who thinks that the Psalms and other songs in the Old Testament (e. g. Ecclesiasticus xxiv., Baruch iii. 9, etc.) were originally processional songs, sung by a choir with instrumental accompaniment and stately gestures, so that the three arts of poetry, music and dancing were united. These songs can be divided into strophe, antistrophe and transition. Where a strophe ends, there stands in seventy-one places in the Book of Psalms the hitherto inexplicable word *Sela* (see p. 286), which certainly is one of the old technical terms in use among the Levites, and indicates a change. Thus Psalm vii. falls into the following parts: verses 1–3, strophe; 4–6, antistrophe; 7–10, transition; 11–14, second strophe; 15–18, second antistrophe. Psalm xc: verses 1–3, strophe; 4–6, antistrophe; 7–10, transition; 11–13 second strophe; 14–16, second antistrophe. This arrangement explains also the alternation of speakers in this psalm. Also among the heathen nations of antiquity it was usual to go round the altar, on which the sacrifices were burnt, in stately processions or dances in honor of the deity.

3. *Versification.* The ordinary verses in Hebrew poetry consist of two lines, but *tristichs* and *tetrastichs* occur, and occasionally verses with five or six lines. Some poems are arranged according to the letters of the alphabet, probably in order to be more easily committed to memory. Such, for instance, are the Lamentations, Psalm cxviii. and Proverbs xxxi.

9. THE PSALTER

1. *Name.* The canon of the Old Testament contains a collection of one hundred and fifty songs, some long and some short, which compose the Book of Psalms (Vulg.: *Psalmorum liber*) or Psalter (C. Trid.: *Psalterium*). The word " psalm " ($\psi\alpha\lambda\mu\acute{o}s$ taken from the Septuagint) means primarily playing on a stringed instrument,[1] and then a song sung to such music. *Psalter* = stringed instrument, and then, by transference, a collection of songs. In Hebrew the psalms are called *tehillim* or *tillim,* songs of praise.[2]

2. *Date of Origin and Authors.* The Psalms were not composed all at one time, nor are they the work of one man, but they were written by various divinely inspired singers and subsequently collected. Most of them have headings containing the author's name, and often also the time and occasion of composition, as well as directions for singing them. These headings are the work of the collectors, not of the composers of the Psalms, and the information that they contain is derived from Jewish tradition.[3] In these headings the following authors are mentioned by name:

---

[1] According to Suidas $\psi\acute{a}\lambda\lambda\epsilon\iota\nu$ is to strike the strings of an instrument with the finger-tips, hence $\psi\alpha\lambda\mu\acute{o}s$ is playing in this manner.

[2] תְּהִלִּים, תִּלִּים from הָלַל, to praise, extol.

[3] Modern critics attach a very slight importance to these headings, and aim at ascertaining the date and origin of the Psalms from internal evidence alone. So Cornill and Reuss. Legarde thought that these headings designated not the composer, but the party of musicians in the Temple, to whom particular psalms were assigned for performance; so that one song was described as assigned to David, another to Solomon, others to Asaph, Core, etc., but tradition is against this theory.

1. *Moses.* The eighty-ninth (Heb. ninetieth) psalm is ascribed to him.

2. *David.* The whole Book of Psalms is often called by his name, and correctly in as far as he began to make the collection; he composed many psalms himself and the rest breathe his spirit. The Hebrew text assigns seventy-three psalms to him, the Septuagint and Vulgate add twelve others, so that in all eighty-five are ascribed to him, or, with Psalm lxxi., eighty-six.

3. *Solomon* is mentioned as having composed two psalms, lxxi. and cxxvi. The heading of the former is in Hebrew, " To Solomon " *lesche-lomo,* and the Seventy render this εἰς Σαλωμών = on Solomon. Most writers, therefore, assume that it was not composed by Solomon, but by David, according to verse 20: " The praises of David, the son of Jesse, are ended." Solomon is extolled as a type of the Messias.

4. *Asaph,* son of Barachias, a Levite and one of David's musicians, is stated in the headings to have written twelve psalms (xlix. and lxxii. to lxxxii.).

5. Eleven of the finest psalms, remarkable for their lyric force (xli., xliii.–xlviii., lxxxiii., lxxxiv., lxxxvi. and lxxxvii.), are ascribed to the *Corahites,* the family of Core the Levite. Psalm lxxxvii. is particularly ascribed to a Corahite named Eman, a descendant of Esdras.

6. Psalm lxxxviii. was composed by Ethan, another descendant of Esdras, and probably also a Corahite.

The remaining thirty-eight psalms bear no indication of their origin, and their authors are unknown. They are called " ownerless " (ἀδέσποτοι), and in the Talmud " orphaned."

Modern critics, such as Hitzig, Olshausen, Reuss and others, regard some psalms as Machabean, i. e. they believe them not to have been composed until the time of the Machabees, viz., in the second century before Christ. To this class belong Psalms lxxiii., lxxviii. and cxviii. Not only the headings, but also the tradition of the Jews refer them to an earlier period, and, moreover, in the time of the Machabees the Book of Psalms had already been translated into Greek.

It is not absolutely impossible that some of the psalms may have been composed in the time of the Machabees, for educated people still used Hebrew, and the Seventy did not complete their work much before 130 B. C. The newly discovered remains of the Hebrew text of Ecclesiasticus prove, however, that the Psalter existed in its present size at the time when Ecclesiasticus was written. *Cf. infra,* p. 353.

3. *Purpose.* As the headings and the final verses of many psalms show, the Psalter was a book containing the songs sung

by the Levites at the public worship of the Israelites. Now the Psalms have become forms of prayer in use in the Church, and especially appointed for recitation by the clergy.

Psalm. xci. has the heading, "Song for the Sabbath day." Psalm c. (in the Hebrew), "Psalm at the thank offering." Several psalms are inscribed "Alleluia" = "Praise the Lord"; an invitation to the congregation. In the headings the word *lamnazzeach* occurs fifty-three times; it is generally translated "to the chief musician"; the Seventy must have pointed the word למנצח differently, as they translated it εἰς τέλος (Itala and Vulgate *in finem*), which may be an indication that the psalm was to be sung at the conclusion of public worship. The expression *sela* (שֶׁלָה) is generally translated *tace* (Imp. P. with ה parag., from שָׁלַת); Maurer renders it "raise" (the voice), so that it means *forte* or *fortius*. The Septuagint has διάψαλμα, music in the interval. Gittith (Ps. viii. and elsewhere) is undoubtedly a stringed instrument (from נָתַת, to strike). Kaulen draws attention to the fact that the liturgical function of many of the psalms that are personal in tone may be discovered from their concluson. For instance, Psalm iii., which is otherwise in the first person, ends with the words: "Thy blessing is upon thy people." Psalm cxxxi. is similar.

The frequently recurring "I" of the Psalms seems to be a kind of answer to the laws of the Pentateuch, which are mostly given with "thou" (as, for instance, in the Decalogue), for God regards His people Israel as one individual. This "I" is also an allusion on the part of the Holy Spirit to both the ancient theocracy and the Messianic kingdom, the Church, which our Saviour describes as a Kingdom of God both on a large and on a small scale, both in mankind in general and in each individual. For this reason the Psalms are adapted to God's universal Church and to each of His servants, and especially for His Servant κατ' ἐξοχήν, the Messias. The enemies against whom complaints are raised in the Psalms are the opponents of God and His Anointed, as well as of His Church and of the faithful individually, who are despised and persecuted for their loyalty to God. The psalms of imprecation (xxxiv., li., lxviii., cviii., Vulgate) are to be judged from this point of view, and not regarded as the imprecations of a single person. This explanation solves the difficult problem how curses can be reconciled with the law of love. Who ever will not turn to God, but attacks God's kingdom and those belonging to it, loses peace, which is a mark of God's favor, and brings down a curse upon himself. He is warned in these psalms of imprecation of the doom that his wickedness deserves. Personal hatred is as little implied as in Noe's curse laid upon his son Cham. Besides, it is not reasonable to apply to the Old Covenant the standard of the New. Strict justice dominated the one, love and mercy the other (see *infra*, p. 357).

The Psalms are, therefore: (1) Prayers of individuals under (*a*) the Old and (*b*) the New Covenant; (2) Prayers of the whole congregation of the faithful under (*a*) the Old and (*b*) the New Covenant; (3) Prayers of the Messias, who speaks not only in His own Name but in the name of each of the faithful and in that of all mankind who believe.

This does not, however, mean that to every psalm this threefold or fivefold description applies. We have here evidence that Holy Scripture must be inspired by God, for no human being would of himself be able to impart such manifold meaning to the sacred songs.

4. *Date of Collection.* The collection of psalms, as we have it, is very ancient, but cannot go back beyond the Captivity, as in it are some psalms which clearly were written either during or after the period of exile (lxxxiv., cv., cvi., cxxv., cxxxvi.). Collections of particular psalms must, however, have existed earlier. We know that David caused religious songs to be sung in the Tabernacle, thus adding to the beauty of the worship there, and for this purpose a collection of such songs was requisite (I Chron. xvi. 41; II Chron. xxiii. 18; I Esdr. iii. 10). This collection and others like it were incorporated in the general collection made after the Captivity. That it consists of parts, some of which are older than others, appears from the words at the close of Psalm lxxi., " The praises of David, the son of Jesse, are ended." All, therefore, that precedes these words belongs to the first collection. The collection as we have it was made at the time when the worship of God was restored by Esdras and Nehemias (II Mach. ii. 13).

5. *Divisions of the Psalter.* On the analogy of the Pentateuch, the Psalter is divided into five parts, or books, which can be distinguished by the doxology at the close of each. The first book contains Psalms i.–xl.; the second, Psalms xli.–lxxi.; the third, Psalms lxxii.–lxxxviii.; the fourth, Psalms lxxxix.–cv.; the fifth, Psalms cvi.–cl. This division corresponds with the five periods in which the different collections were made. The first dates from the time when the ark was set up on Sion (I Chron. xvi. 4); the second, from the close of David's life and Solomon's accession, to which Psalm lxxi. refers; the third belongs to the time of Ezechias (II Chron. xxix. 30). A fourth may have been made during the reign of Josias (II Chron. xxxv. 15). The songs in the fifth book contain many references to the Captivity and the return to Palestine. The general collection of all the psalms was made by Esdras and Nehemias, who did not merely

arrange the five previous collections, one after the other, but inserted in each of them other songs, some old and some new. It is possible that one or two more were added at the time of the Machabees, to bring the number up to 150.

6. *Numbering.* The numbering of the psalms in the Hebrew text differs from that of the Vulgate, which we generally use, and which is derived from the Septuagint. The Seventy put Psalms ix. and x. together, treating them as one. Thus the number assigned to each of the following psalms was one less than in the Hebrew as far as Psalm cxiv., which they put with cxv., so that these two together are numbered cxiii. But in compensation they divided cxvi. into two, so that cxvii. in the Hebrew is cxvi. in the Septuagint, and the number of each psalm in the Greek continues to be one less as far as Psalm cxlvii., which is again divided into two, and in this way the numbering is made to coincide again with that of the original.

7. *Classification according to the Contents.*

(*a*) Songs addressed to God in praise, prayer and thanksgiving form the largest class of the psalms. To it belong also those that refer to nature, such as viii., xviii., ciii.

(*b*) The historical or national psalms also form a numerous class, in which the theme is the glorious past of Israel and its distinctive position above all other nations. In others God's help is besought to prevent it from being oppressed by unbelievers, e. g. Psalms lxxviii., lxxix.

(*c*) Very many of the psalms are didactic, e. g. xxxvi., xlviii., lxxii. give instruction regarding the prosperity of the godless.

(*d*) Some are lamentations; the penitential psalms belong to this class (vi., xxxi., xxxvii., l., cl., cxxix., cxlii.).

(*e*) Several psalms are prophetic, and celebrate the sufferings of the Messias (xv., xxi., lxviii.) and His glory (ii., xliv., cix.). These are called Messianic psalms.

The fifteen psalms numbered cxix.–cxxxiii. are called the Gradual Psalms. In the Hebrew each is headed שִׁיר הַמַּעֲלוֹת = song of the ascent, *canticum graduum.* This name is variously interpreted. It may refer to the return to Palestine from the low-lying lands near the Euphrates, or to the pilgrimages of the Jews to Jerusalem, or to the fifteen steps leading from the Court of the Women to that of the Men, which were ascended by people singing, at the ceremony of drawing water, which

[handwritten marginal notes:]

numbering of psalms ath- Vulg. troti- Heb.

Vulg.	Heb.
1- 8 inc	1-8 inc
9	9 & 10
10	11 &c
113	114 + 115
114 + 115	116
116	117 &c
146 - 147	147

concluded the feast of Tabernacles. At the present time they are said before Matins on the Wednesdays in Lent, on which no feast of nine lessons occurs. There is, however, no special rule enjoining this practice.

More Detailed Statement of Contents

First Book. 1. Theme of the whole Psalter; happiness to those true to God, destruction to the godless. 2. God and Christ triumph over the powers of this world. 3. Morning hymn. 4. Evening hymn. 5. Morning prayer. 6. Cry for help. 7. Help, Lord, for the persecuted! 8. The firmament of heaven. 9. Song of victory — request for further help. 10. Confidence in God. 11. Help, O Lord, for the righteous! 12. Delay not to save us. 13. Alas! godlessness prevails everywhere! 14. Whom will God suffer to approach Him? 15. The suffering Messias cries out for help. 16. Save me from oppression! 17. Hymn of thanksgiving for safety. 18. Glory of God in nature and in the law. 19. Prayer before battle. 20. Thanksgiving for victory. 21. The crucified Messias implores God to save him. 22. God is my shepherd. 23. Hymn to celebrate the bringing of the Ark to Sion. 24. O God, help and pardon me! 25. Chastise me not with the wicked! 26. Courage based on confidence in God. 27. Chastisement only for sinners! 28. God is glorified in the tempest. 29. Thanksgiving for delivery from danger. 30. Save me! 31. Repentance and confession of guilt bring forgiveness. 32. Praise God, the Mighty and Merciful. 33. Fear of God has good results. 34. Punishment be upon our enemies! 35. Wickedness is on all sides, our help is in God. 36. Apparent happiness of the wicked. 37. I am weighed down by sin, Lord have mercy upon me! 38. I suffer, yet I trust in God. 39. I thank thee, O God; help me still further! 40. The merciful shall find mercy.

Second Book. 41. Longing for the sanctuary. 42. Courage and confidence in God. 43. Glorious past and gloomy present, may God help us! 44. Marriage hymn of the Messianic king. 45. God hath delivered Jerusalem from danger of enemies. 46. God hath granted victory to Israel. 47. What God hath accomplished in Sion, shall never be forgotten. 48. The happiness of sinners is fleeting. 49. Not outward sacrifice, but the service of the heart is pleasing to God. 50. David's confession of guilt. 51. God's chastisement falls on the sinner. 52. Like Psalm 13. 53. Save me! 54. Lamentation over the deceits of enemies. 55. Like Psalm 33. 56, 57, 58. Destroy us not, but help us to resist the enemy. 59. After hard fighting came victory; give further aid! 60. Under God's protection will I stand firm. 61. God alone is faithful. 62. Trusting in God, I wait for His help. 63. Evil designs fall back on those who invent them. 64. Thanksgiving for harvest. 65. Thanksgiving for help in time of oppression. 66. Another thanksgiving for harvest. 67. Song of triumph; hope of subjugating all nations. 68. Being oppressed, I cry to God and hope to be heard; the poet speaks thus as a type of the Messias. 69. Like Psalm 39, 14–18. 70. God hath helped us hitherto, may He further assist us. 71. May God abide with Solomon, who is a type of the Messias.

Third Book. 72. The prosperity of the wicked soon passes away. I will not suffer myself to be misled. 73. Lament over the devestation of the sanctuary. 74. Assyria threatens, but our God is stronger. 75. Hymn of thanksgiving after the destruction of the Assyrian army. 76. Is there no escape from the power of the enemies? Remember God's wonderful deeds at the time of Moses and Aaron. 77. The history of Israel from Moses to David teaches us that to fall away from God involves destruction. Remain loyal to the king anointed by God! 78. The heathen have entered, cry to God for help (*cf.* Psalm 73). 79. Israel, God's vine, is hard pressed. 80. Paschal hymn. 81. Unjust judges are judged by God. 82. Many foes are in league against Israel, O God, drive them back! 83. Joy at belonging to the sanctuary (*cf.* Psalm 41). 84. Prayer of the returning exiles for new mercies. 85. O Lord, strengthen thy servant! 86. God's city of Jerusalem is the home of all nations. 87. Prayer for delivery in time of great distress, that has already lasted long. 88. Great promises were made to David, but his race has sunk from its high position. O Lord, be merciful once more!

Fourth Book. 89. Moses considers human misery, the consequence of sin, and implores God's mercy. 90. Trust in God. 91. Much in the life of man is incomprehensible, but God makes all good (*cf.* Ps. 36, 48, 72). 92. God's power over the world. 93. God is our support against unbelievers. 94. Praise and obedience be to the Lord! Otherwise evil will come. 95. Sing praises to the Lord, the most exalted King and Judge! 96. Let us be glad that the glorious King of all the world is our God! 97. Israel and all other nations are to praise God, the judge of the world. 98. All nations must reverence the God of Israel. 99. Praise the Lord, our God, to whom we owe existence and all else. 100. I will lead a blameless life and keep sinners aloof from me. 101. I am wretched and deserted, in deep distress I implore God's mercy. 102. Praise God, who forgiveth all thy sins! 103. God's greatness and providence in the universe. 104. Song of praise prompted by the history of Israel. 105. Israel had made a bad return for God's benefits, and so was punished with exile.

Fifth Book. 106. Thanksgiving for recovery of the Holy Land. 107. Reminiscences of Psalm 56 and 59. God is with us, we fear no foe. 108. Appeal for help against false accusations and persecution. 109. The Messias is king and priest; he conquers all his enemies. 110. Great is God's goodness to Israel. 111. Happiness will follow those loyal to God, the schemes of sinners will be frustrated. 112. God in his greatness welcomes the downcast. (This psalm and the following, as far as 117, were recited when the Paschal lamb was eaten.) 113. God's benefits at the time of the departure from Egypt. 114. God hath helped in time of deep misery. 115. Thanksgiving for the help. 116. Heathen nations also must praise the true God. 117. God heard my prayer, I will trust and thank Him for ever. 118. Utterances of a believer, who proclaims his loyalty to God and the law against all opposition. The sayings are arranged alphabetically, eight times over, and the psalm consists of eight times twenty-two verses; one hundred and seventy-six in all. 119. Former prayers have been granted, therefore I now have confidence. 120. May God protect me. 121. Joy over Jerusalem. 122. Lord, take away our reproach. 123. Had God not been with us, we should have perished. 124. Have trust in God, who will not abandon Jerusalem. 125. Joy at delivery from imprisonment. 126. God's blessing gives prosperity. 127. He who strives in the fear of the Lord, obtains God's blessing. 128. I was often in danger, but God always protected me. 129. The greater the need, the more ready is God's assistance. 130. Humility and confidence cause God to hear our prayers. 131. David had zeal for God's house, therefore David's house shall last forever. 132. Praise of harmony. 133. The priests' evening blessing. 134. Song of praise to God, who has shown His power both in nature and in the history of Israel. 135. God's mercy is over all His works. 136. Israel mourns in exile. Woe to those who destroyed Jerusalem! 137. Thanksgiving for God's benefits, request for further help. 138. God, being present everywhere, knoweth that I have no part with sinners. 139. Keep me safe from the hand of the wicked. 140. Guard me from the snares of the wrong-doer. 141. I cannot help myself, help Thou me, O God! 142. Leave me not, or I shall perish. 143. Song of triumph after a successful contest. 144. Glorious are God's greatness and mercy. 145. Happy is Israel in its trust in God, who ruleth the world. 146, 147. Praise the Lord for all His benefits. 148. All created things in heaven and earth are to announce God's praises. 149. Israel has peculiar reason to praise God. 150. Praise be to God everywhere, in every way and from all living beings!

10. PROVERBS

(31 chapters)

1. *Name.* If we had to deal here only with proverbs in the ordinary sense of the word, the collection would not be included in the canon of Holy Scripture. But the proverbs of Solomon (*proverbia Salomonis*, παροιμίαι Σαλωμόντος, *mishle Shelomo*) [1] differ altogether from our proverbs. They are reflections on the truths of divine revelation, composed in poetical form, and applied to the circumstances of human life. The book also contains maxims of life derived from the author's own experience.

2. *Contents and Divisions.* The book is divided into several parts distinguished by their titles.

It begins with a detailed introduction applying not only to the first part, but to the whole work (i. 1–7). The general meaning of it is: the fear of God is the foundation of all wisdom. "Without it there is in the world nothing but folly, i. e. immorality. Morality is inconceivable without fear of God."

(*a*) The first part consists of chapters i.–ix. It contains not so

---

[1] *Mashal* means primarily comparison, then parable, memento, and also probably song, poem, because of the regular arrangement of the parts.

much a collection of maxims as several continuous instructions and admonitions, intended to inspire love of wisdom.[1]

(b) The second part, chapters x.–xxiv. (or, according to another view, x.–xxii. 16),[2] forms the chief part of the book and contains most of the collection of maxims. There are about 400 of them, expressing very various ideas, but clear and easily understood; e. g. "A wise son maketh the father glad, but a foolish son is the sorrow of his mother," x. 1. "He that loveth correction, loveth knowledge; but he that hateth reproof is foolish," xii. 1. "It is the part of man to prepare the soul, and of the Lord to govern the tongue," xvi. 1. "Pride goeth before destruction, and the spirit is lifted up before a fall," xvi. 18. "A foolish man will clap hands, when he is surety for his friend," xvii. 18.

(c) In chapter xxv. a new collection begins, headed: "These are also parables of Solomon, which the men of Ezechias king of Juda copied out." These proverbs display, on the whole, the same characteristics as the others, so that they afford confirmation of the statement that they also were composed by Solomon. It is quite possible that of the 3000 maxims of this king (III Kings iv. 32) many besides the 400 already collected were commonly on the lips of the people, and the wise and pious counselors of King Ezechias selected a number of these, and added them to the previous collection. They are contained in the next five chapters of the book, xxv.–xxx.

As specimens we may quote: "As clouds and wind when no rain followeth, so is the man that boasteth, and doth not fulfill his promises," xxv. 14. "As a moth doth by a garment, and a worm by the wood, so the sadness of a man consumeth the heart," xxv. 20.

(d) The last two chapters contain additional maxims, — xxx. consists of the sayings of a certain Agur; xxxi. 1–9, advice given to a king named Lemuel by his mother; 10–31, praise of a good housewife in alphabetical form. The names Agur and Lemuel are probably fictitious.[3]

---

[1] The book is often mentioned as "Wisdom," as are also Ecclesiastes, Canticles, the Book of Wisdom, and Sirach or Ecclesiasticus. The "Wisdom" of the Bible is quite unlike the σοφία of Greek philosophy. The latter aims at discovering the ultimate causes of all things by means of human intellect, and knows nothing of revelation; but wisdom in the Hebrew sense proceeds from revelation, and seeks to explain everything in the world by its aid. To the Hebrew sage wisdom is theoretically the knowledge, derived from revelation, of how to live aright, and practically it is living in accordance with this knowledge. In the Hebrew sense wisdom, as it proceeds from revelation, is itself revealed and divine. Even in this book, and especially in chapter viii., wisdom is represented as a person; but in the New Testament it appears fully revealed as Logos, as a divine Person.

[2] A fresh invitation to accept the teaching of wisdom begins in ii. 17.

[3] Cf. however, Kirchenlexikon, 2d ed., article "Agur"; according to this article Agur, son of Jake, was really a Hebrew sage. Kaulen, Einleitung, II, 142, is less sure of it, and says also that we can neither deny nor prove that Lemuel meant Solomon.

3. *Date of Composition.* It is obvious, after a consideration of the contents, that all the parts of the book cannot have been compiled at the same time. The heading of the third part shows that a collection of proverbs existed at the time of Ezechias, and that, at this king's instigation, a further collection was made and appended to the earlier one. The last two chapters also appear to belong to the time of Ezechias. We have, therefore, to distinguish two chief periods in the compilation of this book.

I. Chapters i.–xxiv. date from the time of Solomon, and are to a great extent his composition. (Only the sayings in xxiv. 23–34, are ascribed in xxiv. 23 to other wise men.)

II. Chapters xxv.–xxxi. are in the main of Solomon's composition, especially xxv.–xxix., but the sayings were not collected until the time of Ezechias, when they, with the three additions of unknown authorship, were appended to the book.

4. *Purpose of the Book.* Whoever knows of God's revelation and feels bound to live in accordance with it, but is still weak and wavering in the service of God, may be instructed by this collection of rules of life.

5. *Author.* That Solomon composed most of the sayings is expressly stated in i. 1 and xxv. 1, and has always been acknowledged by Christian and Jewish tradition. The pure and dignified language bears witness to the composition of this book as belonging to the golden age of Hebrew poetry, i. e. to the reign of Solomon.

The Septuagint arrangement of the Book of Proverbs differs in some respects from the Hebrew and the Vulgate, which have been followed in this chapter. It contains a few sayings that are not in the Hebrew, and omits some that are to be found there. — Against admitting the book to the canon of Holy Scripture it is sometimes urged that there are many sayings in it which any uninspired person might have uttered. But the divine revelation contains not only supernatural things but also natural truths, which gain additional weight through this revelation. *Cf.* Vatican Council, III. 2, *De Revel.* The fact that the book is quoted as scriptural in the New Testament justifies its canonical acceptation; e. g. Hebrews xii. 5, " Whom the Lord loveth, He chastiseth " (Prov. iii. 12), and James iv. 6, " God resisteth the proud " (Prov. iii. 34).

11. CANTICLE OF CANTICLES

(8 chapters)

1. *Name.* The names *shir hashshirim,* ᾆσμα ᾀσμάτων, *canticum canticorum,* all express the idea that this song stands as much above all others as a poem above ordinary speech.

2. *Contents.* According to its literal meaning, the song is simply an account of sexual love.

A shepherd in or near Jerusalem loves a maiden who returns his affection with similar feelings. They vie with one another in extolling each other's perfections and in expressions of longing for their union in marriage. The hindrances that they encounter only intensify their love. King Solomon is mentioned by name, but it is more than doubtful whether he is to be identified with the bridegroom, as many assert. It seems better to assume that the bride refuses to accept hospitality in the palace, and rejects the king's overtures, because she wishes to remain faithful to her beloved shepherd. It is left uncertain whether the lovers ever attain to a permanent union, as no further reference is made to it.[1]

3. *Interpretation.* The rationalistic view is that the book is to be interpreted literally, and that the beautiful poem is merely an account of human love.[2] In reply we may say:

(*a*) A mere love-song would never have been admitted to the collection of the sacred books, especially not as the Song of Songs; i. e. as the most exalted and stately canticle.

(*b*) An erotic poem would certainly conclude with a marriage, otherwise the account would be incomplete and unsatisfactory.

(*c*) Tradition not only of the Church, but also among the Jews, is absolutely opposed to the literal interpretation.[3]

(*d*) At the Second General Council of Constantinople (553)

---

[1] Ewald gives a similar account of the contents.

[2] Theodore of Mopsuestia and the more modern rationalists such as Hitzig and Cornill, take this view. The latter remarks that no unprejudiced reader could for a moment doubt "that the theme is the love of man for woman and of woman for man. . . . That it was admitted to the canon was owing to the mistake of interpreting its contents allegorically (as was the case with Ps. xlv. (xliv.)."

[3] That even the Abyssinian Church has always maintained the allegorical interpretation of the Canticle of Canticles has been thoroughly proved in a monograph by Seb. Euringer, Lpz., 1900.

the Church expressly condemned Theodore of Mopsuestia's theory of literal interpretation.

We are not even allowed to suppose that originally a real, human love prompted the composition of the poem, and that later the account of it was taken to symbolize a higher love, so that for this reason the book was included in the Canon. Such a theory would not harmonize with what the Church teaches regarding inspiration, namely that the sacred writers were influenced and guided throughout by God, in fact that God is really the author of the sacred books. They cannot be at first human productions, and then rendered sacred and divine by subsequent inclusion in the Canon. The Council of 553 decided that such an opinion was erroneous.

The correct interpretation is the allegorical; i. e. we must assume that under the cloak and appearance of human love is represented a far higher union, rising above all that is earthly and sensual. There is no reality in this human love, it is only the garment in which a lofty mystery is clothed, to render it intelligible to mankind.[1]

4. The *Mystery* extolled in the Canticle of Canticles is, according to the traditional explanation, the union between God and faithful mankind. This union under the Old Covenant was the bond between God and the people of Israel,[2] under the New Covenant it is the bond between Christ — the Good Shepherd — and the Church. Revelation often represents this union as a marriage; our Saviour speaks of Himself as the Bridegroom

---

[1] We can nevertheless comply with the instructions requiring us to interpret Holy Scripture first literally and then mystically. We must imagine that the divinely inspired poet described an ideal human love, but in doing so had all along a sacred mystery in his mind. We may fix our eyes primarily on the garment or type, but we must consider the higher mystical meaning.

[2] *Cf.* the canticle in Isaias v. 1, 2, that is sung to the "beloved" (דּוֹד). Language very similar to that of Isaias is used by the composer of the Canticle of Canticles, e. g. in ii. 8, 10, 16; v. 1.; vi. 1. Although the bodily perfection and whole form of the bride are extolled, there is nothing sensual in this, for it signifies that by surrender to God, the whole human nature, including the body, is ennobled and spiritualized, filled with supernatural beauty and rendered well pleasing to God. For this reason the body, too, can become worthy to last forever, as the bridegroom is everlasting.

(Matt. ix. 15), and Saint Paul states (Eph. v. 21–33) that human marriage is particularly sacred for the reason that it is a type of that mysterious spiritual union. A relation, resembling that which exists between God and the human beings loyal to Him taken collectively, exists also between God and every soul filled with love and gratitude towards Him, and in a special way between God and every soul which, for love of God, keeps itself in perfect purity and renounces ordinary marriage. For this reason many passages of the Canticle of Canticles are applied by the Church particularly to Mary.[1]

5. *Author*. Tradition ascribes the poem to Solomon. In style and language it belongs to the fairest and happiest period of the national life. It used to be universally believed, by Catholics and non-Catholics alike, that Solomon composed the poem, or that at least it dated from his reign. The most recent criticism, however, on the ground of a few apparently not Semitic expressions, assigns it to a very late period, although in III Kings iv. 32, 33, Solomon is celebrated as a poet of nature, and therefore seems to be referred to distinctly as the author of this, the most beautiful of all Hebrew songs.[2]

---

[1] In a monograph L. Hug puts forward a remarkable interpretation, suggesting that the poem expressed the longing on the part of the kingdom of Samaria for union with that of Juda. In as far as this is to be understood the noble longing felt by God's faithful people in the northern kingdom for the Lord of Israel, dwelling in the Temple at Jerusalem, this interpretation may be accepted. But we must not limit the poem to this one idea.

[2] Reuss thinks that the book was written in the Northern Kingdom, soon after its separation from the Southern, and whilst Thirza was still the capital. But would Solomon have been honored there? Cornill remarks that if it can be said of any book " Thy speech betrayeth thee," this is true of the Canticle of Canticles. He refers particularly to the words *appirjon, litter*, in iii. 9, declaring that it is the Greek φορεῖον, and *pardes*, garden, in iv. 13, which he assumes to be Persian. But Maurer, certainly a Hebrew scholar, derives *pardes* from *padas*, to spread out, and *appirjon* from *para*, to carry. Cornely rightly points out that even in Debora's song (Judges v.) some expressions of the same kind occur, and yet no one questions its antiquity. — A. von Scholz upholds the allegorical interpretation, but thinks the book was composed in the school at Jerusalem.

12. ECCLESIASTES

(12 chapters)

1. *Name.* This book is called in Hebrew *Qohéleth,* which the Seventy translated by *Ecclesiastes* = preacher.

Qohéleth (from *qahal* = to call an assembly, to speak in an assembly) is a feminine form, but probably *qohel* = public speaker. Possibly *chokma* might be supplied, and the name would mean " Speaking Wisdom."

2. *Contents.* The book contains a decidedly melancholy view and description of human life, written in poetical form.

The author surveys all the various ways and pleasures of life, and finds nowhere anything that satisfies the heart; all is vanity, because all is fleeting. Neither life itself, that passes so quickly, nor the so-called good things of life, such as high rank, power, wisdom and knowledge, wealth and pleasure, can bestow happiness, which every man desires. Is man therefore to abandon himself to despair as a pessimist? Or is he, as a materialist, to adopt the principle: Enjoy life whilst it lasts, for all will soon be at an end? No; the author, at the close of the discussion, comes to this decision: he bids man " Fear God and keep His commandments, for this is all man " (i. e. the whole duty of man), and all things that are done, God will bring into judgment for every error, whether it be good or evil (for reward or punishment).

3. *Form.* The writer stands as a spectator amidst the fleeting phenomena of life, and expresses his thoughts as a speaker before an imaginary audience. The style is therefore rhetorical rather than poetical, and yet there is a rhythm throughout that distinguishes the book from the prose writings. Zapletal says (*supra,* 325) : " The book is written in a regular meter."

4. *Author.* Solomon is generally believed to have composed the book, towards the end of his reign, after he had gone astray but had repented. We meet with him here as a penitent.

Reasons for regarding Solomon as the author:

(1) He is mentioned in the heading: " Words of the *Qohéleth,* son of David, king of Jerusalem."

(2) The author speaks of himself several times in terms applicable only to Solomon. He describes the splendor of his court, the abundance of his riches and his wisdom.

(3) On the ground of Jewish tradition, the Rabbis regard Solomon as the author.

(4) The Fathers of the Church speak of the three books of Solomon, so they ascribed to him Ecclesiastes as well as the Canticle of Canticles and Proverbs. Arguments against his authorship are derived from the language of the book, which not only differs very much from that of the Canticle of Canticles and Proverbs, but contains many Aramaic expressions, that suggest its belonging to the period after the Captivity.

We must, however, remember: (1) that a man full of youthful vigor naturally uses vivid language, and in his old age he speaks more calmly and sadly; (2) that the "Preacher" is addressing the people, and so must adopt the popular dialect, which in Solomon's time had absorbed many foreign expressions and forms, in consequence of the constant intercourse with foreign countries.

Ecclesiastical decisions regarding the canon declare the book to be Solomon's, but this may be understood to mean that Solomon's wisdom may be learnt from it, as from Wisdom and Ecclesiasticus. In the decree of Innocent I, v. 405, mention is made of "Salomonis libri V," but the canon of the Council of Trent contains no allusion to its author. On the ground of the language, Kaulen doubts whether Solomon can have been the author. Cornely, like most of the Catholic writers (B. Schäfer, Schenz, Gietmann), follows tradition, and believes that he was. Scholz thinks that it was the work of a number of *Chakamim* (wise men), and that it consists of an original portion with later additions. McNeile (Cambridge, 1904) believes that it was composed about 300 B.C. Peters (*Bibl. Ztschr.*, 1903), after careful comparison with Ecclesiasticus, considers that Ecclesiastes is based upon it, and assigns Ecclesiasticus to a date between 190–180 B.C. and Ecclesiastes to one between 145–130 B.C. Zapletal (*Bibl. Ztschr.*, 1905) lays stress on the fact that it is not possible to trace any influence of Greek philosophy in this book.

13. THE BOOK OF JOB [1]

(42 chapters)

1. *Contents.* Examination into the cause of human suffering, and especially the sufferings of those faithful to God.

Job, a wealthy, respected and pious man, living in the land of Hus (Uz) to the east of Palestine, suddenly becomes very unhappy through the tricks of Satan. He loses his goods and his children, and is attacked by the horrible disease of leprosy. Nevertheless, he long remains submissive to God and patient in his misery. Three friends, Eliphas, Baldad and Sophar, come to comfort him, but they are so much horrified at his state that they for a long time are unable to speak. Job's patience now gives way, and he breaks out into bitter complaints at his lot, that he has not deserved, and he longs for death. His friends rebuke him

---

[1] The Hebrew אִיּוֹב ought not to be written *Hiob* (Luther), but *Jjob* or *Job* (Sept., Vulg.). א is not = *h*, but is a *spiritus lenis*, an inaudible breathing.

for these lamentations, and say he must have drawn down this punishment upon himself by his sins, and so they urge him to do penance, which perhaps may change his fortune. Job persists in asserting his innocence, and all attempts of his friends to convince him of his guilt are fruitless; they finally keep silence and Job remains the victor in this war of words. Eliphas speaks three times and so does Baldad, but Sophar only twice. Job answers each of these speeches, and utters both the introductory and the closing words. There are therefore in all eighteen speeches, or if Job's last utterance which is once interrupted be reckoned as two, there are nineteen. — Now another speaker enters, a young man, named Eliu. He wishes to settle the dispute by explaining that neither Job nor his friends are altogether in the right. To Job he says: "No man is just, but God alone." Job's assertion of his innocence could not be accepted, because it made piety appear useless. To the friends he says it is a mistake to suppose suffering is always the result of sins committed; God often desires by means of suffering to protect man from pride and from the sins proceeding therefrom. — This decision, though given with great assurance, satisfies no one completely because it involves a contradiction; yet there is much truth in it.

It is plain from the speeches made by Job, his three friends and Eliu, that man of himself is incapable of understanding the causes of suffering. Therefore God Himself appears and ends the strife. His judgment is twofold; it is partly *against* Job, who has grumbled at Him, whilst appreciating far too little the power and wisdom with which God guides the destinies of men; and it is partly *for* Job and against his friends, whose harshness is rebuked. After Job has asked forgiveness of God for his complaints, he recovers his prosperity in greater measure than before.

2. *Divisions.* (1) Chapters i.–iii., Job's happiness and his misfortunes. (2) iii.–xxxi., conversation between Job and his friends regarding the causes of his affliction. (3) xxxii.–xxxvii., Eliu's speeches. (4) xxxviii.–xli., appearance of God and His decision. (5) Job's restoration to happiness.

3. *Purpose of the Book.* The Book of Job must not be regarded as an account of the suffering of a single individual, but as giving touching expression to the sorrows of all in affliction. It may be called the lamentation of all suffering humanity and especially of such as are not redeemed.

As long as the believer in God under the Old Dispensation uttered these complaints and cherished at the same time the wish, so often repeated by Job, that God Himself might appear and exert His power, he must have been penetrated with a longing for redemption.

Two causes of suffering are mentioned in the book: (1) At the beginning, and still more clearly at the end, it shows how God's power and wisdom are supreme over mankind and govern their destinies. God allows suffering that He may test men, purify them, and finally reward them generously. We learn from Job's example that every sufferer, though he complain, should still trust calmly to God's providence, for God always turns sorrow to our advantage. It is a law of Divine Providence that joy shall follow sorrow. (2) The more direct cause of suffering is that Satan (chap. ii.) through sin has won a hold upon mankind, and uses his power to drag men with him into misery, as far as he can. When sin is removed by redemption, the power of hell, and with it suffering, will vanish more and more.

This examination has not exhausted all the purpose of the book, for Job has also a typical character. The suffering of the innocent is incomprehensible to man, and yet in the suffering of the most guiltless lies the deepest wisdom. There is namely such a thing as vicarious suffering, and Job is a type of our Redeemer, and a dim foreshadowing of Him who was to endure terrible agony on behalf of others, in order to wipe away sin and conquer the powers of hell (chap. xl., xli.). The patristic explanation has always insisted upon this point.

4. *Historical Foundation.* That the story has an historical foundation and is not merely a work of the imagination seems no less certain than that the details are fictitious. The artfully composed speeches are all fiction.

Reasons for believing the groundwork to be historical are the following: (*a*) In both the Old and New Testament (Ezech. xiv. 14; Tob. ii. 11, etc.; James v. 11) reference is made to Job as to an historical person who was a model of piety and patience. The Talmud, too, assumes that he was a real man, a contemporary of Moses. (*b*) The indications of place in the book point to his being historical, and so does the statement that he was an Arab, and therefore a foreigner. If the author had aimed at describing a fictitious character, he would certainly have made his hero a Hebrew. (*c*) Mere romances seem to have been unknown in the ancient world. Every great poem that has come down from antiquity (such as the Iliad, Odyssey and Æneid) has an historical foundation.

5. *Date and Authorship.* Some critics believe the Book of Job to be as old or older than the Pentateuch; others assign it to the period of the Captivity or even later.

In favor of the first theory is the fact that it contains no allusion to the law of Moses. But the law could not have been mentioned, as the hero is not an Israelite. The description of the perfection of the Creator and Preserver of the world, as given in the book, suggests that the author must have known the Pentateuch, and especially the story of Creation contained in the Book of Genesis. In the same way the enumeration of the sins (xxiv. 2–11) that Job knows he has not committed, seems to allude to parts of the Pentateuch (Ex. xxii. 25; Lev. xix. 9, and xxv. 2; Deut. xxiv. 10). The advanced age to which Job lived — he is said to have lived 140 years after his misfortunes — the mention of star worship (xxxi. 26), from which he held himself aloof, and his position as prince and priest, are all indications of his having belonged to the time of the patriarchs. But though Job himself may have lived at this early period, the book may have been written later.

The date of its composition cannot however have been so late as the Captivity. This is plain from Tobias ii. 15, and Ezechiel xiv. 4, where Job is praised for his virtues; and there are several passages in Amos and Jeremias that are borrowed from the Book of Job.[1] The Aramaic expressions in the book are not numerous, and are quite natural in a work containing the record of events in the east of Palestine, where Aramaic was spoken. No one can prove with certainty that an Aramaic element did not find its way into Hebrew before the Captivity. Political connections and frequent intercourse always have some influence on the speech of a country.

Intercourse with foreign countries was especially frequent in the time of Solomon, whose dominions extended far to the north and south. This period coincides with the golden age of Hebrew poetry, and the Book of Job is perhaps its greatest production. It is therefore probable that the book was written during Solomon's reign, and most of the modern critics are of this opinion.[2]

[1] Amos v. 8 suggest Job ix. 9; Jer. xvii. 1 suggests Job xix. 24; Jer. xx. 14, etc., suggests Job iii. 3, etc., and Jer. xx. 17 suggests Job iii. 11, etc.

[2] Herbst, Welte, Kaulen, Cornely, Danko, Zschokke, Schenz, Knabenbauer, also the Protestant writers Keil, Delitzsch, Hengstenberg,

The resemblance between Job and Proverbs leads us to think that they belong to the same period. — The author is utterly unknown. He may possibly have been Asaph, who composed some psalms containing opinions and subjects not unlike those to be found in Job (Ps. lxxii., lxxxi.). J. Royer tries to show that the prophet Jeremias was the author.

For the meter of the book see page 283. Friedrich Delitzsch, an authority on Assyrian monuments, thinks that the text of Job has been very accurately preserved.

THIRD SECTION

THE PERIOD FROM THE DIVISION OF THE KINGDOMS UNTIL THE END OF THE CAPTIVITY

14. HISTORICAL SURVEY

The following historical events are connected with the composition of the sacred books belonging to the third period of the history of Israel.

1. The separation of the kingdom into two parts: the Kingdom of Juda in the south, where the dynasty of David continued to rule with Jerusalem as the capital of a State consisting of the tribes of Juda and Benjamin; and the Kingdom of Samaria (Israel, Ephraim) in the north, consisting of the remaining ten tribes, having kings of its own and Samaria (Heb., *Schomron* = hill of the watch) as its capital.

2. The overthrow of the northern kingdom by the Assyrians, and the carrying off of the inhabitants to Assyria (722).

3. The overthrow of the southern kingdom, the destruction

etc. It has been assigned to the time of Moses, or earlier, by Goldhagen, Jahn, Ackermann and others. Some ascribe it to Moses; several of the Fathers do this, as well as Saint Jerome, and some more recent commentators, such as Tostatus and Bellarmine. Saint Gregory of Nazianzen, Saint John Chrysostom and Calmet believe Solomon to have been the author. Cornill and Kautzsch, however, think that it is of much later origin, belonging to the Greek period (between 330 and 200), their chief reason being that it is not mentioned in the earlier literature; but *cf.* page 301.

of the Temple, the plundering and burning of the Temple, and the carrying off of the Jews to Babylon (588).

4. The return from the Babylonian Captivity (536).

The chronology in the Books of Kings is not perfectly trustworthy, as data have been stated carelessly and uncritically, but the sequence of the Kings is certain. It is also certain that the year 722 witnessed the overthrow of the northern kingdom, 588 the first destruction of Jerusalem, and 536 the return from Captivity. The duration of the kings' reigns in the two kingdoms cannot be determined until the cuneiform inscriptions in Assyria and Babylonia have been more fully examined. The following dates of the Assyrian and Babylonian kings have been verified from cuneiform inscriptions: Tiglath Pilesar = Phul, 745–727, king of Assyria; Salmanassar IV, his successor, 727–722; Sargon, 722–705 (after 709 king of Babylon also); Sennacherib, 705–682; Assarhaddon, 681–668; Assurbanipal, 668–626; Nabuchodonosor, 605–562.

LIST OF THE KINGS

(a) Of the Northern Kingdom

1. Jeroboam I. 2. Nadab. 3. Baasa. 4. Ela. 5. Zambri. 6. Omri. 7. Achab. 8. Ochozias. 9. Joram. 10. Jehu. 11. Joachaz. 12. Joas. 13. Jeroboam II. Interregnum. 14. Zacharias. 15. Sellum. 16. Manahem. 17. Phaceia. 18. Phacee. Interregnum. 19. Osee, 722.

(b) Of the Southern Kingdom

1. Roboam. 2. Abias. 3. Asa. 4. Josaphat. 5. Joram. 6. Ochozias. 7. Athalia (queen). 8. Joas. 9. Amasias. 10. Ozias (= Azarias). 11. Joatham. 12. Achaz. 13. Ezechias. 14. Manasses. 15. Amon. 16. Josias. 17. Joachaz. 18. Joakim. 19. Jechonias. 20. Sedecias, 588.

The Israelites of the northern kingdom who were carried away to Assyria never returned home, but were lost among the Gentiles. Colonists from the east settled in their land of Samaria, intermarrying with the Israelites that still remained there; but the heathen element was by far the stronger, so that the Samaritans were of mixed race. The Jews who had been taken to Babylon were allowed to go back to their own country by Cyrus, after his conquest of Babylon. Not by any means did all the Jews return to the Holy Land; those who did so were only a small proportion of the people, a " remnant," as the prophets had foretold. Subsequently other companies of Jews came back, chiefly as a result of the exertions of Esdras and Nehemias.

The seventy years of the Babylonian Captivity, foretold by Jeremias (xxv. and xxix.) are not always assigned to the same dates. It seems best to take 606, rather than either 588 or 599, as the first of the seventy years, for it was in that year that Nabuchodonosor first conveyed a great number of Jews, mostly young men of good birth, to Babylon. In this way the seventy years end in 536, which was the date of the Return. Within this period many of the books of the Bible were written; namely, all the prophetic books with the exception of three that belong to the fourth period.

We generally reckon that there were sixteen prophets, four major and twelve minor,[1] or, if Baruch be regarded not as an appendix to Jeremias, but as an independent work, there were seventeen.

To the period before the Captivity belong Isaias and Jeremias, Jonas, Amos, Joel, Abdias, Osee, Micheas, Nahum, Sophonias, Habakuk. To the Captivity itself, Baruch, Ezechiel and Daniel. (Prophets who lived after the Captivity: Aggeus, Zacharias, Malachias.)

The above is the historical order, but that of the Septuagint is: Oseas, Joel, Amos, Abdias, Jonas, Micheas, Nahum, Habakuk, Sophonias, Aggeus, Zacharias, Malachias, Isaias, Jeremias, Baruch, Threni, Letter of Jeremias, Ezechiel, Daniel. The Vulgate has the same arrangement, except that the four major prophets, Lamentations and Baruch are placed before Oseas. In the Hebrew Bible Isaias, Jeremias and Ezechiel stand before the minor prophets, whilst Daniel is placed after Esther among the Ketubim.

15. PROPHECY IN GENERAL

1. Those persons under the Old Covenant, who were called directly by God to proclaim His will, and who received supernatural powers for the purpose, are known as prophets.[2] They

---

[1] The twelve minor prophets collectively form one book. Sirach, writing as early as 200 B.C., if not sooner, speaks of the "twelve prophets" as belonging together (Ecclus. xlix. 12).

The Hebrew name is *nabi*, plural *nebiim* (from *naba*, to gush forth, to speak in a lively and inspired manner) = *inspiratus*, inspired speaker. They are often called also seers, watchmen, shepherds, or men

did not form a class enjoying inherited privileges, as did the priests and kings, but they were chosen and commissioned by God for a time to carry certain messages.

Such were Moses, Josue and Samuel in the earliest period of Jewish national life, and later Nathan, Elias, Eliseus and others. The earlier prophets were conspicuous chiefly for their deeds, the later for their words, many of which were recorded by themselves or by others. The activity of the later prophets lasted from about 800 to 400 B. C.

2. *Functions of the Prophets.* The primary duty of each prophet was to benefit his own generation, to maintain the fidelity of the people towards God, and to threaten sinners with God's chastisement. They were a kind of conscience to the nation. Incidentally, a glance into the future of Israel was often vouchsafed to them, and this they described sometimes in threatening, sometimes in encouraging language. They also took into account the destinies of foreign nations, as far as they came into contact with God's people. To foretell the future was therefore not the only duty assigned to the prophets, although it formed an essential part of their functions. The true prophets were distinguished from the false especially by the fulfillment of their prophecies, although this often took place after their death (Deut. xviii. 21, 22). The most important of their prophetic utterances are the Messianic prophecies, by means of which the people of God were prepared for the coming of the Redeemer, and their longing for Him was awakened, maintained and intensified.

The false prophets, who are so often mentioned, were generally optimists or flatterers, announcing, ostensibly at God's bidding, nothing but what was pleasant, thus encouraging the people in their wickedness, for they relied upon the exalted destiny of Israel as if it made any chatisement on God's part inconceivable (*cf.* e. g. Jer. xxiii. and xxvi.). Our Saviour has warned us that there would be false prophets also under the New Covenant, and said that they might be recognized by their fruits, for suffering and misery were involved in following their doctrines (Matt. vii. 15).

---

of God. The Greek name signifying " one who foretells " does not convey an idea of their whole duty. The root of *nabi* occurs in the form *naba'a*, also in Assyrian and Arabic; in Assyrian it means " to speak, announce "; in Arabic, " to report, make known."

3. *Personality*. The prophets were as a rule holy persons, but sanctity was not a necessary condition of a prophetic vocation. Hence we find among the prophets not only Jonas, who in his disobedience wished to escape from God, but also the Gentile Balaam. Natural qualifications were not absolutely requisite, and therefore people of very different positions in life were intrusted with the work of a prophet. We find in the company of aristocrats, such as David and Daniel, the prophet Amos who was a simple countryman.

We hear of schools of the prophets, but we must not imagine them to have been schools in our sense of the word, places where prophets were trained, as we have schools for physicians or lawyers. The word "school" denotes only a connection such as existed between Christ and His Apostles, though it is possible that in these schools a prophetic vocation was often awakened by the singing and the study of the law (I Sam. (Kings) x. 5; xix. 20). *Cf.* the article *Prophetenschulen* by Welte in the *Kirchenlexikon*.

4. The *Mode of the Divine Communications* varied. As a rule, the prophets received only inward illumination; but often they had visions, perceived by means of the senses. Sometimes they were instructed when in a state of ecstacy, or favored with a vision. They generally speak of the future as if it were present, for they were seers. The present and the future are often confused in their utterances.

5. The spoken word of the prophets was intended for their contemporaries, the written for the future, as witness of the truth and as a testimony against Israel.

6. In order to understand the prophetic books we must always bear in mind: (*a*) that Israel is God's people, and as such exalted above other nations; (*b*) it possesses the kingdom of God on earth and is the bearer of the hopes of redemption; (*c*) it is false to God, and therefore is punished; (*d*) God's kingdom is not to perish on that account, but (*e*) out of Israel shall come the Messias.[1]

---

[1] It is a purely arbitrary assumption on the part of Wellhausen and his followers that all predictions of a better future and of redemption were interpolated into the writings of the prophets after the Captivity. Such critics say that the small remnant of the Israelite nation spent their time in dreaming of a revival of David's kingdom,

PROPHETS PREVIOUS TO THE DOWNFALL OF THE
NORTHERN KINGDOM

16. JONAS

(4 chapters)

1. *Contents.* Jonas,[1] son of Amathi, is commissioned by God
to announce the destruction of the great city of Ninive. The
people of Ninive do penance, and therefore the town is spared.

Jonas belonged to the northern kingdom, having been born at Geth-
Opher, of the tribe of Zabulon (IV Kings xiv. 25). He sought by
flight to avoid carrying out his task of going to Ninive and of announcing the coming destruction of the city, and so he set sail on a Phœnician
ship bound for Tharshish (Tartessus in Spain). A terrible storm arose
at sea on his account, and the sailors, fearing the deity, threw him into
the sea. He was swallowed by a great fish, but remained alive, and
as he repented and prayed to God, he was cast up on the shore still
living after three days. Now he fulfilled God's commission, but as
the Ninivites betook themselves to penance, the sentence was not executed
at that time. Jonas murmured for this reason against God, who rebuked him gently.

2. *Truth or Fiction.* This story is to be regarded as perfectly
true, for our Saviour spoke of Jonas as of an historical person
(Matt. xii. 40–42; Luke xi. 30, 31), thus testifying to the truth
of the story.[2] The occurrences related in the book are certainly

and as their hopes were not realized, they sought consolation partly in
inventing a glorious past, and partly in looking forward to the sub-
jugation of the Gentiles. All that the prophetical books contain regarding the triumph of the kingdom of God over the Gentile world is,
according to these critics, really of very late origin, but has been put
into the mouths of the prophets. Some books, such as Daniel, were
altogether fictitious; to others large additions were made, e. g. Isaias
was more than doubled.

Such theories are inevitable when the supernatural is altogether
denied. Against them Nahum may be quoted, for his book has always
been recognized as genuine, and as belonging to the time before the
Captivity. He speaks in exactly the same way of Assyria as Isaias of
the Gentiles. In chapter ii. he says that Assyria must be overthrown,
because the kingdom of God cannot be allowed to perish. Are we to
suppose that all the Jewish authors after the Captivity were liars and
deceivers, devoid of all conscience?

[1] יוֹנָה = dove.

[2] "For as Jonas was in the whale's belly three days and three
nights, so shall the son of man be in the heart of the earth three

unparalleled, but not therefore incredible. Who will dare to limit the power of the Almighty, and prescribe to Him how far He may go without encountering human unbelief? The fish mentioned in the story was probably a gigantic dog fish (*Canis carcharias*); this species is still found in the Mediterranean, and not unfrequently destroys human life. If it be asked why God chose to work this miracle, Jesus Christ (loc. cit.) Himself suggests that it was in order that Jonas should be a type of His own death and resurrection. This explains also why this story is included among the prophetic books, and is placed at the beginning of them. The size ascribed to Ninive, " a city of three days' journey," is borne out by recent discoveries on the Tigris. From the beginning of the ruins in the north (Sargon's Palace) to the end of them in the south (mouth of the great Zab) is about twenty hours' walk, and one day's journey generally meant from six to eight hours' walk.

3. *Author.* Probably Jonas himself composed the book, being moved to do so by his feelings of contrition for his faults. It may, however, be assumed that his record was arranged by a subsequent writer so as to ·form the present book.

4. *Date.* The prophet must have lived about the year 800 B. C., as, according to IV Kings xiv. 25, he prophesied the successful expedition made by Jeroboam II against Syria.

Strack thinks that the Book of Jonas may have been written at the end of the sixth or the beginning of the fifth century. Cornill assigns it to "the latest period of spoken Hebrew," and refers it to the fourth century. He bases this view chiefly on peculiarities in diction, but the nine expressions on which he relies are not so convincing as to force us to admit so late an origin; they are partly northern provincialisms and partly technical words. The word (iii. 3) *hajetha* ("Nivine *was* a great town") is no proof of a late origin; it may have been inserted into a copy of the book by the editor (Esdras?) in whose time Ninive no longer existed, as his readers could not know the great city. The

---

days and three nights. The men of Ninive shall rise in judgment with this generation, and shall condemn it, because they did penance at the preaching of Jonas; and behold a greater than Jonas here. The queen of the south shall rise in judgment with this generation, and shall condemn it, because she came from the ends of the earth to hear the wisdom of Solomon, and behold a greater than Solomon here." If Solomon and the Queen of Saba were historical personages, Jonas, who preached to Ninive, is so no less.

prayer in ii. 3–10 bears some resemblance to the psalms, but this is no evidence of a very late origin; its contents are quite as well suited to an earlier period, and the Temple (verses 5 and 8) need not necessarily be the second.

17. Amos [1]

(9 chapters)

1. *Date.* Amos probably lived not long after Jonas, for in the introduction to his book the Kings Ozias of Juda and Jeroboam II of Samaria are mentioned. He is the oldest of the prophets whose utterances have been preserved in writing.

2. *Mission.* Amos was a shepherd and caretaker of a sycamore plantation at Thekne, near Bethlehem. God called him to go as a prophet to the northern kingdom, and after fulfilling his mission he returned home and resumed his previous occupation. He seems himself to have written down the prophecies he had uttered as an everlasting testimony against Israel, that had not listened to his warnings.

His time of activity appears not to have been long, as in i. 1 we read that he entered on his mission two years before the earthquake. We do not know what earthquake this was. He probably spoke most of his prophecies at Bethel, the center of the idolatrous worship, for the high priest Amasias of Bethel denounced him to the king (vii. 10).

3. *Contents.* The prophet inveighs against idolatrous worship and the moral corruption connected with it, which showed itself in excessive luxury, partiality in the administration of justice, and oppression of the poor. The whole kingdom is threatened with destruction and the people with exile. Such freedom of speech on the part of a man of the lower classes was intolerable to king, priests and people alike, and Amos was driven out of the country.

4. *Divisions.* Chapters i. and ii., God's chastisement for sin is coming upon all the nations of Western Asia. iii.–vi. It will fall most heavily upon Samaria. vii.–ix. Vision of the punishment to be inflicted upon Samaria.

Chapter i. The neighboring nations have sinned and are being punished by God (through the agency of the advancing Assyrians).

---

[1] עָמוֹס = carrier of burdens.

ii. Samaria, although belonging to God's people, has sinned yet more, and can least of all be spared. iii. God causes the prophets to announce the punishment before He inflicts it; Samaria will be destroyed like a beast torn by a lion, so that nothing remains of it but a few little bones. iv. The punishments inflicted hitherto have been fruitless, destruction is now imminent. v. Song of mourning over Samaria; it could only be saved by penance. vi. The rich and powerful in Samaria as in Juda are chiefly to blame for the decay of morality, therefore the heaviest chastisement shall fall upon them. vii. Three visions, (*a*) and (*b*), show that God has often been induced by prayer to spare His people, but now (*c*) all forbearance is over. The idolatrous priest, Amasias, accused Amos before the king, and received a terrible prophecy concerning his own family; his wife and children were to perish, his property should belong to others, he himself should die in a heathen land and the whole nation go into captivity. viii. Vision of the gathering in of the fruit, meaning that Samaria is ripe for destruction. ix. The Samaritans, on account of their idolatry, are no better than the heathen, but the kingdom of God will not pass away, and salvation will nevertheless come through the Messias.

Strack, Kautzsch and Cornill assign the book to the year 760. The genuineness of some of the verses, which are thought to disturb the connection of ideas, has been questioned, but without sufficient reason (Cornill).

18. Joel [1]

(4 chapters in Septuagint, 3 in Vulgate)

1. *Joel,* son of Phatuel, seems to have labored in the southern kingdom, for he pays no attention to Samaria, but mentions as enemies of God's people the Phœnicians and Philistines (iii. 4) and the Egyptians and Edomites (iii. 19). We know (II Chron. xxvi. 6–8) that King Ozias of Juda fought successfully against such enemies. The *time* of Joel's activity is not stated in his book, but it must have been during the reign of Ozias, and even at the beginning of it, considerably before 760, for the prophet does not allude to the Assyrians who, towards the close of Ozias' reign, penetrated as far as Palestine and made Samaria tributary to them (IV Kings xv. 19).

2. *Contents.* After a short introduction, the prophet speaks of a devastation of the Holy Land by locusts.

i. Palestine has suffered terribly again and again from locusts. ii. This plague is a foreshadowing of heavy chastisement, but if the people

---

[1] יוֹאֵל = the Lord is God.

turn to God and do penance, blessings may come instead of curses.   iii. God's justice threatens those only who do not believe; redemption shall come to the righteous.[1]

3. *Interpretation.*   It is uncertain whether the prophet was speaking of a real plague of locusts or whether he spoke of locusts only as a type of hostile armies.   Most of the later commentators prefer the literal explanation, but the old Rabbis and the Fathers of the Church adopt the figurative interpretation. They may very well be united and we may suppose that Joel saw how the Holy Land was devastated by invasions of locusts in his day, and so he referred to them, when foretelling to the people how the land would be laid waste by foreign hosts, unless Israel returned to its God.

Modern critics assign a late date to this book.   According to Cornill (172), the year 586 (or 588) is the *terminus a quo*, as it was only from this time onward that God had cause to expostulate with the enemies of His people.   Cornill says: " We must go far beyond the year of the destruction of Jerusalem, for the capital is inhabited, the Temple built, and the worship in it organized.   This cannot have been the case until after the return from Captivity.   As the walls of Jerusalem (?) are mentioned in ii. 9, we are brought to the time of Nehemias.   Moreover, Joel knows nothing of moral decadence, he finds fault with nothing [but *cf.* ii. 12, etc.], to him the Jews are infinitely exalted above the heathen. . . . Absolutely convincing is his quotation from Malachias iii. 23 [Vulg. iv. 4] regarding the great and terrible day of Judgment."   But may not Malachias have borrowed from Joel?   There is nothing to oblige us to relegate the book to the period following the Captivity and thus to adopt a view opposed to that of the Canon and to Jewish tradition.   The simple sequence of thought, suited to every period of Jewish history, is this: The Holy Land will be laid waste by the Gentiles (Assyrians, Babylonians, Persians, Greeks, Romans, Mahometans) as a district is eaten up by locusts.   However terrible the visitation may be (though it might be averted if Israel did penance), it cannot put an end to the kingdom of God.   The future belongs to the faithful, whilst unbelievers sooner or later must appear before God's tribunal, especially at the Last Judgment at the end of time.

---

[1] The words in iii. 1, *cum convertero captivitatem Juda et Jerusalem*, which are translated " I shall bring back the captivity of Juda and Jerusalem," contain no reference to the Captivity of the Jews, but mean, according to the original, " I shall change the destiny."   So translates also Kautzsch.

19. ABDIAS [1]

(21 verses)

1. *Abdias* has left on record a short prophecy uttered against Edom or Idumæa, a country near to the Israelites, the inhabitants of which were akin to them in race. He certainly lived in the southern kingdom, as he speaks of Jerusalem and Sion.

Edom is a small country, and its inhabitants, the descendants of Esau, are few in number, but they are proud, and filled with hatred of Juda. But Juda, being the kingdom and people of God, will triumph, and Edom, like all other enemies, will be brought low.

2. *Date.* The contents of the book seem to indicate that at the time of the Babylonian invasion the Edomites made common cause with the enemies of Israel, and openly showed their joy at its misfortunes. This is mentioned as a fact in other places (e. g. Ezech. xxv. 12; Ps. cxxxvi. 7). If this surmise is correct, the prophet must have lived about the year 600, in the time of Jeremias. The position of the book in the canon points to an earlier date, and in v. 18 there is an allusion to the house of Joseph, i. e. to the kingdom of Samaria, that was destroyed in 722.[2] Although Abdias seems (verses 1–9) to have borrowed passages from Jeremias xlix. 7, etc., it is more probable that Jeremias had the earlier prophecy in mind when he wrote.[3] If it be urged that before the time of Nabuchodonosor there was never a day of ruin and desolation for Juda, such as Abdias describes (v. 13), we may reply that great distress fell upon Juda in the reign of King Joram (889–884) when the Arabs and Philistines invaded the country, took the royal family prisoners, and plundered the royal treasury (II Chron. xxi, 16, etc.). Abdias is referring to this event; and we may conclude that he lived at about the same time as Joel (before 760), as the two prophets

---

[1] עֹבַדְיָה = worshiper of Yahweh.

[2] This verse alone is enough to prove the antiquity of the book: "The house of Jacob shall be a fire, and the house of Joseph a flame, and the house of Esau stubble, and they . . . shall devour them, and there shall be no remains of the house of Esau."

[3] In Abdias the speech is connected, whereas in Jeremias parts of it seem to be quoted from memory.

in some places use almost the same expressions. There is no trace in the language of a later origin.

A. Condamin, S.J., in the *Revue biblique* (1900, ii. 261) proves from the structure of the strophes that the whole of Abdias is older than Jeremias.

20. OSEE[1]
(14 chapters)

1. *Osee* was the son of Beeri, of whom we know nothing. His birthplace is uncertain, and it is impossible to decide positively whether he belonged to the northern or the southern kingdom. As, however, he speaks of Juda only incidentally, and refers constantly to the northern kingdom and its circumstances and alludes to its ruler as "our king" (vii. 5), he must have lived in the kingdom of Samaria.

2. *Date.* According to the heading (i. 1), he was a contemporary of Isaias, who was active in the southern kingdom. He must, however, have been older than Isaias, as he was active during the reign of Ozias, and Isaias did not receive his call until the last year of that reign. We may assume that Osee's activity lasted from about 780 to 720.

3. *Contents.* The northern kingdom is going to ruin. Israel is like an adulteress who deserves rejection.

Chapters i.–iii. are a narrative. Osee tells of his domestic misery; his wife is frequently false to him. This marriage was a type of God's relation towards His people. iv.–xiv. A collection of disconnected speeches, strung together, depict the anarchical condition of the northern kingdom. Like Amos, the prophet rebukes the idolatry, immorality and deceit prevalent among all classes. These disorders are leading to the downfall of the State, upon which God has already determined. Reliance is placed upon Egypt and Assyria (xii. 1), but no one notices that the heathen are bringing about the destruction of Israel, — a just punishment for yielding to their vices. By way of consolation a glance into the Messianic future is vouchsafed, in order that those of the people who are pious and willing to do penance may find encouragement. In conclusion (xiv. 5, 6, 10), God says: "I will heal their breaches, I will love them freely. . . . Israel shall spring up as the lily, and his root shall shoot forth. . . . Who is wise, and he shall understand these things? prudent, and he shall know these things? For the ways of the Lord

---

[1] הוֹשֵׁעַ, helper.

are right, and the just shall walk in them; but the transgressors shall
fall in them."

Wellhausen (*Isr. u. jüd. Gesch.*, 80) declares that the prophet was
mistaken, and that Israel vanished from the face of the earth. This
is true of the kingdom of Samaria, but not of the whole nation, and
the two kingdoms were intimately connected.

4. *Symbolical Marriage.* The prophet's marriage, described
in the early chapters, is variously explained. The question
whether he is speaking of real occurrences or relating a parable,
cannot be decided. Most of the Fathers and older commentators
take the former alternative.

21. MICHEAS [1]

(7 chapters)

1. *Micheas,* born in Moresheth of the tribe of Juda, prophesied
under Joatham, Achaz and Ezechias until about the time of the
destruction of the northern kingdom. He was therefore a contemporary of Isaias. His prophecies were addressed to both
kingdoms, but especially to the southern.

2. *Contents.* The prophecies of Micheas bear much likeness
to those of Isaias. They can be divided into three sections, each
ending with a Messianic promise.

I. (Chapters i. and ii.) God is on the point of punishing His people
for their disloyalty. The chastisement is to fall first upon the northern
kingdom, and the southern may take warning from it.

II. (Chapters iii.–v.) The kingdom of Juda will fare no better;
Sion will be taken and destroyed; but still God's kingdom will not
perish; a glorious time will follow a ruler who proceeds from Bethlehem,
but who has been from eternity.

III. (Chapters vi. and vii.) Punishment must inevitably fall upon
Israel because of the wickedness of the people, who cannot fail to
recognize this fact. But the consequence of the punishment need not
be the final rejection of Israel; a peaceful future may and must be
anticipated. The book ends with a touching prayer offered by the
prophet for his people.[2]

---

[1] מִיכָה = מִיכָיָה, who is like the Lord. Septuagint, *Μιχαίας*.

[2] "Who is a God like to thee, who takest away iniquity, and passest
by the sin of the remnant of thy inheritance? he will send his fury in
no more, because he delighteth in mercy. He will turn again, and have
mercy on us; he will put away our iniquities; and he will cast all

The Book of Micheas is probably a collection of the essential portions of the prophecies uttered by him at various times.

Ewald, Stade and Cornill try to prove that several portions of Micheas are not authentic, but a very thorough defense of the genuineness of the book is contained in a work by V. Ryssel, *Untersuchungen über Text*, etc., *des Micha*, Leipzig, 1887.

22. ISAIAS [1]

(66 chapters)

1. *Isaias.* The prophet who bore this name lived in the kingdom of Juda, and prophesied during the reigns of Ozias, Joatham, Achaz and Ezechias. His father, Amos, is not to be identified with the prophet of that name. Isaias was called by God about 757 to undertake his special work, and he probably lived until about 680. According to tradition, King Manasses had him sawn asunder (Heb. xi. 37; Justin., *Dial. c. Tryph.*, 120).

2. *Contents.* The Book of Isaias consists of two very different parts: chapters i.–xxxvii. and chapters xxxviii.–lxvi. The first part deals with the present, the second with the future of Israel.

First part. Chapter i. Words of rebuke for disloyalty introduce the prophetic utterances, — the keynote of the whole book is thus struck. ii.–iv. The Messianic future is indeed in prospect, but it can be realized only after God's chastisement has been inflicted upon His degenerate people. v. Israel is an unfruitful vineyard. vi. The prophet relates that, when he received his mission, he learnt from God that only a small part of Israel could be saved, the great majority must perish. vii.–xii. At the present time the Assyrian power is pressing hard upon Israel, being the instrument used by God for its chastisement; but the Messianic future will come nevertheless; the Messias will be born of the Virgin (blessed by God); He will appear in the north of the country and found a new dominion, a remnant of Israel will be saved, but the power of the heathen will be overthrown. xiii.–xxiii. All the forces of the heathen will be subjugated by the kingdom of God, which alone will last forever. Then follow twelve prophecies of punishment to be inflicted on the heathen nations (Babylonians, Philistines, Moabites, Damascenes, Ethiopians, Egyptians, etc.). Juda, too, as a kingdom will suffer chastisement, but will not perish, for being God's kingdom it is everlasting. xxiv.–xxvii. The world will finally be judged, and

---

our sins into the bottom of the sea. Thou wilt perform the truth to Jacob, the mercy to Abraham; which thou hast sworn to our fathers from the days of old " (vii. 18–20).

[1] יְשַׁעְיָהוּ (Sept., 'Ησαΐας) = the Lord helpeth.

a people who truly worship God will come forth. xxviii.–xxxv. Even though in the immediate future the Assyrian yoke may press heavily upon Juda, all the enemies of God's people must eventually succumb, and the kingdom of God will prevail. Chapters xxvi. and xxxvii. contain an historical account of the invasion of the Assyrians; and this concludes the first part. Chapters xxxviii. and xxxix. are introductory to the second part; [1] they described the sickness and recovery of King Ezechias, as a type of the exile and return of Israel. The second part begins with chapter xl., and forms a closely connected whole, the purpose of which is to announce the coming redemption. This part is divided into three sections, each of nine chapters. With indescribable exultation the prophet foretells a threefold salvation of Israel, i. e. of God's faithful followers in general: (1) It shall be rescued from Captivity, xl.–xlviii.; (2) The Saviour will come, the Servant of God, the Messias, xlix.–lvii.; (3) There shall be salvation for eternity, lviii.–lxvi. (The prophet can scarcely find words in which to make known with exultant joy the salvation of the faithful, — he is truly a *nabi* = a speaker overpowered by divine inspiration.)

3. *Unity of the Work.* The first part is a collection of various utterances of the prophet; the second is, on the contrary, a dissertation, arranged on a definite plan and incapable of division, which we can scarcely imagine was ever proclaimed by mouth. The whole book constitutes the consistent work of a man who is filled with the spirit of God, and aims first at rousing his people for their own good, and then at consoling them. We may follow Kaulen and call the first part the Book of Sorrow, and the second the Book of Comfort. We must therefore believe that not only isolated portions of this book were composed by Isaias, but that he compiled the whole.

4. *Authenticity.* The Babylonians are several times mentioned in the Book of Isaias as being the enemies of God's people, and even the name of Cyrus [2] occurs (xliv. 28, xlv. 1), as that

---

[1] Chapters xxxvi.–xxxix. occur also in IV Kings xviii.–xx.; in many places the two passages are word for word the same. The author of Kings seems to have taken these accounts from Isaias (if Isaias was put to death by Manasses, he must have outlived King Sennacherib, xxxvii., xxxviii., who was murdered in 682).

[2] Heb., כּוֹרֶשׁ, Pers. *Kosru*, in the cuneiform inscriptions *Kurus*, born 598. Even before Cyrus appeared in person, the Israelites seem to have attempted to discover an etymology for the name, deriving it either from קָרַשׁ, to cut off, or חָרַשׁ, to cut into; so that Cyrus = cutter, a characteristic name for a man who cut his way so remarkably into the history of the world. The Seventy gave the name as Κῦρος. As a common noun κῦρος means supreme power, authority.

of the deliverer of the Jews from the Babylonian despotism. For these reasons many critics have assumed that the whole of the second part was the work, not of Isaias, whose active life belongs to about 760 or 780, but of one or more later authors, and was added to the real Book of Isaias. They maintain that Isaias could not have spoken of the Babylonians as existing enemies, because in his lifetime the power of Babylon was still insignificant, and it did not come into conflict with Israel for another hundred years. In the same way he could not possibly have known the name of Cyrus. Probably some Jew about the year 538 tried to encourage and console his people, still groaning under the Babylonian yoke, by means of prophecies directed against Babylon.

Cornill declares the following passages not to be genuine and to have been written by a later hand than Isaias': ii. 2–4; xi. 10; xii. 6; xiii. 2–xiv. 23; xv. 1–xvi. 12; xxi. 1–10 and xxi. 11–17; xxiii.; xxiv.–xxvii.; xxxii. and xxxiii.; xxxiv. and xxxv.; xxxvi.–xxxix., with some small exceptions, and finally xl.–lxvi., which is generally designated the Deutero-Jesaja.[1] Those who maintain that the book is not authentic base their arguments on internal evidence and on the presumption that the future was as obscure to the prophet as it is to us. Marti believes the whole book to be a collection of speeches and disserations, some of which were composed by Isaias. Similar views are expressed in Guthe's *Bibellexikon;* he speaks of there being several constituent parts of the book, varying in age from the eighth to the fourth, or even the third century.

However, for a man who believes in the existence of God and the possibility of an enlightenment of the human intellect by the spirit of God, there appears to be no reason why the book should not really have been composed by Isaias, whose mission it was to announce the triumph of the faithful and of God's kingdom over the unbelievers and the powers of this world. His glance penetrated far beyond his immediate surroundings, beyond Juda and Assyria.

[1] By the " servant of God " in chapters xlix.–lvii. E. Sellin formerly understood Zorobabel, but afterwards Jojachin (Jechonias); Smend, König, Giesebrecht, Marti and Budde think it is a collective name, denoting the people of Israel. Bertholet and Duhm, on the strength of Isaias l. 4 (" The Lord hath given me a learned tongue "), think some teacher of the Thora is meant. Rothstein declares the expression not to be collective, and says that it refers to an individual.

Tradition is in favor of the authenticity of the book, and knows nothing of a second Isaias, whilst Holy Scripture itself bears testimony to it.[1] Internal evidence, too, points to its having been composed before the Captivity. The people are repeatedly warned against idolatry, and this is declared to be the reason for God's chastisement. Such statements would be unnecessary after the Captivity. In chapters lvi. and lvii. the circumstances preceding it are so vividly described that many commentators feel constrained to ascribe these passages to a " Pseudojesaja," living at that period.

PROPHETS LIVING BETWEEN THE DOWNFALL OF THE NORTHERN AND THAT OF THE SOUTHERN KINGDOM

23. NAHUM [2]

(3 chapters)

1. *Nahum's Personality.* This prophet, who, like Jonas, had to prophesy the destruction of Ninive and Assyria, was a native of Elcush, a village in Galilee (Hieron., *Comm. in l. Nahum*). He probably lived in the Holy Land, although his countrymen were in captivity in Assyria, for he mentions places in Palestine, especially Basan, Carmel and Lebanon (i. 4).

In the first part of the third volume of *Beiträge zur Assyriologie* by Delitzsch and Haupt (Leipzig, 1895, pp. 87–188) many reasons are brought forward in support of the theory that Nahum was an Israelite exile, a native of some other Elcush or Alcush near Ninive.

2. *Subject of the Book.* Ninive's destruction.

i. God has determined that Ninive and the kingdom of Assyria shall perish. ii. This destruction is effected by a hostile army, which overruns the city and the kingdom, and puts an end to the latter. iii. The destruction is inevitable, and fully justified.

3. *Date.* Nahum knows that the city of No-Ammon,[3] i. e. Thebes in Upper Egypt, has been destroyed, and reproaches the

---

[1] " [God] purified them by the hand of Isaias, the holy prophet . . . with a great spirit he . . . comforted the mourners in Sion. He showed what should come to pass forever, and secret things before they came " (Ecclus. xlviii. 23–28).

[2] נָהוּם = comforter or comfort. The name is very suitable to this prophet, who comforted God's people when they were in fear of the cruel Assyrians.

[3] The Latin text reads Alexandria, but there can be no doubt that Thebes is meant. *Cf.* the commentaries.

Assyrians for having devastated it (iii. 8). Recent investigations
in Assyria show that King Assurbanipal, who came to the throne
in 668, took and plundered this city about 662. The prophet
refers to this event as something fresh in men's remembrance,
and therefore he seems to have been prominent soon after Assurbanipal's campaign, perhaps about 660. His prophetic threats
were fulfilled in 606.[1]

The authenticity of this work, which is full of the loftiest inspiration, is almost universally acknowledged. The exalted language and the
heartfelt joy that the people of God will soon have nothing more to fear
from the cruel Assyrians, are recognized even by rationalists as tokens
of authenticity.

Happel, *Das Buch d. Proph. Nahum*, 1902, thinks that the book
was not written until after the Captivity, and that Ninive is a fictitious
name for the Syrian empire under Antiochus IV, Epiphanes.

24. SOPHONIAS [2]

(3 chapters)

1. *Personality of Sophonias.* The genealogy of this prophet
is given at the beginning of his book, which is not done in the
case of any other prophet. He seems to have been a descendant
of Ezechias, and this must have been the well-known king of
that name, for no other reason can be discovered for tracing his
genealogy. It is in keeping with his high rank that he addresses his prophecy especially to the princes and king's sons
(i. 8).

2. *Date.* According to the heading of the book, he lived
under King Josias (639–608). He must have been active in

[1] The Medes, in alliance with the Scythians, put an end to the kingdom of Assyria, according to the ordinary reckoning in 625, but according to more recent historians in 606. Kaulen gives the date as 606,
so do Sayce (" Fresh Light from Ancient Monuments," 132) and H. Winckler. The latter mentions an inscription discovered in Babylon in 1894,
which refers to Nabonaid, the last king of Babylon (555–538), and says
that the king of the Medes and Scythians had conquered Assyria, and
thus had helped the Babylonian king Nabopolassar (626–606) out of
his difficulties. We must therefore abandon the theory that the allied
armies of the Medes and Babylonians put an end to the Assyrian kingdom, and believe that the conquest was effected by the Medes and
Scythians.

[2] צְפַנְיָה = the Lord's protection.

the early part of the reign, because he complains bitterly of the prevalence of idolatry in Juda, and as Josias put it down with a strong hand this complaint would have been unnecessary later on. The allusion to the Assyrians as still dangerous (ii. 13, etc.) and the absence of all mention of the Babylonians also are in agreement with the beginning of Josias' reign.

3. *Contents.* Announcement of God's just vengeance being about to fall on Jews and Gentiles.

i. God is ruler and judge of all mankind. Now, in our day, He is judging Juda (the prophet is undoubtedly referring to the invasion of the Babylonians, though he does not speak of these enemies by name). ii. The Gentiles are subject to the same God as the Israelites and will be punished for their cruelty to them. All the empires of the heathen will perish, and mighty Assyria in particular will soon be cast down. iii. Jerusalem should learn from this, and submit loyally to God. But every warning is in vain; and so God's vengeance will light upon it, whilst the heathen nations will turn to the true God. There is, however, still a prospect of mercy for Jerusalem, if Israel will be converted.

According to Cornill, chapter ii. shows a few traces of a later hand, and iii. a great many, and the concluding portion (verses 14–20), in which Israel is called upon to rejoice, is particularly suspicious. This appeal is, however, quite in harmony with the preceding promise that a remnant of Israel shall be saved (verses 10–13).

25. HABAKUK, OR HABACUC [1]

(3 chapters)

1. *Contents.* God sends grievous punishments upon Juda through the Babylonians, who will one day in their turn be exterminated by Him because of their rapacity.

The book begins (chapter i.) with laments over the wickedness prevailing in Juda, and the long delay in God's interference. God declares that chastisement will shortly be inflicted through the Chaldeans (Babylonians), who will cause terrible suffering, acting as His instruments. The prophet is filled with horror, and fears the worst for God's people and kingdom, which is not to be subjugated by the godless heathen. He is ordered (chapter ii.) to write down a prophecy, the fulfillment of which is still far in the future, so that the faithful may read it and be comforted. It states that the idolatrous Chaldeans will in their turn fall a prey to others, and the faithful shall be saved. All merely earthly greatness is to vanish from the kingdom of God. The prophet

---

[1] חֲבַקּוּק, from חָבַק, to grasp, fold = he that foldeth the hands. Septuagint, 'Αμβακούμ.

is (chapter iii.) astonished and alarmed at these communications, but then he extols God in a magnificent song of praise, as being the almighty Judge who guides the course of events for men, destroys the godless, in spite of their apparent prosperity, and saves His own people. Cornill and others deny the authenticity of chapter ii. 9–20 and of the whole of chapter iii., but they are indispensable to a comprehension of the whole! Happel thinks the book is an apocalypse belonging to the period after the Captivity. (*Cf.* Nahum, p. 318.)

2. *Date.* No definite statement occurs in the book as to the time of this prophet's activity; we must therefore have recourse to its contents and try to obtain some chronological inferences from them. We find: (*a*) that Juda was in a state of disloyalty to God; (*b*) that the Chaldean power already existed, but (*c*) Juda had no fear regarding it. These indications point to the rise of the Babylonian Empire, 625; and Habakuk may have been a contemporary of Jeremias, and have labored in the early years of King Joakim's reign.[1]

It is possible that he was active before Sophonias and Jeremias, for he speaks of the Chaldeans as still an almost unknown nation; we should then have to believe that he thought of them still as the race mentioned in Job. i. 17, of no great political importance. The place of the book in the canon suggests, however, that it is of later origin.

3. *Personality of Habakuk.* The history of his life is unknown, nor is it certain whether this prophet is identical with the Habakuk who, according to Daniel xiv., was so miraculously carried from Palestine to Babylon.[2] Several of the Fathers identify them, but in this case Habakuk must have appeared only a short time before the Captivity and have lived throughout its duration, thus reaching a very great age.

[1] Kaulen and Cornely assign the beginning of his activity to the reign of King Manasses, because the news of the Chaldean power still seemed wonderful (i. 5). According to Caspari the book was written between 626 and 605. Cornill dates it after 605.

[2] Kaulen thinks they were different persons, and that some confusion was made by the Seventy, who call both Ambakum. Cornely takes the same view.

26. JEREMIAS [1]

(52 chapters)

1. *Personality*. We can derive a fairly full account of this prophet from his book, which, in addition to his prophecies, contains many details as to his life.

Jeremias was born at Anathoth, one of the priests' cities, north of Jerusalem. His father was a priest named Helcias. In the thirteenth year of King Josias (about 626) the first divine communication was made to the young man in the words: "Before thou camest forth out of the womb, I sanctified thee and made thee a prophet unto the nations," i. e. against the heathen who were attacking the kingdom of Juda, and still more against the heathenish minded Jews themselves. Jeremias was afraid on receiving this communication, and pleaded that he was too young for the task, but in vain. For a generation and a half he had to reproach the Jews, mostly to no purpose, for their sinful folly, announce the destruction of the holy city and the Temple, and with his own eyes behold it, and then proclaim that the only means left to the nation of recovering God's favor was to submit humbly to the heathen, who were commissioned by God to chastise them.

Although Jeremias undertook his difficult task with reluctance, he performed it most faithfully in spite of all obstacles. His chief opponents were the false prophets who, in answer to his threats of punishment, reminded the people of God's mighty protection in the past, of Israel's high destiny and of the impossibility of God's abandoning His people. Jeremias had to undergo much suffering and persecution.

Under the pious king Josias his lot was endurable, but after Josias fell in battle in 608, the hated preacher of truth had to encounter open hostility. Joakim disliked him, and when the Babylonians first invaded the country in 605, and Jeremias wrote down the prophecies of the past twenty years and caused his disciple Baruch to read them in the Temple to convince men of their truth, the king gave orders that Jeremias should be imprisoned and his writings burnt. The prophet escaped, and wrote out his prophecies again, adding to them a denunciation of Joakim. Soon after the king rebelled against the Babylonians, and fresh misfortunes fell upon Juda. Joakim died, and so he did not suffer in his own person the vengeance of the Babylonians, but the new king Jechonias, who with part of the people was carried off into exile at Babylon, and Nabuchodonosor made the weak and incapable Sedecias king. During his reign Jeremias wrote to those already in exile, comforting them and exhorting them for the present to submit to the Babylonian bondage, which would end in seventy years (chapter xxix.). He warned King Sedecias not to rebel against Babylon, as he would only bring down greater misery upon the country. Sedecias did not heed the warning, but was induced to revolt, and Nabuchodonosor hurried to Jerusalem, besieged and de-

---

[1] יִרְמְיָהוּ = appointed by God.

stroyed it. The king was blinded and dragged into captivity with the rest of his people. During these events, Jeremias suffered much at the hands of Jewish fanatics, and was finally imprisoned in the royal palace, being released only after the Babylonians had entered the city. They treated him with respect, and at his own request left him in the country where he could still be of service to the few remaining Jews.

The Babylonians had appointed Godolias (Gedalja), a Jew by birth, to be governor, but he was murdered by an ambitious man who was in league with others, and in their fear the Jews now fled to Egypt, forcing the prophet to accompany them. On the way he uttered his last prophecies. According to tradition he was stoned to death in Egypt by his own countrymen.

2. *The Book of Jeremias,* as we have it, was plainly composed not by Jeremias himself, but by some one else, probably by his disciple Baruch. It bears traces of the period when it was compiled, — an age of disorder and confusion. We cannot find in it any exact chronological arrangement, but the utterances are so confused that it is difficult, if not impossible, to state with regard to each chapter the date to which it belongs. There is, however, a method in the arrangement, for the various parts are ordered so as to bring out more and more clearly the justice in God's dealings with His faithless people. According to the Hebrew and the Latin texts, the book falls into two chief parts. The *first* contains addresses to the Jews, interspersed with historical information (i.–xlv.) ; the *second* consists of prophecies concerning heathen nations, Egyptians, Philistines, Phœnicians, Moabites, Ammonites, Edomites, Damascenes, Elamites and finally also Babylon (xlvi.–li.). Chapter lii. is an historical addition dealing with the fulfillment of the prophet's words.

Introduction: chapter i., God's commission to the prophet. *Part I,* (*a*) chapter ii.–xx., six admonitions regarding the approaching destruction of Juda, on account of its obstinate persistence in wrongdoing. (*b*) xxi.–xxiv., prophecies regarding the faithless leaders of the people. (*c*) xxv.–xxix., Juda, like other nations, will fall a prey to the Babylonians. (*d*) xxx.–xxxiii., nevertheless the people of God shall come back from slavery. (*e*) xxxiv.–xlv., work and sufferings of the prophet at the time of the siege and capture of Jerusalem. *Part II*, xlvi.–li., prophecies regarding the heathen. lii., appendix, history of the fate of Sedecias, who died as a prisoner in Babylon, and of that of his predecessor Jechonias, who was pardoned. This appendix agrees almost word for word with the conclusion of the Fourth Book of Kings.

Saint Jerome arranged the Vulgate text in accordance with the Hebrew, but from chapter xxv. onward the Septuagint order is different, as the prophecies regarding foreign nations are interpolated (xxvi.–xxxii.). The Septuagint text is also about an eighth shorter than the Hebrew and the Latin. Both the Hebrew and the Greek texts are to be regarded as authentic; the passages omitted by the Septuagint should be retained in accordance with the Masorete version, and the Greek arrangement of the text is preferable to the Hebrew.[1]

Streane, "The Double Text of Jeremiah," Cambridge, 1896, considers the text used by the Seventy to have been the original, and prefers the Greek text to the Masoretic, which he believes to be a later expansion of it. A. Scholz, like Workman and Streane, prefers the Septuagint text, but Schneedorfer, Kaulen and Strack think the Masoretic text better. That both are considered authentic may be inferred from the practice of the Eastern and the Western Church. In the East the Septuagint, and in the West the Masoretic text (Vulgate) is in use, just as in Matt. ii. 18 the Masoretic text is followed, and in Heb. viii. 9 the Alexandrian Septuagint.

Rationalistic criticism accepts the prophecies of Jeremias as being on the whole genuine, but it professes to detect several later interpolations on the strength of internal evidence; e. g. xvii. 19, etc., where stress is laid on the observance of the Sabbath, appears to the critics to belong to the time of Nehemias, and l. 51, the prophecy against Babylon, that resembles the "Deuterojesaja" and earlier passages in Jeremias, but is out of place where it stands, seems to be the work of a later hand. But if the commandment about the Sabbath is older than Jeremias (Ezech. xx. 12, etc.), if there is no "Deuterojesaja," and if every writer is prone now and then to repeat himself, we have here no reason at all for denying such passages to be the work of Jeremias.

---

[1] *Arrangements according to the Septuagint.* Chapters i.–xxv., as in the Hebrew and the Latin texts. xxvi. (xlvi. Heb.), prophecy against Egypt; xxvii. (l.), against Babylon; xxviii. (li.), ditto; xxix. (xlvii. 1–7 and xlix. 7–22), against the Philistines, Phœnicians and Edomites; xxx. (xlix. 1–5; 23–27; 28–33), against the Ammonites, Damascenes and Arabs; [the prophecy against Elam, xlix. 34–39, is missing] xxxi. (xlviii.), against Moab; xxxii. (xxv. 15–38), God's indignation against the wicked; xxxiii. (xxvi.); xxxiv. (xxvii.); xxxv. (xxviii.), etc., as far as li., which corresponds to xliv. and xlv. of the Hebrew. lii. is the same in both the Greek and the Hebrew. That the Greek order is preferable appears from xxv. 14, where, after the punishment coming upon Juda has been announced, it is stated that God will chastise also the heathen.

The origin of this different arrangement of the text is obscure. Kaulen thinks that a short copy of the book was made hastily in Egypt at the time when Jeremias was carried thither, or when he died. Cornely, on the contrary, thinks that the book existed from the beginning in two different forms, one of which gave rise to the Masoretic text, and the other, which was shorter, was used by the Greek translators. The latter view is taken also by Workman, "The Text of Jeremiah," Edinburgh, 1889.

27. The Book of Lamentations

1. *Name and Position.* These songs, five in number, are called in the Hebrew *Qinoth* = lamentations,[1] in Greek θρῆνοι, in the Vulgate *lamentationes*. In the Hebrew Bible they are classed with the Ketubim, but in the Septuagint and the Vulgate they follow the Book of Jeremias, as tradition names him as their composer.

Against the tradition that Jeremias was the author of the Lamentations, it is urged that their position among the Ketubim in the Hebrew canon makes it plain that they were not in ancient times ascribed to him, as otherwise they would have been put with his other book. Their position in the Septuagint cannot, it is said, have been the original one, as the language shows that they were not translated by the same person as the Book of Jeremias. These considerations, however, cannot stand against an unbroken tradition and the fact that the contents of Lamentations savor greatly of Jeremias. The Septuagint and the Vulgate express the traditional view at the beginning of the book, with the words: " And it came to pass, after Israel was carried into captivity, and Jerusalem was desolate, that Jeremias the prophet sat weeping, and mourned with this lamentation."

Its poetical character probably caused the book to be classed with Psalms and Proverbs among the Ketubim.

2. *Subject.* The singer complains that Jerusalem has fallen into the hands of cruel enemies, who have plundered and destroyed the Holy City. Many of its inhabitants have been slain, others ill treated and carried away into captivity. Misery and famine prevail in the country. These descriptions suit the period of the first destruction of Jerusalem in 588. The songs express the sorrow felt at this event.

3. *Form.* The first, second, fourth and fifth songs each contain twenty-two verses, corresponding to the number of the letters of the Hebrew alphabet. The third song has $3 \times 22 = 66$ verses. With the exception of the fifth, they are alphabetical, i. e. in the Hebrew text the first verse begins with Aleph, the second with Beth, the third with Gimel, etc. In the third song, verses 1–3 each begins with Aleph, 4–6 each with Beth,

---

[1] קִינוֹת, from קוּן or קִין, to strike, to sound the strings, to sing, especially to sing something sad. The book is also often called אֵיכָה, from the first word in it.

etc. This system occurs also in other poems in the Old Testament (e. g. Ps. cxviii. and Prov. xxxi. 10–31); it probably served as an aid to the memory, for the songs were intended to be sung.[1]

4. *Liturgical Significance.* The Church has adopted Lamentations for use in the Divine Office, and orders some portions to be sung publicly in Holy Week. In doing so, she is not intending to mourn over the destruction of the Jewish Temple and the Holy City, but rather to remind the faithful of the punishments inflicted upon disloyalty, and that our Saviour's sufferings on behalf of mankind were even greater than those of Jerusalem. The Lamentations in Holy Week, therefore, are the voice of our Mother, the Church, calling upon us to do penance and to be faithful to God.

PROPHETS WHO LIVED DURING THE CAPTIVITY

28. BARUCH [2]

(Deuterocanonical; 6 chapters)

1. *Personality.* In both the Vulgate and the Septuagint the little Book of Baruch is appended to the prophecies and lamentations of Jeremias, and the Fathers occasionally refer to it by the name of Jeremias. Baruch was his disciple and faithful companion; he followed his master to Egypt (Jer. xliii. 3, 6) and after his death he went to join the exiles in Babylon. Whilst there he used his prophetic gifts and met with more success than Jeremias had had in Palestine. The Israelites, being now made submissive by their misfortunes, gladly listened to the words of the disciple, although they had persecuted the master. In fact, Baruch's admonitions seemed to them so important that they sent the record of them, written by the prophet in the fifth year after the destruction of Jerusalem, together with a letter of

---

[1] J. K. Zenner, S.J., comes to the conclusion that the Lamentations are made up of monologues and dialogues, and form a dramatic dirge over the fall of Jerusalem. Strack says that a long section of a verse is always followed by a shorter one, and this indicates that they were to be sung.

[2] בָּרוּךְ = blessed, benedictus.

introduction to the Jews left behind in the Holy Land. The
prophet himself conveyed the book as well as some vessels taken
from the Temple.

2. *Contents and Divisions.* Chapter i. contains the above-
mentioned letter of introduction, with an historical preface.
Then follow Baruch's prophetic utterances in chapters i.–v.
Chapter vi. is an appendix, containing a letter addressed by
Jeremias to the unfortunate Jews.

i. 1–14, King Jechonias and other exiles are moved by hearing Baruch's book read aloud to send it and certain gifts to Jerusalem, with
a letter asking that sacrifices might be offered for them on the poorly
restored altar of holocausts. i. 15–iii. 8, prayer acknowledging guilt, composed by the prophet in the name of the penitent nation. "We have
deserved the punishment which even Moses foretold; may God now
fulfill also His comforting promises." iii. 9–v. 9, the prophet's admonition: "The people have fallen into misery because they despised God's
commandments. May they henceforth be faithful to God. Our troubles
are not to cause our destruction, but God will send us help." vi. 1–7,
Jeremias warns those who are going into captivity against the Babylonian idolatry, the errors and folly of which he describes.

3. *Position in the Canon.* The Book of Baruch is deuterocanonical, it is not in the Hebrew Bible. Saint Jerome took the
Latin text from the Itala, because he found no Hebrew version
of the book, but Origen was acquainted with one, as in his
Hexapla he marked the Greek text with obels and asterisks in
the same way as the protocanonical books. That the original was
in Hebrew is proved (*a*) by the unmistakably Hebrew diction,
(*b*) the admission of the book into Theodotion's translation, (*c*)
the repetition of the fourth and fifth chapters in the eleventh of
Solomon's Psalms, which, although now extant only in Greek,
were composed in Hebrew (*supra*, p. 209).

Jeremias' letter could not be added to the Book of Jeremias, because
it was no longer extant in Hebrew, and so it was joined to the work of
Baruch, his disciple. Against its authenticity it is urged that it had
a Greek tone and is in contrast with the general style of Jeremias. But
it contains some unmistakable Hebraisms, e. g. vi. 1, ἁμαρτίας ἡμαρτήκατε ;
vi. 2, ἐξάξω ὑμᾶς μετ᾽ εἰρήνης ; vi. 6, ἐκζητῶν τὰς ψυχὰς ὑμῶν, etc. The
contrast with Jeremias seems to be in vi. 3, where the captivity is said
to be destined to last seven generations, whereas Jeremias speaks of
seventy years. But the Hebrew word דור does not only mean a generation, but also a period. That Jeremias had reason enough for giving such

a warning appears, e. g., from Jer. xliv. 17. The Israelites said to the prophet that as long as they, like their fathers, served other gods, they had bread enough and were prosperous, but since they ceased to do so, they lacked everything and suffered from the sword and from famine. Another evidence of authenticity is the knowledge shown of the state and especially of the cultus of the country near the Euphrates, as Kaulen has shown (*Assyrien und Babylonien*), e. g. an idol is mentioned with sword and battle axe; Layard found a representation of such a deity.

29. EZECHIEL [1]

(48 chapters)

1. *Personality.* Ezechiel belonged to an honorable priestly family; his father's name was Busi. In 597 he was carried away to Babylon into captivity, with King Jechonias, and spent the rest of his life there. In the fourth year of his residence in Babylon, 593, he received his vocation as prophet, and for twenty or thirty years he was actively at work. His usual residence was Tel-Abib, a little town on the river Chabor, a channel of the Euphrates. His grave is still shown in the neighborhood of ancient Babylon. According to tradition, he was killed by an idolatrous Jew, whom he had rebuked for his wickedness.

2. The *Book of Ezechiel* proclaims (*a*) that God is about to inflict a fearful punishment upon His faithless people by means of the Babylonians, but (*b*) He will then restore the Covenant with them.

Four parts may be distinguished in the book.
(1) Chapters i.–iii. Call of the prophet.[2] (2) Chapters iv.–xxiv. Ezechiel, being a captive in Babylon, sees how Jerusalem is besieged and captured, and then destroyed, with the Temple which is abandoned by God. The Holy Land is a wilderness, the false prophets are exterminated, and intercession is vain, for Israel is like a withered vine. In past ages Israel was espoused to God, but fell into adultery through following after the heathen and their idols, wherefore it is now punished by means of the heathen. (3) Chapters xxv.–xxxii. The neighboring nations, Ammonites, Moabites, Edomites, Philistines, Phœnicians and Egyptians, on which Israel relied, are likewise to be plundered by the

---

[1] יְחֶזְקֵאל = mighty is God, or יְחַזְקֵאל, God strengthens. Septuagint, Ἰεζεκιήλ.

[2] In ii. 3 the word גוֹיִם has probably been interpolated by later Jews, who would not acknowledge the apostasy of Israel. It is not in the Septuagint version.

Babylonians, for such is God's will. (4) Chapters xxxiii.–xlviii. After the chastisement God Himself will replace the wicked shepherds, and watch over His flock, arousing His people from death and showing mercy towards them. The prophet beholds and describes a complete change of circumstances, a new Temple, a new form of worship, a new and far more numerous nation having God dwelling in their midst. This description is not to be taken as referring only to the period after the Captivity, but it embraces the Messianic age, to which the vision in chapter i. also seems to point.

3. *Author.* The prophet speaks of himself mostly in the first person; we may therefore assume that he recorded his prophecies himself, and bequeathed them to the Jews at the end of his life. The whole work is remarkably uniform from the first word to the last, so that criticism has scarcely found any cause to doubt or deny anything, and its authenticity has hardly ever been questioned.

Even Cornill acknowledges its authenticity; he says: "If any book of the Old Testament bears on its surface the mark of authenticity, and exists still in the form in which it passed from the author's hand, it is the book of Ezechiel. No other displays a uniformity so magnificently conceived and so clearly executed; no other reveals from the first letter to the last the same hand, the same spirit and the same well-marked individuality." Cornill has attempted to correct the Hebrew text of this book, using for the purpose the oldest translations: R. Krätzschmar thinks that the work of an editor can be detected in the book as we have it. He is supposed to have united two different texts, one longer than the other; in the longer version Ezechiel speaks in the first person; in the shorter, which seems to be an abridgment of the longer text, he is spoken of in the third person. But tradition is opposed to this theory.

4. *Style.* The style of this prophet is full of vivid descriptions and is highly picturesque; the book contains an account of several visions, yet is not very difficult to understand.

The most remarkable vision is that of God's chariot (chapter i.). When the prophet received his commission he saw God Himself in all His glory seated on a throne, which did not stand still, but was carried like a chariot to the four quarters of the heavens by four creatures of wonderful appearance. They resembled respectively a man, a lion, an ox and an eagle. On account of this vision (and of Apoc. iv.) these four symbols have been assigned to the Evangelists.

30. Daniel [1]

(14 chapters)

1. *Personality.* Daniel was in Babylon before Ezechiel, having been sent thither as a hostage in 605; he was brought up at Nabuchodonosor's court, and carefully educated, being known by the Babylonian name of Baltassar. In consequence of this training and of his own extraordinary wisdom, he won great respect and influence at the court of the pagan king, and even under the Medo-Persian government he constantly held high offices. His great authority over both Jews and Gentiles appears not only from his own work, but also from passages in Ezechiel (xiv. 14; xxviii. 3), and to the present day he is spoken of with the greatest respect in Oriental stories. He must have lived to a very advanced age, as his last prophecy (x. 1) belongs to the third year of Cyrus' reign. His grave is shown in Shuster, formerly Susa, and is held in great honor by the Mahometans.

2. *Contents.* Daniel was not a prophet exclusively for the Jews, but he addressed the Gentiles more especially, as it was his task to make known to them the power of the true God and the indestructibility of His kingdom.

Daniel's prophecies are intimately connected with his own life, and from his book we can learn most of his history.

Chapter i. Daniel comes to Babylon and is educated at the king's court. ii. Nabuchodonosor has a wonderful dream of a great statue, the head of which is of gold, the breast and arms of silver, the lower parts of the body of brass, the legs of iron, and the feet partly of iron and partly of clay. Daniel interprets the dream as referring to the various empires, that follow one on the other, but will all finally be made subject to God's dominion.[2] iii. Erection of a great idol. Three friends of Daniel refuse to worship it, and are condemned to death by fire, but are miraculously delivered. iv. Nabuchodonosor has another dream in which it appeared to him that he was to have the heart of a beast for seven years. Daniel interprets this to mean that the king would be mad for a

---

[1] דָּנִיֵּאל = God is my Judge.

[2] According to Düsterwald, the first empire was the Babylonian, the second the Medo-Persian, the third the Græco-Macedonian, the fourth the Roman, and the fifth the Messianic, that is to outlast all the empires of the world.

long time and behave like a beast. v. Feast of King (i. e. Prince) Baltas-sar,[1] and the divine sentence, *Mene, Thekel, Phares.* vi. King Darius, the Mede, who is governing Babylon on behalf of Cyrus, is well disposed to Daniel, but by his courtiers' intrigues is induced to cast him into a den of lions. Daniel is miraculously preserved. vii. Vision of four beasts of prey, representing the four empires, on the ruins of which the rule of the Messias is to be established. viii. Vision of a ram and of a he-goat that overcomes the ram. The ram represents the Persian, and the goat the Græco-Macedonian Empire. ix. Revelation concerning the seventy weeks of years, after which redemption is to come.[2] x.–xii. Visions regarding the Persian Empire, Alexander the Great and the wars following his death, and also Antiochus Epiphanes, who is a type of Antichrist. xiii. Story of Susanna. xiv. Account of the idol Bel, the Babylonian serpent worship, and Daniel's preservation in the den of lions.

It is remarkable that in the Hebrew Bible the Book of Daniel is not placed with the prophetical books, but in the last section, among the Ketubim. This arrangement, however, dates only from about 100 B. C., when the Jewish canon was finally fixed. According to the earlier arrangement of the sacred books, Daniel followed Ezechiel, and the Septuagint has preserved this order.

3. *Divisions.* The book may be divided into two parts, one (chap. i.–vi. and xiii. and xiv.) historical, and the other (vii.–xii.) prophetical. If it is divided according to the language, six chapters (i. and viii.–xii.) are in Hebrew; six (ii.–vii.) in Aramaic; two (xiii. and xiv.) and part of chapter iii. are preserved only in the Greek, and so are reckoned deuterocanonical.

The Septuagint text of Daniel is acknowledged to be very faulty, and for this reason the Church did not use it, but adopted Theodotion's version. The Septuagint text exists in two manuscripts, one Greek and one Syriac. *Cf. supra,* p. 237, note.

4. *Authenticity.* Modern Protestant critics deny Daniel's authorship, and believe that the book was written long after the Captivity. Many go so far as to declare the book an absolute forgery, on account of the detailed prophecies that it contains. As no one in the sixth century before Christ could know what Alexander the Great would do in the fourth century and Antiochus Epiphanes in the second, it is maintained that the book cannot have been in existence before the time of the Machabees. It may have been composed during the conflicts of the

[1] King Nabonaid had fled before the approach of Cyrus.
[2] See Fraidl, *Die 70 Wochen Daniels,* 1883. (The reckoning ought certainly to begin from 458, the seventh year of King Artaxerxes.)

Jews with the Syrians, with the purpose of encouraging the Jews, by showing them, from Daniel's great example, that no worldly power can withstand the dominion of God and His people.

But in answer we may say: (1) The language indicates that the book was written during the Captivity. Being partly in Hebrew and partly in Aramaic, it is well suited to a time when the older language was gradually falling out of use among the Jews, and giving place to Chaldee. These languages were equally familiar to Daniel, as a ruler, and so he left his prophecies on record in both.[1] (2) The contents, too, show that the book belongs to the time of the Captivity. The author was evidently well acquainted with the events of that period and with the customs of the Medo-Persian rulers, in a way that would have been impossible for a Jew in the second century before Christ.[2] Mathathias when dying reminded his friends particularly of things recorded in the Book of Daniel (Matt. ii. 59; cf. Dan. iii. and vi.). Our Saviour Himself (Matt. xxiv. 15) referred to the "abomination of desolation which was spoken of by Daniel the prophet" (Dan. ix. 27).

5. The deuterocanonical portions of the book belong to the same period as the protocanonical, and in all probability were written by Daniel. In style and contents they completely agree with the historical passages in the first part. Many critics regard them as imitations of the book, because (1) no Hebrew original

[1] If stress be laid on the fact that the language of chapters ii.–vii. is not the Eastern, but the Western Aramaic, that was used in Palestine, we may argue that a book intended to be frequently read would have to be adapted to the ordinary speech of the people, and that in this way the text, as originally written by Daniel, has suffered some modification. P. Riessler tries to prove that chapters ii.–vii. were also written in Hebrew in the first instance. In his commentary on Daniel (Vienna, 1902), Riessler comes to the conclusion that the book was certainly written before the downfall of the Persian Empire, and most of it by Daniel himself, although many glosses were added in the time of the Machabees. The language of the book bears traces of Babylonian influence.

[2] A great many of the statements in this book have been confirmed by recent discoveries in Babylon, e. g. the name of the plain Dura (iii. 1), and the name Baltassar (Belshazzar, v. 1). The description of Nabuchodonosor's palace is accurate, and so is the remark that Cyrus did not assume the government of Babylon in person immediately after his conquest.

of them is extant, and (2) in the Greek Bible they are not connected with the protocanonical Book of Daniel, i. e. they are not inserted after chapter i. and chapter vi. respectively, where, according to their contents, they ought to stand.

That a Hebrew text originally existed seems probable from the fact that not only the Seventy, but also Theodotion and Symmachus admitted these portions to their translations, and a study of the Greek text enables us easily to recognize that it is a translation.[1] The Book of Daniel, like that of Jeremias, certainly existed in two forms among the Jews; the Greek translators made use of the longer version, while the Jews in our era recognized only the shorter, probably through dislike of the Christians who had accepted the longer Greek text.

FOURTH SECTION

THE PERIOD FROM THE CAPTIVITY TO THE CLOSE OF THE OLD TESTAMENT REVELATION

31. HISTORICAL SURVEY

The following events belong to this period:

1. In 536, after Cyrus had conquered Babylon, the Jews returned from the Captivity and rebuilt the Temple and city of Jerusalem.

2. An orderly government and mode of life were restored in the Holy Land, in consequence of the exertions of the prophets Aggeus, Zacharias and Malachias, the priest Esdras and the Persian official Nehemias. The claims made upon the Jews by the Persians were trifling and not oppressive.

3. The rise of western influence, first from Greece (Alexander the Great), and then from Egypt and Syria (settlement of many Jews in Egypt); the Septuagint, Antiochus Epiphanes.

4. The struggle of the Machabees to maintain the Jewish religion and independence, and to secure the appointment of native rulers (175–140).

---

[1] C. Julius tries to prove that they did not originally form part of the Hebrew-Aramaic book of Daniel, but were written in Alexandria.

5. More peaceful times under native princes of the tribe of Levi, who were at the same time high priests. Simon, 140–135; John Hyrcanus, 135–106; Alexander Jannæus, 106–78; regency of Alexandra and rule of her sons Hyrcanus II and Aristobulus.

6. Roman supremacy (from 63 onwards).

The books of Holy Scripture that belong to this period are:

(*a*) *Historical writings:* Kings, Chronicles, Esdras and Nehemias, Esther, Tobias, Judith, Machabees.

(*b*) *Prophetical writings:* Aggeus, Zacharias, Malachias.

(*c*) *Didactic works:* Sirach or Ecclesiasticus, Wisdom.

HISTORICAL WRITINGS

32. The Books of Kings [1]

(According to the Vulgate, III and IV Kings)

(22 and 25 chapters)

1. The Books of Kings were originally not divided; they deal with the history of Israel and its kings from Solomon's accession to the Babylonian Captivity, i. e. with the history, in round numbers, of the years 1000–600.

Three parts may be distinguished: (*a*) Solomon's reign, I, i. to xi. (*b*) The two kingdoms, I, xii. to II, xvii. (*c*) The kingdom of Juda, II, xviii. to xxv.

Book III: i., Solomon becomes king; ii., David's death; iii., iv., Solomon's wisdom, his court; v., agreement with Hiram of Tyre; vi., the Temple is begun; vii. to ix., it is finished and dedicated, other buildings; x., Solomon' splendor, his trade, his power; xi., his wives, idolatry and punishment, his death; xii., Roboam becomes king, ten tribes revolt and establish the northern kingdom of Israel; xiii. to xvi., the successive kings of both States; xvii. to xix., the prophet Elias and his work; xx., Eliseus, war against Syria; xxi., Naboth's vineyard, his unjust murder by Achab and Jezabel, Elias' prophecy against them; xxii., Achab falls in war.

Book IV: i., wonders wrought by Eliseus; ii., the kings of the two States fight successfully against King Mesa of Moab; iii. to viii., the worship of Baal prevails in the northern kingdom, and is opposed by Eliseus; viii. to x., as idolatry is spreading also in the southern kingdom, the kings and people are chastised by means of the Syrian King Hasael, and subsequently both kings and Jezabel are killed by Jehu, who

---

[1] The beginning is abrupt; the author continues the second Book of Samuel (second of Kings).

ascends the throne of Israel; xi., xii., Joas reigns in the southern kingdom; xiii., xiv., death of Eliseus, war between the two kingdoms; xv.,
Ozias, King of Juda, has a prosperous reign of fifty-two years, but in
Israel there are frequent changes in the government, and the Assyrians
are already demanding tribute; xvi., xvii., Juda too fears the Assyrians,
who seize the northern kingdom; xviii. to xx., Juda, under the pious
King Ezechias, is miraculously saved from the Assyrians, and the king
recovers from a severe illness (*supra*, p. 316); xxi., Manasses is godless,
and Amon not much better; xxii. to xxv., Josias is faithful and energetic,
but his successors Joachaz, Joakim, Jechonias (Joachin) and Sedecias
become more and more subject to the Babylonians, who finally put an end
to the kingdom of Juda and carry away the Jews into captivity.

2. *Date and Authorship.* The last event recorded in IV
Kings, xxv. 27, is the kindness shown to Jechonias by King
Evilmerodach in the thirty-seventh year of his imprisonment,
i. e. in 560. If the author had known of the release of the
people from Captivity, he would certainly have added this as a
fitting conclusion to his work, which must have been written
during the Captivity. The author is unknown. Judging from
the style and spirit of the book, we may believe it to be the
work of a prophet. Its aim unmistakably is to impress upon the
people of God that happiness is to be found only in confidence
in God and in serving Him, that misery always follows worldli-
ness. The Talmud names Jeremias as the author, and this statement may very well be correct, as the book closely resembles the
prophet's work in spirit and in language. This would, however,
involve our assuming that he began to write it under Josias,
before the downfall of the kingdom of Juda, and carried it on
under the last kings, but that another hand, perhaps Baruch's,
wrote the conclusion.[1] In any case it is impossible that the
books of Samuel and of Kings are by the same author. The
writer of the former describes events in a more objective way,
without showing any such design as is apparent in the Book
of Kings. Moreover, in the latter reference is frequently made
to authorities,[2] and never in the former. Finally, in the Hebrew

---

[1] It is possible that Jeremias, of whose death we know nothing certain,
went to Babylon, and finished the book there at an advanced age.
Holzhey says that the author, or at least the finisher, of the work was an
exile, living between Jeremias and Ezechiel.

[2] The author refers once to the chronicles of Solomon, and frequently
to the chronicles of the kings of Israel and of Juda.

canon the Books of Kings and Samuel were always separated, so that those who collected the books regarded them as being of different authorship. It is only in the Greek and Latin Bibles that the four books were put together.

3. *Object.* The author wishes to show that God has fulfilled the promise given in II Samuel vii. 12, etc. God commissioned Nathan to tell David that his kingdom should not perish like Saul's, but should last forever. If the kings of his line fell into sin they would be punished, but David's kingdom should nevertheless endure.

33. The Books of Chronicles (Paralipomena)
(29 and 36 chapters)

1. *Name.* In Hebrew these two books are called *dibre hajja-mim* = words of the days, records of events arranged according to the time = annales. The Seventy call them Παραλειπόμενα = completions, supplements, because they supplement the books of Kings. St. Jerome followed the Itala version in calling them Chronicon, Chronicles, which name, corresponding as it does both with the Hebrew and with the contents, has passed into general use.

2. *Contents.* The Seventy divided the book, that was originally one, into two parts; the first contains twenty-nine chapters, and consists of two distinct portions. (*a*) Chapters i.–ix. contain genealogies from Adam to the Jews, who returned from Captivity.[1] (*b*) Chapters x.–xxix. contain the history of David, but his fall into sin is not mentioned. The second book consists of thirty-six chapters and contains the history of the kingdom of Juda from the time of Solomon to the Captivity. Whatever is praiseworthy in the Kings is emphasized, and the only source

[1] The genealogies are intended to supply the Israelites, and especially their teachers, the priests and Levites, with information regarding the place of Israel in the history of the world. Ever since the time of Adam one race of believers has been chosen by God from among all other nations, and from this race redemption and the Redeemer are to come. Seth, Noe, Sem, Abraham, Isaac, Jacob, Juda and David are the chief representatives of this blessed line, and they are the ancestors of the Messias. *Cf.* Matt. i. and Luke iii.

of happiness is shown to be fidelity towards God. Nothing is said of the northern kingdom and its rulers, because they have alienated themselves from the blessed line of David, and so have no share in the salvation that is to come.

Book I: i., genealogy of Jacob; ii. genealogy of Juda; iii., pedigree of David; iv., descendants of Juda and Simeon; v., of Ruben and Gad; vi., of Manasses and Levi; vii., of Issachar, Benjamin and Nephtali; viii., of Ephraim and Aser; ix., Saul's pedigree; families in Jerusalem; x., Saul's death; xi., David and his heroes; xii., David's Army; xiii., xiv., David's wars; xv., xvi., bringing of the Ark to Sion; xvii., David determines to build a temple; xviii. to xx., fresh victories; xxi., numbering of the people, and the punishment for it; xxii., preparations for building the Temple; xxiii. to xxvii., arrangement and duties of the persons concerned with the Temple worship; xxviii., xxix., last directions for the building, Solomon's accession, David's death.

Book II: i., Solomon's wisdom; ii. to iv., building of the Temple; v. to vii., the Ark is brought into it; Solomon's prayer; viii., other buildings; ix., the Queen of Saba, Solomon's wealth and magnificence; x. to xii., Roboam, division of the kingdom; xiii., Abia; xiv. to xvi., Asa; xvii. to xx., Josaphat; xxi., Joram; xxii., Ozochias; xxiii., xxiv., Joas prospers as long as he serves God, but falls into idolatry and misery; xxv., Amasias has a similar fate and xxvi., Ozias; xxvii., Joatham is happier because he fears God; xxviii., Achaz is godless, and therefore unhappy; xxix. to xxxii., Ezechias is a good king; xxxiii., Manasses and Amon; xxxiv., xxxv., Josias is faithful; xxxvi., downfall of Juda.

3. *Author*. According to tradition these books were written by Esdras, although this is disputed by many critics, who believe them compiled in the fourth or third century before Christ. The language and style, however, really resemble those of the Book of Esdras, which forms an immediate sequel to it. In any case it was not written until after the Captivity. This is shown by the exalted religious consciousness and by the absence of all mention of the history of Samaria, for the northern kingdom was then occupied not by Israelites, but by hostile Samaritans, who were to have no interest in the work. Another mark of its late composition is the mention in I, xxix. 7 of darics as current coins; they would become so only under the Persian supremacy. The mention of them precludes the possibility of its belonging to the period of Greek influence, because the Macedonians introduced talents and drachmas.

4. *Object*. Esdras had one chief and one secondary object in

writing. The former was to compile a history of the Israelite nation and its kings viewed in their best and laudable aspect, so that the religious and national feelings of the people might be roused, and that they might be convinced of their being the most important nation in the world, because of God's revelations to them.[1] His secondary object was to supplement the Books of Kings. Closely connected with Chronicles are the following:

34. THE BOOKS OF ESDRAS AND NEHEMIAS

(10 and 13 chapters)

In the Vulgate the former is called the First and the latter the Second Book of Esdras. The similarity in their contents enables us to discuss them together, and they have always been regarded as closely connected, both by the Jews and the Church.

1. *Contents.* These books contain an account of the restoration of civil and religious order in the Holy Land after the return of the Jews from Captivity. Esdras and Nehemias were especially active in promoting this restoration.

Contents of the Book of Esdras. Chapters i.–vi. Return of the Jews from Captivity in Babylon (536 B. C.) ; rebuilding and dedication of the Temple (515). Chapters vii.–x. Return of another large body of Israelites under the priest Esra or Esdras, who was zealous in restoring orderly government and protested against the evil practice of marrying heathen women.

Contents of the Book of Nehemias. Chapters i.–vii. Account of the rebuilding of the walls of Jerusalem, and of settling a fixed government among the Jews who had returned. This was particularly the work of Nehemias, an official at the Persian court. Chapters viii.–x. Esdras reads the Law of Moses to the people, and makes them solemnly renew their covenant with God. Chapters xi.–xiii. Supplement added by Nehemias

---

[1] The obvious existence of this object has led critics to question the historical accuracy of this book. Bleek-Wellhausen, Vatke and Stade consider that the author falsified history, and left out or altered whatever did not harmonize with his own views regarding the Temple worship, as being the only one sanctioned by God. Stade even thinks the whole book more or less untrustworthy, but the reasons stated as grounds for this serious charge are insignificant. That the author has omitted a good deal that is found in the Books of Kings is to be explained as in keeping with his object, but he cannot on that account be charged with falsification of history.

regarding his own special work in the Holy Land. All the information given in the books is fragmentary in form.

Many critics have questioned the trustworthiness of the various letters and lists in the books, and especially of the correspondence with the Persian court. In *Entstehung des Judentums* (Halle, 1896), Eduard Meyer, an historian by no means inclined to Yahwism, furnishes proof that the documents are undoubtedly genuine, a fact that surprised no one more than the author himself.

2. *Date of Esdras and Nehemias.* The two men were contemporaries and supplemented each other's work. Esdras devoted his attention more to religious matters; Nehemias to external and political arrangements. The reign of Artaxerxes I Longimanus, King of Persia, is generally said to coincide with the period of their activity (465–425), and this is probably correct.[1] It is objected that the King Artaxerxes to whom Nehemias was cupbearer, could not have been Artaxerxes I, because the Samaritan governor Sanaballat, mentioned in Nehemias ii. 19 and xiii. 28, was still alive, according to Josephus Flavius (*Ant.*, XI, vii. 2), when Alexander the Great appeared upon the scene. As Nehemias (xiii. 6) alludes to the thirty-second year of Artaxerxes' reign, this cannot have been Artaxerxes III Ochus (362–339), and so it must have been Artaxerxes II Mnemon (405–362); and in this way Nehemias and Esdras were not at work until after 400; the activity of Esdras may be dated as beginning in 398, and that of Nehemias in 384 (Kaulen, *Einl.*, II, 73). Josephus Flavius is, however, not a trustworthy authority regarding the history of Esdras and Nehemias, and very probably he has made a mistake here.[2]

3. *Authorship.* The books are not the work of one man, but consist of a collection of official documents and private records.

---

[1] So Welte, *Kirchenlexikon*, Art. Esra (1st ed.), also Loch and Reischl, ii., p. 2; Reusch, *Einleitung*, 125; Cornely, *Introd. Comp.*, 266; Father A. Hammerschmid in the *Passauer Monatschrift*, 1894; Hoonacker, *Nehemie et Esdras:* id. *Zorobabel et le second temple;* id. *Nouvelles études sur la restauration*, etc., Paris et Louvain, 1890, 92, 96; Guthe, *Bibellex.* Esdras began work in 458, Nehemias in 445, and continued until 433 or 432.

[2] In matters of chronology not much confidence can be placed in Josephus, as appears from his confusing King John Hyrcanus (135–106) with his grandson, Hyrcanus II (63–40), as he does in his "History of the Jewish People."

Of the latter, those in Esdras vii.–x. were written by Esdras, and those in Nehemias i.–vii. and xi.–xiii. by Nehemias; the others are of unknown authorship. It is very likely that Esdras made the whole collection, as Jewish tradition has always affirmed; though a later hand may have given the books their present form.

This is inferred from Neh. xii. 22, where " Darius the Persian " may be understood to be Darius Codomanus; the addition of the word " Persian " implies that other, viz., Greek kings, were already recognized. In the same passage there is mention of a high priest named Jeddoa, who, according to Josephus, met Alexander the Great (*Ant.*, XI, viii. 4). But too much stress must not be laid on these speculations. Darius the Persian may be Darius Nothus, who ascended the throne in 425, and was therefore contemporaneous with Esdras and Nehemias. Cyrus and Artaxerxes are repeatedly called " Kings of the Persians," and the Jews spoke of them thus to distinguish them from their own former kings. The high priest, who went to meet Alexander, was not necessarily Jeddoa; Josephus seems to have made a mistake in his chronology here as elsewhere. It is quite likely that the whole work, as we have it, was written by Esdras.[1]

35. THE BOOK OF ESTHER

(16 chapters: i.–x. 3, protocanonical; x. 4–xvi. 24, deuterocanonical)

1. *Contents.* This book relates how a pious Jewish maiden, named Esther,[2] became the wife of the Persian King Assuerus (Achaschwerosch), and how she frustrated a plan formed by Aman, a proud official at court, to have all the Jews in the Persian empire massacred. In memory of this event the feast of Purim[3] was instituted, and it is still kept by the Jews at the end of February or the beginning of March. The king, whose

[1] In most editions of the Vulgate there are two other books, called the third and fourth of Esdras, which at one time were regarded as sacred, but now belong to the apocrypha, not having been declared canonical by the Council of Trent (*supra*, p. 208). The third Book, called in the Septuagint the first, contains nine chapters supplementary to our first Esdras; the fourth, also known as the Apocalypse of Esdras, contains prophecies and visions of Esdras, in sixteen chapters.

[2] The Hebrew name was Hadassa (Myrtle), Lat. Edissa; the Persian Esther = ἀστήρ, star.

[3] *Pur*, a Persian word (Assyr., *puru*) = lot, pl. *Purim* = lots. Aman had chosen the day for the massacre by lot; it was to be the thirteenth Adar.

wife Esther became, and who is called in the Hebrew text
Achaschwerosch, is probably Xerxes I (485–465), known to us
from the wars between Greeks and Persians.[1] The Greek text
calls him Artaxerxes; in the Vulgate, from chapter i.–x., he
is Assuerus; from xi.–xvi., Artaxerxes (Luther wrote the name
Ahasverus). Most ancient commentators identified this king
with Artaxerxes Longimanus (465–425).

Contents according to the Vulgate: i., Feast of Assuerus; rejection of
Queen Vashti. ii., Esther becomes queen, but at the bidding of her uncle
Mardochai is silent as to her origin. Conspiracy of two courtiers is discovered by Mardochai. iii., Aman, a foreigner, is exalted above all the
king's servants, and all, with the sole exception of Mardochai, kneel down
at his approach. Aman procures from the king orders for the massacre
of all the Jews in the empire. iv., v., Mardochai and Esther are horrified. Esther goes to the king, but at first only asks that he and Aman
will come to a feast at her house. The request is granted, and the feast
is to be held on the following day. Aman prepares the gallows for
Mardochai. vi., the king wishes to reward Mardochai for saving his
life, so he orders Aman to lead the hated Jew, dressed in gorgeous rai-
ment, about the city, and to proclaim him everywhere to be the king's
favorite. vii., Aman is overthrown and hanged on the gallows that he
has prepared. viii., ix., the Jews receive permission to use arms in
self-defense. Institution of the Feast of Purim. Mardochai becomes
chief official at court and records all these events. x., xi., Mardochai's
dream and its interpretation. xii., the king's decree against the Jews.
xiii., Mardochai's prayer. xiv., Esther's prayer. xv., account of
Esther's appearance before the king. xvi., the king's decree in favor of
the Jews.

2. *Canonicity.* In the Hebrew text the book has ten chapters;
in the Latin sixteen. The Septuagint also has ten chapters, like
the Hebrew, but they are very much longer. Saint Jerome, from
whom our Latin text has come down to us, supplied from the
Septuagint those passages which do not occur in the Hebrew
text. There are many Hebraisms in these deuterocanonical portions, and this fact, as well as the existence of another Greek
text, independent of the Septuagint,[1] but of the same length,
proves that the present Hebrew text is only an extract from an

---

[1] In the cuneiform inscriptions at Persepolis, the name of Xerxes appears as " Chsajarsa, son of King Darius." In this form it bears some
resemblance to Achaschwerosch. See Kaulen, *Ninive und Babyl.*, p. 112.
Xerxes I was the only king of that name who ruled more than seven
years; in ii. 16 the seventh year of the king's reign is mentioned.

[2] See Fritzsche, *Libri apocr. Vet. Test. græce*, Lips., 1871.

older Hebrew work, which the Seventy translated *in extenso*, and thus have preserved.

The present Hebrew text bears no mark of religion; the name of God does not occur once in it. It was probably mutilated, because gradually the Feast of Purim came to be regarded by the Jews as a kind of Saturnalia or Carnival. Hence the Greek and Latin text is preferable.

3. *Author.* We might be inclined to regard Esther's uncle and guardian, Mardochai, as the author, for, according to ix. 20,[1] he recorded at least the chief points of the history. But in ix. 23, 26 the author of the whole book seems to be clearly distinguished from Mardochai;[2] he must have been a Jew, living somewhat later, who used Mardochai's writings and the Persian annals as his sources of information. Possibly Esdras or Nehemias may have been the author. The book was read aloud at the Feast of Purim.

4. *The Date of Composition* certainly coincides with the existence of the Persian Empire. The book was written whilst the events recorded in it were still fresh in the author's memory, and it reveals a very detailed knowledge of the Persian court and of the habits of the people, and speaks with great respect of the ruling family in Persia.

5. The *Object* of the book is to express thanks for the providential preservation of God's people.

36. THE BOOK OF TOBIAS [3]

(Deuterocanonical, 14 chapters)

1. *Contents.* As a reward for his deeds of mercy Tobias is delivered from great misery. This at once indicates the object of the book, which is intended to inculcate the duty of charity

[1] "Mardochai wrote all these things, and sent them comprised in letters to the Jews that abode in all the king's provinces."

[2] "The Jews undertook to observe with solemnity all they had begun to do at that time, which Mardochai by letters had commanded to be done. . . . And since that time these days are called Phurim, that is, of Lots."

[3] In the Vulgate, father and son are both called Tobias = Tobjâ = "Good is the Lord." In the Greek, the father is Tobit and the son Tobias. In the Chaldee, the father is Tobi, and the son Tobjâ.

towards one's neighbors, and especially towards those of the same faith (*cf.* Gal. vi. 10).

Chapter i.–iv., Tobias, a pious Israelite of the tribe of Nephtali, was taken into captivity by the Assyrians and carried to Ninive, with many of his countrymen from the northern kingdom. He won respect and became wealthy, so that he was often able to help men of his own nation, and he provided for the burial of many Israelites when they died. Later he fell into poverty and became blind, and in his sorrow prayed for death. The same prayer was offered at the same time in Ecbatana by a young woman named Sara, who was suspected of being a murderess. Both prayers are answered in a most unexpected way, for an angel is sent to their help. v.–vii., Tobias, the son, undertakes a journey to ask for the payment of money owing to them; he is accompanied on the way by the angel Raphael in human form, and by means of the angel's help, the fortunes of the family are restored. viii., ix., young Tobias not only recovers the loan, but obtains Sara, a rich and God-fearing woman, as his wife. x.–xiv., the elder Tobias recovers his eyesight; the angel reveals his rank and vanishes.

2. *Text.* The book has not come down to us in the original, but only in translations, which to some extent differ from one another. It was written at first in Chaldee or Hebrew. Saint Jerome had a Chaldee text and made his translation from it in the space of one day, as he tells us in the preface. This haste did not detract from the value of his work, for he read the Chaldee with a Rabbi, and then dictated the translation to a skillful scribe. The Jews and Protestants do not admit this book to the canon, because the original text is not extant, but all the five texts that we have (viz. three Greek versions besides the Itala and the Vulgate) show distinctly an Oriental and even a Semitic character. Recently a Chaldee text has been discovered, but scholars do not regard it as the original, and believe it is a translation from the Hebrew. A Hebrew text was actually published in 1897.[1]

Of the Greek texts, the one used in the Greek Church holds the first rank. The *Codex Sinaiticus* contains another, on which the Itala version,

---

[1] Numerous Hebraisms can easily be detected, e. g. chap. iii. 1 and 9, *dicens* (לאמר); iii. 15, *desuper terram* (מן על הארץ); iii. 24, 25, *in conspectu* (לפני); vi. 15, *deponam senectutem illorum cum tristitia ad inferos* (והורדתם את-שיבתי ביגון שאולה), as in Gen. xlii. 38. *Cf.* also xii. 8, 15, etc. The Chaldee text was published in 1878 by Neubauer, the Hebrew in 1897 by Gaster.

that is quite complete, is based. A third Greek text was the foundation for the Syriac text in the Peshitto.

3. *Date of Composition.* The book was probably written in captivity, either in Assyria or in Babylonia, to console the exiled Israelites.

4. *The Author* is unknown. According to the Greek texts (Sept., xii. 20) both father and son wrote down their story. Some later author made use of these accounts and added information gathered from the lips of the people.

Vetter thinks that the book was written between 250 and 150 B. C., and was composed in Hebrew during the Assyrian-Babylonian dispersion. The material is a family history, preserved on the lips of the people, and made use of by the author for a didactic purpose.

A manuscript (ninth century) from Freising, and now in Munich, contains a Latin text of Tobias, Judith and Esther. It is an Itala text, and varies considerably from the Vulgate.

37. THE BOOK OF JUDITH

(Deuterocanonical, 16 chapters)

1. *Contents.* In the time of Eliachim, the high priest, divisions of the Assyrian army penetrated into the north of the Holy Land and besieged the little mountain stronghold of Bethulia.[1]

Chaper i., supremacy of Nabuchodonosor. ii., campaign of Holofernes, iii., iv., preparations of the Jews for resistance. v., Achior, the Ammonite, reports to Holofernes that the Jews are invincible whenever they are faithful to their God; they are so at this time, and therefore he has no prospect of success. vi., Achior is given over to the Jews that he may perish with them. vii., Holofernes besieges Bethulia. viii., the inhabitants are disposed to surrender. Judith encourages the leaders. ix., Judith's prayer. x. to xii., her visit to Holofernes, who receives her kindly. xiii., after a feast she cuts off his head and carries it to Bethulia. xiv., xv., horror of the Assyrians, their defeat. xvi., Judith's song of praise.

2. *Text.* This book also is not in the Jewish canon, because the original text has perished. It can scarcely be determined

---

[1] Now Beit Ilva. The inhabitants, constrained by want of water, were on the point of surrendering the town, when a pious widow, named Judith, killed the heathen general, Holofernes, by a stratagem, and so delivered her native place.

whether it was in Hebrew or Chaldee. That in the fourth century a Chaldee text still existed is proved by the fact that Saint Jerome made his translation from one.[1] Besides the Vulgate text we have the Septuagint Greek version, which is plainly a translation and not the original, as it is quite at variance with the genius of the Greek language. From it the texts of the Itala and Peshitto have been derived.

3. *The Author* is unknown. He must have written the book either just before or during the Babylonian Captivity. This is indicated both by the use of the Chaldee language and by references in the text (xiv. 6; xvi. 30) to the time that elapsed between the occurrence and the recording of the events.

4. *Difficulties.* The chief arguments against the historical character of the book are derived from the fact that we do not hear elsewhere of any high priest named Eliachim, nor of any Assyrian king named Nabuchodonosor. However, in IV Kings xviii. 18 and Is. xxii. 20, xxxvi. 3, etc., we read of an Eliachim who was son of the high priest Helcias in the reign of King Ezechias, and he no doubt in time succeeded his father. If it is thought surprising that the high priest, rather than the king, should take measures for the defense of the country, it should be remembered that, according to II Chronicles xxxiii. 11, King Manasses, son of Ezechias, was taken prisoner by the Assyrians and kept in captivity for some time. We may therefore assign the events in the story of Judith to his reign. The name Nabuchodonosor was more familiar to the Jewish scribes who copied the sacred books, than the names of the Assyrian kings, and it might easily happen that an uneducated Jew fancied that he ought to substitute the better known name for Assurbanipal. The same remark applies to the name of Arphaxad,

---

[1] See his preface to the book of Judith: "Among the Hebrews the book of Judith is classed with the apocrypha, and its authority is considered less in settling disputed points. It was written in the Chaldee language and is reckoned among the historical books. Because it is asserted that the Council of Nicæa placed this book among the Holy Scriptures, I have yielded to your demand or rather compulsion, and, laying aside some work on which I was deeply engaged, I have produced a little explanation (translation) rendering it more according to the sense than to the letter."

king of the Medes (i. 1; i. 5); we probably ought to read Arbaces.

5. *Authority.* Apart from the testimony of the Church, the truth of the whole story is vouched for by the existence of several Midrashim, i. e. Jewish commentaries upon the book, and also by the institution of a festival, resembling the feast of Purim, in honor of the victory. The festival is mentioned in the Vulgate xvi. 31, but in the Greek text the last verse in omitted, probably because at the time of the Seventy the celebration of it had fallen into disuse.[1]

6. *Object.* The author wished to prove that God's people were safe under His protection as long as they were faithful to Him (v. 25).

38. The Books of Machabees [2]

(Deuterocanonical, 16 and 15 chapters)

1. *Contents of the First Book.* It records the history of the wars waged by the Jews against the kings of Syria (175–140). Under the Seleucidæ the Jews had been much oppressed, and Antiochus IV Epiphanes (175–163) had shown himself particularly cruel. He wished to establish his supremacy by securing religious uniformity, and ordered the Jews to take part in the Græco-Syrian worship; but they steadfastly refused to do this. A terrible persecution followed, and God had chosen Mathathias the priest and his sons to be the instruments of saving His people. They laid ambuscades and attacked the Syrians first in one place, then in another, winning more and more adherents among the people, until finally they recovered the Temple that the Syrians had desecrated. The greatest glory of this achievement fell to Mathathias' son Judas, who was surnamed *maggaba* = hammer; he carried on the work that his father had begun,

---

[1] Bellarmine, *De Controversiis Fidei,* defends the book. Like Kaulen and Cornely, he places the story of Judith in the time of Manasses. Scholz regards the book as allegorical (see *infra,* p. 455), and N. Peters agrees with him.

[2] The Vulgate spelling of the name is Machabæus, probably with reference to the Talmud form מכבי. The Septuagint has Μακκαβαῖος.

and brought the whole country under his sway. From him the name Machabæus passed to the whole family of Mathathias. When Judas was killed in battle in 161 B. C., his equally heroic brother Jonathan took his place as leader, and he again was followed by Simon, who restored peace to the land. The Jews in their gratitude bestowed upon him (140 B. C.) the crown, to be hereditary in his family. He was succeeded by his son John Hyrcanus (135–106).

Chap. i., ii., cause of the wars; iii.–ix., acts of Judas (166–161); ix.–xii., acts of Jonathan (161–143); xiii.–xvi., acts of Simon (143–135).

2. *The Author* was a Jew, for the book was written originally in Hebrew, as Saint Jerome testifies.[1] As towards the end (chap. xvi.) King John Hyrcanus is mentioned in terms of the highest praise, many people have supposed him to be the author. But no writer is in the habit of extolling himself, and it is better to assume that whoever wrote the book knew John Hyrcanus, and composed it during his reign. The author was very likely a priest.

3. *Text.* The Hebrew original text has perished, and we know the book only through the Septuagint translation; it was the source of the Vulgate version, for the Itala was translated from the Septuagint, and Saint Jerome accepted it without alteration.

4. *Contents of the Second Book.* This book has no right to the name "Machabees," and is not a continuation of the first.

It contains (chapters i. and ii.) two letters sent by the Jews in Palestine to their fellow countrymen in Egypt, inviting them to join in keeping the feast of the Dedication of the Temple. Then follows a preface and then some additions to the first book, viz. (chapter iii.) an account of Heliodorus, who robbed the Temple, (chapter iv.) some wicked high priests, (chapter v.) the cruelty of Antiochus and (chapter vi.) of his companions, displayed especially in the case of the aged scribe Eleazar and (chapter vii.) of a Jewish mother with seven sons. Then

---

[1] *Prologus galeatus: Machabæorum primum librum hebraicum reperi. Secundus græcus est, quod ex ipsa quoque phrasi probari potest.* The language of the two books differs greatly; the first contains a number of unmistakable Hebraisms, while the second is absolutely Greek in character.

follow accounts of (chapter viii.) the victories of Judas, (chapter ix.) the death of Antiochus, (chapter x.) the purification of the Temple, and finally (chapters xi.–xv.) further successes of the Jews against the Syrians and other neighboring nations.

5. *The Author* is unknown. He is generally believed to have been a Jew, living either in Egypt or in Palestine.

In the preface or prologue (ii. 24), the author states that a certain Jason of Cyrene, who is otherwise unknown, but was certainly a Jew (Jason, Greek = Josue), wrote in five books a history of God's people during the Syrian persecution, and he himself aimed at making a careful abridgement of it. As in the case of the First Book of Machabees, the history begins with the year 175, but it ends with 161. Like the work from which it is abridged, this Second Book of Machabees was composed in Greek, as Saint Jerome rightly perceived. Greek was spoken at that time at Cyrene in North Africa, where Jason lived, and the compiler of our book seems also to have lived in Africa, and probably in Egypt, as the two letters at the beginning indicate. He knew the Holy Land very well, however (see iii. 15 and vi. 2), and consequently many people believed that he wrote his book there. This theory finds support from his using the Syrian method of dating events (i. 7 and 10), which could hardly have been familiar in Africa.

6. *Date of Composition.* The work cannot have been written much before 100 B. C., as in i. 10 the year 188 of the era of the Seleucidæ is mentioned. This era began in 312 B. C., so 188 in it would correspond with 124 B. C.

PROPHETIC WRITINGS

39. AGGEUS [1]

(2 chapters)

This prophet is known to us only by name; he came into prominence at the time of Zorobabel, in the second year of the reign of Darius Hystaspis (520). His task was to encourage the Israelites to continue the building of the Temple, that had been interrupted for many years, and he succeeded in his undertaking. Only four short speeches of his have come down to us; they are closely connected and contain the essence of his exhortations. Their authenticity is not questioned.

---

[1] חַגַּי = festivals, festive. Saint Jerome: *Festivus.*

Aggeus addressed his words to Zorobabel, who then governed the country, and to Josue, the high priest. (i.) He reproaches the Israelites with building their own houses and leaving the house of God neglected. They seem to have feared that the poor imitation of Solomon's Temple, which was all that the impoverished Jews could build, would not please God, and that He would not be willing to dwell in it. For this reason the prophet assures them (ii.) that this Temple will surpass the other in splendor, for a great change will take place among all nations, so that all eyes will turn with reverence towards Jerusalem, whence peace shall proceed. (iii.) A third speech declares that God can take no pleasure in His people, as long as they display no zeal for the Law and for building the Temple. (iv.) The fourth speech is addressed particularly to Zorobabel, and contains the promise that the house of David, to which he belongs, may look for God's protection, although all other royal races shall perish.

40. ZACHARIAS [1]

(14 chapters)

1. *Personality.* Zacharias was the son of Barachias and the grandson of Addo, one of the most respected priests, who had returned with Zorobabel from captivity. He came forward about the same time as Aggeus, in 520, but as he is spoken of as *na'ar* (youth) in ii. 4, he seems to have acted as a prophet while still very young.

2. *Contents.* Like the Book of Isaias, which it to some extent resembles, the Book of Zacharias falls into two parts: in one the prophet speaks of the present and the immediate future of God's kingdom in the Holy Land, in the other of the more distant future of God's reign in the Church. The first part consists of chapters i.–vi., the second of ix.–xiv., and vii. and viii. serve to connect the two.

In the first part there are several visions regarding God's watchful care for Israel, now restored to be a nation, and at the close there is a symbolical act. Chapter i. Introductory: Before the Captivity God often gave warnings to his people by means of the prophets, but they would not hear, so punishment came upon them. Now mercy shall again be shown them. i. 7–17, mankind is awestruck, and great changes are made in the national life through God's intervention. i. 18–ii. 4. All enemies who have risen up against Israel are destroyed. ii. 5–17. In God's kingdom there must be room for Jews and Gentiles. iii. 1–10. The high priest Josue is mediator between God and the people, and a type of the Messias. iv. Zorobabel will restore the Temple. v. When the

---

[1] זְכַרְיָה = remembrance of the Lord.

Temple worship is revived, the people will again become pleasing to God. vi. 1–8. God has power to turn aside, chastise and destroy the enemies of His kingdom. vi. 9–15. Symbolical act: The prophet has to crown Josue, the high priest, as a type of the Messias.

In chapter vii. the question is raised whether fasting pleases God. That it does so, is not denied, but at the same time we are told that right dispositions, and especially charity towards one's neighbor, are more important than merely exterior forms of religion. viii. "If this rule is observed, the nations of the Gentiles will have recourse to you."

The next six chapters contain two speeches, ix.–xi. and xii.–xiv. The first is addressed to the powers of the Gentiles, the second to Israel itself. First speech, ix. All the enemies of God's kingdom must be humbled and made to serve it, but its ruler shall be gentle, and shall enter Jerusalem on a she-ass. x. The people of Israel, though long subject to the powers of the world, will in the end be gathered together by God from all parts, and will receive mercy. xi. Unhappily Israel rebels against its Lord and Shepherd, and values him at no more than 30 pieces of silver. Second speech, xii. Jerusalem will be for all nations the center of the world's history. xiii. The Jewish nation will despise the salvation and the Saviour offered them by God, and the majority of them must therefore perish, — only a small remnant will find mercy, and become God's people. xiv. The new institution, intended to give salvation, will meet with much opposition, but will be a source of happiness for all nations.

The second part is obscure, and its language differs somewhat from that of the first. This fact, and also the allusion to idolatry and false prophets, of whom we hear nothing after the Captivity,[1] have led many to think that Zacharias did not write these chapters, but that they belong either to a much earlier or to a later period. Jewish and Christian tradition are opposed to such a theory. The collection of the Minor Prophets was made not long after the time of Zacharias (Ecclus. xlix. 12) and they were translated into Greek; if these chapters were added to the first part without comment, it must have been because no uncertainty was felt as to their origin.

41. MALACHIAS [2]

(4 chapters, in Hebrew 3)

1. *Contents.* (1) Reproof addressed to the priests for their negligence and rapacity in the sacrifical worship. The prophet

---

[1] The words refer only to Israel's former transgressions.

[2] Heb. מַלְאָכִי, i. e. probably מַלְאָכִיָה, the ambassador of the Lord.

takes occasion to proclaim the new and more perfect sacrifice on behalf of the whole world. (2) Reproof addressed to the people for their evil practices with regard to marriage. (3) Announcement of the Messias and His Forerunner.

i. God speaks through Malachias: Jacob and Esau were brothers, and had therefore equal claims upon God's providence. Jacob and his descendants were always favored, but they showed no gratitude or love in return. The priests in particular display very little respect for God when they sacrifice lame, blind and diseased animals. Such gifts would be rejected by the Persian governor (*pecha*). Moreover, there is carelessness about the sacrificial worship. The offerings of the Jews do not please God, who chooses instead a pure sacrifice, that shall be offered in all parts of the world. ii. In the past, people, priests and Levites were far more zealous in observing the covenant with God. Israel is now rejected for its indifference. Marriage is not what it should be, and God is displeased with the mixed marriages and frequency of divorce. (This points to the new marriage law to be given by the Messias.) iii. The forerunner of the Messias will soon appear, and be followed by the Ruler Himself, the angel of the Covenant, whom all await. Almost the whole Jewish nation will show itself incapable of understanding and accepting the salvation that is to come through the Messias.

2. *Personality.* We know nothing of the prophet who wrote this little book. In chapter iii. 1 mention is made of a "messenger" of the Lord (*mal'ak*) who is to precede the Messias, and the Messias Himself is called the "messenger of the covenant"; and hence we may infer that the prophet who uttered these words was not known by name, and that his prophecy was described as that "of the messenger," from its contents. Some think that Esdras was the author. The Seventy believed the name to be fictitious, and so wrote as a heading in their translation: Λῆμμα λόγου κυρίου ἐπὶ τὸν Ἰσραὴλ ἐν χειρὶ ἀγγέλου αὐτοῦ. The Vulgate, however, reads: *Onus verbi Domini ad Israel in manu Malachiæ.* Most people agree with the Vulgate and assume that there really was a prophet named Malachias, who was the author of this little book.

3. *Date.* Malachias is the last of the prophets; hence the position of the book in the canon. The Temple seems to have been built when he wrote, but as he rebukes the same evils as are mentioned in the books of Esdras, viz. carelessness in the sacrificial worship, and abuses connected with marriage, he may be regarded as contemporaneous with Esdras and Nehemias.

We may agree with Cornill in thinking that his activity began rather earlier than the time of Esdras and Nehemias, as afterwards there was some improvement on the points that he censures.

DIDACTIC WRITINGS

42. Sirach, or Ecclesiasticus

(Deuterocanonical, 51 chapters)

1. This sacred book is called Sirach, after its author, and Ecclesiasticus (*liber*), probably because it was believed to be modeled on Ecclesiastes. Others have thought that its name, "Book of the Church," was derived from its frequent use in the worship of the church. The Seventy call it "The Wisdom of Jesus, son of Sirach," or "Wisdom of Sirach." The Peshitto title is "Wisdom of Sirach's son."

2. *Contents.* The book is a collection of proverbs, admonitions and instructions, resembling the Proverbs of Solomon. The contents are strung together without any definite arrangement. It may be divided into a preface [1] and the following four parts: (*a*) Instruction on wisdom in general (chap. i.); (*b*) collection of proverbs, constituting the chief part of the book (ii.–xliii.); (*c*) survey of the history of the people of revelation and praise of the great men belonging to that nation xliv.–l.); (*d*) the author's thanksgiving for God's protection and for the gift of wisdom (li.). Parts (*b*) and (*c*) are connected by considerations of God's greatness revealed in nature (xlii. 15–xliii. 37).

(*a*) i., origin and fruits of wisdom; its connection with the fear of God.

(*b*) ii. 1–iv. 11, the spirit of humility and beneficence are essential conditions to wisdom. iv. 12–v. 18, wisdom is the highest good in life. vi. 1–ix. 25, instructions for intercourse with other people. x. 1–xi. 36, behavior in wealth and poverty, in prosperity and affliction. xii. 1–xiii. 32, prudence in acts of charity and in dealing with the powerful. xiv. 1–xvii. 31, do good in the fear of God, and all will be rewarded. xviii. 1–xxiii. 38, warnings against various sins. xxiv. 1–47, God's wisdom is a model for man's. xxv. 1–xxvi. 28, instructions on every-day life and family matters. xxvii. 1–xxxi. 42, instructions regarding anger, revenge,

---

[1] The preface was not written by the author, but by his grandson, who translated the book into Greek.

education and temperance. xxxii. 1–xxxv. 26, instructions for those in authority. xxxvi. 1–19, may God have mercy on His people. xxxvi. 20–xlii. 14, behavior towards counselors; in sickness, in death; the wise man ever seeks to learn, thus he obtains much happiness even amidst the changing circumstances of life. xlii. 15–xliii. 37, all creation bears witness to God's power and glory.

(c) xliv., praise of Henoch, Noe, Abraham, Isaac and Jacob. xlv., of Moses, Aaron and Phinees. xlvi., of Josue and Caleb; of Samuel. xlvii., of Nathan, David and Solomon. xlviii., of Elias, Eliseus, Ezechias and Isaias. xlix., of Josias, Jeremias, Ezechiel, Zorobabel and Nehemias. l., of the high priest Simon.

(d) li., thanksgiving of Jesus Sirach.

Holy Scripture itself, i. e. the earlier books in it, is the chief source of these instructions. It is suggested in the preface that the author, after reading and piously meditating upon the sacred books, had himself derived the benefit of being filled with the Holy Spirit. Deep study of Scripture led up to inspiration — a hint for all who have to make known the word of God.

The author seems to have read and studied especially the book of Solomon's Proverbs, for which reason this book also used to be ascribed to Solomon. This is true in as far as Solomon's wisdom is one of its chief sources. In the liturgy it is referred to as " Liber sapientiæ."

3. *Language.* The book was written originally in Hebrew, but for a long time the Septuagint had to replace the original, and the work was known only in translations. That the Greek is not the original appears from the many Hebraisms that it contains, and from the frequent parallelism in the parts of the verses. Saint Jerome says (*Præf. in libros Sal.*) that he had seen the Hebrew text.[1] The fact that a portion of these proverbs has been preserved in the Talmud is clear proof of their having been written in Hebrew;[2] but the Hebrew text was lost, perhaps because people believed it to have been tampered with, and it is only recently that a considerable part of it (xxxix. 15–xlix. 11, and some other fragments) has been recovered, so that now

[1] *Fertur et Panaretos* [πανάρετος = virtuous] *Jesu filii Sirach liber et alius pseudepigraphus, qui Sapientia Salomonis inscribitur. Quorum priorem hebraicum reperi; non " Ecclesiasticum," ut apud Latinos, sed " Parabolas " prænotatum.*

[2] The proverbs in the Talmud have been collected and edited by Delitzsch: *Zur Geschichte der jüdischen Poesie*, Leipzig, 1836.

we have the Book of Sirach in Hebrew, with the exception of about fifteen chapters and some shorter passages.[1] The Latin texts of the Itala and the Vulgate are based not upon the Hebrew, but upon the Greek, as appears from the retention of many Greek words, such as *agonizari, thesaurizare, eucharis, acharis,* etc. Saint Jerome did not make a Latin translation of this work, probably because the text of the Septuagint and the Itala pleased him better than the Hebrew. The Septuagint text has suffered in course of time; the Itala was translated from an earlier and more correct version.

4. *Author.* The book was composed in Hebrew about the year 190 by Jesus, son of Sirach, a native of Jerusalem. His grandson and namesake made a very free translation of it into Greek about the year 130, in Egypt.

The date may be ascertained in the following way: The author's grandson says in his preface that in the thirty-eighth year, in the reign of Ptolemy Euergetes, he came to Egypt, found that the Jews there had a valuable literature, and determined to add to it a translation of his grandfather's book. The thirty-eighth year may refer either to the grandson's age or to the king's reign. Two kings bore the name Euer-

---

[1] "The original Hebrew of a portion of Ecclesiasticus [xxxix. 15–xlix. 11] together with the early versions and an English translation . . . edited by Cowley and Neubauer," Oxford, 1897. The other portions have also been published. *Cf.* Schechter, "The Wisdom of Ben Sira, portions of the Book Ecclesiasticus from Hebrew Manuscripts," Cambridge, 1899. The fragments were found in Cairo. Professor Margoliouth tried to prove that these discoveries were not parts of a Hebrew original, but of a translation made in the eleventh century. His theory was, however, contradicted and disproved by Ed. König, in his *Originalität des neulich entdeckten hebräischen Sirachtextes,* Frbg. i. B., 1899. The Hebrew text, as far as it has been discovered at present, has been edited with notes and vocabulary by H. L. Strack (Lpz., 1903, VI, and 74 pages). It has also been edited with a translation and critical notes by N. Peters, Frbg., 1902, who brought out in 1905 what is intended to be a supplement to our editions of the Hebrew Bible: *Liber Jesu filii Sirach hebraice secundum codices nuper repertos vocalibus adornatus addita versione latina cum glossario hebraico-latino. Edidit Norbertus Peters,"* Frib. The Hebrew text with a Latin translation may be found also at the beginning of Knabenbauer's "Commentary on Sirach." The fragments show that the Greek translation is very free. Like Schechter ("The Wisdom of Ben Sira"), Knabenbauer draws attention to the fact that Sirach's numerous allusions to all parts of the book of Psalms make it almost impossible for us to accept the theory of Machabeean Psalms.

getes, Ptolemy III, 247–222, and Ptolemy VII, also called Physcon, who ruled at first conjointly with his brother Ptolemy Philometor (170–145) and afterwards alone (145–117). A further clue is given us by the mention of Simon, the high priest, the son of Onias, of whom the author speaks in a way (l. 1–21) that shows he must have known him personally. There were two high priests named Simon, each being a son of Onias. Simon I was high priest, 310–291; Simon II., 219–199. The references in Ecclesiasticus are probably not to Ptolemy III Euergetes, nor to the first Simon, but to Ptolemy VII Euergetes and the second Simon. Now Ptolemy VII reigned over thirty-eight years, and the thirty-eighth year refers, not to the grandson's age, but to the king's reign, i. e. 132 B. C. It is possible, however, that it may mean the thirty-eighth year after the book was composed in Hebrew.

In the third and second centuries B. C. Hebrew was no longer commonly spoken, but it was known and used by the educated classes.[1]

43. The Book of Wisdom

(Deuterocanonical, 19 chapters)

1. By *wisdom* (*chokma*) the Old Testament understands the insight and knowledge how to act aright, that a man may obtain by studying divine revelations and especially Holy Scripture (*cf.* p. 292). This is the wisdom with which the book of that name deals. It is an admonition supposed to be addressed by King Solomon to the rulers of the earth, whom he urges to cultivate a religious mode of life, rather than to follow the principles of false wisdom. In this book there is an unmistakable reference on the part of the Holy Ghost to the New Testament revelation, as the author (1) speaks of a just man as the Son of God, who is hated by the wicked and condemned to a shameful death (chap. ii.); (2) lays stress on the merit of a pure and perfectly temperate life (chap. iii., iv.); and (3) alludes to everlasting rewards and punishments in far plainer terms than the earlier sacred writers (e. g. iv. 19; v. 16).

2. *Divisions.* Four sections may be distinguished: (*a*) i.–v.: General admonition to wisdom: life passed in accordance with the

---

[1] Some people have doubted whether the Jews in Egypt during the third and second centuries B. C. were numerous enough to have developed a Græco-Jewish literature. Schürer draws attention to an inscription from Shedia near Alexandria, which proves that a number of synagogues existed in Egypt in the third century. *Cf. Revue biblique*, 1898, i. 58.

faith secures the advantages of quiet and peace on earth, and of safety at the judgment. (*b*) vi.–ix.: As the mighty must anticipate a stricter examination than others, they should follow Solomon's example, and strive to obtain wisdom, and pray to God for it. (*c*) x.–xix.: The advantages of wisdom are shown from history, as recorded in Holy Scripture. (*d*) xiii.–xv.: Episode; condemnation of idolatry as a contrast to wisdom.

i.–iii., the wicked, who mock the righteous, bring ruin upon themselves. iv., v., the virtuous enjoy inward peace and are justified at the judgment. vi., ye rulers, promote the service of God! a strict trial awaits you. vii.–ix., seek, like Solomon, true wisdom, that is most precious and contains sweet fruits; pray, as I do, for wisdom. x.–xii., in every age God has protected the wise, and punished the wicked. xiii.–xv., how foolish is the idolatry of the heathen! xvi.–xix., the heathen Egyptians, who oppressed the servants of the true God, were grievously afflicted, but the Israelites found help.

3. *Language.* The book was composed in Greek, though the author refers to Hebrew documents. Its composition in Greek is apparent from the purity of the language and the writer's familiarity with Greek ways of thought. The frequent parallelism in the verses and the style, savoring of Hebrew, suggest his having used Hebrew documents.

In i. 14 mention is made of Hades, in xvi. 11 of the river Lethe, in iv. 2 of the games customary among the Greeks, in xix. of ambrosia, the food of the gods. Some of the Hebraisms are, e. g., ix. 6, "children of men," ix. 9, "agreeable to thy eyes."

The old Latin translation and the Peshitto were certainly based on a Greek original.

4. *The Author* is unknown. At one time the book was often ascribed to the Jew Philo, but this theory has long been abandoned, for the book is in direct antagonism to Greek philosophy, which Philo esteemed highly. Moreover, it is never mentioned in the list of his writings. The Greek title σοφία Σολωμών, does not mean that Solomon is to be regarded as the author, but that the wisdom extolled in the book is found also in Solomon's writings and is in harmony with the wisdom obtained by this king from God.[1] It seems certain that the book was written by

---

[1] Hence Saint Jerome says (*Prol. in Libr. Sal.*): (*liber*) *pseudepigraphus, qui Sapientia Salomonis inscribitur.*

a Jew in Egypt, as there are several allusions to that country (the plagues of Egypt, the passage of the Red Sea, and the destruction of the Egyptian army).

5. *Date.* The numerous allusions to the cruelty of the ancient Egyptians to Israel seem to suggest that the monotheism professed by the author and his fellow countrymen displeased the authorities in Egypt, and that the Jews met with hostility in consequence. This was the case under King Ptolemy Philopator (220–204).[1] The book was written during his reign or not long after.[2]

If we consider the OLD TESTAMENT as a whole, we have to acknowledge that among mankind from the time of Adam, Noe, Abraham and Moses, a community belonging particularly to God has always existed, sharply distinguished from the wicked, and kept firm by bonds of justice and fear. The members of this community have often been hated, despised, persecuted and oppressed, but they could never be completely overcome. Wisdom xix. 20, "Thou didst magnify thy people, O Lord, and didst honor them, and didst not despise them, but didst assist them at all times and in every place." Destruction and wickedness prevailed not only outside this race, but often penetrated into it. The faithful servants of God had a hard task to stand firm, and were often reduced to a very small number, and these few were frequently devoid of influence, wealth and power. Beset both from without and from within they besought God's intervention, God's help and redemption, and they awaited it not merely for themselves, but for all mankind, for this was the prospect presented to them in promises and types. Redemption came through JESUS CHRIST. He transformed the little community into one embracing the whole world, and in order to facilitate the spread of Christianity God in His providence had caused the Roman Empire to extend over the world. Now all mankind possesses the blessing of redemption in the great kingdom of Christ, where mercy and love reign supreme. John i. 17, "the law was given by Moses, grace and truth came by Jesus Christ." Before Christ came man was a servant, now he is a son. These are the tidings conveyed in the NEW TESTAMENT.

---

[1] Josephus Flavius, *Contra Apion*, II, 5. The apocryphal third Book of Machabees, generally to be found at the end of editions of the Septuagint, gives a similar account.

[2] Lagrange gives the date 145–150 B.C. That date harmonizes with the author's knowledge of Græco-Alexandrian philosophy, in opposition to which he sets the wisdom derived from revelation.

THE BOOKS OF THE NEW TESTAMENT

1. CLASSIFICATION

THE New Testament Canon may be divided into three parts: historical, didactic and prophetic. The *historical part* comprises the four Gospels and the Acts of the Apostles; the *didactic* the Epistles written by the apostles, viz. fourteen by Saint Paul (Romans, first and second Corinthians, first and second Thessalonians, Philippians, Ephesians, Colossians, Galatians, Philemon, first and second Timothy, Titus, Hebrews), and seven by other apostles (first and second Peter, first, second and third John, James, Jude). The only *prophetic* book of the New Testament is the Apocalypse of Saint John. There are in all twenty-seven sacred books.

FIRST SECTION

HISTORICAL BOOKS

A. THE GOSPELS

2. THE GOSPELS IN GENERAL

1. *Name.* The early Christians gave the name Εὐαγγέλιον, good tidings, the account of life everlasting, forfeited through Adam and restored through Christ. The Evangelium, or Gospel, is therefore the news of the Redemption and the Redeemer, which the apostles were commissioned by Christ to make known in all parts of the world. As all our Lord's teaching was oral, they understood by the gospel oral instruction. The first meaning of the word gospel was therefore the oral preaching of the apostles, and as, with reference to its contents, this preaching

was unanimous, people knew originally of only one gospel. When the preaching of some of the apostles was written down, men began to speak of "gospels," but the various gospels were regarded only as various versions of the same good tidings, viz. of the Redemption by Jesus Christ. One original gospel underlies the four canonical gospels, the first three of which resemble one another closely, while the fourth supplements them. Like the written gospels, all the books of the New Testament are based upon already given oral teaching concerning salvation.

2. *Order of the Books.* The usual arrangement of the gospels, in which Matthew always stands first, then Mark and Luke, and lastly John, occurs in all old translations and in every list of the canonical books, and in most Greek manuscripts. Saint Matthew's Gospel was always believed to be the first, and Saint John's the latest, in order of composition, so that the gospels are placed not in any order of merit, but according to their age.

3. *Origin.* In examining the gospels and all Holy Scripture, D. Fr. Strauss and his followers, and especially Renan, start from the assumption that there are no such things as miracles or prophecies, and that therefore all accounts of such are either intentional fictions, or legends, which in course of time have grown up, as an unhistorical accretion, round an historical fact. It is often asserted that the gospels, as we know them, cannot have originated in the first century. The apostles or their pupils may have perhaps written down a few statements for their own use, and have left these to their followers, but all kinds of additions had been made before these records passed into use among Christians.[1] F. Chr. Baur (ob. 1860) was willing to believe that intentional falsification and actual deception had been practiced. At the present time the Rationalists regard the growth of myths as an important factor. Harnack is of opinion that Christ's personality made so great an impression upon His disciples, and awakened such enthusiasm in them, that they imputed to him fictitious miracles

---

[1] Modern criticism is busily engaged in discovering such "additions," "misunderstandings" and "interpolations" in almost every chapter.

and prophecies. Jülicher, B. Weiss, Pfleiderer and others profess similar views.

All these assertions may be disproved (*a*) by internal evidence, i. e. by the nature of the gospels; (*b*) by external evidence, i. e. by documents from the earliest times of Christianity; (*c*) by the history of the text; (*d*) by the history of the earliest Christian communities.

(*a*) *Internal Evidence.* The Greek of the gospels, abounding in Hebraisms, suggests that they were the work of Greek-speaking Jews; the intimate acquaintance displayed with the geography of the Holy Land indicates that the writers were natives of Palestine; their knowledge of the history of Palestine in the first century shows that they were contemporaries of Christ and the apostles.

Linguistic evidence. Hebrew is on the whole a poor language, and this poverty reveals itself in the Greek New Testament. If Greek writers in the second century had composed the gospels, they would have used many expressions drawn from the wealth of the Greek vocabulary, where the meager Hebrew makes the meaning obscure. For instance, instead of " to see life," they would have said " to enjoy life "; instead of " love or hate a master," they would have said " prefer "; where we find " heart," they would often have written " conscience "; and where we read " flesh," they would have put " body." Only two authors of books in the New Testament have a less Hebrew and more Greek coloring; they are Saint Paul and Saint Luke, both of them born outside Palestine.

Geographical evidence. After the year 70 A. D. Palestine was practically a wilderness. Fifty towns and nearly one thousand other places were completely destroyed. A writer living a century later would not have been able to give with so much accuracy the names of so many places, their distances and other geographical data.

Historical evidence. Four kings named Herod are mentioned in the New Testament: Herod I, the Great; Herod Antipas; Herod Agrippa I, and Herod Agrippa II. Nowhere in the gospels, or in the New Testament as a whole, is there any mistake in the history of these rulers. It would have been impossible for a writer of not much education, and living a century later, to describe the events of their reigns so correctly as is done in the New Testament. After the death of Herod the Great, Palestine was divided into tetrarchies. The evangelists know this. In Luke iii. we hear not of the tetrarch Archelaus, but of the procurator Pontius Pilate; the author knows therefore that Archelaus was deposed, a fact which a later writer might hardly have remembered. Salome's dance after the banquet might cause surprise, as in the Holy Land women were excluded from such festivities, but just at that time dances were common at the conclusion of a meal, as we learn from Suetonius (*Caligula*, c. 57; *Nero*, c. 54). Herod and his courtiers belonged to the "best" Roman society. In the gospels the inhabitants of Palestine, the relation borne by the Jews to the Samaritans, and the Jewish sects are depicted exactly, as we know from other sources, as they were in the first century. An author writing a hundred years after the time of our Lord would certainly have blundered. The tribute in the Temple was at that time still required to be paid in Jewish coinage, although Greek and Roman money was current all over the country. A later author would not have been likely to know this.

In Matt. xx. 2, a denarius is mentioned as the pay of a day laborer. In the time of Augustus this was the ordinary sum, but later the value of money decreased until in 300 A. D. 25 denarii were a day's wages.

Hug expresses himself in similar terms on the subject of this internal evidence; he asks if any one unexpectedly discovered the historical books of the New Testament without previously knowing anything about them, and if, being equipped with the necessary training, he opened them, what opinion would he form of their origin, age and authorship? He would say: "They are written in Greek, in fact in a degenerate sort of Greek that is very suggestive of Hebrew. We seem forced to think that the authors were Greek-speaking Jews. They are written with no regard to elegance of style; the authors must have been common people, who show no sign of education or literary training beyond having read some Jewish books. The Jewish State is everywhere represented as still existing. The story is told in such a way as to prove the authors to have seen and heard the things that they record. . . . Throughout we can perceive a very precise knowledge of facts and perfect familiarity with the period to which the life of Christ belongs; such knowledge can be expected only of contemporaries. . . . The more we examine the gospel story in detail, the more do we find revealed what we know from other sources respecting the character of the Pharisees, Sadducees and Samaritans, and the Roman system of farming taxes, with all its attendant oppression. Reference is made to Greek and Roman coins as well as to early Jewish money."

(b) *External Evidence.* The assertion that no proof of the existence of the gospels before the year 150 can be found is now seldom heard. It is acknowledged that they must have been written, in the form in which we have them, before the year 110.[1] Ignatius, Polycarp and other apostolic fathers not only quote passages from the gospels,[2] but Justin Martyr, in his first "Apology," [3] written about 150, refers expressly (chapter 67)

[1] Jülicher supposes that Christ's words and deeds were handed down orally between the years 30 and 60; that the synoptic gospels were written between 60 and 100; the fourth gospel is not the work of an eyewitness, but was composed after 100 A.D., in accordance with a definite design.

[2] For details, see the separate gospels.

[3] J. A. Cramer tries to show that various extraneous additions have been made to this apology, and that especially chapter 67 is not genu-

to the "memoirs of the apostles, that are called gospels," and states that they were read aloud regularly at public worship. According to this author, therefore, the Christians used these gospels constantly, and knew their contents well, so that it would have been impossible to alter and falsify them, or to set new or forged gospels in circulation.

Not long ago the "Apology" of a Greek philosopher named Aristides was discovered.[1] According to Eusebius (*Hist. Eccl.*, IV, iii. 3, *Chron. ad ann. 2140*), this "Apology" was dedicated to the Emperor Hadrian (117–138), but most likely it was to his successor Antoninus Pius (138–161). In it (II, 6, 7) Aristides writes thus: "Jesus the Messias is called the Son of the Most High God, and it is said that He came down from heaven through the Holy Ghost, took and put on flesh from a Hebrew maiden, and the Son of God dwelt in the daughter of man. This is taught in what they [the Christians] term the Gospel, which was preached not long ago, and *if you read it*, you will recognize the force that there is in it."

Tatian's Harmony of the Gospels, called διατεσσάρων, is a proof that in 170 the four gospels not only existed, but had long been recognized as sacred books.[2] Still older is the Syriac translation of the gospels contained in the Lewis Codex, that was discovered in 1892 (*supra*, p. 245).

(*c*) *History of the Text.* The oldest texts of the Bible that have come down to us, Greek, Latin, Syriac, etc., all show unmistakable traces of being based upon older documents, some of which must have been earlier than the second century. Tischendorf has proved this in his work: *Wann wurden unsere Evangelien verfasst?* Leipzig, fourth edition, 1880.

(*d*) *The Earliest Communities.* At the beginning of the second century the Christians were not isolated individuals, left to look after themselves, but they lived in well-organized commu-

ine. Even if this were the case, it would still be true that Justin mentions facts in our Lord's life recorded by the synoptic writers, and that he speaks of the Logos in terms suggestive of Saint John.

[1] Seeberg is of opinion that this "Apology" was not written until 140, and was dedicated therefore to Antoninus Pius.

[2] Ciasca, *Evangeliorum harmoniæ arabice et latine*, Romæ, 1888. See p. 210.

nities, under rules and teachers, who protected them from all
dangers to their faith. This appears from the epistles of the
apostles, which are universally received as genuine, and from the
writings of the Apostolic Fathers. According to these documents, innovations in matters affecting the faith were regarded
with suspicion and accepted with the greatest caution among the
Christian communities. Forged epistles and forged gospels could
not find admission or credence among them. Marcion, who
wished to alter Saint Luke's Gospel in 142, met with the keenest
opposition, as we learn from Tertullian's work *Adv. Marcion.*

In answer to this testimony nothing can be alleged against the historical character of the gospels, except that, "at the present time, the accounts
of our Lord's miracles are not adapted to secure for Him any special
importance, as all depends upon what He taught rather than upon what
He did. The miracles therefore, as owing their origin merely to the
'enthusiasm' of the disciples, would have to be eliminated from the
gospels (Harnack). In particular the virgin birth of Christ, the intervention of angels during His childhood, the Temptation, all the miracles
of His active life, and the Resurrection . . . must be regarded as late
interpolations in the account of His presumably Messianic work." There
is, however, no proof at all that the miracles are fictitious.

4. The accounts of the four evangelists may best be harmon-
ized, and a lifelike picture of our Saviour can best be produced,
if we take as our basis the fourth gospel and four paschal festivals during His public life (John ii. 13; v. 1; vi. 4; xi. 55),
and fit into this framework first Saint Luke's account, — for he
says (i. 1) that he states events in chronological order, — and
then those of Saint Matthew and Saint Mark. Saint Matthew
often departs from the chronological order, for he had another
object in writing (see page 365).

Both in ancient and modern times attempts have been made to show
that the public life of Christ lasted only one year.[1]
Reasons for this theory, (1) In Isaias' prophecy, lxi. 2, one year and
one day are mentioned. The prophet, speaking as a type of the Messias,

---

[1] J. van Bebber. His views were accepted fully by J. E. Belser. E.
Nagl showed that no tradition from apostolic times exists, but that from
Holy Scripture it is extremely probable that our Lord's active life
lasted three years. L. Fendt believes that the active life lasted only one
year, but he does not state this as a definite conclusion. J. B. Zellinger
thinks that it must be assumed to have lasted two years.

says: "He hath sent me . . . to proclaim the acceptable year of the Lord [reference to the year of Jubilee] and the day of vengeance [day of judgment]." In Luke iv. 19 our Lord quotes this passage and applies it to Himself. He says (John viii. 56): "Abraham . . . rejoiced that he might see my day." (John xi. 9): "Are there not twelve hours of the day?" (John ix. 4): "I must work . . . whilst it is day." Caiphas is spoken of as "the high priest that year" (John xi. 49), i. e. the year of our Lord's active life.

In support of this theory it is said that we hear of only two Paschs in our Lord's public life (John ii. 13 and xi. 55). In John v. i., where we read: "After these things was a festival day of the Jews, and Jesus went up to Jerusalem," the festival may have been Purim or Pentecost. In John vi. 4 the words τὸ πάσχα are believed to be an interpolation. These assumptions are not, however, well founded. (1) In John v. 1 we must understand the Pasch, because shortly before (iv. 35) we read that there were still four months to harvest, which began with the Pasch. The words τὸ πάσχα are found in John vi. 4 in all old manuscripts and translations, and the *Codex Sin. Syr.* that belongs to the first half of the second century has "the feast of the unleavened" in this place.

(2) If the literal meaning of "year" or "day" is to be pressed, we may with equal right refer to our Lord's words in Luke xiii. 7: "For these three years I come seeking fruit on this fig-tree," i. e. on the people of Israel. *Cf.* also Luke xiii. 32: "to-day and to-morrow and the third day."

(3) It seems impossible that all the events recorded in the four gospels took place in one year. The apostles must have been gradually led to understand the dignity of our Lord Himself and His kingdom. He often complained of the weakness of their faith and the dullness of their minds, and if He had been crucified so soon after His first appearance, His disciples would probably have lost faith in Him; the world would not have been transformed and Judaism and heathendom overthrown by their preaching. If only *one* gospel existed, it might be possible to regard one year as covering the whole of our Lord's active life, but taking them collectively, they contain so much that a longer period is plainly necessary.

(4) Knabenbauer aptly refers to our Lord's words in Matt. xxiii. 37: "Jerusalem, . . . *how often* would I have gathered together thy children, . . . and thou wouldest not?" According to Belser our Lord spent no more than eight days in all at Jerusalem.

An appeal is made sometimes to the views of early Christian writers. Belser says: "The Fathers and authors of the ancient Church almost without exception believe that Christ's activity lasted only one year." This opinion, however, was by no means universal. It was received by the followers of Valentinus, but they were opposed by Irenæus, one of the earliest witnesses, being a pupil of Polycarp, Saint John's disciple (Iren., *Adv. Hær.*, II, xxii. 3). Theodoretus of Cyrus (in Dan. ix.) refers to the Messianic prophecy of the seventy weeks of years, after which redemption is to come. The allusion to the half week of years, which led up to the Redeemer's death, is decisive in favor of our Lord's active life having lasted three and a half years. "From Saint John's Gospel it appears that the Lord spent three years and a half in preaching, in instructing the disciples and strengthening their faith by miracles, and then He suffered." Eusebius (*Demonstr. Ev. Lib.*, 8) appeals to "the tradition that the period of teaching and miracles in our Redeemer's life lasted three and a half years, for this is half a week of years, and this is apparent especially in Saint John's Gospel."

The Gospel according to Saint Matthew

(28 chapters)

3. CONTENTS, PURPOSE AND ARRANGEMENT

The first volume contains three parts: (1) Our Lord's childhood, (2) His life and miracles in Galilee, (3) His Passion and Death.

In the introduction (chapter i., ii.) an account is given of the childhood of Christ (Genealogy, the Magi, Flight into Egypt, Massacre of the Innocents, Return). The author then passes on to Christ's public life (iii.–xviii.), the preparation for which were His baptism and temptation (iii.). He describes Christ's first appearance in public, his preliminary choice of apostles (iv.), and the Sermon on the Mount (v.–vii.). Some miracles of healing, and the raising of Jairus' daughter are recorded (viii., ix.), and the experimental sending out of the apostles (x.). Chapters xi. and xii. deal with Christ's relations with John the Baptist and with the Pharisees, chapter xiii. contains parables about the new kingdom of God. The next three chapters, xiv.–xvi., contain the instructions given to the apostles, who are to be the rulers of the new Messianic kingdom (feeding of five thousand, walking on the sea, eating with unwashed hands, the Chanaanite woman, miracles of healing, second feeding of a multitude, request for a sign, Saint Peter's confession). In chapters xvii. and xviii. Christ is gradually preparing the disciples for the necessity of His death (prophecy regarding it, transfiguration, the lunatic boy, second prophecy of his death, teaching about humility and scandal). The history of Christ's sufferings now begins. Chapters xix. and xx., journey to Judea and the teaching given on the way (marriage, the rich young man, workers in the vineyard, third prophecy of the passion, Salome's request). Chapters xxi.–xxv., entry into Jerusalem, dispute with the Pharisees, parables containing warnings (wise and foolish virgins, talents), teaching concerning the judgment. The last three chapters (xxvi.–xxviii.) record the institution of the Eucharist, the Passion, Death and Resurrection of Christ.

In the arrangement of his materials the evangelist had a particular aim in view, viz. to adapt his book to serve Jews by birth as proof of Christ's being the Messias. It is obviously intended for people well acquainted with the Old Testament, and for this reason it refers frequently to the Old Testament prophecies and types, pointing out how they have been fulfilled in Christ.[1] The author has to some extent sacrificed chronological order to his desire to display Christ as the Messias, long foretold but rejected by the ruling class among the Jews. He says very little about our Lord's work in Judea, where the influence of the Synedrium prevented Him from being welcomed, and where He found few followers. But we have a full account of His successful Messianic activity in Galilee, which had been foretold by Isaias, ix. 1, etc. This was insulting to the capital and the Temple, and to the Jewish priesthood, which, being blinded by pride, anticipated not a poor but a politically powerful Messias, who should establish the throne of David in Jerusalem. To shame the unbelief of these men the Messias withdrew almost completely from the capital, and only went thither to die, on the throne of the Cross. Most of His followers were Galileans; the writer of the gospel had probably preached in Galilee, and composed it primarily for Galileans. Traditon declares the author to have been Saint Matthew the apostle.

4. Saint Matthew the Apostle

Before our Saviour took him as a companion, Matthew had been a tax collector at Capharnaum on the Lake of Genesareth, and was probably very wealthy (Luke v. 27). His name is the seventh in the lists of apostles given in Mark iii. and Luke vi., but it is the eighth in the first gospel (x.), as there that of Saint Thomas precedes it. His call is recorded in the first three gospels (Matt. ix., Mark ii., Luke v.), but in Mark and Luke the name of the man called is given as Levi, son of Alpheus, whilst it is given as Matthew only in the first. As all the circumstances are identical in the three accounts, we cannot doubt that Matthew is the same person as Levi. After his call, in his joy and gratitude, Levi may have changed his name to Matthew (i. e. probably " gift of God "). It was not unusual for Jews to

---

[1] Cf. i. 23–ii. 15, 23–iv. 14–viii. 17–xiii. 14. Especially in the account of the Passion, xxi. 4–xxvi. 24, 54, 56–xxvii. 9, 35.

change their names. The New Testament tells us nothing as to his later history. According to tradition he was engaged for twelve years in preaching the gospel to his countrymen in Judea,[1] and then went on to the Gentiles. He is believed to have been particularly active in Ethiopia, as the Roman Breviary states; and he is said to have suffered martyrdom there.[2]

5. AUTHENTICITY OF THE GOSPEL

If traces of the author be sought in the gospel itself (*internal evidence*), they will be found to be very slight and not perfectly certain. It is striking that in the list of apostles in chapter x. the humiliating designation of " publican " follows the name of Matthew; also that in this list Matthew is the eighth name, whereas it is the seventh in Mark and Luke. Moreover, Mark and Luke both record the great feast given to our Lord and His friends by the publican after his call, whereas in the first gospel the feast is mentioned only incidentally, and the giver of it is not named. The inference is that the writer of the gospel put himself in the background from motives of humility and modesty.

External evidence is much stronger.

(*a*) Papias (75–150), a disciple of Saint John the Apostle, and bishop of Hierapolis in Phrygia, says that Matthew wrote a history of Christ in Hebrew: Ματθαῖος μὲν οὖν ἑβραΐδι διαλέκτῳ τὰ λόγια τοῦ κυρίου συνεγράψατο, ἡρμήνευσε δὲ αὐτὰ ὡς ἦν δυνατὸς ἕκαστος.[3]

(*b*) In the same way Irenæus (*Adv. Hær.*, III, 1).[4] Clement

---

[1] Euseb., *Hist. Eccl.*, V, 18.

[2] By Ethiopia we should probably understand a district in what is now Armenia.

[3] Euseb., *Hist. Eccl.*, III, 39. The work of Papias (λογίων κυριακῶν ἐξηγήσεις) is no longer extant. The last words of the quotation refer to Gentile Christian readers.

[4] Irenæus, a native of Asia Minor, was a disciple of Saint John's follower Polycarp. He was bishop of Lugdunum (Lyons) in Gaul from 177 to 202, the year of his death. He says: Ὁ μὲν δὴ Ματθαῖος ἐν τοῖς Ἑβραίοις τῇ ἰδίᾳ αὐτῶν διαλέκτῳ γραφὴν ἐξήνεγκεν εὐαγγελίου τοῦ Πέτρου καὶ τοῦ Παύλου ἐν Ῥώμῃ εὐαγγελιζομένων καὶ θεμελιούντων τὴν ἐκκλησίαν. Μετὰ δὲ τὴν τούτων ἔξοδον Μάρκος, ὁ μαθητὴς καὶ ἑρμηνευτὴς Πέτρου, καὶ αὐτὸς τὰ ὑπὸ Πέτρου

of Alexandria (*Strom.*, I, 21), Origen (*ap.* Euseb., *Hist. Eccl.*, VI, 25) and Tertullian (*De Carne Christi*, 22), all mention Matthew as the author of a gospel.

(*c*) Quotations from the first gospel occur in still earlier writers. Ignatius (*Ad Ephes.*, XIX) speaks of the appearance of the star at the coming of the Magi, and this is recorded nowhere but in Matthew ii. Polycarp (*Ep.*, c. 2) quotes from the Sermon on the Mount (Matt. v.–viii.). Justinus (*Dial.*, 100) says emphatically that Saint Peter's confession (Matt. xvi. 16) exists *in writing*, thus referring to a book recognized as sacred. Very many quotations, chiefly from the Sermon on the Mount, occur in the *Didache* or teaching of the apostles, compiled in the first century (*cf. supra*, p. 210).

(*d*) The earliest heretics, too,[1] especially the gnostics Basilides and Valentine, who lived in the first half of the second century, quote passages from this gospel.

(*e*) It is quoted also by Celsus, a pagan and bitter opponent of Christianity, who lived in the second century under Marcus Aurelius. His attack upon Saint Matthew's Gospel shows that it was recognized by the Christians as a canonical book.[2]

6. OBJECTIONS

It is only since 1824 that the authenticity of the first gospel has been denied. The allegations against it are:

1. That the gospel contains what is legendary, composed with reference to passages in the Old Testament, e. g. ii. 1–18,[3]

κηρυσσόμενα ἐγγράφως ἡμῖν παρέδωκεν, Λουκᾶς δὲ, ὁ ἀκολουθὸς Παύλου, τὸ ὑπ' ἐκείνου κηρυσσόμενον εὐαγγέλιον ἐν βιβλίῳ κατέθετο (*apud* Euseb., *Hist. Eccl.*, V, x. 3).

[1] *Tanta autem est circa evangelia hæc firmitas, ut et ipsi hæretici testimonium reddant eis.* Irenæus, *Adv. Hær.*, III, xi. 7.

[2] This writer is known only from Origen's eight books against him. The conviction of the apostolic origin of this gospel must have been so deeply rooted in ancient times that even so malicious and crafty an antagonist as Celsus did not dare to deny its authenticity, but used its contents in his polemic against the Christians. It would have been both simpler and more effective to say that the sacred books of the Christians were not genuine, if he had been in a position to point out any falsification or deception in them.

[3] According to one critic the story of the Magi is mythical, and has been developed out of a journey made in 66 B. C. by Tiridates, an Asiatic,

xxi. 5 (*cf.* Zach. ix. 9), xxvii. 9 (*cf.* Jer. xxxii. 6, xviii. 2, etc.; Zach. xi. 12), and is moreover not written in so detailed and vivid a style as we should expect from an eyewitness. These are arbitrary assertions, without any solid foundation. The statement that the stories are fabulous and purely imaginary could have weight only if the impossibility of miracles and prophecies could be proved. The other assertion, that an eyewitness would have written otherwise, appears groundless when we bear in mind the purpose and task of the evangelist, who did not aim at being an historian so much as at proving Christ to be the Messias, and who systematically kept that end in view.

2. "All positive evidence of the authenticity of Saint Matthew's Gospel is based upon the testimony of Papias. This is untrustworthy, because, according to Eusebius (*Hist. Eccl.*, III, 40), Papias was a very simple man, who probably let himself be deceived by heretical Jewish Christians, if they showed him a Hebrew book and said it was the gospel of Saint Matthew. Moreover, his words do not refer to our gospel, but only to a collection of Christ's sayings (λόγια)." [1] In answer we may say (*a*) that Papias' testimony is by no means the only statement in support of later evidence. Irenæus says more than Papias, for he implies that Matthew wrote his gospel in Palestine, whilst Peter and Paul, the chief apostles, were preaching in Rome, so that their gospels originated in that city. Origen never mentions Papias, and seems to have had no knowledge of his writings; he appeals for confirmation of his statements, not to Papias, but to tradition — "ὡς ἐν παραδόσει μαθών."

(*b*) It is true that Eusebius (*Hist. Eccl.*, III, 40) describes Papias as σφόδρα σμικρὸς τὸν νοῦν; but this unfavorable opinion refers not to his character and trustworthiness, but to his Chiliastic views. A man who was a bishop and a pupil of the apostles must have had common sense enough not to

to Rome, to visit the Emperor Nero. Dio Cassius gives an account of it in Book lxiii. 1–7. He came with a large escort and did homage to Nero. But how different are the two stories!

[1] Thus Schleiermacher, Harnack and others.

have allowed himself simply to be deceived in a matter where the most superficial investigation would have sufficed to reveal the truth.

(c) The word λόγια does not necessarily mean a mere collection of speeches. This is plain from Papias, who says that Saint Mark wrote down the words and deeds of Christ, and that his record[1] is called κυριακοὶ λόγοι.[2] Moreover, Papias named his own book λογίων κυριακῶν ἐξηγήσεις, although it must have contained accounts of events as well as speeches. Finally the Fathers of the Church even later often allude to Holy Scripture, and especially to the gospels, as λόγια τοῦ κυρίου,[3] just as we still occasionally speak of the gospels as the Word of God, for they contain more speeches and instructions than records of events.[4]

7. Readers

Saint Matthew wrote his gospel primarily for Northern Palestine, where our Lord had been particularly active, and secondarily for the communities of Jewish Christians throughout Palestine. This may be inferred partially from the contents. The author deems it unnecessary to give his readers any information regarding the geography, the provincial peculiarities, the manners and customs of the Jews, although the other evangelists tell us a good deal on these points (e. g. Mark v. 41, vii. 3; Luke i. 26, vi. 4; John ii. 6, xi. 18).

---

[1] Corresponding to the Hebrew word *dabar*, which designates both the word and the subject-matter. *Cf. dibre hajjamim* = chronicles.

[2] Euseb., *Hist. Eccl.*, III, 39.

[3] Clem. Rom., *Ep. I ad Cor.*, 53.

[4] In 1897 it was reported that Papias' important work on the "Sayings of Jesus" had been recovered in the course of excavations in Egypt. This was a mistake. All that was found was one sheet of papyrus measuring about 6 inches by 3½ inches, and containing six phrases very like those recorded in the canonical gospels. It dates probably from the beginning of the third century and so can have nothing to do with Papias. The discoverers (Grenfell and Hunt) published their find in a little work with the title: Λόγια Ἰησοῦ, "Sayings of our Lord," London, 1897 (see *supra*, p. 239). In 1904 the same scholars discovered some further λόγια at Oxyrhynchus, which they published as "New Sayings of Jesus," London (*Bibl. Ztschr.*, 1905, pp. 176, 222).

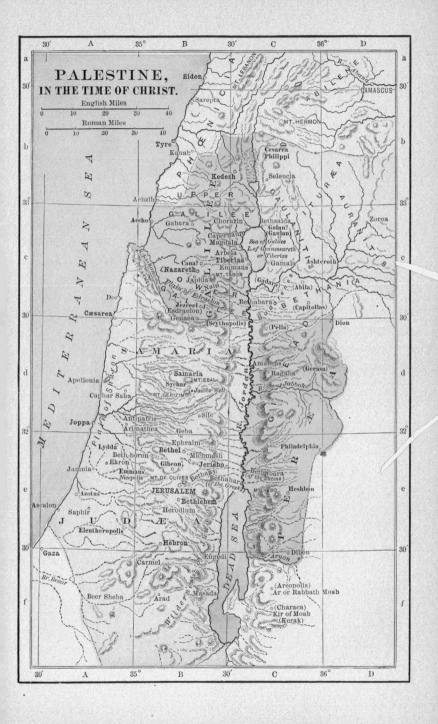

PALESTINE,
IN THE TIME OF CHRIST.

English Miles
0   10   20   30   40

Roman Miles
0   10   20   30   40

MEDITERRANEAN SEA

PHŒNICIA

MT. LEBANON

ABILENE

R. Abana

DAMASCUS

Sidon

Sarepta

MT. HERMON

Tyre

Kanah

Cesarea Philippi

UPPER

Kedesh

Seleucia

GAULANITIS

ITURÆA

AURANITIS

Achzib

GALILEE

Aecho

Gabara

Chorazin

Bethsaida

Golan? (Ganlan)

Zoroa

Capernaum

Magdala

Sea of Galilee
or L. of Gennessareth
or Tiberias

Arbela

Ashteroth

Canaʔ

Tiberias

Emmaus

Gamala

MT. TABOR

(Gadara)

(Abila)

BETHANIA

Nazareth

Japhia

W. Nain

Bethabara

(Capitollas)

Plain of Esdraelon

Dor

Jezreel (Esdraelon)

(Scythopolis)

(Pella)

Dion

Cæsarea

Genaea

SAMARIA

Amathus

Plain of Sharon

Apollonia

Ragaba

(Gerasa)

Samaria

MT. EBAL

Sychar

Jacob's Well

R. Jabbok

Caphar Saba

MT. GERIZIM

Antipatris

Silo

GILEAD

Joppa

Arimathea

Geba

Ephraim

Philadelphia

Lydda

Bethel

Michmash

Beth-horon

Jericho

Ekron

Gibeon

PERÆA

Jamnia

Emmaus

Bethany

Bethabara (of the Greeks)

Neopolis

MT. OF OLIVES

Bethabara (the Turns)

MT. NEBO

Heshbon

JERUSALEM

Azotus

Bethlehem

Ascalon

Herodium

Saphir

JUDÆA

Eleutheropolis

Hebron

DEAD SEA

Gaza

Carmel

Engedi

R. Arnon

Dibon

Br. Besor

(Areopolis)
Ar or Rabbath Moab

Beer Sheba

Arad

Masada

Wilder

(Characa)
Kir of Moab
(Kerak)

R. Jordan

PHŒNICIA

GALILEE

LOWER GALILEE

The frequent references to the Old Testament, that have already been mentioned, show that the writer assumed his readers to be well acquainted with it. In the first gospel there are over seventy quotations from it, more than in the other three together, and the quotations are not merely from the Greek, but they often show a special rendering of the Hebrew text (e. g. iv. 15, 16; cf. Is. viii. 23, ix. 1). The other evangelists use the Septuagint exclusively. The gospel gives altogether the impression of being a work intended for Jews, or rather Jewish Christians. External evidence adds certainty to this supposition. Eusebius (*Hist. Eccl.*, III, 24) states that Saint Matthew, having labored long amongst his fellow countrymen in Palestine, determined to go to other nations, but before leaving the Jews, he wrote down for them his gospel, i. e. the tidings that he had preached regarding the Messias, to make what compensation he could for his absence.[1] Saint Jerome (*De Vir. Illustr.*, III) says that Saint Matthew, first in the land of the Jews, wrote the gospel of Christ for the Jews who had accepted the faith. Similar statements occur in the earlier writers: Irenæus,[2] Origen,[3] Tertullian, Gregory Nazianzen and John Chrysostom.[4]

8. Language

Saint Matthew wrote his gospel in the language commonly spoken in Palestine at that time, viz. in the Chaldee or Aramaic dialect, which is called Hebrew in the New Testament. Just as the Targumim were necessary in the case of the Old Testament, so an Aramaic text was indispensable when the gospel had to be read at public worship. This fact has been much

---

[1] Ματθαῖος . . . πρότερον Ἑβραίοις κηρύξας, ὡς ἔμελλεν καὶ ἐφ' ἑτέρους ἰέναι, πατρίῳ γλώττῃ γραφῇ παραδοὺς τὸ κατ' αὐτὸν εὐαγγέλιον τὸ λεῖπον τῇ αὐτοῦ παρουσίᾳ τούτοις, ἀφ' ὧν ἐστέλλετο, διὰ τῆς γραφῆς ἀνεπλήρου.

[2] *Adv. Hær.*, III, i. 1. "Matthew published among the Hebrews an evangelical work in their language. *Cf. supra*, p. 367.

[3] According to Eusebius (*Hist. Eccl.*, VI, xxv. 4) Origin said that this gospel was written for the Jewish Christians (τοῖς ἀπὸ τοῦ Ἰουδαϊσμοῦ πιστεύουσιν).

[4] For the precise words of each writer see Reithmayr, *Einl. in d. N. T.*, 353, etc.

questioned in recent times, especially by Protestants. Erasmus of Rotterdam was the first to deny it and to pronounce the Greek to be the original. L. Hug is of the same opinion, especially because Greek was well understood in Palestine. But all the evidence of Christian antiquity is unanimous in stating that the original of Saint Matthew's Gospel was in Hebrew.[1] Papias learnt it from John the Presbyter in Ephesus (Euseb., *Hist. Eccl.*, III, 39) ; Irenæus and Origen say the same (see *supra*, page 367). Eusebius gives the further information (*Hist. Eccl.*, V, 10) that Pantænus, head of the school of catechists at Alexandria (179–212), had found the Hebrew original of Saint Matthew's Gospel in India, i. e. in the eastern part of Arabia. Important evidence in support of the truth of these statements is furnished by the fact that the Jewish Christians certainly possessed a Hebrew gospel, called *Evangelium ad Hebræos*. Some of the remaining fragments of it bear considerable resemblance to our gospel, but it appears to have been shorter.[2] The Hebrew original has perished, and the Church knows Saint Matthew's Gospel only in Greek. No certain answer can be given to the question who translated the Hebrew into Greek. Ancient writers were at a loss on this subject and acknowledged their ignorance.[3] Some think that not only the original but also the translation ought to be ascribed to Saint Matthew; others say Saint Mark; and Saint James the Less, bishop of Jerusalem, and Saint John the Apostle might also

---

[1] Kaulen and Schegg are inclined to think that it was in ancient Hebrew, and Resch agrees with them (Gebh. u. Harnack, *Texte u. Unt.*, X, i., p. 107). Cornely believes it was in Aramaic. In the words "τῇ ἰδίᾳ αὐτῶν διαλέκτῳ" Irenæus is probably referring to the Aramaic dialect, as Eusebius by the expression " πατρίῳ γλώττῃ."

[2] We may suppose this gospel to have the first written record of the teaching that the apostles agreed to give in preaching salvation. A tax collector would certainly be able to write well, and so he was employed by Saint Peter and the other apostles to reduce it to writing. The synoptic gospels are an expansion of this teaching adapted to suit the various requirements of Jews, Romans and Greeks. *Cf. infra*, p. 390.

[3] Saint Jerome (*Catalogus Script. Eccl.*, c. 3), *Matthæus, qui et Levi, ex publicano apostolus primus in Judæa propter eos, qui ex circumcisione crediderant, evangelium Christi hebraicis literis verbisque composuit: quod quis postea in græcum transtulerit, non satis certum est.*

be suggested as possible translators. But whoever translated it, it is certain that the Greek text of the first gospel has always been recognized in the Church as a faithful rendering of Saint Matthew's record, whilst the probably shorter Hebrew original ceased to be regarded as canonical, for the reason that it had suffered alterations at the hands of heretical Jewish Christians. As to the date of the translation, we know that it was made in the time of the apostles, because the apostolic fathers quote the Greek text, and Papias alludes to a translation, saying that originally each one interpreted the Hebrew text for himself as best he could.[1]

9. PLACE AND DATE OF COMPOSITION

From what has been said, we learn that Saint Matthew's Gospel was written in the Holy Land, perhaps in Capharnaum, where he had been employed as a publican. With regard to the date, we know that, according to all ancient writers, Saint Matthew was the first of the Evangelists to compose his work.[2] He cannot have done so, however, until several years had elapsed after our Lord's Ascension, for in xxvii. 8 he says: "That field was called Haceldama, that is, the field of blood, even to this day." And again in xxviii. 15 (the report that the disciples had stolen our Lord's body) "was spread abroad among the Jews even unto this day." At the same time he must have written before 70 A.D., for the Jewish State is everywhere described as still existing. To arrive at a more precise date, we may refer to Eusebius, who says (see *supra,* p. 371) that Saint Matthew wrote before going into foreign lands to preach to the Gentiles. If he taught in Palestine from eight to fifteen years,[3] he may have composed his gospel soon after the year 40. Eusebius (*Chron. a. 41*) gives the year 41 as the date, and so do other Greek authors.

---

[1] Belser believes that the translation was made about the year 70.

[2] Orig. *ap.* Euseb., *Hist. Eccl.,* V, 10; Eusebius himself, *Hier. Catal. Scr. Eccl.,* c. 3.

[3] Ancient authorities differ as much as this with regard to the duration of his work in Palestine.

This does not agree with the statement made by Irenæus (*Adv. Hær.*, III, 1, see p. 367), who says that Saint Matthew wrote his gospel whilst Saint Peter and Saint Paul were preaching at Rome. If this were correct, the date of composition would be after 60 A. D., as Saint Paul did not go to Rome earlier.[1]

It seems likely that when Irenæus wrote these words, he did not intend to fix a date, but simply to state that the first gospel originated in the parent community in Palestine, and not like the second and third gospels, in Rome.[2]

The Gospel According to Saint Mark

(16 chapters)

10. Contents and Author

The keynote is struck at the beginning of the book (i. 1–15), — Jesus Christ, the Son of God, proclaimed at His baptism, founds the Messianic kingdom. (1) i. 16–viii. 30, Through His work in Galilee Christ proves Himself to be the Messias and Son of God. (2) viii. 31–xiii. 37, Instructions given to the apostles, men chosen from among the people, to introduce them to their special duties. (3) xiv.–xvi., Passion, Death and Resurrection of Christ. (Cornely gives a similar division of the book.)

More detailed examination. i. John the Baptist appears as the forerunner of the Messias, foretold by the prophets; the Messias Himself, Jesus of Nazareth, at once comes to the Jordan for baptism. It is followed by His fasting and temptation, and then His Messianic activity begins with the call of some disciples. Healing of one possessed by a devil, of Peter's mother-in-law, and of many sick persons, including a leper. ii. Cure of a paralytic, call of Levi, the disciples pluck ears of corn. iii. The man with the withered hand. Pharisees and Herodians oppose Jesus. Choice of the apostles. His enemies declare Him to be possessed. His mother and brethren. iv. Parables of the seed, the sower and the grain of mustard seed. Calming of a storm at sea. v. Cure of

[1] A. Schäfer and Schanz accept this date on the authority of the passage in Irenæus, and believe that the Jewish Christians were in danger, as the Epistle to the Hebrews shows. No suggestion of it can be found in the gospel, however, though the epistle is plain enough on the subject.

[2] Kaulen suggests that the name of Saint Paul, the Apostle of the Gentiles, crept into the text of Irenæus through a copyist's error, and that he really mentioned only the foundation of the Church at Rome by Saint Peter about the year 42. *Cf.* note on page 379, *infra*.

a demoniac on the other side of the lake. Jairus' daughter and the woman with the issue of blood. vi. Unsuccessful preaching in Nazareth. Mission of the Twelve. Herod's alarm. Miraculous feeding of the people. Walking on the sea. vii. Eating with unwashed hands. Dispute with the Pharisees. The Chanaanite woman. Cure of a deaf mute. viii. Feeding of four thousand persons. Cure of a blind man. Saint Peter's confession. Christ foretells His death. ix. Transfiguration. Cure of a boy. Strife for precedence among the disciples. x. Instruction regarding marriage. Blessing of children. The rich young man. Another prophecy of death. Request made by two apostles. Cure of a blind man in Jericho. xi. Entry into Jerusalem. Buyers and sellers in the Temple. xii., xiii. Conflicts with the ruling parties. Allusions to the rejection of the Jews, the destruction of Jerusalem, and the end of the world. xiv. The Paschal Supper. Agony on the Mount of Olives. Seizure by the Jews. Denial by Peter. xv. Scourging. Crucifixion. Death and burial. xvi. Resurrection. Ascension into Heaven.

Who was the author of this book? According to tradition it was Mark; but who was he? He is not to be found in the lists of the apostles, but if his work is to possess the apostolic authority, he must have been very closely connected with them. Among the assistants of the first preachers of the faith, we often [1] hear of a man named Mark or John Mark, belonging to a family of Levites in Jerusalem. Mark is a Roman prænomen that he assumed, and gradually, as he came much in contact with Latins, it took the place of his national name John, although the latter was not quite forgotten. His mother's name was Mary (Acts xii. 12), and his uncle was Joseph, the Levite (Col. iv. 10), who, on account of his wonderful eloquence in preaching the faith, received the name of Barnabas, i. e. son of consolation or prophecy; *bar nebua* = divinely inspired speaker. Barnabas introduced his nephew to the work of the apostles, and about the year 46, in the company of his uncle and Saint Paul, Mark made a missionary journey from Antioch to Cyprus and thence to Asia Minor. At Perge in Pamphylia, however, he left them, and returned to Jerusalem, at which Saint Paul was very much hurt. For several years nothing more is recorded of him in the Acts, and we know nothing of his movements until in 50 we hear of him at Antioch, again with Paul and Barnabas. Another missionary

[1] Acts xii. 12, 25, xiii. 5, 13, xv. 37, 39; Col. iv. 10; II Tim. iv. 11; Philemon 24.

journey had to be undertaken, as they were to attend the council of the apostles, and Barnabas wished to take Mark with him; Paul would not agree to this proposal, and they separated in consequence. Paul, taking Silas as his companion, set out for Asia Minor, whilst Barnabas and Mark revisited Cyprus. Here we again lose sight of Mark. In Col. iv. 1 and Philemon 24, both of which epistles were written during Saint Paul's first imprisonment in Rome, about the year 63, his presence in Rome is mentioned, and he is said to have the intention of visiting the east. In II Tim. iv. 11, Timothy is commissioned to bring him with him to Rome, where Saint Paul then was.

The two great gaps in Mark's history (42–50 and 50–63) may be filled up most suitably in the following way: 1. In I Peter v. 13 Saint Peter calls Mark his son. This must undoubtedly mean that he had converted him to Christianity and baptized him. The Fathers describe Mark as Saint Peter's interpreter. The question has been raised whether this designation denotes that verbal or written assistance was given to Saint Peter by Mark. It is a common word and more often refers to oral than written explanation; hence we must not limit it here to the latter meaning, as some persons do. Saint Peter did not need an interpreter in Palestine or the surrounding countries, where Greek was spoken, but he might have done so where Latin prevailed, i. e. in Italy. About the year 42 Saint Peter fled from Jerusalem during the persecution under Herod Agrippa (Acts xii. 17), and according to tradition he went to Rome; so we may suppose that Mark, after leaving Paul and Barnabas, went to Rome either with or to Saint Peter in order to help him.

2. According to the Fathers,[1] Mark was the founder of the church and bishopric at Alexandria. He may have gone on thither from Cyprus about the year 54 and have remained there until 62, when he appointed Anianus to succeed him,[2] and went to rejoin the apostles (Col. ii. 10). The history of

---

[1] Hieronymus (*De Viris Ill.*, 8), Epiphanius (*Hær.*, cli. 6), Eusebius (*Hist. Eccl.*, II, 16).

[2] Hier.: *usque ad octavum Neronis annum.*

the end of his life is unknown. According to tradition, he suffered martyrdom at Alexandria under Trajan.

11. AUTHENTICITY

Ecclesiastical tradition ascribes the second gospel to this follower of the apostles, and it is supported by testimony and quotations from the earliest times. Justin Martyr (c. Tryph., 106) quotes the name "Boanerges" from Mark iii. 17. Irenæus (Adv. Hær., III, x. 6) gives the beginning and end of this gospel.[1] There is also a good deal of external evidence, going back to the apostolic age.

Papias (Euseb., Hist. Eccl., III, 39) refers to still earlier testimony, that, namely, of John the Presbyter in Ephesus, and says: "Mark, who was interpreter to Peter, wrote down very accurately what he stated regarding the words and deeds of Christ. But he did not write them in chronological order (οὐ μέντοι τάξει) because he had neither heard the Lord nor followed Him. . . . He paid particular attention to one point, viz. to omit nothing of what he had heard, nor to add any falsehood to them."[2]

The testimony of Irenæus is given on p. 367.

Clement of Alexandria (150–217) also refers to earlier witnesses ("the record of the elders from the beginning") and says: "When Peter was preaching in Rome his hearers went to Mark with the request that he would write down what was said, for he had long followed Peter, and remembered his words. After writing the gospel, he handed it to those who

---

[1] *Marcus interpres et sectator Petri initium evangelicæ conscriptionis fecit sic: Initium Evangelii Jesu Christi, Filii Dei, quemadmodum scriptum est. . . . In fine autem Evangelii ait Marcus: et quidem Dominus Jesus, postquam locutus est, receptus est in cœlos et sedet ad dexteram Dei.*

[2] καὶ τοῦτο ὁ πρεσβύτερος ἔλεγε · Μάρκος μὲν ἑρμενευτὴς Πέτρου γενόμενος ὅσα ἐμνημόνευσεν ἀκριβῶς ἔγραψεν, οὐ μέντοι τάξει, τὰ ὑπὸ τοῦ Χριστοῦ ἢ λεχθέντα ἢ πραχθέντα · οὔτε γὰρ ἤκουσε τοῦ κυρίου, οὔτε παρηκολούθησεν αὐτῷ . . . ἑνὸς ἐποιήσατο πρόνοιαν τοῦ μηδὲν ὧν ἤκουσε παραλιπεῖν ἢ ψεύσασθαί τι ἐν αὐτοῖς. (ἐμνημόνευσεν may refer to Mark = "what he remembered," or to Peter = "what he stated." The remark at the end seems to require the latter interpretation.)

had made the request, and Peter, knowing of it, neither hindered nor encouraged him" (Euseb., *Hist. Eccl.*, VI, 14).

Numerous other witnesses might be mentioned, but it will be enough to refer to Saint Jerome, who sums up all our traditional knowledge of this gospel in the words: "Mark, the disciple and interpreter of Peter, at the request of the brethren in Rome, wrote a short gospel in conformity with what he had heard Peter say" (*De Viris Illustr.*, c. viii. 9).

Against the authenticity of this gospel, it is maintained that the earliest and most important testimony, that, namely, of Papias, is untrustworthy, for, apart from his own character (see *supra*, p. 369), he must have been thinking of some quite different book, and not of the second canonical gospel, as he says that Mark wrote *not in order*, whereas there is certainly a chronological order in our gospel, for it begins with John the Baptist and ends with the history of our Lord's Passion.

It is quite obvious, however, that Papias only meant that Mark had not intended or been able to give a complete account of the life of Christ, for he had not been an eyewitness of it. He merely wrote down from memory the chief events in that life, as Peter had spoken of them. John the Presbyter in Ephesus, who most likely ought to be identified with Saint John the Apostle, and who certainly was well acquainted with the history of Christ, detected many omissions in the work. Our Lord's words were not fully reported, and in the story of His life events are left out to which Peter had not alluded in his discourses. The incompleteness of this gospel was one reason why Saint John in his old age determined to write a gospel himself to supplement the others.

12. PLACE OF COMPOSITION AND SOURCES OF INFORMATION

The quotations already made prove incontestably that Saint Mark wrote his gospel in Rome at the request of the faithful, who wished to possess in writing what Saint Peter had preached. Confirmation of these facts may be derived from internal evidence. (1) Saint Mark is fond of explaining Hebrew words by giving the Greek equivalents, e. g. v. 41, xv. 22, 34, 42. In the same way he adds remarks concerning Jewish customs; e. g. v. 41, vii. 3, xiv. 12, xv. 22, 34, 42. These things suggest that he is writing for people who are not Jews and who live far from Palestine. (2) The occurrence of many Latin words in a Greek form, such as $\pi\rho\alpha\iota\tau\acute{\omega}\rho\iota o\nu$, $\kappa\tilde{\eta}\nu\sigma o\varsigma$, $\sigma\pi\epsilon\kappa o\upsilon\lambda\acute{\alpha}\tau\omega\rho$, $\kappa\epsilon\nu\tau\upsilon\rho\acute{\iota}\omega\nu$ (Matthew and Luke read $\acute{\epsilon}\kappa\alpha\tau\acute{o}\nu\tau\alpha\rho\chi o\varsigma$), κοδράντης (= *quadrans*), etc., points to Latin being the usual language of the readers. (3) Some passages refer directly to Rome, especially xv. 21; *cf*. Romans xvi. 13. If it be asked why Mark, writing for the Romans, did not use the Latin language,[1] we may reply that he was obliged to use the language of his master; St. Peter preached in Greek, and could not have approved of the written gospel unless he had understood it thoroughly himself. "Peter's interpreter" would probably take care that a translation was supplied.

That Saint Peter took some share in the work is also apparent from the contents. (1) The events are related as by an eyewitness; *cf*. e. g. i. 29 with Matthew. viii. 14 and Luke iv. 38. (2) There are more references to Saint Peter and his family in the second gospel than in the others. (3) Though other events are recorded very briefly by Saint Mark, he gives the most detailed account of Saint Peter's denial, but he passes over Saint Peter's special commission. (4) In Acts i. 21, before the election of Matthias, Saint Peter says that they must choose a man who had been an eyewitness of our Lord's life, from the time of His baptism to that of His Ascension. These are the events with which the second gospel begins and ends.

13. DATE OF COMPOSITION

This gospel must have been written some time after our Lord's Ascension, as in the last verse (xvi. 20) we read: "They going forth preached everywhere." The apostles had betaken themselves to the Gentiles, thus fulfilling the command to go and "teach all nations" (Matt. xxviii. 19). It is generally believed that Saint Mark did not write earlier than 67 or even 70 A. D.[2] This theory is based upon a passage in Irenæus, who, after speaking of Saint Matthew, adds:[3] "After the departure of Peter and Paul, Mark, the disciple and interpreter of Peter, who had written down what had been preached by Peter, trans-

---

[1] Ephrem the Syrian says that the gospel was composed in Latin.

[2] A. Schäfer thinks that the gospel was written in 66 and published in 67.

[3] *Adv. Hær.*, III, 1; Euseb., *Hist. Eccl.*, V, 10. See p. 367.

mitted it to us." The two apostles suffered martyrdom in Rome in the year 67. The gospel cannot well have been written later than 70, because the evangelist records Christ's prophecy regarding the destruction of Jerusalem without any comment (Mark xiii. 2).

However, it is not unlikely that the date of composition was much earlier. In the Canon this gospel generally stood second, so that in the ancient Church it must have been considered older than that of Saint Luke. Now we know that Saint Luke wrote between 61 and 63. Further, from the quotations given *supra,* on p. 377 (authenticity from Clement of Alexandria and Saint Jerome), we must infer that the gospel existed during the lifetime of Saint Peter, who gave his sanction to it. We may even suppose that the faithful in Rome desired to have his discourses recorded in writing, on the occasion of his leaving them at the end of his first sojourn in that city. The subscriptions in the manuscripts generally mention the tenth year after our Lord's Ascension as the date of the composition of this gospel.[1] If these indications be accepted, we may believe it to have been written between 42 and 50. The words of Irenæus may mean that after the apostles' death Mark published the gospel outside as well as inside Rome. It is, however, more probable that the word ἔξοδος denotes not the death of the two apostles, but their departure from Jerusalem.[2]

---

[1] See Reithmayr, p. 386. Kaulen (*Einl.*, III, 50) suggests 42–44 as the date.

[2] ἔξοδος means "departure," hardly ever "death," as will be seen in referring to a lexicon. The only exception seems to be II Peter i. 15. If this be borne in mind, what Irenæus means is: "Whilst all the apostles were still in Palestine, Matthew wrote the first gospel in the Hebrew language, because he had long been working amongst the Hebrews. Peter and Paul displayed their greatest energy outside Palestine, especially in Rome. When they had left Palestine, their written gospels were composed, namely Peter's through the instrumentality of Mark, and Paul's through that of Luke in Rome." Knabenbauer (*Comm. in Luc.*, p. 9) thinks that ἔξοδος does not mean the death or martyrdom of the two apostles. Cornely (*Introd.*, III, 76) is of the same opinion. Kaulen (*Einl.*, III, 51) proposes to read ἔκδοσιν instead of ἔξοδον, but in this context it would be difficult to assign a suitable meaning to it.

14. Relation to Matthew and Luke

Saint Mark's Gospel is the shortest of all. It resembles Saint Luke's in many respects, but still more Saint Matthew's; in fact the first two gospels contain several passages that are almost word for word the same. This uniformity cannot be accidental, and it is generally assumed that one of the evangelists used the work of the other. It is more probable that Saint Mark used Saint Matthew's than the reverse. For, as we have seen, Saint Matthew left Palestine soon after 40 A. D., when it is certain that Saint Mark's Gospel did not yet exist. On the other hand Saint Mark, being a native of Jerusalem, must have very early become acquainted with Saint Matthew's Gospel, written for use in Palestine, and he may very probably have taken a copy of it with him to Rome. Even if the gospel of Saint Matthew at that time existed only in Hebrew, it may have been used by Saint Mark, when he wrote down Saint Peter's discourses; and whoever translated Saint Matthew must have referred to Saint Mark, that was written originally in Greek. In fact there seems reason for supposing that Saint Mark himself translated Saint Matthew's Gospel into Greek (*supra*, p. 372). In this case the resemblance between the two gospels is quite explicable. Saint Luke may have used both gospels when writing his own, and this would account for the likeness between Saint Mark and Saint Luke.

Against this theory that one evangelist used the writings of another is the weighty argument that the Fathers never suggest anything of the kind. The three synoptic gospels reproduce probably the first catechesis, i. e. the outline which the apostles agreed to use in preaching, the primitive oral gospel to which (according to Gal. ii. 2) Saint Paul also adhered. We may suppose that Mark, or rather his master Saint Peter, took from Saint Matthew, and so from this primitive gospel, as much as was necessary for use in preaching salvation in Rome. Saint Luke, according to his statement in i. 2, added a good deal from other sources to supplement what Saint Paul taught. This is a more satisfactory account of the relation borne by the three gospels to one another than is supplied by the hypothesis mentioned above (*cf. supra*, p. 372, note, and *infra*, p. 390).

15. CONTROVERSY REGARDING THE END OF THIS GOSPEL

The last twelve verses, in which our Lord's appearances after His Resurrection and His Ascension are recorded (xvi. 9–20), are missing in the very ancient Syriac *Lewis Codex*, and in the important Greek manuscripts B and ℵ. Several of the Fathers say that the end of the book is absent in many manuscripts, and in some of the more recent manuscripts before verse 9 stand the words: ἐστὶν δὲ καὶ ταῦτα φερόμενα μετὰ τὸ ἐφοβοῦντο γάρ · ἀναστὰς δὲ κτλ. There is, however, a good deal of evidence in favor of its being genuine. Except those mentioned above, all the older Greek manuscripts contain this conclusion, and so do most of the old translations (Itala and Peshitto, also the Coptic version). Quotations from these verses occur in Irenæus, who knows the nineteenth verse as Saint Mark's, and perhaps in Justinus and Hippolytus. There is also some internal evidence, for Saint Mark could not have ended his gospel with the words ἐφοβοῦντο γάρ. We are not justified in rejecting these verses. It is probable that this section was omitted, first from the portions read in the churches, and then from the manuscripts, because of the exegetical difficulty presented by the apparent discrepancy between Mark xvi. 9, etc., and Matthew xxviii. 1, etc.[1]

---

[1] Westcott and Hort have examined the matter very carefully, and have come to the conclusion that the last verses did not originally form part of the gospel, but were a later addition. They are, however, very old and embody an extremely ancient apostolic tradition. These critics acknowledge that Irenæus quotes Mark xvi. 19 as being Saint Mark's words, and they recognize the testimony of Justinus, though they question that of Hippolytus.

In an article in the *Bibl. Ztschr.*, 1905, pp. 269–272, Mader ascribes this passage to Aristion, mentioned by Papias (*apud* Euseb., *Hist. Eccl.*, III, 39) and possibly one of our Lord's disciples. In doing so, Mader attaches importance to an Armenian translation of the gospels, of the year 989, in which Mark xvi. 9–20 bears the heading " by Ariston the Presbyter." However, Papias does not call Ariston a " Presbyter," nor is Ariston the same name as Aristion.

Reithmayr and Aberle refer to the persecution under Diocletian, when

The Gospel According to Saint Luke

(24 chapters)

16. SUBJECT, CONTENTS AND AUTHOR

Subject. The Messias has appeared, namely Jesus, the Son of God, and has established an everlasting kingdom for the salvation of all nations, such as his forefather Jacob announced, and David in a slight degree possessed (i. 32).

Contents. 1. (Chapters i.–iv.) History of our Lord's childhood and His preparation for His Messianic work. 2. (iv.–ix.) Teaching and miracles in Galilee. 3. (ix.–xix.) Continuation of the above and instruction of the apostles. 4. (xx.–xxiv.) Sufferings and exaltation of the Messias.

Chapters i., ii. Early history of Christ, which the third gospel gives most fully. (Birth of Our Lord's precursor, John the Baptist; Birth of Christ in Bethlehem; Presentation in the Temple; Jesus when twelve years old at the Pasch.) iii. Baptism of Christ. iv. Temptation. Our Lord begins His ministry in Galilee. v., vi. The first apostles. Instructions and miracles. vii. The centurion at Capharnaum, *the young man at Naim,[1] *Christ is anointed by a sinful woman. viii. Further ministry. Jairus' daughter. ix. Feeding of five thousand. Peter's confession. Prophecy of the Passion. Transfiguration. x. *The Good Samaritan. *Martha and Mary. xi. Denunciation of the Pharisees. xii. Warning against anxiety about temporal goods. Treasures in heaven. The lord of the household and his servants. xiii. Leaven, grain of mustard seed, the narrow gate. xiv. Other parables. xv. *The lost sheep, the lost drachma, the Prodigal Son. xvi. *The unjust steward, *Dives and Lazarus. xvii. Instruction on scandal, on pardoning offenses, on the power of faith. xviii. *The Pharisee and the Publican. Blessing of children.

the Christians were forced to get rid of their sacred books. After the persecution ceased, new books had to be procured, and Alexandrian booksellers were foremost in supplying them. In Alexandria it was the custom to fast before Easter only until midnight, because from Matt. xxviii. 1–7 it was inferred that the Resurrection took place at midnight, but in Rome the fast continued until the morning, because Mark xvi. 9 speaks of " early." Hence the final verses of Saint Mark's Gospel were omitted in the Alexandrian Bibles. The *Lewis Codex,* which also ends with the words " they were afraid " may have been based likewise upon an older Alexandrian manuscript. *Cf.* also *Innsbr. Ztschr.,* 1895, i. 187. For us the testimony of the Church secures to these verses a place in the Canon. *C. Trid.,* S. 4, *supra,* p. 254.

[1] Sections marked with an asterisk are peculiar to the third gospel.

The rich young man. Prophecy of the Passion. The blind man at Jericho. xix. *Zacheus. Entry into Jerusalem. Purification of the Temple. xx. Discourse against the Pharisees. xxi. The widow's offering; the destruction of Jerusalem and the end of the world. xxii.–xxiv. Account of Our Lord's Passion and Death, Resurrection and Ascension.

Author. The Church has at all times ascribed this gospel and the Acts of the Apostles to *Lucas,* a disciple and companion of Saint Paul, and frequently mentioned in his epistles. We can gather some information regarding his life from the Acts of the Apostles. Lukas or Lucas [1] was born at Antioch in Syria (Euseb., *Hist Eccl.,* III, 4). He was undoubtedly of Gentile origin, as Saint Paul (Col. iv. 14) carefully distinguishes him from others who were circumcised. By profession he was a physican.[2] He must have become a Christian early, for in the Acts, when he begins to speak of himself (xvi. 10), he does not make any remarks by way of introduction, as he does in the case of Timothy (xvi. 1), but comes forward as already well known to his readers. He accompanied Saint Paul on his second missionary journey from Asia Minor to Macedonia, remaining in the latter country, while Saint Paul went on southwards to Achaia. He seems to have stayed a long time in Macedonia, for we do not hear of his being with Saint Paul again until the latter was leaving Macedonia on his third missionary journey and going to the East, and then Saint Luke joined him at Philippi (Acts xx. 5, 6). They did not again part company. Luke was with Saint Paul during his two years' imprisonment at Cæsarea, traveled with him thence to Rome and remained faithful to him during both his first and second imprisonment there (II Tim. iv. 11). He died at Pataræ in Achaia between the ages of seventy-four and eighty-four.[3]

---

[1] The name is probably an abbreviated form of Lucanus or Lukianos.

[2] Greg. Naz., Sedulius. Hug draws attention to some technical expressions occurring in Saint Luke, especially $\pi\upsilon\rho\epsilon\tau\grave{o}\varsigma\ \mu\acute{\epsilon}\gamma\alpha\varsigma$ (iv. 38); $\dot{\alpha}\chi\lambda\grave{\upsilon}\varsigma\ \kappa\alpha\grave{\iota}\ \sigma\kappa\acute{o}\tau o\varsigma$ (Acts xiii. 11, — $\dot{\alpha}\chi\lambda\grave{\upsilon}\varsigma$ = a mist before the eyes). Harnack too refers to these expressions as evidence of the authenticity of the gospel.

[3] Hieronymus (*De Script. Eccl.*): *vixit octoginta et quatuor annos, uxorem non habens; sepultus est Constantinopoli.* The Church venerates him as a martyr.

17. AUTHENTICITY

That this gospel existed in the first century and was recognized as apostolic, we learn from Clement of Rome, who succeeded to the see of Saint Peter in the year 90. In his letters to the Corinthians (i. 46 and ii. 8) there twice occurs the passage: "The Lord says in the gospel, 'He that is faithful in that which is least, is faithful also in that which is greater'" (Luke xvi. 10).[1] Polycarp, a disciple of the apostles, quotes (Phil. ii.) the words: "Be ye therefore merciful, as your Father also is merciful" (Luke vi. 36). Justin Martyr, who was almost a contemporary (*c. Tryph.*, 103, 105), speaks of our Lord's bloody sweat (Luke xxii. 44) and of His last words: "Jesus cried with a loud voice, 'Father, into thy hands I commend my spirit'" (Luke xxiii. 46).

In the *Didache* there are several quotations from Luke vi. 28–32 on love of one's neighbor and one's enemies. The heretic Basilides, who lived under Hadrian, knew[2] the angel's words: "The Holy Ghost shall come upon thee" (Luke i. 35).

What evidence have we that Saint Luke was the author?

The writer was a Greek, not a native of Palestine. This is quite certain from the comparatively pure Greek of the gospel and of the Acts, which is surpassed by no book in the New Testament, except the Epistle to the Hebrews. Saint Luke was a native of Antioch. He does not actually name himself anywhere as the author of the two books ascribed to him, but we have abundant justification for believing that he wrote them.

In the Acts the author often speaks of himself and Saint Paul in the first person plural: "We journeyed," etc. Therefore he was a companion of Saint Paul. His name is given by other witnesses.

1. Irenæus, who through his master Polycarp, Saint John's disciple, had been well instructed in the apostolic tradition, says: "Luke, the companion of Paul, recorded in writing the gospel

---

[1] The first of these letters is undoubtedly genuine ; it was written about the time of Domitian. The second is spurious.

[2] *Philosophumena*, VII, 26, — generally supposed to be the work of Saint Hippolytus of Rome (beginning of third century).

preached by him." [1] This testimony shows us what was the traditional belief in the churches of Asia and Gaul.

2. *The Muratorian Fragment* (see p. 205), written in Rome during the second century, contains the words: *Tertium evangelii librum secundum Lucam. Lucas iste medicus,"* etc.

3. From *Africa* we have the evidence of Clement of Alexandria (*Strom.*, I, 21) and of Origen (in Matt. i.), as well as of Tertullian (born about 160 in Carthage), who defended the third gospel, on the grounds of tradition, against the heretic Marcion. He constantly speaks of Saint Luke as the author. We can see from his defense that at that time no one, not even Marcion's own followers, questioned the authorship of the book; all that the heretics desired was to cast out certain passages that did not agree with their doctrines. It would be easy to multiply witnesses. There is no trace of suspicion ever having been cast on the authorship of the book in ancient times.

18. AUTHORITIES

Saint Luke was not himself a follower of Christ but his work has nevertheless been admitted to the Canon like the writings of the apostles. This is due to the connection between Saint Luke and Saint Paul, who is called by Tertullian (*Adv. Marc.*, IV, 2) the *magister* and *illuminator* of his disciple. Irenæus (l. c.) states that Luke, being Paul's companion, wrote down the gospel preached by him. The Fathers therefore sometimes refer to the third gospel as that of Paul, in the same way as they speak of the second as that of Peter. Eusebius (*Hist. Eccl.*, III, 4) and Saint Jerome (*De Vir. Ill.*, 7) allude to the belief that Saint Paul is always referring to Saint Luke's Gospel whenever he speaks of " my gospel." The similarity in language between the third gospel and the Acts on the one hand and Saint Paul's epistles on the other, is undeniable. Already in the first chapter of Saint Luke there are at least ten words peculiar to him and Saint Paul. Still more striking is their agreement on subject matter, such as the

---

[1] *Adv. Hær.*, III, i. 1–xiv. 1 (*ap.* Euseb., *Hist. Eccl.*, V, 10).

words of institution of the Holy Eucharist (*cf.* I Cor. xi. 24 and Luke xxii. 19), and the successive appearances of Christ (*cf.* I Cor. xv. and Luke xxiv. 34).

Saint Luke derived much information from Saint Paul, but, as he tells us in the introduction to his book, he also used other authorities, and he mentions those "who from the beginning were eyewitnesses and ministers of the word," i. e. our Lord's own disciples. We must think primarily of those who had also to do with Saint Paul, — Barnabas, formerly a follower of Christ,[1] Saint Peter, who must have made his acquaintance in Antioch; perhaps Saint John; certainly Saint James the Less, bishop of Jerusalem (Acts xxi. 18, etc.). The last named, who was closely related to our Lord, would be in a position to give Saint Luke the exact details concerning the childhood of Christ that are recorded in his gospel. Many think also that he knew Mary, our Lord's Mother. In fact Saint Luke says emphatically that Mary kept in her heart all the words and incidents connected with the childhood of Christ. As, however, Saint Luke says (i. 2) that he had recourse only to "eyewitnesses and ministers of the word," it seems likely that Saint James, having been instructed by Mary, was the source of his knowledge of these events.

19. READERS. DATE. PLACE OF COMPOSITION

Saint Luke dedicates his gospel (i. 3) and the Acts (i. 1), which is a continuation of it, to a certain Theophilus, to whom he gives the title κράτιστος. As is stated in the preface, Theophilus, after being orally instructed in the principles of Christianity, is to be still further established in them by this book, and is to recognize how trustworthy the doctrines are that have been imparted to him. For this end Luke has carefully inquired what he could ascertain about Jesus Christ.

We know nothing of Theophilus, and ancient writers could only suggest that he may have been a Gentile Christian, greatly respected and holding some high office, for this may be inferred

---

[1] Clem. Alex., *Strom.*, II, 20.

from the use of the word κράτιστος.[1] The book is certainly dedicated to him only as a mark of respect, and is intended for a wide circle of readers, as it aims at supplementing the already existing gospels (i. 1, etc.). Its readers were primarily those Christians to whom Saint Paul had preached, viz. both Jews and Gentiles in Achaia, Macedonia and Asia Minor. No gospel had yet been written for converts in this part of the world. Hence Saint Jerome says (*Ep. 20 ad Damasum*): "Luke, who of all the evangelists best understood the Greek language, being a physician, wrote the gospel for the Greeks." As the author (ii. 30, etc.) emphasizes the universality of salvation through the Messias, as Saint Paul was always accustomed to do, it appears that this gospel was not intended exclusively for the Greek-speaking nations, but for all Christians.

We may say with certainty that the date of composition is between 50 and 63. The book cannot have been written before 50, as it was only about this time that Saint Luke can have come into contact with Saint Paul. Neither the third gospel nor Acts can have been written after 63, as at the close of the latter book we read of Saint Paul's arrival in Rome as a prisoner, but nothing is said of his release, which, according to tradition, took place in 63. The author would not have passed over so important an event if he had known of it. We probably ought not to go back far beyond 63 in fixing the date. The years of the Apostolic journeys afforded but little leisure for the compilation of such a work, but the time of Saint Paul's imprisonment may well have been employed in this way. Possibly the work was arranged in Cæsarea and actually written in Rome, between the years 61 and 63.

According to Holtzmann (*Einl. i. d. N. T.*), 386, 405, the third gospel and the Acts were both written after the year 70: "for the author in his preface reveals himself as a man of a later generation, working on the basis of tradition, as *many* before him have written similar accounts." But it is precisely in the preface (i. 1) that Saint Luke de-

---

[1] Some suppose that the name Theophilus is altogether fictitious, like Saint Francis of Sales' Philothea. But the designation κράτιστος, i. e. reverend, mighty, is not in keeping with a merely fictitious personage; it is given chiefly to high officials (Acts xxiii. 26; xxiv. 3; xxvi. 25).

scribes himself as our Lord's contemporary ($\dot{\epsilon}\nu$ $\dot{\eta}\mu\hat{\iota}\nu$) and refers to his authorities as eyewitnesses ($a\dot{\upsilon}\tau\dot{\upsilon}\pi\tau a\iota$).[1]

From Acts xxviii. 14, 15 it appears that Theophilus lived in Rome; we read: "The brethren . . . came to meet us as far as Appii Forum and the Three Taverns." These words seem intended for readers in Rome, for these small places would be unknown to others.[2]

20. THE AUTHOR'S REASON FOR WRITING

In the preface (i. 1) Saint Luke intimates that the already existing gospels seem to him not fully to satisfy the desires of the new converts to Christianity, and therefore he has determined to supplement them. There were already several accounts extant of our Lord's life and works; we possess only two of them, — the gospels according to Saint Matthew and Saint Mark; the rest have perished, not having apostolic sanction and authority. There are indeed many omissions in the first two gospels; Saint Matthew tells us very little, and Saint Mark nothing at all, about the childhood of Christ. Both bring in Saint John the Baptist abruptly, having told their readers nothing of his origin and early history. In his intercourse with Christ's disciples Saint Luke learnt further details, and felt himself qualified to compose a fuller account of our Saviour and the history of the redemption. Theophilus and others may have requested him to do so. It was plain

[1] Other commentators (Hausrath, Keim, Clemen, Jülicher and Krenkel) agree with Holtzmann, and think that the books were not written until after 100 A.D., because they profess to detect a reference to Josephus Flavius, who wrote between 80 and 104. Belser has critically examined the alleged traces of reference to Josephus, but the result at which he arrives is that Josephus was acquainted with both Saint Luke's works, and intentionally omitted or distorted various things in them.

[2] Theophilus was certainly not a native of Palestine, for in mentioning Nazareth (i. 26) and Capharnaum (iv. 31) Saint Luke thinks it necessary to add that they are in Galilee, and he calls Arimathea (xxiii. 51) a town in Judea. He describes the position of the Mount of Olives and gives its distance from Jerusalem (Acts i. 12) and also states the distance of Emmaus (Luke xxiv. 13). Theophilus seems not to have been a Greek, as in that case the Athenians would hardly be mentioned as they are in Acts xvii. 12. The nearer the actors in the story come to Rome, the fewer are these descriptive touches.

that Saint Paul and his companions were able to give fuller information on many points, than could be found in the gospel of Saint Mark, already known in Rome.

21. THE SYNOPTIC WRITERS

The first three gospels resemble one another in a remarkable degree, whilst Saint John's stands quite apart. For this reason Matthew, Mark and Luke are called the Synoptic Evangelists.[1] The likeness between the three gospels appears (1) in the choice of the same subjects, (2) in similarity of language.

(1) With regard to their subject matter, the three evangelists confine themselves almost exclusively to our Lord's preaching in Galilee and to the history of His Passion. Their accounts and statements are parallel; what occurs in one gospel occurs also in the other two. Saint Luke's order often differs from that of Saint Matthew and Saint Mark, because he is more accurate in his chronology. Saint Mark has the fewest peculiarities. His gospel contains only twenty-seven verses that do not occur in either of the others.

(2) With regard to their style, it often happens that all the three synoptic writers, at least two of them, report an event or a discourse in the same way, so that their accounts agree almost word for word for several sentences in succession. This cannot be due to chance. It is no less striking, however, that often in the same account there are variations, additional circumstances being mentioned, or other motives assigned to the utterances reported.

Besides what has been said on page 381, *infra*, regarding the relation in which the three evangelists stand to one another, we may notice that all difficulties are not removed by the hypothesis that they used one another's writings. If Saint Matthew wrote down what he himself had taught, if Saint Mark recorded Saint Peter's doctrine and Saint Luke Saint Paul's, — we should expect considerable differences in the mode of statement, as the three apostles differed greatly in character, position and work. The similarity, however, is so great that it must have a deeper source than mere reference to one another's writings on the part of the apostles. Apparently they agreed amongst themselves how they would preach the gospel in conformity to the commission given them by Christ. Just as He associated mostly with the common people, so did the apostles everywhere address them first. A simple account of our Lord's teaching and works in Galilee was better suited for purposes of instruction than were His disputes with the Rabbis in Jerusalem, recorded later by Saint John. All who preached the faith, and consequently all the three evangelists, adhered to this first outline of apostolic doctrine, which was regarded almost as sacred and not to be tampered with. We can hardly decide whether this first form was kept in writing or orally; there is less difficulty in believing that it was oral.

---

[1] The name probably means "agreeing," but it is not well chosen. Συνοπτικός means otherwise "far-sighted," "comprehensive."

Saint Paul says (Gal. ii. 2) that about the year 51 he communicated the gospel, which he preached among the Gentiles, to the other apostles at Jerusalem, and they were satisfied with it. He does not say that it was written down. If the three evangelists derived their information from a common source, the similarity in their accounts is explained, and if the source was only oral, being less exact than if it had been written, this would explain also the differences in their forms of statement.

The existence of an *oral* primitive gospel, i. e. a form agreed upon by the apostles for preaching salvation, and serving as the foundation of the first three canonical gospels, is assumed by Kaulen, Cornely, Knabenbauer, Le Camus, Langen, Aberle-Schanz and Al. Schäfer. Belser, on the other hand, believes that there was a *written* primitive gospel, viz. the Hebrew original of Saint Matthew.

The Gospel According to Saint John

(21 chapters)

22. CONTENTS OF THE FOURTH GOSPEL

The synoptic writers lay most stress upon proving the God-Man, Jesus Christ, to be the Messias, but though the fourth gospel is also concerned with this topic, it is intended chiefly to teach the divinity of Christ (xx. 31).

Introduction. (i. 1–18) From all eternity the Logos has existed and has been active, but it was only in our time that He appeared on earth, clad in our human nature, but unhappily He found but few among His own people to believe in Him, although He made those who received Him children of God. An eyewitness (i. 14) intends to relate how He, being both God and Man, lived amongst men, and taught them.

Part I. (i. 19–xii.) Jesus of Nazareth revealed Himself in His public life as the Messias and Son of God.

1. (i. 19–iv.) His dignity was recognized by John the Baptist and many who believed in Him in Judea, Samaria and Galilee. (First miracle at Cana, purification of the Temple, Nicodemus, the Samaritan woman, the ruler's son.)

2. (v.–xi.) In spite of His miracles (healing of the lame man, feeding of the five thousand, discourse on the bread from heaven, teaching in the Temple, the woman taken in adultery,[1] the man born blind, the Good

---

[1] This section, vouched for by Saint Jerome, is omitted in the manuscripts B, ℵ, A, C, and in the Lewis Codex. There can be hardly any doubt that it was left out because, for reasons of discipline, it was not read in the churches. The object that the Pharisees had in view on this occasion was to throw discredit on our Lord, since they assumed that He would, as usual, give a merciful judgment, in which case they would be able to charge Him with violating the law of Moses (John viii. 6).

Shepherd, the raising of Lazarus) He was opposed by the sect of the Pharisees and they determined that He must die.

3. (xii.) In consequence of His solemn entry to Jerusalem as Messias, the Pharisees arranged to put a violent end to His activity.

Part II. (xiii.–xix.) He revealed Himself as Messias and Son of God also in His Passion and Death.

1. (xiii.–xvi.) The Last Supper and the last discourse to the disciples, whom He, as Son of God, comforted before His departure.

2. (xvii.) Christ's prayer for His own disciples.

3. (xviii., xix.) His Passion and Death.

Part III. (xx., xxi.) The Messias and Son of God revealed His dignity finally (1) in His glorious resurrection, (2) in His repeated appearances, during which He arranged for the forgiveness of sins and bestowed upon Saint Peter the office of chief pastor.

This evangelist writes with inimitable ardor, with the deepest inspiration. He betrays unspeakable joy that he, with others, was chosen to go about with the Son of God, and to be loved by Him even more than others. "The Word was made flesh and dwelt among us, and we saw his glory, the glory as it were of the only-begotten of the Father," etc.

23. SAINT JOHN THE APOSTLE

We have a fairly detailed knowledge of this apostle's life from the synoptic gospels and the Acts of the Apostles. John [1] was the son of Zebedee, a fisherman living near the Lake of Genesareth, and his wife Salome. He had a brother, who as an apostle is known as Saint James the Great. Their parents must have lived in comfortable circumstances (Mark i. 20; Luke viii. 3; Matt. xxvii. 56). At first John followed his father's calling, but when John the Baptist appeared he became his disciple, and was sent by his master to Jesus (John i. 35, etc.). After the first meeting near the Jordan he returned to Galilee with our Saviour, and resumed his occupation, but he and his brother were soon called by our Lord to be His constant companions. Saint John was our Lord's favorite disciple, and with Saint Peter and Saint James he received special marks of honor (Tabor, the Last Supper, Mount of Olives, Calvary). The Fathers tell us that his remarkable innocence was the reason for this preference. After Christ's Ascension he was one of the most energetic apostles (*cf.* Acts iii. and viii.). With Peter and James the Less he was regarded as a "pillar of the Church" (Gal. ii. 9).

[1] Hebrew *Jochanan* = the Lord is gracious (יוֹחָנָן).

He afterwards left Jerusalem, and we hear of him subsequently as bishop of Ephesus (Euseb., *Hist. Eccl.*, III, 20, 24), but he seems to have gone there after Paul and Timothy.[1] Towards the end of his life he was banished to the island of Patmos in the Ægæan Sea, as several of the Fathers state. Tertullian (*De præscr.*, 36), Saint Jerome and others say that he was first taken to Rome, and there dipped into a barrel of boiling oil, but was taken out uninjured. These events occurred in the reign of Domitian; Nerva, a more merciful ruler, allowed Saint John to return to Ephesus, and he died a natural death there in extreme old age, in the year 100.

24. AUTHENTICITY OF THE FOURTH GOSPEL

According to the tradition of the Church, Saint John is the author of the fourth canonical gospel, but, even more than in the case of the synoptic gospels, negative criticism has striven to disprove its authenticity. It is alleged [2] that the book cannot have been written before about 170, as it is not mentioned earlier, contains historical and geographical inaccuracies, pre-

[1] Papias (*apud* Euseb., *Hist.. Eccl.*, III, 39) speaks of a presbyter named John at Ephesus. He is probably identical with the apostle, who was then very old, for the writer of the second and third epistles of Saint John describes himself simply as ὁ πρεσβύτερος. See also A. Schäfer, 259. Most Catholic commentators identify them, e. g. Cornely, Knabenbauer, Felten, Poggel and Bludau, and so do many Protestants, such as Zahn, Olshausen, Hengstenberg.

[2] So Breitschneider and Strauss. They were followed by Baur, Zeller, Schwegler, all of them adherents of the Tübingen school, and many more recent critics, e. g. J. Réville, *Le quatrième évangile, son origine et sa valeur historique.* Paris, 1901. This writer denies all historical value to the fourth gospel, and believes it to be the work of a mind penetrated with Philo's speculation regarding the Logos. He thinks that John can hardly ever have worked in Asia Minor, and that the gospel is not in harmony with what we know from the New Testament of John, son of Zebedee, etc. In ancient times this gospel was rejected only by the Alogi = "Αλογόι, those who would not accept the Logos. The name, which originated with Epiphanius (*Hær.*, 51, 3), also means " unreasonable." The Alogi lived in the second century, and members of the sect existed in many parts of Asia Minor, especially in Phrygia. Their denial, however, actually serves as a testimony to the universal belief of Christians at that time, for they strove to show that the gospel could not be the work of John the Apostle.

sents us with long and subtle discourses that plainly cannot have been uttered by Christ, and in short consists of a Logos doctrine that was not developed before the second century.

In answer to these statements we may mention as:

(*a*) *Internal Evidence.* (1) The author generally explains Hebrew expressions and Jewish customs, e. g. x. 1–16, x. 22, 23; he was therefore a Jew by birth, writing for readers not living in Palestine. This would agree with Saint John's residence in Ephesus. (2) The author, from motives of humility, does not give his name anywhere, but describes himself as an eyewitness (i. 14, i. 35, etc.; xix. 35, xxi. 24) and as our Lord's beloved disciple (xiii. 23, xix. 26, xx. 2). These are undoubted references to Saint John.[1]

(*b*) *External Evidence.* (1) Quotations from this gospel or from the First Epistle of Saint John, which has always been connected with it, occur in Acts x. and in the works of Ignatius, Polycarp and Papias. (2) The epistle to Diognetus, written, according to chapter xi., by a disciple of the apostles, belonging probably to the first half of the second century as he speaks of Christianity as a new religion, contains expressions regarding the Logos that are similar to those in the fourth gospel. (3) In the same way Justin Martyr (*circa* 140, *supra*, p. 361), in his doctrine of the Logos, assumes a knowledge of the fourth gospel, and says that he bases his teaching concerning Jesus Christ, the Son of God, upon the "Memoirs of the Apostles, viz. the Gospels" (*Dial. c. Tryph.*, 105). In another place (*Apol.*, I, 61) he quotes from John iii. 5: "Unless a man be born again," etc. (4) The gnostic Basilides, writing about 120, refers to John i. 9: "the true light which enlighteneth every man," etc. (*Philosophumena*,

---

[1] The name John occurs twenty times in the fourth gospel, but each time the Baptist is meant; the apostle John and his brother James the Great are often mentioned in the synoptic gospels, but in this gospel never by name. The writer, however, declares himself to be a highly favored apostle; such were only Peter and the sons of Zebedee. Peter cannot have been the author, as he is expressly (xiii. 24, xxi. 21) distinguished from the Beloved Disciple, and it cannot have been James the Great, as the writer was (xxi. 23) very old, whereas James was the first of the apostles to be put to death, 42 A. D. (Acts xii. 2).

VII, 22). (5) Theophilus, bishop of Antioch (about 170–180), quotes (*Ad Autol.*, II, 22) the gospel bearing the name of John as a sacred book, long and universally recognized. " We are instructed by the sacred books and all the inspired writers, of whom John says, ' In the beginning was the Word,' " etc. (6) Irenæus, who lived almost at the same time,[1] whose master, Polycarp, was St. John's own disciple, gives evidence to the same effect, and says that Saint John wrote his gospel during his residence in Ephesus (*Adv. Hær.*, III, i. 1; II, xxii. 5; III, xi. 1).

(*c*) No one can deny that towards the close of the second century the fourth gospel was universally known in the Church, and ascribed to Saint John. This would be impossible, if it had been a recent forgery, for the various Christian communities and their rulers would certainly have resisted the introduction of a work not contained in previous texts, and particularly if it had not stood in the Latin and Syriac versions.

(*d*) It is easy by means of correct exegesis to remove the alleged historical and geographical inaccuracies.

In xi. 49 and xviii. 13 we read that Caiphas was high priest in that year; now Josephus Flavius says (*Antiq.*, XVIII, ii. 2) that Caiphas was high priest for a period of ten years. But in matters of chronology Josephus is known to be untrustworthy. Moreover the gospel does not state that Caiphas held office *only* for one year, but that he was high priest in *that* ever-memorable year.

Sychar (John iv. 5) is not a mistake for Sichem, but there was really a place of that name near Sichem; it is now called Askar. There may very well have been a Bethania beyond the Jordan (John i. 28),[2] besides the better known town of that name near Jerusalem; names compounded with Beth were very common. Saint John knew the Bethany near Jerusalem quite well, for he says it was fifteen furlongs distant from the capital (xi. 18).

(*e*) With regard to the often long and sublime discourses of our Lord, it is probable that Saint John wrote down many

[1] The value of this irrefutable witness is shown in a monograph written by Gutjahr (Graz, 1903) in reply to Harnack, Corssen and others. See also *Revue biblique*, 1898, I, 59; Corluy, *Comm. in ev. s. Joannis*, p. 4.

[2] The ruinous place called Betane (= Betonim in the tribe of Gad, Jos. xiii. 26) may be identified with this Bethania beyond the Jordan.

of His sermons and instructions at once. We can hardly imagine that he would not wish to communicate to his parents, friends and relatives many of the Messias' divine lessons, which he had heard with heartfelt enthusiasm. We must remember, too, that in performing his task as an apostle, Saint John was obliged frequently to repeat Christ's teaching — so that it remained fresh in his memory, and even as an old man he could still reproduce it correctly.

(*f*) The author designates our Saviour as the Logos. About the year 100 both Jews and Gentiles spoke much of the Word of God; and the doctrine of the Logos did not develop as late as the second or third century, but goes back to the first. As far as we know, our Saviour did not speak of Himself as Logos, but soon after the year 100 we find complete systems of a false Logos doctrine existing among the gnostics. The doctrine must have originated in the first century, and Saint John had reason enough to oppose the misuse of the word with the true doctrine of the Logos. He found the name in use not only among his opponents, but also in the Old Testament, where there is frequent allusion to the Word of God as to a person (e. g. Ps. xxxii. 6; Prov. viii. ix.; Wisdom ix. 1, xviii. 15; *cf.* I Cor. viii. 6; Phil. ii. 6, etc.; Col. i. 15; Apoc. xix. 13).[1]

Many recent non-Catholic writers acknowledge now that the fourth gospel was written not later than 110 (see *supra*, p. 361). Jülicher thinks it was not written by Saint John, but as to its date he merely says it cannot be earlier than 100. Zahn, on the contrary, declares himself in favor of the old eclesiastical tradition. Resch thinks it was written soon after 70 A. D., Wuttig about 62, H. Gebhardt soon after 60, and Rutgers, a Dutch scholar, assigns it even to the year 34. Küppers is of opinion that John wrote soon after 44, Luke between 53 and 57, Matthew about 60 and Mark soon after 64.[2]

---

[1] John was able therefore to explain thus to the Gentiles by birth: " What the Alexandrian Greek philosophers imagined about the Logos, we Christians understand far better; it is the divine messenger, long promised and now become fl sh, that we call with perfect right the Logos, because He has spoken to men at all times as God, and now also as Man."

[2] If no attention were paid to tradition we might believe the fourth gospel to be older than the synoptics, as a good deal of internal evidence would seem to justify this view, e. g. chapters ix. and xi.

25. Time and Place of Composition

It is unanimously agreed by early Christian writers that Saint John was the last of the evangelists to write his gospel, and this is borne out by internal evidence. (1) In xxi. 18 there is a reference to Saint Peter's crucifixion, hence the year 67 was over. (2) In speaking of places in or near Jerusalem, the apostle always uses the past tense, $\mathring{\eta}\nu$ (xi. 18, xviii. 1, xix. 41), hence Jerusalem must have been destroyed before the gospel was written. (3) At the end of the book (xxi. 23) there is an allusion to the belief among the Christians that Saint John was not to die. Such an idea could have arisen only after most or all of the other apostles were dead, and when Saint John himself was very old. (4) The party hostile to Christ is always designated οἱ Ἰουδαῖοι; at the time, therefore, when the book was written, Gentile Christians were in the majority, and Jews were scarcely known in the Church except as adversaries. (5) The whole arrangement of the book points to the existence of the other gospels (see below). (6) The author's style savors of Hebrew, and shows that he was a Jew by birth, but the Greek is purer than that of the Apocalypse. He must therefore have written his gospel later than the Apocalypse, having in the interval improved his knowledge of Greek through his intercourse with Greek-speaking Christians. As Saint John (according to Apoc. i. 9, etc.) received and wrote the Apocalypse on the island of Patmos, during the reign of Domitian, we may take the year 100 as the approximate date of his writing the gospel. We know from Irenæus that it was composed at Ephesus.[1]

26. Object and Motive

We may take it for certain that Saint John assumed in his readers an acquaintance with the other gospels (i. 15, 32, iii. 24, xviii. 33, etc.). He mentions very briefly what the synoptic

---

[1] Iren.: καὶ αὐτὸς ἐξέδωκε τὸ εὐαγγέλιον ἐν Ἐφέσῳ τῆς Ἀσίας διατρίβων (see *supra*, p. 395, (*b*), (6)).

writers have already recorded, and then adds some fresh information to their accounts. Hence we are often told that his object was to supplement the other gospels, and this no doubt was part of what he intended to do; but he tells us himself (xx. 30 and 31, xxi. 25) quite plainly what his main object was. " Many other signs also did Jesus in the sight of his disciples, which are not written in this book." If any man were to write in detail all that the Infinite One has done, "the world itself would not be able to contain the books that should be written." Therefore a selection has been made, and only " these are written, that you may believe that Jesus is the Christ, the Son of God, and that believing you may have life in His name."

John felt himself impelled to give this testimony, written with great enthusiasm, to the divinity of Christ and to bequeath it to the Church, as already some were beginning to deny His divinity, among whom Irenæus mentions particularly Cerinthus,[1] and also because it was easy to foresee that others would follow their example.

The immediate impulse prompting Saint John to write was a request addressed to him by many bishops and communities,[2] who begged him to supplement the corporal gospels with a spiritual gospel, i. e. to record his own memories of our Lord in a special work, in which His divinity should be more conspicuous than in the first three gospels.

The historical character of this gospel is denied by many commentators. Some assert that the author was influenced by Philo, and was an idealist, not a genuine historian. However, the fact that he supplements the synoptic writers shows that he paid attention to history, and the discourse that he records (chapter vi.) on the Holy Eucharist is a very suitable introduction to what they tell us concerning its institution. He often gives details of time and circumstance in connection with events, as only an eyewitness could do. No one could describe the incidents of our Lord's Passion so accurately as Saint John, who never left Him even in His sufferings; and therefore he gives minute information regarding Annas, Pilate and the Crucifixion (cf. Knabenbauer in Stimmen aus Maria-Laach, 1904, 361, in answer to Loisy and others. Also the replies given by the Papal Biblical Commission of May 29, 1907).

---

[1] Adv. Hær., I, 26; III, 11.
[2] Frag. Mur.; Clem. Alex., ap. Eus., Hist. Eccl., VI, 14; Hier.

"God, who at sundry times and in divers manners spoke in times past to the fathers by the prophets, last of all in these days hath spoken to us by his Son, whom he hath appointed heir of all things, by whom also he made the world." Heb. i. 1.

The gospels tell us of this last and highest revelation; they are the written reproductions of the oral teaching given by the apostles in fulfillment of their commission to go into the whole world and preach the gospel to every creature (Mark xvi. 15). These four books are the crown of all the inspired writings, and if we may still further discriminate among these divine disclosures, the gospel of Saint John is the chief jewel in this crown, as the Muratorian Fragment suggests, for the writer believes the fourth gospel to be the outcome of a particular revelation.

The gospels contain the teaching that conquered Rome, the capital of the world, Italy and Greece, and soon the whole known world. They are of interest to the antiquarian, who may learn from them how religious subjects were discussed in the times of the first emperors, and by what means paganism was overthrown; they are of interest to the historian, more important than all the excavations at Troy or in Egypt, Assyria and Babylonia, more important even than all the Greek and Latin classics; for Plato and Cicero never induced the inhabitants of a single village to live in accordance with their doctrines, but the gospel has transformed mankind. In the highest degree they are of interest, or rather they are objects of veneration, to the Christian. The gospel is truly a "power of God" (Rom. i. 16), subduing everything to itself, and penetrating the souls of men like a two-edged sword,[1] for it is the word of God in the highest sense. This is why we stand when the gospel is read; this is why candles and incense are brought, for we are dealing with a most high and divine announcement.

How great and joyful a thing it is that the Church has handed down to us the word of God, God's message to men for their salvation in time and in eternity! Can there be any more noble and more honorable occupation than to read and study Holy Scripture in general, and particularly the teaching of Christ, as imparted to us in the gospels! But just as even in Paradise God's words were misinterpreted, so can it be with the written word of God, and therefore it is of the greatest importance to follow with regard to it the rules laid down by the Church, for Holy Scripture is her property (*cf. infra*, p. 458).

B. THE ACTS OF THE APOSTLES
(28 chapters)

27. CONTENTS

The Acts of the Apostles (πράξεις ἀποστόλων, *actus apostolo-rum*) in its *first part* (chapters i.–vii.) deals with the early

---

[1] Heb. iv. 12. "The word of God is living and effectual, and more piercing than any two-edged sword."

history of the Church of Christ and its propagation amongst
the Jews. Most of the incidents recorded took place at Jerusalem. The *second part* (viii.–xii.) describes the extension of
the Church from the Jews to the Gentiles, and Antioch becomes the chief center of activity in the Church. In both these
parts Saint Peter is the chief actor. The *third part*, which is
the longest (xiii.–xxviii.), contains the early history of the
Church amongst the Gentiles; the work of Saint Paul occupies
most of this part, and the center of activity is Rome. Hardly
any other book has come down to us from ancient times that
gives so vivid a picture of the state of the Græco-Roman world
in the time of the apostles.[1]

Part I. i. Ascension of Christ. Choice of Matthias. ii. Descent of
the Holy Ghost at Pentecost. Peter's discourse. iii. The man born lame.
iv. Arrest of Peter and John. Community of property among the Christians. v. Ananias and Saphira. Gamaliel. vi., vii. Stephen.

Part II. viii. Persecution. Conversion of Samaria. Philip and the
eunuch. ix. Conversion of Saul. Peter at Lydda and Joppe. x. Cornelius. xi. The church at Antioch. xii. Peter in prison at Jerusalem,
his miraculous delivery, his departure.

Part III. xiii., xiv. Journey of Paul and Barnabas to Cyprus and Asia
Minor. xv. Council of the apostles. Paul's second missionary journey.
xvi. His activity in Asia Minor and Macedonia. xvii., xviii. Paul in
Athens and Corinth. His third missionary journey. xix. Paul in Ephesus. xx. His journey to Macedonia and Achaia. His return. He takes
leave of the elders from Ephesus at Miletus. xxi.–xxiii. Journey to
Jerusalem. He is taken prisoner and sent to Cæsarea. xxiv.–xxvi. Imprisonment at Cæsarea. Felix and Festus. Agrippa. xxvii. Journey to
Rome. Shipwreck at Malta. xxviii. Arrival in Rome.

Data for the chronology of this book are supplied by II Cor. xi. 32,
and by Josephus Flavius (*Antiq.*, XVIII, 5), who says that King Aretas,
an Arabian prince, made war upon his son-in-law, Herod Antipas, towards
the end of the reign of Tiberius, because Herod had divorced his daughter. Herod appealed to Rome for assistance, which was granted. It was

---

[1] Fr. Blass in 1895 edited the Acts, with a short commentary, and in
1896 he brought out a text edition of it, according to Codex D (see
p. 230). He is of opinion that Saint Luke compiled two versions of the
Acts of the Apostles, a fuller one for the Christians in Rome, and a
shorter one especially for Theophilus. The former is preserved in Codex
D, the latter in our traditional text. In the main Belser agrees with
Blass, but other commentators oppose this theory, e. g. Kaulen and Harnack. W. Ernst tried to show that the Codices B and א are themselves
secondary, but still stand nearest to the original text of Saint Luke (also
with regard to the gospel).

during this war, probably in the year 37, that the governor appointed by Aretas was in command at Damascus, and tried to seize Saint Paul, so that he was obliged to escape secretly. Saint Paul's conversion took place three years before this event, viz. in 34, and the Council of the Apostles was held fourteen years after it, viz. in 51 (Gal. i. 18; ii. 1). Saint Paul's first missionary journey was made before the Council, perhaps in 46–49; the second immediately after the Council, probably 52–55, and the third lasted from 56 to 59. Then the apostle was kept in prison at Cæsarea for two years (59–61), and in Rome for another two years (62 and 63). The book ends at this point.

Harnack gives different figures, because he thinks Saint Paul was converted as early as the year 30.

Weber gives the date of his conversion as 32. It is well known that there is some uncertainty about the chronology of our Lord's life. According to the chronology of Dionysius, Christ was born in the year 754 after the building of Rome. But now commentators are generally agreed in fixing an earlier date; 748 seems to be the safest; and then our Lord's death occurred in 782. (*Cf.* Cornely, *Synopses Script. Sacr.*, pp. 337 and 365.)

28. AUTHOR. AUTHENTICITY

The author of the Acts of the Apostles does not mention himself by name, but gives indications by means of which he may be identified.

1. At the beginning of the book (i. 1) he says that he has already written a treatise concerning what Jesus said and did; in other words, he had written a gospel. We have therefore a choice of four men.

2. He often expressly speaks of himself as Saint Paul's assistant and companion. Of the four evangelists this description applies to Saint Luke alone. It is true that Saint Mark came in contact with Saint Paul, but the author of the Acts says that he accompanied him first on his second missionary journey, which Saint Mark did not make on account of the differences that had arisen between them.

3. The style of the book and the dedication to Theophilus also suggest the third gospel. The book of Acts is therefore the second part of Saint Luke's historical work. He himself (i. 1) calls his gospel the " first book."

The Acts of the Apostles was read in the churches less frequently than the gospels, hence it was separated from the " first book " and put with the epistles. This explains the regret, expressed by Saint John Chrysostom, that many Christians in his day did not know the book (*Hom.*, I, 1, *in Acta Apost.*).

Being less used than the gospels, allusions to and quotations from it are not of frequent occurrence, but it is quite certain that the Apostolic Fathers were well acquainted with it. Polycarp (*Ep. ad Philad.*, c. 1) quotes Acts ii. 24: "whom God hath raised up, having loosed the sorrows of hell." Ignatius (*Ad Smyrn.*, c. 3) quotes Acts x. 41. In the *Didache* (ed. Schlecht, VI, 2) the word ζυγὸν is used of God's law, as it is in Acts xv. 10. Other references to Acts occur in the *Didache* (IX, 2 and 3, X, 6. The book is mentioned by name in the *Fragm. Murat.*, by Irenæus (*Adv. Hær.*, III, xiv. 1), Clement of Alexandria (*Strom.*, V, 12), Origen (*c. Cels.*, VI, 11), and Tertullian (*De Jejun.*, c. 10).

Rationalistic commentators challenge the authenticity of the work, chiefly because they arbitrarily assume it to be the outcome of a dispute between Jewish and Gentile Christians, and intended to reconcile the Jews, who adhered to Saint Peter, and the Gentiles, who relied upon Saint Paul. The writer, having this intention, falsified the early history of the Church by representing it in such a way that the gulf separating the two parties should seem to be bridged over, and unity restored. This could not have been done by a disciple and contemporary of Saint Paul, but a later author must have composed the book. But if such had been the writer's intention, he would not have allowed the obstinacy of the Jews to be so conspicuous as it is throughout the work. The real object with which the book was written is stated plainly in Acts i. 8. It is to show how our Lord's words were fulfilled; "You [apostles] shall receive the power of the Holy Ghost coming upon you, and you shall be witnesses unto me in Jerusalem, and in all Judea, and Samaria, and even to the uttermost part of the earth."

29. READERS

Like the third gospel, this book also is dedicated by Saint Luke to Theophilus, who, as we have seen, must have been a man of high position in Rome. But this Christian was not intended to be the only reader, for at the beginning of the gospel Saint Luke shows plainly that he meant to supplement the existing gospels, and so he must have had a wide circle of readers in view. We may believe that he wrote the Acts, as he did the gospel, primarily for the communities of Greek-speaking Christians, amongst whom he had labored with Saint Paul, and then for the whole Church.

30. Sources of Information

At least a third of the incidents related in the book were matters of personal experience to Saint Luke. In describing other things he had to rely upon the accounts given by others. The same men who supplied him with information for the gospel, furnished him with it for the Acts of the Apostles. He refers to them as eyewitnesses and ministers of the Word, so they were our Lord's apostles and disciples, especially Saint Peter and Saint James the Less; perhaps Saint John, and certainly Saint Barnabas. On some points he must have used written documents, particularly for Saint Stephen's discourse (chapter vii.) and the speeches at the Apostolic Council (xv.). Of course he derived a great deal of information from Saint Paul. Some few speeches, such as Saint Paul's farewell discourse (xx. 18–35), he seems to have written down when they were uttered.

31. Time and Place of Composition

The Acts must have been written whilst Saint Peter was still alive. His abode is not specified, as to do so might involve him in danger. Where we read of his delivery from the power of Herod Agrippa, we are only told that "he went into another place" (xii. 17). The date of the book is therefore before 67, and the conclusion of it gives us another indication of time. The writer leaves his readers in uncertainty as to the result of Saint Paul's trial in Rome. He mentions their arrival there, but says nothing about either an acquittal or a condemnation. It is only from tradition that we know that Saint Paul regained his liberty after being in prison for two years in Rome.[1] We must conclude, therefore, that Saint Paul was still in prison when the book was finished, for otherwise

---

[1] This view is generally accepted.

Saint Luke, who reports everything with accuracy and in detail, would not have omitted to inform his readers of his sentence. We have therefore reason to believe that the Acts of the Apostles was written in Rome between the years 61 and 63, whilst Saint Luke was encouraging Saint Paul in his captivity (Col. iv. 14). This was the opinion formed by Saint Jerome (*De Viris Illustr.*, c. 7).

SECOND SECTION

DIDACTIC BOOKS OF THE NEW TESTAMENT

SAINT PAUL'S EPISTLES

32. SAINT PAUL THE APOSTLE

1. Paul, or, as he was called before his missionary journeys, Saul,[1] was by birth a Jew of the tribe of Benjamin. His birthplace was the city of Tarsus in Cilicia. His parents brought him up according to strictly orthodox principles (Acts xxiii. 6), and it was probably whilst he was still at home that he learnt the business of weaving tent-covers, by which he generally had to support himself on his apostolic journeys. It was a matter of principle among the Pharisees that every man should have his son taught a trade. His parents must have occupied a good position and have been well-to-do, for their son from his birth enjoyed full Roman citizenship and was sent to complete his education at Jerusalem,[2] where he was attached to the school of Gamaliel, a famous teacher of the law, and acquired rabbinical learning and that strict conformity to Jewish customs which was regarded as a special ornament to a zealous Israelite. He must have received some instruction

---

[1] Saul: Sha'úl. This Jewish name was unfamiliar to Greeks and Romans, but Paulus, resembling it in sound, was in frequent use. Perhaps the apostle adopted the latter name as a token of respect to the Roman proconsul Sergius Paulus (Acts xiii. 7), and perhaps also from motives of humility. Παῦλος, paulus = παῦρος = insignificant, little.

[2] From Acts xxiii. 16 it appears that Saint Paul had a married sister in Jerusalem, as her son assisted him when he was in prison.

in the literature of western nations, probably before he left
Tarsus, for he shows in his writings that he was familiar with
Greek authors (Acts xvii. 28; Titus i. 12; I Cor. xv. 33).

2. Being an ardent enthusiast for the Jewish law, young
Saul took part in stoning Saint Stephen, and it is not improbable that he wrote down Saint Stephen's discourse, which
Saint Luke gives very fully in Acts vii., with a view to using
it in further persecutions of the Christians. Saint Stephen's
last prayer may have won for him the grace of conversion,
although for a time his hatred of the followers of the Crucified
seemed intensified (Acts viii. 3, xxii. 4). Not contented with
persecuting them in Jerusalem, he sought and obtained from
the Synedrium letters authorizing him to seize all the disciples
of Christ who were in Damascus, and bring them as prisoners
to Jerusalem. Not far from Damascus he had a vision of our
Lord, which agitated him to a terrible degree and changed
him from an enemy to a most zealous champion of Christianity
(Acts ix., also xxii. 6; xxvi. 13, etc.).

3. He was baptized in Damascus, and at once began to
proclaim Christ as the Messias and as divine. Then for a time
he withdrew to Arabia (Gal. i. 17),[1] probably that by prayer
and penance he might prepare himself for a wider sphere of
action. He returned to Damascus and continued his work,
promoting Christianity with the greatest zeal, so that the Jews,
in their indignation, tried to seize him, and he had to flee
at the risk of his life (Acts ix. 23). He went at first to
Jerusalem in order to make acquaintance with Saint Peter.
This was three years after his conversion, probably in the year
37 (Gal. i. 18). Being persecuted here also by the Jews, and
having received special signs from Christ (Acts xxii. 18), he
went to Tarsus, his native city, and remained there some years
(Gal. i. 21). About this time the first community of Gentile
Christians was formed in Antioch, Barnabas being its ruler,

---

[1] It has been proposed to read "Αραβα in this passage, instead of
'Αραβία. "Αραβα (ערבה) was a place in Galilee, but, being so obscure,
it would have required some further designation. We might perhaps
read ἐρημίαν (araba = solitude). There was actually a place called Beth-
Araba in the neighborhood of the Dead Sea (Jos. xv. 6).

but as he alone could not accomplish all that had to be done, he summoned Saul from Tarsus to be his assistant, perhaps in the year 42. After both had received their ordination as apostles (Acts xiii. 2), they proceeded, like the others, on missionary journeys for the purpose of preaching the gospel.

33. Continuation. First and Second Missionary Journeys of Saint Paul

Saint Paul's three missionary journeys, recorded in the Acts of the Apostles, began at Antioch.

4. The *first journey* (Acts xiii., xiv.) was the shortest. It took place in the years 46–49. With Barnabas and his young nephew, Mark, the apostle traveled first to Seleucia and thence to Cyprus. They crossed the island from east to west, preaching the gospel everywhere. Then they sailed to Asia Minor. Mark left them at Perge in Pamphylia and went to Jerusalem, whilst Paul and Barnabas visited the interior of the country (Antioch in Pisidia, Iconium, Lystra and Derbe in Lycaonia), founding communities of Christians. Then they took ship at Attalia and returned to Antioch, where the Christians were at that time in great excitement regarding the question whether Gentile Christians were bound to keep the Jewish law. On account of this dispute both Paul and Barnabas attended the Council of the Apostles at Jerusalem (Acts xv.), where it was decided that the Gentiles were free from the Mosaic Law, but were to refrain from all participation in heathen worship (e. g. from sacrificial feasts), from incest (marriage between near relatives) and from blood, which included anything strangled. These regulations were made chiefly for the sake of the Jews, to facilitate their entrance into the Church. After the Council, the two apostles returned to Antioch.

5. *Second missionary journey.* Not long afterwards, perhaps in the year 52, Saint Paul undertook another journey (see Acts xv. 36, etc.). Barnabas and Mark again proposed to accompany him, but Saint Paul refused to take Mark with him and they separated, though they did not cherish any resentment against one another, for later on we find Mark with Saint Paul in Rome (Col. iv. 10). Barnabas determined to go with Mark to visit the communities in Cyprus, whilst Saint Paul went to Asia Minor with Silas (Silvanus) whom he had summoned from Jerusalem. They traveled on foot through Syria and Cilicia, then through Pisidia, Lycaonia, where they were joined by Timothy, Phrygia, Galatia and Mysia. At Troas in Mysia, where Saint Luke became one of the apostle's companions,[1] he had in a dream a vision of a Macedonian, imploring help. Taking this as an indication of God's will

---

[1] From this point onwards in Acts we read: "*we* traveled."

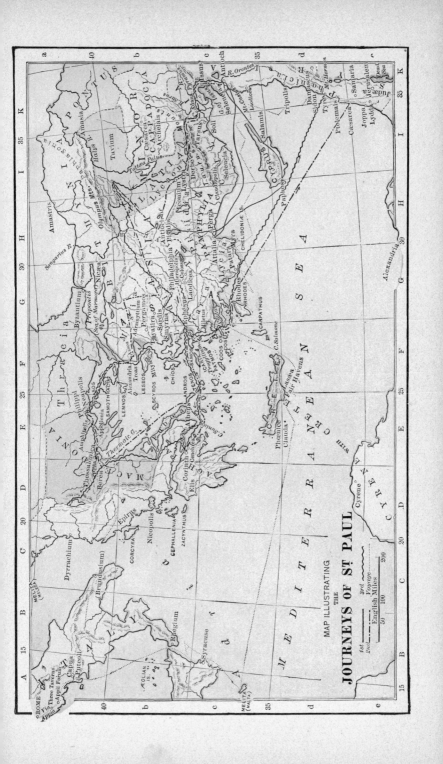

MAP ILLUSTRATING
THE
JOURNEYS OF ST. PAUL

1st ———
2nd -------- Voyage
3rd ....

English Miles
50   100   200

that he should go still farther west, and first to Macedonia to preach the gospel, he at once set out on the way.

6. The city of Philippi was the first place in Europe where he began to preach. He succeeded in establishing a Christian community there, which remained devoted to him, showing him much love and loyalty. From Rome he subsequently addressed a letter of consolation, that we still possess, to this community. Saint Luke seems to have remained in Philippi until he rejoined Saint Paul on his third journey at this point, as it is only in Acts xx. 6 that he resumes the use of the first person plural in his account. St. Paul was forced to leave Philippi after suffering scourging and imprisonment, and Thessalonica was the next scene of his apostolic labors. He could stay here only a short time, as the Jews raised a disturbance, and he had to flee from the city. The two letters written soon afterwards from Corinth to the Thessalonians, prove, however, that he had worked in Thessalonica with success, and that the community there was deficient in instruction but not in firmness of faith. He had a similar experience in Berea, a neighboring town; there was again an uproar among the Jews, and he had to take flight. Then having left Silas and Timothy behind, that they might continue to work in Macedonia, a not unfavorable field for missionary enterprise, he himself went southwards to Athens, where very few would hear him, and on to Corinth, then the capital of Greece. Here he succeeded in establishing a numerous community, consisting chiefly of Gentile Christians, and he stayed with them for a year and a half. It was at Corinth that he learnt to know Aquila and his wife Priscilla, Jewish Christians, who had been driven away from Rome, and they were of great service to him in his apostolic work. Silas and Timothy rejoined him in Corinth. He seems to have gone on one occasion to Illyria from Corinth, as in Rom. xv. 19 he says that he has preached the gospel as far as Illyria, and in 2 Cor. xii. 14 and xiii. 1, he says that before writing that epistle he had already been twice in Corinth. The journey to Illyria is not mentioned in the Acts, and no more suitable date for it can be found. Saint Paul was finally obliged to quit Corinth, on account of a tumult stirred up by the Jews, and he returned to the East. He first visited Ephesus, but did not stay there long, though he left Aquila and Priscilla there and promised to return at a later time. He sailed to Cæsarea in Palestine and went thence (most probably) to Jerusalem in order to fulfill a vow that he had made (Acts xviii. 18, etc.). In the year 55 he revisited Antioch. In the meantime Apollos, an Alexandrian Jew by birth, who had received only the baptism of John, had appeared in Ephesus, preaching Christ as the Messias. Having been more accurately instructed in Christianity by Aquila and Priscilla, he too went to Corinth, and by means of his ardent zeal and great eloquence he won extraordinary popularity, so that many of the Corinthians esteemed him even more highly than Saint Paul (1 Cor. iii. 4, etc.).

34. CONTINUATION. SAINT PAUL'S THIRD MISSIONARY JOURNEY. HIS IMPRISONMENT [1]

7. After some time Saint Paul again traveled through Asia Minor, revisiting especially the communities of Christians in Galatia and Phrygia, and encouraging new converts. Then, as he had promised, he went to Ephesus, and remained there nearly three years. The gospel made such progress in and near Ephesus that the heathen worship suffered in consequence, and the pilgrimages to the Temple of Artemis diminished. This caused Demetrius the silversmith, who maintained himself and a large number of workmen by making little representations of the Temple of Diana, to stir up a tumult against Saint Paul, who was obliged therefore to leave Ephesus.

8. He traveled first to Macedonia, then to Achaia, where he stayed three months (Acts xx. 3), and he undoubtedly visited Corinth. On his return to Macedonia he was rejoined by Saint Luke. He had for a long time been wishing to go once more to Jerusalem and then to Rome (Acts xix. 21). His plan was carried out, but not in the way he had intended. He began his journey by sailing to Troas and going thence on foot to Assus. He went on with his companions by way of Mitylene, Chios and Samos to Miletus, where the elders of the church at Ephesus met him, and he took a touching farewell of them (Acts xx. 17–38). Sailing on, they passed Cyprus on the left, and landed at Tyre, and thence, in spite of all the warnings given by the Christians, Saint Paul went on to Jerusalem. Although he was as cautious as circumstances allowed, he was recognized on the eighth day by some Jews from Asia Minor, and was only saved from the violence and fury of the Jews by the prompt interference of the Roman watchmen. As his life was not safe even in prison (*supra*, p. 404, note 2) he was conveyed by a strong escort of soldiers to Cæsarea, and given into the charge of Felix, the procurator, who kept him in an easy kind of captivity, but did not release him, hoping for a large ransom from the Christians. Two years later Felix transferred the prisoner to his successor Festus.

9. Festus showed some inclination to give the apostle up to the Jewish Synedrium, and Saint Paul, perceiving this, and knowing what cruel vengeance he would have to expect, used his rights as a Roman citizen, and appealed to the emperor (Acts xxv. 9). The result of this action was that his case had to be transferred to Rome, and he had to be taken thither as a prisoner. This was in the autumn of the year 61. His companions were Saint Luke and Aristarchus, a Macedonian. After a long and stormy voyage, the ship was wrecked on the coast of Malta, but all on board were saved. They had to pass the winter in Malta, and were only able to continue their journey in the spring of 62. They landed at Puteoli, and proceeded on foot to Rome.

10. Saint Paul's imprisonment in Rome was comparatively easy; he was allowed to go out, and found opportunities of spreading the gospel.[2]

---

[1] Acts xix. 1, etc.

[2] "He remained two whole years in his own hired lodging, and he received all that came in to him, preaching the kingdom of God, and

At this point the account of Saint Paul given in the Acts of the Apostles ends abruptly. Tradition, however, tells us that after two years he was acquitted, and then undertook a fourth journey, first to Spain, which he had long intended to visit (Rom. xv. 24, 28), then again to the East, and afterwards to Rome, where he was imprisoned again, and in the year 67 on June 29, at the same time as Saint Peter, he suffered martyrdom, dying by the sword as befitted his Roman citizenship.

We know nothing with certainty as to Saint Paul's age. At the time of Saint Stephen's death by stoning, he was (Acts vii. 57) still a young man, certainly under thirty, as he was not allowed to take part in the actual stoning, for a man under thirty could not perform any public action. Saint Stephen's death may be assigned to the year 34; soon after it Paul was employed by the Synedrium and sent to Damascus, so he must then have attained the age of thirty. He was converted on his way, and for about thirty-three years he worked as a Christian and as an apostle, so that it was at the age of sixty-three that he ended his life, witnessing to the faith with his blood.[1]

35. CHARACTER OF SAINT PAUL AS A MAN AND AS A WRITER

1. In outward appearance Saint Paul was, according to all ancient accounts, very insignificant;[2] and he tells us this himself in II Corinthians x. 10. The external gifts of a rhetorician seem to have been denied him, such as a clear, strong voice, a bright and lively glance, assurance and resolution. The absence of these gifts explains why Apollos, being a fluent speaker, won more favor than Saint Paul in many quarters in Corinth.

teaching the things which concern the Lord Jesus Christ with all confidence, without prohibition " (Acts xxviii. 30, 31).

[1] Reithmayr denies that the apostle was ever released, and that he made a fourth journey. Kaulen, Spitta, oppose this view. Eusebius (*Hist. Eccl.*, II, 22) and Saint Jerome (*De Viris Illustr.*, c. 5, *Comm. in Amos*, V, 8) state definitely that he did regain his freedom. Saint Clement of Rome (*Ep.*, I, c. 5) says that Saint Paul went to the limits of the West. In the Muratorian Fragment, where the Acts of the Apostles is mentioned, there is an allusion to a journey of St. Paul *ab urbe ad Spaniam proficiscentis*. It is probable that Saint Paul did not stay long in Spain, and traveled thence to Crete, where he left Titus, and then to Ephesus, where he left Timothy. He visited various communities in the interior of Asia Minor, went by way of Miletus (2 Tim. iv. 20) to Macedonia and Achaia, then to Nicopolis in Epirus, whither Titus was to follow him (Titus iii. 12), and finally back to Rome.

[2] Niceph., *Hist. Eccl.*, II, 37 (Migne, *Patres Gr.*, 145–147).

Moreover Saint Paul purposely avoided trying to please by means of human artifices and especially by rhetorical tricks of speech, for he did not wish the glory to be his, but God's, and he was unwilling that any one should ascribe his success to his own human exertions.[1] He was content to be the humble instrument of the Holy Ghost. Like Jonas after his wonderful rescue, he was always anxious when preaching, and feared lest he should fail in his task and be rejected because of his former sins (I Cor. ix. 16, etc., and 27). Our Saviour had commissioned him, in compensation for the injury he had done the Church, to spread the gospel among the Gentiles, and this duty he fulfilled more abundantly than all the other apostles (I Cor. xv. 10), for he not only attained greater success, but incurred more trouble and suffering.[2] Amidst it all he showed himself so absolutely unselfish that in spite of all the pressure of his apostolic work and the care for so many churches, he nevertheless earned his own living by his trade, and was a burden to no one. He regarded his labors merely as reparation for his former faults, and he expected a reward only because he worked "without charge" (Acts xx. 34; I Cor. ix. 18).

2. Saint Paul wrote no special instructions on matters of faith and morals intended for Christians in general, nor did he compose any strictly historical works, unless we ascribe the third gospel and the Acts of the Apostles to him. We have, however, written remains of his work, for his zeal impelled him to do what he could to serve the faithful with his written words where he could not be with them in person.[3] We possess fourteen epistles by him, of various lengths. Although most of them are occasional pamphlets, they are priceless jewels from the rich treasury of his divinely gifted intellect. In them Saint

---

[1] I Cor. ii. 1–4; II Cor. x. 10: "For his epistles indeed, say they, are weighty and strong, but his bodily presence is weak and his speech contemptible."

[2] In II Cor. xi., being suspected, he is compelled to speak of his labors and sufferings, and what he tells us of them in that passage is certainly not all.

[3] Other apostles did the same, and so did the Fathers of the Church, and our bishops still continue the practice.

Paul shows himself a master of the art of bringing conviction home to the understanding, of touching the heart and of rousing the will. The zeal of this man, amidst his manifold occupations, the vigor and fullness of his thoughts, the ardor of his heroic faith are so great that the reader is often unable to follow his thought, and so many passages remain obscure, a fact that already Saint Peter regretted (II Peter iii. 16). The topics that he deals with most frequently are Christ and His relation to the world, the reconciliation of mankind with God through Christ's Blood, salvation at the day of judgment, possible to all through submission to Christ, and the advantages of the new covenant in comparison with the old, that is now at an end.

36. Sequence of Saint Paul's Epistles

Saint Paul's epistles were generally read at public worship in the communities to which they were addressed, and collections of them were made at a very early date. The first trace of a collection is in II Peter iii. 15. By the middle of the second century the heretic Marcion reckoned that there were ten epistles, for he omitted the pastoral letters and the epistle to the Hebrews. Most of the Fathers of the Church recognized thirteen as by Saint Paul, for they ascribed Hebrews to another author. The collection in our Canon is arranged with reference not to the date of origin but to the importance of the churches to which the epistles were addressed. If they are put in chronological order they stand thus:

(1), (2) and (3). The two epistles to the Thessalonians and the epistle to the Galatians were written during Saint Paul's first residence in Corinth, about the year 53, so they belong to his first missionary journey. Three epistles belong to his third journey; viz. (4) the first epistle to the Corinthians was written at Ephesus in 58; (5) the second to the Corinthians from Macedonia, also in 58, and (6) the epistle to the Romans during the apostle's second visit to Corinth, probably in 59.

Saint Paul wrote four epistles whilst he was a prisoner in Rome for the first time; viz. (7) the epistle to the Philippians, about 62, and in 63 those to (8) the Ephesians, (9) the Colossians and (10) Philemon. (11) The epistle to the Hebrews is generally believed to have been written in Italy in 63 or 64, after Saint Paul had been set at liberty. It is generally assumed that (12) the first epistle to Timothy and (13) the epistle to Titus were written about 65, when Saint Paul was on his fourth journey in the East, and, finally, (14) the second epistle to Timothy was written during his second imprisonment in Rome in 66 or 67.

37. THE EPISTLE TO THE ROMANS

(16 chapters)

1. *Motive.* We know from Horace and other Roman authors that even before the time of Christ there were many Jews in Rome, the capital of the world, and that they possessed several synagogues, which were frequently visited by Gentiles. It is possible, therefore, that some account of our Saviour reached Rome as early as the reign of Tiberius or that of Caligula. It is certain that a congregation of Christians existed there in the earlier part of the reign of Claudius, and the epistle is addressed to readers assumed to be well instructed and steadfast in Christianity. Every early Christian writer names Saint Peter as the founder of this church; he had left Palestine because of the persecution under Herod Agrippa and came to Rome soon after the accession of Claudius.[1] It is probable that he converted first some Jews to Christianity, but they were soon joined by Gentiles. In his life of the Emperor Claudius (chapter xxv.), Suetonius says that he expelled all the Jews from Rome because of their incessant quarrels.[2] He mentions a certain " Chrestos " as the instigator of these disputes, so we may suppose that the pagan writer was not accurately informed, and had heard of quarrels about Christ, and that disturbances had broken out among the Jews concerning the

---

[1] Acts xii. 17, where the author cautiously writes: ἐπορεύθη εἰς ἕτερον τόπον. Cf. also *War Petrus in Rom?* Münster, 1872; *Kirchenlex.*, art. Petrus; Schmid, *Petrus in Rom*, Lucerne, 1879 (see p. 438).

[2] *Judæos impulsore Chresto perpetuo tumultuantes Roma expulit.* (In acordance with iotacism, η may be pronounced like ι, so that χρηστός = χριστός. But even if this pronunciation was not usual in Rome, it would be very natural to put a well-known word like χρηστός = *probus*, honest, instead of the still unfamiliar χριστός. Cf. Tertullian, *Apolog.*, 3.) Of the expelled Jews probably many returned, as did Aquila and Priscilla (Rom. xvi. 3). Saint Peter too seems to have been amongst those driven out; he probably went at first to Asia Minor, whither he afterwards sent his epistles.

Christian religion. It was perhaps in consequence of the expulsion of the Jews that the majority of the Christians in Rome were Gentiles by birth, as we read in the epistle.[1] For a long time a bond of mutual esteem and love had existed between Saint Paul and this community, and he had greatly desired to be able to visit Rome;[2] but as this was not possible just then, he sought to benefit the Roman Christians by means of a written communication, and he also wished to see the principles that he insisted upon duly appreciated at the center of the whole civilized world.

What caused the quarrels was the discussion whether salvation through the Messias was limited to the people of Israel, as the Jews preferred to think, or was intended to be within reach of all nations. In the first case all Gentiles, in order to attain to salvation, would have to begin by submitting to the Mosaic Law, and could only thus obtain a share in the benefits of redemption. If this Jewish opinion had prevailed, as far as human reason can judge, Christianity could scarcely have become common to all nations. The correct doctrine and practice was stated clearly at the Apostolic Council, but for a long time there were great difficulties in carrying the rules into execution.

2. *Contents.* In this epistle Saint Paul gives his opinions fully regarding paganism, Judaism and Christianity. The contents of the book are therefore chiefly *dogmatic* (chapter i.–xi.) though at the end they become *ethical* (xii.–xvi.).

Dogmatic portion of the epistle. In the introduction (i.–iii.) Saint Paul speaks of the universal sinfulness of mankind, and the need of redemption. All, not only the Gentiles, who did not know the law of Moses, but also the Jews, who were under the law, have merited rejection by God through their sins.

Argument. The doctrine of salvation. The way to be justified before God has been opened to all men by faith in Jesus Christ. This way has been all along the only possible one; for man could never please God otherwise than by faith. David and Abraham were justified not by the law, but by faith in a future Redeemer (iv.). This same justification is now won through faith in and devotion to the Son of God, appearing in our flesh, who, being Himself free from sin, by His obedience even to the death of the Cross, has removed the guilt which was brought upon mankind by Adam's disobedience (v.). Henceforth it is possible for every man justified through Christ to live in a manner pleasing to God, for by

---

[1] Rom. i. 5, 6, 13; vi. 17, etc.; xi. 13; xv. 5, etc. That there were Jews amongst them appears from Rom. ii. 17; iv. 1, etc.; vii. 1, etc.

[2] Acts xix. 22; Rom. i. 13; xv. 22–24.

baptism the malice inherited from Adam is destroyed, and the Christian is brought under the influence of the grace that proceeds from Christ (vi.). The Mosaic Law could not confer this capability upon man, but left him powerless against sin, because grace was wanting (vii.). But through the spirit of Christ man can overcome sin and the flesh, and, being chosen by God in the freedom of His grace, can bear with joyful hope all the sufferings of earthly life (viii.). In reply to the question how matters now stand with regard to Judaism, Saint Paul says that for the moment the Jews have been rejected by God, and their place has been taken by the Gentiles, but in the fullness of time (xi. 25, 26) Israel shall find mercy by adhering to Jesus Christ (ix.–xi.). *Cf*. Is. xi. 11, xliii. 5–7; Jer. iii. 18, etc.

In *the ethical part of the epistle*, Saint Paul speaks of the fruits that the faithful ought to bring forth in their life. Following our Lord's example, they should bring forth chiefly humility and love, which shows itself in loyal fulfillment of duties, and in good will even towards enemies (xii.), and further in obedience to the government. They must also act with consideration towards the weak and imperfect (xiv.), and preserve harmony by the utmost submission to one another (xv.).

The closing chapter (xvi.) contains personal communications and greetings.

3. *Time and Place of Writing.* According to xv. 23, etc. (*cf*. I Cor. xvi. 1, etc.; II Cor. viii. 14; Acts xix. 21), Saint Paul wrote this letter when he was in Achaia on his third journey. There can be no doubt that he wrote from Corinth, for he recommends to the Romans (xvi. 1) a Corinthian deaconess named Phœbe, who was going to Rome, and probably took the letter with her, and he also conveys greetings from Corinthian Christians (Caius, xvi. 23; *cf*. I Cor. i. 14; Timotheus and Sopater, xvi. 21; *cf*. Acts xx. 4). The date must be the spring of the year 59, as the apostle was in Philippi on his way back from Achaia at Easter, and wished to celebrate Pentecost in Jerusalem (Acts xx. 6–16).

The epistle is generally regarded as authentic, although some modern critics, like Marcion of old, would reject the last two chapters (xv. and xvi.), because they contain some expressions favorable to the Jews and apparently not in Saint Paul's style. He was, however, by no means hostile to the Jews, and only regretted their antagonism to Christ. (*Cf*. i. 16; iii. 2; ix. 1–5; x. 1.) Spitta thinks that the epistle consists of two letters put together, both written by Saint Paul. The longer may have been written in 58 at Corinth, but the shorter, containing the last few chapters, was not written before 63 or 64, after the apostle's release from prison. Tradition, however, from the earliest times has accepted the unity of the epistle.

ambitious, untrustworthy and dishonest. The tendency, too, to follow heathen practices still existed, and showed itself in participation in idolatrous feasts (II Cor. vi. 14–18); moreover the adherents of the Jewish party were more embittered than ever against Saint Paul. All these facts impelled the apostle to write a second letter, which Titus, who was glad to return to Corinth, took with him.

2. *Object and Contents.* Defense of himself and exhortation to charity.

The epistle falls into three parts; the first contains Saint Paul's self-defense addressed to the community in general, the second his self-defense addressed to the Judaizing party, and the third his exhortation to good works.

1. (i.–vii.) Saint Paul speaks of himself in relation to the church at Corinth, and explains the misunderstandings that had disturbed it. As a pledge of the restoration of harmony, he desires that the incestuous man, who is now penitent, shall be re-admitted to the congregation (ii. 5–11). He repeatedly expresses his joy that the Corinthians have been won over to him and so to true Christianity. (*Cf.* especially vii. 4, etc.)

2. (viii., ix.) The Corinthians are again urged to collect money for the Jewish Christians in Jerusalem — works of mercy always ought to be performed.[1]

3. (x.–xiii.) Arguments against the Judaizing party. Defense of Saint Paul's person and doctrine. Announcement of his coming.

In this epistle, more than in any other, Saint Paul speaks from his heart. On reading it, we can feel that he had not merely won the new converts to Christ, but had done so almost with violence, and had filled them at the same time with wonderful affection for himself, since they saw with what unselfishness he endured all that was painful in his laborious work as an apostle, without ever relaxing his zeal.

3. *Time and Place.* The epistle was written in Macedonia (viii. 1, ix. 4), according to several subscriptions at Philippi, in the summer months of the year 58.[2]

---

[1] Saint Paul laid so much stress on this matter because he considered (Rom. xv. 27) that the Gentile Christians were bound to show their gratitude for the gift of Christianity to the parent church at Jerusalem. We learn from Gal. ii. 10 that he had personally undertaken to look after the poor on the occasion of the Apostolic Council. The Jewish Christians, hated and despised by their own nation, and for the most part reduced to poverty, were in danger of falling back into unbelief and Judaism. See *infra*, Epistle to the Hebrews, 5.

[2] If Saint Paul left Ephesus at Pentecost (I Cor. xvi. 8), and if he left Philippi again about Easter, 59 (Acts xx. 6), in order to go to

The authenticity of both epistles to the Corinthians is universally recognized. The first particularly is expressly mentioned in Saint Clement's first letter to the Corinthians, c. 47.

40. THE EPISTLE TO THE GALATIANS

(6 chapters)

1. *Galatia,* in Asia Minor, took its name from the Galatæ = Galli = Kelts, who settled there in 257 B. C. Some offshoots of the great Gallic race from the far West gradually made their way through Pannonia and Illyria to Asia Minor, and there entered the army of King Nicomedes of Bithynia, receiving from him, in return for their services, part of ancient Phrygia, with the addition of a portion of Bithynia, to be their dwelling place. Their chief towns were Ancyra, Tavium and Pessinus. From 24 B. C. onwards Galatia was a Roman province.

At the time of the apostles the name Galatia was given not merely to the territory occupied by the Galatæ, but to the whole Province, which contained, besides Galatia proper, Lycaonia, Pisidia and Pamphylia lying to the south of it. Saint Paul visited these districts on his first missionary journey (Acts xiii. 13, etc., xiv.), but did not reach Galatia proper. It is possible that he went there on his second and third journeys, but it is more likely that this epistle is addressed to the inhabitants of the Roman Province of Galatia, and not to the Galatæ, or at least not to them alone. Cornely takes this view, and V. Weber and Belser agree with him. (1) According to Gal. ii. 5, Saint Paul, at the Council, resisted his opponents, "that the truth of the gospel might continue with you." This seems to show that Christianity had been preached in Galatia before the Apostolic Council. (2) In the epistle Saint Paul speaks of Barnabas (ii. 1, 9, 13) as of a well-known person, but it was only on the first missionary journey that Barnabas could have become known there. (3) Saint Paul always follows the Roman usage in speaking of places — he means by Achaia, Macedonia and Asia, the Roman provinces of those names, and not the older regions to which they once applied.

2. *Motive.* On his missionary journeys in Asia Minor Saint Paul visited this province and preached the gospel there with

Jerusalem, having previously spent three months in Achaia, we may believe that the epistle was written in August or September, allowing some months for traveling. Kaulen thinks it was written at the end of June, Cornely in the autumn of the year 58.

success. But after his departure Jews came to Galatia, who tried to mislead the people and rouse them to hostility against Saint Paul, calling upon them to submit to the Jewish law as well as to Christianity, if they would be saved. We are not told by whom Saint Paul was informed of the danger threatening his Galatian converts, but he sought to avert the evil by means of this epistle, which must be regarded as a circular letter, for it is not addressed to one particular church, but "to the churches of Galatia" (i. 2).[1]

3. *Contents and Object*. Rejection of the unjustifiable demands of the Judaizing party.

The epistle consists of three parts, each of two chapters: i. and ii. Saint Paul's apostleship and doctrine are of divine origin, and he is in complete accord with the other apostles. iii. and iv. The doctrine that he preaches harmonizes with the history of the old covenant, which bears the same relation to the new as Agar to Sara. v. and vi. To accept the Mosaic Law, or to add it to the gospel, is unnecessary and reprehensible.

4. *Time and Place*. It is generally assumed that the epistle was written in 56, during Saint Paul's visit to Ephesus on his third missionary journey. The contents, however, point to its having been written during the second journey, for the vivid description of the proceedings at the Apostolic Council, and of the dispute with Saint Peter concerning the *legalia* at Antioch, indicates that these events were still fresh in Saint Paul's memory. It may have been written at Corinth, in 53 or 54, not long after the epistles to the Thessalonians.[2]

The authenticity of this epistle was formerly unquestioned, but has recently been challenged by some non-Catholic critics.

---

[1] "Paul, an apostle . . . and all the brethren who are with me, to the churches of Galatia."

[2] Val. Weber in discussing this epistle tries to prove not only that the Galatians to whom the epistle is addressed were the inhabitants of the Roman province of Galatia, and so were the southern Galatians, converted on Saint Paul's first journey, but also that the epistle was written in 48 or 49, before the Apostolic Council; this would make it the earliest of all the Pauline epistles. Belser, like Weber, thinks it is addressed to Southern Galatians, and was written perhaps at Antioch in Syria, in the year 49. Steinmann believes it to be addressed to the Galatians in the north of the province, and to have been written at Ephesus in 54 or 55.

41. The Epistle to the Ephesians
(6 chapters)

1. *Ephesus* is situated on the seacoast of Ionia, at the mouth of the Caystrus, somewhat to the south of Smyrna. It was a very ancient city of high reputation. The Temple of Diana was especially famous; it was burnt down by Herostratus in 356 B. C., but was rebuilt, and ranked as one of the seven wonders of the world. In 133 Ephesus became the capital of the Roman province of Asia. In early Christian times (431 A.D.) the third general Council against Nestorius was held here. Ephesus was destroyed by the Turks and is now a village, called Aja Soluk.

2. *Motive.* On his second missionary journey Saint Paul went on to Ephesus from Corinth, and found a community of Christians there (Acts xviii. 21). On his third journey, after traveling through Galatia and Phrygia, he again visited Ephesus, and remained there from two to three years. He was forced to leave, owing to Demetrius' revolt, but he always retained particular affection for the faithful in and near Ephesus, and the touching words that he spoke in Miletus when he bade them farewell are a witness to it (Acts xx.). When he was in prison he still tried, by means of the epistle preserved to us, to encourage the faithful in living a Christian life, for they were in danger of being led astray by those who wished to sow the seed of later Gnosticism. The doctrine concerning angels, strongly emphasized and accurately stated, is aimed at these enemies (i. 21, iii. 10, vi. 12).

3. *Place.* Saint Paul wrote the epistle from prison (iii. 1, iv. 1, vi. 20), but it is uncertain whether it was from Cæsarea or from Rome that he addressed the Ephesians. He is generally believed to have written it in Rome, and to have dispatched it with the letters to the Colossians and Philemon. If this be the case, it was written in 63.

4. *Difficulties.* It is remarkable that there are no personal touches in this epistle; the wording is very general, and almost suggests (i. 15, iii. 1, 2) that Saint Paul had not come into

contact with his readers. Commentators have doubted, therefore, whether this epistle was really intended for the Ephesians.
It is true that in the first verse the words ἐν Ἐφέσῳ occur,
but in the earliest manuscripts it is still possible to see that
they have been inserted by a later hand. In Codex B they
are in the margin, in Codex ℵ they are wanting. We may
therefore suppose that it was intended primarily for Ephesus,
but was to be sent as a circular letter to all the other churches
of the province of Asia, viz. Smyrna, Pergamus, Thyatira, Sardes,
Philadelphia and Laodicea.

5. The *contents* are partly doctrinal, partly ethical.

Chapters i.–iii. are doctrinal, for Saint Paul states how great is the
happiness of those Gentiles who now belong to the Church, the spotless
Bride of Christ. God's intention to save not only His own people, but
also the morally corrupt Gentiles, through Jesus Christ, was formerly
concealed, but is now manifest, and Saint Paul has the commission and
the will to bring the tidings of it to the Gentiles. Chapters iv.–vi. are
ethical. He states that all the faithful collectively form one body, and
they must show themselves to be one, by the harmony between the
various limbs. They must no longer live as heathen, but must practice
Christian virtues, and by goodness of life correspond to God's loving
intention. Admonitions to Christian families.

6. *Carrier of the Epistle.* Tychicus, a friend and assistant
of Saint Paul in his work of teaching, was to carry this epistle
(vi. 21). The same man conveyed also the epistle to the
Colossians (Col. iv. 7). These two epistles resemble one another closely, and we can hardly doubt that Tychicus conveyed
them both from Rome towards the end of the year 63, taking
with him at the same time the short letter to Philemon, a
Christian living at Colossæ.

The authenticity of this epistle is beyond question, for in
support of it we have the evidence of the *Fragm. Mur.,* Irenæus,
Origen, Tertullian and Clement of Alexandria, all of whom
know it only as addressed to Ephesus. Even if the words
ἐν Ἐφέσῳ in v. 1 are missing in the manuscripts they undoubtedly occur in the title.

42. The Epistle to the Philippians

(4 chapters)

1. *Philippi* in Macedonia was the first city on European soil
in which Saint Paul preached the gospel. It was formerly only
a village known as Krenides,[1] but was enlarged and fortified
by Philip II of Macedonia, and thenceforth bore his name. A
Roman colony was established there in 42 B. C., and the inhabitants enjoyed immunity from taxation and the privileges
of Roman citizenship. At the present time a little village
called Filiba stands on the ruins of the former city. Saint
Paul visited Philippi on his second missionary journey and
founded a Christian church there. He returned thither on his
third journey (Acts xx. 6). The faithful in this town were
particularly loyal to their teacher, and were more steadfast
than many others, both in faith and morals. This is plain
from the epistle addressed to them by Saint Paul, which reveals the existence of a very close bond between him and them,
and contains almost no rebukes, nor any suggestion of wrongdoing on their part.

2. *Motive.* The Philippians had heard that Saint Paul was
in prison, so with loving anxiety they made a collection
of money, and sent the proceeds by one of the chief men in
the community, by name Epaphroditus ('Επαφρόδιτος), to Saint
Paul (iv. 18). The apostle gave the messenger the letter
that we possess to carry back with him.

3. *Contents.* Expression of gratitude and warning.

Chapter i. Joy at the proof of the Philippians' loyalty to the gospel.
He tells them how he fares in his imprisonment; he is willing either to
live or to die. ii. He recommends them to be subject to one another according to the example of Christ. iii. He warns them against Judaizing
teachers. iv. He thanks them for their affectionate offering that he has
received.

4. *Time and Place.* Saint Paul speaks of his bonds (i.
7, 13), so the epistle was written in prison, but on which oc-

[1] i. e. springs, from the number of springs and watercourses in the
neighborhood (κρηνίς = κρηνή).

casion? He refers to his recognition in the Prætorium
(i. 13), the headquarters of the imperial bodyguard, and he
sends greetings from persons attached to the emperor's household (iv. 22). These are plain indications that he was in
prison in Rome. We have three other epistles belonging to
the same period, viz. those to the Ephesians, Colossians and
Philemon. In all he expresses the hope of being set at liberty, so they were written during his first imprisonment; but
whereas in the epistle to Philemon (verse 22) he orders a lodging to be prepared for himself, he writes here less confidently
(i. 20, ii. 17). This epistle therefore is probably earlier than
the other three, and may have been written in the year 62.

It is almost universally acknowledged to be authentic. In his epistle
to the Philippians (iii. 5, 9) Saint Polycarp refers to this work of the
apostles.

43. The Epistle to the Colossians

(4 chapters)

1. *Colossæ* (or Kolassai) was a town in Phrygia, on the
Lycus, about forty hours' journey inland and eastward of
Ephesus. It has perished under Turkish rule, and now there
is only a village, called Konon or Chonas, in the neighborhood.

2. *Motive.* The Christian church at Colossæ was not founded
by Saint Paul himself (i. 4, ii. 1), but it is not improbable
that one of his disciples preached the gospel here during the
apostle's long sojourn in Ephesus. The chief teacher of the
Colossians, Epaphras ('Επαφρᾶς), visited Saint Paul when a
prisoner in Rome, and took him news of the condition of that
and the neighboring churches (i. 7, iv. 12). In consequence
of this, Epaphras himself was imprisoned (Philemon 23). The
tidings that he brought included the fact that there were
dangers threatening the faith (ii. 4, 8); false teachers with
gnostic tendencies were trying to lead the Christians astray,
partly into Judaism and partly into heathenism, and were
spreading a false doctrine about angels. Saint Paul wrote this
epistle with reference to these matters, and as Epaphras was
in prison, he sent it by Tychicus (iv. 7), probably at the same

time as the epistles to the Ephesians and Philemon, in the year 63.

3. *Contents.* Of the four chapters, the first two contain instructions, the last two admonitions.

i. The blessings of Christianity, far surpassing all the wisdom of Jews and Greeks. ii. Suffer not yourselves to be led astray by the words of philosophers and Rabbis. The worship of angels and a perverse use of mortification cannot take the place of Christianity. iii. Sanctify yourselves by purity of life, lay aside the old man more and more, and put on the new, by becoming like unto Christ. iv. Tychicus and Onesimus will give you further news. Greetings.

At the conclusion of the letter, Saint Paul orders it to be read in Laodicea, and that which he sent to that city to be read also at Colossæ (iv. 16). We know nothing of any epistle at Laodicea; probably that to the Ephesians is meant, of which Marcion asserted that it was intended for Laodicea. (Harnack, *Altchristl. Lit.*, p. 4, suggests that it was the epistle to the Ephesians.) These two epistles are very much alike, as they were both written with a view to opposing the rise of gnosticism, and to stating the true doctrines of Christianity.

The authenticity of the epistle is vouched for by Ignatius (Eph. x.), Clement of Rome (I Cor. xlix.), Polycarp (Phil. v. and xi.), but against it may be urged that gnosticism could not have appeared at so early a date. If, however, soon after 100 A. D. Basilides and Valentinus came forward with comprehensive gnostic systems, the beginning of the heresy must have existed long before. In his first epistle to the Corinthians, i. 18; ii. 6, etc.; viii. 1; xii. 8, Saint Paul gives warnings against what is assumed to be wisdom, very much as he does in the epistle to the Colossians.

44. First Epistle to the Thessalonians

(5 chapters)

1. *Thessalonica* (Θεσσαλονίκη), the largest city in Macedonia, lying southwest of Philippi on the Sinus Thermaicus, was a flourishing commercial town. It is now called Salonik, and is, next to Constantinople, the most important place in Turkey in Europe. Of the seventy thousand inhabitants a third are Jews, and in ancient times there were many Jews here. Saint Paul addressed them first, when, on his second missionary journey, he came hither from Philippi with Silas and Timothy, to bring tidings of the Messias. They did not long listen to him with patience, but soon showed their hostility, although they were unable to hinder the growth of a church

consisting chiefly of Gentile Christians. Being forced to take flight, Saint Paul sent Timothy, probably from Berea, to Thessalonica to look after the new converts and then to bring him news of them to Achaia. Timothy rejoined Saint Paul at Corinth, and gave him a report of the condition of the newly founded community.

2. *Motive of the Epistle.* The church in Thessalonica was suffering in consequence of not having received sufficient instruction (iii. 10). The converts were firm in the faith, but morally they were not much changed, and their careless, heathenish mode of life had not been discarded. Several deaths, too, had occurred, in consequence of which many Christians abandoned themselves to discouragement, being badly instructed regarding the future life and the resurrection. These facts led Saint Paul to write them an epistle.

3. *Contents.* Saint Paul seeks to strengthen his converts in the gospel; he warns them against the heathen vices of fornication, dishonesty, hard-heartedness and indolence, and instructs them on the second coming of Christ.

i. To my joy you have become Christians. ii. Remember my sojourn amongst you. With the greatest earnestness I preached salvation to you, and you asccepted it with zeal. iii. Timothy, whom I sent to you, has brought me good news of you. iv. Practice the virtues of Christians; be moral, love your neighbors, and be diligent at your work. With regard to those who have passed away, be without anxiety; they will rise again at Christ's second coming. v. The time of the judgment is uncertain, the Lord will come like a thief in the night.

4. *Time and Place.* This epistle is the earliest of all Saint Paul's writings that have come down to us. It was written at Corinth in the year 53.

45. Second Epistle to the Thessalonians
(3 chapters)

1. *Motive.* After a short time further news of the church at Thessalonica reached Saint Paul. His epistle had made a deep impression and had had a good result; to some extent it had served to soothe men's minds, but as he had spoken of

the second coming of Christ and the end of the world, and had declared the time of the judgment to be uncertain, the Thessalonians fancied that the end of all things was imminent, and they were giving themselves up to the greatest alarm. Their excitement had been aggravated by a forged letter ostensibly written by Saint Paul. Some, probably of the lower classes, were refusing to work and living in idleness, allowing themselves to be supported by the charity of their fellow Christians. On receipt of this news, Saint Paul sent a second epistle to Thessalonica.

2. *Contents.* Admonition to lead the life of honest Christians. Completion of his instruction regarding the end of the world and the Last Judgment.

i. At the last day God will reward your zeal for the faith. ii. But we must not expect the end of the world immediately; there must first be a great falling away on the part of Christians (Matt. xxiv. 23), and the man of sin (Antichrist, I John ii. 18; Acts xx. 7) will appear and rule with the utmost arrogance. Then, when wickedness has reached its climax, Christ will come and put a speedy end to it. iii. The apostle warns the people against idleness, and bids them break off all intercourse with those who deliberately live on alms. Every man should try to support himself by his own work. On the other hand, Saint Paul urges them not to desist from helping the really poor.

3. *Time and Place.* Like the first epistle, the second was writen at Corinth, about the year 54.

We possess very ancient testimony vouching for the authenticity of both epistles. The Muratorian Fragment, and even Marcion, set them in the Canon. Irenæus knew both (*Adv. Hær.*, V, vi. 1; III, vii. 2), and so did Clement of Alexandria (*Strom.*, IV, 12; V, 3). Justin Martyr speaks of the "Man of apostasy, who speaketh terrible things against the Most High" (*c. Tryph.*, 32, 110, *cf.* II Thess., ii. 3, 4). It is only in modern times that the authenticity of the first epistle has been questioned, chiefly because of its resemblance to the epistles to the Corinthians, as if the apostle might not have addressed two churches in a similar fashion. The authenticity of the second epistle is challenged because it contains the doctrine of Antichrist, which resembles the Apocalypse, and the arbitrary assumption is made that this epistle therefore was written after the time of Saint Paul.

PASTORAL EPISTLES

For about a century this name has been given to three
epistles; the first and second to Timothy and that addressed
to Titus. They resemble one another in motive and contents,
and all contain instructions for fulfilling the duties of a
bishop. They have always been classed together.

There is very ancient evidence for the authenticity of these three
epistles. They occur in the Itala and Peshitto and in the Muratorian
Canon. Polycarp (*Ad Phil.*, c. 4 and 9) clearly quotes I Tim. vi. 7 and
10; II Tim. iv. 9; Irenæus (*Adv. Hær.*, III, iii. 3) refers to II Tim.
iv. 21.

46. THE FIRST EPISTLE TO TIMOTHY

(6 chapters)

1. *Timothy*, the son of a Gentile father and a Jewish
mother, was born at Lystra in Lycaonia. He was a faithful
disciple and companion to Saint Paul, who, on quitting
Ephesus, left him behind in charge of the church there. From
other points on his journey Saint Paul continued to send him
instructions and admonitions regarding his duties as bishop.

2. *Contents.* i.–iv., Principles; v. and vi., their application.

i. The reason for Saint Paul's leaving Timothy at Ephesus was the
appearance of heresy, that endeavored to substitute a distorted form of
Judaism for the gospel. The fundamental principle of the gospel teaching, which must constantly be emphasized, is that Christ came to save
sinners. ii. For the further spreading of the gospel, prayer is needed as
well as preaching. iii. Moreover, the right men must be chosen as
clergy; and the qualities are stated which must chiefly be kept in view
in selecting them. iv. Timothy must oppose the teachers of so-called
wisdom, that is only a fiction, and although still young, he must be an
example to all. v. Instructing and guiding men of every rank and age,
and even the priests. vi. No self-interest is to influence him, but he is
always to turn his thoughts to the judgment of Christ and to life
everlasting.

3. It is difficult to fix the *date* of this epistle, since it seems
to fit no situation in Saint Paul's life, as far as we know
it from the New Testament. For this reason the authenticity
of the epistle has been denied, but we find that it was used
by the earliest Fathers; the oldest translations, viz. the Itala

and Peshitto, contain it, and it is included in every ancient list of the canonical books.

The following hypotheses have been put forward regarding the date of its origin:

1. "During his long residence at Ephesus (56–58) Saint Paul made a journey not mentioned by Saint Luke in the Acts, and in the course of it wrote this epistle" (*Ad Maier,* Reithmayr). But the epistle assumes the existence of an already well organized community, such as we cannot believe was formed at so early a period.

2. "Saint Paul, being driven away from Ephesus through the disturbances caused by Demetrius, traveled to Macedonia and Achaia, leaving Timothy behind, and it was from Macedonia or Achaia that he sent him these written instructions" (Aberle-Schanz). But on that occasion Saint Paul sent Timothy before him into Macedonia (Acts xix. 22; II Cor. i. 1). If we assume that Timothy soon returned, the peaceful tone of the letter does not agree with this period; it is not thus that a man writes who has just emerged from a most difficult contest, and knows that his friend is in the midst of dangers threatening his life (II Cor. i. 8).

3. The usual supposition is that Saint Paul, being released from his first imprisonment in Rome (63), first visited Spain, and then made a journey to see the churches in Greece and Asia; and it was then that he left Timothy as bishop in Ephesus, and during his further travels, perhaps in the year 65, wrote this epistle to him (Kaulen, Cornely). Old subscriptions to the Epistle give Laodicea in Phrygia as the place of composition. Against this theory is the fact that Saint Paul had previously (Acts xx. 25) told the Ephesians that they would see his face no more. We may, however, limit these words to the majority of those who went to meet him at Miletus. The passage in I Timothy iv. 12, "Let no man despise thy youth," causes less difficulty, for if Timothy was about twenty when he was converted in 51 or thereabouts, in the year 65 he would certainly still be very young to hold the office of a bishop.

47. The Second Epistle to Timothy

(4 chapters)

1. *Time and Place*. Saint Paul wrote this epistle when he was imprisoned in Rome for preaching the gospel (i. 8, 17; iv. 16, etc). He had but little hope of regaining his freedom and was looking forward to a speedy death. As he expresses himself quite otherwise in the epistles to the Philippians, Ephesians, Colossians and Philemon, which he also wrote when a prisoner in Rome, as he even orders a lodging to be prepared for himself in Colossæ, we must regard this epistle as belonging to a later date, and as written during his second imprisonment in Rome, when he had no prospect of release, for it ended with his execution. The second epistle to Timothy was therefore written in Rome in 66 or 67 A. D.

2. *Contents*. Saint Paul asks Timothy to come to him. He lays down rules for his guidance in his office, particularly with regard to heretics. Personal information.

i. How gladly would I again see my beloved Timothy! But it is possible that you will not find me alive; so receive now my instructions and last exhortations. Remember the grace of your consecration, and discharge manfully and steadfastly the duties of a good shepherd. Be not ashamed of your master, though he is a prisoner, but take him as an example. Work fearlessly for the gospel, and strive to train up others as teachers of it. ii., iii. Do not dispute with heretics. The appearance of wicked men does not injure the sanctity of the Church. Win over the wavering by gentleness and patience. Prepare for suffering. Let it cost what it may, you must hold fast to tradition and to Holy Scripture. iv. Be zealous. You will have to take my place, as my course is nearly ended. I am abandoned by most of my friends, and only Luke is with me. Bring me the cloak that I left behind at Troas, and my books, and come with Mark to join me. Greetings to my friends in Ephesus.

48. The Epistle to Titus

(3 chapters)

1. *Titus*. Saint Paul's disciple and companion was left by him on the island of Crete to arrange the still confused circumstances of the Christian communities there, and especially to appoint rulers of the churches. From a distance the apostle gave him further instructions for his guidance.

It is scarcely possible to ascertain when Titus came into contact with Saint Paul. According to the *Menologium* of the Emperor Basilius (August 25, Migne, *P. Gr.*, 117, p. 604, etc.), Titus was a native of Crete, and went to Jerusalem as a young man. Whilst there, he saw our Lord and accepted the faith. If this be true, he may have become acquainted with Saint Paul soon after the latter's conversion.

2. *Contents.* A statement of what Titus has to do, and after he has accomplished his task he is to return to Saint Paul.

i. His chief business is to select suitable men to act as elders, i. e. as priests and bishops. They must possess a good reputation, virtues and knowledge, and be capable of defending the doctrines of Christianity. The Cretans are acknowledged to be very difficult people to deal with, and false teachers with Judaizing tendencies have already found a footing amongst them. Zeal and prudence are therefore particularly necessary. ii. Titus is to display these qualities towards all classes, — men, women and servants, — and insist upon the works of the faith. iii. False teachers are to be left alone, after a few rebukes have been given them. Saint Paul intends to send some one to Crete as a substitute for Titus (iii. 12), that he may be able to join him at Nicopolis, where he intends to pass the winter. (Whether this town is Nicopolis in Cilicia or Nicopolis in Epirus, over against Actium, is not clear; the former was a long way from Saint Paul's earlier sphere of activity, but he might pass the latter on his way from Macedonia and Achaia through Illyricum (*cf.* Rom. xv. 19) back to Rome. Hence we should probably understand Nicopolis in Epirus).

3. *Date.* Nothing is told us in the Acts of Saint Paul's visit to Crete and his work there. Some suppose that he founded the church in Crete before his long sojourn in Ephesus, perhaps on his way thither; or else he interrupted his work in Ephesus to go with Titus to Crete, and left his disciple there. The usual theory is that it was only on his fourth missionary journey, after his visit to Spain, that Saint Paul preached the gospel in Crete and left Titus there, sending him the letter of instructions from some point farther on his journey. The circumstances are therefore approximately the same as those connected with the first epistle to Timothy, and the date of composition may be taken as 65 or 66. The epistle was perhaps written at Corinth.

Whilst he was on his last missionary journey and after it was over, Saint Paul knew well that his work was drawing to its close; in II Tim. iv. 6 he speaks plainly of the end of his life. It was therefore very natural that he felt bound to give his friends and disciples, who were to take his place, rules for the maintenance and propagation of true Christianity.

49. THE EPISTLE TO PHILEMON

(25 verses)

This short letter is addressed to a prominent Gentile Christian at Colossæ, whom Saint Paul had converted. A slave, named Onesimus, had run away from him, and, learning to know Saint Paul, who was then in prison in Rome, was brought by him to the Christian faith. The apostle induced him to return to his master, and he traveled with Tychicus (Col. iv. 7–9), who was conveying the epistles to the Ephesians and Colossians. Saint Paul gave Onesimus at the same time a letter recommending him to his master. This epistle therefore, like those mentioned above, was written in the year 63.

Contents. Recommendation of Onesimus.

Philemon is requested to receive Onesimus kindly, for he has now become a brother, and to forgive him. At the same time Saint Paul asks Philemon to prepare him a lodging, for he hopes soon to come to Colossæ. The oldest authorities vouch for the authenticity of this epistle; Itala, Peshitto, Tertullian (*Adv. Marcion*, V, 21), Clement of Alexdria, *Fragm. Mur.*, Eusebius and others.

50. THE EPISTLE TO THE HEBREWS

(13 chapters)

1. *Contents.* The advantages of Christianity over Judaism.

The writer, without the customary greeting by way of introduction, begins at once with his *expositio:* i.–iii. In Jesus Christ the fulfillment of all the Old Testament prophecies has taken place. The covenant instituted by Him is far better than that of Moses, for Christ is the Son, Moses only the servant of God. iv. Christ offers peace and everlasting rest, which no one can despise save at the cost of being rejected, as was the first generation of Israelites in the wilderness. v., vi., vii. Christ is the true high priest, appointed by God, of the order of Melchisedech, and, having been exalted into Heaven, He stands far above the Levitical priesthood. viii., ix. The place also of worship (Heaven) and the sacrifice of Christ stand far higher than the old form of worship in the earthly sanctuary. x. Exhortation to perseverance. xi. Reference to former models of faith: Abel, Henoch, Noe, Abraham, Moses. xii., xiii. Exhortation to concord and sanctity. Request for a friendly reception of the epistle. Greetings.

2. *Readers.* The contents show that the Hebrews addressed in this epistle were not Jews, but Jewish Christians in Palestine, and particularly in Jerusalem, for they loved the Mosaic ritual and saw it still in use.

3. *Canonicity.* In ancient times opinions were divided with regard to this epistle. Whilst some valued it very highly, others either rejected it altogether or denied that it was the work of Saint Paul. It is remarkably unlike his other epistles; the thoughts show a resemblance, but the language is different. One result of the peculiarities of this epistle was that it was not everywhere admitted for use in the churches, and it was only in the East that it was always and everywhere regarded as canonical. We can see this from Origen, Cyril of Jerusalem and the Peshitto. In the West the Fathers before the fourth century scarcely quote it at all. Saint Jerome, Saint Ambrose and Saint Augustine were the first who made use of it, relying upon its reputation in the East, like the other canonical books. The Councils of Hippo (393) and Carthage (397) included it in the Canon, as did Innocent I (405). The long-continued opposition offered to this book in the West may be explained in connection with the Montanists and Novatians, who asserted that there was no hope of pardon for a Christian who apostatized, — a view that seemed to find some support in Hebrews vi. 4 and x. 26.

4. The book was regarded with suspicion also, because the *authorship* of it is not quite certain, even at the present day. The *language* [1] is not that of Saint Paul, although the subject matter is unmistakably his; and as this is the case

---

[1] The author writes pure, classical Greek, and shows great skill in expression, but he makes use of a peculiar form of speech which occurs nowhere else in the New Testament, and especially not in Saint Paul's epistles. As early a writer as Eusebius (*Hist. Eccl.*, III, 38) drew attention to the likeness between this epistle and Saint Clement's first epistle to the Corinthians.

it is pretty generally assumed [1] that Saint Paul employed one of his fellow workers to write it. Some ascribe the composition to Barnabas, others to Luke, some few to Apollos, but most to Clement of Rome. The statements of ancient writers preponderate in favor of Clement.[2] (Reithmayr, *Einl.*, p. 681; Cornely, *Comp.*, 571). It may be that Saint Paul intentionally put himself somewhat in the background, because many of the Jewish Christians disliked him.

5. *Time and Place.* According to xiii. 24 the epistle was written in Italy, probably in Rome.[3] It may have been composed during Saint Paul's first imprisonment, but as it contains no allusion to his being in captivity, it is more likely that it was written after his release, about the year 63 or 64. At this time the Christians in the Holy Land were in great danger of relapsing into Judaism, since they had lost their chief support, the Apostle Saint James the Less, in the year 62.[4]

---

[1] B. Heigl, relying on the tradition of the East, maintains the theory that Saint Paul himself wrote the epistle. It should be noticed that Saint Jerome (*Catal. Scr. Eccl.*) believed that Saint Paul wrote it in Hebrew, and that it was translated into Greek by Barnabas or Luke or Clement. It would be remarkable, however, if the Hebrew original had vanished so that no trace of it remained.

[2] That Clement knew the epistle to the Hebrews is at least probable. Irenæus (*Adv. Hær.*, III, iii. 3) says that he had intercourse with the apostles. According to Origen (*Comm. in Jo.*, VI, 36) and Eusebius (*Hist. Eccl.*, III, 15), he is identical with the Clement whom Saint Paul calls his fellow worker (Phil. iv. 3). We do not know whether he was a Jew or a Gentile; the character of his first (authentic) epistle to the Corinthians leads us to infer that he was a convert from Judaism. He probably became Pope under Domitian (81–96).

[3] "Italy" includes Rome and does not exclude it. Caution may have been necessary owing to persecutions.

[4] It is remarkable that this revered head of the Church is not mentioned in the epistle, but the words (xiii. 7) "Remember your prelates who have spoken the word of God to you; whose faith follow, considering the end of their conversation," are probably a reference to the two apostles named James, both of whom died as martyrs for the faith in Jerusalem.

CATHOLIC EPISTLES

51. These Epistles in General; their Name

From the very earliest times this name has been given to seven epistles written by apostles, viz., three by Saint John, two by Saint Peter, one by Saint James the Less and one by Saint Jude Thaddeus. It is not quite clear why these seven epistles were called Catholic.

First Theory: We have here the apostles collectively, not merely one apostle, Saint Paul, as in the other fourteen epistles. But against this theory is the fact that here too only a small proportion of the apostles (four out of twelve) are concerned.

Second Theory: These epistles are not, like those of Saint Paul, addressed to single churches or to individuals, but to all men, or at least to many. But against this is the fact that the epistles to the Galatians, Ephesians and Colossians are also intended for several churches, but are not on that account called Catholic.

Correct Theory: Catholic means here "recognized by the universal Church." This is the explanation given by Eusebius (*Hist. Eccl.*, III, 3), who says: "The first epistle of Peter is universally recognized, but his acta, his gospel, his preaching and his apocalypse are not among the Catholic books." The expression is not quite synonymous with ὁμολογούμενα, — the universal Church recognized these epistles as apostolic, but the apostolicity of some was opposed by a few churches.

52. The Epistle of Saint James

(5 chapters)

1. *The Writer* of this epistle is the Apostle Saint James the Younger or Less, son of Alpheus, Bishop of Jerusalem, and brother (i. e. near relative) of our Lord. Saint James the Elder or Great, son of Zebedee, brother of John, suffered martyrdom in 42 A.D., at which time this epistle certainly did not

exist, as it contains an allusion to the Epistle to the Romans.[1]

2. *Readers.* The epistle is addressed to the twelve tribes of Jews which were scattered abroad; that is to the Jewish Christians outside Palestine. It behooved the Bishop of Jerusalem, as the ecclesiastical head of the Holy Land, to address them.

3. *Motive.* It is plain from the epistle itself that some misunderstanding about Christian liberty had crept in amongst the Jewish Christians. Many interpreted the freedom from the Mosaic law, dating from the time of Christ, to mean that in order to attain to salvation it was enough to believe in Him, and that no good works need be done. They especially regarded themselves as released from all obligation of charity towards their neighbors. Reports of these things could easily be carried from all countries to Jerusalem, as every year many pilgrims went to Palestine to celebrate the festivals, and by their agency the epistle could also be distributed in all directions.

4. *Contents.* Encouragement to have patience in trials affecting the faith. Faith alone is not enough to secure salvation; it is necessary also to carry Christian teaching into practice, particularly active love of one's neighbor.

i. James, the servant of God and of our Lord Jesus Christ, to the twelve tribes in the diaspora, i. e. scattered outside Palestine. There are many dangers and temptations, because the kingdom of God does not appear with the anticipated outward magnificence. Have patience and be not foolish. Pray to God for a right understanding. Let the poor man rejoice in his dignity as a Christian, let the rich humble himself as a follower of Christ. To boast of riches is wrong, because they so soon pass away. We ought always to become more perfect, and not

---

[1] In the New Testament (Matt. xiii. 55; Mark vi. 3; Gal. i. 19) James the brother of the Lord is mentioned. Is he to be identified with one of the above-named or not? Some commentators, both ancient and modern, believe that James, the brother of the Lord, was a third person, not mentioned in the lists of the apostles, and therefore not an apostle, and it is to him that they ascribe this epistle. But James, the brother of the Lord, is certainly identical with James, son of Alpheus, for (1) Saint Paul says in Gal. i. 19, that when he was in Jerusalem he saw none of the *apostles* save James, brother of the Lord; (2) the extremely ancient distinction between Jacobus maior and Jacobus minor indicates that tradition knew of only two men of the name.

only hear Christianity preached, but also practice the works of faith.
ii. In Christianity there is no respect of persons; rich and poor are alike.
The chief duty is practical love of one's neighbor, for as in the case
of Abraham sacrifice must be added to faith. iii. Particularly to be
avoided are the sins of the tongue, which injure charity towards one's
neighbor. iv. The correction of visible faults does not avail much, unless
the bad interior disposition is combated and cured. Beware of desiring
the fleeting goods of this world, of despising one's neighbor and of esteem-
ing oneself too highly. v. Woe to the rich who oppress the poor! blessed
are those who continue patient in suffering! Beware of unnecessary
oaths; never lose confidence in God either in prosperity or adversity;
receive holy unction in sickness; confess your sins honestly and be
zealous in prayer. Seek to bring those that are astray back to the right
path.

5. *Time and Place.* The epistle was written in Jerusalem,
probably not earlier than 60 A. D., as it contains allusions to
misunderstood doctrines of Saint Paul (ii. 23; *cf.* Rom. iv. 3;
Gal. iii. 6), who did not extend his sphere of activity until
between 50 and 60, and whose earliest epistles belong to that
period.

We may assume that Saint James received news, chiefly from Rome
and Galatia, regarding the misunderstanding of Saint Paul's teaching on
the works of the law, when Saint Paul himself was in prison at Cæsarea,
and that he made haste to correct those who were in error.

The *authenticity* of this epistle and its position in the Canon
are vouched for by the Itala and the Peshitto, and by many
quotations in Hermas, Clement of Rome, Irenæus, Hippolytus, etc.

53. THE TWO EPISTLES OF SAINT PETER

(5 and 3 chapters)

1. The first of these epistles was probably written when
persecutions were in prospect (i. 7, iii. 13, etc., iv. 12, etc.).
The faithful are exhorted to stand firm in faith and morals,
the latter particularly, in order that among the heathen the
name of Christian may cease to be synonymous with wrong-
doer (ii. 12). They are urged to pay the greatest possible
obedience to authority (ii. 13), to practice brotherly love,
peaceableness and patience in suffering.

i. Stand fast in the faith. Christ has come, and through Him we attain to everlasting salvation. ii. and iii. In union with Christ lead a holy life; be subject also to authority, so that no one may be able to reproach you with anything. iv. Beware against heathen vices, be full of brotherly love, and despair not in affliction and persecution. v. The rulers of the Church must be an example to all, and every Christian should be humble at heart.

The second, shorter, letter, which is remarkably like the epistle of Saint Jude, is directed against certain false teachers, who, under a pretense of Christian liberty, are trying to spread a spurious spirituality and declare all carnal desires to be matters of indifference.

i. Great are the graces bestowed upon us, but we must zealously co-operate with them, in order that we may be saved through Christ. ii. Beware of false teachers who countenance immorality. iii. The Lord will come to judgment, and the world will be destroyed. Keep yourselves blameless.

This epistle seems to have been written to introduce, ratify and recommend Saint Jude's epistle to a circle of readers outside Palestine, who were in the same sort of danger as those whom Saint Jude addresses. It is possible that it was sent round with Saint Jude's epistle.[1]

2. At the beginning of each letter " Peter, the apostle of Jesus Christ," makes himself known as the author.

His original name was Simon; his father was John (John xxi. 15) or Jonas (Matt. xvi. 17). He was brought to our Saviour by his brother Andrew, and received the name Cephas (= Petrus = Rock) and the first place amongst the apostles. After our Lord's Ascension he was at the head of the Apostolic College and directed the Church first in Jerusalem, then in Antioch, and (from the year 42 onwards) in Rome. From Rome he revisited the East, but returned thither and was crucified in the year 67.

3. *Readers.* Both epistles were intended for Christian communities in Asia Minor, viz. in Pontus, Cappadocia, Galatia, Asia and Bithynia. Several of the Fathers state (Reithmayr, *Einl.*, p. 719) that Saint Peter had preached the gospel in these countries. The readers were chiefly Jewish Christians,

---

[1] A comparison of the text of Jude x. with II Peter ii. 12 shows that Saint Jude's epistle was written first.

for an accurate knowledge of the Old Testament is taken for granted. There must, however, have been Gentile Christians living in these parts, and several passages refer to those who have only just learnt to believe in the true God.

4. *Time and Place.* In the first epistle (v. 13) Babylon is mentioned as the place of writing. This certainly cannot be Belbel (Fostat) near Cairo in Egypt, nor the great city on the Euphrates, but it is undoubtedly the city on the Tiber, which stood in the same kind of antagonism to the Church as Babel of old to Israel. The apostle seems to wish his residence in Rome not to be universally known, and the faithful would easily understand what he meant by Babylon (*cf.* Apoc. xiv. 8, xviii. 1, etc.).[1] Silvanus or Silas is mentioned in verse 12 as the writer of the first epistle; he had probably come to Rome to bring news of the churches concerned, and Saint Paul may have already started for Spain. The first epistle was composed at the time of the outbreak of Nero's persecution (64), and the second belongs to the close of the apostle's life (67), as Saint Peter speaks of his approaching death (i. 13–15).

5. *Canonical Validity.* The first of these two epistles has always been reckoned among the ὁμολογούμενα, but the second was not originally allowed to be read in all churches. According to Eusebius (*Hist. Eccl.,* III, 3), it was only in Alexandria that it had always been read at public worship, not in Syria and the West. In the Fathers there are occasional ref-

---

[1] Saint Peter's residence in Rome was denied first by the Waldenses and later by the Magdeburg Centuriators in the interests of Lutheranism, but now there is scarcely one serious student who questions it. The Anglican Bishop Lightfoot acknowledges that Saint Peter lived in Rome, but denies that he was ever bishop of the Christians there. ("The Apostolic Fathers," London, 1890.) Harnack agrees with him. Dr. H. Lisco, *Roma Peregrina*, Berlin, 1901, tries to show that the headquarters of the earliest Christianity were not in the city of Rome, but in the port of Ephesus, also called Rome. He thinks that Paul and Peter founded the church here, that the epistles were all written here and that Ignatius died in this place. It was only towards the end of the second century that the Church migrated to the Italian city of Rome. But all this is pure fiction! C. Erbes tried to prove that Saint Peter died at Jerusalem, not in Rome. He bases this opinion partly on Matt. xxiii. 34, etc., assuming, without any proof, that the word "crucify" here refers to Peter, and those who crucified him would in that case be the Jews.

erences to and quotations" from it,[1] but still many seem to have been afraid to use it, and some declare it to be a forgery.

The following considerations are in favor of its authenticity: (1) The unbroken tradition of the Alexandrian Church, which must have contained many Jewish Christians for whom the epistle would have had most interest. Mark, who founded this church, is mentioned by name in 1 Peter v. 13, and after Saint Peter's death he may have brought both epistles to Alexandria. (2) Ephrem the Syrian often quotes the second epistle, and calls it a sacred book, written by Peter. (3) Saint Jerome and other Latin Fathers of a later date regard it as authentic. There are also reasons, derived from the epistle itself, for thinking it authentic. The author calls himself Peter, the apostle and servant of Christ. He says that he was an eyewitness of the Transfiguration, and he refers to his previous epistle (iii. 1). If these arguments are not enough to remove all doubt as to its authenticity, it is the duty of the Church in its teaching capacity to decide the matter. This decision has been given, and it is in favor of the authenticity of the second Epistle, so that no one, except heretics, can continue to question it.

54. The Three Epistles of Saint John

1. The *first* of these epistles (five chapters) is doctrinal, and in subject matter and language closely resembles the fourth gospel. The chief thoughts in it are: (a) There is a kingdom of darkness as well as a kingdom of light. (b) Jesus Christ, the son of God, has appeared in the flesh to bring men from darkness into light. (c) We must therefore believe in the divinity of Christ, and adhere by faith to the Son of God; and then (d) through Him we shall become children of God. (e) For this reason the faithful ought to love one another as brethren.

---

[1] Clem. Rom., *Ad Cor.*, I, 7: "Noe preached penance, and those who listened to him were saved." *Cf.* II Peter ii. 5. Also i. 11, "On account of his hospitality and fear of God, Lot was saved from Sodom." *Cf.* II Peter ii. 6. *Pastor Hermœ Vis.*, IV, 3. "You are they who have escaped from this world." *Cf.* II Peter ii. 20.

Analysis. i. 1–ii. 28: The present world is the kingdom of darkness. Warning against love of the world. ii. 29–iii. 22: Necessity of mutual love amongst Christians. iii. 23–v. 17: Importance of faith in the divinity of Christ.

The author nowhere gives his name, but the unmistakable connection with the fourth gospel and the unbroken tradition of the Church point to Saint John.[1]

Date. The epistle is not addressed to any particular church or individual, nor does it end as the circular letters of the apostles usually do; it has, in fact, not the form of a letter at all. This is accounted for by the theory mentioned in the Muratorian Fragment, and generally accepted, that it was intended to accompany Saint John's Gospel and to serve as an encyclical for several churches. It would, according to this hypothesis, have been written, like the gospel, about the year 100, in Ephesus.[2]

---

[1] In his epistle to the Philippians, c. 7, Polycarp quotes I John iv. 2, 3. His disciple Irenæus (*Adv. Hær.*, III, 16) knows the epistle as the work of "John, the Lord's disciple," and it was known also to the author of the Muratorian Fragment, Tertullian (*c. Prax.*, 15), and others. The adversaries were not Docetæ, but Nomists, i. e. adherents of Judaism, who denied both our Lord's divinity and that He was the Messias.

[2] The so-called *Comma Johanneum* did not make its appearance, as many suppose, until after the eighth century, in the Latin Bibles. In I John v. 7, 8 we read: "There are three who give testimony [in heaven: the Father, the Word and the Holy Ghost. And these three are one. And there are three that give testimony on earth]: the spirit and the water and the blood, and these three are one." The words within the brackets are contested. Döllinger especially charges the Western church with forgery, because the passage does not occur in the Greek manuscripts (*Allgem. Zeitung*, 1887, Nos. 88, 89), but it is indispensable for the context. It is quoted by as early a writer as Saint Cyprian (*De Unit. Eccl.*, c. 6), and Tertullian (*c. Prax.*, 25) also refers to it. The question therefore is not how the words came into the Latin Bibles, but how they fell out of the Greek. Instead of charging the Western church with forgery, Döllinger should have accused the Greek church with carelessness. Might not the words have been erased from the Bibles during the disputes with the Arians? It might conceivably be to their interest to suppress such passages. Some theologians of high reputation, such as Franzelin, Heinrich and Scheeben, maintain the authenticity of v. 7; others, e. g. Kaulen and Cornely, think it spurious. Cornely doubts its being genuine chiefly because Saint Augustine did not know it, for the passage generally quoted from the *Speculum* is not in Saint Augustine's

2. The *second epistle* (13 verses) is to an honorable lady named Cyria, and the *third* (14 verses) to some one named Caius. Many think that Cyria may be a name for some Christian community, and that Caius may have been the priest who presided over it. Both epistles express joyful appreciation of the zeal of the Christians to whom they are addressed. In the second (verse 7) is a warning against the errors of the Docetæ, and in both the writer gives utterance to his hope of seeing his friends again. Both seem to have been written after the gospel, as the second epistle (verse 9) contains a reference to John viii. 31 and some allusions to the first epistle. These two short epistles were probably dispatched soon after the gospel and the first epistle.

3. There is no doubt as to the authenticity of the first epistle; it has always been reckoned among the ὁμολογούμενα, but many have questioned that of the two shorter epistles, and it has been suggested that they were written by another John, the presbyter of Ephesus, not the apostle, as the writer of both epistles calls himself ὁ πρεσβύτερος. But we have seen (p. 393) that this presbyter is identical with Saint John the apostle. The language in these epistles resembles that of the first epistle and gospel, and there is plenty of evidence

work of that name, but from a later book bearing the same title, and falsely ascribed to him. It happened that Saint Augustine used the Itala, which was not the version used by Saint Cyprian and Tertullian.

Künstle, *Das Comma Johanneum*, Feb., 1905, tries to prove that the passage originated in Spain, where Priscillian (ob. 384) composed it out of attempted explanations of the words about the three that bear witness on earth. Künstle, however, overlooks the importance of Cyprian's quotation. The latter died in 258, so Priscillian lived over a century later. It should also be noticed that the debated words occur in the Itala MS. from Freising, which goes back to the sixth century (see p. 249). A decision of the Roman *Congregatio s. Officii*, dated Jan. 13, 1897, and ratified by Leo XIII on Jan. 15, 1897, states that the authenticity of the passage cannot be *tuto* either denied or questioned. This does not mean that henceforth all discussion of it must be at an end, as if the words were certainly Saint John's, written under divine inspiration; it merely means that they form part of the text approved by the Church. We may of course hope that further research will remove all doubt on the subject. The decree is intended to secure their position and prevent their being needlessly abandoned.

to show that the apostle was the author.[1] The chief reason for doubting their authenticity seems to be that they were not much used in public worship, but this was owing to their being very short and to the contents apparently being of a personal nature. In later times anything was viewed with suspicion that had not from the beginning been used at public worship.

55. THE EPISTLE OF SAINT JUDE THE APOSTLE

1. *Contents.* This epistle contains admonitions, and briefly but emphatically warns its readers against the attempts made by some opponents of Christianity to lead people astray; and it also describes the serious consequences of such errors (25 verses). The enemies mentioned in this epistle were probably not yet gnostics, but false spiritualists, who, under the pretext of Christian liberty, gave way to all kinds of sensual indulgence.[2] They seem to have resembled the Manicheans of a later date.

2. The *author* calls himself at the beginning "Jude, the servant of Jesus Christ, and brother of James." In the lists of apostles (Luke vi. 16; Acts i. 13) the name occurs of Jude, brother of James the Less, and this must be the author. He has the cognomen Thaddeus (*tad* = breast, therefore the courageous, the stout-hearted). He describes himself neither as an apostle nor as a brother of our Lord, though he was both, a proof of his humility.

3. The *authenticity* of this epistle was generally recognized in ancient times; only the Syrian Church long refused to regard it as apostolic; and on this account Eusebius places it among the ἀντιλεγόμενα. The chief reason for doubting it is that in verse 9 it seems to refer to the apocryphal book known as the *Assumptio Mosis,* and in verses 14 and 15 to *Henoch,*

---

[1] The Murat. Fragment; Iren., I, xvi. 3; III, xvi. 8; Clement of Alexandria, Origen and others.

[2] Rampf mentions the heretics Simon Magus, Menander, Dositheus, Gorthæus, Cleobius and Nicolaus, who were distressing the Church in Palestine.

another apocryphal work. Saint Jerome lays particular stress on this fact.[1] It should, however, be noticed that this reference does not proceed from any belief in these books being genuine records of revelation. The writer derives his statements from Jewish tradition, and uses them not *because* they are in apocryphal books, but *in spite of* that fact. These references give us a clue to the readers to whom this epistle is addressed.

4. Both the Book of Henoch and the *Assumptio Mosis* are Jewish apocrypha, and the circumstance that the author calls himself emphatically " the brother of James " suggests that the Christians addressed were Jews, for he must mean James the Less, who, as bishop of Jerusalem, was the chief support of the Jewish Christians. Further indications that the epistle was intended for them occur in verse 5, where the delivery of the Israelites from Egypt is mentioned, in verse 7, where there is an allusion to Sodom, and in verse 11, where the readers are reminded of Cain, Balaam and Core.

5. *Date.* The Jewish Christians, both in the Holy Land and in the Diaspora, were in a very dangerous position, as the head of their church, Saint James the Less, had suffered martyrdom in the year 62, so that, being deprived of their accustomed support, they were without support and defenseless in face of attempts to lead them astray. According to verse 3 the apostle who wrote this epistle considered it his duty to address it to his countrymen, who were struggling to preserve the faith delivered to them. The circumstances under which it was written were therefore almost the same as those of the Epistle to the Hebrews. Just as the latter warns the Jewish Christians against falling back into Judaism, so does this epistle warn them not to let themselves be drawn into heathenish license, under pretext of its being Christian liberty. It must have been written about 63–65.

6. The place of its composition cannot be ascertained. According to tradition, Saint Jude preached the gospel at Edessa in Mesopotamia. This at least is what Eusebius states (*Hist.*

---

[1] *De Viris Illustr.*, c. 4.

Eccl., I, 13); but others say that the faith was preached there by one of Christ's disciples named Addeus (Addai). Whether there is some confusion here is uncertain. This epistle may have been sent from Jerusalem to Saint Peter, whose second epistle, written in Rome, is plainly connected with it; and he, fearing the same sort of dangers for many churches in Asia Minor, himself wrote to draw attention to what Saint James's brother, who was well known to them, had announced in Palestine.

THIRD SECTION

THE PROPHETIC BOOK OF THE NEW TESTAMENT

56. THE APOCALYPSE

(22 chapters)

1. *Contents.* This revelation (ἀποκάλυψις = disclosure) of mystery gives information regarding the future of the Church of Christ, the struggles for and against Christ, and the final victory of the faithful.

It is divided into four parts:[1]

(1) Chapters i.–iii.: Communications and admonitions addressed by Saint John to the Christian churches in the Roman province of Asia.

(2) Chapters iv.–xi.: Statements as to the future of the Church.

(3) Chapters xiii.–xix.: Description of Christ's warfare with three great powers.

(4) Chapters xx.–xxii.: The end of the world.

i. Christ appears to Saint John at Patmos, and gives him messages to deliver to the communities of the province of Asia (Ephesus, Smyrna, Pergamus, Thyatira, Sardes, Philadelphia, Laodicea) with reference to the righteous life (i.–iii.). The real revelation now begins.

ii. Saint John is caught up to heaven, and sees God on a throne, surrounded by twenty-four ancients and four wonderful beasts. God holds

---

[1] The unity of the Apocalypse is defended by M. Kohlhofer and Belser. Its prophetic character is recognized also by H. B. Swete, "The Apocalypse of Saint John," London, 1906.

in His hand a book fastened with seven seals (denoting the future), which no one but the Lamb can open (iv., v.). One seal after another is broken, and each time appears a judgment coming upon mankind for the purpose of improving them. After the sixth seal is opened there is a great earthquake, so that people believe the last judgment of God has come. But a reprieve is granted, as there are still many of the elect on earth who are not to perish with the wicked. There then appears around the throne of God an innumerable host of people, who owe their salvation to Christianity and praise God for it. There are 144,000 of the Jews, and a countless multitude of Gentile nations (vi., vii.). After the seventh seal is opened, seven angels in succession blow trumpets, and fresh plagues come upon the world; but, as soon as they cease, sin appears again (viii., ix.).

Before the seventh trumpet sounds Saint John has three visions: (a) He receives further communications in the form of a book that he has to swallow (x.); (b) he has to use a measure to mark off the inner part of the Temple from the outer and from the city of Jerusalem. The outer part and the city share the fate of unbelievers. (c) Two witnesses of God are announced who preach penance. They are slain by the unbelievers, but raised to life again by God. They are generally believed to be Elias and Henoch (xi.). Now the seventh trumpet sounds (xi.-xv.). This heralds a struggle between Christ and His enemies, and at the same time announces the victory of Christ.

iii. The enemies of Christ are represented first in types, viz. (a) the dragon, (b) the beast with seven heads and ten horns, (c) the beast with two horns (xiii.). Ecclesiastical commentators generally understand by these enemies, (a) the devil, (b) the powers of the world, antagonistic to Christ, (c) the prophets of unbelievers with their false wisdom. Christ and His followers, especially virginal souls, are opposed to all these, and at once the song of victory is raised (xiv.).

The conflict of Christ is preceded by the coming of seven angels pouring vials of God's wrath upon the earth, thus signifying and heralding the last judgment (xv., xvi.). As these also effect no amendment in the wicked, the conflict proceeds, having as its aim to execute just vengeance. The first to be subdued are the tools of the devil, then the dragon himself. Next Babylon, the power of the world antagonistic to Christ, falls, and then follows His victory over the beast representing the false prophets and wisdom of unbelievers (xvii.-xix.). Finally the dragon is overcome and bound for one thousand years, whilst Christ and His followers rule on earth (xx.).

iv. After one thousand years the dragon is let loose again, and tries to stir up the nations against the saints of God, but He overthrows all His enemies and casts the devil and the two beasts into a pool of fire. Then follows the resurrection and the last judgment. Saint John sees at the end a new heaven and a new earth, and the new Jerusalem, i. e. a vision of the Church of Christ in glory (xxi., xxii.).

2. *Character and Aim of the Book.* The Apocalypse is a prophetic book and foretells the future destiny of the Church

and the faithful. But just as many of the Old Testament prophecies became intelligible only after their fulfillment, so it will probably be with those in the Apocalypse. Failing special instruction by the infallible teaching authority of the Church, it is scarcely possible to have a perfectly sure comprehension of this book.

(*a*) It does not contain an account of events themselves but of their types, which admit of various interpretations. (*b*) We are living in the midst of the events foretold in the book; and just as it is scarcely possible for each combatant in a war to form an opinion as to the general course of it or even of a single battle, so is any complete comprehension of the struggles of the Church denied as a rule to individual Christians. Moreover (*c*) many of the events foretold lie still in the future. It must not be assumed that all the things foretold are bound to happen exactly in the order in which they stand in the book. For instance, in chapter xviii. we read of the fall of Babylon, which primarily means heathen Rome, but we need not suppose that all the incidents described before this chapter belong to the period before the fall of that city, and that only those that stand after it belong to the centuries following the destruction of the pagan city. We cannot as a rule look for sequence of time in prophetic visions.

Even without special instruction on the part of the Church, we can understand much in this book that serves to console Christians in times of persecution, and especially in the period preceding the judgment, and to give such consolation is the chief aim of the book.

Stress is laid particularly on the following points: (1) The future is determined by God and not by man. (2) The future of man depends on Christ and His Church. (3) The various evils of this life are decreed by God as a punishment, but also for the amendment of man. (4) God is long-suffering, He waits long before He permits the judgment to come. (5) Many of the Jews and a countless multitude of the Gentiles will attain to eternal salvation through Christianity. (6) The depravity of the world will not remain limited to mankind outside the Church, but will penetrate even into the Church, that is to say, amongst Christians (Jerusalem), but will not injure it in its essential character. (7) There are three chief enemies to Christ and His Church: the devil, the anti-Christian powers of the world, and false knowledge. (8) The victory of Christ and the Church over these enemies is absolutely certain. (9) A completely new order of things is to follow the resurrection and the last judgment, for heaven and earth are to be transformed and glorified as the dwelling place of God's servants, whilst the wicked are cast out.

3. *Author and Authenticity.* The Apostle Saint John was the author of the Apocalypse. This is plain from internal evidence; he calls himself John, speaks of the island of Patmos as his abode (i. 9)[1] and occupies the position of pastor towards the seven churches of Asia. We have also external evidence. Papias, a disciple of the apostles, knew the Apocalypse and called it the work of Saint John. His writings have perished, but his knowledge of the Apocalypse is mentioned in the Fathers (Cramer, *Catena Patr. Græc.*, VIII, 360). The testimony of Justin Martyr[2] is quite clear, so is that of Hermas[3] and that of Irenæus (*Adv. Hær.*, V, xxx. 3). Melito of Sardes (circa 150) actually wrote a commentary on the Apocalypse.[4]

It was not until a later period that some wished to deny Saint John's authorship. Dionysius of Alexandria, who occupied Saint Mark's see from 248 to 265, laid stress on the fact that Saint John does not mention himself by name in his other writings, and the occurrence of his name here makes the authenticity of the book doubtful, and suggests that it is the work of another author. Eusebius (*Hist. Eccl.,* III, 25) expresses himself very vaguely; as a peace-loving bishop, connected with the court, he may have disliked the book because it foretold the destruction of the Roman Empire. The chief reason, however, why the authenticity of the book was questioned, was that the Chiliastic doctrines, which found their chief support in the Apocalypse (chapter xx.), assumed after the third century a more and more heretical tendency. Cyril of Jerusalem, Chrysostom and Theodoretus did not acknowledge the book, but as soon as Chiliasm lost its reputation, as it did chiefly through Saint Augustine, all doubt regarding the authenticity of the Apocalypse vanished likewise.

[1] According to Pliny (*Hist. Nat.*, IV, 12, 23) Patmos was often used by the Romans as a place of exile.

[2] *c. Tryph.*, 81: " A man named John, one of the apostles of Christ, prophesied in the revelation granted to him of the one thousand years." Eusebius too (*Hist. Eccl.*, IV, 18) says of Justin that he knew and recognized the Apocalypse.

[3] Hermas, who was, according to the *Fragm. Mur.*, brother of Pope Pius I (142–157) derives many of the thoughts and expressions in his *Pastor* from the Apocalypse (e. g. *Vis.*, II, 4; IV, 2).

[4] Euseb., *Hist. Eccl.*, IV, 26.

4. *Time and Place.* It is generally believed that the book was written during the reign of Domitian (81–96), on the island of Patmos, where Saint John was then living in exile. Irenæus (l. c.) says: " The revelation was seen not long ago, almost in our own time, towards the end of the reign of Domitian." It is assumed therefore that the Apocalypse was written about the year 96 (Kaulen, 271; A. Schäfer, 353).

5. It seems, as Kaulen remarks, a special dispensation of Providence that at the end of Holy Scripture stands a book in which a new heaven and a new earth are placed in our anticipation, whereas at the beginning of the Bible the account is given of the creation of heaven and earth. Genesis and the Apocalypse correspond to one another; the one depicts the happiness of the first human beings in their intercourse with God, the other contains the promise of a new Paradise.

FOURTH PART

INTERPRETATION OF HOLY SCRIPTURE

(HERMENEUTICS)

1. INTRODUCTION

THE name "Hermeneutics" (ἑρμηνευτική sc. τέχνη) comes from ἑρμηνεύειν = to interpret, expound, and designates the art of making plain a writer's meaning.

There is the more need to expound a writer the more remote he is in time and place from his readers, and the more the opinions and circumstances of his age and country differ from their own.

The fifty-eight books that the Catholic Church reverences as sacred, have this in common with other ancient writing that they were composed in foreign languages, now long dead, and written under circumstances of time and place differing greatly from our own. The figurative language of the East, and especially of the ancient East, is strange to us, and the numerous illustrations derived from Eastern people are frequently unintelligible to those who live in the colder West under another sky. Hence the comprehension of these sacred books is subject to quite other conditions than those governing our appreciation of modern authors, and it is often impossible without special elucidation.

Not only is an explanation of Holy Scripture indispensable from this merely human aspect of it, but we must remember that its divine origin raises it above the average human judgment, that is often obscured by our passions. It is only when a man allows himself to be guided by the same Spirit who called the sacred books into existence, that they become intelligible to him. The Holy Ghost inspires not each individual reader, but is ever active in the Church, the pillar and stronghold of truth. If, therefore, an individual desires rightly to understand and interpret Holy Scripture, he must find out the opinion of the Church, and be guided by it.

By biblical hermeneutics we mean the sum total of all those principles and rules in accordance with which the sense of Holy Scripture, both in its human and its divine aspect, can be ascertained and expounded.

We have to ask: What are we to understand by the meaning of Holy Scripture, how is it to be discovered, and how explained when discovered? Our subject therefore falls into three divisions:

1. The meaning of Holy Scripture.
2. The discovery of the true meaning of Holy Scripture.
3. The explanation of the text of Holy Scripture.

Hermeneutics differs from exegesis in the same way as theory from practice.

FIRST SECTION

THE MEANING OF HOLY SCRIPTURE

The meaning of Holy Scripture is its true signification, or what the Holy Ghost intended to reveal through the written word. The meaning of the text must not everywhere be limited to the literal meaning, as underlying the letter many a mystery is often concealed. There is therefore more than one meaning of the written word.

2. OF THE MEANING IN GENERAL OF HOLY SCRIPTURE

The Fathers and scholastic writers both distinguish a twofold sense in Holy Scripture: the literal and the mystical, — *sensus literalis* and *sensus spiritualis sive mysticus*.

1. The literal sense is that which the actual words directly convey. This is again twofold, viz. (*a*) the precise and (*b*) the transferred or metaphorical sense.

The precise literal sense is that which the written words,

taken in their own exact signification, convey, e. g. Gal. iv. 22 : " Abraham had two sons, the one by a bondwoman and the other by a free woman." The literal metaphorical sense is that which the words directly convey when taken figuratively. When, for instance, in Holy Scripture, our Lord is called a lion, a lamb or a vine, this is obviously meant not strictly but figuratively, as properties are ascribed or transferred to Him which we know a lion, a lamb or a vine to possess. These designations denote generosity and courage, readiness to be sacrificed, and abundance of life on the part of our Saviour.

2. The literal sense is frequently only the body of the written word, under which the soul or *spiritus* is concealed. The spiritual or mystical sense is that which resides not in the words themselves, but is suggested more or less obscurely by means of the things signified by the words. It is called mystical or mysterious, because it is not plain to view on the surface, but is more hidden, and generally more difficult to discover than the literal sense. So Galatians iv. 22, the passage quoted above, is explained by Saint Paul allegorically of the two testaments : Agar, Ismael = the Old Testament; Sara, Isaac = the New Testament.

The older theological writers distinguish three kinds of this mystical or spiritual sense, viz. an allegorical, a tropological and an anagogical.

The *allegorical* meaning is the reference of some discourse or account in the Bible to a doctrine of the faith, especially to Christ and the Church. If any section of Holy Scripture, in addition to the obvious, literal meaning (for the mystical sense always depends upon the literal, and proceeds from it),[1] admits or requires some reference to Christ or the Church, then the passage possesses, over and above the literal meaning, also a higher and mystical sense, which is called allegorical. Thus, for instance, the story of the rescue of Jonas from the sea is not to be limited to the prophet, but, according to Matthew xii. 39, refers also to our Lord's rest in the grave and Resurrection.

The *tropological* or moral meaning is the application of a

---

[1] Leo XIII., *Encycl. Providentissimus, supra,* p. 167.

passage to moral life, whilst the obvious and literal interpretation gives another meaning. Thus Genesis xv. 6, "Abram believed God, and it was reputed to him unto justice," has, according to Romans iv. 23, reference also to the necessity that mankind should believe in Christ.

The *anagogical* sense of a passage is the application that it allows to the future life, over and above its obvious and immediate meaning. Thus, according to Matthew xxiv. 37 and I Peter iii. 20, the account in Genesis of the ark may be applied also to the faithful who find salvation in the Church.

We may say, therefore, that the allegorical interpretation concerns faith; the tropological, morals; and the anagogical, hope; or the allegorical is *de rebus credendis*, the tropological *de rebus agendis* and the anagogical *de rebus sperandis*. The allegorical may be said to be based upon the past, the tropological refers to the present, and the anagogical points to the future of the faithful. This is all summed up shortly in the lines:

> **Litera** gesta docet, quid credas allegoria,
> Moralis [sc. sensus] quid agas, quo tendas anagogia.

This fourfold interpretation may be found, for instance, in the word *Jerusalem* or *Sion*.

It is *de fide* that there is really a mystical meaning to Holy Scripture, for Jesus Christ and the apostles have given mystical explanations of many passages. Thus our Saviour gave a mystical meaning to the story of Jonas by applying it to Himself. The apostle Saint John (xix. 36), in saying that our Saviour's bones were not broken on the Cross, refers to Exodus xii. 46, where it is forbidden to break a bone of the Paschal lamb. As stated above, in Galatians iv. 24, Saint Paul declares Agar and Sara, Ismael and Isaac to be representatives of the Old and New Covenants.

The early Christians were plainly instructed in the mystical or typical meaning of the Bible by the first preachers of the faith. In the catacombs in Rome, which served the Christians of the earliest ages as places of assembly and worship, Noe is often represented as one person in a floating chest; for, according to I Peter iii. 20, every Christian is saved from destruction by means of baptism, as Noe was saved from the flood. Abraham's sacrifice is often depicted in such a way that Pilate appears as judge, for that sacrifice was a type of the death of Christ on the cross. (*Stimmen aus Maria-Laach*, 1895, VII, 140, etc.).

The Jews too had, and still have, a method of interpreting Holy Scripture in a spiritual sense. It is called the *Midrash* (= investigation), and is an explanation that goes beyond the literal meaning. They give the name Midrash, however, only to those commentaries which go back to the period of the old schools in Palestine and Babylon, that is, between the second and the eleventh centuries. In the Midrashim they distinguish the Halacha (הלכה, way, direction, rule of conduct) and the Haggada (הגרה, story, saying). The Halacha is the authoritative explanation, given originally by a high priest, or by the synedrium or by the scribes in the schools, and so it embodies a tradition affecting manners and mode of life. The Haggada does not possess this official character, and is the work of private individuals, expressing private opinions. In the Haggada the mystical interpretation is prominent.

3. Of the Application of the Literal and Mystical Meaning

1. Only the literal meaning can, as a rule, be used by theologians in proof of doctrinal or moral truths. The reason for this is that the explanation of a passage in the mystical sense depends in a great degree upon personal opinions and the feelings of the individual. The right with which one person claims to explain some passage of the Bible in the mystical sense can be claimed by another for the purpose of overthrowing such an explanation.

The case, however, is different when the Church has pronounced in favor of the mystical interpretation of some passage, or when Holy Scripture or the consensus of the Fathers unmistakably requires a mystical explanation. In these circumstances the mystical meaning constitutes valid evidence, as it is then clear that the Holy Ghost has intended that there should be a mystical meaning, and that therefore God's word is stated mystically. Thus Deuteronomy xxv. 4 serves to prove the right on the part of ministers of the gospel to ask and accept their support from the faithful, because Saint Paul interprets it thus in I Corinthians ix. 9. The same remark applies to Genesis viii. (*cf.* I Peter iii. 20).

2. It is not every passage in Holy Scripture that contains

a mystical sense. Clement of Alexandria, Origen and the Alexandrian exegetical writers in general went too far in this respect,[1] and tried to extract a mystical sense from almost every passage in the Bible. To some extent Saint Ambrose and Saint Gregory the Great did the same.[2] The school of Antioch,[3] the chief representative of which was Saint John Chrysostom, did not go to such extravagant length. What kind of mystical meaning can be discovered in sentences such as: "Thou shalt love the Lord thy God," "Thou shalt not kill," etc.? In the same way it would be wrong to assume that any passage in Holy Scripture possessed only a mystical, and not a literal meaning.[4] Even the Canticle of Canticles admits primarily of a literal interpretation, although it would be wrong to stop short at it. Not a book nor a passage in Holy Scripture can be mentioned in which no literal sense at all is discoverable.

3. Not only in the Old, but also in the New Testament, can we find a mystical sense. Saint Thomas Aquinas tells us (*Summa*, I, qu. 1, art. 10) : *Nova lex est figura futuræ gloriæ,* — "The new law is a type of future glory." In the same way Saint John Chrysostom said that Christ fulfilled the old prophecies, but at the same time brought in others and by His works signified what was in prospect (*Hom. in Matt.* 66). A type of this kind is, for instance, His crucifixion outside Jerusalem, which signified the cutting off of Christianity and Salvation from Judaism, according to Hebrews xiii. 12. Accord-

---

[1] Scholz thinks that they followed the Jewish school, but this is not correct, for they had more resemblance with the pagan philosophers who gave a mystical interpretation to the stories of the gods.

[2] Saint Ambrose, after he had unexpectedly become bishop, having had no theological training, applied himself zealously to the study of Holy Scripture. As he knew Greek well, he took as his guides Philo and Origen, from whom he derived his tendency to mystical interpretations, but to some extent he followed Basilius, who belonged to the school of Antioch. In his commentary on the book of Job, Saint Gregory the Great almost restricted himself to the allegorical and moral sense.

[3] To it belonged also Theodore of Mopsuestia, who is too sober, even dry and rationalistic, in his interpretations, and his orthodox brother Polychronius.

[4] See Origen's opinion, *supra*, p. 192.

ing to Matthew xxiv., the destruction of Jerusalem seems to be a type of the last judgment.

Dr. A. von Scholz,[1] Professor of Old Testament Exegesis at the University of Würzburg, thought he could vindicate the Bible " in the eyes of the learned and cultured classes " by giving an allegorical interpretation to most of the books in the Old Testament. In his rectoral address of the year 1893 and in his very carefully elaborated commentaries, he opened up new lines to Catholic exegesis, which, if they were correct, would lead to the solution of many of the problems in the Old Testament. According to Scholz there are but few strictly historical books; almost all are allegories regarding the struggle between the kingdom of God and His enemies. " The Oriental always speaks in allegories. Our Saviour Himself mostly gave His instruction in parables." [2] He believes the whole of the Old Testament to be the work of a school in the far East, employed in collecting and multiplying the sacred books. " Isaias and Jeremias are a collection made by this school; Ezechiel was a member of it, and so he is the sole author of his book. The book of Daniel originated there also; his name designates not a statesman, but the Messias among His people. Joel, Abdias, Habakuk, Nahum[3] and Jonas were all compiled after the Captivity, as well as Zacharias, Malachias and almost all the Psalms. Joel's grasshoppers are nations. Habakuk mentions the Chaldeans; these first destroyers of Jerusalem represent the last enemies of God's kingdom. The reference is the same in Nahum's Ninive and Abdias' Edom. Jonas is none other than the Messias; the book of that name does not profess to have been written by Jonas, but to give an account of him. The problem of Qohelit (Ecclesiastes) is solved in Is. xlix. 4; Qohelit is the Messias, who has labored in vain, at least as far as many are concerned, and whose kingdom will be attacked and apparently suppressed, as He was Himself." The grammatical and historical interpretation must also to a great extent be given up. " Canticle of Canticles and Tobias, for instance, belong together, as both deal with the same subject, the final conversion of Israel. The same relation exists between Threni and Job. Judith can be proved not historical. Esther, Daniel, Ruth, Tobias, Bel and the Dragon are fantastic stories, incredible in the highest degree, but in reality allegories."

There are many serious arguments against these hypotheses. A few may be mentioned here:

1. Will the " learned and cultured classes " put more faith in these uncertain allegories than in the historical opinions?

---

[1] The following remarks are made with all deference to the zeal and learning of this eminent man, but the matter is much discussed at the present day, and some mention of it seems necessary in a book of this kind. It is only fair to say emphatically that Dr. Scholz aimed at nothing but serving the Church. He died in 1908.

[2] It should be noticed that our Lord's parables are always easily recognizable as teachings; they do not profess to be historical (such as Judith, Tobias, Esther, etc.).

[3] Happel and Dornstetter hold similar opinions.

2. If all this be true, who would be in a position to expound the sacred books to the masses? And yet these books are intended for the instruction of the simplest people, as God's word is always to be made known. Or is our Lord's teaching alone the word of God, and not also the Old Testament? *Cf.* Heb. i. 1.

3. Christ speaks of Jonas as an historical person, and contrasts him with Himself (Matt. xii. 40, 41). "A greater than Jonas here!" "As Jonas *was* in the whale's belly three days and three nights, so shall the son of man be in the heart of the earth." Or are we perhaps to give an allegorical interpretation to the account of our Saviour's rest in the grave also?

4. The headings of the Psalms, derived from Hebrew tradition, cannot be simply discarded.

5. Josephus Flavius regards the books of Esther, Daniel, etc., as historical, and so supplies evidence regarding Jewish tradition and exegesis in the first century A. D.

6. The feast of Purim and the feast in honor of Judith's victory (Judith xvi. 31) testify to the historical character of the books of Esther and Judith.

7. In the Church, the exaggerated allegorical interpretation of the Old Testament, due to Origen and the exegetical school of Alexandria, found no favor, although the Alexandrian scholars did not even occupy themselves with the distant future.

8. The order of the Canon, as well as exegetical tradition in the Church, undoubtedly favors the historical view. Neither the Fathers nor later commentators know anything of the theory of so extensive an allegory. *Cf.* the encyclical of Leo XIII.

9. Has not a dread of the miraculous had something to do with the origin and development of these hypotheses? "The miraculous in the history of theocracy, including that of the sacred books, is not exterior, but interior. *Omnis gloria eius, filiæ regis, ab intus.* (Rectoral oration, p. 35.) Where, however, is the limit to be drawn? Are Cain and Abel, Noe, Melchisedech and Samson not historical? Is not the brazen serpent historical? or the manna? Is everything *merely* allegorical? And what are we to say of the miracles of the New Testament, some of which are not less striking? Are we to give only a symbolical meaning to Christ's walking on the sea, to the multiplication of the loaves, and, finally, even to His calling the dead to life?

10. If these hypotheses were correct, all our catechisms of the Catholic religion and all our handbooks of Christian doctrine for schools and colleges would have to be withdrawn and revised. Our children at school must no longer be taught "Bible History" as the truth, but it must be explained to them as a collection of fictions. In the same way the Archangel Raphael's name must be removed from the liturgy, for the Church says, on October 24: *Deus, qui Raphaelem archangelum Tobiæ, famulo tuo, comitem dedisti in via* . . .

11. Is it conceivable that the Holy Ghost in the Church should have kept the true meaning concealed for so many centuries, and only have allowed it to be discovered in our time?

12. The Old Testament with its many types has in the main been

fulfilled in Jesus Christ. See Luke xxiv. 27: "And beginning at Moses and all the prophets, he expounded to them in all the scriptures the things that were concerning him." The Old Testament is the shadow of the New; but now all is relegated to a misty distance, — almost all the Old Testament is supposed to deal with the end of God's kingdom. Is not, however, the Church of Christ now present with us, the final kingdom of God? Fond as Saint Ambrose is of allegories, he generally limits them to Christ and the Church; so, for instance, he interprets the story of Isaac and Rebecca with reference to Christ and the faithful soul. Origen even, who often goes much too far in his allegorical explanations, sees in the fall of the walls of Jericho only an indication of the success of the apostles' preaching. We do not deny that in the Old, as well as in the New Testament, there are allusions to the final destiny of the Church and of the faithful, e. g. Is. xxiv.-xxviii.; Dan. xii.; but such allusions are so clear and unmistakable, that there can be no doubt as to the writer's intention. It is very questionable whether this free interpretation of the sacred books is in accordance with the Biblical Commission of June 23, 1905. (See *Bibl. Ztschr.*, 1905, p. 443.)

4. Of Accommodation

1. By accommodation [1] we understand an explanation by means of which a passage of Scripture, without regard to its real meaning, is, by a kind of extension or reference, applied to something quite foreign to the mind of the sacred writer.

For instance: The words in Ecclus. xliv. 17, *Noe inventus est justus*, are applied by accommodation to other holy men also. Again, Lament. iv. 4, *Parvuli pétierunt panem, et non erat qui frangeret eis*, is often taken to be a play upon words, and applied to the Christian education of the young. Esther v. 12: *Etiam cras cum rege pransurus sum* is referred to the daily sacrifice; Psalm lxvii. 36, *Mirabilis Deus in sanctis suis* means in the original "Wonderful [or fearful] is God in the sanctuary [of the Temple]," but in the translation it can be applied to the saints.

This sort of interpretation is neither directly nor indirectly motived by the Holy Ghost, and has no divine authority; hence it can never be used as a foundation for any proof.

Nevertheless it may be used for purposes of edification, for

---

[1] Accommodation is generally called *sensus accommodatitius*, but Cornely rightly points out (*Comp.*, 127) that we ought not to speak of an applied *sense*, as the word *sense* always refers to the intention in the mind of the writer, and that is not present in this case.

it occurs in Holy Scripture itself, and is used by the Church and the Fathers.

For instance in the Breviary the words which in Ecclus. xliv. 20 refer to Abraham, *Non est inventus similis illi, qui conservaret legem Excelsi,* are applied to every Confessor Pontiff.

2. There are limitations to the use of accommodation, and the following conditions must be fulfilled:

(*a*) Such an interpretation must not be declared to be the true meaning of a passage.

(*b*) It may be applied only in a pious manner, so that there is no lack of the reverence due to Holy Scripture. It would be a misuse of God's word to apply passages of it to profane things or in jest. This is expressly forbidden by the Council of Trent (*Sessio* 4), and bishops are required to punish, if need be, any who act in a contrary way.[1]

(*c*) If we read in Holy Scripture that this or that was done "in order that the Scripture might be fulfilled," we must not understand this by way of accommodation, but either according to the literal sense (*sensus literalis*), if anything that had been foretold actually occurred, or according to the mystical sense (*sensus mysticus*), if some type was realized.

For instance, in Matt. xxvii. 35 is a quotation from Ps. xxi. 19: "They divided my garments among them, and upon my vesture they cast lots." We must not say that the verse of the Psalm is *applicable* to our Saviour, and *can* be used in reference to Him, but we must believe that the Holy Ghost, through the Psalmist, was indicating an event in the Passion of the Messias.

---

[1] (*S. Synodus*) *temeritatem illam reprimere volens, qua ad profana quæque convertuntur et torquentur verba et sententiæ sacræ scripturæ, ad scurrilia scilicet, fabulosa, vana, adulationes . . . mandat et præcipit ad tollendam huiusmodi irreverentiam et contemptum, ne de cetero quisquam verba s. scripturæ ad hæc et similia audeat usurpare, ut omnes huius generis homines temeratores et violatores Dei iuris et arbitrii pœnis per episcopos coerceantur.*

SECOND SECTION

OF DISCOVERING THE MEANING OF HOLY SCRIPTURE
(Heuristics)

The use of biblical criticism is essential to a true knowledge of Scripture. We may distinguish the lower and the higher criticism. The former is concerned with examining and, if need be, with correcting the text. As in course of time, even unintentionally, some corruption of the text may have occurred, we have to try to discover the correct readings, by the assistance of early manuscripts, ancient translations and quotations in the works of the Fathers (*supra*, p. 222, etc.). Higher criticism deals with the age, origin, authenticity and purity of the sacred books. It is aided less by so-called internal evidence than by historical testimony, although the former may often be adduced in confirmation of the latter.

That form of criticism is erroneous which refuses to recognize anything supernatural, and therefore desires to eliminate as spurious whatever appears miraculous or prophetic.

Moral considerations must also be kept in view. Whoever wishes to comprehend the meaning of Holy Scripture must have a good intention and moral purity, for "wisdom will not enter into a malicious soul, nor dwell in a body subject to sins " (Wisd. i. 4), and he must also have humility, for "where humility is, there also is wisdom" (Prov. xi. 2). Reading and study of the sacred books are no less necessary, as Sirach says in the prologue to Ecclesiasticus; and lastly, he must pray for understanding: *quod est præcipuum et maxime necessarium, orent ut intelligant* (Aug., *De Doctr. Chr.*, III, 37).

The rules to be observed in trying to discover the correct meaning of Holy Scripture are partly taken from instructions given by the Church, and partly proceed from certain peculiarities of the sacred books.

5. PRINCIPLES LAID DOWN BY THE CHURCH

Divine revelation itself indicates how we may attain to a correct knowledge of the meaning of Scripture. In II Peter i. 2 we find the following statement: *Hoc primum intelligentes, quod omnis prophetia scripturæ propria interpretatione non fit. Non enim voluntate humana allata est aliquando prophetia, sed Spiritu sancto inspirati locuti sunt sancti Dei homines.*

"Understanding this first, that no prophecy of scripture is made by private interpretation. For prophecy came not by the will of man at any time, but the holy men of God spoke, inspired by the Holy Ghost."

In these words the apostle intends to deny to the individual the right to interpret the prophecies in the Bible according to his private judgment.[1] He bases this prohibition upon the inspiration of the prophets, who were, he says, influenced by the Holy Spirit when they uttered their prophecies. For this reason whoever reads and studies Scripture must not stop short, when he is trying to discover the meaning, at what the writings of the prophets appear to him, in his private opinion, to convey; but he must go further, and have regard to the Holy Ghost working in the prophets. As the same Holy Ghost still guides the Church and protects her from error, and as the Holy Scriptures are the property of the Church, it follows that they can be rightly understood only in and by means of the Church. The apostle is speaking, it is true, only of the prophetic books, but by analogy his words apply equally to the historical, poetical and didactic books. They are all the work of the Holy Ghost that brings about their comprehension no less than their origin. The apostle's rule was developed and explained by the Council of Trent (Sess. 4) in the following decision: *S. Synodus decernit ut nemo suæ prudentiæ innixus sacram scripturam ad suos sensus contorquens contra eum sensum, quem tenuit et tenet s. mater ecclesia, cuius est iudicare de vero sensu et interpretatione scripturarum sanctarum, aut etiam contra unanimen consensum Patrum ipsam scripturam sacram interpretari audeat.*[2]

---

[1] It would be possible to refer the words *propria interpretatione* to the prophet, in which case Saint Peter would mean that it was not the prophet, who by his own insight and penetration perceived and made known the future, but the spirit of God influenced him to do so. But *interpretatio*, Gk. ἐπίλυδις = solution, implies that something is given, and does not mean penetration. If it did, the two sentences would be tautological.

[2] Almost the same language was used by the Vatican Council of 1870, Sess. 3, cap. 2. Particular stress, however, is laid on the fact that this rule applies especially *in rebus fidei et morum.*

"The holy synod declares that no one relying on his own judgment shall dare to wrest[1] Holy Scripture in accordance with his opinion, contrary to that which our holy Mother the Church held and still holds, for to her does it belong to decide upon the true meaning and interpretation of Holy Scripture; nor shall any one dare to expound the same Holy Scripture in a way contrary to the unanimous decision of the Fathers."

In this decree we must notice first of all that "it belongs to the Church to decide upon the meaning and interpretation of Holy Scripture." This is a fundamental principle, containing three important rules, which have been observed in the Church from the beginning, not only since the Council of Trent. The Council merely gave expression to the tradition of the Church on this point.

1. It is a fundamental principle of Protestantism that each person may and must read and interpret Holy Scripture according to his own subjective judgment, but in the Church it is forbidden to regard one's own opinions as the sole standard in examining Scripture. No one is allowed *suæ prudentiæ inniti*, in contradiction to the Church, for private judgment is fallible, but the Church is infallible, for the Holy Ghost was not given to each individual but to the whole Church.

2. The hermeneutist may never go beyond the limits which the Church, guided by the Spirit of God, has set to her teaching; if he lights upon an interpretation not agreeing with the doctrines of the Church, he must recognize it to be false, for the Holy Ghost cannot contradict Himself. For the same reason the commentator may never contradict that particular interpretation which the Church has ever maintained to be the correct interpretation of a passage.

3. The hermeneutist in examining the meaning of Scripture must not depart from the unanimous decision of the Fathers, and he must not pronounce an interpretation to be correct that is at variance with the *consensus unanimis Patrum*. The *consensus* of the Fathers is nothing but the expression of the view taken by the Church. Where all the Fathers are agreed, there we undoubtedly have the apostolic tradition and the

---

[1] *Contorqueo* = to give anything a forced turn.

opinion of the Church. When the Fathers are not all agreed regarding the meaning of a passage, we are free to adopt whichever opinion we prefer, provided that the teaching authority in the Church has not decided the matter.

These rules involve no limitation of a reasonable use of human liberty. For (1) nothing more is required than that man shall submit his opinion to the Holy Ghost, who guides the Church. (2) Holy Scripture is not something apart from, or superior to, but of the Church, i. e. it belongs to the Church, to which Jesus Christ intrusted the whole of revelation, to make it known to mankind. Holy Scripture stands and falls with the Church.[1] The contents of Holy Scripture are thus nothing but the written doctrine of the Church, whose right and duty it is to watch over it, so that human passion and prejudice may not foist upon it an interpretation contrary to her former teaching.

As soon as the Bible is separated from the Church, it ceases to be respected. This is plainly to be seen in the case of the more recent sects. The Reformers wished to recognize the Bible, and not the authority of the Church, and their adherents followed them. But the consequence was that Holy Scripture has gradually lost all value amongst them, and at the present time many learned Protestants regard it merely as the work of men, and consequently in their opinion it is no longer the word of God. They have rejected the idea of inspiration, and now argue only about the letter of the book.

6. HERMENEUTICAL RULES BASED ON THE PECULIAR CHARACTER OF THE BIBLE

In so far as the Bible is the work of men, it has many properties in common with other ancient books, but as God is its author, it has also certain peculiarities belonging to it alone, as the book of revelation. The student of Holy Scripture has therefore to observe the following rules:

[1] "I should not believe the gospel itself, unless the authority of the Catholic Church induced me to do so" (Saint Augustine).

A. *On the Human Side*

1. He must carefully attend to the connection, both grammatical and logical. Both kinds of connection must be kept in view at the same time, and be used to make good one another's deficiences. This is particularly important for the Old Testament. In Hebrew the subject frequently changes; the numerous particles employed in Western languages are wanting; the verb has only the perfect and future tenses; there are frequent ellipses, etc. Thus the connection can often be restored only by means of the laws of logic.

2. Of still greater importance is it to observe the usage of the language. We mean by this the sense of a word, expression or sentence which at the time of some definite author was generally assigned to it.

In order to learn the usage of a language, we must have recourse to witnesses, taking as such the other authors who wrote in the language of that particular writer whom we desire to explain. Witnesses may be classified as direct and indirect. Direct witnesses are authors who used the same language as their native tongue, at about the same period. Indirect witnesses are those who used the same language only in kindred dialects or at another period.

The following rules hold good with regard to the witnesses for the usage of the language in the Bible:

(*a*) We cannot trace any great changes in the development of Hebrew as we know it in the Bible.[1] We find nearly the same language in all the books of the Old Testament; Genesis differs very little from Malachias in language. For this reason all the Old Testament writers are direct witnesses to one another. The same is true of the Greek text of the Septuagint, which almost all belongs to the same period.

(*b*) The language of the New Testament is based to a great

---

[1] The long seclusion of the people of Israel and the respect of later writers for the Mosaic law, were two causes of the preservation of Hebrew. (*Cf.*, however, p. 270, (*e*).) In the same way Arabic changed very little for several centuries, because the Koran was regarded as the model of style.

extent upon that of the Septuagint version of the Old. A
writer of the Septuagint is regarded, therefore, as a direct
witness for the Greek New Testament, and *vice versa*. All
the writers of the New Testament are direct witnesses to one
another, as they all wrote about the same time, viz. in the
first century.

(*c*) The earlier Greek Fathers may be used as direct witnesses for the New Testament and the Septuagint, because they
copied the language of the Septuagint and the New Testament.
The Chaldee, Syriac and Arabic writers are indirect witnesses,
and so are the later Greek Fathers and the Greek profane
authors.

3. Parallel passages of the sacred books serve to throw light
on the usage of the language. In order to discover these more
easily, use is made of biblical concordances, which are either
concordances of words or of subjects.

The former give, in alphabetical order, stating chapter and
verse, all the places where some particular word occurs in the
Bible. The latter do not notice the words, but they state, in
a series of articles arranged alphabetically, all that is to be
found, scattered up and down the Bible, on certain subjects,
such as baptism, sacrifice, prayer, Juda, Sion, etc. Verbal
concordances have been made for the Hebrew as well as for
the Greek and Latin texts of the Bible.[1]

---

[1] The best verbal concordances are: of the *Hebrew* text, Buxtorf,
Bâle, 1632. This important work, revised by Fürst and Bär, is even sur-
passed by the *Hebr.-Chald. Konkordanz des Alten Testaments*, by Sal.
Mandelkern, Leipzig, 1896.

Of the *Septuagint*, there is Tromm's *Concordance*, Amsterdam, 1718,
and an excellent new one by Hatch and Redpath, 6 parts, Oxford, 1897,
in which reference is made also to other early Greek versions. Another
concordance to the proper names in the Septuagint was also published
in Oxford. Of the *Vulgate* there is a useful concordance by Fr. Lucas,
Antwerp, 1618, etc. An abbreviated concordance of the Vulgate, intended especially for preachers, was brought out by Cornaert, Ratisbon,
1897. Based upon the very useful *Manuale concord.* by P. de Raze, is
the comprehensive *Thesaurus concord. scr. s.*, compiled by Peultier, Etienne and Gantois, Ratisbon, 1898.

Of subject concordances we may mention Calmet, *Lexicon biblicum;*
Lueg, *Realkonkordanz* (5th ed., 1900); Winer (Prot.), *Bibl. Wörterbuch;* Riehm, *Bibel-Lexikon;* Guthe, *Kurzes Bibelwörterbuch* (both

B. On the Divine Side

4. We must notice the relation in which the two Testaments stand to one another.[1] The Old Testament is to be regarded as prefiguring what was to come through and after Christ, as the *umbra futurorum bonorum* (Heb. x. 1; Col. ii. 7). It is connected with the New Testament as the bud with the blossom, as the announcement with the fulfillment, as the shadow with the light. Therefore one Testament cannot be properly understood without reference to the other (see H. Weiss, *Messian. Vorbilder im A. T.*, Feb., 1905).

5. Here and there in the New Testament passages are quoted from the Old, which cannot be found there in precisely the same form. We need not think that the text has been tampered with; ancient writers generally quoted according to the sense, disregarding verbal accuracy. On account of the rarity and costliness of manuscripts, it was not always possible to verify quotations. Many are therefore inaccurate from our point of view, but they are not falsified on that account (e. g. Matt. ii. 23; John vii. 38, quoted roughly from Is. xliv. 1–3).

6. We must not be offended by anthropomorphic expressions, which seem to us out of keeping with our conception of God. It is with a well-considered design that Holy Scripture speaks of God as of a Being resembling man, and ascribes to Him a face, eyes, ears, mouth, hands, feet and the senses of smell and hearing. This is done out of consideration for man's power of comprehension; and the same is the case when the Bible

---

Prot.). Also a large but still unfinished work by Vigouroux, *Dictionnaire de la Bible*, Paris; and an English (Prot.) *Dictionary of the Bible* by James Hastings, Edinburgh, 1898–1902, 4 vols., with an extra volume published in 1904; the *Encyclopœdia Biblica* by Cheyne and Sutherland Black, 4 vols., London, 1903. See also the article *Bibelkonkordanzen* in the *Kirchenlexikon*, II, 636.

[1] S. Aug. qu. 30 in Exod.: *In veteri testamento novum latet; in novo testamento vetus patet.* In Luke xxiv. 44, 46, 47, our Lord says to the apostles: "All things must needs be fulfilled which are written in the law of Moses, and in the prophets, and in the psalms, concerning me. . . . Thus it is written, and thus it behoved Christ to suffer, and to rise again from the dead the third day: and that penance and remission of sins should be preached in his name unto all nations, beginning at Jerusalem."

represents God as loving or hating, as jealous, angry, glad
or filled with regret, dispositions which apply to God not *per
affectum* but *per effectum*. They show us that God is not
coldly indifferent to loyalty or disloyalty on the part of men,
but notices them well. Moreover we must not forget that man
is made in the likeness of God, and that therefore in the
divine Being there must be something analogous to the qualities of men, though in the highest perfection.

THIRD SECTION

EXPLANATIONS OF THE TEXT OF HOLY SCRIPTURE

As early as the times of the Fathers much attention was
paid to expounding the sacred books, as a powerful means for
furthering the knowledge and piety of the faithful and for
warding off heresies. Every one knows how much Origen, Saint
John Chrysostom, Saint Ambrose, Saint Jerome, Saint Augustine and Saint Gregory the Great contributed to the elucidation of Holy Scripture. The same activity has continued in
every century, and various methods of explanation have been
developed. It is usual to distinguish four kinds of interpretation, viz. paraphrases, *scholia*, glosses and commentaries.
Every age has produced paraphrases, but scholia belong to the
time of the Fathers, glosses to the Middle Ages, and commentaries to the present day.

Explanations in the form of homilies were usual particularly in the
time of the Fathers, and were intended not only to supply a practical
need, but to promote a better understanding of Scripture. They would
be well adapted for the present time. Saint John Chrysostom and Saint
Augustine have left us models of this method of exegesis.

7. PARAPHRASES

A paraphrase of Holy Scripture is the method of explaining
the meaning of the words, which, while retaining the consecutive
language of the author, inserts in his text whatever may conduce
to its elucidation. Explanations such as seem serviceable are put

into the author's mouth, and his statements are expanded, so that he is made to elucidate himself.

The essential qualities of a good paraphrase are:

(1) *Fidelity.* If any one seeks information from a paraphrase, he wishes to learn from it the author's meaning and not the paraphrast's subjective opinions. Every deviation from the true meaning and contents of the language of a sacred writer would be a fraud practiced on the reader.

(2) *Intelligibility.* The measure of this quality is determined by the amount of education possessed by those for whom the paraphase is intended. It must therefore be more or less detailed, as it is intended for uneducated or educated readers. As a general rule in a paraphrase (*a*) unintelligible and unfamiliar expressions are replaced by words in ordinary use; (*b*) where the meaning is obscure, it must be expressed clearly in accordance with the rules of hermeneutics; (*c*) where there is an obvious omission, it must be supplied by a short interpolation.

(3) *Dignified diction.* The paraphrast must use stately language, doing his best to adapt it to the words of the original, so that the simple and dignified character of Holy Scripture is not destroyed. All words and phrases used only in the vulgar language of everyday life must be avoided, because reverence for the word of God ought to appear equally in the paraphrase.

8. SCHOLIA

Scholia are short notes on the text of a book, and they exist on that of the Bible. They deal with the whole text, and in this way differ from glosses, which single out for explanation only particular words and phrases. They differ from commentaries by their brevity and conciseness, and by their avoidance of every kind of excursus. The requirements of a good exegesis in scholia are: (*a*) a short introduction, (*b*) a continuous explanation, relevant and philological, (*c*) criticism and emendation of the text.

Bibliography. In ancient times the scholia of Theodorus of Mopsuestia enjoyed great reputation, although his jejune and frivolous interpretations often caused annoyance and offense. The textual elucidations of Saint John Chrysostom and of Theodoretus, bishop of Cyrus in Syria, won universal approbation. Saint Jerome too, and Saint Augustine, tried to some extent to expound the Bible by means of scholia. The works of these four scholars are of great value to us, especially because they adhere to the literal meaning, without however excluding the mystical. Procopius of Gaza (A. D. 600) collected earlier Greek scholia. The Greek writers Theophylactus, who became Archbishop of Achris in Bulgaria in 1078, and Euthymius Zigabenus, monk in a religious house near Constantinople in the eleventh century, followed St. John Chrysostom and Theodoretus, for which reason, although they themselves were schismatics, their scholia are still valued and used. Oecumenius, bishop of Tricca in Thessaly, is supposed to have written scholia on the Acts and Epistles about the year 600; they are generally quoted under his name, but it is quite possible that they were the work of some other author. It is certain that Oecumenius wrote an interpretation of the Apocalypse in the form of a commentary; it has been recently discovered by Fr. Diekamp.

9. GLOSSES

1. By *glosses* we mean a form of elucidation that deals only with single obscure words, and does not aim at explaining the subject matter.

The word γλῶσσα means primarily tongue, then language, but the Greek grammarians, who expounded the Greek authors, applied the word γλῶσσα to some obscure word in the text requiring explanation; the remark elucidating it was called γλώσσημα. Soon, however, the usage was reversed; the obscure word in the text was called the γλώσσημα, and its explanation γλῶσσα. The two words were adopted into western languages with these significations. Many glosses written by the earliest readers of the Bible have crept into the sacred text, but they are as a rule easily recognizable.

2. The subjects of the Greek grammarians' glosses were words not generally known, especially those derived from foreign languages, provincialisms, unfamiliar, obsolete and technical expressions. They wrote their remarks or glosses generally in the margin of a copy of the author whom they were studying, but sometimes the glosses were written apart in a separate book. Following this method, Greek ecclesiastical writers composed glosses on obscure words in the Greek of the Old and New Testaments. Subsequent Greek grammarians collected glosses of this kind, adding others of their own, and arranging the whole collection alphabetically, so that the obscure word in the text stood first, and then a word or note by way of interpretation of it. These collections are called *glossaries*, and the author or collector of glosses is a *glossator*. A glossary differs from a dictionary in not containing all the words of a language, but only the obscure words with their interpretation.

3. The chief among the Greek glossators is Hesychius, an Alexandrian grammarian of the fourth century. His glossary (which he himself called a lexicon) has come down to us. That of Suidas, a Greek grammarian who lived about 1000 A. D., is equally important.

Other valuable lexicons or glossaries are those of Zonaras of Constantinople, a Greek monk who lived in the twelfth century, and of Photius, a well-known Patriarch. We ought also to mention the *Etymologicum Magnum*, compiled by an unknown scholar in the eleventh century, and the *Glossarium* of Varinus Phavorinus (ob. 1537), a Benedictine from Camerino in Umbria, who had been a pupil of the Greek scholar, John Lascaris. Most of these glossaries deal with profane works as well as Holy Scripture, but special glossaries, containing only words from the Bible, have been compiled from them and published.[1] A collection of Latin glossaries was made by Löwe and Götz, 1888–1901.

4. In the Middle Ages the word γλῶσσα acquired a somewhat different meaning. It was applied to a collection of short, objective elucidations of Holy Scripture, and particularly of the Vulgate. The mediæval glosses scarcely differ at all from scholia. Glosses of this kind are also called *catenæ*, when several old explanations are, as it were, linked together and given one after the other. The most famous of these is the *Catena aurea* of Saint Thomas Aquinas, a collection in very condensed form of earlier elucidations of the gospels, collected from over eighty Greek and Latin authors (new edition, Turin, 1894). A Jesuit named Cordier, who lived at Antwerp about 1628, did excellent work in editing *catenæ*.[2] We have two especially famous glosses dating from the Middle Ages, viz. Walafried Strabo's *Glossa Ordinaria* and Anselm of Laon's *Glossa interlinearis*.

Walafried Strabo (born 807, died as Abbot of the monastery at Reichenau, near Constance, in 849), taking as his foundation the elucidations of Scripture given by his master Rhabanus Maurus, compiled a glossa of the Vulgate text of the Old and

---

[1] Ernesti, *Glossæ sacræ Hesychii*, etc. Lipsiæ, 1785–86.

[2] We mention also Pearson's *Critici Sacri*, 9 vols., London, 1660, and Frankfurt am Main, 1695–1701, a collection of Catholic and Protestant commentators; also J. A. Cramer's collections of " Catenæ from the Greek Fathers," Oxford, 1838–1844.

New Testaments, which was afterwards called the *Glossa Ordinaria,* partly because it was so generally used, and partly to distinguish it from Anselm's work.   Strabo's explanations are mostly derived from the Fathers, but he added a good many of his own, and for nearly seven hundred years, viz. from the ninth to the sixteenth century, his work was for theologians the ordinary and almost the only exegesis of Holy Scripture. (His complete works may be found in Migne's *Patrologia,* Tom. 113, 114.)   In the twelfth century *Anselm,* dean of the Cathedral at Laon (ob. 1117), attempted to make a still shorter interpretation by writing easily intelligible words or very brief remarks above the obscure words in the Vulgate, between the lines of the text, so that his work received the name of *Glossa Interlinearis.*   From the twelfth century onwards the Vulgate was regularly copied with both these glosses, so that the text stood in the middle of the page, the *glossa ordinaria* on the upper margin and on either side of the text, and the *glossa interlinearis* between the lines of it.   After the fourteenth century the postil [1] by the Franciscan Nicholas of Lyra (Lyranus, ob. 1340) [2] and the additions made by Bishop Paul of Burgos [3] were written on the very broad margin left below the Bible text.   In this form the Vulgate appeared among the first productions of the printing press.

10. COMMENTARIES

1. By a commentary we mean a connected and exhaustive explanation of the meaning of a book.   This form of exegesis belongs to recent times, and is connected with the classical studies that have been carried on in preference to others since the fifteenth century.

2. A biblical commentary may be concerned with the exe-

---

[1] The name comes from the words: *Post illa sc. verba textus,* — the explanation followed the text.

[2] His birthplace was Lyra, a little town in Normandy.

[3] He was by birth a Jew, but was converted in 1390.   His son became bishop of Burgos after him, in 1435, and it was to this son that he had sent his *additiones.*

gesis of the original text or of a translation. In the latter case, a Catholic commentator is bound to use a version that has received the sanction of the Church, but where difficulties occur, he must always compare the original, and if possible by that means throw light on the obscure passage. We generally expound the New Testament in accordance with the Greek text, but reference must always be made to the Vulgate. Most writers expound the Old Testament according to the Vulgate, but with reference both to the Hebrew text and to the various versions, particularly the Septuagint (*cf. supra,* p. 167).

3. The arrangement of a commentary on the Bible is generally the following:

(*a*) The actual commentary is preceded by an introduction to the book, discussing the author and the readers for whom he wrote, the motive, purpose and contents of the book, and the place and date of its composition. In this way the reader is supplied with a preliminary survey of the book, is enabled to form some opinion regarding it, and is prepared to understand its various parts.

(*b*) The text is divided into sections, either corresponding to the chapters in the book, or so that several chapters of kindred contents are grouped together under one heading.

(*c*) To the explanation of each section is suitably prefixed the text under discussion, either in the original or in a translation, the latter being more usual.

(*d*) The commentator has to practice textual criticism, i. e. where different readings occur he must state which he regards as correct, and for what reasons.

(*e*) In the exegesis of the various sections, for the purpose of elucidating obscure passages, the commentator must avail himself of all the resources of scholarship in the domains of philology, history and theology, and also use his own opinions, provided always that he attends to the fundamental principles of the Church (*cf.* p. 167, etc.).

(*f*) Finally we expect of a commentator that he should mention the chief explanations put forward by others with whom he does not agree, giving at the same time his reasons for refusing to assent to them.

11. STUDY AND READING OF THE BIBLE

As it is of the utmost importance that the Word of God should remain pure and free from all falsification, Leo XIII issued the following rules on Jan. 25, 1897:

1. The use of editions of the original text and of early Catholic versions that are published by non-Catholics but profess to be faithful and pure, is permitted only to those who are engaged in theological or biblical studies, provided that Catholic doctrines are not attacked in the prolegomena or notes.

2. In the same way and under similar conditions other translations of the sacred books, whether in Latin or in some other language, but not in the vernacular, are permitted though published by non-Catholics.

3. Translations of the sacred books into the vernacular, even if made by Catholics, are absolutely forbidden unless they are approved by the apostolic See, or, under the supervision of the bishops, are provided with explanatory notes taken from the Fathers or some approved Catholic authors.

4. All translations of the sacred books into the vernacular which are the work of non-Catholics are forbidden, especially those distributed by the so-called Bible societies. They are permitted, under the conditions stated above (1),[1] only for the purposes of theological or biblical study.

These rules laid down by the Church have called forth much adverse criticism from non-Catholics. Protestants go so far as to declare the reading of the Bible to be a duty, but this is a mistake.

Reasons for the Catholic regulations: 1. Nowhere in Holy Scripture is Bible reading prescribed. Jesus Christ gave instructions to preach, and consequently also to hear, the gospel. If every one were bound to read the Bible, many could not be saved. The early Christians did not possess the whole of the Sacred Scriptures, and according to Protestant teaching it is not certain which books belong to them. *Cf.* p. 208.

2. Such a precept was unknown throughout all the early ages of the Church. The Fathers recommend the reading of the sacred books, but

---

[1] Gregory XVI issued very similar rules on Jan. 7, 1836, and May 8, 1844.

know nothing of a command enjoining it; and their recommendation is addressed to priests and clerics. At the present time laymen are also recommended to read long or short portions of Holy Scripture, or, under certain conditions mentioned above (3), the whole Bible.

3. The Bible, being the written teaching of the Church, is intended primarily for those who teach in the Church, and only through them for those who hear. It was thus under the Old Covenant. The book containing the law of Moses was given over to the priests; only the king was to have a copy of it, and the people were required, not to read, but to hear. (Deut. xxxi. 9, etc.; *cf.* Deut. xvii. 18.)

4. The Bible is by no means easy for every one to understand, but is frequently obscure (*supra*, p. 168), and even scholars are not agreed as to the meaning of many passages. Disastrous results have often followed Bible reading by young persons and inaccurate interpretation by unqualified people.

5. The schismatic Greek Church, and even many Protestants, agree with the rules laid down by the Catholic Church.[1]

APPENDIX

EXEGETICAL BIBLIOGRAPHY

Of the time of the Fathers special mention must be made of Justin Martyr (ob. 167) and Irenæus (ob. 202), who explain many parts of the Bible in the course of their works; but systematic commentary originated in Alexandria, through Clement of Alexandria (ob. 217) and Origen (ob. 254), who were followed by Athanasius (ob. 373). In the fourth century the exegetic school at Antioch and Nisibis arose, which, unlike that of Alexandria with its fondness for allegory, always examined the literal meaning first, without, however, excluding the mystical interpretation. The chief representatives of this school are John Chrysostom (ob. 407) and Ephrem (ob. 379). Basilius (ob. 379) and Gregory of Nyssa (ob. 395) occupy a position about midway between the Alexandrian and Syrian schools. Theodore of Mopsuestia (ob. 428) went even further than the school of Antioch, for he refused to admit any mystical interpretation at all. The most noted Greek commentators in the fifth century are Cyril of Alexandria (ob. 444) and Theodoretus (ob. 458). Among the Latin writers Ambrose (ob. 397), Jerome (ob. 420), Augustine (ob. 430) and Gregory the Great (ob. 604) are conspicuous above all others.

In the Middle Ages we have the Venerable Bede (ob. 735), Walafried Strabo (ob. 849), Rhabanus Maurus (ob. 856), Rupert of Deutz (ob. 1135), Thomas Aquinas (ob. 1274), Bonaventure (ob. 1274), Alphonsus Tostatus (ob. 1454) and Dionysius the Carthusian (ob. 1471).

Nearer our own times, commentaries of the whole Bible have been writ-

---

[1] Even Protestants have recently felt the necessity of using only extracts from the Bible in schools, instead of, as hitherto, allowing the whole Bible to be read.

ten by Fr. Vatablus (ob. 1547 in Paris), Emanuel Sa, S.J. (ob. 1596), James Tirinus, S.J. (ob. 1636), Cornelius a Lapide, S.J. (= van den Steen, born near Liège, 1566, died in Rome, 1637),[1] Stephen Menochius, S.J. (ob. 1655), Aug. Calmet, Abbot of the Benedictine monastery at Sennones in Lorraine, died 1757.

Wilhelm Estius (ob. 1613) wrote notes on the most important passages in Holy Scripture. The commentaries of Sa, Tirinus and Estius were put together and united in John de la Haye's editions of the Bible in 1643 and 1660.

The following have written commentaries on single parts of the Bible: Jansen (ob. 1576) annotated the books of Psalms, Proverbs, Ecclesiasticus and Wisdom, and wrote a harmony of the gospels. Maldonatus, S.J. (ob. 1583), annotated Jeremias, Baruch, Ezechiel, Daniel, and especially the gospels; Salmeron, S.J. (ob. 1585), the gospels and the Acts of the Apostles; Agellius (ob. 1608), Psalms, Proverbs, Lamentations, Habakuk. Serarius, S.J. (ob. 1609), annotated most of the historical books of the Old Testament and the Epistles. Pererius, S.J. (ob. 1610), wrote on Genesis and Daniel; Estius (ob. 1613), on the epistles; Fr. Lucas (ob. 1619), on the gospels; Bellarmine, S.J. (ob. 1621), on the Psalms; Pineda, S.J. (ob. 1637), on Ecclesiastes and Job; Bonfrère (ob. 1643), on the Pentateuch, Josue, Judges, Ruth, Kings and Chronicles; Corderius, S.J. (ob. 1650), on Job.

The best of these older commentaries have been printed in J. P. Migne's great work: *Scripturæ s. Cursus completus*, 28 vols., Paris, 1839, etc., an almost inexhaustible storehouse of information.

The most important and comprehensive modern commentary on Holy Scripture is the one appearing in Latin at Paris, under the superintendence of the Fathers of the Society of Jesus; its title is *Cursus sacræ Scripturæ*, and over thirty large octavo volumes of it have already been published. The chief collaborators are the Fathers Cornely, v. Hummelauer and Knabenbauer. Belonging to it (besides the *Introductio*, see p. 475) is the *Lexicon biblicum* by M. Hagen, S.J., of which three large volumes have appeared, but it is still unfinished.

---

[1] A new edition of his commentary on the gospels appeared at Turin, 1896–99, in 4 volumes, edited by A. Padovani.

WORKS TO WHICH REFERENCE HAS BEEN MADE

(Protestant authors are marked with an asterisk)

Aberle, M. v., Einleitung in das Neue Testament, edited by P. Schanz. Freiburg i. Br., 1877.

Allioli, J. Fr., Handbuch der biblischen Altertumskunde, conjointly with Gratz and Haneberg. 2 vols. Landshut, 1844.

Allioli, J. Fr., Die Hl. Schrift des A. u. N. Test. übersetzt und erläutert. 3 vols. Ratisbon, 1897.

Bardenhewer, O., Patrologie. Freiburg i. Br., 1901.

Belser, J. E., Einleitung in das Neue Testament. 2d ed. Freiburg i. Br., 1905.

*Benzinger, J., Hebräische Archäologie. Freiburg and Leipzig, 1894. 2d revised edition. Tüb., 1907.

Boese, H., S.J., Die Glaubwürdigkeit unserer Evangelien. Freiburg i. Br., 1895.

Cornely, Rud., S.J., Historica et critica introductio in U. T. libros sacros. Paris, 1885 *seqq.* 4 vols. Ed. 2. 1893–1897.

Cornely, Rud., S.J., Compendium introductionis in s. Scripturas. Paris, 1889. Ed. 5. 1905.

Cornely, Rud., S.J., Synopses omnium librorum sacrorum utriusque Test. Paris, 1899.

*Cornill, C. H., Einleitung in das Alte Testament. Frb., Tüb., 1891, 1895.

*Delitzsch, Fr., Babel und Bibel. Leipzig, 1902, 1903. This little work has attracted great attention. It originated in some lectures given in Berlin in the presence of the German Emperor, on Jan. 13, 1902, and Jan. 12, 1903, by Professor Delitzsch, who is well known as an Assyriologist. He believes that the most important records in the Bible were derived from Babylonian and Assyrian sources, this being particularly the case with Genesis. His theory gave rise to a lively debate and the publication of many articles that were noticed at the time in Göttsberger and Sickenberger's " Biblische Zeitschrift," 1903–1906. Most of these works do not agree with Delitzsch's hypothesis. See also Delitzsch, " Mehr Licht," Leipzig, 1907; *cf. supra*, p. 272.

*Driver, S. R., Introduction to the Literature of the Old Testament, 1891.

*Duhm, B., Die Entstehung des Alten Testamentes. Freiburg i. Br. and Leipzig, 1897.

Gla, D., Repertorium der Kath.-theol. Literatur von 1700–1894. Vol. I, sect. 1. Paderborn, 1895.

Grimm, Jos., Die Samariter. Munich, 1854.

Grimm, Jos., Einheit der vier Evangelien. Ratisbon, 1868.

Guthe, H., Bibelwörterbuch. Tüb. and Lpz., 1903.

Haneberg, D. B., Die religiösen Altertümer der Bibel. Munich, 1869.

Haneberg, D. B., Geschichte der bibl. Offenbarung. 4th ed. Ratisbon, 1876.

Herbst, J. G., Einleitung in die Schriften des Alten Testamentes, edited by B. Welte. Carlsruhe and Freiburg, 1840–1844.

Hilprecht, H. V., Excavations in Bible Lands during the Nineteenth Century. Philadelphia, 1903. Hilprecht was born in 1859 at Anhalt, and is now professor at the University of Philadelphia, U. S. A. He has devoted much time to the excavations on the Euphrates, and in 1903 published the above-mentioned work on the subject. Its contents are briefly as follows: In 1802 Grotefend found the key to the cuneiform inscriptions, and afterwards the regions of the Euphrates and Tigris were visited by Rich, Botta and Rawlinson; the last-named discovered Sargon's palace in Ninive in 1842. In 1854 the town of Ur (now Mugheir or Muqajir), the home of Abraham, was discovered in South Babylonia, and in 1878 the town of Sippar. Since 1888 American expeditions have carried on excavation work in the lower Euphrates, and have succeeded in finding at Nippur the kings' library. At Nippur remains of the civilization of various periods have been discovered in layers, one below the other: Roman, Greek, Parthian, and, lowest of all, Babylonian. Hilprecht takes care not to destroy the respect paid to the Bible. His work is not limited to the country near the Euphrates, and many scholars have collaborated with him. Benzinger writes on the excavations in Palestine, the Mesa stone and the inscription at Siloe. P. Jensen discusses the Hethites, Steindorff the excavations in Egypt, and Hommel the discoveries made in Arabia.

Hoberg, G., Moses und der Pentateuch, 1905. ("We possess a Mosaic Pentateuch, but not in an edition prepared by Moses.")

Holtzmann, H. J., Lehrbuch der historisch-kritischen Einleitung in das Neue Testament. 3d enlarged and improved edition. Freib. i. Br., 1892.

Hommel, Fr., Die altisraelitische Überlieferung in inschriftlicher Beleuchtung. Munich, 1897.

Höpfl, H., Die höhere Bibelkritik. Paderborn, 1905.

Hug, L., Einleitung in das Neue Testament. 2 vols. Freib. i. Br., 1846.

Hug, L., Gutachten über das Leben Jesu von Strauss. Freib. i. Br., 1846.

v. Hummelauer, Fr., S.J., Der biblische Schöpfungsbericht. Freib. i. Br., 1877 and 1898.

v. Hummelauer, Fr., S.J., Commentarius in Pent. Paris, 1895, etc.

Jeremias, A., Monotheist, Strömungen innerhalb der babyl. Religion. Lpz., 1905. ("There are suggestions of monotheism, but it is impossible to maintain that monotheism was invented and discovered in Babylon. Israel always occupies the foremost position.")

Jülicher, Ad., Einleitung in das Neue Testament. 5th and 6th ed. Tüb. and Leipzig, 1905.

Kaulen, Fr., Einleitung in die Heilige Schrift des Alten und Neuen Testamentes. 4th and 5th ed. Freiburg i. Br., 1898, 1905.

Kaulen, Fr., Der biblische Schöpfungsbericht. Freiburg i. Br., 1902.

*Kautzsch, E., Die Heilige Schrift des Alten Testamentes übersetzt und herausgegeben. Freiburg i. Br., 1894.

*Kayser, Aug., Theologie des Alten Testamentes. 2d ed., by Marti. Strassburg, 1894.

Keil, P., Zur Babel- und Bibelfrage. Reprinted with additions from the Pastor Bonus. Trèves, 1903. A careful work throwing considerable light on the subject in question.

*Keil, K. F., Handbuch der hebr. Archäologie. 2 vols. Leipzig, 1858.

Keppler, P., Wanderfahrten und Wallfahrten im Orient. Freiburg i. Br., 1894, 5th ed., 1905.

Kihn, H., Encyklopädie und Methodologie der Theologie. Freiburg i. Br., 1892.

Kirchenlexikon by Wetzer and Welte. Freiburg i. Br., 1847–1854.

Kirchenlexikon (Wetzer and Welte), re-edited by Hergenröther and Kaulen. Vol. I–XII. Freiburg i. Br., 1882–1901.

*Kirchhoff, A., Palästinakunde. Halle, 1899.

Kley, J., Die Pentateuchfrage. Münster, 1904.

*Krüger, G., Entstehung des Neuen Testamentes. Freiburg i. Br. and Leipzig, 1896.

Künstle, K., Das Comma Johanneum. Freiburg i. Br., 1905.

Langen, J., Grundriss der Einleitung in das Neue Testament. Freiburg i. Br., 1868.

Loch, V., and Reischl, W., Die hl. Schriften des Alten und Neuen Testamentes übersetzt und erläutert. Ratisbon, 1851.

*Maurer, Fr., Hebr. u. chald. Handwörterbuch zum A. T. Stuttgart, 1851.

Mayer, Bon., Das Judentum. Ratisbon, 1843.

*Meyer, Ed., Entstehung des Judentums. Halle, 1896.

Migne, J. P., Scripturæ sacræ cursus completus. 28 vols. Parisiis, 1839.

*Nestle, E., Einführung in das Griech. Neue Testament. Göttingen, 1897.

Nikel, J., Der Monotheismus Israels in der vorexilischen Zeit. Paderborn, 1893.

Nikel, J., Genesis und Keilschriftforschung. Freiburg i. Br., 1903.

Pawliki, M., Ursprung des Christentums. Mayence, 1885.

Pörtner, B., Die Autorität der deuterokanonischen Bücher des Alten Testamentes. Münster, 1893.

Reithmayr, Fr. X., Einleitung in das Neue Testament. Ratisbon, 1852.

Reithmayr, Fr. X., Lehrbuch der biblischen Hermeneutik, edited by V. Thalhofer. Kempten, 1874.

Reusch, Fr. H., Lehrbuch der Einleitung in das Alte Testament. 3d ed. Freiburg i. Br., 1868.

*Reuss, E., Die Geschichte der heil. Schriften des Alten Testamentes. Brunswick, 1881.

*Riehm, E. K. A., Wörterbuch der bibl. Altertümer. 2 vols. Bielefeld and Leipzig, 1875, etc.

*Sayce, A. H., Fresh Lights from Ancient Monuments. London, 1883.

Schäfer, B., Altertümer der Bibel. 2d ed. Münster, 1891.

Schäfer, B., Kurzgef. wissenschaftl. Kommentar zum Alten und Neuen

Testament, mit mehreren herausgegeben von B. Schäfer. 12 and 7 vols. Vienna, 1901, etc.

Schegg, P., Biblische Archäologie, edited by Wirthmüller. Freiburg i. Br., 1886.

Schenz, W., Einleitung in das Alte Testament. Ratisbon, 1887.

*Schleusner, J. Fr., Lexicon gr. lat. in N. T. Lips. 1792.

Schöpfer, Am., Geschichte des Alten Testamentes. 4th ed. Brixen, 1906.

Scholz, P., Die heiligen Altertümer Israels. 2 vols. Ratisbon, 1868.

*Schürer, E., Geschichte des jüdischen Volkes im Zeitalter Jesu Christi. 3 vols. and one vol. containing index. 3d ed. Leipzig, 1898–1902.

Sellin, E., Die alttestamentliche Religion in Rahmen der andern altorientalischen. Leipzig, 1908. The author compares the ritual, customs, laws, pious practices, faith and doctrine as set forth in the Old Testament with those of other Oriental religions. Points of resemblance are discovered and examined. The result is to prove them not the same, but totally different. The religion of Israel stands alone, and is far above that of neighboring nations.

*Siegfried and Stade, Hebräisches Wörterbuch zum A. T. Leipzig, 1893.

*Smend and Socin, Die Inschrift des Königs Mesa von Moab. Freiburg i. Br., 1886.

*Stade, Bernh., Geschichte des Volkes Israel. 2 vols. Berlin, 1888, etc.

*Stade, Bernh., Entstehung des Volkes Israel. Giessen, 1899.

*Steuernagel, C., Allg. Einleitung in den Hexateuch. Göttingen, 1900.

*Strack, H. L., Einleitung in das Alte Testament. 6th ed. Munich, 1906.

Trenkle, Fr. Sal., Einleitung in das Neue Testament. Freiburg i. Br., 1897.

*Volck, K. J., Entwicklungsgeschichte der alttest. Religion nach der Graf-Wellhausenschen Hypothese. Carlsruhe, 1891.

Weinhart, B., Das Neue Testament. 2d ed. Freiburg i. Br., 1899.

*Wellhausen, Jul., Prolegomena zur Geschichte Israels. Berlin, 1886.

*Wellhausen, Jul., Israelitische und jüdische Geschichte. Berlin, 1894.

Welte, B., Nachmosaisches im Pentateuch. Freiburg i. Br., 1841.

*Winer, G. B., Biblisches Realwörterbuch. 2 vols. 3d ed. Leipzig, 1847.

*Winckler, H., Die Tontafeln von Tell el Amarna. Berlin, 1896.

*Zahn, Th., Geschichte des neutestamentlichen Kanons. 2 vols. Erlangen and Leipzig, 1888, 1890.

Ziegler, L., Die lateinischen Bibelübersetzungen von Hieronymus und die Itala des Augustinus. Munich, 1879.

*Zimmern, H., Biblische und babylonische Urgeschichte. Leipzig, 1901. Contains opinions similar to those expressed by Delitzsch in the work mentioned above. Contents: Creation, Paradise, Patriarchs, story of the Deluge.

CONCLUSION

IN Holy Scripture God Himself tells us how His kingdom was established among men as a protest against godlessness, and was maintained in the times of the prophets in spite of the great powers of the world; how it was transformed by His Son to be the kingdom of the Messias, which was originally like a grain of mustard seed, but has spread more and more among all nations, and for over nineteen hundred years has stood firm as the power of God amidst mankind. This kingdom, the Church, has fought its way through paganism in Western Asia, Greece and Rome, has prevailed over the barbarism of savages, has endured in spite of all sects and divisions, and still at the present day stands as firmly on the rock, its foundation, as it ever did in antiquity or in the Middle Ages. If now the struggle against the Church is carried on with more violence and arrogance than ever before, we are certain, from God's promises contained in the sacred books, and from the experience of so many centuries, that no power in the world, no malice and no pretended wisdom will ever succeed in destroying that kingdom which God intended to be for the salvation of all who desire to avoid temporal and eternal ruin. If a man has fathomed the secret of God's kingdom on earth, — and it is an open secret, — scales seem to fall from his eyes when he reads Holy Scripture, but if he has not understood it, and does not know and recognize the divine institution of the Church, Holy Scripture remains to him a book sealed with a sevenfold seal. It was only to those of His disciples who believed in Christ that the Holy Ghost gave understanding (Matt. xiii. 11).

Unbelief may proclaim as loudly as it will that it has discovered the key to a correct understanding of the Bible; it is mistaken, as certainly as God is everlasting truth. For

> " Opinionum commenta delet dies;
>   sed veritas manet et invalescit in æternum."
>
> 3 Esdr. iv. 38.

INDEX

INDEX

Israel, coins, 120
—— cubit measure, 69
—— holy persons in, 90
—— measures for liquids, 118
—— Monotheism and Polytheism, 56
—— priests in, 94
—— religious institutions, 66
Israelites, 21
—— history of, 37
—— in Egypt, 65
—— sects, 103
—— worship of idols, 61, 62, 63
Issachar, 22
Istar, 61
Itala, 247
Itinera hierosol., 4
Itinerarium Burdigalense, 4
Ituræa, 33

Jabbok, 9
Jacob, 21, 37
Jaffa, 29
Jealousy offerings, 119
Jebus, 20, 22
Jebusites, 20
Jeremias, book of, 322
Jericho, 28, 60
Jeroboam, 53
Jerusalem, destroyed, 38
—— named Jebus, 20
—— situation of, 22, 24, 25
Jethur, 33
Jewish sects, 103
Jews, 38
Job, book of, 298
Joel, book of, 310
John Hyrcanus, 89
John the Baptist, place of death, 33
Joiada, 52
Jonas, 29
—— book of, 307
Joppe, 29
Jordan, 6, 10, 22
Josaphat, see Valley
Joseph, 21, 37
Josephus Flavius, 22, 32, 33, 66, 67
Josias, 47
Josue, 21
—— book of, 275

Jubilee, year of (Mosaic), 145
Juda, 21
Juda Hakkadosch, 67
Judæa, 22
Judas Machabæus, 63, 86
Judges, book of, 277
Judith, book of, 344
Junilius, 188
Juno, 61
Justin Martyr, 361

Kana-Eldschelil, 32
Kana-Galil, 32
Kanatha, 33
Kaphtor, 21
Kapporeth, 79
Kariathiarim, 29
Kefr-Kana, 32
Kemosch, 42
Ken, 75
Kenites, 19
Ketura, 37
Kidron, 26
Kijjim, 59
King Anu, 63
Kings of the Northern Kingdom, 303
—— of the Southern Kingdom, 303
Kinnor, 136
Kison, 9
Kronos, 59, 64
Kubeibeh, 29
Kulonieh, 29
Kutu, 65

Lais, 21
Lake Genesareth, 10, 13, 22
Lake Merom, 10
Lamentations, book of, 325
Langton, Stephen, 219
Languages, biblical, 212
Laws concerning food (Mosaic), 131
Lebanon, see Mount Lebanon
Legal defilement (Mosaic), 121
Leprosy, 14
—— uncleanness due to, 122
Levi, 21
—— tribe of, 90
Levites, as judges, 93
——in charge of worship, 91

194